THE ECONOMICS OF WORLD WHEAT MARKETS

Fred,

Thank you for your support.

John Antle

The Economics of World Wheat Markets

Edited by

J.M. Antle

and

V.H. Smith

Department of Agricultural Economics and Economics and Trade Research Center, Montana State University–Bozeman, USA

CABI *Publishing*

CABI *Publishing* is a division of CAB *International*

CABI Publishing
CAB International
Wallingford
Oxon OX10 8DE
UK

Tel: +44 (0)1491 832111
Fax: +44 (0)1491 833508
Email: cabi@cabi.org

CABI Publishing
10 E 40th Street
Suite 3203
New York, NY 10016
USA

Tel: +1 212 481 7018
Fax: +1 212 686 7993
Email: cabi-nao@cabi.org

A catalogue record for this book is available from the British Library London, UK

Library of Congress Cataloging-in-Publication Data
The economics of world wheat markets / edited by J.M. Antle and V.H. Smith.
p. cm.
Papers from a symposium held at Montana State University in May 1997.
Includes bibliographical references and index.
ISBN 0-85199-360-5 (alk. paper)
1. Wheat trade Congresses. 2. International trade Congresses.
I. Antle, John M. II. Smith, Vincent H.
HD9049.W4E27 1999
382′.41311--dc21 99–16709
CIP

Typeset in 10/12pt Melior by Columns Design Ltd, Reading.
Printed and bound in the UK by Biddles Ltd, Guildford and King's Lynn.

Contents

Contributors

Robert Ackrill, Department of Economics, University of Leicester, Leicester LE1 7RH, UK.

John M. Antle, Department of Agricultural Economics and Economics and Trade Research Center, Linfield Hall, Montana State University–Bozeman, PO Box 172920, Bozeman, MT 59717–2920, USA.

Eugenio S.A. Bobenrieth, Departamento de Economica, Universidad de Concepcion, Casilla 1987, Concepcion, Chile.

Susan M. Capalbo, Department of Agricultural Economics and Economics and Trade Research Center, Linfield Hall, Montana State University–Bozeman, PO Box 172920, Bozeman, MT 59717–2920, USA.

Colin A. Carter, Department of Agricultural and Resource Economics, University of California–Davis, One Shields Avenue, Davis, CA 95616, USA.

Bruce L. Dahl, Department of Agricultural Economics, North Dakota State University, PO Box 5636, Fargo, ND 58105–5636, USA.

Eugenio Diaz-Bonilla, International Food Policy Research Institute (IFPRI), 2300 K St NW, Washington, DC 20036, USA.

Murray Fulton, Centre for the Study of Cooperatives, Department of Economics, University of Saskatchewan, 101 Diefenbaker Centre, Saskatoon, Saskatchewan S7N 5B8, Canada.

Bruce L. Gardner, Department of Agricultural and Resource Economics, University of Maryland, 6902 Chansory Lane, University Park, MD 20782, USA.

Barry K. Goodwin, Department of Agricultural and Resource Economics, North Carolina State University, PO Box 8109, Raleigh, NC 27695–8109, USA.

Richard S. Gray, Department of Agricultural Economics, University of Saskatchewan, 51 Campus Drive, Saskatoon, Saskatchewan S7N 5A8, Canada.

Thomas J. Grennes, Department of Agricultural and Resource Economics, North Carolina State University, PO Box 8109, Raleigh, NC 27695–8109, USA.

Dermot Hayes, Department of Economics, Iowa State University, 568 Heady Hall, Ames, IA 50011, USA.

Robert W. Herdt, The Rockefeller Foundation, 420 5th Avenue, New York, NY 10018, USA.

Robert Hine, Department of Economics, University of Nottingham, Nottingham NG7 2RD, UK.

Jikun Huang, Centre for Chinese Agricultural Policy, Beijing, China.

D. Gale Johnson, Department of Economics, University of Chicago, 1126 E 59th Street, Chicago, IL 60637, USA.

James B. Johnson, Department of Agricultural Economics and Economics and Trade Research Center, Linfield Hall, Montana State University–Bozeman, PO Box 172920, Bozeman, MT 59717–2920, USA.

Stanley R. Johnson, Extension Administration, Department of Economics, 218 Beardshear Hall, Iowa State University, Ames, IA 50011–2020, USA.

Won W. Koo, Department of Agricultural Economics, North Dakota State University, PO Box 5636, Fargo, ND 58105–5636, USA.

Timothy Lloyd, Department of Economics, University of Nottingham, Nottingham NG7 2RD, UK.

Tigran A. Melkonian, Center for Agricultural and Rural Development (CARD), Department of Economics, 578 Heady Hall, Iowa State University, Ames, IA 50011, USA.

Samarendu Mohanty, Department of Economics, Iowa State University, 568 Heady Hall, Ames, IA 50011, USA.

Anthony Rayner, Department of Economics, University of Nottingham, Nottingham NG7 2RD, UK.

Cesar Revoredo, Department of Agricultural and Resource Economics, University of California–Davis, One Shields Avenue, Davis, CA 95616, USA.

Scott D. Rozelle, Department of Agriculture and Resource Economics, University of California–Davis, One Shields Avenue, Davis, CA 95616, USA.

Vincent H. Smith, Department of Agricultural Economics and Economics and Trade Research Center, Linfield Hall, Montana State University–Bozeman, PO Box 172920, Bozeman, MT 59717–2920, USA.

Pavel Vavra, Department of Agricultural Economics and Economics and Trade Research Center, Linfield Hall, Montana State University–Bozeman, PO Box 172920, Bozeman, MT 59717–2920, USA.

William W. Wilson, Department of Agricultural Economics, North Dakota State University, PO Box 5636, Fargo, ND 58105–5636, USA.

Brian D. Wright, Department of Agricultural and Resource Economics, University of California–Berkeley, 207 Giannini Hall #3310, Berkeley, CA 94720, USA.

Walter E. Zidack, Department of Agricultural Economics and Economics and Trade Research Center, Linfield Hall, Montana State University–Bozeman, PO Box 172920, Bozeman, MT 59717–2920, USA.

Preface

The Trade Research Center at Montana State University–Bozeman convened a research symposium on 'The Economics of World Wheat Markets: Implications for North America' in May 1997. The purpose of this symposium was to assemble leading agricultural economists in the field from the USA, Canada, Europe and Latin America to present and discuss current research on the economics of world wheat markets. A summary of the conference proceedings was published in October 1997 by the Trade Research Center. This volume contains the full set of papers from the conference, all of which were the subject of critical discussion at the symposium, subsequent peer reviews, and detailed revisions by the authors. In addition, to make this volume a more complete statement of what is known about world wheat markets, Chapter 4 on stocks by Carter, Revoredo and Smith was commissioned subsequent to the symposium. The editors also prepared the first chapter, which reviews data and trends in world wheat markets, and the last chapter, which summarizes the volume and raises questions for future consideration by researchers in the field.

The editors wish to thank all of the authors, commentators and other participants in the symposium for their thoughtful and creative inputs, which have vastly improved the quality of the book. Particular debts of gratitude are owed to Colin Carter, Jim Johnson and Linda Young for their contributions to this work. Amanda Cater, Jim Johnson and Linda Young also deserve special recognition for their contributions to the organization and management of the symposium. This project could not have been completed without the support of Montana State University, including the College of Agriculture and its then dean, Dr

Tom McCoy; the Department of Agricultural Economics and Economics and its faculty; and the Extension Service and its then dean, Dr Charles Rust. Important contributions were also provided by the Montana Grain Growers Association, the Louis Dreyfus Company, Con Agra, the Canadian Wheat Board and the Minneapolis Canadian Consulate General, and through the Henry Schaefer Fellowship Program, University of Western Australia. We are most grateful to all of them for their help and contributions. In addition, the preparation of this book has been greatly facilitated by CABI *Publishing* and, in particular, Tim Hardwick, our editor at CABI *Publishing*. Finally, we are happy to acknowledge the debts we owe to Kitty Sue Squires for her wonderful work in coordinating, organizing, and processing the manuscript, and to Joan Macdonald and Alison Todd for their contributions to its production and the preparation of the index.

John M. Antle
Vincent H. Smith

Introduction

Wheat is one of the three major grain commodities – wheat, maize and rice – produced on a worldwide basis by farmers. It is consumed by households in rich, middle-income and low-income countries in the form of bread, pasta, breakfast cereals, cakes and other bakery products. Lower-quality wheat is also used for animal feed in many countries. In a very real sense, therefore, wheat is a crucial staff of life for many communities and a major food commodity for many others. Wheat is also one of the agricultural products most heavily traded on world international commodity markets. In 1997, world production and consumption of wheat were both just over 600 million tonnes. Approximately 105 million tonnes of that output, approximately 17%, was traded between approximately 20 exporting nations and 80 importing nations. The functioning of world wheat markets is therefore fundamentally important to the economic welfare of consumers and agricultural producers throughout the world.

In the 1990s, world wheat markets have been the subject of increasing scrutiny by both policy makers and academic economists. The most obvious reason has been an increase in the year-to-year variability of world wheat prices relative to the 1980s. Between 1993 and 1996, the average price of wheat exported by the USA increased from about \$118 to about \$207 per tonne. In contrast, by May 1998, the price of wheat had declined from its 1996 peak to about \$140 per tonne. In 1996, there was widespread concern that wheat prices would continue to increase well beyond \$200 per tonne, in part because of adverse climate effects on production and in part because of concerns about growing demand in large developing countries such as China and India. Some organizations such as World Watch were even claiming that China would shortly 'starve the world' by increasing wheat and other grain imports by as much as 50 or 60 million tonnes (about a tenth of current world wheat production and half of current world wheat exports). In contrast, in 1998, many wheat producers in Canada and the USA were concerned that wheat prices would continue to decline to well below $110 per tonne, creating serious economic and social disruption through farm foreclosures and bankruptcies in rural communities ranging from the Great Plains to the eastern seaboard of North America.

Given the recent volatility of world wheat markets, and the substantial changes in economic conditions and agricultural policies that have taken place in major wheat-importing and exporting countries since the late 1980s, a careful examination of the economic forces that drive the behaviour of world wheat markets and the current status of economic research on wheat is both timely and necessary. This volume provides such an examination. In 1997, the Trade Research Center at Montana State University organized a symposium on the economics of world wheat markets in the 1990s and beyond, and future implications for North American grain markets. Presenters and discussants at the symposium included leading agricultural economists from North and South America, Europe and Australia. The symposium began with a keynote address by D. Gale Johnson, widely recognized as the world's leading authority on international commodity markets. This book consists of peer-reviewed and edited versions of the papers presented at the symposium. While discussants' comments from the symposium are not published, the authors have taken the discussants' comments into account in revising their papers.

The book provides a detailed overview of recent and future likely developments in worldwide wheat markets among major exporting countries and importing countries. Country-specific developments are then investigated for Russia and China, the two countries whose roles in world wheat markets have been changing most rapidly since the late 1980s and 1990s, and for major exporting countries, including the USA, the European Union (EU), Canada, Argentina and Australia. In addition, the effects of the General Agreement on Tariffs and Trade (GATT), North American Free Trade Agreement (NAFTA), and MERCOSUR international trade agreements, which have been particularly important for developments in world wheat markets, are examined. The consequences of developments in both international markets and the USA and Canada for US grain producers are then evaluated. The primary goal of the book, therefore, is to provide the reader with a detailed understanding of the key economic issues concerning world wheat markets and to provide insights about the consequences of current and future developments in the economic performance of those markets.

An important secondary goal of this volume is to introduce the reader to analytical techniques currently being developed to analyse wheat commodity market behaviour. For the most part, authors include technical discussions in appendices or guide the reader to other sources for more technical material and are targeted towards the more general reader. Two of the chapters included in the volume develop new methods and models to examine the short-term (day-to-day) dynamics of wheat (Chapter 5) and the behaviour of state trading companies (Chapter 11). These two chapters are targeted towards a more technical audience.

The first part of the volume consists of six chapters. These chapters provide the reader with insights into the general behaviour of world wheat markets. In Chapter 1, the editors provide the reader with an introduction to the economics of world wheat markets and describe their performance using recent data. D. Gale Johnson (Chapter 2) outlines the historical development of world wheat markets and explains the long-term behaviour of real (inflation-adjusted) world wheat prices. He argues, in contradistinction to the suggestions of some commenters, that there is considerable scope for expansion in world wheat production and that world wheat prices are more likely to fall than to increase in real terms over the next 20 to 40 years. This is especially the case in Africa where shifts in domestic agricultural and general economic policies to improve incentives for farmers, by reducing agricultural taxation and improving the functioning of markets, could have substantial effects on both planted areas and yields.

Professor Johnson's optimism about the availability to the world's poor, at declining rather than increasing prices, of grains in general and wheat in particular is to some degree buttressed by the insights provided by John Antle *et al.* (Chapter 3). These authors observe that, despite occasional spikes associated with periods of shortage, world wheat prices have steadily declined in real terms since the 1860s. They then consider whether the price increases that occurred in 1995 and 1996 presage the beginning of a watershed period in which wheat prices will steadily increase over the next 10 to 20 years. They review the predictions of four major international agricultural forecast models – the Food and Agricultural Policy Research Institute (FAPRI) baseline model, the Organization for Economic Cooperation and Development (OECD) AGLINK model, the United States Department of Agriculture (USDA) baseline projections, and the International Food Policy Research Institute (IFPRI) IMPACT model. All of these models indicate that in real terms wheat prices will either remain relatively constant or decrease over the next 5 to 20 years. There are considerable uncertainties, however, about developments on both the supply side and the demand side of world wheat markets. The authors therefore adjust the FAPRI model to look at two extreme cases. The first assumed that import demand growth would be more rapid and supply growth less rapid than in the FAPRI baseline; the second assumed exactly the opposite. In neither of these 'extreme' cases do forecasted long-run trend prices change more than about 15% relative to the baseline, a finding that suggests a new and persistent upward trend in world wheat prices is unlikely to occur over the next 10 to 20 years. The analysis leads to the conclusion that real wheat prices are likely to fluctuate with the range predicted by a simple time-trend model estimated with wheat price data for the latter half of the 20th century.

World wheat stocks appear to have had important implications for world wheat prices since the 1950s. Carter *et al.* (Chapter 4) examine the relationship between the ratio of stocks to world consumption and price levels. They provide evidence that, in common with other grain commodities such as rice and maize, in world wheat markets declines in stocks-to-use ratios have had smaller (although still substantial) effects on prices in the 1990s than in previous decades. They hypothesize that the moderate decline in the link between stocks and prices is associated with (a) the increased integration of world markets in the 1990s as a result of regional and multilateral trade agreements such as the GATT, NAFTA and MERCOSUR, and (b) changes in the domestic policies of major grain exporters such as the USA that have reduced government-held stocks and at the same time reduced interventions that stabilize domestic market prices but destabilize international market prices. The paper by Bobenrieth and Wright (Chapter 5) examines the link between stocks and very short-run (hour-to-hour and day-to-day) movements in wheat prices. Their results indicate that stocks may also be important in this setting.

The first part of the book concludes with an examination by Robert Herdt of the potential for expanded food grain (wheat, maize and rice) production through biotechnology research and development (Chapter 6). He notes that currently over 90% of all agricultural investments in genetic research and other biotechnologies are being made in industrialized countries such as the USA. If biotechnology is to provide substantial contributions to increases in yields in developing countries then much larger investments will have to be made to fund biotechnology research and development relevant to those countries. In the short to medium term, however, conventional technological innovations are likely to continue to be the basis of most yield gains in grains, with the possible exception of rice.

Part II of the book examines state trading and import demand stability in two countries that were major wheat importing regions in the late 1980s and early 1990s, China and the former Soviet Union. Scott Rozelle and Jikun Huang (Chapter 7) appraise future trends in wheat production, consumption, and net imports in China utilizing an econometric model of China's grains market. While their conclusions are contingent on the rate at which China continues to invest in agricultural research and technology development and the continued rate of urbanization of the Chinese population, Rozelle and Huang find that under the most likely scenarios China's role in world wheat markets will remain that of a net importer whose purchases from other countries will be similar to what they were in the early and mid-1990s. In a typical production year, China is likely to import between 6 and 14 million tonnes per year (5–13% of total world wheat exports), although in some years China's wheat imports may be considerably lower than 6 million tonnes. This contrasts with some predictions that China may import as much as 30 to 40 million tonnes by 2010.

The future role of Russia in world wheat markets is examined by Barry Goodwin and Thomas Grennes (Chapter 8). In the late 1980s and early 1990s, Russia and other member countries of the former Soviet Union were large net importers of wheat, purchasing between 9 and 15% of total world exports. Goodwin and Grennes provide compelling evidence that Russia's role has changed dramatically since then. They provide evidence that, since the liberalization of market forces in the early 1990s, price and income elasticities of demand for food products have increased. The removal of price subsidies, coupled with declining real incomes, has therefore reduced the demand for livestock and other food products in the mid-1990s. The result has been the liquidation of considerable proportions of both the national cattle and pig herds with the result that domestic demand for wheat as feed has declined sharply. Russia is now, therefore, no longer a major importer of wheat and in the late 1990s its annual net imports have declined to between 1 and 2 million tonnes from 10 to 12 million tonnes in the early 1990s. Nor is Russia likely to return to its role of a major net exporter. Goodwin and Grennes argue that economic reform has had little effect on agricultural productivity in the early and mid-1990s but that Russian agricultural producers have considerable potential to increase yields if economic incentives improve as efficient transportation and marketing systems develop. Thus it is quite possible that the former Soviet Union will be a net exporter of wheat in the first decade of the third millennium.

The papers presented in Part II provide strong supporting evidence for the conclusions by Johnson (Chapter 2) and Antle *et al.* (Chapter 3) that world wheat prices are unlikely to increase persistently in real terms over the next 10 to 20 years. One of the two countries that were major importers in the early and mid-1990s, China, is unlikely to expand its wheat imports and the other, Russia, may completely change its role from that of a major importer to a net exporter.

Part III of the book focuses on three of the five major exporting countries – Canada, Australia and the EU – and the potential effects of current provisions and possible future innovations in the GATT on wheat exports from those countries. Wheat exports from Canada and

Australia are in both cases managed by state trading enterprises organized as monopoly export marketing boards: the Canadian Wheat Board (CWB) and the Australian Wheat Board (AWB). Colin Carter and William Wilson (Chapter 9) examine changes in the structure and operation of these export marketing agencies since the late 1980s. They argue that both of these export marketing boards have operated inefficiently, with atypically large marketing and other grain-handling costs, at least in part because of political objectives. These inefficiencies undermine the benefits that may accrue to producers in those countries from the practice of monopoly price discrimination by those agencies. In Australia, over the past decade, the AWB has largely removed itself from the control and management of grain movements within the country. This has resulted in improved grain-handling efficiency. This has not been the case in Canada. Both countries' export marketing boards may face difficulties in the next round of multilateral trade policy negotiations under the World Trade Organization if price discrimination by state trading enterprises is addressed in the agricultural negotiations.

The EU has contributed between 15% and 22% of total world exports in the early and mid-1990s. Tony Rayner *et al.* (Chapter 10) examine the implications of the 1994 GATT agricultural provisions for EU wheat exports. Utilizing a small-scale econometric model of the EU cereals market, Rayner *et al.* show that the EU is on a 'knife edge' with respect to meeting its obligations under the 1994 GATT agreement to reduce the volume of EU-subsidized wheat exports by 20% and the value of the export subsidies paid to wheat producers by 36%. They conclude that if the EU is to comply with these commitments under the current GATT then further reform of the Common Agricultural Policy will be needed to reduce incentives for farmers to produce wheat.

The final paper in Part III provides a theoretical analysis of optimal strategies by monopoly state trading export agencies. Tigran Melkonian and Stanley Johnson (Chapter 11) argue that the operations of monopoly wheat export agencies such as the CWB can be modelled effectively using a game theory approach. Their results suggest that CWB strategies to differentiate Canadian wheat on the basis of quality may be optimal over the long run but may also impose significant welfare costs on different groups within the country.

Part IV of the book is concerned with the effects of economic integration and policy convergence and harmonization on wheat markets within the Western Hemisphere, both in North America and in South America. Bruce Gardner (Chapter 12) examines the issue of how far North America currently is from establishing a single continent-wide market for wheat. He concludes that, as a result of the Canada–US Free Trade Agreement implemented in 1989 and the North American Free Trade Agreement implemented in 1994, in many respects the Canadian and US grain sectors are well integrated. However, while aggregate measures of government support for wheat producers are quite similar in the two countries, the policies used to provide that support are very different. The result is that the wheat markets in the two countries are not integrated in the sense that wheat prices differ only by market-driven forces such as transportation costs.

The effects of economic integration under MERCOSUR and other Latin American country trade liberalization initiatives are examined by Eugenio Diaz-Bonilla (Chapter 13). In the 1980s and 1990s South America has generally been a net importer of wheat and wheat products such as flour. Diaz-Bonilla's analysis indicates that this is likely to continue to be the case over the next decade largely because increases in production within the region will be matched by increases in consumption driven by both population growth and increasing per capita incomes. The main effects of MERCOSUR are likely to be on the patterns of trade in wheat between Brazil and Argentina. Historically, Argentina has exported considerable amounts of feed wheat to the former Soviet Union. In the 1990s, as this market has diminished, MERCOSUR has provided Argentina with a tariff advantage over Canada, the USA and the EU in the Brazilian market. As a result, trade between Argentina and Brazil has expanded in the mid-1990s and this trend is likely to continue.

Part V examines the linkages between domestic and international trade policies and markets for wheat producers in the North American Great Plains. Prices received at the farm gate for wheat are not port-of-exit prices. Farmers confront a basis problem; the prices they receive are net of the costs of storing, cleaning, transporting and marketing wheat to domestic and international consumers. The basis paid by both US and Canadian farmers in the Northern Great Plains amounts to between \$30 and \$40 a tonne or between 15 and 30% of export prices (depending on the variety and class of wheat and the general level of wheat prices). A substantial portion of this basis consists of rail, road and/or barge transportation costs from farm to port. In many cases, both in Canada and the USA rail transportation is the only viable means of shipment but in the USA the lines along which wheat is shipped are monopolized by one company. In Canada, currently two railroads ship wheat – freight rates on those routes are regulated by the government, and proposals for rate deregulation have been proposed. Murray Fulton and Richard Gray (Chapter 14) examine alternative regulatory regimes that would separate ownership of track, the source of the monopoly, from access to the track by competitive operators. They conclude that such an approach may potentially result in lower freight rates than the private monopoly market structure that currently prevails in the USA.

Quality premiums are also important in world wheat markets. Protein premiums, for example, have steadily increased since the early

1980s as milling and baking techniques have become more sophisticated. William Wilson and Bruce Dahl (Chapter 15) investigate the extent to which export markets have become more concerned with quality attributes. Their findings indicate that export markets for US wheat have shifted towards higher-quality varieties and classes of wheat, although the implications for quality premiums are unclear.

The final two chapters in this part examine the linkages between changes in international market conditions and domestic policies and farm-level behaviour, utilizing the FAPRI 'optimistic' and 'pessimistic' scenarios to conduct farm-level simulations. Won Koo (Chapter 16) presents a representative farm framework for evaluating the impact of changes in market conditions and policies on the profitability and financial viability of grain producers in North Dakota. John Antle *et al.* (Chapter 17) examine how changes in world wheat market conditions may affect cost of production, net returns, and land use in Montana wheat and barley production. Both analyses conclude that long-term trends in grain prices will continue to put smaller, marginal producers at economic risk, but that wheat and barley production will remain profitable for larger-scale, efficient producers. Thus, the Northern Great Plains region will continue to be a major source of US wheat exports for the foreseeable future. The volume's final chapter, by the editors, synthesizes the findings and raises questions that need to be addressed by future research.

John M. Antle
Vincent H. Smith

1

An Overview of Future Development of World Wheat Markets

1

An Overview of World Wheat Markets

John M. Antle and Vincent H. Smith

Department of Agricultural Economics and Economics and Trade Research Center, Montana State University–Bozeman, USA

1. Introduction

Wheat is consumed and produced in almost every country in the world. Globally, along with rice, wheat is one of the world's two most important food grains, consumed by households in a myriad of different types of breads, biscuits, cakes and other baked goods, breakfast cereals, noodles and pasta. As a feed grain, wheat is an important source of animal nutrition. Wheat is also produced on a global basis, both north and south of the equator, in a wide variety of agroclimatic zones. Major producing areas include semiarid regions such as the Great Plains of North America, the Steppes of the Ukraine, the Mediterranean rim of North Africa, and some provinces in China. It is also raised in much wetter and cooler environments in Northern Europe and Central Europe, in many South American countries, and in the perpetually warm environments of tropical Africa and India.

Perfect matches between domestic wheat production and consumption within a country are relatively rare. Moreover, wheat is not simply wheat. Different classes of wheat generally have different end uses, are grown in different regions and countries, and are far from perfect substitutes. Soft white wheats tend to have a relatively low protein content and are widely used for cake and biscuit products. Hard red and hard white wheats tend to have a higher protein content and are widely used for bread making and noodles. Durum wheats are used to make pasta products. These different wheats also tend to be raised in different countries and regions. As a result, international trade in wheat is extensive. In the 1990s, total world wheat exports have averaged about 100 million tonnes per year, representing approximately one-sixth of total world wheat production, which, in 1997/98, was over 600 million tonnes.

World trade in wheat is substantial and world wheat markets are complex. Wheat's importance as a major food grain, and extensive political activity on the part of producer interest groups, has led many governments to implement widely varying domestic and international trade policies that have significant impacts on domestic and international wheat markets. The objective of this book is to examine the economics of world wheat markets and how policy interventions by individual countries affect the ways in which those markets function through sixteen studies of key aspects of the world's wheat economy. The purpose of this introductory chapter is to provide an overview of world wheat production, consumption and trade, and the institutions through which world wheat markets function. These include the major commodity exchanges on which trades in wheat are implemented and the grain-handling system that transports wheat from the producer to the processor and, eventually, the final consumer. We begin by examining trends in world wheat production, consumption, trade and end-of-year stocks since 1960. Next, we investigate the competitive structure of the world wheat market in terms of major wheat producers, exporters, and importers. We then describe the institutions involved in wheat handling, wheat marketing and the process by which wheat is marketed and transported.

2. Recent Trends in World Wheat Production, Consumption, Trade, Stocks and Prices

Data on world production, consumption, trade and end-of-year stocks for the period 1960/61 to 1997/98 are presented in Table 1.1 and Fig. 1.1. In the 1960/61 production year, world production of wheat was 233.5 million tonnes, world consumption was 230.9 million tonnes, total world exports were 41.9 million tonnes (approximately 18% of world production), and world end-of-year stocks were 82.8 million tonnes, implying a stocks-to-use ratio of 35.8%. By 1997/98, world production had increased by 261% to 609.4 million tonnes at an annual rate of about 2.6%, world consumption had increased by about the same proportion to 585.7 million tonnes, total world exports were 98.2 million tonnes (approximately 16% of world production) and world end-of-year stocks were 147.6 million tonnes, implying a stocks-to-use ratio of 28%.

Most of the increase in world wheat production over the past 40 years has resulted from improved yields. Data on harvested wheat areas and average per hectare yields are presented in Table 1.2. In the 1960/61

Table 1.1. World production, consumption, trade and stocks, 1961–1998 (in million tonnes).

	Production	Consumption	Trade	Stocks
1961	234	231	42	83
1962	220	233	47	70
1963	247	241	44	76
1964	230	236	56	70
1965	265	257	52	79
1966	259	277	61	61
1967	301	274	56	88
1968	292	282	51	98
1969	324	300	45	121
1970	304	322	50	104
1971	307	330	55	81
1972	344	335	52	89
1973	338	352	70	75
1974	366	358	63	83
1975	355	357	64	81
1976	353	347	67	87
1977	414	374	63	127
1978	378	396	73	109
1979	439	413	72	135
1980	418	432	86	121
1981	436	444	94	114
1982	445	445	101	114
1983	473	456	99	131
1984	484	469	104	147
1985	509	489	106	166
1986	495	490	85	171
1987	524	516	91	179
1988	496	527	116	148
1989	495	524	105	118
1990	533	533	104	119
1991	588	562	101	145
1992	543	556	111	133
1993	562	550	112	145
1994	559	562	100	142
1995	525	548	98	118
1996	538	551	96	105
1997	583	578	98	110
1998	609	586	98	133

Source: USDA, 1998.

production year, globally 202.3 million ha of wheat were harvested; by 1997/98, this figure had increased by 229.2 million ha, an expansion of only about 13% in land area allocated to wheat production. In contrast,

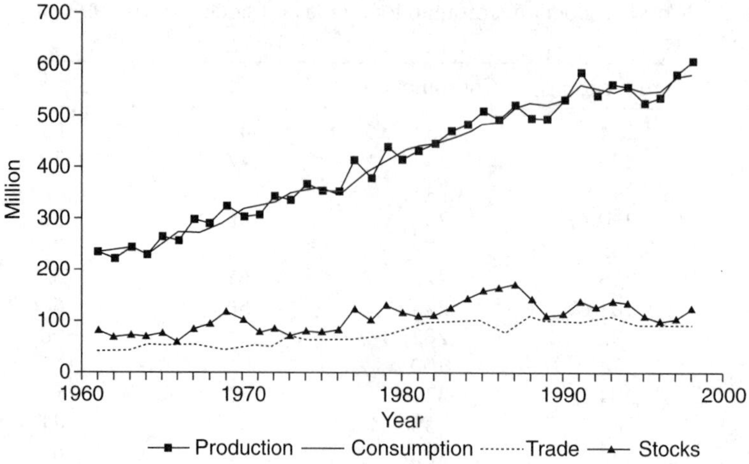

Fig. 1.1. World wheat production, consumption, trade and stocks, 1961–1998.

over the same period, globally wheat yields more than doubled, increasing from an average of 1.15 tonnes per ha (17.1 bushels per acre) in 1960/61 to 2.66 tonnes per ha (33.61 bushels per acre) in 1997/98. These yield increases can be largely attributed to an ongoing series of technical innovations resulting from public and private agricultural research, including the development of semi-dwarf and hybrid wheat varieties during and subsequent to the green revolution of the 1960s, innovations in machinery and equipment (for example, air seed drills and computer technologies), improvements in the quality of agricultural chemicals (fertilizers, fungicides and pesticides), and improved management practices (Alston *et al.*, 1998). The impacts of technical innovation on world wheat markets and the potential for further gains in yields are discussed in some detail by D. Gale Johnson in Chapter 2 and Robert Herdt in Chapter 6.

It is not surprising that increases in world wheat production have been matched by similar increases in world wheat consumption. If world wheat markets operate with any reasonable degree of efficiency, adjustments in prices will bring quantities demanded into line with quantities supplied. An interesting question, therefore, is what has happened to wheat prices over the past 40 years. World wheat prices, represented by the US dollar-denominated free-on-board (f.o.b.) Gulf of Mexico export price for US Hard Red Spring No. 2, are presented in Fig. 1.2, where they have been converted to constant 1996 dollars using the US gross domestic product (GDP) deflator price index. Figure 1.2 shows that, in real (inflation-adjusted) terms, world wheat prices have fallen over the past 40 years while exhibiting considerable year-to-year variability closely associated

Table 1.2. World production, planted acres and average yields.

Crop year	Planted acres (million ha)	World production (million tonnes)	Yield (tonnes per ha)
1960/61	202.3	241.1	1.15
1970/71	207.0	306.5	1.48
1975/76	225.3	352.6	1.56
1980/81	237.1	436.3	1.86
1985/86	229.9	494.9	2.15
1990/91	231.4	588.0	2.54
1995/96	219.8	538.1	2.45
1997/98[a]	229.6	609.7[a]	2.66[a]

[a] Estimated yields and output and repeated for 1997/98.
Source: USDA, 1999.

with yield and output variability. In years when average yields and world production rise much above their long-run trends, prices tend to decrease quite sharply; when average yields and world production fall much below their long-run trends, prices tend to rise quite sharply. Over the long run, however, increases in supply have outstripped increases in demand, resulting in lower real prices for wheat and improvements in consumer welfare. John Antle *et al.* provide a detailed examination of current and likely future world wheat price trends in Chapter 3.

Much has been made by some market analysts of the relationship between wheat stocks and wheat prices. Figure 1.2 also shows the end-of-year world stocks-to-use ratio for wheat. When wheat stocks decline

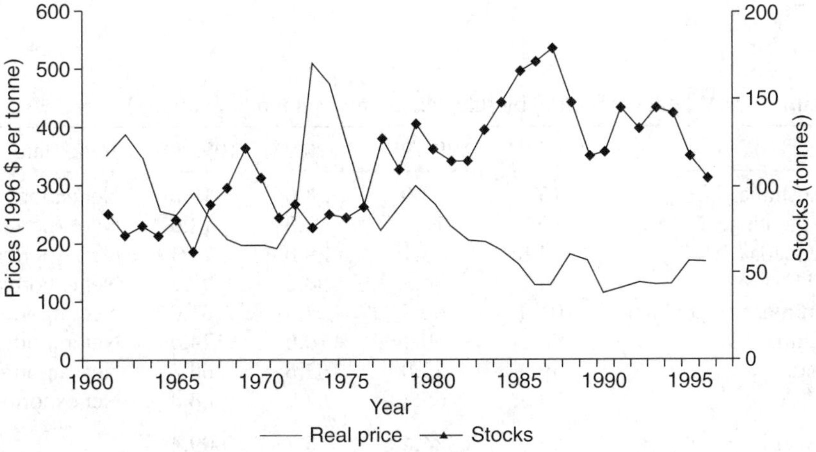

Fig. 1.2. Real world wheat prices and world stocks-to-use ratio, 1961–1996.

sharply relative to use, Fig. 1.2 suggests that wheat prices tend to increase. However, the relationship between stocks-to-use ratios and prices does not appear to have been stable over the past 40 years. In the early 1970s, a decrease in the world stocks-to-use ratio from about 33% to 22% was associated with a more than 300% increase in wheat prices. In the mid-1990s a similar decrease in the world stocks-to-use ratio was associated with only a 60% increase in wheat prices. The issue of the role of stocks is addressed in detail by Colin Carter, Cesar Revoredo, and Vincent Smith in Chapter 4 while the role of wheat stocks in the short run is discussed by Eugenio Bobenrieth and Brian Wright in Chapter 5.

Countries that are major producers of wheat are also, for the most part, major consumers of wheat. Table 1.3 shows wheat production and trade status for selected countries in 1995 and 1998. In both years, China was both the largest producer and consumer of wheat in the world, followed by India, the European Union (EU), the former Soviet Union and the USA. China plays a particularly important role in world wheat markets, producing over 100 million tonnes of wheat in most years and usually consuming somewhat more than that. The extent to which increases in China's wheat consumption outstrip increases in its production will have important ramifications for world wheat markets and world wheat prices. Some analysts have suggested that China will be importing as much as 40 million tonnes of wheat by 2010; others are more sceptical. Scott Rozelle and Jikun Huang provide a careful evaluation of China's current and future role in world wheat markets in Chapter 7. Russia and other former Soviet Union countries are also major producers and consumers of wheat whose role in world wheat markets is changing. Barry Goodwin and Tom Grennes examine recent developments and likely future trends in the former Soviet Union in Chapter 8.

Table 1.3. Wheat production by selected countries (in million tonnes).

	1990/91	1994/95	1996/97	1997/98	Trade status
Australia	15.1	8.9	23.6	19.0	Net exporter
Argentina	10.9	11.3	15.9	13.9	Net exporter
Canada	24.8	23.1	29.8	24.3	Net exporter
EU	89.1	84.5	98.6	95.2	Net exporter
Former Soviet Union	101.9	60.7	4.3	81.0	Net importer
China	98.2	99.3	110.6	124.0	Net importer
India	49.9	59.8	62.6	68.7	Net importer
USA	74.3	65.2	62.2	68.8	Net exporter
World	588.0	524.6	578.2	609.4	

Source: USDA, 1998.

3. The Structure of World Wheat Trade

Since at least the 18th century international trade has been an important component of the world wheat economy, although patterns of trade in wheat have not been stable over the very long run. In the late 18th and early 19th centuries, for example, most trade in wheat took place between European countries, with Britain, France and Russia most often being net exporters. Beginning in the 1860s, however, the world wheat economy experienced an important shock as the expansion of the railway system in the USA and Canada opened up the Northern Great Plains to dryland wheat production, and Canada and the USA became important sources of world exports. In the first half of the 20th century, Communism and collectivization devastated the functioning of grain markets and grain production in the former Soviet Union and, after World War II, in other central European countries such as Poland. As a result, instead of being a major net exporter of wheat, as it was in the early 1900s, Russia and its satellite countries had become frequent large net importers by the 1960s and 1970s. In addition, during the 19th century, increases in population and per capita incomes, decreases in grain prices associated with the western expansion in North America, and very modest agricultural productivity growth rates turned Northern European countries such as Britain from net exporters to net importers of wheat.

More recently, over the period 1960 to 1998, annual world exports and imports of wheat have increased by almost 250% from 41.9 million tonnes to about 100 million tonnes (Table 1.1) at a slightly slower rate than world production and the share of annual total world wheat production traded between countries declined from 18% to 16%. During this entire period, the USA, Canada and Australia have consistently been important wheat exporters. In the late 1970s and 1980s, however, the EU shifted from being a small net importer of wheat to a large net exporter and Argentina's wheat exports also increased. The EU's pivotal role in world wheat markets is investigated by Anthony Rayner *et al.* in Chapter 10, while recent developments in Argentina and other South American wheat markets, including the importance of MERCOSUR (the Southern Common Market that currently consists of Brazil, Argentina, Uruguay and Paraguay), are discussed by Eugenio Diaz-Bonilla in Chapter 13. Another feature of the period 1960 to 1998 has been the increasing importance of developing countries as consumers in world wheat markets. This issue is taken up by D. Gale Johnson and John Antle *et al.*

Exporting countries

Exports by the five major countries and their export market shares for the crop marketing years 1996/97 and 1997/98 (which run from 1 July to 30 June) are presented in Fig. 1.3. In both years, these five countries jointly provided about 90% of total world wheat exports. The USA had the largest share of total world exports (27% in 1996/97 and 28.1% in 1997/98), followed by Canada (18.2% in 1996/97 and 21.3% in 1997/98), Australia (18.2% in 1996/97 and 15.5% in 1997/98), the EU (17.8% in 1996/97 and 15.5% in 1997/98) and Argentina (10% in 1996/97 and 9.4% in 1997/98).

There is no systematic link between the relative importance of a country as a wheat producer and its status as a major wheat exporter. Table 1.3 shows that the USA and the EU produce substantial proportions of total world wheat output (11.3% and 15.6% respectively in 1997/98) but that Argentina, Australia and Canada each produce less than 5% of world output. Australia, Canada and Argentina are all countries with relatively small domestic populations and relatively low levels of domestic wheat consumption that export most of the wheat they produce. The USA and the EU both have much larger populations and utilize much larger proportions of their domestic wheat output for human consumption and animal feed but still export substantial

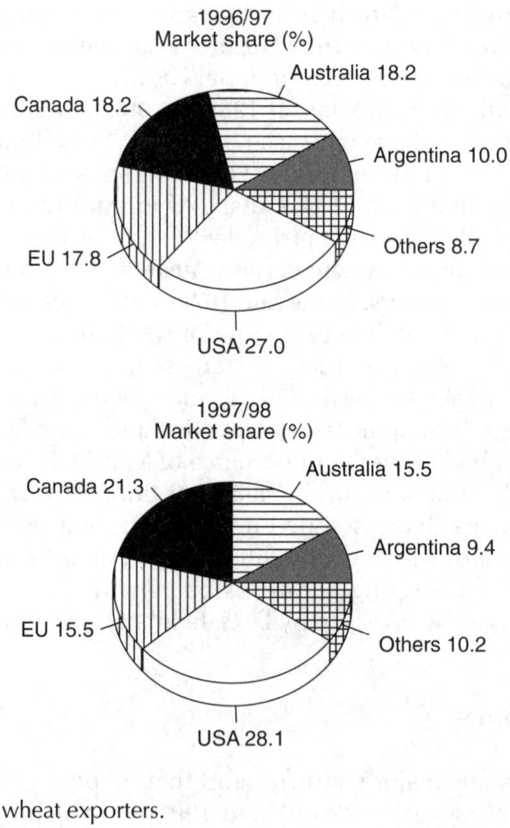

Fig. 1.3. Major wheat exporters.

amounts of wheat (about 40% of domestic production in the USA and about 30% of domestic production in the EU).

The export side of the world wheat market is now, therefore, dominated by five countries and, as noted above, in the 1960s and 1970s used to be dominated by three countries. Some economists have therefore been concerned that international trade patterns in wheat have been distorted through the exercise of market power in an oligopoly market setting. Alouze *et al.* (1978) for example, argued that in the 1960s and 1970s the world wheat market could be characterized as a monopoly operated by a three-country cartel consisting of Australia, Canada and the USA while, earlier, McCalla (1966) suggested that the world wheat market could be viewed as a duopoly consisting of the USA and Canada. More recently, others have suggested that Canada, through the Canadian Wheat Board (the single-desk export and domestic marketing agency for western Canadian wheat and barley), and Australia, through the Australian Wheat Board (AWB, which is also an export marketing board), have exercised some market power *vis-à-vis* importers, albeit in the context of an oligopoly market structure. Ironically, the Canadian Wheat Board (CWB) has itself laid claim to such market power in order to justify its continued existence (Kraft *et al.*, 1996) although others are more sceptical about the degree of that market power and the extent to which either the CWB or the AWB has been able to obtain monopoly profits from its operations in world wheat markets (see, for example, Carter and Loyns, 1996). The functions and roles of the AWB and the CWB in world markets are described and discussed by Carter and Wilson in Chapter 9.

Importing countries

Import market shares for major wheat-importing countries are presented in Fig. 1.4 for the crop years 1996/97 and 1997/98; import volumes for these countries are presented in Table 1.4 for these and early years. The structure of the import side of the world wheat market is very different from the structure of the export side. In 1997/98, over 80 different countries imported wheat and the market share held by the largest importer, Japan, was only 6.2%. Moreover, only ten countries had import market shares in excess of 2%, and over 53.3% of total world exports were purchased by about 70 countries with market shares of less than 2%. A similar pattern pertained in 1996/97 although during the early and mid-1990s both the former Soviet Union and China imported substantial quantities of wheat and had import market shares in excess of 10%.

These data suggest that the import side of the world wheat market is competitive. However, appearances can be deceptive. At the

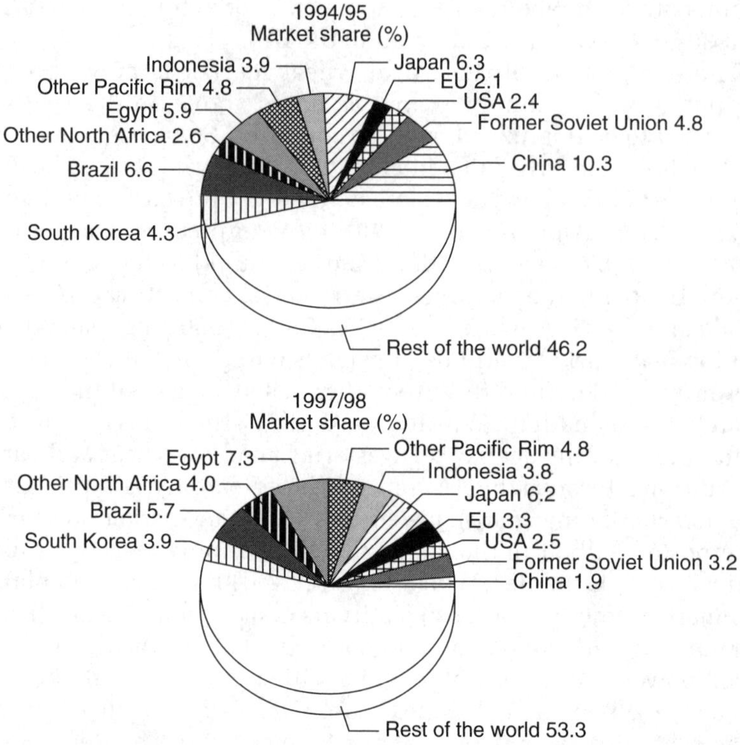

Fig. 1.4. Major wheat importers.

beginning of the 1990s many wheat-importing countries purchased grain through monopsony state trading agencies in the form of import marketing boards. While the prevalence of state-operated import marketing agencies has declined in the 1990s, monopsony import purchasing agencies still operate in some relatively important wheat-importing countries including China, Japan, South Korea, and Russia. Several economists have suggested that some of these agencies have been quite successful in utilizing their market power as single purchasers in world markets and monopoly sellers in domestic markets both in raising revenues for the government and in increasing market prices for domestic producers (see, for example, Love and Murningtyas, 1992). Tigran Melkonian and Stan Johnson examine the incentives and optimal purchasing and marketing strategies of such state trading enterprises in Chapter 11.

Another interesting feature of the import side of the world wheat market has been the growth of wheat imports by Pacific Rim countries such as Indonesia and Thailand in the early and mid-1990s and the relative stability of wheat imports in the Pacific Rim region between

Table 1.4. Wheat imports by selected countries (in million tonnes).

Importing country	1994/95	1995/96	1996/97	1997/98
EU	2.1	2.5	2.4	3.0
Former Soviet Union	7.7	9.4	6.3	6.0
Japan	6.3	6.1	6.3	6.2
Eastern Europe	1.9	1.6	3.6	1.3
China	10.2	12.5	2.8	2.0
Algeria	5.7	3.4	3.6	4.8
Brazil	6.5	5.5	5.2	5.7
Egypt	5.9	5.9	7.0	7.2
South Korea	6.3	2.6	3.5	3.8
Morocco	1.2	2.4	1.5	2.4
Indonesia	3.8	3.6	4.2	4.5
Philippines	2.1	2.0	2.2	2.1
USA	2.4	1.7	2.6	2.5
Others	36.1	36.3	46.5	46.7
World	98.2	95.5	97.7	98.2

1996/97, the marketing year immediately prior to the 1997 Asian financial and economic crisis, and 1997/98. Table 1.4 shows that wheat imports by Pacific Rim countries (other than China) changed very little between those two years, suggesting either that income effects on the demand for wheat in those countries are very small or that a hysteresis effect exists; that is, increases in income in those countries may have resulted in increases in wheat demand but, because of somewhat permanent shifts in taste and preferences, subsequent decreases in incomes may have very modest short-run effects on wheat demand.

Finally, it should be noted that, as on the export side of the market, there is no obvious link between a country's relative importance as a wheat producer and its role as a wheat consumer. China is the largest wheat-producing country in the world but, in the 1990s, has also frequently been the largest importer. Similarly, both India and the former Soviet Union are major wheat producers but also net wheat importers. On the other hand Japan and Egypt produce relatively small proportions of world wheat output but are relatively important wheat importers. What matters in all of these countries is simply that domestic wheat production is smaller than domestic wheat consumption in most years.

Summary

In general, the world market for wheat can be characterized as consisting of a few large wheat exporters and many relatively small wheat importers.

13

…nce of single-desk selling and buying on the part of …mporters may have resulted in some degree of …the export and the import sides of the market.

…ket Institutions

Wheat is sold for processing into commodities for human consumption – milling wheat – and for use as animal feed – feed wheat. Feed wheat is usually of much lower quality than milling wheat, generally containing less protein and gluten while including higher proportions of broken kernels and foreign matter or trash. Milling wheat is generally of higher quality, with higher protein and more desirable gluten content and, because of more thorough cleaning, fewer broken kernels and a lower trash content. This section examines the nature of the marketing chain for wheat and the ways in which prices for wheats with different characteristics are established.

The marketing chain

The United States Department of Agriculture (USDA) estimates that in the USA only nine cents of every dollar spent by households on products that include wheat are received by producers. Similar relationships also hold in other developed countries. This implies a complex set of relationships in the marketing chain that links the wheat farmer and the final consumer through a grain-handling and processing sector that uses many inputs.

The marketing chain for export wheat can be viewed as having four sections, each of which has several links.

1. Transportation from the farm to the port of exit, including storage and cleaning of the exportable product and, in some cases, milling into flour or other semi-finished products for export.
2. International shipment from the port of exit to the port of entry in the importing country.
3. In-country shipment to the domestic milling facility.
4. Processing, distribution and marketing of final products.

The marketing chain for wheat to be consumed in the country of origin can be viewed as having two sections.

1. Transportation from the farm to the domestic processing facility, including storage and some cleaning of the wheat.
2. Cleaning, processing, distribution and marketing of final products.

In both cases, the marketing chain provides important services that change the time, space and form dimensions of wheat. The focus here is on the first links of these chains: storage and transshipment from the farm to the port of exit or the domestic milling facility.

The concept of *basis* is important in commodity markets. The basis is the difference between the price paid by purchasers of an agricultural commodity at the port of exit or on a major commodity exchange that identifies a common delivery point (such as the Chicago Board of Trade, the Kansas City Board of Trade, or the Minneapolis Grain Exchange) and the price received by the farmer at the local county elevator. In the case of wheat, the basis represents the charges levied for storage, transportation and cleaning of the product before delivery to either a domestic buyer or a foreign buyer at a specified physical location. The basis faced by farmers in different locations is often very different. Within the USA, for example, wheat farmers in the state of Washington are much closer to the Pacific North West export ports of Portland and Tacoma than farmers in central Montana. Producers in the state of Washington therefore face a much lower basis than producers in central Montana because of substantially lower transportation charges.

In many developed countries, wheat produced by farmers is usually first placed in on-farm storage facilities to facilitate their marketing strategies (it often pays to wait a while between harvesting and marketing grain). When farmers market their grain, usually they sell their wheat to local storage facilities, called country elevators in the USA and Canada, rather than through direct contracts with milling companies (although some niche marketing of grain does occur and has expanded in the 1990s as the organic food market has grown). These storage facilities may be owned by independent operators, farmer cooperatives, or large grain-handling corporations. In most situations, farmers have the option of selling their wheat to several competing country elevators and this section of the wheat marketing chain is not usually characterized by monopsony market power. In Canada and the USA, country elevators are located either along rail lines or navigable rivers so that wheat may be shipped by rail or barge, both of which are modes of transport with considerable cost advantages over trucking for longer-haul shipments to export terminals or domestic milling facilities.

Competition among and within alternative long-haul transportation modes for wheat is an important issue for wheat producers in North America. Currently, there are only four major long-haul rail companies in the USA and only two in Canada, where grain haulage rates are regulated by the government. In the USA, in regions where the big four rail companies compete with one another or with barge companies, rail freight rates (on a km per tonne basis) are as much as 50% lower than in other regions where one rail company operates and faces no barge competition. Freight charges account for the bulk of the basis deduction faced by most US and Canadian wheat producers. In many locations in the Northern Plains states of the USA, for example, basis deductions amount to as much as $40 per tonne, of which between $20 and $30 are accounted for by rail freight charges. Given that wheat prices at US ports of export range from about $120 to about $180 per tonne in most years, reductions or increases in basis charges of between $5 and $15 per tonne would lead to changes in farm-gate prices of between 4% and 12%. The issue of competition in the grain transport industry and its implications for basis charges are examined by Murray Fulton and Richard Gray in Chapter 14.

World wheat prices

Wheat is not a homogeneous commodity. Different countries have different systems for differentiating wheats with different quality characteristics. In the USA, for example, wheat is divided into six major classes: Hard Red Spring, Hard Red Winter, Hard White, Soft Red Winter, Soft White, and Durum. Soft wheats tend to be closer substitutes for one another's uses than for hard wheats because of some differences in end uses. Durum wheats tend to be used for pasta products rather than bread, cakes, biscuits and other baking products.

Within each class, wheat is assigned to one of several different grades (in the USA, for example, wheat is classified into six grade categories). The grade assignment for any given shipment is based on several characteristics including test weight, moisture content, damaged kernels and purity. Within each class and grade, wheat is also evaluated for its gluten and protein content. At any given point in time, the price paid for a shipment of wheat varies with its class, grade and protein content; that is, different prices are quoted for wheats of the same class and grade but with different protein contents and for wheats of different classes and grades with the same protein contents. Table 1.5 provides examples of different cash or spot market prices for different classes and grades of wheat with different protein content quoted on the same day for exports from Pacific North West ports. William Wilson and Bruce Dahl examine the changing role of wheat quality in world demand for wheat exports from North America in Chapter 15.

In countries where wheat prices are linked to world market conditions, prices change from day to day in response to changes in prices quoted on major commodity exchanges where commodity traders, acting on behalf of grain-handling companies, milling companies, farmers, non-farm investors and speculators, and themselves, carry out extensive trades on a daily basis. The prices quoted on these commodity exchange markets are also influenced by off-commodity exchange trades between major buyers and sellers. For example, if the CWB signs a contract to ship 0.5 million tonnes of wheat to China's grain-importing state trading enterprise, prices on the

Table 1.5. Spot (cash) market prices for different varieties of wheat in the Pacific North West (Portland), 21 January 1999.

Class and grade of wheat		Price	
		$ per tonne	$ per bushel
Number 1	Hard Red Winter		
	Ordinary	129	3.51
	10% protein	129	3.51
	11% protein	129	3.51
	12% protein	137	3.72
	13% protein	143	3.88
Number 1	Dark Northern Spring		
	13% protein	148	4.02
	14% protein	160	4.30
	15% protein	163	4.43
Number 1	Soft White Wheat	112	3.05
Number 1	White Club Wheat	120	3.27

Source: *Billings Gazette*, 1999.

commodity exchanges will probably move upwards once the details of the deal become general knowledge.

Wheat is traded internationally on three major commodity exchanges in the USA: the Chicago Board of Trade, the Kansas City Board of Trade, and the Minneapolis Grain Exchange. These three commodity markets are generally regarded as establishing world wheat prices and wheat price movements across these markets are closely linked. All three commodity markets handle wheat as well as other agricultural and natural resource commodities.

Futures and options contracts for wheat are bought and sold on all three exchanges. A futures contract is a promise to deliver a fixed amount of a specific commodity at a fixed price to a specified place at a specified *future* point in time; for example, a contract signed on 1 September, 1999 may require delivery of 5000 tonnes of 14% protein Hard Red Wheat No. 2 to Kansas City on 15 June, 2000 at a price of $145 per tonne. An options contract provides the holder with the *option* to sell or buy a fixed amount of a specified commodity at a specified price at any time between the date on which the options contract is signed and the date on which the options contract expires. A 'sell' options contract is described as a *put*. A 'buy' options contract is described as a *call*.

The prices at which wheat is to be exchanged in both futures and options contracts reflect the consensus 'best guesses' of participants in the markets about what wheat prices will be at the time the contractual obligations must be fulfilled. If, on 1 September 1999, the price for 14% Hard Red Wheat is being quoted as $145 per tonne on 15 June, 2000 futures contracts, then $145 per tonne represents the market's best guess about what the price of that wheat will be on 15 June, 2000. If many traders in the market believed that futures price to be either too low or too high, they would either buy or sell the futures contract, driving the futures price to the level expected by most traders in the market. Futures markets therefore serve as important price discovery mechanisms for wheat producers.

Futures and options contracts are used by many farmers and processors to protect themselves against unexpected movements in wheat prices; that is, they allow farmers and processors to avoid price risk through hedging. Farmers who expect to have grain to sell from their harvests can use futures and/or options contracts to 'lock in' guaranteed prices at the time of planting or between planting and harvesting. Processors can also use futures and options contracts to lock in the prices they will have to pay for future deliveries of grain using these contracts. Some traders operate as speculators, taking gambles that actual prices will move above or below those offered in futures contracts. Others operate as arbitragers, seeking small per unit profits on relatively large-volume trades that exploit small discrepancies in prices offered for wheat across exchanges and across time.

Longer-run movements in world wheat prices are discussed in some detail by John Antle *et al.* in Chapter 3. Short-run movements in prices and the roles of futures and options contracts are examined by Bobenrieth and Wright in Chapter 5. Longer-run movements in international prices have important implications for local production decisions. The impacts of changes in world market conditions and domestic policies, as reflected by movements in world prices, input costs, and production options, on wheat producers in Northern America are examined by Won Koo in Chapter 16 and by John Antle *et al.* in Chapter 17.

5. Summary

This chapter has provided a brief overview of the historical development and current structure of world wheat markets. The marketing chains for wheat have been briefly described and key marketing institutions discussed. Particular attention has been given to the role of the storage and transportation system between the farmer and the port of export or domestic milling company. The purpose has been to provide the reader with a context within which to place the detailed research studies that follow. Throughout the chapter, key economic issues for world wheat markets and the studies included in this volume that examine those issues have been identified. The first of these, by Professor D. Gale Johnson, which is presented in the next chapter, provides a broad overview of the future of world wheat markets and their implications for North America.

References

Alouze, C.M., Watson, A.S. and Sturgess, N.H. (1978) Oligopoly pricing in the world wheat market. *American Journal of Agricultural Economics* 60, 173–185.

Alston, J.M., Pardey, P.G. and Smith, V.H. (1998) Financing agricultural R&D in rich countries: what's happening and why. *Australian Journal of Agricultural and Resource Economics* 42:1, 51–83.

Billings Gazette (1999) *The Billings Gazette*, Billings, MT, 21 January.

Carter, C.A. and Loyns, R.M.A. (1996) *The Economics of Single Desk Selling of Western Canadian Grain*. Alberta Department of Agriculture, Calgary, Canada.

Kraft, D.F., Furtan, W.H. and Tyrchniewicz, E.W. (1996) *Performance Evaluation of the Canadian Wheat Board*. Canadian Wheat Board, Winnipeg, Canada.

Love, H.A. and Murningtyas, E. (1992) Measuring the degree of market power exerted by government trade agencies. *American Journal of Agricultural Economics* 74, 546–555.

McCalla, A.F. (1966) A duopoly model of world wheat pricing. *American Journal of Agricultural Economics* 48, 711–727.

USDA (United States Department of Agriculture) (1998) *Wheat Yearbook*. Economic Research Service, WHS-1998, US Department of Agriculture, Washington DC, USA.

USDA (United States Department of Agriculture) (1999) FAS Online. Foreign Agricultural Service, US Department of Agriculture, Washington DC, USA, 15 January.

2

North America and the World Grain Market

D. Gale Johnson

Department of Economics, University of Chicago, Chicago, USA

1. Introduction

Most discussions of prospective world demand and supply of food fail to recognize how much the last half-century differs from all previous history. In the last half-century, both food production and per capita food consumption have greatly increased. The absolute increase in the world's population since World War II has exceeded that of all previous history; in other words, the world's population more than doubled in a half-century. While the population was more than doubling, per capita food consumption increased by more than ever before. Except for famines induced for political reasons, by war, or from enormous mismanagement of resources, the poor people of the world were subjected to far less suffering from famines than in previous history.

What may have been even more remarkable about this half-century was that the most rapid population growth ever recorded occurred while real per capita incomes grew at annual rates that were multiples of any previous historical period, and the real prices of grain fell, not by a little but by a great deal. Slow increases in real per capita incomes and in consumption in the developed countries started in the mid- to late 18th century in Europe, and significant increases in the developing world did not begin until halfway through the 20th century. Until the middle of the 18th century, annual rates of world population growth did not exceed 0.5% (Kremer, 1993). Prior to 1920, population growth rates in the developed world exceeded those of the developing world. Only after 1940 did the developing countries have significantly higher population growth rates than the developed countries.

2. Income and Food Production Growth

Maddison (1995) provides estimates of real per capita gross domestic product (GDP) for most major countries from 1820. His estimates for 11 Asian countries indicate that, from 1820 to 1950, the average per capita GDP increased by only 25% – from $609 to $863 (1990 prices) – while the population increased by 84%, or at an annual rate of less than 0.5%. From 1950 to 1992, the Asian countries increased per capita income to $5300, increasing five times while population increased by 128% for an annual rate of almost 3%. The eleven Asian countries include Taiwan, South Korea and Japan. It may be useful to review the data for the two largest countries – India and China. In the 130 years after 1820, the per capita income in China increased by 17% and that of India by 12%. In 1950, they had nearly the same per capita incomes – $614 and $597.

By 1992, however, the paths of economic growth between the two countries deviated, with China's per capita GDP increasing to $3098 and India's to less than half that amount ($1348), with most of the difference appearing in the last 15 years. Even at its much slower pace, India more than doubled its per capita income while the rate of population growth was about four times greater than in the 1820–1950 period. Clearly, slow population growth was not enough to generate significant economic growth. After 1950, the developing world emulated the growth of the industrial countries a century or more earlier but at a much more rapid pace. In both instances, rapid population growth was associated with rapid growth in real per capita income following a period in which there was low population growth and little or no per capita economic growth, however measured. The growth of both total and per capita food supply in the developing world since 1950 has been unparalleled. During the decade of the 1970s per capita food production in developing countries increased by 8%, and during the 1980s the increase was 13%. While grain production in the world may have stagnated during the 1980s, in the developing countries it increased by 9%. Perhaps the most striking development during the 1980s was the increase of per capita food production in the three most populous developing countries: China (28%), India (20%) and Indonesia (32%).[1]

In developing countries, the most significant variable to consider is the per capita food supply in terms of calories, which increased by 27% from 1961 to 1990 (Table 2.1). The increase in available calories from the beginning of the 1960s to the late 1980s and early 1990s was due, in large part, to the near doubling of world grain production. From 1961 to 1965, world grain production was 985.5 million tonnes, nearly doubling to 1907 million tonnes in 1990/92 (FAO, various issues). The rate of growth in grain production over this period was about 50% greater in the developing countries than in the developed countries.

Table 2.1. Daily per capita supply of calories for major world regions, selected periods, 1961–1990.

	1961–1963	1969–1971	1979–1981	1988–1990
Developing, all	1940	2117	2324	2473
Africa	2117	2138	2180	2204
Latin America	2363	2502	2693	2690
Near East	1825	2029	2245	2442
Other	2116	2292	2425	2626
Developed, all				
North America	3054	3235	3330	3603
Europe	3088	3239	3371	3452
Oceania	3173	3287	3157	3328
Soviet Union	3146	3323	3368	3380
Other	2545	2722	2812	2975

Source: FAO, *Production Yearbook* (various years).

My recital of the achievements of the past half-century has a purpose, believe it or not, and the purpose is to provide a background for my topic, namely a research agenda for better understanding the future of North American grain production in world markets. The background, as I shall argue, is highly relevant in a number of different ways. To begin with, it emphasizes the enormous successes world food producers have achieved during the last half of the 20th century. In addition, those who make their living by presenting the future of food supply in very negative terms should be called upon to show conclusively why the remarkable record of the recent past will not continue.

The record is relevant in calling into question most of the versions of the neoclassical growth theory, which has long provided support for pessimistic views of the relationships between population growth and economic growth, including the food supply. By emphasizing the role of savings and technological change as exogenous variables combined with the diminishing marginal product of labour, the neoclassical growth theory gave implicit, if not explicit, support for those who want to accept the pessimistic prospects for improvement in the quality of life that so concerned Ricardo and Malthus in their early work.[2]

The world of the last half of the 20th century has proven to be far more complex and flexible than depicted by the neoclassical growth theory. The fact that we do not fully understand the interactions between population growth, the creation and utilization of scientific knowledge and invention, and productivity change does not mean that we should cling to a model whose apparent implications have clearly been contradicted by events. Until we are capable of making productivity change and investment, including investment in human capital, endogenous in our models, we fail to provide an appropriate understanding of how our world has generated such enormous economic growth, including improvements in the food supply and numerous measures of human well-being, as has occurred during the 20th century. The New Growth Theorists have clearly pointed us in the right direction, but there is still a lot we need to learn before we know exactly what road is being travelled (Romer, 1986; Lucas, 1988).

3. A Proposed Research Agenda

What are some of the major directions that research on the role of North American grain production in the world market should take? I believe that the following are some of the important areas to be examined:

- the roles of land and diminishing returns in influencing the supply of grain;
- the factors affecting the growth of grain production in the developing countries with special consideration of the effects of governmental policies of market intervention, investment in human capital, and attention to the rural infrastructure;
- the development of supply and demand for grain in Central and Eastern Europe;
- the prospective growth of demand for grain in the world, with particular emphasis on the role of livestock use of grain;
- the effects of the probable increase in grain price variability in world markets due to policy changes in the European Union (EU) and the USA;
- our models of short-run grain price movements; and
- the factors influencing the comparative advantage of grain production in North America.

Admittedly, this research agenda says rather little about North American grain production. This is deliberate since North America's role in grain production will depend at least as much on developments outside the region as within it. In particular, the path of real grain prices will be determined to a large extent by supply and demand developments in the rest of the world. To a considerable degree, the suggested areas of research parallel the agenda topics of this conference. I shall comment on each of these in turn, with most of what follows emphasizing the first three.

Land and diminishing returns

The principle of diminishing returns to changes in factor proportions has had a powerful influence on thinking about the world's food supply. In Ricardo's and Malthus' time as well, the concern was real, and considerable pessimism was justified concerning the future of mankind. However, in second and subsequent editions, Malthus recognized that recent history provided a basis for a degree of optimism (Malthus, 1992). In the late 1700s, perhaps 80% of the population of Europe was engaged in agriculture, with each farm family producing no more than enough food for itself and a fifth of another family. The potential impact of science on productivity had not yet emerged. Knowledge of the processes of agricultural production was based on common or folk knowledge, or based on the experiences of people who farmed or observed farming. This knowledge, accumulated over a very long time, resulted in minimal increases in the ratio of grain output to the seed used and in the productivity of labour over several centuries (Johnson, 1997).

At the beginning of the 19th century, the limitations on increases in food output were to be found primarily in the slow rate of improvement of labour productivity, not in limitations in the supply of land. Land was extensively used in most of Europe until the fairly recent past (Boserup, 1965). Long fallow was a common practice. As the population grew, albeit slowly, the periods of fallow were gradually shortened and practical alternative means of maintaining fertility were increasingly applied – manure, legumes, and field refuse. Labour productivity increased very slowly until well into the 19th century when the mechanical revolution transformed agriculture in Europe and North America. Harvesting methods changed little from at least the 10th century until the introduction of the reaper and the binder at the middle of the 19th century. Labour required to harvest a hectare of wheat declined by 90% in the USA between 1840 and 1900 (Cooper *et al.*, 1972). The yield of wheat and other small grains per unit of cultivated land in the USA and Europe stagnated in the 70 years prior to World War II (Brown, 1965). The increase in the world's food supply from the time the population of the world was a billion in 1815 until 1950, when it was 2.5 billion, came largely from increasing the amount of cultivated land; yield increases had a minor role. The biological and chemical revolutions were not significant factors in agricultural productivity until the introduction of hybrid maize in the mid-1930s and did not significantly impact production until a decade or so later.

These facts are well known, yet the implications are inadequately reflected in much of the discussion of future food supply and demand. The yield revolution resulting from modern science has greatly reduced the importance of land in determining the fate of nations. It is quite surprising, given the limited role that land has had throughout history, that land is so often assumed to be the primary factor limiting food production. If land ever had a limiting role for a significant part of the world, it was perhaps for no more than one or two centuries. Its dominance was brief, except in the minds of those who doubt the ingenuity of mankind, when that ingenuity is not held in check by misconceived policies and misrule.

Of course, the principle of diminishing returns has not been repealed nor will it ever be. If all else is constant, a change in factor proportions changes marginal products. But what seems not to be generally understood is that it takes only a small increase in productivity to offset the effects of a significant change in the ratio of land to all other inputs used in crop production. Nor is it recognized that, while aggregate non-land inputs may increase during certain periods of agricultural development, the success realized in finding effective substitutes for labour may result in little change in the ratio of land to all other inputs.

The growth of grain production in developing countries

There should be serious reconsideration of the commonly accepted assumption that land is a major factor in limiting output growth in the low-income countries. First, there should be reconsideration of the empirical role that diminishing returns to inputs applied to land has in influencing output. Second, the assumption that labour is 'surplus' in the agriculture of low-income countries should be vigorously rejected. Third, the role of policies and institutions in influencing the rate of growth of farm output needs much greater exploration than it has received.

4. Diminishing Returns to Inputs Applied to Land

With respect to the role of diminishing returns to resources applied to land, there needs to be exploration of the magnitude of the changes in factor proportions and the extent to which the non-farm inputs introduced over the past two centuries were labour-saving rather than land substitutes. Actually, many of the non-farm inputs introduced in the last 150 years are both labour- and land-saving, but the degree of labour saving has far outpaced land saving. Perhaps something can be learned from the experience of the USA. If we review the changes in inputs and outputs over the past 80 years, we find that the ratio of non-land inputs – such as fertilizer, machinery and labour – to land inputs has remained unchanged while the ratio of non-labour inputs to labour has increased sharply over the same years. It may be concluded, therefore, that the primary effort of research, development and investment has been to increase the productivity of labour rather than of land.

Japan is considered to be a country in which land has had a dominant role in determining output growth, though currently approximately a quarter of its paddy land sits idle. From 1880 to 1940, the arable land area increased by 29%, contributing substantially to the 96% increase in crop output (Hayami and Ruttan, 1985). During this period, the labour input in agriculture declined by only 13%. The annual growth in labour productivity for these six decades was 1.68%, more than the 1.01% growth in land productivity. Both labour and land productivity increased at greater annual rates in Japan than in the USA since labour productivity in the latter grew at an annual rate of 1.16% and land productivity increased a mere 0.22% (Hayami and Ruttan, 1985).

5. The Productivity of Labour

For the period 1940–1980, the annual growth in labour productivity increased to 3.55% in Japan and 6.1% in the USA while the annual growth in land productivity was very nearly the same, namely 2.12% in Japan and 1.90% in the USA. In Japan, the amount of arable land decreased by 11% while there was no change in the USA. These data do not indicate that land was any more of an obstacle to output expansion in Japan than in the USA. The slower growth of labour productivity in Japan than in the USA since 1940, measured in physical terms, was a predictable result of the differences in the agricultural price policies followed in each country.

I believe that the above comparison of changes in labour and land productivities in such diverse agricultures as Japan and the USA at least raises questions about the relative importance of land in limiting output growth. In terms of the research agendas of the agricultural research institutions in the developing world, including the international centres, is it not perhaps time to consider giving much greater emphasis to finding ways to increase labour productivity rather than allocating nearly all resources to increasing land productivity? After all, the increases in labour productivity will determine the real incomes of future generations of farm people though one could hardly believe this to be the case from the way public research resources are now allocated.

If one accepts the Chinese data on labour used per hectare (1 ha equals 2.5 acres) of maize, rice and wheat, labour in developing countries may well not be readily available in certain peak seasons, such as planting and harvesting. The days per hectare range from 185 for wheat to 293 for rice, with maize being intermediate at 215 (Colby *et al.*, 1992). Farm employment in China appears to have peaked and is now very slowly declining absolutely because of the large difference between the value of the marginal product of labour in agriculture and in other employments, especially in urban areas. If food output is to continue to grow, labour productivity in farming must increase through finding substitutes for labour. This is a well-known phenomenon illustrated by the experience of the industrial countries where labour employment in agriculture has declined while output has continued to grow.

Surplus labour, in the sense that it can be withdrawn from agriculture without an adverse effect on farm output, does not exist in developing countries and it is time that this should be universally recognized. Thus, as I have argued elsewhere, China needs to create an economic environment in which capital will be substituted for labour in the years ahead (Johnson, 1996). Such substitution must occur if two desirable results are to be achieved: continued growth in agricultural production and in labour productivity; and, above all else, in returns per unit of farm labour.

Researchers have neglected emphasizing labour-saving innovations because of the general view that still prevails, even after *Transforming Traditional Agriculture* (Schultz, 1964), that there is surplus labour in agriculture; therefore, increasing labour productivity will only increase the amount of surplus labour and farm output will not increase. But, perhaps more importantly, there is general acceptance of the view that nothing should be done to promote an increase in the flow of rural to urban migrants, which is believed would result from saving labour in farming. After all, cities are overcrowded, and anyway there will not be jobs for them once they leave agriculture, or so it is alleged. Pessimism about job creation seems to be a universal phenomenon in developing countries, as it now also seems to be in the majority of industrial countries.

Land is but one input in the production of food. It is important that there be increases in the efficiency of all resources used in agriculture, not just land. If our interest is in improving the well-being of rural people in developing countries, it is clearly important to increase labour productivity. Such improvement should not be restricted to finding substitutes for labour in farming. Even greater emphasis should be given to increasing investment in human capital so that farm people will enhance their prospects as they continue to shift out of agriculture into non-farm employment.

6. The Role of Government Policies

While there is general recognition that national policies have a significant effect on agricultural production, this is seldom a significant consideration in most efforts to project growth of grain production. In other words, it is seldom asked how policy changes might affect the growth path. Yet there is overwhelming evidence that policies do matter, and they matter a great deal. The World Bank studies of the effects of rates of protection on agriculture in 18 developing countries conclude that national policies have large effects on the growth of agricultural production. These studies show definitively that high rates of negative protection of agriculture not only adversely affect the growth of farm output, but also have major impacts on the growth of gross national product (Schiff and Valdes, 1992).

Strong confirmation of the role of policies on farm production is provided by the effects of the Chinese agricultural policy reforms undertaken since 1978. From about 1955 to 1978, the growth of grain production barely kept pace with population growth. In the first six years of the reforms (1979–1984), farm output grew at an annual rate of 7.6% for an increase of 56% and for the next decade continued to grow at 5.4%, a rate seldom attained elsewhere. These growth rates contrast with the 2.56% for the 1956–1978 period. For the first 6 years of reform, grain production grew at an annual rate of 4.9%; since then, the rate has been only 0.9%. This decline in the growth rate has often been alleged to indicate that the reforms had pretty much run their course by 1984.

Was the use of grain in China constrained by its production from 1984 to 1994? The answer is in the negative. China had net annual grain imports of 13 million tonnes for 1980–1984 and net annual exports of 5 million tonnes for 1992–1994 (State Statistical Bureau of China, 1996). In addition, farmers increased their year-end stocks of grain by more than 150 million tonnes. The probable answer to the apparent inconsistency between the large increase in meat production and the small increase in grain production is that grain production is significantly underestimated. The annual household surveys indicate that the underestimate may be at least 10%.

The land and people of China did not change in some miraculous fashion after 1978. What changed were the policies affecting agriculture: the abandonment of the communes and their replacement by the household responsibility system or private farming, the removal of restraints on markets and non-farm activities of farm people, higher farm prices and increased supplies of non-farm inputs. Up to half of the increase in output from 1978–1984 can be attributed to the change in incentive structure resulting from the institutional changes (Lin, 1992).

The emphasis on understanding the effects of national policies on the growth of grain production is especially relevant to projections of food production in sub-Saharan Africa. It seems to me that the potential of grain and food production in that region may be grossly underestimated by emphasis on recent trends because national policies have definitely been adverse to the growth of agricultural output. What seems to be forgotten is that the decline in per capita food production began after 1970 when the emphasis on taxation of agriculture to support industrialization became the basis for national policies in much of the region.

While the adverse impacts of policies affecting agriculture in sub-Saharan countries have been studied and criticized, I don't believe there has been a systematic effort to indicate what the food production potential of the region would be if more appropriate policies were followed. That the potential is much greater than current realization is suggested by Mitchell and Ingco (1993):

> African farmers have already demonstrated that they can increase production with present resources when there are incentives to do so. Food production in many African countries rose significantly due to the stimulus of higher prices after the drought in 1983–1984. In addition, agricultural growth in countries successfully adjusting economic policies has reached more than 3.5% per annum in 1987--1990, compared to less than 0.5% in countries that maintained poor policies.

I find the data on grain yields in Table 2.2 further striking evidence of what has been achieved in the last five decades and what is likely to be achieved in the developing countries over the next few decades. Grain yields per hectare of seeded area were the same in the developing and developed countries from 1934 to 1938; land and nature were the dominant determinants of yields, and neither the developed countries nor the developing countries had superior resources.[3] The chemical and biological agricultural revolutions had not yet come into play. Over the following half-century, grain yields increased significantly in both groups of countries, though significantly more in the developed than in the developing countries. Is there any reason to believe that yields in developing countries cannot increase to the level in the developed countries? The developing countries have closed the yield differential from 51% in 1969–1970 to 29% in 1990–1992.

Policies and Central and Eastern European agriculture

The future developments in the demand and supply of grain and food in Central and Eastern Europe cannot be understood without an analysis of the potential effects of policy changes now under way. The agricultural policies of these countries, prior to the transition to market economies, had major impacts on the commodity composition of production, on resource use in agriculture, and on the productivity of those resources. Projections based on the pre-reform period, without modifications for the policy and institutional changes that have occurred or are likely to occur as market economies are established, are misleading. Under the old systems, livestock production was heavily subsidized and consumption was significantly greater than would have been the case without subsidies; in many cases the subsidies exceeded the prices consumers actually paid in the retail stores.

Table 2.2. Average grain yields for developing and developed countries and the world, selected periods, 1934–1992 (in tonnes per ha).

	1934–1938	1952–1956	1961–1965	1969–1970	1979–1981	1985–1987	1990–1992
Developing[a]	1.14	1.14	1.21	1.38	1.88	2.17	2.45
Developed[b]	1.14	1.36	1.93	2.13	2.59	3.04	3.14
World	1.14	1.21	1.43	1.68	2.17	2.55	2.69

[a] Includes China for all periods.
[b] Includes former Soviet Union for all periods.
Source: FAO, *Production Yearbook* (various issues).

Of the projections I have seen, other than my own, only Tyers (1994) has emphasized this point, though Brooks (1991) warned us that the transition to a market economy would be extremely difficult due to the enormous distortions in the prior agricultural economy, with particular emphasis on the price distortions related to livestock products. The otherwise excellent 1994 studies of world food developments by researchers at the Food and Agriculture Organization (FAO), the International Food Policy Research Institute (IFPRI) and the World Bank gave limited or no emphasis to the effects of past price distortions or the negative productivity consequences of socialized agriculture (Islam, 1995). Throughout the region, except in Poland, per capita meat consumption has fallen by a third or more primarily because of declining real incomes and the drastic decline in the relative farm prices of meat and milk. The elimination of the subsidies did not result in higher prices of meat relative to consumer prices because farmers bore the full impact of the elimination of the subsidies.

However, as livestock production returns to profitability, retail prices will be much higher relative to other prices than in the past. It will take many years of real per capita income growth to offset the consumption effects of higher retail prices for livestock products. We need much more information than we now have to determine when the two effects will be offsetting and when per capita consumption will once again start to increase. Until that time occurs, the demand for grain for livestock feed will remain low, and any recovery in grain production will find its way into international markets. The future of international grain prices will be greatly influenced by developments during this transitional period.

We should not ignore the potential increases in productivity that are highly probable as the organization of agriculture is stabilized. With respect to the republics of the former Soviet Union, overall productivity may increase due to increases in the productivity of feed, reduction in the high rates of seed use, increased yields due to improvements in seed quality, more effective grain combines, and reduced waste in transportation and marketing. Without any changes in the yield of grain in the field, these changes could increase the available supply of grain by as much as 55 million tonnes (Johnson, 1993). Changes in exportable supplies due to higher yields and reduction in consumption of livestock products would be over and above this figure. The reduction in livestock production could release some 35 million tonnes of grain. In the late 1980s, the former Soviet Union imported as much as 40 million tonnes of grain and 1 million tonnes of meat. If the increases in productivity and decline in livestock production are of the order indicated, the shift in the net trade position of the area might be as much as 75 to 80 million tonnes at some time in the future in contrast to the high imports of the late 1980s.[4] Obviously, these changes are going to take longer, perhaps much longer, than anticipated. Nor do I want to argue that others who address these possibilities should come to the same conclusions as I have. But I do argue that analysis of these issues needs to be addressed if we are to better understand the future of international trade in grains.

It should also be noted that little useful information concerning future levels of agricultural production can be derived from the post-1990 experience of the Central and Eastern European economies. In most countries, agricultural production has been very unprofitable for almost the entire period since 1990. The sharp decline in inputs that has occurred will eventually be reversed when agriculture returns to profitability.

Feed use of grains

As real per capita incomes increase in the developing countries, the per capita demand for livestock products will increase, and the demand for grain and other feeds will expand. Since the income elasticity of demand for livestock products seems to be of the order of unity in developing countries, the growth of per capita livestock production is often thought to result in a rapid growth in the demand for grain and to compete with the production of grain as well. The evidence is very clear that from 1960 to 1993 the world's supply of grain more than kept pace with all sources of the increase in demand, including demand due to expanded livestock production, since real grain prices fell by a great deal over that span of time (Fig. 2.1). Note that the recent increase in real export prices, which has already abated significantly from the last data in the figure, was modest compared with the early 1970s and did not bring prices back to the levels of the 1960s or the late 1970s.

The point I wish to emphasize here is that we need to improve our understanding of the interrelationships between economic growth,

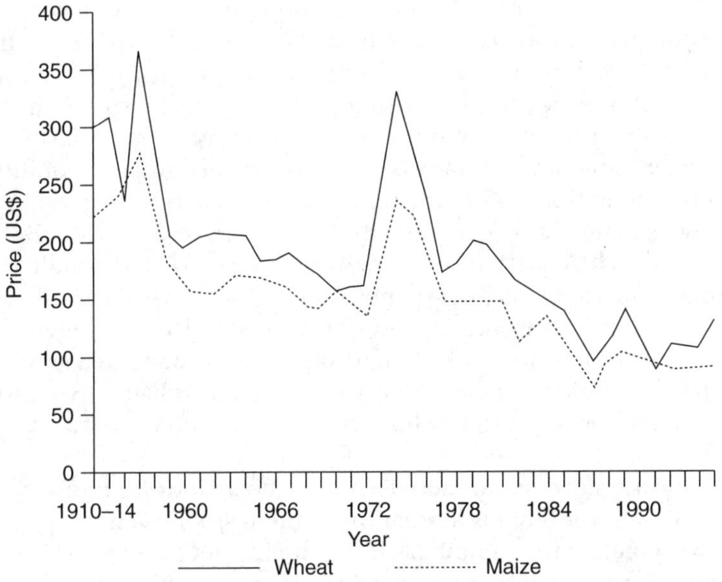

Fig. 2.1. World wheat and maize prices, selected periods, 1910–1995.

policy changes and the productivity of feed used in livestock production. The rapid expansion of livestock production in China since 1978 could not have been achieved without significant changes in feeding efficiency. The average age of slaughter pigs, the major source of meat production, has fallen significantly since the early 1980s as evidenced by the increase in pork output relative to the pig inventory at the beginning of the year. In 1980, the annual pork output per pig in the inventory was 37 kg; in 1995 the output more than doubled to 88 kg (State Statistical Bureau, 1996). This has clearly resulted in reducing the amount of feed required to produce a kilogram of pork though it is not clear how much the use of grain has declined since there has been substitution of grain for other feed sources over time. The other possibility is that grain production is significantly underestimated in China and that the degree of underestimation has increased during the reform period.[5]

Grain price variability

Due to policy changes in the EU and the USA, grain price variability in international markets will be much greater than it has been over the last quarter of the 20th century. Politicians have apparently discovered that grain stocks are very expensive and that price stability is no longer as important to farmers as it was once thought to be. As a result, the holding of grain stocks has been returned to the market, which will hold but a minor fraction of the amount of stocks that resulted from recent governmental price support policies. Consequently, small shocks in either supply or demand will create significant price variability.

Further reductions in trade barriers will reduce price variability, but it will be a long time before the transition to relative free trade in grain will have a significant dampening effect on price variability. Both the EU and the USA still intervene in grain markets through export manipulations, such as export subsidies or the unconscionable action of the EU in imposing export taxes on wheat in 1995 to prevent their domestic grain users from fully participating in the increase in world grain prices. The USA behaved only somewhat less badly by halting its export subsidies on wheat, which it either has renewed or will do so soon.

We clearly need better models of price behaviour for periods of 3 or 4 years. Whenever there is a price spike, there are those who rush to the press with claims that a new period of high prices and stringency has occurred. Since 1970 there have been three such spikes; the first two were dissipated in about 2 years (see Fig. 2.1) and the third has now been reversed. Surely we have the wit to devise a short-term model that at least will reflect the responses to the price spikes and indicate how long it is likely to take to return to the long-term trend. I am not sure we have the wit to create a model that will tell us when the price spikes will occur though I suppose that we should have anticipated that the low level of real grain prices in 1990 to 1993 would not continue. After all, Brown (1997) kept telling us that world per capita grain production declined after 1984 and I fear that we failed to ask why this was occurring – whether the decline was in fact a response to the sharply declining real prices of grain or due to something else. Since real prices were declining, most of us apparently assumed that slow output growth would not have any undesirable consequences. In this instance, more of us should have listened to Brown (1997), not because there was a long-run imbalance between the growth of food demand and supply but because we were witnessing too much of a good thing and, like most things that are too good, it came to an end with the sharp, though temporary, grain price increases in 1994 and 1995.

7. Conclusions: Comparative Advantage of North American Grain Production

I come, at long last, to what the editors of this book probably thought I was to discuss. I have saved it to the last because I have the least to say about it. The comparative advantage of North America in grain production rests on efficient organization of farm operating units and intelligent, well-educated and experienced farm operators combined with bountiful supplies of land well adapted to grain production. This is the first basis; the second basis is that North America is probably blessed with the world's best infrastructure supporting grain production. This covers the gamut: research, transportation, marketing institutions, repair services (including prompt availability of spare parts), and competitive input suppliers who have a tradition of adapting to change whether it be in seeds, fertilizers, pesticides or farm machines.

While, during the last few decades, there have been government interventions that limited the gains in trade that could have been achieved, grain production overall was probably more responsive to market forces than anywhere else in the world. Mostly, North American grain producers operate in a highly supportive policy structure. If US farmers cannot maintain their comparative advantage in grain production, they do not warrant any expressions of pity. For the next several years, grain producers each year will receive a significant sum of money for every hectare that they have devoted to grain over the past years. While these payments will not directly contribute to either lowering marginal costs of production or increasing marginal revenue, the payments will provide a nice cushion against many of the adversities that farmers face. In this world of money for nothing, their only rivals will be the farmers of the EU who will receive even larger payments. But in the rest of the world, few producers will be able to match such an economic and policy environment.

How well North American grain producers will fare, as measured by land prices, will depend primarily on what happens to world market prices and the rate of farm productivity improvement compared with producers elsewhere. If the trend of real prices since 1980 reasserts itself, then grain farmers should not be encouraged to hold unattainable expectations concerning the future economic environment. Departments or ministries of agriculture present a biased view of the world to their farmers. When the news is good, such news is trumpeted, but when the news is bad, speech is muffled. There is a political incentive to foster a sense of good feeling even if it is obvious that the not-so-good is only just over the horizon or around the proverbial corner.

Notes

1. In the 1970s, per capita food production increased in China by 16%, India 2%, and Indonesia 18%. The increase in per capita food consumption increased in the 1980s and generally favourable trends in per capita food production continued into the 1990s. Comparing per capita food production in 1992–1994

with 1982–1984, the increases were: China 27%, India 16% and Indonesia 36%. The data are from FAO, *Production Yearbook* (various years).

2. Malthus (1992) modified his views concerning the role of food in limiting population growth after his first edition, but one almost never sees a reference to what he said in the second and subsequent editions. Only the first, pessimistic edition is noted. After noting the recent growth in Europe's population, he wrote:

> ... fewer and fewer famines and fewer diseases arising from want have prevailed in the last century than in those that preceded it. On the whole, therefore, though our future prospects respecting the mitigation of the evils arising from the principle of population may not be as bright as we could wish, yet they are far from being entirely disheartening and by no means preclude the gradual and progressive improvement in human society which, before the late wild speculations on the subject, was the object of rational expectations.
>
> (Malthus, 1992, pp. 330–331)

He failed to note that he had been largely responsible for the '... late wild speculations on the subject ...'.

3. The developed countries include the former Soviet Union in all time periods. The other developed regions consist of Europe, Oceania and North America, except for the area south of the Rio Grande, and Japan. China is included with the developing countries. In 1934–1938 the average grain yield in the former Soviet Union, according to FAO, was 1.02 tonnes per ha. In 1990–1992 the average yield on the territory of the former Soviet Union was 1.80 tonnes per ha, well below the developing country average.

4. The change in net trade is not quite the sum of the reduction in feed use and productivity improvements in livestock production, since the estimated effect of the productivity improvements are based on the previous level of livestock production.

5. The rural household surveys in China indicate that in recent years national grain output has exceeded the estimates published by the State Statistical Bureau by at least 50 million tonnes or about 10%.

References

Boserup, E. (1965) *The Conditions of Agricultural Growth: The Economics of Agrarian Change Under Population Pressure.* Aldine, Chicago, USA.

Brooks, K. (1991) *Decollectivization in East/Central Europe.* Draft. The World Bank, Washington DC, USA.

Brown, L.R. (1965) *Man, Land, and Food: Looking Ahead at World Food Needs.* Foreign Agricultural Economic Report No. 11, US Department of Agriculture, Economic Research Service, Washington DC, USA.

Brown, L.R. (1997) Facing the Prospect of Food Scarcity. *State of the World.* Worldwatch Institute in association with W.W. Norton & Company, New York, pp. 23–41.

Colby, W.H., Crook, F.W. and Webb, S.E. (1992) *Agricultural Statistics of the People's Republic of China, 1949–1990.* Statistic Bulletin No. 844, US

Department of Agriculture, Economic Research Service, Washington DC, USA.

Cooper, M.R., Barton, G.T. and Brodell, A.P. (1972) *Progress of Farm Mechanization.* Miscellaneous Publication No. 630, US Department of Agriculture, Washington DC, USA.

FAO (Food and Agricultural Organization) (various issues) *Production Yearbook.* United Nations, New York, USA.

Hayami, Y. and Ruttan, V. (1985) *Agricultural Development: an International Perspective,* revised. Johns Hopkins University Press, Baltimore, USA, pp. 480–481, 486–487.

Islam, N. (1995) *Population and Food in the Early Twenty-First Century: Meeting Future Food Demand of an Increasing Population.* International Food Policy Research Institute, Washington DC, USA.

Johnson, D.G. (1993) Trade effects of dismantling the socialized agriculture of the former Soviet Union. *Comparative Economic Studies* 36:4, 21–31.

Johnson, D.G. (1996) *China's Rural and Agricultural Reforms: Successes and Failure.* Working Paper No. 96/12, Chinese Economy Research Unit, University of Adelaide, Australia.

Johnson, D.G. (1997) Agriculture and the Wealth of Nations. *American Economic Review* 87:21, 1–11.

Kremer, M. (1993) Population growth and technological change: one million B.C. to 1990. *Quarterly Journal of Economics* 108:3, 681–716.

Lin, J. (1992) Rural reforms and economic growth in China. *American Economic Review* 82:1, 34–51.

Lucas, R.E., Jr (1988) On the mechanics of economic development. *Journal of Monetary Economics* 22, 3–42.

Maddison, A. (1995) *Monitoring the World Economy 1820–1992.* OECD, Paris, France.

Malthus, T.R. (1992) *An Essay on the Principle of Population.* Selected and introduced by David Winch. Cambridge University Press, London/New York, pp. 325–332.

Mitchell, D.O. and Ingco, M.D. (1993) *The World Food Outlook.* Mimeo, World Bank, Washington DC, USA, p. 130.

Romer, P. (1986) Increasing returns and long-run growth. *Journal of Political Economy* 94, 1002–1037.

Schiff, M. and Valdes, A. (1992) A synthesis of the economics in developing countries. In: *The Political Economy of Agricultural Pricing Policy,* Vol. 4, Part 2. Johns Hopkins University Press, Baltimore, USA, pp. 59–81 and 199–232.

Schultz, T.W. (1964) *Transforming Traditional Agriculture.* Yale University Press, New Haven, USA.

State Statistical Bureau of China (1996) *China Statistical Yearbook.* China Statistical Publishing House, Beijing, China, p. 377.

Tyers, R. (1994) *Economic Reform in Europe and the Former Soviet Union: Implications for International Food Markets.* Report No. 99, International Food Policy Research Institute, Washington DC, USA.

3

Long-term Supply and Demand Trends: Whither the Real Price of Wheat?

John M. Antle,[1] Dermot Hayes,[2] Samarendu Mohanty,[2] Pavel Vavra[1] and Vincent H. Smith[1]

[1] *Department of Agricultural Economics and Economics and Trade Research Center, Montana State University–Bozeman, USA*
[2] *Department of Economics, Iowa State University, Ames, USA*

1. Introduction

In late 1995 and throughout a good part of 1996, many voices joined together in predicting a new era of higher prices for food and feed grain commodities as world stocks of wheat and maize declined and world market prices for those commodities increased substantially. For a brief period, in May 1996, wheat prices were even in excess of $220.44 per tonne and maize prices in excess of $157.47 per tonne. Moreover, instead of subsidizing wheat exports, the European Union (EU) was taxing them to ensure the availability of feed wheat supplied for domestic livestock producers. At the same time, as is still the case, some analysts were arguing that China would be likely to increase imports of food grains substantially over the next few decades. In addition, on the supply side it has been claimed that the end of the green revolution is at hand and that growth rates for yields of wheat and other crops are beginning to decline. Thus, over the past 2 years, many observers and some models of agricultural commodity markets have been predicting that the world prices of wheat and some other major food and feed grains will increase over both the medium and longer term.

In contrast, the historical evidence on the direction of the long-run behaviour of wheat yields and the real price of wheat is clear and presents a very different picture. During the 19th century and the first three decades of the 20th century wheat yields in major wheat-producing countries such as the USA, Canada and Europe increased at between

0.5% and 1% per year. Between 1935 and 1996, they increased much more rapidly, with annual growth rates ranging from just over 1% to more than 3.5% in major producing regions. The result of these supply-side shocks, as Professor D. Gale Johnson has consistently emphasized for many years (Johnson, 1975, 1985, 1997), has been that since at least 1866 the long-run trend in world wheat prices has been downward and accelerating. Moreover, the rate of decline in real world wheat prices has been accelerating. Between 1866 and 1996 world wheat prices declined at an annual average rate of 0.89% per year; between 1920 and 1996 they declined at an annual average rate of 1.1%; and between 1955 and 1995 they declined at an annual average rate of 2.69%.

These empirical observations do not accord with either the views of the Club of Rome in the early 1970s or the current prognostications of some world watch organizations, so the following question arises. Is the market for wheat (along with some other agricultural commodity markets) confronting a watershed period over the next 10 to 15 years, as a result of which there will be an important change in the direction of the long-run trend in world wheat prices so that they rise over the next 30–50 years? Alternatively, as Professor D. Gale Johnson has correctly predicted at other times, are world wheat markets going to experience business as usual over the long run and generate further declines in the real price for wheat? The major purpose of this chapter is to address this question. The evidence we examine suggests that the historical trend is likely to be reversed only if there is a dramatic shock to productivity (say because of climate change) or a dramatic shock to demand (say because of very large increases in per capita incomes in developing countries).

The chapter is organized as follows. Section 2 presents a brief history of world wheat production, prices and trade, in which particular attention is given to developments since 1960. In the third section potential sources of uncertainty about medium-term and long-term wheat supply and demand trends are examined. Section 4 describes four alternative well-known forecast models of future wheat market conditions and compares and contrasts the forecasts of those models and the assumptions on which those forecasts are based. In section 5, alternative forecasts of future wheat market conditions are obtained from the Food and Agricultural Policy Research Institute (FAPRI) under 'optimistic' high-price and 'pessimistic' low-price scenarios about future exogenous supply, demand and policy shocks. A conclusion is presented in the final section.

2. A Brief History of World Wheat Production, Prices and Trade

Wheat has been cultivated for human consumption and animal feed since at least the earliest of biblical times, possibly originally in the fertile crescent delineated by the Tigris and Euphrates rivers in the Middle East. Today many different varieties of wheat are produced commercially in most regions of the world. The relatively recent history of wheat production has been heavily influenced by the phenomenon of sharply rising yields. In this section, we describe this phenomenon and its consequences for world wheat output and prices. We then briefly describe the regional patterns of world wheat production and trade that have developed over the past 40 years.

Data on wheat yields in the USA (which produces between 12 and 14% of total world wheat output) for the period 1865 to 1996 are presented in Fig. 3.1. From the perspective of the history of yields, this 130-year period can be divided up into two sub-periods, 1865–1936 and 1936–1996. In the first 70-year period, wheat yields in the USA increased slowly from about 0.5 tonnes per ha in the 1860s to just under 1 tonne per ha in the early 1930s at an annual growth rate of about 1% per year. In the second 60-year period, wheat yields in the USA increased more rapidly from about 1 tonne per ha in the mid-1930s to about 2.5 tonnes per ha in the 1990s at an annual growth rate of 1.6%.[1] The increases in yields in the USA accomplished since the 1930s are in large part due to the development of semi-dwarf wheat varieties in the 1950s and subsequent varietal innovations by many scientists both within and outside the USA (Dalrymple, 1986; Pardey *et al.*, 1996).

Yields have also increased substantially in other major wheat-producing countries and regions over the past 40 years. Data on yields in the EU (which also produces between 12 and 14% of world wheat output), China (with about a 20% share), and the former Soviet Union (with about a 13% share) are presented in Fig. 3.2 for the period 1960–1995. Over this period, yields in the EU have increased from just under 2 tonnes per ha to about 5.5 tonnes per ha at an annual growth

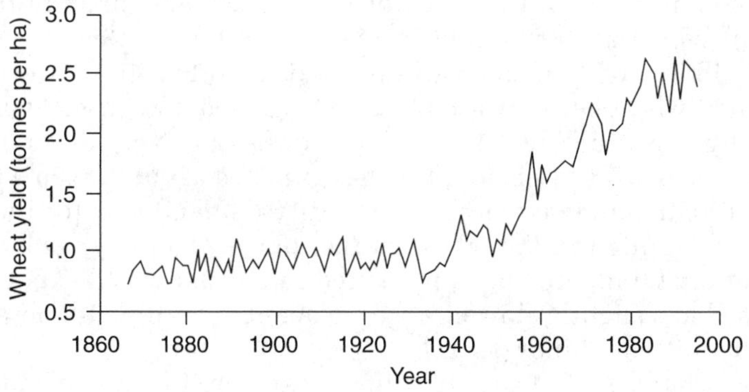

Fig. 3.1. US wheat yields, 1866–1995.

Fig. 3.2. Wheat yields in selected major wheat-producing countries, 1960–1995.

rate of just under 3%. Yields in China have increased even more rapidly from about 0.8 tonnes per ha to about 3.5 tonnes per ha at an annual growth rate of 4.3%, but yields in the former Soviet Union have increased more slowly from about 1 tonne per ha to about 1.3 tonnes per ha at an annual growth rate of about 0.8%.[2]

The general increases in wheat yields in major production regions such as the USA, the EU, China and the former Soviet Union have largely been responsible for increases in world wheat production since 1960. Figure 3.3 presents data on the area planted to wheat worldwide between 1960 and 1995. While there has been some variability over this period, there has been no dramatic or even substantial upward trend in the area planted to wheat which, since 1970, has averaged about 240 million ha. Data on world production, consumption and trade in wheat are presented in Fig. 3.4. Between 1960 and 1995, roughly in line with the increases in yields reported above, world production of wheat has increased by a factor of about 2.3 from about 235 million tonnes to about 540 million tonnes per year at an annual growth rate of 2.4%. Consumption has grown at about the same rate as price adjustments have brought quantity demanded into line with quantity supplied in the world market place. Over the same period international trade in wheat, measured by annual world exports, has increased at a slightly slower rate from about 45 million tonnes to just over 100 million tonnes per year.

The relative size of supply shifts as compared with demand shifts in the world wheat market are reflected by movements in the real price of wheat. Data on real (inflation-adjusted) wheat prices in the USA,

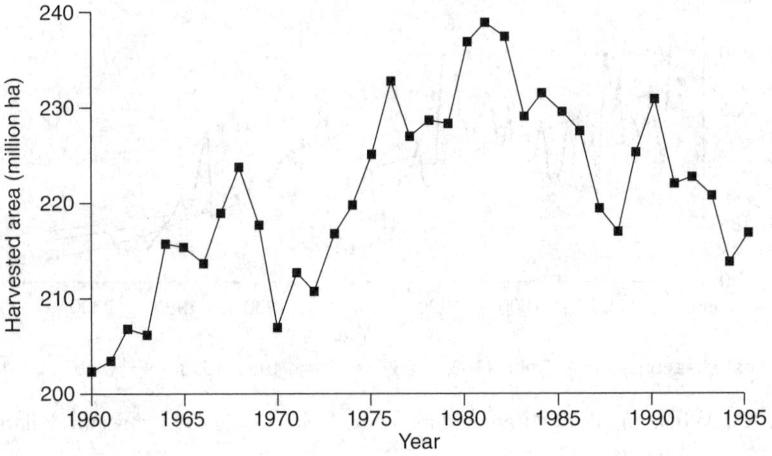

Fig. 3.3. World wheat harvested area, 1960–1995.

chosen as proxies for world wheat prices, over the period 1866 to 1995 are presented in Fig. 3.5. The evidence is graphic and speaks volumes for the contributions of technological change in agriculture over the past 130 years to the welfare of consumers. Despite occasional blips, typically associated with periods of war, world wheat prices have steadily fallen over this period. When the data on real wheat prices are fitted to a simple exponential trend line (which performs quite well),

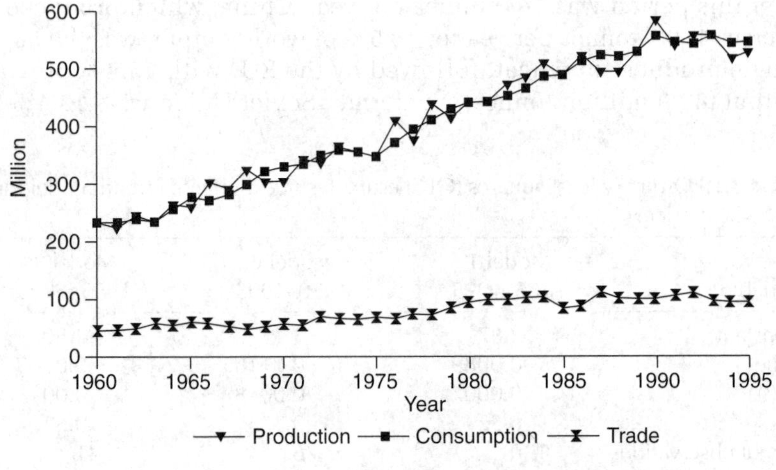

Fig. 3.4. World wheat production, consumption and trade, 1960–1995.

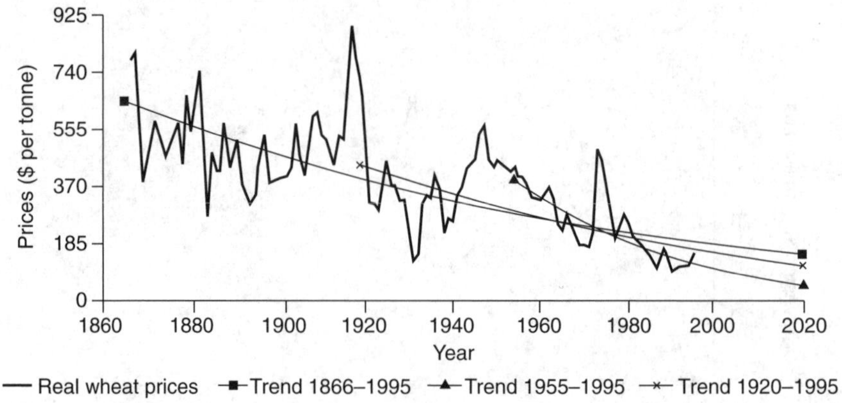

Fig. 3.5. Wheat prices and trends in the USA, 1866–1995 (1995 constant dollars).

the coefficient on the trend term is −0.0089, implying that over the past 130 years the real price of wheat has declined at an average annual rate of 0.89%. For the 1920–1995 period, price declined at a 1.2% annual rate, and during 1955–1995 the annual rate of decrease was 2.7% (see Table 3.1). Some of the forecast models discussed in section 4 suggest that the real price of wheat will rise over the next 20 to 30 years. An important issue is whether or not those models are right; that is, in contrast to the past century, is it really the case that, over the next three decades, increases in the demand for wheat will outstrip increases in its supply?

Data on the average production of wheat worldwide and in major wheat-producing countries and average shares are presented for the period 1991–1995 in Table 3.2. Average total world wheat production over this period was 544 tonnes per year. China, which produced on average 100.7 tonnes per year or 18.5% of world output, was the largest single producer of wheat, followed by the EU[3] with 15.4% of world output (83.9 million tonnes), the former Soviet Union with 13.4% (73

Table 3.1. Ordinary least squares (OLS) estimates of exponential trend model for real wheat price.

Variable	Model 1 1866–1995	Model 2 1920–1995	Model 3 1955–1995
Constant	2.87	3.13	4.80
Time	−0.0089	−0.0118	−0.0269
(SE)	(0.0007)	(0.0018)	(0.0033)
R^2	0.52	0.37	0.62
No. of observations	130	76	41

Model estimated is ln price = $\alpha + \beta \times$ time.

Table 3.2. Wheat output and output shares in major wheat-producing countries, 1991–1995.

Country	Production (million tonnes)	Share (%)
China	100.7	18.5
EU-12	83.9	15.4
Former Soviet Union	73.0	13.4
USA	61.7	11.4
India	58.7	10.8
Canada	27.5	5.1
Australia	13.8	2.5
Argentina	9.9	1.8
Others	114.7	21.1
World	544.0	100.0

Source: USDA, 1996; FAO, 1997.

million tonnes), the USA with 11.4% (61.7 million tonnes) and India with 10.8% (58.7 million tonnes). Canada, which produced 5.1% of world output (27.5 million tonnes), has only a relatively modest share of world production even though, as discussed below, it is a major wheat net exporter. Similarly, Australia's share of world output, 2.5%, is even smaller.

Major wheat producers may be either net exporters (as is the case for the EU and the USA) or net importers (as is the case for China and the former Soviet Union) depending on domestic demand for wheat for human consumption and animal feed. In addition, the roles played by individual countries in world wheat markets may change over time. Data on average exports and shares of total world exports enjoyed by current major exporting countries are presented in Table 3.3 for the periods 1960–1964, 1980–1984 and 1991–1995. Corresponding data are presented for major importing countries in Table 3.4. The data are averaged over five-year periods to smooth out the effects on imports and exports of the vagaries of year-to-year changes in production conditions on export capabilities and import needs.

Table 3.3 shows that total world exports of wheat increased substantially between 1960 and 1995, more than doubling over this period. However, the market shares of current major exporters have not been constant. The export market enjoyed by the USA, for example, fell only very slightly between 1960–1964 and 1980–1984 from 39% to 38.7%, but declined quite sharply over the next decade to under 30% by 1991–1995. Canada's share of world markets also declined over the 35-year period, from 22.2% in 1960–1964 to 17.7% in 1991–1995, though most of this decline had occurred by 1980–1984. Market shares for Australia and Argentina also moderated between 1960 and 1995.

Table 3.3. World wheat trade and wheat export market shares, 1960–1995.

	1960–1964		1980–1984		1991–1995	
Exporters	Volume[a]	Share (%)	Volume[a]	Share (%)	Volume[a]	Share (%)
USA	19.5	39.0	41.6	38.7	34.4	29.1
EU-12[b]	4.2	8.4	23.3	21.7	34.3	29.1
Canada	11.1	22.2	19.1	17.8	20.9	17.7
Australia	6.4	12.8	11.2	10.4	10.2	8.6
Argentina	3.1	6.2	6.9	6.4	6.0	5.1
Others	5.7	11.4	5.4	5.0	12.3	10.4
World	50.0	100.0	107.5	100.0	118.1	100.0

[a] Volumes are in million tonnes.
[b] Includes intra-EU trade.
Source: USDA, 1996.

Table 3.4. World wheat trade wheat import market shares, 1960–1995.

	1960–1964		1980–1984		1991–1995	
Importers	Volume[a]	Share (%)	Volume[a]	Share (%)	Volume[a]	Share (%)
China	4.4	9.3	11.4	11.0	9.8	8.3
Japan	3.1	6.6	5.7	5.5	6.0	5.1
Egypt	1.7	3.6	5.8	5.6	5.9	5.0
South Korea	0.6	1.3	2.3	2.2	4.2	3.5
Algeria	0.4	0.8	2.6	2.5	4.0	3.4
Indonesia	0.1	0.2	1.5	1.4	3.0	2.6
Eastern Europe	6.0	12.7	4.7	4.5	2.0	1.7
EU-12[b]	11.0	23.3	11.9	11.4	17.0	14.4
Former Soviet Union	3.0	5.5	21.0	20.0	16.0	13.2
Others	17.4	36.8	37.1	35.6	50.6	42.8
World	47.3	100.0	104.1	100.0	118.1	100.0

[a] Volumes are in million tonnes.
[b] Includes intra-EU trade.
Source: USDA, 1996.

In contrast, the share of the export market enjoyed by the EU increased substantially from 8.4% in 1960–1964 to 29.1% in 1991–1995. The EU's expansion of wheat exports was driven by the rapid increases in yields experienced by EU producers over this period, which have been attributed by many commentators to the high prices guaranteed to EU producers during this period under the Common Agricultural Policy (CAP). Many of the same commentators expect this trend to be reversed over the period 1995–2005 as a result of the 1992 CAP reforms and the provision of the 1994 General Agreement on Tariffs and Trade (GATT). Evidence provided by Vavra and Smith (1996) about cereal-planting decisions in the UK raises questions about whether or not this is in fact likely to be the case. In their model, yields were expressed as a function of time (a proxy for technical innovations). They found that wheat-planted area had not been significantly affected by the set-aside and price provisions of the 1992 CAP reforms. Regardless of how market shares enjoyed by the five major wheat-exporting countries have changed, however, it has remained the case that these five countries have consistently provided and continue to provide about 90% of total world wheat exports.

The data presented in Table 3.4 on world wheat imports paints a substantially different picture. While the former Soviet Union, China and Japan have consistently been important importers of wheat, in most years their market shares have been much smaller than those enjoyed by major wheat exporters. While the former Soviet Union purchased about 20% of all wheat imports between 1980 and 1984, its import market share was only 5.5% in the early 1960s and had decreased to 13.2% by 1991–1995. China has been a more consistent importer in this respect, purchasing between 8.3 and 11% of world imports between 1960–1964 and 1991–1995. Among other importers, South Korea's import market share steadily increased from 1.3% in 1960–1964 to 3.5% in 1991–1995. Algeria's import market share followed a very similar path, as did Indonesia's market share. Interestingly, intra-EU trade in wheat has become somewhat less important on a relative basis. EU member country imports (including intra-EU trade) declined from 23.3% of world imports in 1960–1964 to 14.4% in 1991–1995. Finally, it is worth noting that the import side of the world wheat market is much less concentrated than the export side of the market; at no time over the period 1960–1965 did the top five wheat-importing countries purchase more than 45% of total world imports and more often their aggregate market share was less than 35% of total imports.

3. Uncertainties about Medium- and Long-Term Supply and Demand Trends

The preceding section described the historical record on long-term trends in world wheat supply and demand. For more than 100 years, although there have been some short-term fluctuations in real wheat prices caused by weather and political factors, the simple fact is that supply has increased faster than demand with the result that the real price has declined. This has been true in the latter half of the 20th century despite unprecedented increases in global population and income. Whatever increases in demand these factors brought forth were more than offset by increases in productivity and cropped area. The basic economics of these long-term trends in shifts in supply and demand is well understood.

What is less clear is whether these long-term trends in supply and demand will persist into the foreseeable future. Can we reasonably expect that the real price of wheat will continue to decline in the medium to long term, or are there possible changes in the underlying driving forces – unforeseen surprises – that could reverse these trends and result in a higher real world price for wheat? In this section we discuss uncertainties on the supply side and the demand side of the market that could lead to a reversal of the long-term downward trend.

Supply-side uncertainties

Using the fact that total production is the product of area in production and yield per unit of area, we can organize the discussion in terms of factors affecting land in wheat production and factors affecting productivity. However, it is important to note that the two may be interrelated in important ways, as we shall discuss below.

Area in wheat production depends on two factors: availability of new land to be brought into production, and the relative profitability of wheat versus other uses of land. According to recent estimates by the Food and Agriculture Organization (FAO, 1993), there are about 1.5 billion ha of crop land in the world, and about 3.4 billion ha of land in permanent pasture. Table 3.5 shows the breakdown by region of the world. These data show that land in wheat production is quite evenly distributed around the world, and in no region is it much more than about 20% of total cropland.

Table 3.5. World agricultural land use (thousands of ha), 1993.

	Total cropland (% of total)		Total land in wheat production (% of total cropland)		Total pasture (% of total)	
Africa	166,963	(12.5)	8,348	(5)	883,569	(26)
North and Central America	264,473	(19.5)	36,911	(14)	362,051	(11)
South America	90,816	(6.5)	6,590	(7)	495,404	(14.5)
East Asia	242,248	(18)	53,407	(22)	792,189	(23.5)
South Asia (India and Pakistan)	186,900	(14)	33,551	(18)	16,800	(0.5)
Europe	122,021	(9)	26,392	(21.5)	79,445	(2.5)
Oceania	49,854	(4)	9,891	(18.5)	428,602	(13)
Former Soviet Union	225,400	(17)	47,242	(21)	327,000	(10)
Total	1,348,675		220,605	(16.5)	3,368,260	

Source: FAO, 1994.

In many wheat-producing regions of the world there are substantial opportunities for substitution among crops depending on relative profitability. For example, in the warmer and more humid areas of the US wheat belt, substitution between wheat, maize and soybeans is possible, and in the drier and colder parts of the wheat belt livestock production is a competitive alternative. Thus, one source of uncertainty about wheat production and the future of the real price of wheat arises because of uncertainty about the prices for substitute crops and livestock. In the long term, the prospect of climate change augments uncertainties about the availability of suitable land for wheat production.

Another significant uncertainty factor is in the conversion of the wheat area to other agricultural and non-agricultural uses. Long-term land conversion programmes such as the Conservation Reserve Program (CRP) in the USA have had, and may continue to have, a significant impact on the amount of land in crop production in certain regions of the world. In 1996 there were 89.95 million ha of land in the CRP in the USA, with 46.4% of those hectares in the wheat belt. A large proportion of CRP land falls in the wheat belt because that is where a large share of the economically marginal land is found. Other supply-control programmes kept about 37 million additional hectares out of production. Relative to total land in wheat production in the world, the amount taken out by these policies will probably remain relatively small, but could have some impact on world markets at the margin.

Despite possibilities for substitution between wheat and other uses, the total area in wheat has been quite stable over time. There is probably much greater uncertainty about productivity than about the amount of land in wheat production. The greatest uncertainty probably lies in sustaining the positive trends in productivity that have been obtained in the second half of this century. Ruttan (1995) observes that in the medium term productivity growth will continue to depend on conventional plant breeding and the use of associated mechanical and chemical inputs, with the contribution of genetic engineering several decades away and very uncertain.

An important source of uncertainty about long-term productivity trends is the impact of modern agricultural technology on the natural resource base. Pingali (1994) presents evidence that rice yield potential is reaching a plateau because of problems associated with long-term use of monoculture and other factors. Similar concerns have been raised about long-term effects of crop production on soil productivity (Bouma *et al.*, 1995) and the long-term degradation of groundwater supplies in irrigated areas (FAO, 1993). On the other hand, resource quality has improved in many areas because of better land and water management. One need only compare the quality of resource management in US agriculture today with that of earlier decades, for example the management of soil erosion with minimum tillage, to realize this fact. Research by

Lindert (1996) indicates that in parts of China and Indonesia the quality of agricultural land may have improved rather than deteriorated over the past 50 years. The debate among agricultural scientists and sustainable agriculture advocates over the long-term effects of modern agricultural practices on soil quality and productivity remains unresolved at this time. The most reasonable assumption is perhaps that resource degradation in agriculture is a location-specific phenomenon that varies substantially from place to place, but it remains unclear if there is a long-term trend around the world towards resource degradation and associated reductions in productivity.

One could also question whether the scale of production that has been achieved in wheat and other grain production in the USA and other high-technology areas can be relied upon to achieve further gains in productivity and reductions in average costs of production. If these productivity-enhancing, cost-reducing trends are being played out, then we could see the rate of productivity growth and production growth slow in future decades.

The possible exhaustion of the productivity gains associated with the Green Revolution, and possible trends towards resource degradation, also coincides with an era of a decreasing rate of growth in investments in agricultural research in the high-income countries where much of such investment takes place, despite evidence that public-sector research remains highly productive (Fuglie *et al.*, 1996). There has been continued growth in private-sector research, which to some degree substitutes for public investment. Private research, however, is much more applied and orientated towards product development than public research, perhaps with the exception of investments in biogenetic research. Research investment by the Consultative Group on International Agricultural Research (CGIAR) has stagnated and in some cases declined in recent years, and investment in many developing countries has declined or remained at very low levels. Thus, there remains considerable uncertainty about whether the world will continue to invest successfully in agricultural research that will provide the foundation for future productivity growth at rates comparable to those achieved in the past 50 years.

One reason why there is particularly great uncertainty about future productivity growth is our limited ability to forecast or predict technological innovation and productivity growth (Antle, 1996). Whereas we have a solid foundation of theory and data to forecast how price changes and policies have an impact on land allocation between crops, livestock and other uses, we do not have equally well-developed theories or methods to forecast technology and productivity. None of the models used to forecast future production or prices incorporates endogenous technology, despite the substantial literature providing evidence that technological innovation is endogenous to prices. Models of endogenous technology would predict, for example, that research investment in wheat productivity would be positively related to the price of wheat. Consequently, long-term forecasts of agricultural supply that assume technology is exogenous to prices would be likely to over- or underestimate prices significantly, depending on whether the assumed rate of productivity growth was too high or too low. The topic of endogenous productivity also raises the issue of policy impact on productivity. As D. Gale Johnson points out in his chapter of this book, policies on the former Soviet Union, China and Africa have significantly and adversely affected production and productivity. China has reformed its policies. Whether or not the former Soviet Union and Africa will be able to do so remains a significant question.

An additional source of long-term uncertainty about production and productivity trends is associated with possible climate change and its impacts on agriculture. Even if we take at face value the Intergovernmental Panel on Climate Change's (1990) consensus prediction of global warming, there remains tremendous uncertainty about how climate will change on a scale that matters for agriculture. Different general circulation models produce very different predictions of average temperatures, temperature extremes, and precipitation patterns (Schimmelpfennig *et al.*, 1996). These models are also unable to provide data at a spatial or temporal resolution that is meaningful for climate-sensitive biological processes such as crop production. Current climate models generate predictions at a scale of 50 km^2 or greater. Moreover, most climate change analyses provide estimates of climate with some increased CO_2 level (typically, doubled CO_2), but do not provide information about the rate of change of temperature or precipitation patterns over time. Therefore, most of the existing climate change analyses have been incapable of providing information that would be needed to assess how well climate-sensitive activities such as agriculture would be able to adapt.

Demand-side uncertainties

The market level demand for wheat in any given region includes demand for wheat as food for human consumption and as feed for livestock. In general, at least with respect to basic commodities such as food grains, predictions about shifts in food demand are usually driven by predications about population growth and income growth. Relative price movements, though very difficult to forecast, are often viewed as less important determinants of food demand for major grains, because estimated own-price and cross-price elasticities tend to be quite small. However, many food grains such as wheat and barley can be, and are, also used as feed grains. The demand for feed grains is a derived demand, driven in large part by demands for livestock products, which again, to a large degree, are driven by income and population growth. The feed demand for a particular grain such as wheat is influenced by relative price movements among substitute feed grains to a much greater degree than is the demand for food grains because of more obvious substitution possibilities in feed mixes. Thus relative price movements can be expected to be more important determinants of the demand for wheat as feed than the demand for wheat as food.

The above discussion indicates potential sources of uncertainty on the demand side of the world market for wheat with respect to forecasts of future market developments. Per capita consumption of wheat for food and feed is affected by income growth, which influences the demand for wheat as food directly and for wheat as feed by increasing the demand for livestock and poultry products such as beef and chicken. Changes in market demand are therefore strongly influenced by per capita income growth (and the distribution of income) and population growth. Uncertainties about future levels of food demand for wheat therefore derive from uncertainties about per capita income growth rates, both in the aggregate and among important sub-aggregates of the population (for example, low-income versus high-income households and rural versus urban households). By and large, economists are likely to place more confidence in aggregate forecasts of per capita income than in forecasts for population sub-aggregates, although even forecasts of aggregate per capita incomes have relatively large standard errors, especially in developing countries.[4] In developed economies such as the USA, where estimated income elasticities are very small, errors in per capita income forecasts are relatively unimportant. In developing countries, where income elasticities are considerably larger, errors in forecasts of future economic growth rates and the distribution of income among different population sub-groups are likely to lead to important errors in estimates of the demand for wheat for direct human consumption.

Population growth in all countries is important in determining increases in the demand for wheat for human consumption. Uncertainties about future changes in population therefore lead to uncertainty about future changes in the demand for wheat and, in consequence, the future price of wheat. With respect to developing countries, which currently are faced with relatively high population growth rates, it should be noted that errors in income growth estimates may lead to offsetting errors in population growth rates. To the extent that population growth rates are inversely related to per capita incomes, underestimates of the latter may be associated with overestimates of the former and, therefore, in the context of the demand for wheat, the errors may be offsetting.

Predictions of future food demand for wheat may not be heavily affected by errors in forecasts of relative prices. The same may not be the case for feed demand. Substitution elasticities here are not linked to relatively rigid human preferences for particular wheat-based products such as bread and pasta. Rather, they are determined by technical substitution possibilities in feed diets between wheat, maize, barley and other crops such as oilseeds and lucerne. Predictions of relative price movements are particularly difficult, especially in the medium- to long-term context. In fact, forecasting feed demand is generally more difficult, not least because income elasticities for livestock products are larger and errors in forecasting economic growth are therefore likely to lead to significant errors in forecasting feed demand. In addition, feed demand depends not only on total meat consumption and livestock production but also on the mix of livestock products, which itself depends on the relative prices of red meats, poultry and fish. Thus forecasts of feed demand for wheat, and therefore aggregate wheat demand depend on relatively speculative explicit or implicit assumptions about movements in livestock product prices and, by implication, the size and composition of national livestock industries.

Finally, in the context of world markets, country-specific domestic and trade policies may be important, at least in the short to medium term.[5] For example, radical changes in the economic policies (including agricultural policies) in the former Soviet Union have led to sharp reductions in cattle herds and, therefore, equally sharp reductions in the demand for wheat as feed. The result has been a substantial reduction in former Soviet Union wheat imports. Shifts in agricultural policy regimes in China, including agricultural research policy, may also have substantial short- and medium-term implications for future Chinese import demand for wheat.

4. Alternative Forecast Models of Future Wheat Prices, Production and Consumption

In this section, we review predictions about future wheat market prices obtained from four general models designed to predict future agricultural commodity market conditions. These models include three forecast models that focus on short- and medium-term (1–10-year) predictions and one forecast model that has a longer-term focus. The three short- to medium-term forecasts include:

1. the FAPRI baseline forecast model to the year 2005;
2. the Organization for Economic Cooperation and Development (OECD) AGLINK forecast model to the year 2000; and
3. the US Department of Agriculture (USDA) Baseline Projections to 2005.

The longer-run forecasts are from the International Food Policy Research Institute (IFPRI) International Model for Policy Analysis of Agricultural Commodities and Trade (IMPACT) model developed by Rosegrant *et al.* (1995).

The FAPRI model, which is discussed in more detail in section 5, is a multi-commodity, multi-country econometric model. FAPRI forecasts are developed through an iterative process involving the estimated parameters of the model and input from commodity market experts. Baseline FAPRI forecasts are developed under the assumption that existing agricultural policies will remain in place (including the provisions of the 1996 Federal Agricultural Improvement and Reform (FAIR) Act for the USA and the current EU CAP). Potential revisions of the World Trade Organization (WTO) are not taken into account, but existing provisions of the 1994 GATT agreement are assumed to be binding. With respect to China and the former Soviet Union, two net importers about which there is considerable uncertainty, the FAPRI model does not constrain Chinese imports of all grains to be less than or equal to 5% of domestic consumption (the stated objective of Chinese policy makers) and assumes that wheat yields in the former Soviet Union reach but do not exceed the historical highs achieved in the late 1980s and 1990. In developing baseline forecasts, the FAPRI model adopts fairly optimistic assumptions about gross domestic product (GDP) growth. World GDP is assumed to grow at 3% per year, GDP growth is assumed to be 2.4% in developed economies, 5.7% in developing economies and 4–6% in transition economies.

The USDA (1997) develops baseline projections for many commodities, including wheat. Its current baseline projections track commodity prices through 2005. The projections are made under the assumption that the provisions of the FAIR Act remain in place until then. In addition, China, the former Soviet Union and Taiwan are assumed not to accede to the WTO, the EU is assumed to continue to consist only of its current 15 member countries, the North American Free Trade Agreement (NAFTA) is assumed not to expand, and major countries' agricultural policies are assumed to evolve along their current paths. Economic growth is assumed to be 2.5% per year in developed countries, 5% between 1997 and 1999 and 4.7% thereafter in transition economies, 5.5% in most developing countries, and, in China, 9% until 2000 and 8.4% between 2001 and 2005. Population growth in developing economies and globally is assumed to slow down over the entire period. These assumptions imply relatively strong per capita income growth in developing countries, indicating a shift towards products with relatively large income elasticities such as red meats, poultry and bread. The USDA points out that its baseline projections are conditional rather than unconditional forecasts of commodity market conditions. However, presumably its baseline forecasts represent the outcomes it expects to occur under the most likely policy, income growth and population growth scenarios.

The OECD (1996) provides short-term forecasts of commodity prices through 2000. These forecasts are generated by the OECD AGLINK model of major temperate zone agricultural commodities. The AGLINK model consists of 'dynamic economic' models for seven major agricultural producing regions within OECD. The OECD approach to forecasting is similar to that used by FAPRI. Initially, information is obtained from OECD member countries on market developments with a view to determining the key assumptions that underpin the formal model. Initial projections are then obtained and commented on by experts in member countries. Subsequently, a second baseline projection is developed under modified key assumptions.

The OECD projections reported here assume that existing agricultural policies remain in place for most member countries (including the EU) but that in the USA the provisions of the 1990 FACT Act rather than the 1996 FAIR Act are implemented. The annual economic growth rate is assumed to increase from 2.4% to 2.9% per year over the period 1995–2000 among OECD countries (developed economies), to be about 6% in the dynamic Asian economies (such as Taiwan and Korea), about 9% in China, about 3.3% in Central and South America, about 5–5.5% in Africa and the Middle East, and between 2 and 4% in transition economies. Population growth in sub-Saharan Africa is assumed to be sufficiently rapid to result in lower per capita incomes. It is not clear what is being assumed about population growth in other regions.

The IFPRI IMPACT (Rosegrant *et al.*, 1995) is built upon existing global trade models such as the OECD model, the FAO model (Alexandratos, 1995), and the Texas A&M based IFPSIM and SWOPSIM models, which have been extended to permit the development of longer-term forecasts. The modelling approach is partial equilibrium, in that interactions between agricultural and other sectors of the economies are ignored, but it does account for interactions between agricultural commodity markets.

The model accounts for 35 separate countries, and for crop and livestock markets. Crop area decisions and yields are modelled separately and markets are cleared through endogenous price adjustments. Demand is determined by largely exogenous changes in income and population, migration from rural to urban areas, and endogenous shifts in agricultural commodity prices. Crop supply shifts are largely determined by assumptions about trends in yields. For the purposes of making projections, the global population growth rate is assumed to be 1.7% with considerable variation across regions. In sub-Saharan Africa, the assumed annual population growth rate is 2.9%, in South Asia 1.8%, in India 1.7%, in China 1%, and in developed economies 0.4%.

Over the forecast period, the economic growth rate (as measured by GDP) is assumed to range from 4.4% to 5.5% in developing countries, to be over 6% in the dynamic Asian economies, 6% in China, 5.5% in India, 3% in Latin America, 3% in the former Soviet Union and the transition economies and 2.4% in the developed economies. These assumptions are generally quite similar to those adopted in the short-run models discussed above with the exception of China. The IFPRI model assumes a lower growth rate for the Chinese economy because, over the longer-run 25-year forecast period, China's current rapid economic growth rate is expected to moderate.

The price forecasts obtained from the FAPRI, USDA, OECD and IFPRI models over the various relevant time horizons are presented in Fig. 3.6. In addition, Fig. 3.6 also includes two 'sophisticatedly simple' sets of price forecasts obtained from exponential regressions of the US price of wheat against time over the periods 1920–1995 and 1955–1995. Regression results for these models are reported in Table 3.1. Both the FAPRI and USDA baseline forecasts indicate that world wheat prices will initially decline from relatively high levels of more than \$202.07 per tonne in 1995 to about or just less than \$146.96 per tonne in 1998. Thereafter they are forecast to increase fairly steadily to between \$169 and \$180.03 per tonne by 2005. The OECD forecasts indicate that per tonne prices will drop fairly rapidly from about \$202.07 in 1995 to about \$156.15 over the period 1996–1998 and to just below \$146.96 by 2000. The IFPRI IMPACT model forecasts a decline in per tonne wheat prices from about \$180.03 in 1995 to about \$154.31 in 2020. Data on the actual time path of price changes predicted by the IFPRI IMPACT model were not available. Thus, in Fig. 3.6, annual price movements are assumed to follow a linear path.

Clearly, the different forecast models result in quite different predictions about the future time path of wheat prices. The IFPRI IMPACT model incorporates assumptions that result in wheat supply shocks that exceed wheat demand shocks over the longer run. Two possible explanations of this outcome are as follows. On the demand side, the IFPRI IMPACT model assumes a lower economic growth rate for China than do the FAPRI and USDA models. On the supply side, the IFPRI model may incorporate more optimistic assumptions about yield trends for both wheat and other grains. In the following section, the FAPRI model is adjusted to consider the effects on FAPRI model forecasts of different yield and demand growth assumptions.

It is also interesting to compare the forecasts obtained from the commodity market models with the naïve forecasts obtained from simple exponential trend models of wheat. Predictions from two models are reported, the first estimated using US data over the period 1920–1995 and the second estimated using US data for the period 1955–1995 following the Korean war. Both models forecast much lower

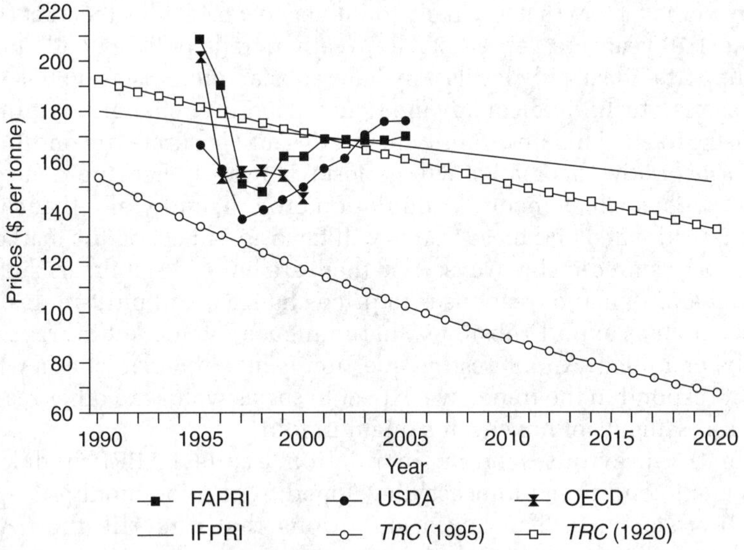

Fig. 3.6. Alternative forecasts of future world wheat prices (1995 constant dollars). TRC, Trade Research Center.

prices by 2020 than does the IFPRI model. In the first naïve exponential model, per tonne wheat prices are predicted to fall from just under \$183.70 in 1995 to about \$135.94 in 2020 at an annual rate of 1.18%; in the second model, they are predicted to decline from \$152.47 in 1995 to \$64.30 in 2020 at annual rate of 2.7%. The difference between the two naïve forecasts derives from the fact that there are only data from the post-war period in the second model, during which the effects on wheat prices of rapid technical advance associated with varietal improvement were particularly important. These naïve models do indicate the importance of alternative assumptions about yield trends for price forecasts, and again they raise the issue of whether it is plausible to believe that demand shifts will outstrip supply shifts over the next 30–50 years, in contrast with the previous 130 years.

5. Alternative Scenarios and Their Implications for FAPRI Model Wheat Price Forecast

This section presents a more detailed discussion of the FAPRI model and presents two alternative forecasts to the FAPRI baseline forecast for the price of wheat developed using the FAPRI model with, from the point of view of wheat producers, first more 'optimistic' assumptions and then more pessimistic assumptions about general market trends. Many of the factors that are likely to influence world wheat markets over the next 10 years are unpredictable. Weather, trade policies, and domestic support and subsidy levels may have substantial impacts on this market, as may technological advances and structural changes within the industry itself. This uncertainty precludes any accurate unconditional forecasts of how this market will perform. However, there are some general trends, such as income, population growth, and yield, that can at least be estimated and these trends will have an impact on the market in more or less predictable ways. Also there are built-in stabilizers such as supply and demand, responses to price changes, and built-in destabilizers, such as export subsidies, that influence the market in ways that can be modelled. An interesting question is how the market as a whole might respond to the trends we expect to see as well as to other reasonable assessments of how events might unfold.

In the previous section, in relation to the FAPRI model, we presented conditional forecasts developed from a commonly accepted baseline scenario. The key assumptions that underlie the FAPRI baseline analysis, such as, on the import side, the role of China and, on the export side, yield growth and/or land use in major net exporting countries such as Australia and the EU, were then subjected to a critical review. Next, reasonable and plausible alternative assumptions were identified and organized into two scenarios, an 'optimistic' scenario that would lead to higher world and US prices, and a 'pessimistic' scenario that would lead to lower world and US prices.

As noted above, the baseline is the FAPRI baseline, which is developed as follows: a group of about 30 US-based policy analysts gather each year in November. Universities represented include Iowa State, University of Missouri, Texas A&M, Arizona State, and the University of Arkansas. Individuals within this group have specific commodity or country/regional expertise. This group uses expert opinion and a set of multi-commodity, multi-country commodity models to make guesstimates as to where world markets are going over the next 10 years. Care is taken to ensure that intra-country and intra-commodity results are mutually consistent, and that various trade policies are properly embedded in the model structure.

These preliminary results are distributed to about 150 recognized experts, and these experts are then invited to provide critical evaluation at a baseline review that is held in Kansas City in mid-January. Valid criticisms are incorporated into the analysis at a subsequent meeting of the trade modellers in February. The final report is then published in April or May. Because of the emphasis on consensus-forming as well as the interaction with individuals from other modelling groups, the resulting baseline is usually similar to those issued by other groups such as USDA and OECD.

The authors examined the FAPRI baseline assumptions and suggested the following as viable alternatives.

The optimistic scenario

1. Australian wheat exports were reduced to 11–11.5 million tonnes from the FAPRI baseline assumption of 13.5–15 million tonnes. The reasoning here was that FAPRI was allowing more land to shift from wool to wheat than could reasonably be accomplished. Also important was the expectation that more Australian land would be devoted to feed grains than FAPRI had assumed.
2. Chinese wheat imports were increased by about 3 million tonnes per year. Here the differences revolve around estimates of the level and recent changes in Chinese wheat stocks. The FAPRI model implicitly acknowledges that low Chinese wheat imports in 1996/97 were caused by greater Chinese production. The contrary view expressed here is that this relatively low import level was a response to high wheat prices and was achieved by drawing down Chinese stocks.
3. The FAPRI baseline shows India changing from a small net wheat exporter to a small net importer. The authors felt that consideration of some additional demand-side growth was warranted.

The pessimistic scenario

1. The FAPRI baseline somewhat conservatively assumes that EU yield growth will slow to 1% per year. This is motivated by the recent decoupling of EU price supports and the relatively high level of wheat yields in the EU. The alternative view considered in this scenario is that EU yield growth will continue at 1.5% per year.
2. In the baseline scenario, it is assumed that the EU meets all of its GATT obligations because the predicted world price exceeds the CAP price for wheat. In this scenario, the EU is assumed to exceed its GATT-constrained wheat exports if necessary; that is, we assume that if the EU is faced with mounting stocks of wheat, it will find some alternative interpretation of its GATT commitments that allows it to export all of its surplus. Hence, the pessimistic scenario assumes that the EU acts as if it is indifferent to its GATT commitment on wheat.
3. One possible US reaction to the EU response discussed in pessimistic scenario 2, above, would be to increase US Export Enhancement Payments (EEP). However, because this is a pessimistic scenario we assumed that this would not occur.

Forecasts of world wheat prices (measured as US free-on-board (f.o.b.) Gulf prices) for the baseline, optimistic and pessimistic scenarios are presented in Fig. 3.7. Details of forecasts for wheat production, consumption, trade and stocks for major countries involved in world wheat markets are presented in Tables 3.6–3.11 in the Appendices.

The individual optimistic and pessimistic scenarios represent reasonable and acceptable alternatives. However, if all of the pessimistic or optimistic outcomes occurred simultaneously, one might expect some major impacts. This did not turn out to be the case. To see why, consider that adjustments occur in 30 separate countries and among 14 different commodities. The sheer size of the model causes shocks to be dissipated among hundreds of different markets – much as they would be in the real world.

In the optimistic scenario, US wheat prices rise in the range of $3.67 to $9.19 per tonne – a typical day's move on the Chicago Board of Trade (CBOT). This is not an aberration of the model that is used. It shows simply that world agriculture can respond to substantial shocks, particularly if they occur in only one commodity. Consumers adjust along demand curves, and producers adjust area planted and move along elastic long-term supply curves.

Also, policy endogeneity with respect to both the US and the EU export subsidy programmes actually tends to reduce some variations in world wheat prices over the longer term. For example, in the optimistic scenario, relatively high world prices cause the USA to reduce EEP subsidies. The result is that US producers do not receive all of the benefits of the price increases (some of those benefits accrue to US taxpayers). Thus, in the alternative forecasts, US wheat exports in

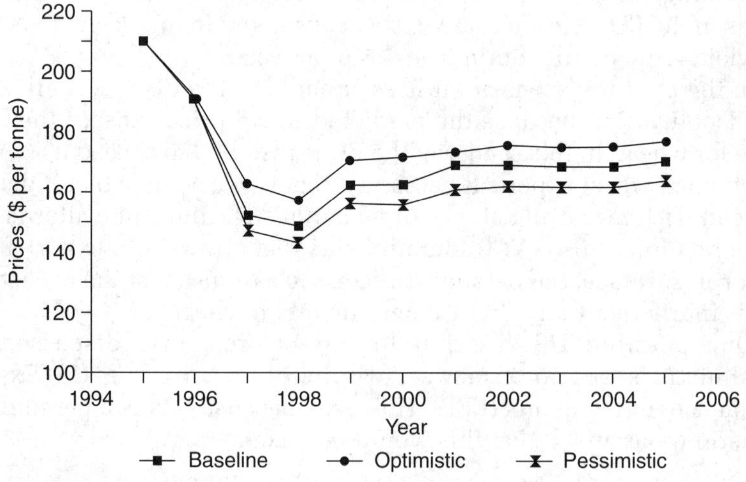

Fig. 3.7. Alternative FAPRI world wheat price forecasts.

2005–2006 in the baseline equal 30.3 million tonnes and in the optimistic scenario equal only 33.13 million tonnes. US market share rises from 31% in 1996–1997 to 37% in 2000 but falls back to only 32.7% in 2005–2006.

It is interesting to observe how, because of policy endogeneity, US and EU policies that, within any particular year, serve to isolate domestic markets and destabilize world prices, can act to stabilize world prices *over time*. In the optimistic scenario the policies are not used as much as in the baseline and, through the removal of these destabilizers, markets are stabilized.

In the pessimistic scenario, we have purposely disconnected some of the endogenous policy changes; that is, we do not change US EEP policy in the face of distortionary EU behaviour. As might be expected, these new rules of the game have a significant impact on the EU share of world markets – EU exports rise by almost 4 million tonnes by 2005–2006 from a baseline value of 20.56 million tonnes. However, the impact on other variables is again small. US exports are 1.5 million tonnes lower because non-US wheat exporters adjust to EU expansions. US wheat prices fall in the range of \$3.67 to \$5.51 per tonne. Again this shows the resilience of the models and, by extension, the markets to reasonable shocks. Bad behaviour on behalf of the EU allows them to capture market share (at some cost to their taxpayers) but does not alter equilibrium prices substantially.

Time constraints prohibited us from running the pessimistic scenario with a US EEP response. However, recent history would suggest that a price war between the USA and EU *would* have an impact on world prices but not on market shares.

These experiments suggest two general results. First, the model and, if the model is to be believed, world wheat markets are robust in the long run. This is true simply because demand and supply responses for wheat (and for other commodities) act to dampen the effects of a wheat-specific shock. If this is the case, then the flat lines obtained for price projections from large-scale commodity models seem reasonable. This result stands in direct contradiction to the hysteria that has accompanied the possibility that China might emerge as a large wheat importer, or the cross-Atlantic and intra-North-American wars that accompany changes in wheat policies. We did not examine a multi-commodity shock (that is, a shift in worldwide income growth) but it is likely that without a cross-commodity stabilizing influence the price impact of such as shock would be much larger.

Second, the US and EU policies operate in ways that are more complicated than we thought. For example, a series of positive events (from the perspective of a US wheat producer) would act to disconnect EU and US export subsidies. Without these supports, the US producer does not capture all of the benefits of the favourable trends.

Also, when world prices rise above the EU intervention price so that the EU does not subsidize exports, then consumers and producers in the EU respond to world prices and dampen the favourable impact of favourable trends. Given that these discretionary policies are in place, they can add stability to multi-year models when prices rise because the distortions are automatically removed. The pessimistic scenario shows how a single country can capture market share at taxpayer expense but also shows that the world price impacts of such behaviour are small. For large price impacts we may need two of those large competing countries (the USA, the EU and Canada) to compete in a subsidy war.

6. Conclusion

Over the past 130 years, the per tonne real price of wheat, in terms of 1995 dollars, has steadily declined from over $808.28 in 1866 to about $146.96 in 1997 at an average annual rate of 0.9%. As D. Gale Johnson has already pointed out (Johnson, 1997), despite massive increases in world population and per capita incomes since the 1950s, the rate of technological innovation in wheat production has been sufficiently large to ensure that the world wheat supply curve has shifted outward sufficiently rapidly to speed up the rate at which real world wheat prices have been declining. Thus the crucial question is whether, over the next 5–10 years, the pattern of supply shocks and demand shocks will change enough to alter this trend.

The three short- to medium-term forecast models examined in section 4 – the FAPRI model, the OECD AGLINK model and the USDA baseline forecast model – all predict that wheat prices will increase over the next 5–10 years. However, it is worth noting that they assume relatively rapid economic growth in developing countries (upwards of 5% per year) and in China, where economic growth is assumed to be between 8 and 9% per year over the forecast periods. Moreover, yield growth is forecast to be quite modest. In contrast, the IFPRI 2020 forecast model predicts that wheat prices will decline over the next 25 years, largely much in line with long-term trends. However, the IFPRI forecast is based on a slower economic growth rate for China of 6% per year over the forecast period and, possibly, more optimistic assumptions about yield growth rates.

The results of the small-scale simulation exercise utilizing the FAPRI model are interesting in the following context. Reductions in yield growth trends (which drive supply shifts) and/or increases in demand would be needed to reverse the long-run direction of the trend in the world wheat market. The simulations presented in section 5 suggest that relatively large shocks are needed to alter world wheat prices and so relatively large changes in the relative shifts in supply and demand are likely to be needed to result in increases in real world wheat prices. It is difficult to see why the long-run trends in world wheat demand and supply shifts should be expected to experience substantial changes. Without dramatic events such as those predicted by some climate change models, there is no compelling evidence that an end to agricultural productivity is imminent. Even with climatic change, the overall impact on global food production is not expected to be large, and for some crops could be positive.

Nor is it obvious that positive shocks to demand are likely to be exceptionally large. Perhaps, then, a better bet is to accede to the view that the medium- to long-run future of real wheat prices is likely to be much like their past; they are going to fall, not rise. Of course, exactly how fast they are going to fall is entirely another question.

Notes

1. Khatri (1994) reports a similar general pattern of growth rates for wheat yields in the UK. Between the mid 1800s and the 1930s wheat yields in the UK increased by between 0.5% and 1% per year. Between 1945 and 1990, wheat yields increased much more rapidly at an annual rate of close to 3% per year.
2. The relatively poor performance of yields in the former Soviet Union is largely accounted for by a sharp decline in per hectare yields between 1990 and 1995 from 2 tonnes to 1.3 tonnes. This decline is associated with the radical changes in the agricultural policy and market environment in the former Soviet Union that took place during the early 1990s.
3. During this period the EU consisted of 12 member countries: Belgium, Denmark, France, Germany, Greece, Ireland, Italy, Luxembourg, The Netherlands, Portugal, Spain and the UK.
4. The experience of the republics of the former Soviet Union and other Eastern European countries provides a salutary warning about the difficulties associated with predicting medium-term and long-term income growth. In the mid-1980s, very few social scientists would have predicted the breakup of the Soviet Union, the development of Poland, the Czech Republic and other former COMECON countries as independent nations with radically different economic systems. Nor would they have predicted radical decreases in per capita incomes in Russia and other former Soviet Union republics.
5. In the longer term, country-specific policy choices may not matter very much because of the endogeneity of policy with respect to economic conditions (see, for example, Becker, 1983; Gardner, 1983; Alston and Hurd, 1990).

References

Alexandratos, N. (1995) *World Agriculture: Towards 2010*. Food and Agriculture Organization of the United Nations and John Wiley & Sons, New York, USA.

Alston, J.M. and Hurd, B.H. (1990) Some neglected social costs of government spending in farm programs. *American Journal of Agricultural Economics* 72, 149–156.

Antle, J.M. (1996) Methodological issues in assessing the potential impacts of climate change on agriculture. *Agricultural and Forest Meteorology* 80, 67–85.

Becker, G.S. (1983) A theory of competition among pressure groups for political influence. *Quarterly Journal of Economics* 98 (August), 371–401.

Bouma, J., Kuyvenhoven, A., Bouman, B.A.M., Luyten, J.C. and Zandstra, H.G. (1995) *Eco-Regional Approaches for Sustainable Land Use and Food Production.* Kluwer Academic Publishers in cooperation with International Potato Center, Dordrecht, The Netherlands.

Dalrymple, D.G. (1986) *Development and Spread of High-Yielding Wheat Varieties in Developing Countries.* Agency for International Development, Washington DC, USA.

FAO (Food and Agriculture Organization) (1993) *The State of Food and Agriculture, 1993.* Food and Agriculture Organization of the United Nations, Rome, Italy.

FAO (Food and Agriculture Organization) (1994) *Yearbook.* United Nations, Rome, Italy.

FAO (Food and Agriculture Organization) (1997) *Ag Database*, United Nations, Rome, Italy.

Fuglie, K., Ballenger, N., Day, K., Klotz, C., Ollinger, M., Reilly, J., Vasavada, U. and Yee, J. (1996) *Agricultural Research and Development: Public and Private Investments Under Alternative Markets and Institutions.* Agricultural Economic Report No. 735, Economic Research Service – NASS, US Department of Agriculture, Washington DC, USA.

Gardner, B.L. (1983) Efficient redistribution through commodity markets. *American Journal of Agricultural Economics* 65, 225–234.

Intergovernmental Panel on Climate Change (1990) *Climate Change: The IPCC Scientific Assessment.* Houghton, J.T., Jenkins, G.J. and Ephraums, J.J. (eds) Cambridge University Press, New York, USA.

Johnson, D.G. (1975) *World Food Problems and Prospects.* American Enterprise Institute, Washington DC, USA, pp. 3–4.

Johnson, D.G. (1985) World commodity market situation and outlook. In: *US Agricultural Policy: The 1985 Farm Legislation.* American Enterprise Institute, Washington DC, USA, pp. 19–50.

Johnson, D.G. (1997) North America and the world grain market. Paper prepared for presentation at conference The Economics of International Wheat Markets: Implications for Northern Rockies and Great Plains, Montana State University–Bozeman, USA, May 29–31.

Khatri, Y.J. (1994) Technical change and the returns to research in UK agriculture, 1953–1990. PhD thesis, Department of Agricultural Economics and Management, University of Reading, UK.

Lindert, P. (1996) Soil degradation and agricultural change in two developing countries. In: *Global Agricultural Science Policy for the Twenty-First Century: Invited Papers.* The Conference Secretariat of Global Agricultural Science Policy for the Twenty-First Century, Melbourne, Australia.

OECD (Organization for Economic Cooperation and Development) (1996) *The Agricultural Outlook: Trends and Issues to 2000.* Organization for Economic Co-operation and Development, Paris, France.

Pardey, P.G., Alston, J.M., Christian, J.E. and Fan, S. (1996) *Summary of a Productive Partnership: The Benefits from US Participation in the CGIAR.* EPTD Discussion Paper No. 18, International Food Policy Research Institute, Washington DC and Department of Agricultural Economics, University of California, Davis, USA.

Pingali, P.L. (1994) Technological prospects for reversing the declining trend in Asia's rice productivity. In: J.R. Anderson (ed.) *Agricultural Technology: Policy Issues for the International Community.* CAB International, Wallingford, UK, in association with the World Bank.

Rosegrant, M.W., Agcaoili-Sombilla, M. and Perez, N.D. (1995) *Global Food Projections to 2020: Implications for Investment.* International Food Policy Research Institute, Washington DC, USA.

Ruttan, V.W. (1995) Constraints on sustainable growth in agricultural production: into the twenty-first century. In: Antle, J.M. and Sumner, D.A. (eds) *The Economics of Agriculture*, Vol. 2, *Papers in Honor of D. Gale Johnson.* University of Chicago Press, Chicago, USA.

Schimmelpfennig, D., Lewandrowski, J., Railly, J., Tsigas, M. and Parry, I. (1996) *Agricultural Adaptation to Climate Change: Issues of Long-run Sustainability.* Ag Economic Report 740, Economic Research Service, US Department of Agriculture, Washington DC, USA.

USDA (US Department of Agriculture) (1996) *Wheat Yearbook.* Economic Research Service, US Department of Agriculture, Washington DC, USA.

USDA (US Department of Agriculture) (1997) *Agricultural Baseline Projections to 2005, Reflecting the 1996 Farm Act.* Staff Report WAOB-97–1, US Department of Agriculture, Washington DC, USA.

Vavra, P. and Smith, V.H. (1996) *Cereal Area Supply Response in the UK: the Effects of CAP Reform.* Research Discussion Paper No. 3, Trade Research Center, Montana State University–Bozeman, USA.

Appendices

Table 3.6. Wheat trade: baseline scenario.

Wheat trade	1995/96	1996/97	1997/98	1998/99	1999/2000	2000/01	2001/02	2002/03	2003/04	2004/05	2005/06
						Million tonnes					
Net exporters											
Argentina	4.42	10.47	8.70	8.85	9.15	9.42	9.68	9.91	10.11	10.30	10.49
Australia	13.28	18.69	12.97	13.02	12.61	12.27	12.09	12.08	12.19	12.38	12.65
Canada	16.21	19.23	18.30	17.69	18.17	19.30	19.45	19.65	19.79	19.91	20.02
EU	9.61	14.61	13.62	12.38	13.43	14.15	16.27	17.70	18.86	20.24	21.87
Eastern Europe	3.34	−3.03	1.50	1.32	1.38	1.56	1.67	1.77	1.78	1.76	1.72
Ukraine	0.90	0.30	0.95	1.24	1.49	1.24	1.13	1.03	0.91	1.04	0.97
Total non-USA	47.76	60.27	56.04	54.77	56.99	58.79	61.17	63.00	64.48	66.42	68.40
USA	31.93	24.74	26.81	25.35	27.55	29.13	29.97	30.51	31.04	31.21	31.46
(Trade share %)	40.1	29.1	32.4	31.6	32.6	33.1	32.9	32.6	32.5	32.0	31.5
Total net exports	79.69	85.01	82.84	80.12	84.53	87.93	91.13	93.51	95.51	97.63	99.86
Net importers											
Japan	5.54	5.86	5.80	5.87	5.93	5.96	5.98	6.00	6.03	6.05	6.08
Russia	5.13	2.51	0.05	−0.27	−0.75	−0.85	−0.87	−0.87	−0.83	−0.78	−0.69
Other former Soviet Union	−0.23	1.75	1.74	1.47	1.53	1.55	1.58	1.59	1.62	1.66	1.72
Other Western Europe	0.31	0.38	0.46	0.53	0.54	0.55	0.56	0.62	0.65	0.66	0.66
Developing	68.98	68.62	74.88	71.78	76.06	79.40	82.54	84.81	86.73	88.76	90.90
China	12.34	2.60	1.80	2.23	4.51	5.50	6.49	6.87	6.91	6.86	6.70
High-income East Asia	4.12	5.04	5.46	5.03	5.10	5.37	5.66	5.97	6.29	6.64	6.99
India	−0.55	−0.45	1.50	0.58	1.28	2.03	2.30	2.25	2.11	2.08	2.19
Other Asia	12.14	13.91	15.51	14.68	15.29	15.72	16.22	16.76	17.29	17.83	18.37
Brazil	5.47	5.18	5.70	5.62	5.62	5.65	5.72	5.80	5.88	5.97	6.05
Mexico	1.28	1.94	1.50	1.51	1.61	1.69	1.76	1.85	1.95	2.06	2.16
Other Latin America	6.88	7.21	7.89	7.93	8.10	8.26	8.43	8.62	8.82	9.03	9.27

Algeria	3.40	3.11	4.30	4.18	4.24	4.31	4.41	4.53	4.66	4.80	4.94
Egypt	5.91	7.00	7.20	7.26	7.28	7.33	7.41	7.52	7.65	7.80	7.97
Morocco	2.43	1.46	2.40	1.60	1.72	1.89	2.08	2.17	2.28	2.40	2.53
Tunisia	0.94	0.87	1.40	1.09	1.13	1.18	1.24	1.30	1.36	1.43	1.51
Other Africa and Middle East	14.62	20.77	20.23	20.06	20.19	20.47	20.81	21.19	21.52	21.87	22.21
Rest of world	0.34	0.41	0.43	0.46	0.47	0.47	0.48	0.48	0.48	0.49	0.49
Residual	−0.38	5.48	−0.51	0.00	0.00	0.00	0.00	0.00	0.00	0.00	0.00
Total net imports	79.69	85.01	82.84	80.12	84.53	87.93	91.13	93.51	95.51	97.63	99.86
Wheat prices	US dollars per tonne										
US Gulf Ports	209.00	184.33	154.94	149.52	151.22	156.56	158.64	160.18	162.10	163.89	166.31
Canada (Thunder Bay)	232.16	204.17	170.70	164.46	166.29	172.22	174.47	176.14	178.27	180.26	182.97
Australian (export unit)	231.00	182.48	153.91	148.76	150.38	155.44	157.48	158.98	160.86	162.61	164.98

Note: Totals may not equal the sum of the individual regions because of changes in trade position (net exporter or importer) and because of rounding error.

Table 3.7. Wheat trade: optimistic scenario.

Wheat trade	1995/96	1996/97	1997/98	1998/99	1999/2000	2000/01	2001/02	2002/03	2003/04	2004/05	2005/06
					Million tonnes						
Net exporters											
Argentina	4.42	10.47	8.68	8.78	9.07	9.39	9.66	9.96	10.23	10.54	10.80
Australia	13.28	18.98	12.47	13.28	13.05	12.72	12.47	12.37	12.37	12.45	12.56
Canada	16.21	19.23	17.80	16.97	16.96	17.48	17.42	17.24	17.12	16.84	16.67
EU	12.39	16.42	10.35	10.89	11.81	14.52	16.43	17.40	18.59	21.54	22.99
Eastern Europe	3.34	−3.11	1.50	1.16	1.23	1.31	1.39	1.39	1.09	0.74	0.43
Ukraine	0.90	0.30	0.95	1.57	2.07	2.16	2.32	2.70	2.86	2.99	3.16
Total non-USA	50.55	62.28	51.75	52.73	54.66	58.37	60.52	61.98	63.13	65.93	67.38
USA	31.93	24.74	26.67	29.54	32.75	33.18	35.21	36.87	37.97	38.40	39.78
(Trade share %)	38.7	28.4	34.0	35.9	37.5	36.2	36.8	37.3	37.6	36.8	37.1
Total net exports	82.47	87.02	78.42	82.27	87.41	91.55	95.73	98.85	101.10	104.33	107.16
Net importers											
Japan	5.54	5.86	5.80	6.04	6.05	6.06	6.08	6.10	6.13	6.15	6.18
Russia	4.81	1.40	0.00	−0.09	−0.47	−0.79	−0.85	−0.92	−0.87	−0.84	−0.78
Other former Soviet Union	−0.23	1.75	1.74	1.69	1.43	1.45	1.42	1.35	1.30	1.26	1.24
Other Western Europe	0.31	0.38	0.46	0.53	0.54	0.55	0.56	0.62	0.65	0.66	0.66
Developing	68.98	68.65	73.80	73.55	78.93	83.03	87.21	90.32	92.56	95.79	98.62
China	12.34	2.60	1.80	3.60	6.74	7.97	9.59	10.69	11.32	12.58	13.34
High-income East Asia	4.12	5.12	4.41	4.99	5.03	5.31	5.57	5.87	6.18	6.52	6.86
India	−0.55	−0.61	1.80	1.74	2.73	4.07	5.11	5.45	5.42	5.52	5.92
Other Asia	12.14	14.03	15.11	14.56	14.77	14.88	14.95	15.05	15.04	15.08	15.02
Brazil	5.47	5.20	5.40	5.33	5.35	5.43	5.54	5.67	5.80	5.94	6.08
Mexico	1.28	1.95	1.50	1.32	1.65	1.77	1.89	2.01	2.14	2.29	2.44
Other Latin America	6.88	7.39	7.86	7.89	8.03	8.20	8.32	8.46	8.57	8.73	8.87

Algeria	3.40	3.20	4.30	4.19	4.24	4.32	4.39	4.53	4.64	4.80	4.94
Egypt	5.91	7.00	7.20	7.91	8.11	8.42	8.72	9.05	9.41	9.80	10.22
Morocco	2.43	1.50	2.40	2.41	2.53	2.65	2.72	2.77	2.88	3.00	3.01
Tunisia	0.94	0.78	1.40	1.07	1.10	1.15	1.19	1.25	1.30	1.37	1.43
Other Africa and Middle East	14.62	20.50	20.63	18.55	18.64	18.87	19.21	19.54	19.86	20.16	20.49
Rest of world	0.34	0.41	0.43	0.46	0.46	0.46	0.46	0.46	0.46	0.47	0.47
Residual	2.73	8.58	−3.80	0.00	0.00	0.00	0.00	0.00	0.00	0.00	0.00
Total net imports	82.47	87.02	78.42	82.27	87.41	91.55	95.73	98.85	101.10	104.33	107.16
Wheat prices					US dollars per tonne						
US Gulf Ports	209.00	184.33	159.42	160.25	168.46	171.72	182.24	187.12	191.88	194.82	202.18
Canadian (Thunder Bay)	232.16	204.17	175.81	173.16	182.32	185.86	197.87	203.44	211.03	214.32	223.80
Australian (export unit)	231.00	182.48	158.27	156.20	164.04	167.14	177.47	182.30	188.85	191.71	199.85

Note: Totals may not equal the sum of the individual regions because of changes in trade position (net exporter or importer) and because of rounding error.

Table 3.8. Wheat trade: pessimistic scenario.

Wheat trade	1995/96	1996/97	1997/98	1998/99	1999/2000	2000/01	2001/02	2002/03	2003/04	2004/05	2005/06
						Million tonnes					
Net exporters											
Argentina	4.42	10.47	8.68	8.76	8.88	9.07	9.27	9.43	9.62	9.82	10.04
Australia	13.28	18.98	12.47	13.28	12.98	12.54	12.16	11.89	11.71	11.71	11.87
Canada	16.21	19.23	17.80	17.35	17.89	18.95	18.86	18.99	18.79	18.78	18.60
EU	12.39	16.42	10.35	11.47	11.46	12.40	14.84	16.12	20.41	21.58	22.62
Eastern Europe	3.34	−3.11	1.50	1.13	1.05	1.35	1.69	1.97	2.03	2.15	2.40
Ukraine	0.90	0.30	0.95	1.27	1.00	0.85	0.93	0.90	0.84	1.05	1.44
Total non-USA	50.55	62.28	51.75	54.23	55.69	58.15	61.11	62.93	67.24	69.06	71.10
USA	31.93	24.74	26.67	24.89	25.08	25.46	25.06	25.72	24.21	25.02	24.55
(Trade share %)	38.7	28.4	34.0	31.5	31.1	30.5	29.1	29.0	26.5	26.6	25.7
Total net exports	82.47	87.02	78.42	79.12	80.77	83.62	86.16	88.65	91.45	94.08	95.64
Net importers											
Japan	5.54	5.86	5.80	6.04	6.05	6.06	6.08	6.10	6.13	6.15	6.18
Russia	4.81	1.40	0.00	−0.95	−2.42	−2.99	−3.37	−3.63	−3.84	−3.97	−4.13
Other former Soviet Union	−0.23	1.75	1.74	1.74	1.60	1.68	1.70	1.70	1.71	1.72	1.73
Other Western Europe	0.31	0.38	0.46	0.53	0.54	0.55	0.56	0.62	0.65	0.66	0.66
Developing	68.98	68.65	73.80	70.34	72.09	74.84	77.34	79.73	82.46	85.03	86.55
China	12.34	2.60	1.80	1.42	0.85	1.34	1.37	1.36	1.28	1.64	1.52
High-income East Asia	4.12	5.12	4.41	5.05	5.13	5.41	5.72	6.02	6.37	6.70	7.07
India	−0.55	−0.61	1.80	0.14	0.51	0.81	1.10	1.27	1.76	1.72	1.17
Other Asia	12.14	14.03	15.11	14.82	15.35	15.70	16.13	16.52	16.89	17.17	17.42
Brazil	5.47	5.20	5.40	5.35	5.38	5.47	5.60	5.73	5.88	6.02	6.17
Mexico	1.28	1.95	1.50	1.35	1.73	1.86	2.00	2.15	2.30	2.45	2.60
Other Latin America	6.88	7.39	7.86	7.99	8.28	8.54	8.79	9.06	9.31	9.56	9.80

Algeria	3.40	3.20	4.30	4.25	4.33	4.41	4.54	4.69	4.85	5.01	5.19
Egypt	5.91	7.00	7.20	7.91	8.11	8.42	8.72	9.05	9.41	9.80	10.22
Morocco	2.43	1.50	2.40	2.42	2.57	2.70	2.79	2.86	2.99	3.12	3.15
Tunisia	0.94	0.78	1.40	1.08	1.13	1.17	1.23	1.29	1.35	1.41	1.48
Other Africa and Middle East	14.62	20.50	20.63	18.55	18.73	19.00	19.35	19.74	20.08	20.43	20.75
Rest of world	0.34	0.41	0.43	0.47	0.48	0.49	0.49	0.50	0.50	0.51	0.51
Residual	2.73	8.58	−3.80	0.00	0.00	0.00	0.00	0.00	0.00	0.00	0.00
Total net imports	82.47	87.02	78.42	79.12	80.77	83.62	86.16	88.65	91.45	94.08	95.64
Wheat price	US dollars per tonne										
US Gulf Ports	209.00	184.33	159.42	143.19	142.95	146.52	144.50	146.89	142.27	147.05	145.40
Canadian (Thunder Bay)	232.16	204.17	175.80	153.12	152.27	156.16	153.60	156.25	153.91	159.31	159.16
Australian (export unit)	231.00	182.48	158.27	139.06	138.35	141.74	139.61	141.94	140.00	144.66	144.57

Note: Totals may not equal the sum of the individual regions because of changes in trade position (net exporter or importer) and because of rounding error.

Table 3.9. World and US wheat supply and utilization.

	1995/96	1996/97	1997/98	1998/99	1999/2000	2000/01	2001/02	2002/03	2003/04	2004/05	2005/06
World											
Area harvested (million ha)	219.80	231.10	229.01	227.82	226.77	226.16	226.25	226.33	226.52	226.80	226.96
Yield (tonnes per ha)	2.45	2.52	2.64	2.59	2.62	2.66	2.69	2.73	2.76	2.80	2.83
	Million tonnes										
Production	537.53	582.47	603.51	590.91	595.14	601.11	609.28	617.36	625.89	634.80	643.36
Beginning stock	118.38	104.18	107.00	126.93	129.45	129.77	129.18	128.77	128.56	128.52	128.40
Total supply	655.92	686.65	710.50	717.84	724.60	730.88	738.47	746.13	754.45	763.32	771.76
Consumption	551.74	579.66	583.57	588.38	594.83	601.70	609.70	617.58	625.93	634.93	643.72
Ending stocks	104.18	107.00	126.93	129.45	129.77	129.18	128.77	128.56	128.52	128.40	128.04
Total use	655.92	686.65	710.50	717.84	724.60	730.88	738.47	746.13	754.45	763.32	771.76
Trade[a]	79.69	85.01	82.84	80.12	84.53	87.93	91.13	93.51	95.51	97.63	99.86
Stocks-to-use ratio (%)	18.88	18.46	21.75	22.00	21.82	21.47	21.12	20.82	20.53	20.22	19.89
USA											
Area harvested (million ha)	24.65	25.44	26.14	25.38	25.24	27.07	26.82	27.08	27.04	26.98	26.89
Yield (tonnes per ha)	2.41	2.44	2.67	2.59	2.61	2.62	2.65	2.67	2.68	2.70	2.72
	Million tonnes										
Production	59.40	62.19	68.76	63.94	64.48	65.47	66.44	66.97	67.57	68.09	68.56
Beginning stocks	13.79	10.23	12.07	18.47	20.69	20.78	20.37	20.11	19.83	19.54	19.23
Domestic supply	73.19	72.42	80.83	82.42	85.17	86.25	86.81	87.08	87.40	87.63	87.80
Food, other	24.03	24.28	24.76	25.46	25.89	26.27	26.69	27.12	27.57	28.06	28.56
Seed	2.83	2.80	2.63	2.64	2.67	2.69	2.70	2.71	2.71	2.72	2.72
Feed, residual	4.13	8.54	8.16	8.28	8.27	7.78	7.34	6.92	6.54	6.41	6.18
Ending stocks	10.23	12.07	18.47	20.69	20.78	20.37	20.11	19.83	19.54	19.23	18.87
Domestic use	41.23	47.69	54.03	57.07	57.62	57.11	56.84	56.57	56.36	56.42	56.34
Net trade	31.93	24.73	26.81	25.35	27.55	29.14	29.97	30.51	31.04	31.21	31.46

[a] Excludes intra-regional trade.

Table 3.10. US wheat supply and utilization: optimistic scenario.

	1995/96	1996/97	1997/98	1998/99	1999/2000	2000/01	2001/02	2002/03	2003/04	2004/05	2005/06
Area (million ha)											
Contract area	n/a	31.03	31.02	31.16	31.03	30.94	30.91	30.91	30.91	30.91	30.91
CRP idled	4.34	4.12	4.05	3.78	4.03	4.21	4.27	4.27	4.27	4.27	4.27
Planted area	27.98	30.61	28.73	29.03	29.22	29.76	29.77	30.56	30.79	30.97	31.04
Harvested area	24.66	25.43	25.73	25.69	25.86	26.33	26.33	27.02	27.22	27.37	27.43
Yield (tonnes per ha)											
Actual	2.40	2.44	2.66	2.60	2.62	2.64	2.65	2.67	2.69	2.70	2.72
Programme	2.30	2.32	2.32	2.32	2.32	2.32	2.32	2.32	2.32	2.32	2.32
					Million tonnes						
Supply	75.06	74.94	83.44	87.36	89.47	90.84	90.89	92.05	92.76	93.26	93.55
Beginning stocks	13.81	10.24	12.08	17.79	19.10	18.72	18.58	17.68	17.42	17.06	16.77
Production	59.41	62.20	68.77	66.99	67.92	69.67	70.14	72.46	73.44	74.29	74.88
Imports	1.85	2.50	2.59	2.59	2.45	2.45	2.18	1.91	1.91	1.91	1.91
Domestic use	31.03	35.63	36.39	36.54	36.08	37.16	36.08	35.82	35.72	35.99	35.39
Feed, residual	4.16	8.55	8.79	8.26	7.25	7.82	6.20	5.40	4.71	4.36	3.16
Seed	2.83	2.80	2.78	2.82	2.89	2.91	3.01	3.05	3.09	3.11	3.18
Food, other	24.03	24.28	24.81	25.45	25.94	26.43	26.87	27.38	27.93	28.52	29.05
Exports	33.78	27.25	29.26	31.72	34.66	35.10	37.14	38.81	39.98	40.50	41.98
Total use	64.81	62.87	65.65	68.26	70.74	72.26	73.21	74.63	75.70	76.49	77.37
Ending stocks	10.24	12.08	17.79	19.10	18.72	18.58	17.68	17.42	17.06	16.77	16.18
FOR Special Program	0.00	0.00	0.00	0.00	0.00	0.00	0.00	0.00	0.00	0.00	0.00
CCC inventory	3.21	2.53	2.53	2.53	2.53	2.53	2.53	2.53	2.53	2.53	2.53
9-Month loan	0.35	1.96	2.29	2.08	1.74	1.69	1.35	1.29	1.21	1.20	1.06
'Free' stocks	6.67	7.59	12.96	14.49	14.45	14.35	13.80	13.60	13.32	13.04	12.59

Continued

Table 3.10. US wheat supply and utilization: optimistic scenario (*Continued*).

	1995/96	1996/97	1997/98	1998/99	1999/2000	2000/01	2001/02	2002/03	2003/04	2004/05	2005/06
Prices and returns (US$)											
Farm price per tonne	167.17	157.98	130.69	131.39	138.37	141.14	150.09	154.24	158.29	160.79	167.04
Loan rate per tonne	94.79	94.79	94.79	94.79	94.79	94.79	94.79	94.79	94.79	94.79	94.79
Contract payment per tonne	n/a	32.11	23.18	24.00	23.26	21.35	17.22	16.71	16.71	16.71	16.71
Contract payment per ha	n/a	63.70	45.86	47.47	46.01	42.24	34.06	33.06	33.06	33.06	33.06
f.o.b. Gulf price per tonne	209.08	184.33	159.42	143.19	142.95	146.52	144.50	146.89	142.27	147.05	145.40
Variable expenses per ha	188.49	196.79	197.67	194.80	195.70	198.28	201.04	204.55	207.23	209.71	212.94
Market net returns per ha	225.13	202.75	163.25	159.25	179.25	186.76	210.31	220.73	231.54	238.42	254.81

CRP, Conservation Reserve Program; FOR, Farmer Owned Reserve; CCC, Commodity Credit Corporation; f.o.b., free-on-board.
Note: Totals may not equal the sum of the individual components because of rounding error.

Table 3.11. US wheat supply and utilization: pessimistic scenario.

	1995/96	1996/97	1997/98	1998/99	1999/2000	2000/01	2001/02	2002/03	2003/04	2004/05	2005/06
Area (million ha)											
Contract area	n/a	31.03	31.02	31.16	31.03	30.94	30.91	30.91	30.91	30.91	30.91
CRP idled	4.34	4.12	4.05	3.78	4.03	4.21	4.27	4.27	4.27	4.27	4.27
Planted area	27.98	30.61	28.73	29.03	27.75	27.83	28.02	27.85	28.07	27.65	28.08
Harvested area	24.66	25.43	25.73	25.69	24.57	24.64	24.80	24.65	24.84	24.47	24.84
Yield (tonnes per ha)											
Actual	2.40	2.44	2.66	2.60	2.61	2.63	2.65	2.66	2.68	2.69	2.71
Programme	2.30	2.32	2.32	2.32	2.32	2.32	2.32	2.32	2.32	2.32	2.32
					Million tonnes						
Supply	75.06	74.94	83.44	87.36	87.48	87.82	87.92	87.63	88.01	87.64	88.26
Beginning stocks	13.81	10.24	12.08	17.79	20.58	20.30	19.82	19.81	19.30	19.60	18.82
Production	59.41	62.20	68.77	66.99	64.45	65.07	65.92	65.91	66.80	66.14	67.54
Imports	1.85	2.50	2.59	2.59	2.45	2.45	2.18	1.91	1.91	1.91	1.91
Domestic use	31.03	35.63	36.39	39.71	40.19	40.70	41.64	41.88	43.62	43.49	44.67
Feed, residual	4.16	8.55	8.79	11.36	11.23	11.22	11.56	11.23	12.31	11.56	12.08
Seed	2.83	2.80	2.78	2.68	2.71	2.74	2.74	2.78	2.76	2.82	2.83
Food, other	24.03	24.28	24.81	25.67	26.25	26.74	27.33	27.87	28.55	29.11	29.76
Exports	33.78	27.25	29.26	27.07	26.99	27.29	26.47	26.45	24.79	25.33	24.69
Total use	64.81	62.87	65.65	66.78	67.18	68.00	68.10	68.33	68.41	68.82	69.36
Ending stocks	10.24	12.08	17.79	20.58	20.30	19.82	19.81	19.30	19.60	18.82	18.90
FOR Special Program	0.00	0.00	0.00	0.00	0.00	0.00	0.00	0.00	0.00	0.00	0.00
CCC inventory	3.21	2.53	2.53	2.53	2.53	2.53	2.53	2.53	2.53	2.53	2.53
9-Month loan	0.35	1.96	2.29	3.28	3.23	3.02	3.26	3.13	3.59	3.23	3.47
'Free' stocks	6.67	7.59	12.96	14.76	14.54	14.27	14.02	13.64	13.47	13.06	12.90

Continued

Table 3.11. US wheat supply and utilization: pessimistic scenario (*Continued*).

	1995/96	1996/97	1997/98	1998/99	1999/2000	2000/01	2001/02	2002/03	2003/04	2004/05	2005/06
Prices and returns (US$)											
Farm price per tonne	167.17	157.98	130.68	116.88	116.68	119.72	118.00	120.03	116.10	120.17	118.76
Loan rate per tonne	94.79	94.79	94.79	94.79	94.79	94.79	94.79	94.79	94.79	94.79	94.79
Contract payment per tonne	n/a	32.11	23.18	24.00	23.26	21.35	17.22	16.71	16.71	16.71	16.71
Contract payment per ha	n/a	63.70	45.86	47.47	46.01	42.24	34.06	33.06	33.06	33.06	33.06
f.o.b. Gulf price per tonne	209.08	184.33	159.42	143.19	142.95	146.52	144.50	146.89	142.27	147.05	145.40
Variable expenses per ha	188.49	196.79	197.67	194.80	195.70	198.28	201.04	204.55	207.23	209.71	212.94
Market net returns per ha	225.13	202.75	163.24	121.42	121.81	129.41	124.15	127.94	116.62	126.71	121.63

CRP, Conservation Reserve Program; FOR, Farmer Owned Reserve; CCC, Commodity Credit Corporation; f.o.b., free-on-board.
Note: Totals may not equal the sum of the individual components because of rounding error.

4

The Longer-run Dynamics of World Wheat Prices: the Role of Stocks

Colin A. Carter,[1] Cesar Revoredo[1] and Vincent H. Smith[2]

[1]*Department of Agricultural and Resource Economics, University of California–Davis, USA;*
[2]*Department of Agricultural Economics and Economics and Trade Research Center, Montana State University–Bozeman, USA*

1. Introduction

On 10 October, 1997, the *Wall Street Journal* reported that: '[Grain] futures prices soared Friday on the Chicago Board of Trade after the US Agriculture Department suggested that US inventories may barely be able to meet world demand.'

The above quotation may have exaggerated the circumstances of the time but does reflect the fact that market concern over the potential for low grain stocks has become more frequent in the past few years. It has been almost 25 years since public attention and debate have focused on the fears of low grain stocks and food security implications. Public interest in this issue seems to wax and wane along with cyclical swings in stocks-to-utilization ratios. The issue has surfaced again recently but resulted in less intense debate than in the early 1970s. It is, nevertheless, a question of considerable importance in relation to the behaviour of world wheat markets. In 1973, when world wheat stocks declined to less than 20% of world utilization, world wheat prices more than tripled. In contrast, in 1995, when the world wheat stocks-to-use ratio declined to even lower levels, although world wheat prices increased by about 60% they did not respond to the same degree. Moreover, the duration of the period of high wheat prices in the mid-1990s was much shorter than in the early 1970s. The changing role of stocks in world wheat markets, therefore, presents an important practical and intellectual question.

The purpose of this chapter is to discuss the role of stockholding in world wheat and other grain markets. We attempt to uncover any strong and obvious trends in stockholding behaviour and we discuss potential impacts of domestic production disturbances on changes in carryout stocks. Trends in wheat and other grain stocks are analysed relative to stock behaviour in other agricultural commodities such as sugar, cotton and coffee. We attempt to address the question of whether or not stockholding behaviour in grains differs significantly from stockholding behaviour for other major agricultural commodities.

The role of wheat and other grain stocks has long been a topic of interest to agricultural economists because grain represents the single most important component of world food consumption, accounting for around 60% of all calories consumed. Grain is also a special commodity for other reasons. For example, it has been used as an economic weapon in the recent past. The 1980 grain embargo against the former Soviet Union was initiated by the USA to punish the Soviet Union for its invasion of Afghanistan. In 1985, the US Export Enhancement Program (EEP) was introduced to enable the USA to use export subsidies to punish the European Union (EU) for its own use of grain export subsidies. Stocks played an important role in both the 1980 embargo and the 1985 EEP.

Given the staple nature of grain and the vagaries of nature, it is possible that a near stock-out and a serious grain shortage could occur, although it should be recognized that the probability of this event is very low. Over the past 30–40 years, world carryover stocks of cereals have averaged about 2–3 months of global utilization. However, for the past few years, end-of-season stocks amounted to less than 2 months' utilization. This is largely because governments in both the USA and the EU have reduced stock holdings from the levels that pertained in the mid-1980s. At the same time, some analysts believe that stocks have increased in some countries such as China. There is considerable ambiguity about the actual world stock situation. In fact, the differences in various US and international agency estimates of China's stocks exceed some estimates of total world cereal stocks. The US Department of Agriculture (USDA), for example, estimated that end-of-year stocks in China were about 400 million tonnes in 1997 (USDA, 1998) while the Food and Agricultural Organization (FAO) estimated that China's stocks were only 54 million tonnes (FAO, 1997). The 350 million tonne difference between these two figures exceeds FAO's estimate that total world cereal grain stocks were 280 million tonnes.[1]

Given the changes that have taken place in US and EU cereal policies since the early 1990s, it is reasonable to ask whether we have entered a new era in which average end-of-season global stocks will be lower than in the past. Alternatively, it may be the case that the relatively low stocks-to-use ratio that has prevailed in the mid-1990s may only be a short-term deviation – an aberration – from the long-term stocks-to-utilization ratio. If the latter is the situation, will world grain stocks be rebuilt in the USA, in the EU, or in some other regions? If they are not re-established, what are the implications, if any, for world grain markets and the volatility of world grain prices?

After China, the USA is the second largest grain-producing country and by far the largest grain exporter, producing about 15% of the world's grain supply and exporting about 40–45% of total grains traded. Until the 1996 farm bill (the Federal Agriculture Improvement and Reform Act – the FAIR Act), US farm policy involved considerable government intervention in commodity stockholding, including stock procurement and disbursement. The USDA's Commodity Credit Corporation (CCC) was established in 1933 and acted as the government stockholding agent, among its other tasks. CCC stock policy applied mainly to wheat, rice and feed grains, but not soybeans. The US government believed that farmers were prone to overproduction and stock-holding programmes were therefore introduced to remove grain from the market following bumper harvests in order to boost prices. Simultaneously, at various times the US government paid farmers to idle cropland (most recently under the US Conservation Reserve and Acreage Reduction Programs).

Under the 1996 FAIR Act, farm subsidies were to a considerable extent 'de-coupled' from production and the US government largely removed itself from the business of stockholding. It has been argued by some analysts that in future years this shift in US policy will tie movements in grain prices more closely to changes in supply and demand conditions. The potential impact of low government stocks became evident in 1996 when, in the spring, US wheat prices hit record levels, averaging $261.96 per tonne in May of that year, largely because market participants anticipated very low stocks-to-use ratios. In 1996, US wheat stocks were at their lowest level in 20 years. Worldwide supplies of wheat and coarse grains were at their lowest level in 35 years, and annual consumption surpassed production, drawing down reserves even further. Figure 4.1 shows the decline in US stocks of wheat since the early 1980s.

In many ways, in 1996, the reactions of market participants were very different from those of market participants to similar declines in stocks-to-use ratios that occurred in the early 1970s. The duration of the 1996 price surge was very short and the overall tight stock situation attracted far less attention than that of the early 1970s. This may have been because the price surge in the early 1970s was driven by different factors, including crop shortfalls and strong import demand in the former Soviet Union. However, some observers did choose to become alarmed in 1996. The United Nations Food and Agricultural Organization (FAO, 1997), for example, warned that 1996 grain carryover stocks were below minimally acceptable levels and that food security was being jeopardized in some parts of the world. Commenting on the 1997 harvest, the FAO claimed that reserve stocks 'will remain

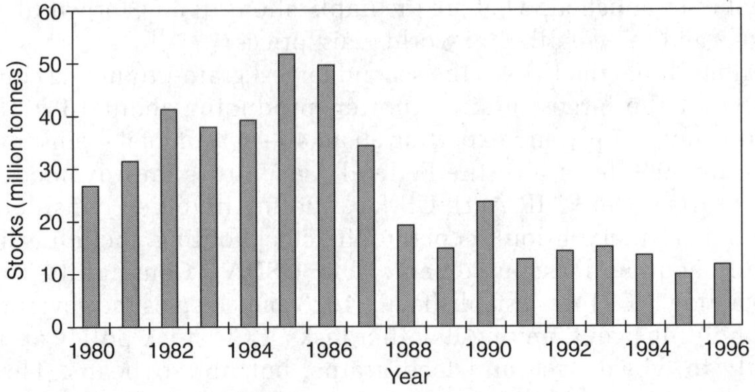

Fig. 4.1. USA: end-of-year stocks of wheat, 1980–1996.

at 15% of expected consumption, considerably less than the 17–18% considered necessary by the FAO'. The FAO went on to suggest that: '[T]he low level of reserve stocks means that even a relatively minor deterioration in crop outlook could lead to sharp price rises with serious consequences for the food security of many low-income food-deficit countries' (FAO, *Food Outlook*, July/September 1997). The FAO's concern was partly fuelled by the drop in stocks, shown in Fig. 4.2, and partly by somewhat extreme forecasts of the effects of El Niño on agricultural production. El Niño is a climatic feature characterized by warm water moving back and forth across the Pacific Ocean between the coast of South America and Indonesia. Some scientists believe El Niño can significantly influence climate, and in 1997 it was predicted that El Niño would play a major role in reducing grain production in Latin America.

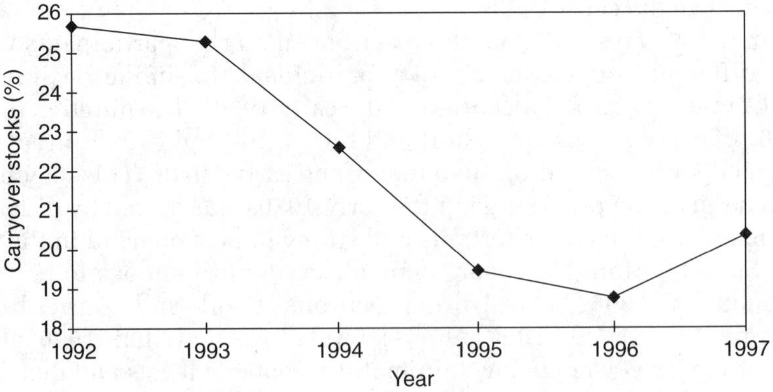

Fig. 4.2. World wheat carryover stocks as percentage of production.

2. Recent History and Evidence of the Role of Stocks in World Grain Markets

In the 1970s, world grain markets and world grain prices exhibited considerable volatility, raising important questions about why the international markets for grain commodities were so unstable during that period. While several potential sources of this price volatility were identified, the volatility of grain stocks was highlighted as one of the major contributing factors to the problem. A good proportion of these stocks were controlled by domestic policy choices on the part of the USA and the EU, a fact that was also regarded as important. D. Gale Johnson suggested that domestic stabilization policies were largely responsible for the instability of world grain markets at that time (Johnson, 1975). Most governments, he argued, were more interested in the stability of grain prices within their own countries than the external consequences of their domestic policy decisions and the stability of international grain prices. Grennes *et al.* (1978) also examined the potential quantitative effects of domestic policies on price stability. They demonstrated that policies such as the variable import levy/export subsidy programme implemented by the EU in the 1970s and 1980s, which insulates domestic wheat markets from international market conditions, export substantial price instability to the world market.

Domestic price stabilization is usually obtained through two mechanisms. The first is the use of trade policies to isolate a country's domestic grain markets from changes in international market conditions (the approach adopted by the EU). The second is the use of storage policies to offset the effects of either supply or demand shocks. However, managing domestic markets via trade policies may have different effects upon prices in international markets compared with managing domestic markets via storage programmes.

Trade policies that restrict imports and exports may increase price variability elsewhere in the world. Suppose, for example, a given country or region chooses to neutralize the domestic effects of all variations in domestic and world supply or demand conditions through policy responses that do not involve storage. It then follows that all the price effects associated with these changes in underlying market conditions must be absorbed by other countries. In contrast, if domestic prices are stabilized through storage programmes, then changes in stocks will absorb most of the effects of international supply and demand shocks, albeit at some (perhaps considerable) cost to the governments implementing these programmes. D. Gale Johnson noted that during the 1960s, despite substantial year-to-year variations in world grain production, the grain storage policies of the USA, Canada and Australia effectively stabilized world prices. These countries, which accounted for over 70% of world exports in the 1960s, effectively managed their substantial grain stocks as if those stocks represented a world reserve to be used to reduce the volatility of international grain prices. However, these countries reduced their holdings of grain stocks at the beginning of the 1970s, partly because of the high costs of physically storing the grain and partly because of opportunities to dispose of those stocks through quasi-commercial sales to the Soviet Union.

D. Gale Johnson also suggested that, in relation to the objective of international price stability, there is a trade-off between trade openness and storage. Danin *et al.* (1975) showed that, under free trade, the volume of grain reserves required to achieve a given degree of price stability is much smaller than under a system with trade barriers. The main reason is that trade can be an offset device for supply shocks. One implication of this finding is that if trade barriers decrease as a result of trade negotiations then any given decrease in world grain reserves will have smaller effects on the volatility of world grain prices.

Ironically, during the 1970s and early 1980s, levels of domestic agricultural protection were very high and significant reductions in agricultural trade barriers appeared to be most unlikely. Most economists, therefore, were concerned about the effects of changes in world grain reserve policies on international grain price stability rather than the issue of whether, and to what degree, trade liberalization would reduce price volatility in international markets (see, for example, Adams and Klein, 1978; Lee and Blandford, 1980; Newbery and Stiglitz, 1981; and Bigman, 1982). Zwart and Meilke (1979), however, explicitly considered whether modifying domestic policies that insulated domestic markets from changes in world market conditions would increase international price stability. Their results indicated that modifying such policies would be a viable alternative policy to the use of buffer stocks to reduce the volatility of international grain prices.

In related studies, Blandford (1987) and Sharples and Goodlow (1984) examined the responses of individual countries to domestic and international production and price shocks. Both studies reported that there was an important difference in the way that individual countries reacted to such shocks. Most appeared to transmit fluctuations in domestic grain supply and demand conditions to the world market. Only the USA appeared to respond by implementing policy responses that stabilized world market prices. Sharples and Martinez (1993) also examined the responses of individual countries to changes in domestic and world grain market conditions using more recent data for the 1980s and early 1990s. They too concluded that the USA pursued policies that served to reduce price volatility in international grain markets. In contrast, some countries, including the former Soviet Union and Argentina, were substantial sources of world grain market instability.

3. A Simple Conceptual Framework

In an international setting, depending on the domestic policy environment, stock-holding policies implemented by one country may stabilize or destabilize the world price. The point can be illustrated in a simple two-country model in which production is stochastic in both countries. Figure 4.3, in a standard back-to-back supply and demand framework, shows normal demand (D_A), supply (S_A), excess demand (ED_A) and excess supply (ES_A) curves in the net exporting country, country A, and the net importing country, country B. In the absence of stock-holding by the government, in a normal production year the international market clearing price will be P_N.

Suppose initially that production shocks in each country are negatively correlated; that is, if country A has low yields then country B has high yields. The effects of abnormal production conditions in each country will then be offsetting. Poor yields in country A shifts both its supply curve and its excess supply curve to the left to S'_A and ES'_A but good yields in country B shift its supply curve and its excess demand curve to the right to S'_B and ED'_B. In the example, because the production shocks in each country are exactly offsetting, there is no change in world output and no change in the world price but trade between country A and country B declines from M_0 to M_1.

Now suppose that country A, the exporting country, operates a guaranteed minimum price or price floor programme in which the domestic minimum price, P_M, is set above the world price. Country A is also assumed to follow a simple stock-holding rule. When domestic production exceeds normal expected levels the government acquires stocks and when production falls below normal expected levels it releases stocks. The effects of the policy are illustrated in Fig. 4.4, in which normal supply and demand curves for both countries and the excess demand curve for country B remain unchanged (and the domestic market for country B is omitted for simplification). Under

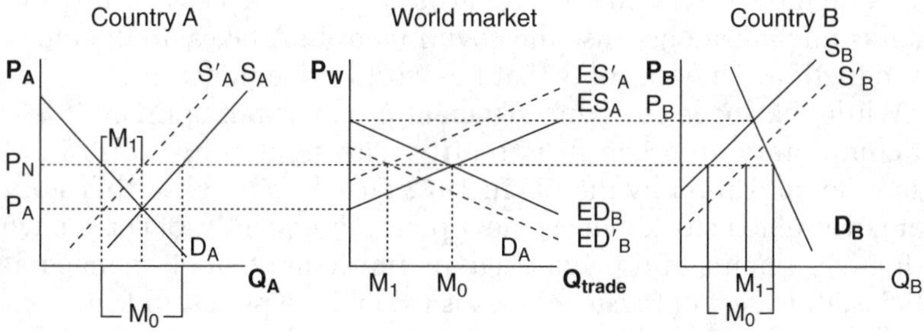

Fig. 4.3. A two-region world commodity market model.

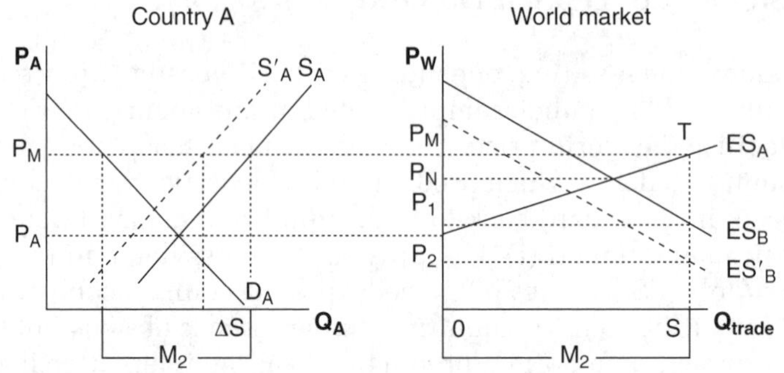

Fig. 4.4. The effect of production shocks in the two-region world commodity market model.

normal market conditions, given country A's price floor programme, the excess supply curve for country A becomes ST ES_A because at any world price below P_M, as a result of the minimum price policy, country A will export M_2 units of the commodity. As a result, the equilibrium market price falls to P_1 because, at any world price below P_M, the minimum price policy in country A increases world production.

Given the minimum price policy, when country A has a bad production year and, commensurately, country B has a good one, as in the previous case the excess demand curve for country B shifts inwards. However, assuming country A's government holds sufficiently large stocks, its excess supply curve will remain unchanged because the government will release stocks in the amount equal to ΔS, the horizontal shift in the domestic supply curve that represents the shortfall in normal production. Thus country A maintains the amount of product available for export at each world price through its stock adjustment policy. The consequence of this type of stock-holding policy is that the world price declines to P_2. A symmetrical result, not illustrated in Fig. 4.4, holds when A has a good year and B has a bad year. In this case, B's excess demand curve shifts outwards while A's excess supply curve remains unchanged because the government in A takes up the increase in production. The upshot is that the world price increases.

While the above stock management policy is not optimal, it is also not completely divorced from reality. The great grain sell-off to the former Soviet Union by the EU in 1972 closely mimicked this story of poor government stock-management policy. Frequently, of course, when both governments and private agents implement stock-management policies, the effect of those policies is to stabilize prices. In fact, even in the above example, if supply shocks in the two countries were positively correlated instead of being negatively correlated, country A's stock-management policy would stabilize prices. The purpose of the above example, however, is to illustrate that stock-holding, perhaps especially by government agencies, does not necessarily result in more stable world prices. Thus reductions in world stocks for specific commodities that are driven by changes in government policies may or may not lead to more volatile prices.

4. Who Holds the Stocks?

In recent years, the data on cereal stocks have displayed some striking changes. Here we attempt to highlight these changes and discuss their implications for the world market.

1. The stocks-to-use ratio has fallen.
2. The USA and the EU have reduced annual carryover, due to changes in farm policies. In the EU, as in the USA, farm policy has moved towards decoupled payments. Growth in cereals production has slowed and stocks have fallen.[2] Figure 4.5 shows that EU cereal grain stocks declined from 34.2 million tonnes to 28.5 million tonnes from 1987 to 1996.
3. Stocks are now mainly held by grain-exporting countries in the developed world, with the notable exception of China.
4. China may hold as much or more grain in storage as the rest of the world put together.[3]
5. In both the EU and the USA, until recently the government, not the private sector, has held most of those countries' grain stocks.

Developments in the EU and the USA are important because together these two exporters account for over 50% of world trade in cereals. In

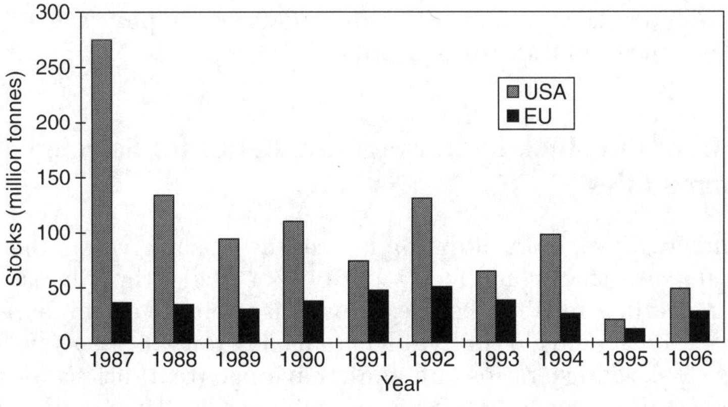

Fig. 4.5. USA and EU: end-of-year stocks of grain, 1987–1997.

addition, a large number of grain importers have relied on a handful of exporters (including the USA and the EU) to carry stocks from one year to the next. On average, over the years 1992–1997 major grain-exporting countries appear to have held more than 37% of world cereal stocks. However, FAO (1997) data suggest that China's stocks may have been understated and, therefore, that the above data may overstate the role of stock-holding by the main exporting countries in the developed world.

The pattern of stock-holding varies somewhat by type of grain. Over the same time period, in the case of wheat, the main exporting countries (the USA, the EU, Canada, Australia and Argentina) have carried a larger share of total world stocks (48%) than is the case for other cereals (FAO, 1997). Wheat stocks were concentrated primarily in the USA, the EU and Canada. For coarse grains, the figure was 43%, also larger than the overall average. In the case of rice, the main exporters carry a smaller share of stocks, with an average carryover of 30%. However, it should again be noted that there is considerable ambiguity about the amount of stocks for each of these commodities held in China. More accurate data on China's grain stocks could lead to substantial changes in the estimates reported here.

Interestingly, when stock-holding is examined for major non-grain commodities that are traded internationally, there is no clear-cut pattern with respect to which countries hold stocks. Exporting countries can also be major stock-holders in the coffee market, where Brazil and Colombia carry about 60% of the world's stocks. However, the situation is very different for both cotton and sugar, where importing countries tend to hold the majority of world stocks. As with grains, China complicates any generalization of this sort because of the country's erratic trading patterns and its tendency to hold large stocks. China typically holds large stocks of sugar and cotton and is usually a net importer of both of these commodities. The EU is a large importer of cotton and also an important stock-holder. However, the EU both exports and imports sugar (but is a net exporter) and also carries significant sugar stocks.

5. Trends in Stock-to-consumption Ratios for Selected Commodities

As noted above, more attention has recently been given to the role of cereal grains stocks (and food security concerns), primarily because of sharp declines in stocks-to-use ratios. It is useful to examine trends in stocks-to-use ratios for individual grains. Figures 4.6–4.9 show end-of-year stocks-to-use ratios and annual average (real) prices for wheat, coarse grains, rice and soybeans over the period. Time periods for the different commodities vary due to data availability.

Figure 4.6 shows that the stocks-to-use ratio for wheat has ranged from 35% in the late 1960s to about 20% in the late 1990s. In the late 1960s the stocks-to-use ratio for wheat was relatively high. However, in the early 1970s, a combination of export policies that reduced production (for example, the Canadian government paid farmers to remove acreage from production) and coincident crop failures led to a sharp decline in the wheat stocks-to-use ratio and, in 1973, wheat prices tripled.

This event drew global attention to the sensitivity of market prices to the stocks-to-use ratios and served as a rallying point for commentators and international organizations' agencies concerned about the possibility of widespread famine (Club of Rome, 1972). In fact, famine did not occur on an international basis. When wheat prices tripled, production responded very quickly and the stocks-to-use ratio increased quite rapidly until, by the mid-1970s, it reached 30%. The stocks-to-use ratio for wheat then fluctuated within a fairly narrow band of 20–30% until the mid-1980s. There were then two major decreases in the stocks-to-use ratio during the periods 1986–1987 and 1992–1997.

The data presented in Fig. 4.6 highlight an important issue. It seems surprising that wheat prices did not respond more sharply when, in the mid-1990s, the stocks-to-use ratio for wheat fell to around 20%. This decline did not result in a rapid and sustained price rise. Even though the stocks-to-use ratio was lower in the mid-1990s than in 1972, in real terms wheat prices only increased to about one-third the level attained in 1973.

Why, in the mid-1990s, did wheat prices fail to repeat the pattern exhibited in the early 1970s? Several hypotheses have been considered. While world wheat trade grew rapidly during the 1970s, it levelled off

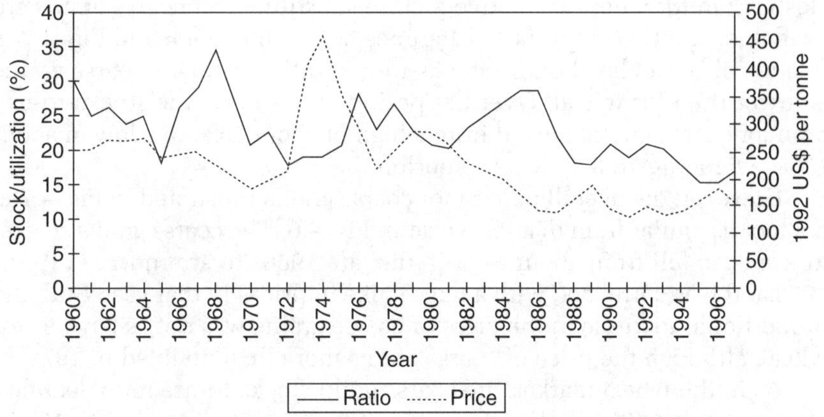

Fig. 4.6. World: wheat, stock/utilization and average price 1960–1997. Correlation coefficient (ratio, price): 0.08. Source: USDA, 1998.

during the early 1980s and 1990s. This suggests that one reason why prices did not react to the drop in the stocks-to-use ratio was that import demand growth was stagnant in the mid-1990s. Import demand levelled off because of the economic collapse in the former Soviet Union. China and the former Soviet Union were large wheat importers during the 1970s and they drove demand growth, at one point accounting for one-third of imports. However, their combined role as importers has since declined because the former Soviet Union's imports have dropped off sharply. China remains a significant importer but one whose role is highly variable from year to year.

A second possible explanation is that, in contrast to the situation in the 1990s, the 1973 surge in world wheat prices was one component of an overall commodity boom that took place during a highly inflationary period. Prices for most primary commodities were increasing at the time and there may have been a speculative price bubble in agricultural and other commodity prices, including wheat. In contrast, the supply shock in the 1990s was more or less confined to grains.

Figure 4.7 presents data on the stocks-to-use ratio and annual average world prices for coarse grains. The correlation coefficient between the stocks-to-use ratio and the price of coarse grains for the data presented in Fig. 4.7 is −0.26, higher (in absolute value) than for wheat (0.08) obtained using the data presented in Fig. 4.6. In fact, the correlation coefficient between the wheat stocks-to-use ratio and wheat prices does not even have the expected sign. These correlation coefficients suggest that coarse grain prices are more responsive than wheat prices to changes in stocks-to-use ratios. In fact, the larger correlation coefficient for coarse grains (compared with wheat) seems surprising, given that, a priori, we might expect more sluggish price responses for coarse grains because demand 'ought' to be more price-elastic than for wheat as relatively close substitutes for coarse grains are available. Another important difference between Fig. 4.6 and Fig. 4.7 is that the absolute level of the stocks-to-utilization ratio for coarse grains is lower than for wheat. Over the period 1967–1997, the stocks-to-use ratio for coarse grains ranged from a high of about 25% to a low of about 12%, averaging 18.3% over the period.

However, the overall pattern for coarse grains illustrated in Fig. 4.7 is not too dissimilar from that for wheat in Fig. 4.6. The coarse grains stocks-to-use ratio fell from about 17% in the late 1960s to around 12–13% in 1973 and was correlated with a large spike in prices in that year. Still, the proportional increase in the price of coarse grains was not as large as for wheat, although the price of coarse grains more than doubled in 1973.

As in the wheat market, the coarse grain stocks-to-use ratio declined after the mid-1980s, falling from about 25% in 1986 to about 11% in 1995. As in the case of wheat, this decline in the stocks-to-use ratio for coarse grains also did not result in price increases that were as large as

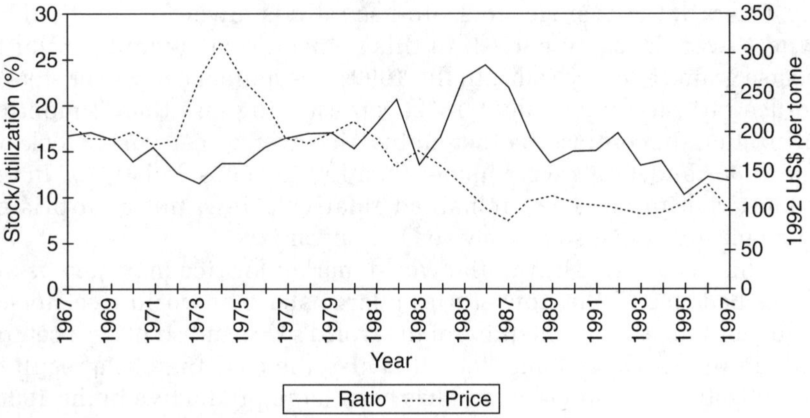

Fig. 4.7. World: coarse grains, stock/utilization and average price 1967–1997. Correlation coefficient (ratio, price): −0.26. Source: USDA, 1998.

in the early 1970s. Even though the coarse grain stocks-to-use ratio in 1995 was lower than that in 1973, in the mid-1990s, the real price of coarse grain increased to only about 40% of its 1973 peak.

Figure 4.8 presents similar data for rice. As noted above, the relationship between the stocks-to-use ratio and world market price for coarse grains exhibited a slightly different pattern from that for wheat. The same is true for rice. The spikes in wheat and coarse grain prices that occurred in 1973 also occurred in the price of rice, which more than tripled. This coincided with a decrease in the rice stocks-to-use ratio (as was the case for the other cereals). The estimated correlation coefficient between the stocks-to-use ratio and the price of rice over the entire period is −0.25, about the same as for coarse grains.

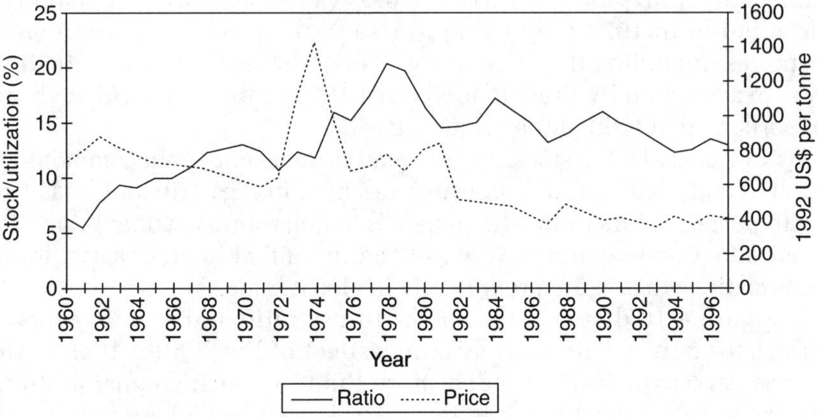

Fig. 4.8. World: rice, stock/utilization and average price 1960–1997. Correlation coefficient (ratio, price): −0.25. Source: USDA, 1998.

Overall, the average stocks-to-use ratio is lower for rice than for wheat over the same period. In this respect, rice is more similar to coarse grains and soybeans. In the 1990s, the annual carry-over stocks-to-use ratio has been about 15%, representing less than 2 months' utilization. In contrast to other grains, rice average carryover stocks in the 1980s and 1990s were higher than in the 1960s and 1970s. In the 1990s, rice prices have remained relatively low, not a surprising outcome given that stocks have edged upwards.

This structural shift in the world market for rice may have taken place because China now carries a large share of world rice stocks. China produces over one-third of the world's rice and so plays a central role in the world rice markets. It is also the case that, as a result of privatization, China's rice land has been more productive in the 1980s and 1990s relative to the period 1960–1979 when, for the most part, farms were collectivized.

On average, rice stocks are still lower than wheat stocks (relative to use) and one possible explanation is that a smaller percentage of global rice production is traded internationally (about 3%) compared with either wheat (about 15%) or coarse grains (about 10%). The higher level of national self-sufficiency in the case of rice suggests that perhaps the market prices may not be so responsive to changes in world stocks. It is also worth noting that, in the case of wheat, the percentage of global production that is traded has been slowly falling. This may partially account for the fact that recent low levels of carry-over stocks have not elicited dramatic price responses in world wheat markets.

Figure 4.9 presents stocks-to-use ratios and prices for soybeans over the period 1964 to 1997. Soybean stocks-to-use ratios appear to be lower than for any other grains, averaging around 11.1% since the early 1970s. Soybean stocks were extremely high in the late 1960s but the situation changed rapidly in the early 1970s. A sharp decline in fishmeal production in 1973 led to a rapid rise in the prices of protein meal supplies, including the price of soybeans. The world market situation was exacerbated by President Nixon's 1973 embargo on US soybean exports, which fuelled the price surge.

Now consider the stocks-to-use trend in some non-grain commodities such as coffee and sugar. These are presented in Figs 4.10 and 4.11. The main purpose of including these data is to determine whether or not the stock situation in grains is very different from that in other agricultural commodities that figure prominently in global trade.

Figure 4.10 displays the stocks-to-use ratio and annual average prices for coffee. The most striking aspect of Fig. 4.10 is that world coffee carryover has exceeded more than one year's consumption. Stocks were extremely high in the 1960s (over 130% of annual utilization). The coffee market experienced a price spike in the early 1970s but the spike occurred a few years after a similar spike in grains. Visual

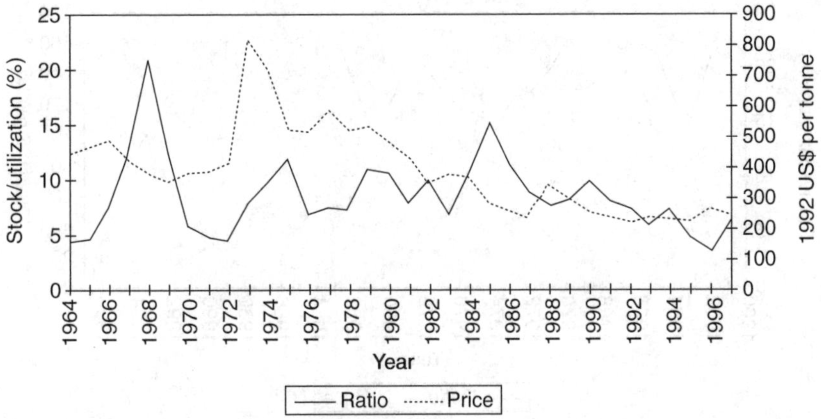

Fig. 4.9. World: soybeans, stock/utilization and price 1964–1997. Correlation coefficient (ratio, price): 0.02. Source: USDA, 1998.

inspection of Fig. 4.10 suggests that the price spike in coffee does not appear to have been as closely related to a reduction in stocks.

Coffee exporters have historically limited exports through a system of quotas and limiting exports resulted in higher prices. However, a comparison of Fig. 4.10 and Fig. 4.6 suggests that coffee prices are no more stable than wheat prices. For the time period covered in Fig. 4.6, the coefficient of variation for the price of wheat is 0.33, while the coefficient of variation for the price of coffee over the same period is 0.52.

Figure 4.11 shows that sugar prices exhibited a strong reaction to the 1973 commodity boom, and the price response was greater than for any other commodity examined in this chapter. Sugar prices increased about sevenfold in a very short time period. As was the case with

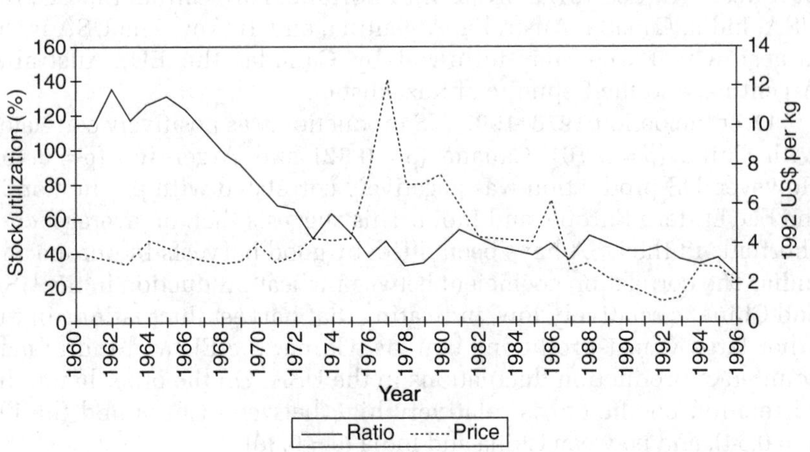

Fig. 4.10. World: coffee, stock/utilization and average price 1960–1997. Correlation coefficient (ratio, price): −0.20. Source: USDA, 1998.

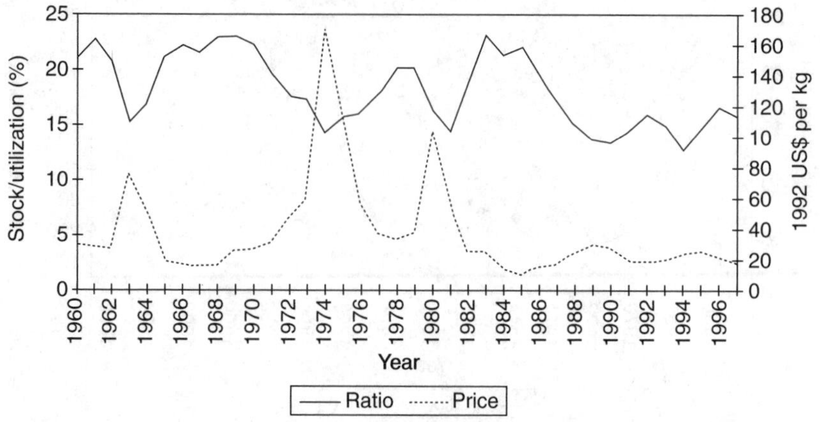

Fig. 4.11. World: sugar, stock/utilization and average price 1960–1997. Correlation coefficient (ratio, price): −0.40. Source: USDA, 1998.

wheat, sugar stocks declined rapidly in the early 1970s but then recovered again after the price surge. Since the mid-1970s, world sugar stocks have remained relatively constant at an average 20% of production and world prices have remained relatively low.

6. Adjustments to Domestic Supply Shocks and the Role of Stocks

Correlation coefficients were estimated for domestic wheat production for the world's main wheat producers and exporters. The largest wheat producers (in declining order of importance) are China, the EU, the USA, India, Canada, Australia, Argentina, and Turkey. The USA is the largest wheat exporter, followed by Canada, the EU, Australia, Argentina, and the Republic of Kazakhstan.

Over the period 1978–1997, US production was positively correlated with China ($\rho = 0.16$), Canada ($\rho = 0.32$) and Argentina ($\rho = 0.46$). However, US production was negatively correlated with production in the EU, Eastern Europe, and India. This suggests that, on average, crop shortfalls in the USA have been offset by good harvests in Europe and India. The correlation coefficient between wheat production in the USA and China is relatively low, indicating that harvest fluctuations in the other large wheat-producing regions (China, the EU and India) may counteract production fluctuations in the USA. On the other hand, the correlation coefficient is relatively high between China and the EU ($\rho = 0.54$), and between China and India ($\rho = 0.30$).

Cross-country correlation coefficients were not computed for all commodities examined in this chapter. However, it is useful to compare wheat with rice, partly because the average stocks-to-use ratio for rice is lower than for wheat. The main producers of rice (in decreasing order of importance) are China, India, Indonesia, Vietnam, Thailand, Japan, Brazil and the USA. Over the period 1978 to 1997, rice production in China was negatively correlated with rice production in India ($\rho = -0.15$), Vietnam ($\rho = -0.19$) and the USA ($\rho = -0.62$). These results are of interest because China and India together account for about 60% of the world's rice production. The main exporters of rice are Thailand, Vietnam, the USA, India, and China. Over the period 1978–1997, production in Thailand was negatively correlated with Vietnam ($\rho = -0.39$) and the USA ($\rho = -0.32$), but positively correlated with the other exporters India ($\rho = 0.18$) and China ($\rho = 0.56$). Overall, these findings indicate the potential importance of trade as a vehicle for stabilizing international price movements.

Sharples and Martinez (1993) examined the linkage between grain stocks and world price variability. One of their main findings was that stock-holding by the USA provided stability in world grain markets. On the surface, this seems surprising because, in part, the US stock build-up in the early 1980s also led to the export enhancement programme, which may have destabilized world grain markets. One reason why the findings by Sharples and Martinez could be misleading is that their methodology is problematic because it is not based on a complete structural supply-and-demand model for each commodity that explicitly accounts for the effects of each country's policy regime.

Following Sharples and Martinez, while recognizing the limitations of the approach, we examine stocks behaviour for selected countries and selected commodities. For each major producing country, we address the same questions raised by Sharples and Martinez; that is, to what extent are domestic production shocks absorbed by changes in domestic stocks and domestic consumption, and to what extent are the effects of domestic production shocks transferred into the international market? In their analysis, Sharples and Martinez begin with the following identity:

$$\Delta Q = \Delta C + \Delta S + T \qquad 4.1$$

where ΔQ is the year-to-year change in domestic production, ΔC is the change in domestic utilization, ΔS is the adjustment in stocks (i.e. the change in stocks in the current period minus the change in stocks in the previous period)[4] and T is net exports (exports minus imports).

This identity simply indicates that domestic production shocks (ΔQ) can be absorbed in any of three ways: through changes in domestic utilization (ΔC), through changes in domestic stocks (ΔS), or through international trade (T). For instance, suppose China experiences a drought that significantly reduces its wheat production. China can respond to this event by dipping into domestic stocks (if they exist), by cutting back on domestic utilization, or by importing more wheat. We estimate a series of regressions to obtain a preliminary idea of how major producing countries actually respond to production shocks within their own borders.

We estimate three equations for two different time periods, 1960–1977 and 1978–1997 (except in the case of soybeans for which data are available only over the period 1978–1992). These periods correspond to the two periods examined by Sharples and Martinez, with the exception that their data ended in 1991. The three estimation equations are as follows:

$$\Delta C = \alpha_1 + \beta_1 \Delta Q + \epsilon_1 \quad 4.2$$

$$\Delta T = \alpha_2 + \beta_2 \Delta Q + \epsilon_2 \quad 4.3$$

$$\Delta S = \alpha_3 + \beta_3 \Delta Q + \epsilon_3 \quad 4.4$$

However, unlike Sharples and Martinez, we included an intercept in equations 4.2, 4.3 and 4.4. The intercept term is included because the left-hand-side variables have different means while the identity in equation 4.1 implies they have the same mean. Sharples and Martinez failed to account for this fact and as a result their estimated coefficients may be biased.

Results are reported in Tables 4.1–4.6 for wheat, rice, maize, soybeans, coffee and sugar. In each table, countries or regions are identified in column 1. Columns 2, 3 and 4 report summary statistics for annual production and production variability (mean, standard error, and coefficient of variation [cv]). The last three columns – 5, 6 and 7 – present the regression results from equations 4.2–4.4.

The results for wheat are reported in Table 4.1. For the period 1978–1997, the estimated coefficients of variation (cv's) for wheat production indicate that China (cv = 6.68%), the EU (cv = 7.35%) and India (cv = 4.68%) enjoy relatively low production variability compared with other major wheat-producing regions. China, the EU and India are currently the largest, second largest and fifth largest wheat producers in the world. The annual average production from 1978 to 1997 was 86.7 million tonnes in China, 80.5 million tonnes in the EU and 48.5 million tonnes in India. The largest degrees of wheat production variability are exhibited in Australia (cv = 25.57%), Argentina (cv = 22.45%), Canada (cv = 16.75%), the new independent states (NIS) (cv = 15.52%) and the USA (cv = 12.35%). The regression results of most interest are those for high-variability countries that are also important exporters (Australia, Argentina, Canada and the USA). The model parameter estimates reported in the last three columns of Table 4.1 indicate that Australia, Argentina and Canada respond to domestic production shocks through relatively large trade adjustments. On average, during the period 1978–1997, changes in trade absorbed 59% of Australia's year-to-year

Table 4.1. Allocation of domestic wheat production shocks for the major stockholding countries, 1960–1977 and 1978–1997.

Country or region	Production (million tonnes)			Share of production absorbed by:		
	Mean	Standard error[a]	cv[a] (%)	Trade	Consumption	Stock
Argentina						
1960–1977	6.849	1.972	28.79	0.548	0.049	0.403
1978–1997	10.419	2.339	22.45	0.935	0.079	−0.015
Australia						
1960–1977	9.652	2.237	23.18	0.341	−0.006	0.664
1978–1997	15.488	3.960	25.57	0.595	−0.014	0.419
Canada						
1960–1977	16.303	3.962	24.30	0.154	0.016	0.830
1978–1997	25.218	4.223	16.75	0.462	0.074	0.465
China						
1960–1977	29.751	3.289	11.06	0.319	−0.027	0.707
1978–1997	86.752	5.798	6.68	0.490	−0.070	0.580
Eastern Europe						
1960–1977	23.194	5.683	24.50	0.305	0.427	0.268
1978–1997	33.491	5.010	14.96	0.356	0.463	0.181
EU						
1960–1977	47.340	3.678	7.77	0.303	0.243	0.453
1978–1997	80.461	5.912	7.35	0.239	0.072	0.689
India						
1960–1977	17.892	2.635	14.73	0.429	0.278	0.292
1978–1997	48.482	2.267	4.68	0.027	0.282	0.690
Mexico						
1960–1977	1.990	0.322	16.18	0.629	0.110	0.261
1978–1997	3.489	0.632	18.11	0.457	0.369	0.174
NIS[a]						
1960–1977	75.869	12.797	16.87	0.279	0.007	0.714
1978–1997	79.229	12.300	15.52	0.164	0.198	0.638
South Africa						
1960–1977	1.294	0.217	16.77	0.697	0.053	0.250
1978–1997	2.142	0.550	25.68	0.697	0.048	0.254
Turkey						
1960–1977	8.825	1.210	13.71	0.198	0.145	0.657
1978–1997	14.390	0.964	6.70	0.827	0.052	0.120
USA						
1960–1977	41.648	4.029	9.67	−0.311	0.004	1.307
1978–1997	62.753	7.747	12.35	0.011	0.181	0.807
World						
1960–1977	307.197	15.971	5.20	0.000	0.036	0.964
1978–1997	511.573	22.276	4.35	0.000	0.261	0.739

[a] Standard error with respect to a linear trend; cv, coefficient of variation; NIS, new independent states.

Source: USDA, 1998.

production variability, 93% of Argentina's production variability and 46% of Canada's production variability. However, the USA appears to have behaved very differently from the other three major exporters. During the period 1978–1997, US trade absorbed an estimated 1% of annual production shocks.

In contrast to the USA, Australia and Canada have state trading agencies with monopoly rights over exports.[5] Argentina also had a state trading agency during part of this time period. One possible explanation for the results on trade absorption is that the state traders simply try to sell as much as they can irrespective of market conditions. The state traders are government bureaucracies that do not have a strong incentive to maximize profits, but rather they maximize their own objective functions. Australia and Argentina tend to carry very low levels of stocks from year to year. Canada sometimes carries large stocks when transportation is constrained but these stocks are held by farmers and not by the state trading agency. However, the full explanation behind these results on trade absorption is probably much more complicated than discussed here, given the historical role of the USA government in stock-holding.

The utilization coefficients in Table 4.1 are not as interesting as the trade and stock adjustment coefficients, because domestic utilization tends to be quite price-inelastic. To a large extent, stock adjustment coefficients mirror trade adjustment coefficients for wheat. The USA has a very high stock adjustment coefficient (81%). However, the figures are much smaller for Canada (46%), Australia (42%) and Argentina (−1%).

In the case of rice, the four largest producers are China, India, Indonesia and Vietnam. Table 4.2 indicates that each of these producers exhibits less production variability (measured by the coefficient of variation) than, say, the USA or Thailand. Vietnam, Thailand and the USA, which have relatively high stock adjustments, are relatively small rice producers, but figure prominently in trade. Overall, across all countries, production variability is estimated to be much less for rice than for wheat.

In the case of maize, the USA dominates world output, with an average annual production of 196 million tonnes out of a world annual average total of 471 million tonnes. China is the second largest producer, with an average annual output of 83 million tonnes. Maize production in the USA is more than twice as variable as maize production in China. The results presented in Table 4.3 indicate that, as with wheat, the US stock changes have absorbed most of the production shocks. In China, on average stocks have absorbed about 57% and trade has absorbed about 21% of production shocks.

The USA, Brazil, China and Argentina are the four largest producers of soybeans. The results presented in Table 4.4 indicate that over the period 1978–1997 production variability was remarkably similar among

Table 4.2. Allocation of domestic rice production shocks for the major producers, 1960–1977, 1978–1997.

	Production (million tonnes)			Share of production absorbed by:		
Country	Mean	Standard error[a]	cv[a] (%)	Trade	Consumption	Stock
Argentina						
1960–1977	0.174	0.032	18.39	0.296	0.081	0.62
1978–1997	0.352	0.101	28.69	0.570	0.038	0.39
Australia						
1960–1977	0.194	0.026	13.40	0.057	0.204	0.73
1978–1997	0.622	0.107	17.20	0.801	−0.034	0.23
Burma						
1960–1977	5.030	0.384	7.63	0.239	0.761	0.00
1978–1997	7.710	0.455	5.90	0.162	0.334	0.50
China						
1960–1977	68.585	3.850	5.61	−0.017	0.667	0.34
1978–1997	119.763	5.830	4.87	0.084	0.205	0.71
Egypt						
1960–1977	1.456	0.218	14.97	0.494	0.506	0.00
1978–1997	2.014	0.320	15.89	0.115	0.708	0.17
EU						
1960–1977	0.996	0.097	9.74	0.805	0.087	0.10
1978–1997	1.290	0.131	10.16	0.704	0.109	0.18
India						
1960–1977	39.449	3.668	9.30	−0.002	0.413	0.58
1978–1997	65.907	4.348	6.60	0.011	0.547	0.44
Indonesia						
1960–1977	12.275	0.700	5.70	0.287	0.990	−0.27
1978–1997	27.508	1.372	4.99	0.145	0.387	0.46
Pakistan						
1960–1977	1.899	0.173	9.11	−0.028	0.890	0.13
1978–1997	3.438	0.303	8.81	−0.023	0.198	0.82
South Korea						
1960–1977	3.999	0.422	10.55	0.331	0.642	0.02
1978–1997	5.297	0.490	9.25	0.945	0.195	−0.14
Taiwan						
1960–1977	2.158	0.105	4.87	0.140	0.241	0.62
1978–1997	1.841	0.093	5.05	0.604	0.123	0.27
Thailand						
1960–1977	8.141	0.674	8.28	0.339	0.723	−0.06
1978–1997	12.758	0.871	6.83	0.377	0.053	0.57
Uruguay						
1960–1977	0.083	0.011	13.25	−0.199	−0.137	1.33
1978–1997	0.372	0.078	20.97	0.668	0.086	0.24
USA						
1960–1977	2.845	0.338	11.88	0.036	0.216	0.74
1978–1997	4.986	0.645	12.94	0.211	0.083	0.70
Vietnam						
1960–1977	6.419	0.491	7.65	0.307	0.693	0.00
1978–1997	12.226	0.690	5.64	0.301	0.699	0.00
World						
1960–1977	197.783	5.439	2.75	0.000	0.488	0.51
1978–1997	325.787	7.674	2.36	0.000	0.497	0.50

[a] Standard error with respect to a linear trend; cv, coefficient of variation.
Source: USDA, 1998.

Table 4.3. Allocation of domestic maize production for the major producers, 1960–1977, 1978–1997.

	Production (million tonnes)			Share of production deviations absorbed by:		
Country	Mean	Standard error[a]	cv[a] (%)	Trade	Consumption	Stock
Argentina						
1960–1977	7.165	1.423	19.86	0.771	0.110	0.119
1978–1997	9.875	2.461	24.92	0.806	0.146	0.049
Brazil						
1960–1977	13.382	1.308	9.77	0.440	0.271	0.290
1978–1997	26.192	2.729	10.42	0.083	0.370	0.548
Canada						
1960–1977	2.156	0.259	12.01	0.505	0.143	0.352
1978–1997	6.390	0.777	12.16	0.540	0.284	0.176
China						
1960–1977	31.268	2.739	8.76	0.045	0.490	0.465
1978–1997	83.228	6.602	7.93	0.215	0.212	0.573
France						
1960–1977	5.695	1.462	25.67	0.789	0.197	0.014
1978–1997	11.978	1.298	10.84	0.417	0.258	0.325
Hungary						
1960–1977	4.484	0.582	12.98	0.433	0.567	0.000
1978–1997	6.150	0.969	15.76	0.478	0.199	0.322
India						
1960–1977	5.531	0.661	11.95	0.001	0.625	0.374
1978–1997	8.065	0.806	9.99	0.041	0.867	0.093
Indonesia						
1960–1977	2.834	0.534	18.84	−0.006	1.006	0.000
1978–1997	5.061	0.442	8.73	0.055	0.737	0.208
Italy						
1960–1977	4.382	0.394	8.99	1.177	−0.283	0.106
1978–1997	7.009	0.887	12.66	0.389	0.629	−0.017
Mexico						
1960–1977	7.848	0.777	9.90	0.643	0.258	0.098
1978–1997	12.929	2.280	17.63	0.691	0.213	0.096
Romania						
1960–1977	7.468	0.977	13.08	0.063	0.937	0.000
1978–1997	10.123	1.572	15.53	0.235	0.402	0.362
USA						
1960–1977	120.327	11.046	9.18	0.178	0.475	0.348
1978–1997	196.123	35.382	18.04	0.022	0.198	0.780
World						
1960–1977	270.914	12.278	4.53	0.000	0.692	0.308
1978–1997	471.596	37.148	7.88	0.000	0.179	0.821

[a] Standard error with respect to a linear trend; cv, coefficient of variation.
Source: USDA, 1998.

Table 4.4. Allocation of domestic soybean production shocks for the major producers, 1964–1977, 1978–1997.

	Production (million tonnes)			Share of production deviations absorbed by:		
Country	Mean	Standard error[a]	cv[a] (%)	Trade	Consumption	Stock
Argentina						
1964–1977	0.451	0.513	113.75	0.984	0.092	−0.076
1978–1997	8.544	1.076	12.59	0.707	0.317	−0.024
Brazil						
1964–1977	4.775	1.727	36.17	0.489	0.289	0.222
1978–1997	19.085	2.221	11.64	0.441	0.489	0.071
Canada						
1964–1977	0.297	0.073	24.58	0.491	0.337	0.172
1978–1997	1.301	0.211	16.22	0.537	0.230	0.233
China						
1964–1977	7.640	0.827	10.82	−0.004	1.004	0.000
1978–1997	11.038	1.328	12.03	0.178	0.822	0.000
Colombia						
1964–1977	0.098	0.024	24.49	0.142	0.748	0.110
1978–1997	0.119	0.040	33.61	0.797	0.118	0.085
India						
1964–1977	0.059	0.033	55.93	0.000	1.000	0.000
1978–1997	1.910	0.469	24.55	0.032	1.025	−0.057
Indonesia						
1964–1977	0.497	0.038	7.65	0.323	0.677	0.000
1978–1997	1.146	0.171	14.92	0.280	0.758	−0.038
Japan						
1964–1977	0.152	0.020	13.16	1.141	−4.820	4.680
1978–1997	0.196	0.051	26.02	−0.475	1.965	−0.489
Mexico						
1964–1977	0.289	0.096	33.22	0.289	0.591	0.120
1978–1997	0.518	0.224	43.24	0.803	0.185	0.012
NIS[a]						
1964–1977	0.484	0.136	28.10	−0.896	0.451	1.445
1978–1997	0.598	0.176	29.43	0.504	0.447	0.049
Paraguay						
1964–1977	0.132	0.046	34.85	0.784	0.216	0.000
1978–1997	0.311	0.249	80.06	0.984	0.016	0.000
Romania						
1964–1977	0.126	0.045	35.71	1.407	−0.407	0.000
1978–1997	0.251	0.087	34.66	0.245	0.672	0.083
South Korea						
1964–1977	0.239	0.021	8.79	0.176	0.792	0.032
1978–1997	0.212	0.022	10.38	2.018	−1.007	−0.012
USA						
1964–1977	32.335	3.424	10.59	0.252	0.324	0.424
1978–1997	55.512	7.424	13.37	0.330	0.219	0.451
World						
1964–1977	48.175	3.593	7.46	0.000	0.543	0.457
1978–1997	104.866	7.174	6.84	0.000	0.538	0.462

[a] Standard error with respect to a linear trend; cv, coefficient of variation; NIS, new independent states.
Source: USDA, 1998.

these four countries, with coefficients of variation for production ranging from 12.6% in Argentina to 11.6% in Brazil. Argentina exports most of its production shock (70% on average). Among the major producers, the USA has the largest estimated stock coefficient; on average, in the USA, stock adjustments have accounted for 45% of production variability.

Over the period 1978–1992, the three largest producers of coffee were Brazil, Colombia and Indonesia. Brazil exhibits the largest production variability (cv = 22.9%), followed by Colombia (cv = 13.1%) and Argentina (cv = 6%). The trade adjustment coefficients presented in Table 4.5 are 13% for Brazil and 14.8% for Colombia. These are very similar and may reflect the effects of the International Coffee Agreement (ICA), which operated over most of this time period. Indonesia has a larger trade coefficient (39%), which reflects that country's greater willingness to sell outside the coffee agreement.

Results for sugar are presented in Table 4.6. The largest sugar producers are the EU (16 million tonnes), India (10.7 million tonnes), Brazil (9.4 million tonnes), the NIS (6.9 million tonnes), Cuba (6.6 million tonnes) and the USA (6.0 million tonnes). The NIS displays the greatest production variability. Cuba, India and Brazil are also characterized by relatively high production variability. The EU and the USA are at the other end of the spectrum, with relatively low production variability. The estimated coefficients of variation for the EU and the USA are 5.97% and 5.01%, respectively.

Cuba (81%) and the USA (70%) have the largest estimated trade coefficients for sugar. Historically, Cuba has been heavily dependent on sugar export revenues and, like Australia and Canada with respect to wheat, Cuba may have an implicit policy of selling as much of the crop as they possibly can in a given year, regardless of market signals. On the other hand, the high trade coefficient for the USA in sugar reflects a highly protective import policy administered through tight import quotas: if US production increases, import quotas fall and vice versa.

7. Summary

The relationship between world wheat and other grain stocks and world market prices has changed quite substantially over the period 1967 to 1997. The earlier part of the period (from the 1960s to the mid-1980s) was an era in which the governments of the major grain-exporting countries (the USA, Canada and the EU) held substantial stocks of grain. During this period, low stocks-to-use ratios tended to result in sharp increases in world grain prices. In the late 1980s and 1990s, however, while it was still the case that decreases in stocks-to-use ratios generally resulted in price increases, the price increases tended

Table 4.5. Allocation of domestic coffee production shocks for the major producers, 1960–1977, 1978–1992.

	Production (million 60 kg bags)			Share of production deviations absorbed by:		
Country	Mean	Standard error[a]	cv[a] (%)	Trade	Consumption	Stock
Brazil						
1960–1977	22.522	7.119	31.61	0.044	0.029	0.927
1978–1992	26.043	5.988	22.99	0.133	0.023	0.844
Cameroon						
1960–1977	1.175	0.156	13.31	0.202	−0.004	0.802
1978–1992	1.672	0.334	19.95	−0.231	0.018	1.212
Colombia						
1960–1977	8.200	0.643	7.84	0.092	0.022	0.886
1978–1992	13.157	1.500	11.40	0.148	0.002	0.850
Costa Rica						
1960–1977	1.228	0.122	9.90	0.344	−0.001	0.657
1978–1992	2.223	0.274	12.33	0.578	−0.004	0.426
El Salvador						
1960–1977	2.221	0.374	16.85	0.624	0.000	0.376
1978–1992	2.623	0.346	13.21	0.479	0.011	0.511
Ethiopia						
1960–1977	2.381	0.244	10.26	0.223	0.005	0.772
1978–1992	3.138	0.257	8.20	0.747	0.030	0.223
Guatemala						
1960–1977	1.972	0.151	7.66	1.248	−0.003	−0.245
1978–1992	2.876	0.217	7.54	1.684	−0.001	−0.683
India						
1960–1977	1.363	0.199	14.57	0.292	−0.029	0.738
1978–1992	2.517	0.525	20.87	0.044	0.035	0.921
Indonesia						
1960–1977	2.470	0.331	13.40	1.018	−0.002	−0.016
1978–1992	6.030	0.332	5.51	0.390	0.078	0.532
Ivory Coast						
1960–1977	3.831	0.794	20.71	0.319	−0.314	0.994
1978–1992	4.116	0.937	22.77	−0.076	−0.001	1.076
Mexico						
1960–1977	3.092	0.282	9.14	0.992	0.069	−0.062
1978–1992	4.486	0.438	9.77	1.370	−0.024	−0.345
Papua New Guinea						
1960–1977	0.355	0.056	15.76	0.828	0.005	0.167
1978–1992	0.891	0.128	14.41	0.445	0.001	0.554
Uganda						
1960–1977	2.778	0.624	22.45	0.168	0.000	0.832
1978–1992	2.667	0.286	10.72	1.081	0.000	−0.081
Zaire						
1960–1977	1.124	0.190	16.89	0.262	−0.001	0.739
1978–1992	1.569	0.211	13.46	0.617	0.018	0.365
World						
1960–1977	68.829	7.512	10.91	0.000	0.163	0.837
1978–1992	91.600	5.847	6.38	0.000	0.159	0.841

[a] Standard error with respect to a linear trend; cv, coefficient of variation.
Source: USDA, 1998.

Table 4.6. Allocation of domestic sugar production for the major producers, 1960–1977, 1978–1997.

	Production (million tonnes)			Share of production deviations absorbed by:		
Country	Mean	Standard error[a]	cv[a] (%)	Trade	Consumption	Stock
Australia						
1960–1977	2.325	0.183	7.88	1.101	0.064	−0.16
1978–1997	3.785	0.404	10.66	0.881	0.053	0.06
Brazil						
1960–1977	4.860	0.424	8.72	0.697	−0.167	0.47
1978–1997	9.405	1.396	14.84	0.402	0.049	0.54
China						
1960–1977	1.630	0.228	14.00	0.530	0.215	0.25
1978–1997	5.165	0.806	15.60	0.740	0.162	0.09
Cuba						
1960–1977	5.666	1.022	18.03	0.674	0.013	0.31
1978–1997	6.695	1.120	16.73	0.815	0.035	0.14
EU						
1960–1977	10.534	0.747	7.09	0.649	−0.075	0.42
1978–1997	16.661	0.995	5.97	0.351	0.066	0.58
India						
1960–1977	3.979	0.594	14.94	0.003	0.116	0.88
1978–1997	10.721	1.670	15.58	0.161	−0.038	0.87
Indonesia						
1960–1977	0.773	0.122	15.73	0.068	0.529	0.40
1978–1997	1.879	0.161	8.56	0.965	−0.222	0.25
Mexico						
1960–1977	2.260	0.153	6.77	0.481	−0.104	0.62
1978–1997	3.592	0.325	9.05	0.258	0.020	0.72
NIS[a]						
1960–1977	8.095	1.314	16.24	0.575	0.147	0.27
1978–1997	6.898	2.446	35.46	0.566	0.186	0.24
Philippines						
1960–1977	1.901	0.203	10.70	0.153	0.122	0.72
1978–1997	1.952	0.297	15.20	0.258	0.058	0.68
South Africa						
1960–1977	1.503	0.166	11.06	0.394	0.117	0.48
1978–1997	2.075	0.331	15.96	0.781	−0.011	0.23
Thailand						
1960–1977	0.563	0.310	54.98	0.904	0.149	−0.05
1978–1997	3.315	0.556	16.76	0.926	0.028	0.04
USA						
1960–1977	5.505	0.367	6.67	0.326	−0.181	0.85
1978–1997	6.018	0.302	5.01	0.696	0.016	0.28
World						
1960–1977	66.899	2.274	3.40	0.000	0.526	0.47
1978–1997	103.792	4.800	4.62	0.000	0.436	0.56

[a] Standard error with respect to a linear trend; cv, coefficient of variation; NIS, new independent states.
Source: USDA, 1998.

to be smaller. A similar pattern of change has taken place with respect to coarse grains.

Several explanations have been put forward to account for the changing relationship between observed stocks-to-use ratios for wheat and coarse grains and world market prices. One is that governments in major wheat-exporting countries are no longer managing large stocks as a part of their domestic price stabilization and farm income support programmes. Another is that grain markets have become somewhat more integrated as government grain income and price support policies have been moderated in the 1990s. The importance of domestic trade and stock-holding policies for wheat is reflected by the regression results. Over the period 1978–1997, Canada, Argentina and Australia have mainly responded to production shocks through trade. In contrast, the USA has responded to production shocks by adjusting stocks. However, it is not clear whether changes in US policy since the mid-1980s have led the USA to respond to production shocks in the mid-1990s through trade rather than by changing domestic stocks.

The evidence with respect to other traded commodities indicates that the role of stocks in determining world prices varies considerably. One important element appears to be the share of world production that is traded. In markets where the share of world production that is traded is relatively small, the link between stocks-to-use ratios and price movements seems to be weaker. This may be another reason why world wheat prices have been less closely tied to wheat stocks. In the 1960s, approximately 25% of world wheat production was traded; in the mid-1990s, only about 17% of world wheat production was traded.

In summary, substantial changes have taken place in the role of stocks in world grain markets over the past two decades. This study provides evidence that suggests these changes may be linked to shifts in government stock-holding, price and farm income support programmes and trade policies. In addition, changes in the relative importance of trade in world grain markets may be important. However, no clear-cut evidence has been provided as to the relative importance of these factors. Providing answers to this question represents an important agenda for future research.

Notes

1. Even though the USDA acknowledges that China's grain stocks could be in the neighbourhood of 400 million tonnes in the 1990s (see Crook, 1996), the stock figures published by the USDA in their *Production, Supply and Distribution (PS&D) View Database* (1998) are much lower than the 400 million tonnes figure. We use the PS&D database for the figures reported in this chapter and we warn the reader that the stock figures for China could be very different, but there is no consensus on this data problem.

2. See Chapter 10 (this volume) by Rayner *et al.* They discuss EU cereal stocks and suggest that, even though stocks are low now, they may well rebuild, according to both the Organization for Economic Cooperation and Development (OECD) and official EU projections.
3. Crook (1996) compares the USDA's stock estimates with those from sources in China. In 1990, published reports in China estimated 490 million tonnes of grain stocks, while the USDA estimated stocks to be only 82 million tonnes.
4. $\Delta S = (E - B) - (E_{-1} - B_{-1})$, where E is ending stocks this period, B is beginning stocks this period, and E_{-1} and B_{-1} are for the previous period.
5. See Chapter 9 (this volume) by Carter and Wilson. They discuss the Australian and Canadian state trading agencies.

References

Adams, F.G. and Klein, S. (1978) *Stabilizing World Commodity Markets.* Lexington Books, Lexington, Massachusetts, USA.

Bigman, D. (1982) *Coping with Hunger: Toward a System of Food Security and Price Stabilization.* Ballinger Publishing Company, Cambridge, Massachusetts, USA.

Blandford, D. (1987) Instability in world grain markets. *Journal of Agricultural Economics* 34, 379–395.

Club of Rome (1972) *Proceedings of a Conference on the Limits to Growth.* Sponsored by the Club of Rome, Potomac Associates, the Smithsonian Institution, and the Woodrow Wilson International Center for Scholars. Smithsonian Institution, Washington DC, USA.

Crook, F.W. (1996) China's grain stocks: background and analytical issues. In: *China: Situation and Outlook Series.* Technical Report No. WRS–96–2, US Department of Agriculture, Washington DC, USA, pp. 35–39.

Danin, Y., Sumner, D. and Johnson, D.G. (1975) *Determination of Optimal Grain Carryovers.* Paper No. 74:12, Office of Agricultural Economic Research, University of Chicago, Chicago, USA.

FAO (Food and Agricultural Organization) (1997) *Food Outlook*, 30 September. United Nations, Rome, Italy.

Grennes, T., Johnson, P.R. and Thursby, M. (1978) Insulating trade policies, inventories and wheat price stability. *American Journal of Agricultural Economics* 60, 132–134.

Johnson, D.G. (1975) World agriculture, commodity policy and price variability. *American Journal of Agricultural Economics* 57, 823–828.

Lee, S. and Blandford, D. (1980) *Buffer Stocks and the Stabilization of International Commodity Markets: an Application of Optimal Control Theory.* Search: Agriculture, No. 11, Cornell University Agricultural Experiment Station, Ithaca, New York, USA.

Newbery, D.M.G. and Stiglitz, J.E. (1981) *The Theory of Commodity Price Stabilization: a Study in the Economics of Risk.* Clarendon, Oxford, UK.

Sharples, J.A. and Goodlow, C.A. (1984) *Global Stocks of Grain: Implications for US Policy.* Staff Report No. AGES 840319, US Department of Agriculture, Economic Research Service, Washington DC, USA.

Sharples, J.A. and Martinez, S. (1993) *The Role of Stocks in World Grain Market Stability.* Foreign Agriculture Economic Research Report No. 248, US Department of Agriculture, Washington DC, USA.

USDA (US Department of Agriculture) (1998) *PS&D (Production, Supply & Distribution) View Database.* Economic Resource Service, US Department of Agriculture, Washington DC, USA.

Zwart, A.C. and Meilke, K.D. (1979) The influence of domestic pricing policies and buffer stocks on price stability in the world wheat industry. *American Journal of Agricultural Economics* 61, 434–447.

5

The Short-run Dynamics of World Wheat Prices

Eugenio S.A. Bobenrieth[1] and Brian D. Wright[2]

[1]*Departamento de Economia, Universidad de Concepcion, Chile;* [2]*Department of Agricultural and Resource Economics, University of California–Berkeley, USA*

1. Introduction

The price of wheat has long been of interest to farmers, merchants, speculators and economists. Agricultural economists have focused largely on the spread between spot and futures prices, and the relation between that spread and current stockholdings, on the one hand, and rational price forecasts, on the other. Speculators, on the other hand, largely focus on the high-frequency price movements relevant when a day is a long time to hold a position.

In this chapter, our focus is on these daily changes in the spot price of wheat. Assuming that the reported spot price series for the Kansas City Board of Trade (KCBT) and the Minneapolis Grain Exchange (MGE) are accurate measures of the current price, daily changes appear to be unpredictable and to have a non-Gaussian probability distribution, with 'fat tails' and a volatility that appears to fluctuate over time.

Similar stylized facts about financial assets prices have been the motivation for a growing empirical literature on the estimation of price variation processes in financial securities markets (Gallant *et al.*, 1991; Engle and Ng, 1993; Hamilton and Susmel, 1994).

This chapter estimates the price variation process for daily wheat using a structural dynamic model of price formation that generates implications consistent with the above facts about the sample distribution of price changes. The approach is based on Bobenrieth (1996), which generalizes the standard rational expectations storage model of commodity prices, offering a structural explanation along lines suggested in Khim (1994) for differences and persistence in volatility across time, non-Gaussian distributions for price variations, price correlation, and continuously positive storage.

The possibility of storage introduces some fundamental qualifications in the way commodity prices should be modelled. Modern attempts to uncover the main factors behind interharvest commodity price fluctuations include Gustafson (1958), Scheinkman and Schechtman (1983), Williams and Wright (1991), and Deaton and Laroque (1991, 1992, 1994a, b). Scheinkman and Schechtman (1983) proved that for a competitive commodity market with risk-neutral, forward-looking, profit-maximizing agents, the commodity price process should be nonlinear if stockouts can occur, that is, if the non-negativity of storage is a binding constraint with probability 1 in finite time. Therefore, simplistic empirical estimations based on AR models should be discarded as not reflecting the nonlinearity in prices resulting from the agent's intertemporal optimization. Deaton and Laroque (1991, 1992) indicate that, at least for commodities where the weather plays a major role in price fluctuations, a random-walk hypothesis for price behaviour seems very implausible. They estimate a version of the storage model with stockouts for several commodities, with yearly observations over an extended period of time (a model with independent and identically distributed harvest shocks and deterministic, stationary demand), finding that their estimates fit well some of the stylized characteristics of empirical commodity price series, but with a price autocorrelation that is too low (particularly for high prices), as compared with those implied by the model. Miranda and Rui (1995) perform an estimation of the commodity price process by directly assuming away the possibility of stockouts, postulating a convenience-yield-based autocorrelation process, according to which the intertemporal price relation is always present, with the qualification that the level of such an autocorrelation is changing, as a function of the empirical supply of storage function. Also based on the convenience-yield hypothesis, Pindyck (1993, 1994) tests a present-value model for commodity prices, according to which the current price of a commodity is the present value of future convenience-yield benefits, a flow of benefits that are obtained directly by the ownership of stocks. Purely empirical studies of commodity prices offer a variety of approaches with different implications. Cuddington and Urzúa (1989) and Gersovitz and Paxson (1990) fit autoregressive integrated moving average (ARIMA)-type time series models, finding it difficult to reject these parsimonious specifications.

This chapter addresses price behaviour at daily frequencies, and explores the consequences of allowing for heterogeneously distributed shocks. The explanation for price correlation and volatility differences relies on the distinction that is made between the (ergodic) unconditional probability density function for prices and the density that is conditional on information available at every period. A full integration with studies of annual data awaits further work.

The chapter is organized as follows: section 2 discusses the theoretical model, section 3 presents the empirical model, in section 4 we discuss the data and present the estimation, in section 5 non-parametric densities are estimated and section 6 concludes the chapter.

2. A Model of Conditional Price Autocorrelation

This section describes the dynamic model of price formation. Details are given in Bobenrieth (1996).

Suppose a competitive wheat market, where agents are profit-maximizers, risk-neutral speculators, with the 'speculative' activity being the holding of stocks when a 'sufficiently large' price increase is expected. Price forecasts are made as equilibrium forecasts, i.e. the expected price is common to all agents, and the actions of speculators generate the expected price as the equilibrium price. Equivalently, the model price expectations are internally consistent in the sense of Muth (1961).

Storage at time t is a reversible decision at $t + 1$, and it is therefore associated with a planning horizon of only one period. Let $x_t \equiv$ quantity stored from period t to period $t + 1$, $z_t \equiv$ (total) availability of the commodity at t, availability can either be consumed or stored, and consists of storage carried from last period plus the tth period realization of exogenously distributed supply shock. Let $P_t^c \equiv$ (inverse) consumption demand function, and $p_t \equiv$ price at t. Define the state variable H_t as determining the prediction for next period's 'harvest' distributions and suppose that H_t is an exogenous markovian process. Thus H represents day-to-day excess supply to the market, rather than the annual harvest familiar in inter-year models. Equilibrium price is thus given by $p_t = P_t^c(z_t - x_t)$, and can be shown to be a function of the information at time t, which includes the value of H_t.

The rational expectations equilibrium implies a set of Euler optimality conditions. In words, these necessary conditions mean that, in equilibrium, expected profits from the marginal unit of storage cannot be positive. If they were, speculators would increase their storage level, thus increasing current price and reducing the expected price for next period. If the market is uncertain about the arrival date of harvests, and if reductions in consumption imply a sufficiently large increase in price, then stocks are positive for every period, because of the intertemporal arbitrage relation that forces the discounted expected price not to be higher than the current price, thus implying price autocorrelation. Moreover, it is possible to show that storage (and therefore price) reacts to news on the next period's supply probability distribution:

storage is low under 'positive' news, and high otherwise, for any given availability level.

Given that the market adjusts so that the price at any period remains equal to the (discounted) expected price for the next period, the conditional expected return $r_{j+1} \equiv \dfrac{\beta E_t p_{j+1} - p_j}{p_j}$ is zero, where β is the discount factor. The second conditional moment is affected by information changes: the transformation in distribution of future shocks transforms the function that defines the second moment of $r_{t-\tau+k+1}$, conditional on current information at every period, because the storage function is transformed. In particular, conditional on a first-order stochastic transformation of the next period's shock probability distribution, the variance of the return is high or low, thus determining the relevant conditional density for the return.

3. Empirical Model

The central piece of the empirical model is the speculative real return r_t, upon which the rational expectations hypothesis places strong restrictions: intuitively, the main implication of the model can be understood in a gambling context. The speculator is betting on a fair game (otherwise arbitrage opportunities would be realized by risk-neutral agents); therefore it is not possible to make systematic profits and, if the gambling is stopped at any point in time, then expected total wealth (expected as of the initial date) is equal to the initial fortune. In terms of the real return r_t, this intuition is translated into the 'martingale difference property', which states that, at any point in time, the expected return for the next period, conditional on all information available at that time, is zero.

The martingale difference property of returns drives limiting results for the empirical model, by making use of laws of large numbers and central limit theorems that are appropriate to martingale difference sequences. Conditional on the price regime, an appropriately chosen transformation of the sample average of the returns converges asymptotically to a limiting normal distribution with zero mean and a limiting variance that depends on the regime itself. The null value of the asymptotic mean is a consequence of the null value that is assumed by each conditional expectation of r_t, and the difference in variances is a consequence of the differences in conditional variances, where the term 'conditional' means in this context conditional on the full information available at the specific time, information that includes the particular volatility regime. Following this argument, the long-run, unconditional probability density function of the returns – i.e. the density where all returns (regardless of which regime they come from) are mixed together – is a mixture of the probability density functions that are attached to each of the regimes. In the context of two regimes, the unconditional density would thus be a mixture of two Gaussian densities.

Define $H_t^* = \begin{cases} 1 \text{ if } I_t = I_t^F \\ 2 \text{ if } I_t = I_t^G \end{cases}$

and suppose the following transition probabilities:

$$p_{11} = \Pr\{H_t^* = 1 | H_{t-1}^*, p_{12} = \Pr\{H_t^* = 2 | H_{t-1}^* = 1\} = 1 - p_{11},$$
$$p_{22} = \Pr\{H_t^* = 2 | H_{t-1}^* = 2, p_{21} = \Pr\{H_t^* = 1 | H_{t-1}^* = 2\} = 1 - p_{22}.$$

The density of r_t conditional on the value of the state variable H_t^* is:

$$f(r_t | H_t^* = j; \theta) = \frac{1}{\sqrt{2\pi\sigma_j}} \exp\left\{\frac{-(r_t - \mu_j)^2}{2\sigma_j^2}\right\}, \; j = 1, 2;$$

where θ represents the relevant vector of parameters.

The unknown parameters σ_1^2, σ_2^2, p_{11}, p_{22}, μ_1, μ_2 are estimated numerically by maximum likelihood, following the iterative procedure of Hamilton (1989). Considering that the theory predicts that the mean return is zero (both conditional and unconditional), the estimates for the mean parameters μ_1, μ_2 provide a test for that prediction. The states are unobservable, so that an inference needs to be made regarding their likelihood at each time period. In particular, the state probabilities at each t are obtained iteratively as follows:

$$\Pr\{H_t^* = j\} = \sum_{i=1}^{2} \Pr\{H_t^* = j, H_{t-1}^* = i, \text{ with } \Pr\{H_t^* = j, H_{t-1}^* = i\} =$$

$$\Pr\{H_t^* = j | H_{t-1}^* = i\} \times \Pr\{H_{t-1}^* = i\} = p_{ij} \times \Pr\{H_{t-1}^* = i,$$

and the state-unconditional density of r_t is given by

$$f(r_t; \theta) = \sum_{j=1}^{2} f(r_t, H_t^* = j; \theta),$$

with $f(r_t, H_t^*; \theta) = f(r_t | H_t^* = j; \theta) \times \Pr\{H_t^* = j$, so that the log-likelihood function is given by

$$\log f(r_1, \ldots, r_{T-1}, r_T; \theta) = \sum_{t=1}^{T} \log f(r_t; \theta).$$

This log-likelihood function is maximized numerically with respect to all unknown parameters in the model, and a range of initial values is tried in the estimation. Ergodic state probabilities are used to start the algorithm and filtered state probabilities are calculated for each subsequent date.

4. Data and Empirical Results

The estimation was conducted on daily real returns for wheat at the KCBT market (from 12 April, 1976 to 31 March, 1995) and wheat at the MGE market (from 7 February, 1983 to 29 March, 1995). The real return is calculated as

$$\left(\frac{p_{t+1}\beta_t - p_t}{p_t}\right) \times 100,$$

where p_{t+1}, p_t are cash prices, and β_t is the daily discount rate, for which the daily-equivalent interest rate implicitly paid on 3-month treasury bills is used.

The basic features of the empirical series considered in this work are summarized in Table 5.1. The sample means are close to zero, and they are statistically not significant magnitudes. Moreover, the median, a more robust estimator of location, is also close to zero. Skewness is very low in absolute value, and the real return series exhibit some (moderate) degree of kurtosis.

We now present the estimation of the Markovian–Gaussian mixture model: maximum likelihood estimates are presented in Tables 5.2–5.5. The covariance matrix of estimated parameters is positive definite in all cases.

The results show a mean that is not statistically different from zero, two significant variances, and persistent states with significant estimates for transition probabilities, as the theoretical model predicts. The model estimations with two means show that both estimated values for the means are not different from zero, a result that is also obtained in the single-mean models. Notice that, for all of the commodities considered, the estimates for variances and transition probabilities are robust with respect to the model specification. In addition, the parameter estimates are fairly robust with respect to initial parameter values used in the estimation of each model.

Table 5.1. Wheat daily real returns facts.

Wheat at KCBT		Wheat at MGE	
Statistic	Value	Statistic	Value
Mean	−0.01089	Mean	−0.00208
SD	1.27924	SD	1.61434
Median	−0.01500	Median	−0.01544
Skewness	−0.07169	Skewness	−0.60948
Kurtosis	4.68220	Kurtosis	15.19212

KCBT, Kansas City Board of Trade; MGE, Minneapolis Grain Exchange.

Table 5.2. Maximum likelihood estimates of parameters and asymptotic standard errors, wheat daily real returns at the KCBT. Two estimated means and two estimated variances (number of observations 4727).

	Estimate	Standard error
Mean 1	0.00204	0.01377
Mean 2	−0.05474	0.08715
Variance 1	0.71015	0.02711
Variance 2	4.76471	0.32553
p_{11}	0.96458	0.00518
p_{22}	0.87341	0.02075
Log-likelihood	−2955.31742	

KCBT, Kansas City Board of Trade.

Table 5.3. Maximum likelihood estimates of parameters and asymptotic standard errors, wheat daily real returns at the KCBT. One estimated mean and two estimated variances (number of observations 4727).

	Estimate	Standard error
Mean	−0.00190	0.00938
Variance 1	0.72036	0.02698
Variance 2	4.94541	0.35465
p_{11}	0.96747	0.00467
p_{22}	0.86389	0.02276
Log-likelihood	−2956.80936	

KCBT, Kansas City Board of Trade.

Table 5.4. Maximum likelihood estimates of parameters and asymptotic standard errors, wheat daily real returns at the MGE. Two estimated means and two estimated variances (number of observations 2939).

	Estimate	Standard error
Mean 1	0.00879	0.02115
Mean 2	−0.05019	0.10885
Variance 1	0.74444	0.36209
Variance 2	10.84485	0.86373
p_{11}	0.96919	0.00596
p_{22}	0.86317	0.02472
Log-likelihood	−2034.6048	

MGE, Minneapolis Grain Exchange.

This Markovian–Gaussian mixture model was also tried for estimation with more than two states, with poor results in terms of significance and values of the parameters. We conclude it is not possible to identify more than two states for the empirical time series that are used in the estimations.

Table 5.5. Maximum likelihood estimates of parameters and asymptotic standard errors, wheat daily real returns at the MGE. One estimated mean and two estimated variances (number of observations 2939).

	Estimate	Standard error
Mean	0.00718	0.01479
Variance 1	0.74508	0.03614
Variance 2	10.85524	0.86481
p_{11}	0.96926	0.00595
p_{22}	0.86335	0.24735
Log-likelihood	−2034.68422	

MGE, Minneapolis Grain Exchange.

The rational expectations hypothesis is central to the model developed in this work, and it implies the martingale difference property for speculative returns, which is the main feature that drives the limiting results upon which the empirical model is constructed. We now test the martingale difference property by considering autocorrelations for daily returns. We calculate sample autocorrelations $a(\tau)$ for $\tau = 1, 2, \ldots, 10$; where τ represents the number of lags. As shown in Hamilton (1994), sample autocorrelations are consistent estimators of population autocorrelations. We test for uncorrelatedness by comparing the estimated value of $a(\tau)$ with the $\left|\frac{N_\alpha}{\sqrt{T}}\right|$ asymptotic bound, where N_α is the critical value of a standardized normal distribution for an α% level of significance, and T is the sample size (the justification for the use of this test as an autocorrelation test for non-normal series is provided in Harvey (1993) and Hamilton (1994)).

Results are reported in Tables 5.6 and 5.7, showing low absolute values for all of the sample autocorrelations, with most of the estimated autocorrelations statistically not different from zero at the 5% level of significance.

Tables 5.6 and 5.7 also present the portmanteau test statistic for autocorrelation. This statistic is defined by

$$Q = T\sum_{\tau=1}^{P} a^2(\tau).$$

where, as before, $a(\tau)$ are the sample autocorrelations, T is the sample size, and P is the maximum number of lags considered to construct the test. Q is asymptotically χ^2_P distributed for data from a white noise process, therefore providing an additional criterion for testing the uncorrelatedness hypothesis. As discussed in Harvey (1993), there is no specific rule for choosing the number of lags P in the Q statistic, but higher levels of P generate a loss of power of the test.

Table 5.6. Sample autocorrelations and portmanteau test statistic Q, wheat at the KCBT (sample size 4727).

Lags	Autocorrelation	Q test statistic
1	−0.01787[a]	1.50975[a]
2	−0.02534[a]	4.54591[a]
3	0.02061[a]	6.55425[a]
4	−0.02704[a]	
5	−0.04008[b]	
6	−0.03567[b]	
7	0.02593[a]	
8	0.02113[a]	
9	0.00557[a]	
10	0.01472[a]	

[a] Fails to reject the null hypothesis of no autocorrelation at the 5% significance level.
[b] Fails to reject the null hypothesis of no autocorrelation at the 1% significance level.
KCBT, Kansas City Board of Trade.

Table 5.7. Sample autocorrelations and portmanteau test statistic Q, wheat at the MGE (sample size 2939).

Lags	Autocorrelation	Q test statistic
1	−0.03604[a]	3.81694[a]
2	0.00188[a]	3.82732[a]
3	−0.05185[b]	11.72814
4	−0.03358[a]	
5	−0.05393	
6	−0.03847[b]	
7	−0.03789[b]	
8	0.01997[a]	
9	−0.02185[a]	
10	0.02807[a]	

[a] Fails to reject the null hypothesis of no autocorrelation at the 5% significance level.
[b] Fails to reject the null hypothesis of no autocorrelation at the 1% significance level.
MGE, Minneapolis Grain Exchange.

The portmanteau test statistic Q is computed for both data sets with P being alternatively 1, 2 and 3. Results show that the white noise hypothesis cannot be rejected at the 5% or 1% significance level in most cases.

The Markovian–Gaussian mixture model implies that the unconditional probability density function of the returns, as a mixture of two normal probability density functions, is not normal itself. This is a hypothesis with empirical content, as it is possible to test for normality based on the market return series. We now present two normality tests: the Anderson–Darling test (Shapiro, 1990) and the asymptotic Bowman–Shenton test (Bowman and Shenton, 1975).

The Anderson–Darling normality test belongs to the class of 'distance tests'. The specific test statistic is performed as follows: given the sorted sample of standardized variates

$$w_t = \frac{r_t - \bar{r}}{s},$$

where

$$\bar{r} = \frac{1}{T}\sum_{t=1}^{T} r_t,\ s = \sqrt{\frac{T\sum_{t=1}^{T} r_t^2 - (\sum_{t=1}^{T} r_t)^2}{T(T-1)}};$$

transform the w_t values to their equivalent standard normal cumulative probability as follows: $Z_t = \Pr\{Z < w_t\}$, $t = 1, \ldots, T$, and compute the test statistic

$$A^2 = A^2\left(1 + \frac{0.75}{T} + \frac{2.25}{T^2}\right),$$

where

$$A^2 = -\frac{\left\{\sum_{t=1}^{T}(2t-1)[\ln(Z_t) + \ln(1 - Z_{T+1-t})]\right\}}{T} - T;$$

the 'ln' notation stands for natural logarithm.

The test statistic A^{2^*} is compared with the critical level given in Shapiro (1990). For a 5% significance, the critical value is 0.752.

The Anderson–Darling test statistic A^{2^*} is computed for all return series. Results are reported in Table 5.8, implying rejection of the normality hypothesis at the 5% significance level for all cases considered.

The asymptotic Bowman–Shenton test is based on the skewness and kurtosis magnitudes, as compared with those of a normal distribution. The test statistic is given by:

$$BS = \frac{(\sqrt{b_1})^2}{6/T} + \frac{(b_2 - 3)^2}{24/T},$$

Table 5.8. Anderson–Darling test statistic.

Wheat at KCBT	54.42951
Wheat at MGE	98.32456

KCBT, Kansas City Board of Trade; MGE, Minneapolis Grain Exchange.

where $\sqrt{b_1}$ and b_2 are the sample skewness and kurtosis, and $6/T$, $24/T$ are the asymptotic variances of $\sqrt{b_1}$ and b_2, respectively. The Bowman–Shenton test statistic is asymptotically χ^2_2.

The Bowman–Shenton test statistic is reported in Table 5.9, with values that imply rejection of normality at the 1% significance level.

With the purpose of comparison, we compute the maximum likelihood estimation of the return series for each of the wheat markets considered, specifying a Gaussian joint density for the returns. Results are reported in Tables 5.10 and 5.11.

The eigenvalues of the covariance matrix are all strictly positive in every estimation, implying a positive definite covariance matrix.

Several observations follow from Tables 5.10 and 5.11: all estimated means are statistically not different from zero, as was the case for the Markovian–Gaussian mixture model estimation. In addition, the estimated variances are in the range of the variances that are estimated in both versions (i.e. two estimated means and one estimated mean) of the Markovian–Gaussian mixture model.

A student's t distribution can be interpreted as the mixture of normal distributions, thus providing an alternative specification for the

Table 5.9. Bowman–Shenton test statistic.

Wheat at KCBT	561.40075
Wheat at MGE	18385.11600

KCBT, Kansas City Board of Trade; MGE, Minneapolis Grain Exchange.

Table 5.10. Gaussian maximum likelihood estimates of parameters and asymptotic standard errors, wheat daily real returns at the KCBT (number of observations 4727).

	Estimate	Standard error
Mean	−0.01088	0.01306
Variance	1.63611	0.03366
Log-likelihood	−7870.92060	

KCBT, Kansas City Board of Trade.

Table 5.11. Gaussian maximum likelihood estimates of parameters and asymptotic standard errors, wheat daily real returns at the MGE (number of observations 2939).

	Estimate	Standard error
Mean	−0.00207	0.02245
Variance	2.60519	0.06796
Log-likelihood	−5577.3167	

MGE, Minneapolis Grain Exchange.

joint density of the returns. Based on this interpretation, we now present a maximum likelihood estimation of the model with a student's t distribution.

Under the student's t structure, the density of the real return r_t can be written as:

$$f(r_t|k) = \frac{\Gamma[(k+1)/2]}{\Gamma[k/2]} \frac{1}{\sqrt{k\pi}} \frac{1}{(1 + r_t^2/k)^{(k+1)/2}}, \; k > 0;$$

where Γ is the gamma function, defined by:

$$\Gamma(t) = \int_0^{=\infty} \mu^{t-1} e^{-\mu} d\mu \text{ for } t > 0,$$

and k is the only parameter of the density, the number of degrees of freedom of the student's t. For this distribution, the mean of the return r_t is zero for $k > 1$, and the variance implied by the degrees of freedom parameter k is given by

$$\frac{k}{k-2},$$

for $k > 2$. Results are reported in Tables 5.12 and 5.13.

While the asymptotic results developed imply a Gaussian distribution of returns conditional on any given state, the basic structure of the unconditional density of returns being a Markovian mixture of two

Table 5.12. Student's t maximum likelihood estimation, wheat daily real returns at the KCBT (number of observations 4727).

	Estimate	Standard error
Degrees of freedom (k)	4.59438	0.22614
Implied variance	1.77089	
Log-likelihood	−7481.27	

KCBT, Kansas City Board of Trade.

Table 5.13. Student's t maximum likelihood estimation, wheat daily real returns at the MGE (number of observations 2939).

	Estimate	Standard error
Degrees of freedom (k)	3.03242	0.14400
Implied variance	2.93791	
Log-likelihood	−4926.4355	

MGE, Minneapolis Grain Exchange.

densities (both with zero mean) is a result that is robust to the particular density specification taken to obtain the mixture. To show this point, we present the estimation of the Markovian mixture model with logistic probability distributions; i.e. the density of the return r_t conditional on the state j, $j = 1, 2$ is now specified as:

$$f(r_t | H_t^* = j, \theta) = \frac{\pi}{\sigma_j \sqrt{3}} \frac{e^{-\pi(r_t - \mu_j)/\sigma_j \sqrt{3}}}{\{1 + e^{-\pi(r_t - \mu_j)/\sigma_j \sqrt{3}}\}^2}$$

The σ_1, σ_2 parameters are the two standard deviations, and the μ_1, μ_2 parameters are the two means. The unknown parameters σ_1, σ_2, μ_1, μ_2 are estimated numerically by maximum likelihood, for both the two means and two variances and the one mean and two variances specifications. Results are reported in Tables 5.14 and 5.15.

The covariance matrix of the estimated parameters is positive definite in all cases.

Table 5.14. Logistic maximum likelihood estimates of parameters and asymptotic standard errors, wheat daily real returns at the KCBT. Two estimated means and two estimated variances (number of observations 4727).

	Estimate	Standard error
Mean 1	0.00099	0.02151
Mean 2	−0.05005	0.03528
Variance 1	0.73647	0.03594
Variance 2	3.87221	0.36457
p_{11}	0.96552	0.00744
p_{22}	0.91138	0.02317
Log-likelihood	−7268.57984	

KCBT, Kansas City Board of Trade.

Table 5.15. Logistic maximum likelihood estimates of parameters and asymptotic standard errors, wheat daily real returns at the KCBT. One estimated mean and two estimated variances (number of observations 4727).

	Estimate	Standard error
Mean	−0.00201	0.01834
Variance 1	0.73522	0.03611
Variance 2	3.87464	0.36572
p_{11}	0.96567	0.00735
p_{22}	0.91143	0.02292
Log-likelihood	−7268.88079	

KCBT, Kansas City Board of Trade.

5. Non-parametric Density Estimations

Non-parametric (kernel) density estimations were performed using Gaussian and Epanechnikov kernels. These estimations correspond to the construction of an estimate for the probability density of the daily return without stating any parametric assumption about the density. Several estimation strategies are available for these estimations, including kernel estimators and nearest-neighbour methods (a standard reference is Silverman (1986)). The kernel estimator uses a kernel function K, usually satisfying the condition $\int_{-\infty}^{\infty} K(r)dr = 1$, with the density estimation at an arbitrary point R in the support of the random variable given by

$$\hat{f}(R) = \frac{1}{Th} \sum_{j=1}^{T} K\left(\frac{R - r_j}{h}\right),$$

where T is the number of observations, h is the window width, and r_j, $j = 1, \ldots, T$ is the sample. The window width h is a smoothing parameter, controlling for the noise variability of the estimation. Many common parametric probability density functions are used as kernel functions in the estimation of $\hat{f}$; and in particular both Gaussian and Epanechnikov kernels have comparatively good efficiency properties, in terms of minimizing the mean integrated square error, $MISE(\hat{f})$, given by $MISE(\hat{f}) = E\int \{\hat{f}(R) - f(R)\}^2 dR$. The window width used in the estimations of this work is the optimal window width proposed by Silverman (1986: 46–47).

Graphs corresponding to these estimations (Figs 5.1–5.4), show unimodal estimated distributions, centred at zero, with an approximately symmetric shape. The leptokurtic characteristic of these distributions can be explained by the theory presented in this work, as the consequence of mixing two normal densities, both with the same zero mean, but each with a distinct variance.

The Markovian–Gaussian mixture model generates as a by-product the filtered probability of each observation belonging to any given state. We now exploit these probabilistic guesses, by partitioning the full sample of real returns for each commodity into two subsamples, each subsample corresponding to the predicted state of the returns (the rule is to take r_t as being a state 1 observation if $\Pr\{r_t \in \textit{state } 1\} \geq 0.5$, taking r_t as corresponding to state 2 otherwise). Based on these subsamples, we perform a Gaussian kernel non-parametric density estimation for each of them to check the predictions implied by the estimated model. Combined graphs are presented in Figs 5.5 and 5.6, showing (for each wheat market) two estimated conditional densities centred at zero, one with a distinctly higher variance than the other, with a variance of the unconditional density that is in between the variances for the estimated conditional probability density functions.

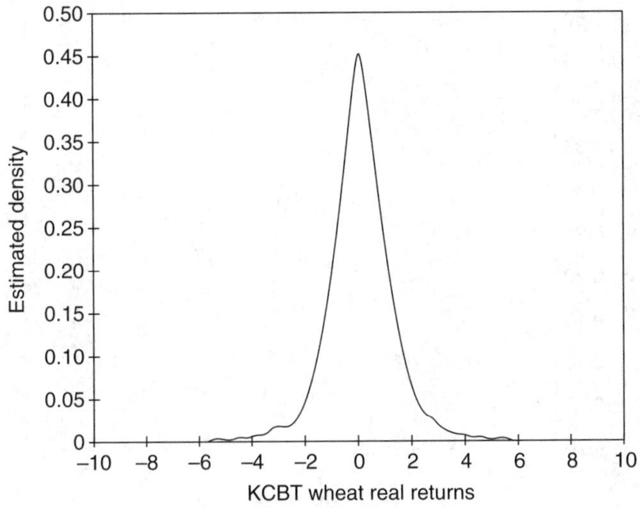

Fig. 5.1. Gaussian kernel density estimation, KCBT wheat real returns.

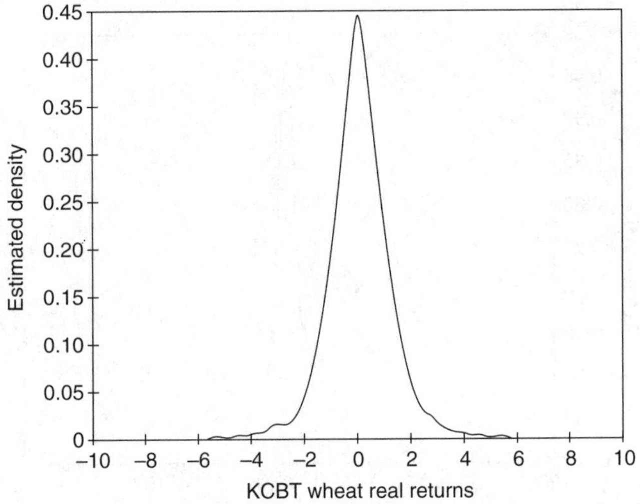

Fig. 5.2. Epanechnikov kernel density estimation, KCBT wheat real returns.

6. Conclusion

This chapter explicitly generalizes the standard i.i.d. rational expectations model for the case of wheat prices, to encompass news. The subject of market reaction to news is strongly appealing, and it has been addressed in the literature at least since the works of Working (1934, 1948) and Cootner (1960), but it has been absent from the modern literature on commodity price determination. The standard implicit

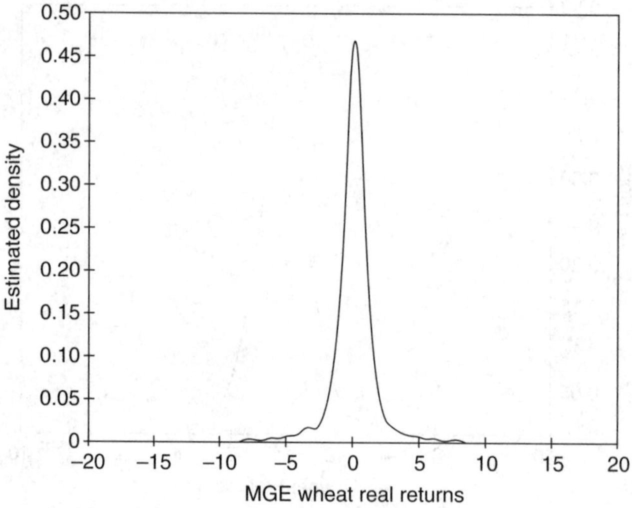

Fig. 5.3. Gaussian kernel, MGE wheat real returns. Full sample.

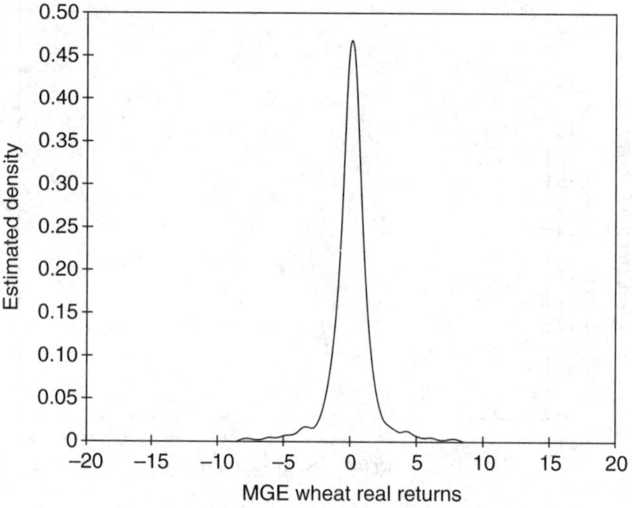

Fig. 5.4. Epanechnikov kernel, MGE wheat real returns. Full sample.

assumption is that the agent always faces the same future, no matter what the market conditions are. Day-to-day trading does not easily accommodate such modelling restrictions, as most of the practical speculator's attention concentrates on how to respond optimally to a changing perception of the future as information changes in real time. We conclude that when the distinction is recognized between the unconditional return distribution (a concept related to the long-run behaviour) and the conditional return distribution (which is the rele-

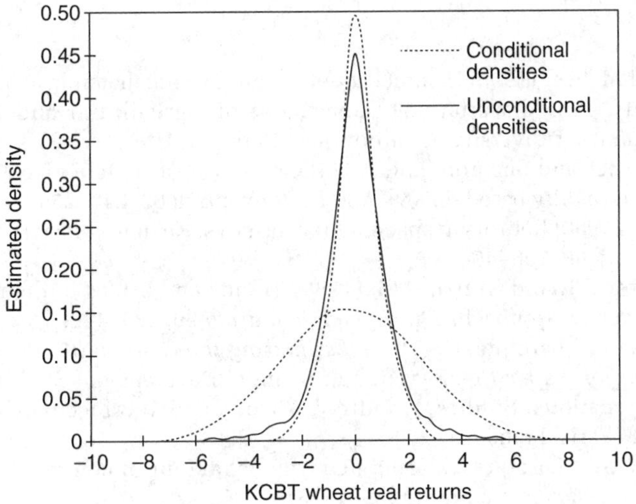

Fig. 5.5. KCBT wheat returns: unconditional and state-dependent densities.

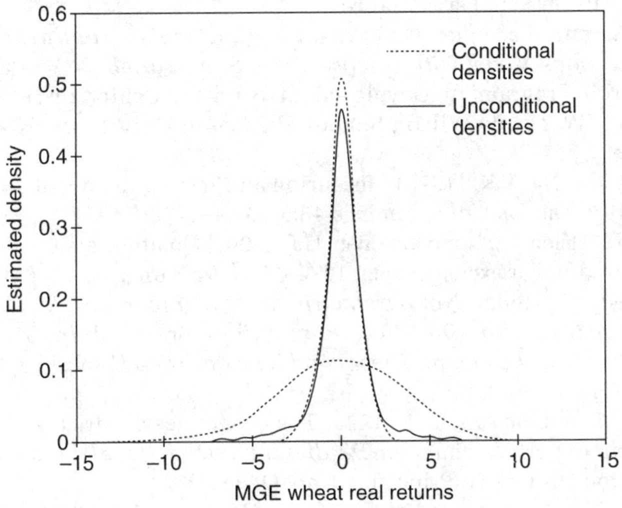

Fig. 5.6. MGE wheat returns: unconditional and state-dependent densities.

vant object for the period-by-period recursive decision-making), a much richer empirical characterization of wheat price series can be achieved. The empirical relevance of this new modelling approach is shown by parametric estimations of the first two moments of the return function, as well as non-parametric density estimations, for two wheat price series. Integration with results from annual models is a task that awaits further investigation.

References

Bobenrieth, E.S.A. (1996) Commodity prices under time-heterogeneous shocks density. PhD dissertation, Department of Agricultural and Resource Economics, University of California at Berkeley, USA.

Bowman, K.O. and Shenton, L.R. (1975) Omnibus test contours for departures from normality based on $\sqrt{b_1}$ and b_2. *Biometrika* 62, 243–250.

Cootner, P. (1960) Returns to speculators: Telser vs. Keynes. *Journal of Political Economy* 68, 396–404.

Cuddington, J.T. and Urzúa, C.M. (1989) Trends and cycles in the net terms trade: a new approach. *The Economic Journal* 99, 426–442.

Deaton, A. and Laroque, G. (1991) *Estimating the Commodity Price Model, Discussion Paper 154.* Research Program in Development Studies, Center of International Studies, Woodrow Wilson School, Princeton University. INSEE, Paris, France.

Deaton, A. and Laroque, G. (1992) On the behaviour of commodity prices. *Review of Economic Studies* 59, 1–23.

Deaton, A. and Laroque, G. (1994a) *Competitive Storage and Commodity Price Dynamics.* Working paper, Research Program in Development Studies, Center of International Studies, Woodrow Wilson School, Princeton University. INSEE, Paris, France.

Deaton, A. and Laroque, G. (1994b) *Estimating a Nonlinear Rational Expectations Model with Unobservable State Variables.* Working paper, Research Program in Development Studies, Center of International Studies, Woodrow Wilson School, Princeton University. INSEE, Paris, France.

Engle, R.F. and Ng, V.K. (1993) Measuring and testing the impact of news on volatility. *The Journal of Finance* 48:5, 1749–1778.

Gallant, A.R., Hsieh, D.A. and Tauchen, G.E. (1991) On fitting a recalcitrant series: the pound/dollar exchange rate, 1974–1983. In: Barnett, W.A., Powell, J. and Tauchen, G. (eds) *Nonparametric and Semiparametric Methods in Econometrics and Statistics: Proceedings of the Fifth International Symposium in Economic Theory and Econometrics.* Cambridge University Press, Cambridge, UK.

Gersovitz, M. and Paxson, C.H. (1990) The economies of Africa and the prices of their exports. *Princeton Studies in International Finance No. 68.* Princeton University, Princeton, New Jersey, USA.

Gustafson, R.L. (1958) *Carryover Levels for Grains: a Method for Determining Amounts that are Optimal under Specified Conditions.* USDA Technical Bulletin 1178, USDA, Washington DC, USA.

Hamilton, J.D. (1989) A new approach to the economic analysis of nonstationary time series and the business cycle. *Econometrica* 57, 357–384.

Hamilton, J.D. (1994) *Time Series Analysis.* Princeton University Press, Princeton, New Jersey, USA.

Hamilton, J.D. and Susmel, R. (1994) Autoregressive conditional heteroskedasticity and changes in regime. *Journal of Econometrics* 64, 307–333.

Harvey, A.C. (1993) *Time Series Models*, 2nd edn. The MIT Press, Cambridge, Massachusetts, USA.

Khim, J. (1994) *Asymmetric Effect of Storage on Price and Backwardation in Commodity Futures*. Department of Economics, University of Chicago, Chicago, Illinois, USA.

Miranda, J.M. and Rui, X. (1995) *An Empirical Reassessment of the Commodity Storage Model*. Working paper, Ohio State University, Columbus, Ohio, USA.

Muth, J.F. (1961) Rational expectations and the theory of price movements. *Econometrica* 29, 315–335.

Pindyck, R.S. (1993) The present value model of rational commodity pricing, *The Economic Journal* 103, 511–530.

Pindyck, R.S. (1994) Inventories and the short-run dynamics of commodity prices. *RAND Journal of Economics* 25, 141–159.

Scheinkman, J.A. and Schechtman, J. (1983) A simple competitive model with production and storage. *Review of Economic Studies* 50, 427–441.

Shapiro, S.S. (1990) *How to Test Normality and Other Distributional Assumptions*. Statistics Division, American Society for Quality Control, Milwaukee, Wisconsin, USA.

Silverman, B.W. (1986) Density estimation for statistics and data analysis. *Monographs on Statistics and Applied Probability*. Chapman and Hall, New York, USA.

Williams, J.C. and Wright, B.D. (1991) *Storage and Commodity Markets*. Cambridge University Press, Cambridge, UK.

Working, H. (1934) Price relations between May and new-crop wheat futures at Chicago since 1885. *Wheat Studies* 10, 183–228.

Working, H. (1948) Theory of the inverse carrying charge in futures markets. *Journal of Farm Economics* 30, 1–28.

6

The Future of the Green Revolution: Implications for International Grain Markets

Robert W. Herdt

The Rockefeller Foundation, New York, USA

1. Introduction

The term 'Green Revolution' has been used by many different people to mean many different things. Some mean modern agriculture in the developing world, others mean export agriculture in the developing world, still others mean high-chemical-input agriculture anywhere. I use the term in a more limited way, to mean the rapid, widespread adoption of semi-dwarf rice and wheat varieties and chemical fertilizer that occurred between 1965 and 1985 in the countries of Asia and, to an extent, in Latin America.[1] Asia has been an important player in the international grain market throughout the past 35 years, and the Green Revolution had an important impact on Asia's participation over that period.

Given what is now extremely broad acceptance of semi-dwarf varieties and fertilizer, documented below, any future Green Revolution would have to be generated by a new wave of technological change, presumably generated from biotechnology.

The chapter begins with a recapitulation of the Green Revolution record, then considers crop biotechnology and its promise, examines the prospects for significant impact from crop biotechnology, reviews information on donor assistance to biotechnology research in the developing world, and concludes with observations on the impact all this may have on international grain trade.

2. Green Revolution

According to the US Department of Agriculture (USDA) data, in the 1961–1965 period, world wheat output was 251 million tonnes; by the 1986–1990 period it had doubled to 531 million tonnes (USDA, 1996). Over the same period, South Asia increased its wheat production from 15.5 to 63.5 million tonnes and China increased its wheat production from 19.1 to 90.1 million tonnes. Wheat yields increased about 240% from 825 kg per ha to about 2000 kg per ha in South Asia and by 390% from 775 to 3025 kg per ha in China. Thus, while South Asia increased wheat production by 300% and China by 370%, the rest of the world increased production by 70%. This was one of the main reflections of the Green Revolution.

In 1961–1965 world rice production averaged 240 million tonnes. It increased to an average of 492 million tonnes over the period 1986–1990. South Asia's rice production went from 72.7 to 135.9 million tonnes, China's went from 72.2 to 176.9 million tonnes over the same period, and South East Asia's went from 49.1 to 106.9 million tonnes. Yield increased by about 160% from 1530 to 2425 kg per ha in South Asia, by about 220% from 2550 to 5450 kg per ha in China, and by about 180% from 1650 to 2950 kg per ha in South East Asia. South Asia's rice production increased 90%, China's increased 140%, South East Asia's increased 120%, while the rest of the world's increased 60%. The Green Revolution in rice was clearly less dramatic than in wheat.

Maize is much less important in Asia than either rice or wheat, and many would say there has been no Green Revolution in maize – at least, it has not been generally acknowledged by the community that comments on world food issues. World maize production averaged 214 million tonnes in the 1961–1965 period and 456 million tonnes in the 1986–1990 period. South Asia's production was only 10 million tonnes in the second period, up from 6 in the first. Maize is moving somewhat more rapidly in China, going from 20 to 80 million tonnes. Data for Africa and Latin America also fail to show much dramatic movement in maize production.

Asia dominates global rice production, while it is just another player in world wheat production and has been insignificant on the maize scene. Asia's production increases have been much more rapid in wheat than in rice, driven by more rapid increases in yields. Wheat yields averaged 836 kg per ha in South Asia in the early period and increased by 130% to 1978 kg per ha in 1986–1990; they averaged 774 kg per ha in China in 1961–1965 and increased to 3045 kg per ha later – an increase of almost 300%. Rice yields, on the other hand, increased by 60% in South Asia, by 80% in South East Asia, and by 110% in China.

'Modern' semi-dwarf varieties of both wheat and rice were key to the yield increases that drove the Green Revolution. Adoption rates of modern varieties have been tracked by Dana Dalrymple and the international agricultural research centres associated with their production (Dalrymple, 1986). China invented semi-dwarfs slightly before and independently of the international centres. The new varieties came out of the centres in the mid-1960s and by 1982 had spread to about 80% of the wheat area in South Asia and to 50% of the rice area in South and South East Asia. By that time farmers in China had started planting hybrid rice, building on their already widespread adoption of semi-dwarfs. By 1990 semi-dwarf wheat had spread to 88% of South Asia's wheat area (Byerlee and Moya, 1993) and semi-dwarf rice to 80% of Asia's rice area.

Irrigated land is also associated with the Green Revolution in Asia. In the 1961–1965 period South Asia had 37.6 million ha of irrigated land; that increased to 63.8 million ha by the later period, an increase of 70%. China's irrigated area increased from 31.3 million ha to 45 million, an increase of 40%.

Fertilizer is the third component of the Green Revolution. In 1961–1965 South Asia used only 5 kg per ha of fertilizer and China 12; by the 1986–1990 period South Asia's farmers were applying an average of 65 kg per ha and China's farmers an average of 240 kg per ha (Bumb and Baanante, 1996). Fertilizer use increased by factors of 13 in South Asia and 20 in China. In the rest of the world fertilizer use increased by a factor of less than three.

Observers differ on the extent to which the semi-dwarf varieties of wheat and rice were responsible for Asia's Green Revolution. Clearly, fertilizer was an important factor. It is also clear that the semi-dwarf varieties and fertilizer perform much better with irrigation than under rainfed conditions, especially where rainfall is limiting, although both semi-dwarf varieties and fertilizer are applied on rainfed farms in many areas of Asia. As elsewhere, if rainfall distribution or amount limits crop growth, yields are reduced and farmers tend to apply lower rates of fertilizer.

Despite the importance of fertilizer and irrigation, varietal change was a key factor. An analysis of the differences between the capacity of the best rice varieties in India and the USA to respond to fertilizer before the advent of the Green Revolution showed without question the Indian varieties simply could not productively absorb high rates of fertilizer (Herdt and Mellor, 1964). That ability to convert high rates of fertilizer into grain productively was, in fact, the characteristic of the semi-dwarf varieties that made them so different from earlier varieties. Until that time, low fertilizer use and limited mechanization meant that Asian farm output was generated essentially by inputs produced on farms. Today, fertilizer, produced by the industrial sector, is an important source of food.

On the other hand, through the 1990s, pesticides have been very little used in Asian wheat production. While the application of fungicides on wheat has become routine in Europe, it is not much used in Asia, and the same can be said for insecticides on wheat. Herbicides are beginning to be used for wheat.

Pesticides and rice are a somewhat different story. The first semi-dwarf rices were vulnerable to the attacks of many insects, and by the early 1970s International Rice Research Institute (IRRI) results showed that yields with insecticides were higher than without. But in those early studies costs of the pesticides applied were not considered, so rates in excess of economic optima were sometimes used as illustrations of the effect of pesticides (Herdt *et al.*, 1983). Also, those early pesticide studies failed to account for the natural selection pressure applied to insects that enabled them, in time, to overcome the killing power of the insecticides. By the mid-1980s scientists were developing integrated pest management practices that involved a minimum of insecticide, and today in most Asian countries insecticide application on rice is unnecessary, and often results in lower yields than no application, if used improperly (Kenmore, 1996).

Herbicides were of little importance during the Green Revolution when labour was still relatively low-cost in Asia and rice was transplanted by hand in rows. More recently, with rising wage rates and migration of labour to the bright lights of the cities, farmers are turning to direct seeding of rice. That makes it necessary to control weeds through use of herbicides, and herbicide use in rice is increasing. This trend has, it seems, convinced Monsanto Corporation that there is a market for their products in rice-growing Asia because they are reported to have begun a concerted effort on rice in Asia.

3. What is Biotechnology and What is its Promise?

A decade ago some writers used 'biotechnology' to refer to such techniques as improved fermentation or cheese making, but, while those are biological processes that use technology, most authors now confine their use of the term biotechnology to procedures that use molecular techniques involving DNA. The essence of all DNA is four nucleotides: adenine (A), guanine (G), thymine (T) and cytosine (C). The nucleotides pair up into strands that twist together into the well-known double helix, with A always pairing with T, and G always pairing with C. The entire sequence of base pairs for an organism contains the complete genetic code for that organism, and every cell in the organism contains the entire array of DNA. When cells reproduce, the strands of the double helix separate and, because of the unique pairing, each strand serves as a blueprint for a new strand.

The ability to identify and multiply the DNA sequences that constitute the basic genetic code gives extremely precise ways to identify biological organisms and has led to a number of different kinds of molecular markers and to the capacity to move genetic information from one organism to another without sex – including across species. Heretofore, interspecific crosses have been impossible or, in the rare cases where possible, such as crossing a donkey and a horse to get a mule, have resulted in sterile offspring. In essence, biotechnology can be used to modify the genetic composition of organisms in ways that were not possible using conventional breeding.

Genetic transformation and molecular markers are two of the primary tools of biotechnology. Their application to animal agriculture is diverse and complex, in many cases following applications to humans and in other cases breaking new ground. My knowledge does not extend to those many and varied applications, so the rest of the chapter is confined to plants.

Transformation enables plant scientists to transfer genes from any source into plants and (sometimes, under some conditions) get stable intergenerational expression of encoded traits. Transformation can be achieved with greater efficiency and more routinely in the dicots than in the monocots, but with determined efforts nearly all plants can be transformed, and monocot transformation is becoming more routine. Marker-assisted breeding is used to follow, from one generation to the next, the presence of a particular sequence of DNA and of genes linked to that sequence.

Transformation and marker-assisted breeding have been used towards four broad goals: to change product characteristics, improve plant resistance to pests, increase output, and produce unique metabolites.

Product characteristics

Changed product characteristics are illustrated by one of the first genetically engineered plants to pass regulations and to be made available for general consumption by the public, the FLAVR SAVR™ tomato, whose fruit-ripening characteristics have been modified so as to provide a longer shelf-life (Fray and Grierson, 1993). Biotechnology has also been used to change the proportion of fatty acids in soybeans, modify the composition of oilseed rape (canola) (Voelker *et al.*, 1992), and change the starch content of potatoes (Stark *et al.*, 1992).

Pest resistance

Natural variability in the capacity to resist damage from insects and plant diseases has long been exploited by plant breeders. Biotechnology provides new tools to add to this capacity. *Bacillus thuringiensis* (*Bt*), which produces an insect toxin particularly effective against lepidoptera, has been applied to crops by gardeners for decades. Transformation of tomato plants with the gene that produces *Bt* toxin was one of the first demonstrations of how biotechnology could be used to enhance plants' ability to resist damage from insects (Perlak and Fishoff, 1993). Transgenic cotton that expresses *Bt* toxin at a level to provide protection against cotton bollworm has been developed (Perlak *et al.*, 1990), and a large number of *Bt*-transformed crops are currently being field-tested. Promoters can be associated with transferred genes to ensure expression in particular plant tissues or at growth stages, and this is one of the strategies being used by scientists to manage the exposure of insects to *Bt*.

Other approaches to prevent insect damage include transformation of crops with genes of plant origin for proteins that retard insect growth, such as lectins, amylase inhibitors, and protease inhibitors (Shah *et al.*, 1995).

Genes providing resistance to viral plant pathogens have been derived from the viruses themselves, most notably with coat-protein-mediated resistance (CP-MR); one of the first cases being a yellow squash with CP-MR resistance to two plant viruses, which has been approved for commercial production in the USA (Shah *et al.*, 1995). Practical resistance to fungal and bacterial pathogens has been more elusive, although genes encoding several enzymes that degrade fungal cell walls have been explored.

Increased yield potential

While protecting plants against insects and pathogens promises to increase harvested output by saving a higher percentage of present yield, a number of scientists are seeking to increase the potential crop yield, including the exploitation of hybrid vigour, delayed senescence and increased starch.

Several strategies to produce hybrid seed in new ways are likely to contribute to increasing yield potential. Cytoplasmic male sterility has been widely used even before biotechnology, but other strategies to exploit nuclear-encoded male sterility required biological manipulations that could only be carried out using molecular biology tools, and now several of these are quite far advanced (Williams, 1995). Some entail suppression of pollen formation by exploiting sensitivity to temperature or day length. Delayed senescence or 'stay-green' trait enables a plant to continue producing photosynthate beyond the period when a non-transformed plant would, thereby potentially producing a higher yield (Gan and Amasino, 1995). Potatoes that produce higher starch content than non-transformed controls have been developed (Stark *et al.*, 1992).

Unique plant metabolites

Plants have been designed to produce a range of lipids, carbohydrates, pharmaceutical polypeptides and industrial enzymes, leading to the hope that plants can be used in place of microbial fermentation (Goddijn and Pen, 1995). One of the more ambitious of such applications is the production of vaccines against animal or human diseases. The hepatitis B surface antigen has been expressed in tobacco, and the feasibility of using the purified product to elicit an immune response in mice has been demonstrated (Thonavala *et al.*, 1995).

Gene markers

Far-reaching possibilities for closely identifying genome composition have been made possible through various molecular marker techniques with names like RFLP, RAPD, micro-cassettes, and others. These techniques allow scientists to follow genes from one generation to subsequent generations, adding powerfully to the tools at the disposal of plant breeders. In particular, they enable plant breeders to combine several resistance genes, each of which may have different modes of action, leading to longer-acting or more durable resistance against pathogens. Marker tools also facilitate the combining of a number of genes that individually provide only a weakly expressed desirable trait in order to get strong expression.

4. Prospects for Broad Impact

Research continues to improve the efficiency and reduce the costs of the various means of transformation and the several types of genetic markers. As this research succeeds, it will be applied to more plants and genes.

By far the greatest proportion of current crop biotechnology research is being conducted in industrialized countries on the crops of economic interest in those countries. In 1995 almost 2000 plant biotechnology research projects were under way in the 15 countries of the European Union (EU), with 1300 actually using plants (as opposed to plant pathogens, theoretical work and so forth). Of those, about 210 were for work on wheat, barley and other cereals, 150 on potato, 125 on oilseed rape, and about 90 on maize (Lloyd-Evans and Barfoot, 1996).

Field trials are one of the final stages before seeds are sold to farmers, and reflect the composition of research conducted in earlier years. Between 1986 and the end of 1995, some 3647 field trials had been conducted worldwide, 53% in the USA, 19% in the EU (almost half of which were in France), 13% in Canada, and the balance in 25 other countries (James and Krattiger, 1996). Argentina, Chile, China and Mexico led in numbers of field trials in developing countries, but none had more than 2% of the total. A rough estimate of R&D biotechnology funding for agriculture suggests about $2.5 billion is being spent worldwide, with no more than $75 million being spent in developing countries (A.F. Krattiger, personal communication).

Through 1993 the most field trials worldwide were conducted on potato (19%), with oilseed rape second (18%); tobacco, tomato, and maize each accounted for about 12%, with more than ten trials each on lucerne, cantaloupe, cotton, flax, sugar beet, soybean, and poplar. Nine trials had been done on rice, and fewer than that on wheat, sorghum, millet, and sugar cane, the food crops that, apart from maize, provide most of the food for most of the world's people who live in the developing countries (Dale, 1995). By the end of 1995, maize, with 33% of field trials worldwide, had far surpassed potato (11%), with oilseed rape maintaining second place (21%), and soybean (9%) following potato (1995 data on field trials come from James and Krattiger, 1996).

Herbicide resistance is the simplest trait to incorporate into a plant because application of the herbicide applies ideal selection pressure to the population being screened, killing all susceptible individuals. Thus, a population of cells, some containing DNA that confers herbicide resistance, can quickly be screened. A number of different herbicides are available, and there is a strong self-interest on the part of herbicide manufacturers to encourage farmers to use herbicides. This means that several pressures work to ensure that transgenic crops with herbicide resistance will be produced.

Herbicide tolerance has been the most widely tested trait, accounting for 35% of the field trials for agronomically useful genes through 1995. Twenty per cent of tests were conducted on ten different types of modified product quality – including delayed ripening, modified processing characters, starch metabolism, modified oil content.

About 37% of field trials in developing countries were for herbicide resistance, 21% for virus resistance, 26% for insect resistance, 9% for product quality, fungal resistance or agronomic traits. Maize was the subject of the most tests (27%), cotton was the subject of 18% of the trials, with tomato, tobacco, and soybeans each accounting for about 15%, and potato and canola making up most of the rest.

Incorporation of resistance to pests and diseases has been the objective of much of the crop biotechnology work, accounting for 32% of field tests through 1995. This work, as well as the rest of the field trials, is largely focused on temperate area crop pests. It is possible that genes that address insect or disease problems of temperate crops may be effective in tropical crops. But before they can be used in the tropics there are still business and biological problems associated with getting access to the genes, and transforming plants with those genes.

Intellectual property rights may slow the transfer of genes although, in one case, Monsanto has made available, without cost, the genes conferring resistance to important potato viruses to Mexico, and has trained Mexican scientists in transformation and other skills needed to make use of the genes. The transformed potatoes are now being field-tested in Mexico.

Drought is a major problem for nearly all crop plants, and the prospects of a 'drought-resistance gene' has excited many in the development assistance community. However, plant scientists recognize drought tolerance or resistance as having many dimensions: long, thick roots; thick, waxy leaves; the ability to produce viable pollen under drought stress; the ability to recover from a dry period, and others. Some of these traits can undoubtedly be controlled genetically, but little progress has thus far been made in identifying the genes that control them. Salt tolerance is often discussed with drought tolerance because salt conditions and drought cause plants to react in similar ways, but some of the genes helpful for drought tolerance may be useless for salty conditions and vice versa. Some early workers held out the prospect that by fusing cells of plants tolerant to drought with elite-type plants not tolerant a combination of the two would result, but that has not been demonstrated.

I believe that relatively little attention will be paid to the crops or the pests/diseases/stresses of importance in the developing world unless they are also of importance in the more advanced countries. That is, while the gains in fundamental knowledge that apply to all organisms will, of course, be available to developing countries, the applications in the form of transformation techniques, probes, gene promoters, and genes for specific conditions will not be generated without deliberate efforts aimed at that goal. Hence plant biotechnology progress will be slower in developing than in developed countries.

Pest-resistance genes will raise average yields by preventing damage, but there is little prospect for dramatic changes in yield potential through biotechnology. The reason is simple: few strategies are being pursued that attempt directly to raise yield potential because few strategies have been conceived. Hybrid rice is one exception already mentioned. Discussions of other ways of raising yield potential revolve around increasing the 'sink' size and increasing the 'source' capacity (Kropff *et al.*, 1994). The first requires increasing the number of grains or the average grain size, the latter increasing the capacity of the plant to fill those grains with carbohydrate. Both are desired but, certainly for rice, there are only a few investigators worldwide thinking about how biotechnology might advance each. While there is a community of scientists working to understand basic plant biochemistry, including photosynthesis, this work as yet offers few hints about which genes can be manipulated to advantage using molecular biology.

Assistance to developing-country plant biotechnology

It is estimated that between 1985 and 1994 about $260 million was contributed as grants to agricultural biotechnology in the developing world, with another $150 million in the form of loans, with perhaps an average of $50 million per year in the more recent years (Brunner and Komen, 1994). At least a third and perhaps half of these funds have been used to establish organizations designed to help bring the benefits of biotechnology to developing countries. This compares to about $200 million annually spent by the federal government alone in the USA (Office of the President, 1992), with the private sector more than doubling that.

Maize is the focus of much crop biotechnology work in the USA, and most of the work on maize is directed towards making it better suited for production or more capable of resisting the depredations of pests in the industrialized countries. The International Wheat and Maize Improvement Center (CIMMYT) sponsors the largest concentration of international effort directed at identifying traits of tropical maize that could be improved using biotechnology, but it spends barely $2 million per year on those efforts. The International Rice Research Institute (IRRI) is probably spending as much on rice biotechnology.

I know of five coherent, coordinated programmes directed specifically at enhancing biotechnology research on developing-country crops: one supported by United States Agency for International Development (USAID), one by the Dutch government, one by the McKnight Foundation, one by the Rockefeller Foundation, and one by the Asian Development Bank.

The USAID-supported project on Agricultural Biotechnology for Sustainable Productivity (ABSP), headquartered at Michigan State University, is implemented by a consortium of US universities and private companies. It is targeted at five crop/pest complexes: potato/potato tuber moth, sweet potato/sweet potato weevil, maize/stem borer, tomato/tomato yellow leaf virus, and cucurbits/several viruses. An outgrowth of the earlier USAID-supported tissue culture for crops project, ABSP builds on the network of scientists associated with the earlier project.

The cassava biotechnology network, sponsored by The Netherlands Directorate General for International Cooperation, held its first meeting in August of 1992. It aims to bring the tools of biotechnology to modify cassava so as better to meet the needs of small-scale cassava producers, processors and consumers. Over 125 scientists from 28 countries participated in the first network meeting. Funding to date has been about $2 million. An important initial activity is a study of farmers' needs for technical change in cassava, based on a field survey of cassava producers in several locations in Africa. Funding beyond 1997 is not assured.

The Rockefeller Foundation support for rice biotechnology in the developing world started in 1984. The programme has two objectives: to create biotechnology applicable to rice and with it produce improved rice varieties suited to developing-country needs, and to ensure that developing-country scientists know how to use biotechnology techniques and are capable of adapting them to their own objectives. Approximately $70 million in grants have been made by the programme through 1996. A network of about 200 senior scientists and 300 trainee scientists are participating, in all the major rice-producing countries of Asia and a number of industrialized countries. Researchers in the network transformed rice in 1988, a first for any cereal. Transformed rice has been field-tested in the USA, and a significant number of lines transformed with agronomically useful traits now exist. Molecular maps are being used to assist breeding, and some rice varieties developed by advanced techniques not requiring genetic engineering are now being grown by Chinese farmers.

The McKnight Foundation has provided about $12 million for biotechnology research on agriculturally important problems to a number of teams of researchers from laboratories in advanced and developing countries. This innovative programme used a global call for proposals and a competitive process to award the grants across a range of subject-matter of interest to the investigators. The research under the first set of grants is currently under way and no plans have been announced for further funding.

The Asian Development Bank provides about $300,000 annually (IRRI, 1996) to fund the Asian Rice Biotechnology Network, which links IRRI and Asian countries to share information and cooperate in the development of tools of biotechnology for rice.

It is unlikely that these five focused crop biotechnology efforts, taken together, entail in excess of $35 million annually. Total agricultural biotechnology research in the developing world is on the order of $50 million annually (Brunner and Komen, 1994). China, India, Egypt and Brazil and a few other countries have a reasonable base for plant biotechnology.

5. Implications for Global Grain Markets

What is the likely future of the Green Revolution and what implications does it hold for global grain markets?

First, it is evident that whatever the new tools of biotechnology will contribute towards a future Green Revolution the impact is likely to be gradually spread over a period of years. The impact of the first Green Revolution can barely be discerned in aggregate data; it is unlikely that the impact of molecular biology will be any more dramatic when considered from the global vantage point.

Because the overwhelming majority of plant biotechnology research is being conducted in the industrialized countries, it would seem likely that any changes in comparative advantage that result from the research will work to the advantage of those countries. A massive amount of biotechnology work is being done on maize in the USA. The first wide-scale plantings of genetically engineered maize, borer-resistant maize and genetically engineered herbicide-resistant soybeans were made in the USA in 1996. There is every indication that the use of these varieties will increase quickly and therefore it would appear that North American production would gain relative to other regions.

However, other innovations may have an offsetting effect. For example, mulch-based, no-till systems have spread to over 6 million ha in Brazil, with much of that land planted to maize and soybeans (FEBRAPDP, 1997). It is difficult to determine the relative cost-reducing effects of the no-till and the genetically engineered crops, but that will determine the contribution to any change in comparative advantage across the two regions.

Thus far, relatively little investment has been made in 'downstream' biotechnology on wheat either in the industrialized countries or in the developing world, so little impact on global grain markets is to be foreseen from genetic engineering. Rice, on the other hand, has been the subject of concerted biotechnology efforts, in the expectation that improvements in productivity will result (Herdt, 1991). Most of those investments have been by the public sector, with the gene constructs and methods shared across countries. But some countries are better able to apply the knowledge, so one may see some change in relative efficiency from this source. More recently the Monsanto Corporation is reported to have made a decision to enter the Asian rice business, one supposes at least initially with herbicide-resistant rice, so one might expect some gains in efficiency in countries with high labour costs as herbicide replaces older weed-control methods.

Perhaps more important than changes in comparative advantage across regions may be changes in relative efficiency of crops to provide desired product characteristics or functions. Even prior to genetic engineering, conventional breeding methods on oilseed rape produced canola, which has taken the market share from maize and other vegetable oils. Oilseed rape has been the subject of extensive and successful genetic engineering efforts, with its composition of fatty acids manipulated in a number of ways. Markets once served by coconut and soybeans have been eroded by this rapeseed, and further changes are likely.

One can conceive of productivity or product changes that might cause the substitution of one grain for another, or perhaps even the substitution of cassava for grains, but, as far as I am aware, any such efforts are at an early stage and would not lead to such results in the foreseeable future. On the contrary, most research seems aimed at either offsetting specific pest problems or incorporating specific quality traits.

The discussion of the preceding section shows that the efforts directed at biotechnology for developing country agriculture are small, especially when compared with those directed at the industrialized world. Still, some important contributions should come from the former. Training of developing-country scientists under various programmes means there is a small cadre of plant molecular biologists in a number of developing countries.

The Rockefeller Foundation's support for rice biotechnology is beginning to pay off in the form of new rice varieties available to some Asian farmers. In China, a rice variety produced at the Shanghai Academy of Agricultural Sciences through anther culture, which incorporates genes for resistance to pathogens and cold, has been field-tested on over 3000 ha in Anhui and Hubei provinces, resulting in yields from 6 to 24% higher than the most popular previous varieties.

We expect that the contributions to rice yield increases from biotechnology in Asia will be of the order of 10–25% over the next 10 years. These will come from improved hybrid rice systems largely in China, and in other Asian countries from rice varieties transformed with genes for resistance to pests and diseases.

The speed with which varieties get into farmers' hands depends largely on national conditions – the closeness of linkages between biotechnologists and plant breeders, the ability of scientists to identify the most limiting conditions, identify genes that overcome those constraints and get those genes into good agronomic backgrounds, and the efforts plant scientists and others have put into crafting biosafety regulations.

Developing-country maize yields may be affected by biotechnology if genes useful in tropical countries are discovered in the course of the massive work being done on maize in the USA. Although most of the maize work is being done by private firms, it is not unlikely that some of the discoveries will be made available for application in developing countries either at no cost or at low enough cost to make their use commercially feasible. Biotechnology applications to cassava are further in the future, as are those to smallholder banana and other crops of importance in the developing world.

My own conclusion is that factors other than biology are likely to be more important to future global grain markets, at least more important than the productivity effects of biotechnology. For one thing, the public apprehension about biotechnology, coupled with opportunism, has already led to demands for trade barriers against genetically engineered crops.

Note

1. While modern wheat also spread in North Africa and the Republic of South Africa over that period, the area and production of wheat in sub-Saharan Africa are very small relative to global food production or international trade.

References

Brunner, C. and Komen, J. (1994) *International Initiatives in Biotechnology for Developing Country Agriculture: Promises and Problems.* OECD Technical Paper 100, OECD Development Center, Paris.

Bumb, B.L. and Baanante, C.A. (1996) World trends in fertilizer use and projections to 2020. *IFPRI 2020 Vision Brief* 38 (October), 1–2.

Byerlee, D. and Moya, P. (1993) *Impacts of International Wheat Breeding Research in the Developing World, 1996–1990.* CIMMYT, Mexico, DF, Mexico, p. 26.

Dale, P.J. (1995) R&D regulation and field trialling of transgenic crops. *Trends in Biotechnology* 13, 398–403.

Dalrymple, D.G. (1986) *Development and Spread of High-Yielding Rice Varieties in Developing Country.* US Agency for International Development, Washington DC, USA, p. 110.

FEBRAPDP (Federação Brasileira de Plantio Directo na Palha) (1997) *No-Till Farming.* Federação Brasileira de Plantio Directo na Palha, Brazil.

Fray, R.G. and Grierson, D. (1993) Molecular genetics of tomato fruit ripening. *Trends in Genetics* 9, 438–443.

Gan, S. and Amasino, R.N. (1995) Inhibition of leaf senescence by autoregulated production of cytokinin. *Science* 270, 1986–1988.

Goddijn, O.J.M. and Pen, J. (1995) Plants as bioreactors. *Trends in Biotechnology* 13, 379–387.

Herdt, R.W. (1991) Research priorities for rice biotechnology. In: Khush, G.S. and Toenniessen, G.H. (eds) *Rice Biotechnology*, Vol. 6. CAB International & IRRI, Wallingford, UK, pp. 19–54.

Herdt, R.W. and Mellor, J.W. (1964) The contrasting response of rice to nitrogen: India and the USA. *Journal of Farm Economics* XLVI, 150–160.

Herdt, R.W., Castillo, L. and Jayasuriya, S.K. (1983) *The Economics of Insect Control on Rice in the Philippines.* IRRI Agricultural Economic Department Paper, No. 83–05, p. 34.

IRRI (International Rice Research Institute) (1996) *IRRI 1995–1996: Listening to the Farmers.* International Rice Research Institute, Los Baños, the Philippines.

James, C. and Krattiger, A.F. (1996) *Global Review of the Field Testing and Commercialization of Transgenic Plants: 1986 to 1995, the First Crop of Biotechnology.* ISAAA Briefs No. 1–1996, pp. 1–31.

Kenmore, P.E. (1996) Integrated pest management in rice. In: Persley, G.J. (ed.) *Biotechnology and Integrated Pest Management.* CAB International, Wallingford, UK, pp. 76–96.

Kropff, M.J., Cassman, K.G., Peng, S., Matthews, R.B. and Setter, T.L. (1994) Quantitative understanding of yield potential. In: Cassman, K.G. (ed.) *Breaking the Yield Barrier: Proceedings of a Workshop on Rice Yield Potential in Favorable Environments.* IRRI, 29 November–4 December 1993. International Rice Research Institute, Manila, the Philippines, pp. 21–38.

Lloyd-Evans, L.P.M. and Barfoot, P. (1996) EU boasts good science base and economic prospects for crop biotechnology. *Genetic Engineering News* 16:13, 16.

Office of the President (1992) *Budget of the USA, Fiscal Year 1992g.* US Government Printing Office, Washington DC, USA.

Perlak, F.J. and Fishoff, D.A. (1993) In: Kim, L. (ed.) *Advanced Engineered Pesticides.* Marcel Dekker, New York, USA, pp. 199–211.

Perlak, F.J., Deaton, R.W., Armstrong, T.A., Fuchs, R.L., Sims, S.R., Greenplate, J.T. and Fishoff, D.A. (1990) Insect resistant cotton plants. *Biotechnology* 8, 939–943.

Shah, D.M., Rommens, C.M.T. and Beachy, R.N. (1995) Resistance to diseases and insects in transgenic plants: progress and applications to agriculture. *Trends in Biotechnology* 13, 362–368.

Stark, D.M., Timmerman, K.P., Barry, G.F., Preiss, J. and Kishore, G.M. (1992) Regulation of the amount of starch in plant tissues by ADP glucose pyrophosphorylase. *Science* 258, 287–292.

Thonavala, Y., Yang, Y.F., Lyons, P., Mason, H.S. and Arntzen, C. (1995) Immunogenicity of transgenic plant-derived hepatitis-B surface-antigen. *Proceeding of the National Academy of Sciences USA* 92, 3358–3361.

USDA (US Department of Agriculture) (1996) *World Agricultural Trends and Indicators.* On-line database, Economic Research Service, US Department of Agriculture, Washington DC, USA.

Voelker, T.A., Worrell, A.C., Anderson, L., Bleibaum, J., Fan, C., Hawkins, D.J., Radke, S.E. and Davies, H.M. (1992) Fatty acid biosynthesis redirected to medium chains in transgenic oilseed plants. *Science* 257, 72–74.

Williams, M.E. (1995) Genetic engineering for pollination control. *Trends in Biotechnology* 13, 344–349.

11

State Trading and Import Demand Stability in Major Importing Countries

7

Wheat in China: Supply, Demand and Trade in the 21st Century

Scott D. Rozelle[1] and Jikun Huang[2]

[1]*Department of Agriculture and Resource Economics, University of California–Davis, USA;*
[2]*Centre for Chinese Agricultural Policy, Beijing, China*

1. Introduction

China has played an important role in world wheat markets, accounting for up to 15% of wheat imports in the last decade. Predictions about world wheat markets rest heavily on assessments of China's role; however, the future of China's wheat economy remains difficult to predict due to its unique characteristics. China is the only country in East and South East Asia that has a large wheat-producing, wheat-consuming rural population. China's potential for future productivity increases is difficult to gauge by studying other developing countries since more of China's wheat area is irrigated than in nearly any other large wheat-producing nation in the world (Stone, 1993). China's research system, which traditionally produced some of the world's most advanced wheat technology, is in disarray (Rozelle *et al.*, 1997b).

Looking to the past provides little help since few would have predicted that the rapid expansion of wheat output could have kept up with rising demand. In the past, China's wheat sector was China's most tightly regulated commodity, yet its yield performance surpassed all other major staples. The officially posted sales price of wheat, 355 yuan per tonne, did not change in nominal terms for 23 years between 1970 and 1992. Wheat yield increases, however, exceeded those of rice, maize, and other coarse grains, averaging 5.2% annually in the 1970s and 8.3% annually during the early reform period, 1978–1984. Although wheat imports soared in the early years and have fluctuated since, as leaders relaxed the restrictions of the socialist period, China has met most of the expanding demand from its own supplies.

Currently, wheat producers face serious obstacles for maintaining rates of yield increases. Concerned about stability of domestic staple prices for urban residents (Chen, 1994), leaders continue to intervene with procurement measures and import policies to keep wheat prices low. At the same time, the opportunity cost of labour and chemical fertilizer and pesticide prices have risen relatively faster (Huang *et al.*, 1996). Environmental pressures have added a new concern for leaders charged with keeping agriculture productivity high.

On the demand side, as markets develop, the patterns of demand are changing but pressures move in many directions. Better retail markets provide consumers with more choice – southerners can get better wheat products and northerners have access to high-quality rice (Huang and Rozelle, 1997a). As labour markets expand, northern rural migrants will consume less wheat as they enter urban society; southern migrants, on the other hand, will eat more. Rising incomes may increase demand to some extent; however, it is likely that consumers will also substitute meat, fruits, and vegetables for wheat consumption.

The purpose of this report is to explore the special features of China's wheat economy and to increase our understanding of the nation's domestic wheat sector and its future participation in global markets. It also seeks to establish a more comprehensive, transparent, and empirically sound basis for assessing the future growth of China's wheat supply, demand and trade needs.

The second section assesses trends in China's wheat economy, and the third section examines a series of factors, beyond income and prices, that may have an important impact on Chinese grain demand and supply. An econometric model is used to estimate China's wheat demand, supply, and imports. These estimates are heavily dependent on assumptions about the growth rates of income, population, and investment in research and irrigation, and policy implications are derived from the alternative scenarios. After the baseline assumptions and results are presented, alternative forecasts of these variables and their implications are explored.

2. Wheat Production, Utilization and Imports in China

The growth of agricultural production in China since the 1950s has been one of the main accomplishments of the nation's development policies.[1] Except during the famine years of the late 1950s and early 1960s, the country has enjoyed rates of production growth that have outpaced the rise in population. Even between 1970 and 1978, when much of the economy was reeling from the effects of the Cultural Revolution, grain production grew at 2.8% per annum (Table 7.1, rows 1–3). After accelerating to 5.8% per year in the early reform period, 1978–1984, grain yield growth slowed to 1.8% in the 1984–1995 decade.

Table 7.1. Growth rates of agricultural production, sown area and yields in China, 1970–1995.

Commodity	Pre-reform 1970–1978	Reform period 1978–1984	1984–1995	1978–1995
Grain				
Production	2.8	4.7	1.7	2.4
Sown area	0.0	−1.1	−0.1	−0.4
Yield	2.8	5.8	1.8	2.8
Rice				
Production	2.5	4.5	0.6	1.7
Sown area	0.7	−0.6	−0.6	−0.6
Yield	1.8	5.1	1.2	2.3
Wheat				
Production	7.0	8.3	1.9	3.9
Sown area	1.7	−0.04	0.1	0.2
Yield	5.2	8.3	1.8	3.6
Maize				
Production	7.4	3.7	4.7	4.1
Sown area	3.1	−1.6	1.7	0.8
Yield	4.2	5.4	2.9	3.3
Area sown to cash crops	2.4	5.1	2.1	3.1

Note: Growth rates are computed using regression methods.
Sources: ZGTJNJ (1980–1996) and ZGNYNJ (1980–1996).

Wheat production in China has also grown steadily throughout the last several decades. Production and yield growth rates have exceeded the average for overall grain in most of the subperiods (Table 7.1, rows 7–9). In the 1970s and the early reform period, wheat yields increased at annual growth rates exceeding those of rice and maize. Wheat producers also maintained their sown area, unlike rice producers, whose sown area fell 0.6% per year between 1970 and 1995. Wheat farmers, however, fell behind maize farmers, who increased sown area in the same period.

Farmers plant wheat in every province of China, but cropping patterns and the intensity and importance vary from region to region. Farmers produce all wheat in tight rotations with other crops, except for the single-season spring wheat in the four northern provinces. North China Plain farmers most commonly plant winter wheat in conjunction with maize or cotton. Because cold climates push back harvesting for the wheat and increase the need to plant maize and other crops early to avoid early autumn frosts, wheat farmers typically space their wheat crops such that farmers will sow or transplant their maize or cotton crop before the wheat is harvested. Yangtze Valley farmers, especially those living north of the Yangtze, where two rice crops do not do very well, plant overwintering wheat varieties in tight rotations with their single-season rice crops.

China's wheat production has traditionally been and remains primarily in the North China maize–wheat region. In 1975, 68% of wheat was sown in the North China Plain and the North West. By 1995, this percentage had dropped to 63% primarily due to a slow rise in the rice–wheat acreage. Farmers in the Yangtze Valley increased their proportion of wheat from 29% in 1975 to 33% in 1995.

Total wheat production rose to 99 million tonnes in the early 1990s, but utilization was even higher. With no changes in stocks, and by importing 11 million tonnes, the total annual supply of wheat during this period was 110 million tonnes. Although this supply was used to meet a number of needs – seed, animal feed, and direct consumption for food – wheat used for direct food consumption took up about 96% of the total supply in the early 1990s. Farmers used 4 million tonnes as feed in the early 1990s, in part reflecting the relatively low wheat prices during the period.

On a per capita basis, the average resident in China currently consumes 85 kg of wheat per year. Rural consumers, on average, consumed 90 kg per capita in the early 1990s, more than their counterparts in urban regions, who consumed 67 kg. China's average consumer is in second place in Asia in per capita wheat consumption (FAO, 1991). Only South Koreans, at 105 kg per capita, consume more wheat than the Chinese. Per capita wheat consumption in China surpasses that in Japan (54 kg) and Indonesia (12 kg).

Unlike other relatively high wheat-consuming East and South East Asian countries, China's farmers produce most of the nation's wheat. Between 1985 and 1995, on average, China imported 10 million tonnes of wheat each year, relying on imports during this time for just over 10% of its wheat needs. Japan and Korea, on the other hand, import more than 90% of their wheat (FAO, 1991). Although only a small part of domestic needs, this level of imports still makes China one of the world's largest wheat importers, accounting for 10–15% of world wheat trade.

3. Structural Change and Government Intervention in China's Agriculture

Many forces arising from China's development and transition processes affect the growth and balance of China's wheat economy. China is a country in rapid transition from a socialist system to one where an increasing proportion of its goods and services, including food, are being allocated by market forces (Sicular, 1991; Rozelle *et al.*, 1996). It also is a country that is rapidly developing, where institutions are changing fast and incomes and relative prices fluctuate significantly. In contrast to many reform governments, far from giving up its activist role as a major actor in the economy, China's leaders remain deeply involved in guiding the nation's development process. Any attempt accurately to forecast future wheat supply and demand trends must take into account these economic forces.

Factors influencing demand: market development and urbanization, income growth and demand

Income growth and demand

On the demand side, recent changes in the urban economy have made urban consumers almost entirely dependent on markets for their consumption needs (Huang and Rozelle, 1997b). In urban areas, prices and income changes are most likely to be the fundamental forces driving consumption pattern changes. Urban incomes rose at a steady rate of nearly 8% per year in the early years of reform (Table 7.2, column 1). At that time, rising incomes meant an increasing demand for almost all food products, including wheat. Real income per capita for urban residents continued to rise in recent years, jumping 6–7% between 1985 and 1995. At the current average level of income for most urban residents, consumption of wheat products rises only marginally with new increments in income (Carter and Zhong 1991; Garnaut and Ma, 1992); for urban consumers, when income increases by 1% their demand for wheat increases by only 0.1% (Huang and Rozelle, 1995b). Although rural incomes have grown more slowly since the mid-1980s (Table 7.2, column 2), demand for food grains has still increased as incomes have risen (Fan *et al.*, 1994; Halbrendt *et al.*, 1994). For rural consumers, when income increases by 1% the demand for wheat increases by 0.19%. As income of the urban and rural populations grows over the next several decades, the impact of income increases on demand for wheat should fall, and eventually may become negative, as it has in other rapidly developing countries in Asia.

Rural market liberalization

Rural consumption markets are also less complete, and farmers who face incomplete markets may not be able to consume the quantities they demand. Farmers in many areas face limited choices in their consumption decisions since many of the products they desire on a daily basis, such as meat and fresh fruit, are not always available, even as their incomes rise. In a sample of households drawn from the national household income and expenditure survey by the authors, a strong and significant correlation was found between the level of consumption of primarily purchased goods, such as meat and fruit, and the level of market development, holding income and prices constant (Huang and

Table 7.2. Important factors affecting the supply and demand for grain and rice in China's economy, 1958–1992.

Year	(1) Urban income per capita	(2) Rural income per capita	(3) Market development index	(4) Ratio of urban population	(5) Agriculture research stock	(6) Agriculture research expenditure	(7) Irrigation stock	(8) Irrigation expenditure
1958	n/a	n/a	n/a	16	n/a	165	6,766	3,053
1965	n/a	n/a	n/a	18	n/a	357	17,375	1,314
1970	n/a	n/a	n/a	17	239	401	23,280	3,256
1975	229	101	21	18	352	700	42,928	4,526
1980	372	167	31	19	408	791	47,819	3,209
1985	490	298	42	24	573	1,078	49,928	2,016
1990	593	306	45	26	789	808	53,476	3,006
1992	778	319	46	28	880	977	59,003	5,527

Notes and sources: (1) and (2) are from ZGTJNJ (1980–1993) and are measured in real 1985 million yuan. (3) is from Huang and Rozelle (1995a) and measures the proportion of food purchased by rural households on consumption markets. (4) is from the United Nations (1993). (5) and (6) are in real 1985 million yuan and are from SSTC (1991, 1993). (7) and (8) are in real 1985 million yuan and are from MWREP (1988–1992).

Rozelle, 1997b). Discontinuous free markets, lack of refrigeration, and generally high transaction costs for procuring food affect the consumption patterns of rural consumers.

In the future as markets develop, rural demand patterns may change. Although changes in rural markets have been rapid, in 1992 Chinese farmers still purchased only 46% of the food they consumed. Huang and Rozelle (1997b) predict that as markets develop and rural consumption increases, consumption patterns will be affected. Meat and fruit consumption should rise, and directly consumed food grain and vegetables should fall.

Urban migration

Across Asia, as countries urbanize, the behaviour of consumers changes dramatically (Bouis, 1989; Huang and David, 1993). Outside China, urban dwellers consume more wheat and other convenience foods and less in the way of staples (or fewer preparation-intensive products). Hence, as populations in Asia have shifted from rural to urban, wheat consumption has typically risen.

The ratio of urban to rural residents in China is also changing rapidly; urban population grew from 19% of total population in 1980 to 28% in 1992 (Table 7.2, column 4).[2] The impact of the population shift on food grain demand in China has been documented (Huang and Bouis, 1995). In contrast to other countries in Asia, rural–urban migration's impact on wheat may be different because average rural wheat consumption levels are so high. Since rural demand currently exceeds urban demand, China's future migration should be expected to dampen wheat consumption.[3]

Factors influencing supply

Technology

On the supply side, many sharp transitions are also under way. Above all, technological change needs to be considered explicitly, since it has been the engine of China's agricultural economy, in general, and for fine grains, such as wheat, in particular (Stone, 1988; Rozelle and Huang, 1997). China's technological base grew rapidly during both the pre-reform and reform periods. In one of the best-known cases, hybrid rice, a breakthrough pioneered by Chinese rice scientists in the 1970s, increased yields significantly in many parts of the country and rapidly spread to nearly one-half of China's rice area by 1990 (Lin, 1991). Although less dramatic, continuous and rapid change came to wheat farmers as well. After importing rust-resistant, semi-dwarf varieties from the international agricultural research system in the late 1960s, Chinese breeders incorporated these traits into its own varieties. By

1977, producers cultivated about 40% of China's wheat areas in semi-dwarf varieties; by 1984, this number rose to 70%. Today in China, it is difficult to see anything but dwarf varieties, especially in the main producing provinces. Certainly this rapid expansion contributed to the rapid growth of wheat yields in the 1970s and 1980s.

Robust growth in the stock of research capital has in part been responsible for these dramatic yield increases (Table 7.2, column 5; Fan and Pardey, 1992). There is concern, however, that China's system may be suffering from neglect after more than a decade of reform (Rozelle *et al.*, 1997b). Real annual expenditures on agricultural research fell between 1985 and 1990, before resuming real growth in 1990 (Table 7.2, column 6; SSTC, 1991, 1993). The slow-down in growth in annual investments in the late 1980s will result in slower growth in the overall stock of research in the 1990s. If economic indicators signal tightening supplies and rising prices, officials may respond by increasing current expenditures (Jin *et al.*, 1997).

Irrigation investment

China's progress in water control has been another major source of productivity gain (Liu, 1992). Irrigated area increased from less than 18% of cultivated area in 1952 to nearly 50% in 1992 (ZGTJNJ, 1993). In the initial years, most of the construction was based on both locally organized small-scale projects and publicly financed large-scale surface projects (Stone, 1993). In the late 1960s and 1970s, tube-well development drove the expansion of irrigated area construction, especially in the North China Plain maize–wheat region. Development of the nation's water control infrastructure continued during the 1980s as the government launched a large number of new medium- and large-scale water control projects (Stone, 1993). Even though pump set numbers stagnated in the 1980s, the overall quality of water control equipment has been continually upgraded (ZGNYNJ, 1990). Irrigation was also one of the major factors influencing land and labour utilization in the cropping sector in the 1970s and 1980s, as better water control stimulated the increase in double-cropped area (Stone, 1993).

Although much of the labour for China's irrigation development was contributed by local residents, public irrigation expenditures financed a big part of the construction of the national water control network. Irrigation investment and the stock of facilities have followed patterns similar to those for research (Table 7.2, columns 7 and 8). The investment in irrigation facilities has been by far the largest component of total construction investment in agriculture, and is several times higher than investment in agricultural research. Real annual expenditures on irrigation rose rapidly until 1975, before beginning a ten-year decline. In 1985, however, annual expenditures began to grow again and were at an all-time high in 1992 (Table 7.2, column 8). Changing agricultural strategies and periods of fiscal control have made public expenditure on water control follow a more variable path.

Marketing and pricing trends and policies

Wheat prices, as well as those for rice and maize, have fluctuated throughout the reforms, peaking in 1980, 1988 and 1994, years preceding strong growth in grain output (Table 7.3, columns 2–4; Rozelle *et al.*, 1996). Fertilizer price and other input price trends, however, may offset or amplify the rising and falling output prices (Table 7.3, columns 5–6). For example, although rice and maize prices rose around 30% in real terms between 1990 and 1995, fertilizer prices almost doubled. Under such conditions, aggregate output may not have moved as much as one might anticipate given the rising farmgate prices.

In addition to expected price levels, farmers also respond to the variability of expected price and the level of price risk, and it may be that China's farmers could increase (decrease) output as they face less (more) risk. Sicular (1995), Watson (1994) and Rozelle *et al.* (1996) argue that one of the most significant shifts in China's rural policy in the 1990s, which may have affected price risk, is the effort to liberalize domestic grain markets. Liberalization, in general, is expected to decrease price variability as price variations once caused by local shocks could be dampened by incoming flows of grain from more distant locations not affected by the shock. One of the main results of the early policy efforts in the rice and maize sectors was a sharp and sustained integration of markets as measured by a variety of measures and statistic tests (Rozelle *et al.*, 1996). Output markets became so integrated and competitive that even when the government tried to retrench on its liberalizing reforms, market forces dominated and integration in South China rice markets and coastal grain markets deepened even in the mid-1990s. The governor's responsibility system, a policy that among other objectives was designed to keep grain from flowing indiscriminately among provinces in an effort to keep local grain prices low, was only effective in several inland maize-growing provinces, such as Henan, Shaanxi and Shanxi. In these provinces, it was thought that the regional government could still exercise its control over grain markets by virtue of its ability to monitor the rail transport system, the sole means of moving bulk commodities in and out of the region as opposed to coastal traders that can move grain by rail, boat, ship or truck, making monitoring grain movements difficult, if not impossible.

Major wheat-producing areas appear closely to resemble inland maize-producing regions in terms of the record of being isolated from national grain markets. Larger wheat producers in provinces are the same as those inland provinces – Henan, Shaanxi, and Shanxi – which

Table 7.3. Factors affecting supply in China's agriculture, 1975–1995.

Year	HRS[a]	Milled rice	Wheat	Maize	Fertilizer mixed price (yuan per tonne)	Implicit wage (yuan per day)	Soil erosion land (1000 ha)
		Market price (yuan per tonne)					
1975	0.00	1,040	804	798	484	1.94	119,202
1980	0.14	1,395	1,070	734	455	2.99	118,936
1985	0.99	1,008	755	600	600	4.58	127,112
1990	0.99	1,338	922	690	630	4.48	133,859
1995	0.99	1,685	985	921	1,138	5.72	163,000

[a] HRS variable is reported as proportion of villages that adopted the Household Responsibility System (HRS). Price, wage, and irrigation expenditure/stock are in real 1990 price (deflated by general retail price index).

Sources: ZGTJNJ (1980–1993), State Price Bureau (SPB, 1988–1992), Ministry of Agriculture (ZGNYNJ, 1980–1996) and MWREP (1988–1992).

were not integrated with national markets in the mid-1990s. Integration analysis also found that in the six provinces for which complete wheat price data series were available from 1988 to 1995, the level of integration fell between the early 1990s and mid-1990s. Top government officials were apparently successful in their efforts to blockade the outflow of grain from their provinces, keeping their local markets insulated from outside supply-and-demand forces and forcing down local prices. Interviews with traders and government grain officials in these provinces (who typically are against blockades and other measures that erect barriers reducing their business opportunities) found that they believed policies that fluctuated from closing markets to opening them to closing them again reduced the willingness of farmers to grow wheat (or produce at high yield levels). It may be that grain marketing and pricing policies in some of the major, inland wheat provinces have a distinct negative impact on wheat production.

Other factors

In addition to the factors already discussed, institutional changes, environmental factors, and labour movement out of the agricultural sector induced by rising wage trends may also affect agricultural output. This section briefly reviews these forces.

INSTITUTIONAL CHANGE. Leaders implemented decollectivization policies in the late 1970s, focusing first on poorer regions of the nation and then gradually extending the policy to the whole country. By 1980, 14% of villages had returned land-use rights to farm households, a figure that moved rapidly upward in the early 1980s, reaching and staying at a level of 99% of villages in 1984 (Table 7.3, column 1). McMillan *et al.* (1989) and Lin (1992) argue that the economic reforms generated most of the agricultural growth in the early reform era, although these were one-time effects that were exhausted by the mid-1980s.

ENVIRONMENT. Trends in environmental degradation – including erosion, salinization, and loss of cultivated land – show that there may be considerable stress on the agricultural land base; erosion has increased since the 1970s, although in a somewhat erratic pattern (Table 7.3, column 7). This and other factors (e.g. salinization) have been shown to affect output of grain, rice and other agricultural products in a number of recent studies (Huang and Rozelle, 1994, 1996; Huang *et al.*, 1996).

WAGES, OPPORTUNITY COST AND LABOUR SHIFTS. Increasing opportunities in the non-cropping and off-farm sectors (Table 7.3, column 6) have led to large shifts of labour-use patterns (Table 7.4). After putting ever-increasing amounts of labour into grain production in the 1950s, 1960s and early 1970s, labour use on all crops fell substantially from 1975 to

Table 7.4. Labour use in agricultural production in China, 1975–1994 (man-days per ha).

Year	Rice	Wheat	Maize	Soybean	Cotton	Rapeseed
1975	638	402	375	221	919	453
1980	506	347	360	213	818	442
1985	347	222	238	141	626	317
1990	309	210	259	180	664	279
1994	279	180	220	165	649	253

Sources: Labour utilization by crop computed by authors based on data from ZGTJNJ (1980–1996); SPB (1988–1996).

1994 (SPB, 1988–1992). Wheat farmers use less than half the level of labour used before reform. On a man-day per ha basis, labour fell from 402 man-days in 1975 to 180 in 1994 (Table 7.4, column 2). These results are consistent with recorded trends in other crops (Table 7.4, columns 1 and 3 to 6) and qualitative information on changes in labour-use patterns. Interviews by the authors with agricultural officials, local leaders, and farmers during extensive fieldwork in a number of China's wheat-producing provinces (Hebei, Henan, Hubei, Shaanxi, Shandong and Sichuan) have found that large quantities of labour moved out of wheat farming during the 1980s as a result of an abandonment or transformation of marginal lands where mainly low-yielding wheat and other coarse grains had been produced during the collective era.

There were also shifts of labour from farm to non-farm activities in wheat-producing areas. The increasing gap between the total number of rural labourers and the total number of agricultural labourers demonstrates that labour is flowing out of agriculture (ZGTJNJ, 1980–1996). Higher wages have attracted tens of millions of workers to the industrial and commercial sectors during the reform period. Some of the biggest flows came out of the highest-producing wheat provinces: Anhui, Henan, Hubei and Sichuan (Rozelle *et al.*, 1997a). This sectoral shift has undoubtedly also caused the allocation of time to farming to drop sharply. In the mid-1980s, rural residents allocated 75% of their time to agricultural activities, and the rest went to non-agricultural activities; in 1992, less than 60% of labour went to agriculture (Tong and Huang, 1995).

Characteristics inherent to China's developing and transitional rural economy have both facilitated and constrained labour mobility. The labour-intensive nature of Chinese farm management practices allows labour to enter and exit the cropping sector without incurring high start-up or close-down costs. Employment opportunities in local township and village enterprises and the rapid expansion of the self-employed labour force may make the flow of labour between agriculture and industry more fluid. At the same time, natural barriers, such as moving costs (which exist within all economies), impede flows. China's factor markets also still contain a number of structural imperfections, such as employment priority for local workers, housing shortages, and the urban household registration system (Lin, 1991). One of the costs of these kinds of barriers is that they may slow down the movement of factors among alternative economic activities, reducing the efficiency of the sector's producers.

4. Factors Contributing to China's Wheat Production Growth

Between 1976 and 1995, the output of wheat from the North China Plain maize–wheat region grew on a per annum basis by 4.54%. The relative roles of technology, institutions, output rations, and wages in China's increased grain production was investigated using an econometric model by Huang and Rozelle (1997a).

Within key subperiods, wheat production grew faster during the early reform period, 1978–1984 (8.3%), and slowed in the late reform period, 1984–1995 (1.9%). To identify which factors have made the biggest contributions to the growth of China's wheat sector, the growth rates of wheat during the sample period and key subperiods can be decomposed into their component parts.

The results for the North China wheat decomposition (Table 7.5) show that, although institutional innovations are important, government investments have contributed the most to wheat yield growth during the period 1976–1995. Improvements in technology from research expenditures have contributed by far the largest share, augmenting the annual growth rate of output by 2.82% (62% of the total growth rate). Public investment in irrigation contributed 0.43% per year to the growth rate of total wheat during this period (9% of the total growth rate). Decompositions for rice in South China and maize in the same North China Plain maize–wheat region (Huang and Rozelle, 1997a) show that research investment has created more wheat growth (2.82%) than rice growth (1.38%), but somewhat less than maize growth (4.98%). Part of the explanation may be that the initial growth from new Green Revolution technology for rice had already taken place; semi-dwarf varieties of rice had been introduced in the late 1950s long before use elsewhere in the developing world (Stone, 1988). Although maize improvements had started in the early 1960s with the release of hybrid cultivars, serious maize blight epidemics had reduced yields in the late 1960s, and programmes to develop and release disease-resistant single-cross maize hybrids did not really reach the farm level until the mid-1970s. Thus, the impact of maize research could appear to look larger since it started from a lower base and largely occurred during the study period.

The contribution of irrigation investment to the growth of wheat falls well below the return to research investment (0.43%). Part of this

Table 7.5. Sources of wheat production growth in northern China.

		1978–1984			1976–1995		
			Sources of growth			Sources of growth	
	Output elasticity	Factor growth rate (% per year)	(Rate)	(%)	Factor growth rate (% per year)	(Rate)	(%)
Research stock	0.587	5.53	3.30	43	4.72	2.82	62
Irrigation stock	0.172	2.52	0.43	6	2.49	0.43	9
Institutional innovation		0.99	3.86	51	0.99	1.63	36
Input and output prices			0.86	1		0.16	4
Land and labour prices			−1.34	−18		−0.40	−9
Land	−0.002	20.75	0.04	−1	8.91	0.02	0
Labour	−0.098	13.23	−1.30	−17	3.90	−0.38	−8
Environment factors			0.31	4		−0.10	−2
Disaster	−0.078	−3.84	0.30	4	1.07	0.08	2
Erosion	−0.021	−0.27	0.01	0	0.65	0.01	−2
Residual			0.21	17		0.01	0
Total			7.63	100		4.54	100

The Household Responsibility System (HRS) is measured by the cumulative proportion of households adopting the production responsibility system in any given year. The impact of the HRS on the growth rate of the output is computed by the following two steps: 1) the output change due to the change in the HRS ratio is computed using the estimated coefficient of the HRS variable; 2) these changes in the output are then transformed into changes in annual growth rates.
Note: Short-run elasticities are used in the analysis. Both output and factor growth rates are computed by a least-squares estimate.

somewhat puzzling result may come from a failure to identify the complex interactions and necessary sequencing of agricultural investments (Huang and Rozelle, 1997a). During the early Mao era, much of the initial, high pay-off investment in water control had already taken place, and so the initial high return to irrigation may have already occurred. Also, the contributions from research could be picking up part of the returns from irrigation investment, since modern high-yielding technology requires good water control for realizing its maximum gains.

Between 1976 and 1995, the implementation of the Household Responsibility System was the second most important factor in increasing yields; institutional changes increased the wheat output growth by 0.99% per year (36% of the total). Because its implementation was started in 1978 and completed in 1984, the contribution of the Household Responsibility System is smaller, relative to public investment. The relatively high return to technology, however, has important implications for policymakers in China, who in the 1980s appeared to have believed that China could maintain its rapid growth on the basis of institutional change and thus for a time ignored research and water control investments.

The positive impacts of government investment and institutional reform policies have been partially offset by the rises in land and labour prices. Overall, during the 1976–1995 period, growth would have risen by 9% more had higher wages, primarily, not induced farmers to move out of wheat farming. The net impact was somewhat larger, 18%, in the early reform years when the real wage grew rapidly. However, given the massive shifts of labour out of wheat farming (nearly 50% when measured on a labour-days per hectare basis, Table 7.4), it may be surprising that the impact was as small as it was. In contrast, the stagnation of real wages in the late reform period, 1985–1995, has limited the impact of wheat and non-wheat competition for labour; output growth fell by only 4% for wheat.

Environmental factors have had much less effect on rice and wheat production than elsewhere in China's cropping sector. Whereas drops in growth rates are as high as 8% in the case of maize during the 1976–1995 sample period (Huang and Rozelle, 1997a), and reach 47% in the case of cash crops in the late 1980s (Huang *et al.*, 1996), environmental factors reduced wheat output growth by only 2% during the sample period 1976–1995 (Table 7.6), a rate that was consistent even during the late reform period, 1985–1995. This smaller impact could be expected since rice and wheat are much less likely than maize and some cash crops to be grown in hilly and more ecologically fragile areas. These results suggest that, if policymakers give increased attention to the adverse consequences of environmental stresses, the efforts should be targeted on a crop-by-crop basis.

Table 7.6. Sources of wheat and maize production growth in China, 1984–1995.

	Wheat Sources of growth		Maize Sources of growth	
	Rate	%	Rate	%
Research stock	3.43	162	6.07	124
Irrigation stock	0.47	22	0.50	10
Institutional innovation	0.00	0	0.00	0
Input and output prices	−0.75	−35	−1.14	−23
Land and labour prices	−0.09	−4	0.03	1
Land	−0.01	−0.4	0.00	8
Labour	−0.08	−4	0.36	−7
Environmental factors	−0.04	−2	−0.38	−8
Disaster	−0.02	−1	−0.03	−1
Erosion	−0.02	−1	−0.35	−7
Residual	−0.90	−42	−0.19	−4
Total	2.12	100	4.89	100

Perhaps the most important result of our research for understanding the future supply from China's wheat sector is that in recent years, 1985–1995, almost all growth has come from public investment, especially that in research. Deteriorating price ratios, especially, and rising wages and environmental stress, to a lesser extent, have held back the expansion of wheat production. The benefits of one-time institutional reforms in the early 1980s have been exhausted and have not directly contributed to wheat output growth. Investment in research and irrigation have contributed 184% (162 + 22, baseline assumption) of wheat growth during the past 10 years (Table 7.6). By exceeding 100%, the figures imply that not only can all growth be accounted for by public investment but it compensates for negative factors elsewhere in the economy. If these relationships hold in the future, wheat supply in the 21st century is going to rely heavily on increased investment in agriculture by policymakers.

5. A Framework for Forecasting China's Grain Supply and Demand

This report uses wheat supply and demand models for China and a world trade model to forecast China's imports of wheat. Further discussion of these models is available in Rozelle and Huang (1997).

Demand-side assumptions

Income growth and population growth will remain important determinants of food balance in the future. Population growth peaked in

China in the late 1960s and early 1970s. Since then, fertility rates and the natural rate of population growth have begun to fall. Relying on the United Nations' (1993) demographic predictions, the growth rate during the first decade of the projection period, 1990–2000, is assumed to be 1.3% per annum (Table 7.7). This annual rate falls during the next two decades to 0.7%, a level that is considerably under the world's projected growth rate (about 1.7%).[4]

Alternative scenarios simulate the situation where less control is exercised over the population in the future by the Chinese government, and population growth rates slow to approximately 1% per annum after

Table 7.7. Assumptions on the growth of factors affecting wheat supply and demand in China, 1995–2020.

	Low	Baseline	High
(Growth rate, %)			
Population			
1995–2000	1.1	1.3	1.4
2000–2010	0.5	0.7	0.9
2010–2020	0.4	0.6	0.8
Per capita real expenditure			
Rural	2.0	3.0	4.0
Urban	2.5	3.5	4.5
Agricultural research investment	2.5	3.5	4.5
Irrigation investment	2.5	3.5	4.5
Wheat price	−1.0	−0.5	0.0
Other grain price	−0.5	−0.5	−0.5
Fertilizer price	1.0	1.0	1.0
Environmental factors			
Salinity	0.2	0.2	0.2
Erosion	0.2	0.2	0.2
(%)			
Share of urban population			
2000	34	34	34
2010	42	42	42
2020	50	50	50
(Index number)			
Rural market development index			
2000	0.6	0.6	0.6
2010	0.7	0.7	0.7
2020	0.8	0.8	0.8

Note: Population estimates are based on UN demographic predictions. Agricultural research and irrigation expenditures are derived from the Ninth Five-Year Plan and China's Long-Term Plan to 2010. The trends in the deterioration of the environment are based on extrapolations of past trends (Huang and Rozelle, 1995a).

2000 (Rosegrant *et al.*, 1995). The movement of the population from urban to rural areas is expected to continue, and affects the rate of growth of rural and urban populations. Urban population growth rates are expected to rise by 4% per year in the 1990s, and this rate will continue at a high level, 2.4% per year during the 2010–2020 decade. Rural population growth rates, despite higher fertility, will grow by only 0.2% in the 1990s, reflecting high rates of rural to urban migration. The rate of rural population growth will actually became negative in the decade preceding 2020.

Baseline per capita real expenditures are forecast to average about 3% in the rural sector and 3.5% in the urban sector (Table 7.7, rows 4 and 5). The impact of higher growth rates, 4% per year per capita income growth for rural residents and 4.5% for urban residents, will be simulated.

Wheat price trends are projected to follow those of world prices.[5] World wheat prices are expected to fall by 0.5% annually throughout the projection period (Table 7.7, row 8). Although once far out of line with world agricultural prices, in recent years China's market prices have converged with those in international markets (Huang and David, 1993).

The development of rural consumer markets also affects the future demand for grain and meat in China's economy because farmers, who have access to a greater variety of goods, will adopt different consumption patterns (Huang and Rozelle, 1997b). Currently about 46% of food in rural China is purchased on the market. This is expected to rise to 60% by the year 2000 and increase by 10% in each of the next two decades thereafter (Table 7.7, rows 16–18). The trend will not affect total grain demand as much as the composition of the nation's grain needs. But as markets develop, even with income and prices held equal, the amount of wheat consumption falls. This reduction is offset by the increased demand for feed grain needed to meet the rising demand for meat that accompanies rural market development.

Supply-side assumptions

Commodity price projections for producers' prices are assumed to be the same as those used in the demand-side analysis (Table 7.7, rows 8 and 9). Fertilizer prices are expected to grow by 1% per year, although in recent years trends have included both falling price levels and rapid price hikes (Table 7.7, row 10; World Bank, 1990; ERS, 1995). In relative terms, the grain-to-fertilizer price ratio is expected to continue to deteriorate as it has since the mid-1980s (Ye and Rozelle, 1994). Extrapolation of recent trends in the labour market provided the projection that the opportunity cost of labour for agriculture will continue to rise at 1% per year during the study period. A similar growth rate is assumed for the opportunity cost of land.[6]

Investment in agricultural technology and irrigation should also be expected to have a strong influence in China's future grain supply (Huang and Rozelle, 1996; Huang *et al.*, 1996). As noted previously, annual expenditures on research declined from 1985 to 1990, and irrigation expenditures dropped from 1975 to 1985, but both types of expenditures increased after these periods of decline. The recent recovery in research and irrigation investments, together with the experience of other Asian countries, recent discussions with agricultural leaders and academics, and China's commitment to a strong domestic grain economy, leads to the expectation that China will sustain a long-run rate of increase in these investments (Table 7.7, rows 6 and 7). The baseline projections of investment growth nevertheless remain well below historical rates of growth. Erosion and salinization are expected to continue to increase at a steady but low pace (Table 7.7, rows 11–12).

6. Projection Results

According to our analysis, per capita wheat consumption in China crested in the mid-1990s. From a baseline high of 85 kg, wheat consumption per capita remains at that level for the first 15 years of the forecast period, before falling in 2020 to 82 kg (Table 7.8, row 1). The average rural resident will consume greater amounts up to the year 2020; expenditure elasticities are positive up to 2010, after which falling prices will stimulate demand more than rising incomes will dampen it (Table 7.8, row 2). Urban wheat consumption per capita peaks in the year 2010 and declines over the last 10 years of the projection period (Table 7.8, row 3). Aggregate wheat demand per capita drops faster than either rural or urban demand because the total demand for the product falls as migration occurs.

Although per capita wheat demand is falling in the later projection period, total wheat demand continues to increase through 2020 mainly because of population growth. By the end of the forecast period, aggregate wheat demand will reach 137 million tonnes, over 20% higher than the initial baseline demand (Table 7.9, column 9). During this same period, wheat demand rises at about the same rate as that for rice, but at a much lower rate than coarse grains. Total grain demand is projected to increase by more than 50% (Huang *et al.*, forthcoming). Wheat will fall from making up about 30% of total grain utilization to only a little more than 20%.

Baseline projections of the supply of wheat show that China's producing sector falls slightly behind the increase in demand in the 1990s. Wheat supply is predicted to reach 110 million tonnes by the year 2000. This projection implies a rise in wheat output of only about

Table 7.8. Projected annual per capita wheat food consumption (kg) under alternative income growth scenarios in China, 1996–2020.

Alternative scenario	1995	2000	2010	2020
Baseline				
National average	85	85	85	82
Rural	92	94	96	97
Urban	67	68	69	68
Low-income growth				
National average	85	84	83	80
Rural	92	93	95	95
Urban	67	68	68	67
High-income growth				
National average	85	86	86	83
Rural	92	95	98	98
Urban	67	69	69	68

Note: Base year is 1995.

10% over the early 1990s (99 million tonnes), a figure far below the more optimistic estimates given in recent years by Ministry of Agriculture officials.

The gap between supply and demand is expected to narrow after 2000, however. Production is expected to rise somewhat faster in the second and third decades of the forecast period, mostly as a result of the resumption of investment in agricultural research. Wheat production is expected to reach 122 million tonnes in 2010, an increase of 11% during the preceding 10 years; production will reach 137 million tonnes by 2020, an even slightly higher percentage increase for the decade (12% over the 2010 level).

Under the projected baseline scenario, the initial widening gap between the forecast annual growth rate of production and demand in the late 1990s implies a rising deficit. Wheat consumption rises at about 1.6% per year, 1.3% from the rise in population and only about 0.3% due to rising per capita wheat demand. Wheat production during this period grows only 1.3% annually. Wheat imports rise somewhat in the late 1990s from about 10 million tonnes per year to 13 million tonnes (Table 7.9, row 1, column 3). Wheat imports peak, however, in this time period and then decline to their recent levels by 2010, approaching zero in 2020 (Table 7.9, row 1, columns 6 and 9).

7. Conclusions

This report examines trends in China's wheat economy, reviews the current trends in supply, demand, marketing, and trade, and then

Table 7.9. Projections of wheat production, demand and net imports (million tonnes) under various scenarios with respect to population, income, technology and price policies, 2000–2020.

	2000			2010			2020		
Alternative scenario	Demand	Production	Net imports	Demand	Production	Net imports	Demand	Production	Net imports
Baseline	123	110	13	132	122	10	138	137	1
Low population growth	121	110	11	128	122	6	130	137	−7
High population growth	125	110	15	136	122	14	144	137	7
Low income growth	122	110	12	130	122	8	137	137	0
High income growth	124	110	14	134	122	12	140	137	3
Low investment rate	123	108	15	132	118	14	138	129	9
High investment rate	123	111	12	132	126	6	138	144	−6
Protection domestic	123	111	12	130	123	7	135	139	−4
Liberalizing wheat market	125	110	15	135	120	15	143	134	9

predicts China's future involvement in world grain markets. The authors' framework includes a demand-side model that, in addition to the impacts of income and population trends, accounts for the effects of urbanization and the changing level of the development of rural consumption markets. The supply response model considers the impact of prices, public investment in research and irrigation, institutional change, and environmental factors.

The projections show that under the most plausible expected growth rates in the important factors, China's wheat imports will rise somewhat in the late 1990s before peaking and gradually declining through 2020. Wheat import trends starkly contrast with those of feed grains, which by the year 2000 are expected to expand sharply and continue to rise throughout the first two decades of the next century, eventually reaching 25 to 35 million tonnes, a level many times higher than maize's historic high (Huang *et al.*, forthcoming). Increasing maize imports arise mainly from the accelerating demand for meat and feed grains. Increasing wheat imports are caused by steadily expanding demand and a slowing of supply due to reduced investment in agricultural research in the late 1980s. After 2000, wheat imports are expected to stabilize as demand growth slows due to increasing urbanization, declining population growth rates, and relatively low and falling expenditure elasticities for wheat. As supply growth is sustained with the ongoing recovery of investment in agricultural research and irrigation, supply is projected to speed up and slowly begin to meet most of national demand by 2020.

One of the most important differences between the projections for wheat imports and those for other commodities is in the sensitivity of the predictions (Huang and Rozelle, 1997a; Huang *et al.*, forthcoming). Whereas there are considerable ranges in the projections for total grain, mostly maize, when baseline assumptions are varied in both the short and long run, wheat import projections are fairly robust. Substantially lower rates of agricultural investment lead to higher import predictions, a result that should be expected from the factor that has the largest marginal output response. In the case of almost all other factors, however, there are few changes in the assumptions that result in predictions of China becoming a significantly larger wheat importer than it currently is. Almost all major demand factors – urbanization, income growth and low or negative expenditure elasticities, and market liberalization – are pushing China's consumers to reduce wheat demand over the next 25 years. Without a catastrophic breakdown in supply, which could happen with sharp changes in cropping patterns, or a radical change in agricultural policy and an increase in responsiveness of farmers to prices, supply should be able to keep up with demand, or at least prevent the gap between supply and demand from growing significantly larger than it is at present.

It appears that China will neither empty the world grain markets nor become a major grain exporter. Although China will become a more important player in world grain markets as an importer in the coming decades, its importance will be primarily in world feed markets. In contrast, although in the next several years China should continue to retain its current position as the world's leading wheat importer, if the baseline assumptions hold over the long run, and the structural parameters used in this study remain reliable, China's reliance on world wheat markets may gradually fall. Both potential exporters outside China and those charged with managing China's food needs through domestic production and imports need to be ready. Exporting nations, especially those dealing with wheat and maize, will undoubtedly be those more affected – some positively and others negatively.

If China's policymakers believe the projected level of total imports is too high, either politically or because they see some other physical or economic constraint, then investment strategies need to be devised in the near future due to the long lags between the period of expenditure and the time when such investments can affect production. Continued investment in wheat technology will help ease these trends. On the other hand, China's leaders may find it acceptable or politically expedient to continue to import at current levels of wheat, and may choose to reduce investment in wheat research, allocating more to other crops, such as maize, which ultimately may be in shorter supply domestically. Investment in and preparation of facilities and institutions needed to handle the increased volume of incoming wheat and grain will smooth the shock of production shortfalls in the short and long run, and will reduce the time and expense of importing grain. China's foresight in dealing with the forthcoming challenges will most probably determine whether the production–demand gaps turn into a major agricultural crisis or whether they will become an opportunity to develop the nation's food economy more effectively and to continue to integrate itself into world food markets.

Notes

1. In this chapter, agricultural production refers to grain crops and cash crops only. Other crops (including tea, fruit, vegetables, and other miscellaneous products) are excluded. Grain and cash crops are planted on over 90% of sown area. In accordance with the Chinese definition, in the descriptive section of the chapter, grain includes rice, wheat, maize, other coarse grains, soybeans, and white and sweet potatoes (valued at a ratio of 5:1). Cash crops include cotton, oil-bearing crops (including rapeseed, groundnuts, sesame seed and other oilseed crops); sugar cane, sugar beets, tobacco, hemp-producing crops (such as jute), medicinal crops, and several minor miscellaneous crops. In the empirical analysis, grain is divided between rice and other grains (wheat, maize and

soybeans). These four grain crops accounted for 82% of grain-sown area in 1992. Cash crops are restricted to cotton, rapeseed, groundnuts and sugar cane. These crops accounted for 70% of the total area sown with cash crops in 1992.
2. This measure does not include a large part of the temporary migrant community (the so-called floating population). In the short run, this part of the population must be ignored since little is known about their consumption patterns. Moreover, there is no reason to expect that by adding them on to the urban population at this time the urbanization impact would be increased. It may be that their consumption patterns are more rural than urban in the temporary living conditions. But, to the extent that a part of these residents end up staying in the cities permanently, they will almost certainly eventually adopt some of the urban habits.
3. Although migrants from southern areas may adopt the consumption patterns of their urban counterparts and increase their intake of wheat products as elsewhere in Asia, those from wheat-consuming northern regions will most probably rapidly begin to adopt consumption patterns similar to city residents, a move that will probably mean that wheat demand for this part of the labour force will fall. Based on a recent survey by Rozelle *et al.* (1997a), there are probably about equal numbers of migrants coming from the north and from the south.
4. The baseline assumptions for population growth rates in the three study decades imply an overall projection period population growth rate of 0.89, a level slightly higher than that assumed by Rosegrant *et al.* (1995) (0.74). There are many reasons to believe that, with increasing reform, the government's ability to control fertility may lessen and future rates of population growth may be greater than the baseline rates. Rosegrant *et al.* (1995) use an alternative rate of 1% per year. In this study's scenario of high population growth, it is assumed the growth rate in the first decade is 1.413, the second 0.932, and the third 0.844, implying an overall study-period growth rate of 1.06. In a later section, results are presented showing the sensitivity of the conclusions to the choice of population growth rates.
5. In one sense, the assumption is consistent with China's entry into the General Agreement on Tariffs and Trade (GATT), where in the long run Chinese producers will not be protected or taxed by border restrictions. Since China's grain prices are nearly the same as world market ones, there is also no obvious one-time effect from liberalization. The case would be different if China went the round of its prosperous East Asian neighbours and began to protect its producers with ever-increasing prices. Even the most ardent grain fundamentalists find this scenario plausible given China's severe fiscal problems.
6. The opportunity cost of land is calculated from China's cost-of-production data as real resource per mu (1 hectare = 15 mu), net of variable production costs and wages.

Appendix

Alternative projections

To test the sensitivity of the results to changes in the underlying forces driving the supply and demand balances, a number of alternative scenarios are run, altering the baseline growth rates of the key variables, including income, population and investment in technology. The results, shown in Table 7.9, indicate that low population growth rates would reduce wheat demand by only 8 million tonnes in 2020, compared with the baseline, with wheat imports completely disappearing (actually becoming negative or beginning exports, which probably will never happen because of the existence of high transaction costs). With high population growth, imports increase to 15 million tonnes in 2000 and remain significantly positive through 2020.

Income growth simulations (Table 7.9, rows 4 and 5) generate about the same results as the population growth rate simulations. Since expenditure elasticities for wheat are low, import demand rises but does not explode. This relative insensitivity is in stark contrast to aggregate grain import demand and import demand for maize, which varies sharply with the assumed growth rate because the income elasticity for livestock and the indirect demand for grain are much higher.

Perhaps the most important supply-side simulation result shown in Table 7.9 is the impact of investment in agricultural research and irrigation on wheat production and trade balances (Table 7.9, rows 6 and 7). The variation due to changing the growth of investment assumption is hardly surprising given the large contribution that agricultural research, and the technology it has produced, has made to agricultural productivity in recent years (Huang and Rozelle, 1996; Huang *et al.*, 1996). Increases in the rate of growth in investment in agricultural research and irrigation from 3 to 4% per year are projected to shift China from an import to an export position by 2020. If, instead, growth in annual investment in the agricultural research system and irrigation fell only moderately – from 3% per year, as forecast under the baseline projections, to 2% – then by 2020 total production would only be 129 million tonnes. With no change in the assumption regarding the level of food demand, imports under such a scenario would stay just below the level of current imports (about 8 million tonnes).

Hence, continuing high levels of grain imports could be expected only if there were continued decline in the growth of agricultural investment and if the government did not respond with countervailing policy measures as import levels rose. Such a scenario could unfold only if the government were unwilling or unable to undertake policies to stimulate food production growth. However, agricultural research and irrigation investments have already recovered in recent years, and in recent months, as grain prices have risen in response to short-term tightening of grain supplies, government policymakers have responded with promises of greater investments in agriculture (Mei, 1995). Although most of the investments have been targeted at irrigation, improvements in the operations of research institutes have also been announced. If China's government maintains current investments levels in wheat research, wheat imports under the most likely demand scenario will slowly fall.

In addition to domestic investments, the government could also look to the international arena for technological products that would allow China time to redevelop its agricultural research system. In fact, there are currently several large international seed companies investigating the possibilities of moving into the China market for seeds. Such moves would reduce the expected decline in grain supply and also decrease the expected level of imports even if growth in public investments slowed. The potential for bringing in companies interested in wheat seed production and sales, however, is necessarily going to be less than for maize, since hybrid seeds are easier to protect in a country like China, which has weak intellectual property rights.

Table 7.9, rows 8 and 9, shows that wheat production, demand and imports are relatively insensitive to price trends. This means that government pursuit of either price protection or market liberalization policies will cause little deviation away from the baseline results. Output price trends do affect China's wheat balances, but the effects are small. From the baseline level, for every 0.5% increase (decline) in the annual projected wheat price trend, imports over the next decade fall (rise) by less than 2 million tonnes (row 8). Over the long run, if China supported prices at current levels, demand would fall somewhat, supply would rise as farmers would increase output and, by 2020, China might have annual production levels that exceed supply (but even after 25 years of price supports, the difference between the baseline projections is only 5 million tonnes). Similar magnitudes are observed in the other direction (row 9). If China were to have prices in its own markets integrated with expected world price trends (falling by 1% per year), then, instead of becoming almost self-sufficient (row 1, baseline), China might import about 8 million tonnes annually, a level just slightly under the recent average.

The relative insensitivity of projected imports to price policy depends on low estimated output price-response elasticities and the implicit assumption that current production patterns will continue in the future. Any shift in these assumptions could lead to sharp changes to the predicted supply, demand and imports. China's fairly restrictive policy environment and the subsistence nature of its households may account for the low response of output and demand to prices in the estimations. If the decision-making environment in China evolves as the rest of the economy develops, farmer production and demand responses may vary more with prices in the future. If production were to rise more and demand were to fall more when Chinese leaders implement pricing policies, the projected imports might even be lower than currently projected. Likewise, if the nation's leaders opened the agricultural economy and prices continued falling, as they have throughout the past century, the nation's imports of wheat could be significantly larger than currently projected.

Changes to the current cropping patterns could also lead to lower predicted output levels and higher future imports, as wages rise and the relative prices of crops change. Currently, the intense rice–wheat and wheat–maize rotations in most of China's wheat-producing areas demand large quantities of labour and may not be conducive to mechanized planting and harvesting. As wages continue to increase, pressures will rise to search for labour-saving cropping patterns. It may be that, with a higher projected demand for feed grains, farmers in some areas will abandon two-season rotations and choose to produce single-season maize. If demand for wheat does not change, the concomitant need for wheat imports would increase. The current projections are based on parameters estimated on the basis of past data and historic technologies and cropping patterns. Any fundamental change in the way that wheat farmers cultivate their land may have sharp impacts on future wheat supply, demand and imports.

References

Bouis, H. (1989) *Prospects for Rice: Supply Demand Balances in Asia.* Working Paper, International Food Policy Research Institute, Washington DC, USA.

Carter, C. and Zhong, F. (1991) China's past and future role in the grain trade. *Economic Development and Cultural Change* 39, 791–814.

Chen, X. (1994) The central government's politics and measures are good, but it is difficult to implement them at the local and departmental level. *Liaowang* 18 (2 May), 13–16.

ERS (Economic Research Service) (1995) Projections model for predicting agricultural output: an introduction. In: *Research in China – Issues and Data Sources.* Proceedings of WRCC-101, US Department of Agriculture, Washington DC, USA.

Fan, S. and Pardey, P. (1992) *Agricultural Research in China: Its Institutional Development and Impact.* International Service for National Agricultural Research, The Hague, Netherlands.

Fan, S.G., Cramer, G.L. and Wailes, E.J. (1994) The impact of trade liberalization on China's rice sector. *Agricultural Economics* 11, 71–81.

FAO (Food and Agricultural Organization of the United Nations) (1991) *Demand Prospects for Rice and Other Foodgrains in Selected Asian Countries.* Food and Agricultural Organization Economic and Social Development Paper, No. 97, Rome, Italy.

Garnaut, R. and Ma, G. (1992) *Grain in China: A Report.* East Asian Analytical Unit, Department of Foreign Affairs and Trade, Canberra, Australia.

Halbrendt, C., Tuan, F., Gempeshaw, C. and Dolk-Etz, D. (1994) Rural Chinese food consumption: the case of Guangdong. *American Journal of Agricultural Economics* 76, 794–799.

Huang, J. and Bouis, H. (1995) *Structural Changes in Demand for Food in Asia.* Food, Agriculture, and the Environment Discussion Paper, International Food Policy Research Institute, Washington DC, USA.

Huang, J. and David, C. (1993) Demand for cereal grains in Asia: the effects of urbanization. *Agricultural Economics* 8, 107–124.

Huang, J. and Rozelle, S. (1994) Environmental stress and grain yields in China. *American Journal of Agricultural Economics* 77, 853–864.

Huang, J. and Rozelle, S. (1995a) *Income, Quality, and the Demand for Food in Rural China.* Working Paper, Food Research Institute, Stanford University, Stanford, California, USA.

Huang, J. and Rozelle, S. (1995b) *Urban Life, Urban Consumption.* Working Paper, Food Research Institute, Stanford University, Stanford, California, USA.

Huang, J. and Rozelle, S. (1996) Technological change: rediscovering the engine of productivity growth in China's agricultural economy. *Journal of Development Economics* 49, 337–369.

Huang, J. and Rozelle, S. (1997a) *Agricultural Growth, Reform, and Agricultural Growth in China.* Paper prepared for the World Bank, China Division, Agriculture Section, World Bank, Washington DC, USA.

Huang, J. and Rozelle, S. (1997b) Market development and food demand in rural China. *China Economic Review* 8, 200–220.

Huang, J., Rosegrant, M. and Rozelle, S. (1996) *Public Investment, Technological Change, and Reform: Comprehensive Accounting of Chinese Agricultural Growth*. Working Paper, International Food Policy Research Institute, Washington DC, USA.

Huang, J., Rozelle, S. and Rosegrant, M. (forthcoming). China's food economy to the 21st century: supply, demand, and trade. *Economic Development and Cultural Change*.

Jin, S., Pray, C., Huang, J. and Rozelle, S. (1997) *The Political Economy of Agricultural Research in China*. Working Paper, Department of Agricultural Economics, Rutgers University, New Brunswick, New Jersey, USA.

Lin, J.Y. (1991) The household responsibility system reform and the adoption of hybrid rice in China. *Journal of Development Economics* 36, 353–373.

Lin, J.Y. (1992) Rural reforms and agricultural growth in China. *American Economic Review* 82, 34–51.

Liu, X. (1992) Irrigation investment in China. Unpublished doctoral dissertation, Department of Agricultural Economics, University of Philippines, Los Baños, Philippines.

McMillan, J., Walley, J. and Zhu, L. (1989) The impact of China's economic reforms on agricultural productivity growth. *Journal of Political Economy* 97, 781–807.

Mei, F. (1995) China can feed its population. *China Daily*, 29 April.

MWREP (Ministry of Water Resources and Electrical Power) (1988–1992) *Compiled Statistics on the Development of China's Water Conservancy System*. Ministry of Water Conservancy, Beijing, China.

Rosegrant, M., Agcaoili-Sombilla, M. and Perez, N. (1995) Rice and the global food economy: projections and policy implications of future food balances. Paper presented in the Final Conference on the Medium- and Long-Term Projections of World Rice Supply and Demand, sponsored by the International Food Policy Research Institute and the International Rice Research Institute, Beijing, China, 23–26 April.

Rozelle, S. and Huang, J. (1997) Wheat in China: supply, demand, marketing, and trade in the twenty-first century. Paper presented at The Economics of World Wheat Markets: Implications for North America conference, sponsored by the Trade Research Center, Montana State University, Bozeman, Montana, May.

Rozelle, S., Park, A., Huang, J. and Jin, H. (1996) *Dilemmas in Reforming State–Market Relations in China*. Working Paper, Department of Economics, Stanford University, Stanford, California, USA.

Rozelle, S., Guo, L., Shen, M., Giles, J. and Low, T.Y. (1997a) Poverty, networks, institutions, or education: testing among competing hypotheses on the determinants of migration in China. Paper presented at the 1997 Association for Asian Studies Meetings, Chicago, Illinois, USA, 13–16 March.

Rozelle, S., Pray, C. and Huang, J. (1997b) Agricultural policy in China: testing the limits of commercialization-led reform. *Contemporary Economic Policy* XXXIX, 37–71.

Sicular, T. (1991) China's agricultural policy during the reform period. In: Joint Economic Committee, Congress of the United States (ed.) *China's Economic Dilemmas in the 1990s: the Problems of Reforms, Modernization, and Interdependence*. M.E. Sharpe, Armonk, New York, USA, pp. 340–364.

Sicular, T. (1995) Redefining state, plan, and market: China's reforms in agricultural commerce. *China Quarterly* 143, 1020–1046.
SPB (State Price Bureau) (1988–1992) *Quanguo nongchanpin chengben shouyi ziliao huibian (*National Agricultural Production Cost and Revenue Information Summary – in Chinese). China Price Bureau Press, Beijing, China.
SSTC (State Science and Technology Commission) (1991, 1993) *Zhongguo Kexue Jishu Ziliao Ku*, 1985–1990; 1991, 1993 (China Science and Technology Statistical Yearbook, 1985–1990; 1991, 1993 – in Chinese). State Science and Technology Commission, Beijing, China.
Stone, B. (1988) Developments in agricultural technology. *China Quarterly* 116 (December).
Stone, B. (1993) Basic agricultural technology under reform. In: Kueh, Y.Y. and Ash, R.F. (eds) *Economic Trends in Chinese Agriculture: the Impact of Post Mao Reforms.* Clarendon Press, Oxford, UK, pp. 767–822.
Tong, Z. and Huang, J. (1995) *Agricultural Labor Absorption in China.* Working Paper, International Food Policy Research Institute, Washington DC, USA.
United Nations (1993) *World Population Prospects, 1992 Revisions.* Department of Economic, Social Information, and Policy Analysis, United Nations, New York, USA.
Watson, A. (1994) *China's Agricultural Reforms: Experiences and Achievements of the Agricultural Sector in the Market Reform Process.* Working Paper 94/4, Chinese Economy Research Unit, University of Adelaide, Australia.
World Bank (1990) *Agriculture to the Year 2000.* A World Bank Country Study (Annex 2 to *China: Longer-term Development Issues and Options*), World Bank, Washington DC, USA.
Ye, Q. and Rozelle, S. (1994) Fertilizer policy in China's reforming economy. *Canadian Journal of Agricultural Economics* 42, 191–208.
ZGNYNJ (various years, 1980–1996) *Zhongguo Nongye Nianjian* (China Agricultural Yearbook). Ministry of Agriculture Press, Beijing, China.
ZGTJNJ (various years, 1980–1996) *Zhongguo Tongji Nianjian* (China Statistical Yearbook). China Statistical Press, Beijing, China.

8

Russian Agriculture and World Grain Trade: Lessons from the Past and Implications for the Future

Barry K. Goodwin and Thomas J. Grennes

Department of Agricultural and Resource Economics, North Carolina State University, Raleigh, USA

1. Introduction

Profound changes in the structure of agricultural economies in the republics of the former Soviet Union have occurred in recent years. The collapse of the Soviet system and the reforms that followed in the early 1990s brought about a transitional movement toward a market-orientated economy. Reforms have been slow to occur in many cases, however, and many sectors of the Russian economy, including agriculture, have experienced significant structural shocks, which have resulted in impressive reductions in production, consumption and trade. For example, total grain production in the Russian Federation was 63.4 million tonnes in 1995, down from 116.7 million tonnes in 1990, representing a decrease of 46%. Over the same period, imports have also fallen substantially. For example, grain product imports in 1994 were less than 10% of their 1992 level (USDA–ERS, 1997).

A number of factors are responsible for the fundamental changes realized in the Russian agricultural economy. These include changes in production subsidies, which have made inputs more expensive; significant reductions in gross income, which have shifted consumption patterns and have sharply curtailed consumer spending; higher world prices and diminished US loan guarantees, which have made imported agricultural products relatively more expensive and thus have decreased imports; and poor harvest conditions, which have decreased output in recent years. Many of these changes have been driven by market conditions and policy changes.

The relevance of the republics of the former Soviet Union as important destinations for US grain exports may have diminished somewhat in recent years, especially in light of the relatively small flow of agricultural products. In 1995, Russia imported $1.6 billion worth of bulk agricultural products, of which only 7.1% originated in the USA (USDA–FAS, 1997). Likewise, the potential for Russia and other republics of the former Soviet Union to be significant world exporters of wheat seems limited without more fundamental economic reform. However, a point not often recognized in agricultural trade research is that Russia has been a major wheat exporter. As late as the five-year period ending in 1971, Russia averaged wheat exports of 4.5 million tonnes per year. At that point, Russia was a larger exporter than Argentina and the European Community and their wheat exports were 60% of those of Australia. Furthermore, at the end of the Tsarist period, Russia was the world's largest wheat exporter. Indeed, some of the world's largest grain trading companies had their beginnings as exporters of wheat from the Black Sea regions of Tsarist Russia (Morgan, 1979). The implications of such points for the future of world grain trade are unclear, of course, and any inferences for the future that are based upon market experiences a century ago are tenuous, at best. However, a simple consideration of history demonstrates that the markets, which are in the early stages of a gradual transition, were once well integrated with world agricultural markets and demonstrated the existence of significant comparative advantages as the world's largest grain exporters. Further, of the major grain exporters of the period (Russia, the USA, Canada and Australia), only Russia has lost its role as an important wheat exporter.

Full comprehension of the effects of economic reforms in Russia requires empirical analysis of market parameters such as income and price elasticities. Unfortunately, obtaining such estimates at the present is frustrated by a dearth of available data pertinent to market conditions in republics of the former Soviet Union. In particular, reforms were undertaken only a few years ago and thus there is little experience from which to draw actual observations on market transactions and agents' behaviour. Further, economic conditions in the former Soviet Union are in a state of transition and thus it is not clear that observed market data, even those drawn from the post-reform (i.e. post-1992) period, are pertinent to the market conditions likely to exist after these adjustments and transitional changes produce a new equilibrium.

In light of these limitations, one avenue of research has evaluated market conditions during the last free-market period for Russian agriculture, the Tsarist period (Goodwin and Grennes, 1998). We briefly summarize results of that study in this chapter. Other research has utilized grain production and trade data collected prior to reforms to make inferences regarding the future of Russian grain trade (see, for example, Tyers, 1994; Jones *et al.*, 1996; Leetmaa *et al.*, 1997). These studies provide valuable inferences regarding the possible outcomes of market reforms but are certainly limited by their reliance upon pre-reform data. As a general rule, the results of these studies tend to be quite dependent upon assumptions regarding elasticities and other parameters underlying the inferences.

The objectives of this chapter are twofold. First, the chapter reviews the current agricultural situation in the Russian Federation. The status of current production and consumption patterns in Russia is reviewed and the changing role of the state in agricultural markets in Russia is evaluated. The chapter also summarizes results from related papers (McCurdy *et al.*, 1997; Goodwin *et al.*, 1998) that pursue alternative empirical analysis of reform and its effects on Russian agriculture.

2. Recent Developments in Russian Agriculture[1]

Before reform

Prior to the reforms of the early 1990s, agriculture represented a significant proportion of overall gross domestic product (GDP) in the former Soviet Union. In particular, agriculture accounted for over 20% of total employment and generated over 25% of total GDP before reform (Serova and Melyukhina, 1995). In the former system of central planning, output levels and output and input prices were administered by planners and thus were often not permitted to reflect relative scarcities. The economy was, for the most part, closed to the rest of the world and local markets were not integrated with international market conditions. Further, internal allocations of inputs and outputs were set according to administrative criteria rather than according to local market prices.

Agricultural output growth in the former Soviet Union occurred at a steady rate but did not keep pace with the rest of the world. A consideration of wheat yields over the last century (Fig. 8.1) demonstrates that yield improvements in Russia did not keep pace with those realized by France and the USA. However, the figure also demonstrates that, in the distant pre-Soviet past, Russian wheat yields were trending in a manner very similar to those in the USA and France and, in fact, were trending in a pattern consistent with convergence of yields. Significant breaks in the pattern of yield trends occurred in the mid-1930s, a period of significant changes in the structure of Soviet agriculture, brought about by Stalin's forced collectivization of agriculture and organization of large state and collective enterprises.

The planners adopted a series of policies during the 1970s that simultaneously subsidized the consumption of food commodities and the production of farm products. As von Braun *et al.* (1996) note, subsidies

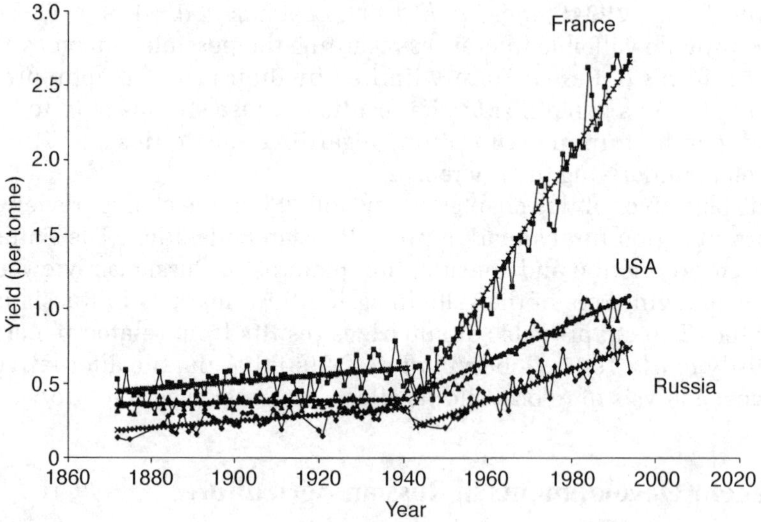

Fig. 8.1. Wheat yields and yield trends: Russia, France and the USA. Source: USDA–ERS, 1997.

to agriculture as a share of total state expenses increased by 77% during the 1980s. Of particular importance to the grain-importing sector was the extensive promotion of the production and consumption of livestock products in the 1960s and 1970s. A commitment on the part of planners to increase the consumption and production of meat, eggs and dairy products significantly increased feed grain requirements. By the mid-1980s, over two-thirds of Russia's grain was directed toward cattle and poultry feed uses. A significant proportion of feed requirements were met through the import of grain products. Russian imports of wheat grew to a high of 17.6 million tonnes in 1992 (USDA–ERS, 1997).

Russian agriculture after collectivization and prior to reform was characterized primarily by large collective farms (kolkhozes) and state farms (sovkhozes). The average size of state and collective farms in 1980 was 10,432 and 7283 ha respectively (USDA–ERS, 1997). Although agriculture was dominated by large consolidated farming operations, free-market conditions developed for small quantities of products produced on private plots during the years preceding reform.

Primary inputs were supplied to the large collective and state farms at heavily subsidized prices. Wädekin (1993/94) notes that output/input price ratios were maintained at levels far below those realized in Western countries. For example, at the end of the 1980s, one grain combine required former Soviet Union farmers to sell only about 160 tonnes of grain while US farmers were required to sell 740 tonnes of grain to purchase a combine. Likewise, the cost of a tractor was equivalent to 26 tonnes of wheat while, in the USA, the corresponding cost was equivalent to 127 tonnes. Fertilizer was also heavily subsidized, with 1 tonne of urea being equivalent to 0.39 tonnes of grain in the former Soviet Union as compared with 1.24 tonnes in the USA. Finally, a similar condition existed for livestock feed, where 1 tonne of feed required 0.06 tonnes of beef in Russia as compared with 0.13 tonnes in the USA. Agricultural credit was also heavily subsidized. The interest rates for short-term and long-term loans were 2 and 0.75% respectively. Debt forgiveness was also commonplace. Fuel prices were held well below international levels.

Consumption patterns in pre-reform Russia reflected the changes in production patterns mandated by planners. Meat consumption rose from less than 30 kg per capita in 1960 to over 60 kg per capita in 1980 (tho Seeth and von Braun, 1995; USDA–ERS, 1997). Food consumption, in terms of total caloric intake, rose to levels comparable to those in Western countries and exceeded levels common to other countries with similar levels of per capita income. For example, in 1980, the typical Soviet consumer took in 3250 calories per day. In comparison, US consumers took in 3410 calories per day (von Braun *et al.*, 1996). It is important to note that, although levels of consumption were similar to those realized in developed Western economies, significant periods of famine and hunger were experienced over the last century in Russia. In particular, widespread famine was experienced during the period of collectivization and during the war years. Further, widespread shortages and rationing of basic commodities were commonplace.

Reform and transition

Disintegration of the Soviet Union brought about significant changes in the policy environment and the structure of agriculture. These changes have been major in some areas whereas, in many other cases, the structure of agriculture retains many of its pre-reform characteristics. In January 1992, in an event known as the 'Big Bang', price support policies were largely dismantled and the transition toward a market-orientated economy began. The rouble became convertible in international markets and thus the Russian economy was, to varying degrees, open to international market influences.

Real income in the Russian Federation has fallen steadily since reforms began. In 1995, real GDP was more than 40% lower than 1991 levels. Reforms also brought about very high levels of inflation throughout the economy. The rate of inflation topped 900% in 1993 (OECD, 1995). The extent to which reported real income decreases and high inflation rates reflect inaccuracies in the reporting of statistics is unclear. There is, however, at least some reason to suspect that pre-reform reporting of income levels by Goskomstat, the state statistical reporting agency, may have overstated actual income levels and thus the actual decreases in income after reform are overstated to some extent (Dobozi and Pohl, 1995). The high inflation is particularly troublesome for segments of the economy such as pensioners whose incomes are not indexed in some way to inflation. Over the last 2 years, inflation fell dramatically and reached levels comparable to that in many developing countries. In July 1996, inflation reached an all-time low of 0.7% per month (USDA–FAS, 1997). However, late 1998 and early 1999 saw considerable financial instability and a resurgence of inflation to levels comparable to those realized in 1995. Another disturbing trend realized in post-reform Russia involves life expectancies, which fell dramatically in the years immediately following reforms.

Federal price controls for agricultural commodities were, for the most part, lifted in January 1992 and nominal prices increased rapidly for many food products. In early 1992, food prices rose by approximately 300% (OECD, 1995). However, price controls were maintained for many basic commodities such as bread and milk, although the authority for price controls was largely shifted from central to regional (oblast) authorities. As a result, a wide range of price controls exist among individual oblasts. Regional authorities use wholesale and retail price controls, subsidies, and barriers to inter-regional commodity trade to regulate prices and food stocks. These regional regulations serve as a significant barrier to inter-regional trade and market integration (Goodwin *et al.*, 1998). The emerging private sector must deal with the high transaction costs associated with inter-regional trade restrictions. Because of the difficulties associated with measuring aggregate prices and the residual presence of price regulations in many oblasts, it is unclear whether real food prices have actually increased or decreased over the transition (DeMasi and Koen, 1996). What is clear, however, is the significant decrease in most consumers' purchasing power.

Prior to reform, most agricultural output was delivered to the state through government procurement channels. State and regional authorities maintained stocks intended to guarantee food supplies. Marketing through state procurement channels was mandatory for production subsidies. In 1993 and 1994, the state procurement system underwent significant changes. In 1993, deliveries to state stocks were no longer compulsory and marketing to the state was placed on a level equivalent to all other marketing channels. The proportion of wheat delivered through state procurement channels has fallen in recent years. In 1990, 37% of wheat production was delivered to state stocks. This had fallen to 21% by 1995. This decrease occurred in part because of a severe lack of funds for the state procurement agency to use in paying producers for their grain. The decreases in state procurement in the grain sector accompanied the significant decreases in the feeding of grain which occurred as the livestock sector diminished in size. At the same time, private grain trading companies such as Ogo gained increasing prominence and gave rise to an emerging private grain-marketing sector.

Prior to reform, Russian agriculture was heavily subsidized, although planners also maintained consumption prices that were significantly beneath those realized in the rest of the world. Indeed, as Fig. 8.2 points out, state support of agriculture increased significantly throughout the 1980s and reached a high point in 1988, when nearly 35% of agricultural revenues were attributable to state support measures (Serova and Melyukhina, 1995). Inputs were heavily subsidized and resulting input usage levels were high, probably reflecting an inefficient allocation of resources.[2] Following reform, however, input subsidies were significantly reduced and input prices increased significantly. Usage levels adjusted in a corresponding fashion (Fig. 8.3) and, although the proportion of arable land in cultivation remained fairly constant (Fig. 8.4), output of agricultural products fell considerably. In 1995, only 30 million tonnes of wheat was produced as compared with over 49 million tonnes in 1990. Although state support of agriculture has decreased significantly in recent years, it remains substantial in many sectors, particularly livestock. In 1993, 84% of explicit state subsidies to agriculture were directed toward livestock sectors. In contrast, only 6.2% of subsidies went for the purchase of fertilizers, chemicals, and machinery (Serova and Melyukhina, 1995).

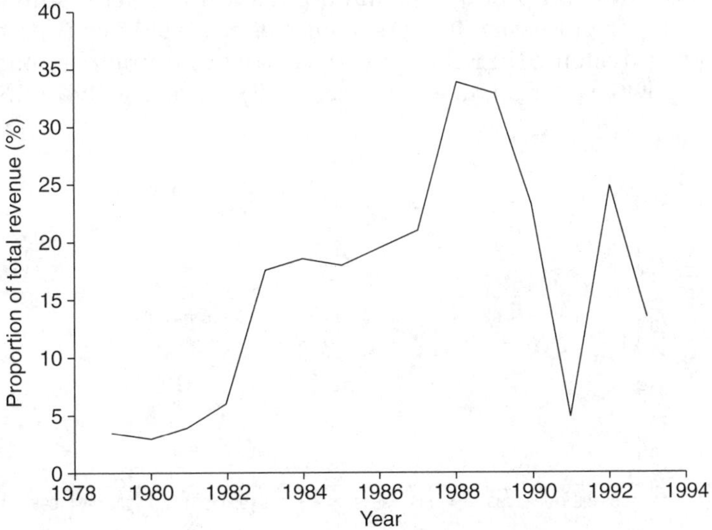

Fig. 8.2. Share of state support in total revenues of agricultural enterprises. Source: USDA–ERS, 1997.

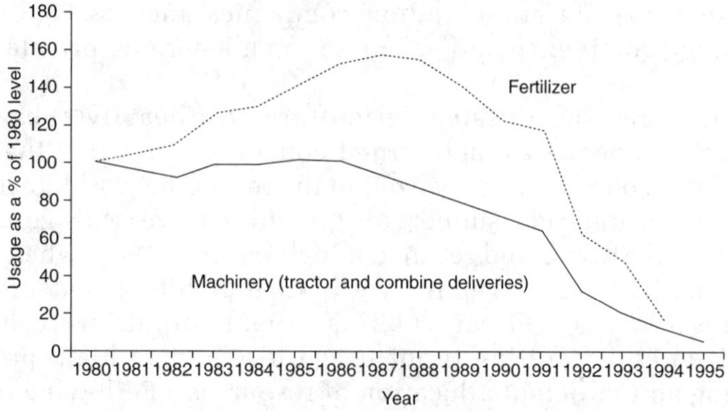

Fig. 8.3. Input usage in agriculture. Source: USDA–ERS, 1997.

As noted above, beginning in the 1970s, Soviet policy reflected a determined effort to boost consumption of livestock products through feed and other input subsidies. However, reforms brought about significant decreases in the size of livestock inventories. Figure 8.5 illustrates the significant declines in cattle and pig inventories that occurred in the early 1990s. Recently, Russia has become a large importer of meat, especially poultry from the USA (USDA–FAS, 1997). Although these imports are formally classified as meat products, they are to some extent an implicit import of US feed grains.

In spite of these substantial levels of support, especially prior to reform, there is evidence that, as a whole, the combination of output price subsidies and production and input subsidies has resulted in a current net tax of Russian farmers. Liefert *et al.* (1996) report producer subsidy equivalents (PSEs) for a variety of agricultural commodities over the 1992–94 period. In every case, the PSEs are negative, implying

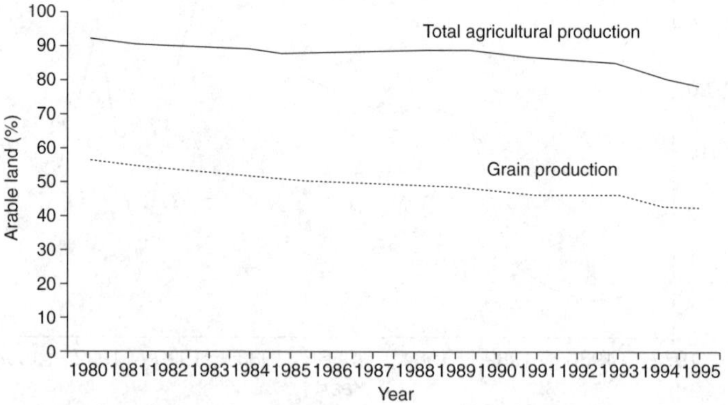

Fig. 8.4. Cultivation of arable land (percentage in cultivation and in grain production). Source: USDA–ERS, 1997.

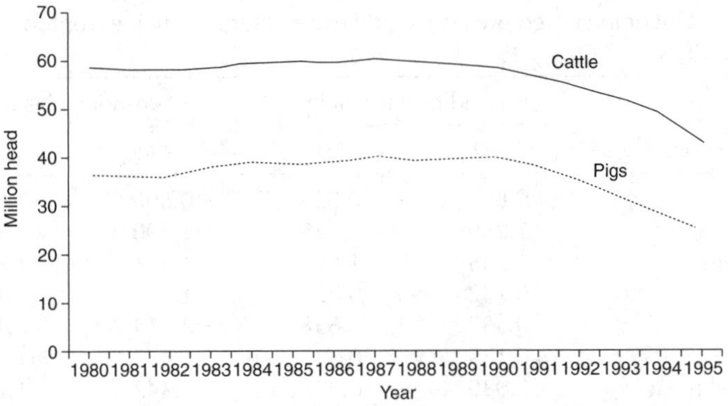

Fig. 8.5. Cattle and pig inventories. Source: USDA–ERS, 1997.

a net taxing effect from government intervention. For wheat in 1994, their results imply a gap of 3% between the imputed domestic prices and the larger world reference prices.[3]

Decreases in real income and changes in food prices led to significant changes in food consumption patterns in post-reform Russia. Personal consumption expenditures in 1995 were only 67% of their 1991 level. Expenditures on food goods in 1995 were only 79% of 1991 levels (Russian Federation, Goskomstat data, unpublished, 1996). Per capita consumption of nearly all food items decreased significantly after reform (Fig. 8.6). Decreases were especially strong for meats, fish, and dairy products.

An analysis of longitudinal household survey data by McCurdy *et al.* (1997) found that demands for most food commodities are relatively price- and income-elastic and, further, that price and income elasticities have tended to increase as reforms have progressed. A summary of their

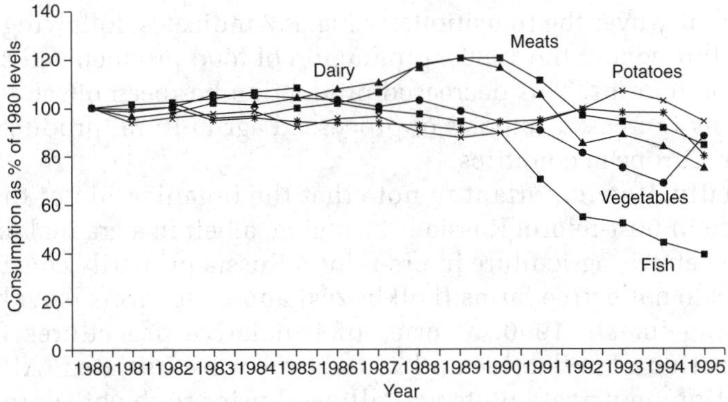

Fig. 8.6. Per capita consumption of selected food items (as a percentage of 1980 levels). Source: USDA–ERS, 1997.

Table 8.1. Uncompensated own-price and expenditure elasticities for food in transition Russia.

	Expenditure elasticity		Own-price elasticity	
Food category	1992	1995	1992	1995
Grains	0.697	0.824	−0.898	−1.001
Fruit	1.289	1.245	−1.290	−1.168
Vegetables	1.245	1.686	−1.281	−1.999
Beef	0.732	0.720	−1.950	−1.126
Poultry	0.552	0.638	−2.114	−0.165
Pork	0.139	0.332	−1.450	−1.183
Processed meat	1.039	0.973	−1.342	−1.372
Dairy	0.783	0.800	−1.259	−1.086
Eggs	0.962	1.044	−1.172	−0.679
Potatoes	1.282	1.712	−1.964	−2.570
Confections	0.998	0.918	−1.393	−1.567
Fats	0.896	0.777	−0.077	−1.140
Fish	4.750	4.232	−2.650	−2.870

Source: McCurdy *et al.* (1997).

elasticity results is presented in Table 8.1. Two characteristics of the elasticity estimates are especially notable. The first is the relatively elastic response associated with food price changes in Russia. Second are the increases in elasticity that have occurred in many cases as the transition has progressed. The expenditure elasticity estimates can be compared with income elasticity estimates by adjusting the estimates using a measure of food expenditure's elasticity to income changes. Suvorov (1997) reported an overall food income elasticity of 0.66, which, when used to adjust the expenditure elasticities reported by McCurdy *et al.* (1997), produces food product income elasticity estimates that are mainly inelastic.

Domestic production of processed food products has fallen substantially over the transition. As Fig. 8.7 indicates, following strong growth throughout the 1980s, production of food products fell sharply following reforms. This decreased production has been offset, to some extent, by increased imports of processed agricultural products from Western European countries.

Finally, it is important to note that the organization of the farm structure in post-reform Russia is changing, albeit in a gradual manner. As noted above, agriculture in pre-reform Russia primarily consisted of large-scale collective farms (kolkhozes) and state farms (sovkhozes). Beginning in late 1990, a series of legislative procedures for the privatization of collective and state farms were initiated. Although production on private plots was allowed prior to the breakup of the former Soviet Union, provisions for privatization of formerly state-owned enterprises have brought about a small expansion in the share of

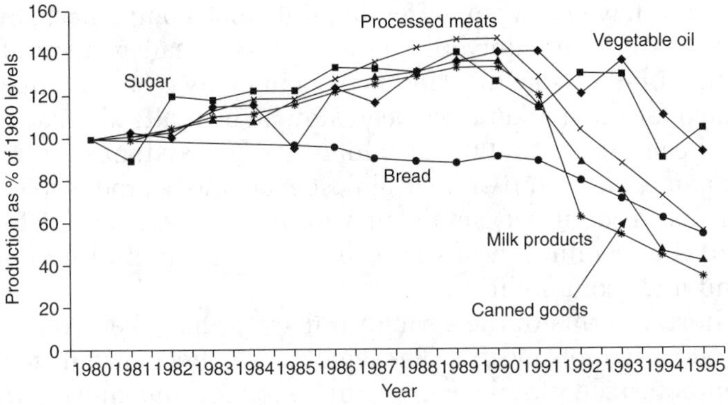

Fig. 8.7. Processed food production (percentage of 1980 levels). Source: USDA–ERS, 1997.

private farm holdings (Fig. 8.8). Beginning in 1991, governmental decrees began reorganizing and reregistering the state and collective farms. Each public farm was required to decide whether to privatize or to maintain its state-owned status. As has been the case with most formerly public enterprises, privatization typically involves the formation of a joint-stock company for which workers and pensioners are granted a share of the company's privatized resources, which are often then leased back to the original enterprise.[4]

As of 1995, about 25% of agricultural land remained with farms retaining their former status as state or collective farms. A larger share

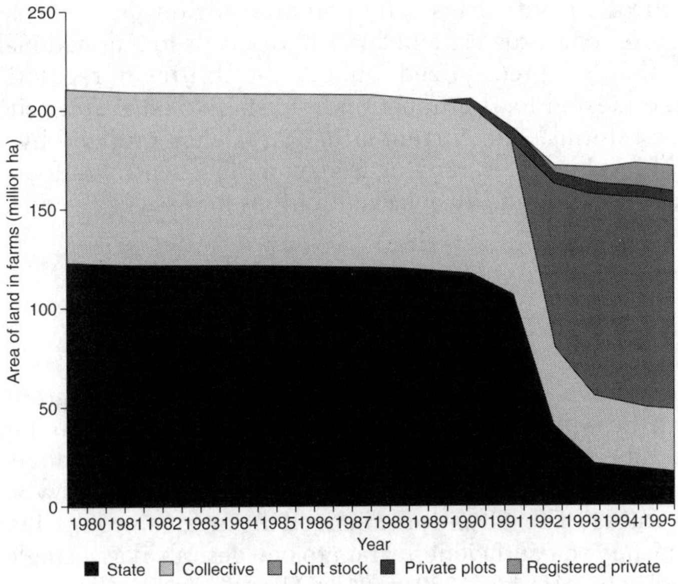

Fig. 8.8. Allocation and area of land in farms. Source: USDA–ERS, 1997.

(nearly 50%) have been converted to joint-stock companies. However, these are changes in name only in many cases. Management of assets remained with the same decision-makers in many cases and incentives to produce for the market have been slow to be realized.[5] The average size of these farms, 26,000 of which are in existence, is 4800 ha (Prosterman *et al.*, 1997). Grain is almost exclusively produced on large-scale farms. In contrast, small, private plots now account for large shares of the production of some commodities, including potatoes, milk, and meat commodities.

In short, reforms in the agricultural sector have been modest and slow to occur in most regards. The large-scale collective and state farms that characterized Soviet agriculture are, for the most part, still operating much as they did before reforms. These large farms account for the largest share of grain production, although private production is becoming increasingly important for many other commodities. Many of these farms have been converted into 'privatized' joint-stock companies, although resources are managed by the same operators that made decisions before reforms. Agriculture has obtained diminished support from the government, especially in input and livestock production subsidies. However, government support has continued to account for a significant share of agricultural revenues in recent years. The high cost of inputs such as fertilizer and farm machinery has led to a decline in both area cropped and yields. In many cases, supplies of important inputs are inefficiently controlled by monopolies that developed as a result of the modest changes that reform brought about in formerly state-controlled industries. The potential for output and yields to expand as reforms progress and farms have access to international input markets should be recognized. Finally, the shifting of regulations on regional trade and food production from state to local authorities has inhibited reforms. The current situation is characterized by a wide variety of local policies, ranging from complete control of food stocks and inter-regional trade by oblast authorities to cases of essentially free trade and production.

3. Tsarist Russia and World Grain Trade

As noted above, the emerging prominence of world grain trade following the repeal of the British Corn Laws in 1846 saw an important role for Russia in world grain markets. Impressive changes were realized in world production, consumption, and trade in wheat and related grains. The situation changed from most countries being approximately self-sufficient in grain to one described as a single world grain market (see Harley, 1980, p. 218; O'Rourke and Williamson, 1994). Grain prices converged among European countries, and new exporters emerged from all over the globe. European grain markets became connected to market conditions in the USA, Canada, Argentina, Australia and India. Links between the world wheat and rice markets were also established (Latham and Neal, 1983).

Sources of these changes involved technological innovations as well as the relaxation of trade barriers. Impressive reductions in both domestic and international transportation costs also took place. Improvements occurred in the storage, grading and milling of grain (Veblen, 1892). Organized commodity markets with cash and futures trading developed. The cost of acquiring information declined with the emergence of the telegraph and related innovations (Metzer, 1974).

Associated with these innovations was rapid growth in world wheat trade and changes in world market shares of exporting countries. Changes in production and trade also occurred within countries as older producing regions lost their comparative advantage to newer regions more distant from consuming centres. The centre of US wheat production moved westward from Indiana, Illinois, and Wisconsin to the Great Plains. The decline in transport costs from Chicago to New York was as great as the decline from New York to Liverpool. The decline in price differences was greatest for farm-level prices in newer producing areas.

An important question of considerable debate involves the extent to which Russian agriculture contributed and responded to developments in the world grain market. One strand of the literature, represented by Gerschenkron (1965), stresses the 'backwardness' of Tsarist Russia, especially its agriculture. A second strand acknowledges some differences in Russian institutions, such as post-emancipation restrictions on peasants, but finds that economic agents in Russia responded to market conditions in the same general way as their contemporaries in the West (see, for example, Kahan, 1973; Metzer, 1974; Gregory, 1980, 1994; Gatrell, 1986). This section of the chapter evaluates Russian grain trade during this period to determine whether Russian behaviour was in some sense different from other participants in the world grain economy. In addition to its historical interest, the question may be relevant to the contemporary issue of the possibility of transforming Russian agriculture from state and collective farms back to market-orientated institutions. This potential relevance derives, in part, from the fact that the Tsarist period represents the last era, excepting a brief experiment with the New Economic Policy, of free-market conditions for agricultural commodities in Russia.

Russian wheat exports grew rapidly during the Tsarist period. At the beginning of World War I, Russia was the world's largest wheat exporter. Russian leadership occurred in spite of major expansion in wheat exports by the USA, Canada, Argentina, Australia and India (see Stern, 1960; Harley, 1980). As trade expanded, price differences between

Odessa and Liverpool diminished sharply (Harley, 1980). Odessa became a major port and the Louis-Dreyfus firm came to dominate the Odessa trade (Rothstein, 1960; Morgan, 1979).

As railways expanded within Russia, regional price differences also narrowed, and the location of production changed to represent the new pattern of comparative advantage (Gatrell, 1986). Wheat production moved to new areas of Western Siberia, and producers in old areas of Russia lobbied for higher rail rates to protect themselves from domestic competition. Farm-level prices in distant locations rose relative to Odessa prices. The decline in domestic and international transport costs allowed farm-level prices of wheat in Russia to rise even when wheat prices were falling in Liverpool.

Russian wheat yields and yield trends during the Tsarist period were somewhat similar to those in Western Europe and North America. Although yields averaged 0.3–0.7 tonnes per ha less than those in the USA, trends showed a narrowing of this difference through the late 1930s. However, during the period that followed the collectivization of Soviet agriculture and World War II, a significant divergence occurred between Russian wheat yields and yields in Western Europe and North America. Figure 8.1 illustrates wheat yields and yield trends between 1872 and 1995. A significant break in the yield trends is apparent following World War II. The most significant break occurred for France, where large increases in yields occurred in response to increased domestic support for grain production in Western Europe. As noted, the gap between US and Russian grain yields showed some evidence of narrowing in the period preceding collectivization. However, a large gap in yields persisted over the post-war period.

Following the abolition of serfdom, the Russian agricultural sector became increasingly integrated with the international economy and differences in Russian and international prices decreased significantly. Figure 8.9 illustrates the difference between annual average prices at Odessa, an important Russian market from which much wheat was exported, and Liverpool, an important international market.[6] The price differential consistently declined over the Tsarist period, reflecting a narrowing of the band between domestic Russian prices and international prices. Convergence of domestic Russian prices and prices in the international market reflects declines in transportation costs that resulted from improvements in the domestic and international shipping infrastructure. Such improvements included the development of the Russian rail system, improved port facilities for ocean shipping and an improved infrastructure for the storage and handling of grain.

As was previously noted, Russian grain exports increased significantly following the abolition of serfdom. Russia was the world's largest exporter of wheat, rye, barley and oats. Russia's share of world exports over the period 1909–1913 was 25% for wheat, 37% for rye,

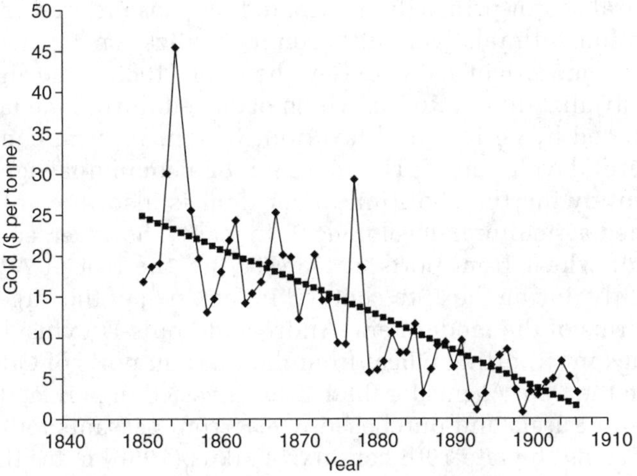

Fig. 8.9. Odessa/Liverpool price difference and trend. Source: USDA–ERS, 1997.

71% for barley, and 43% for oats (Timoshenko, 1932). Figure 8.10 illustrates wheat and coarse grain exports for Russia, the USA and France between 1852 and 1988. Russian grain exports were consistently above those of competitors until the Revolution, after which Russia never regained its prominence as a grain exporter.[7]

The conventional view of the state of Tsarist Russian agriculture following the abolition of serfdom is one of a relatively backward

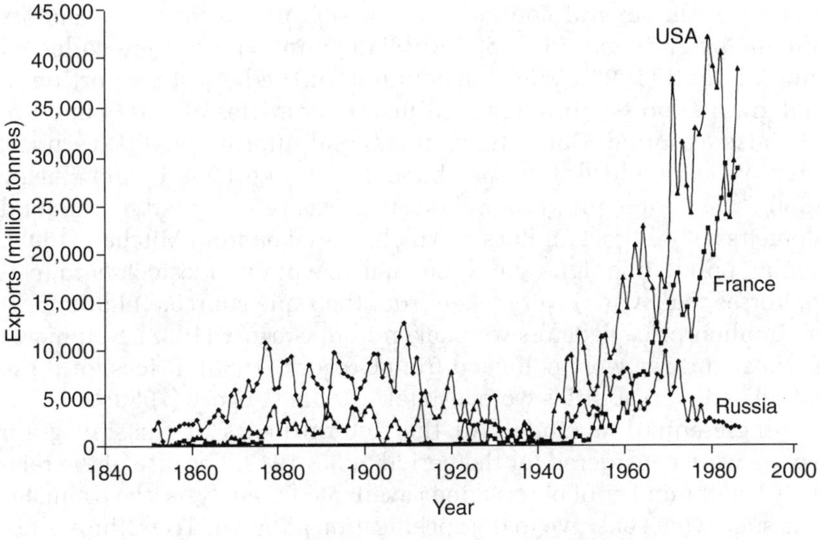

Fig. 8.10. Wheat and coarse grain exports. Source: USDA–ERS, 1997.

agricultural sector primarily dominated by peasant production and consumption with relatively little commercialization or international trade. This view originated with Gerschenkron (1965), who argued that the industrialization of Russia which occurred during the late 1800s was financed by agricultural taxation, which, in turn, constrained agricultural development. The retention of a communal agricultural system following the abolition of serfdom is also thought to have constrained agricultural development. In reality, however, commercial exports of wheat from ports at Odessa and the Sea of Azov grew significantly during the 19th century. In fact, two of the largest grain-trading firms of the modern era, André and Louis-Dreyfus, had their beginnings in exporting wheat from the Russian ports of Odessa and Rostov on the Don. Agents for these firms invested in port facilities and elevators in Russia and purchased wheat from peasants for export to Britain during the late 19th century.[8] Falkus (1966) notes that many Russian agricultural producers began to produce explicitly for export and that regional patterns of wheat production in Russia shifted in response to increased export demand.

Goodwin and Grennes (1998) considered empirical models of grain exports during the Tsarist period to evaluate these two competing views of 19th-century Russian agriculture (i.e. an impoverished, backward agricultural sector versus a commercial agricultural infrastructure exporting to the world market). Of primary interest was the extent to which international prices influenced wheat exports and the extent to which local (peasant) production and consumption were influenced by economic variables. A brief summary of their findings and an extended analysis using their data are reported here.

Data from several sources were assembled to evaluate factors influencing grain exports. Total Russian grain exports were collected from Mitchell (1992). Wheat accounted for the largest proportion of total grain exports, although significant quantities of barley and rye were also exported. Domestic (Odessa) and international (Liverpool) wheat prices (gold dollars per bushel) were collected from Harley (1980).[9] Development of the rail system was represented by the total kilometres of rail track in Russia, which was taken from Mitchell (1992). Russian population figures and the total size of the livestock herd (cattle, horses and swine) were taken from the same source. Total income and implicit price deflators were taken from Gregory (1982). Shipments of wheat and rye were collected from Gregory (1980). Prices for these and related commodities were also taken from Gregory (1980).

Single-equation models of the determinants of Russian grain exports were considered for the period 1885–1913. Because of the relatively small number of observations available for analysis, the estimates were somewhat sensitive to the specification adopted. Thus, three alternative models (differing in their treatment of population and time-lags) are presented. Table 8.2 contains parameter estimates and summary statistics. The models are estimated in a linear-in-logarithms form such that parameter estimates correspond directly to elasticities. The estimates indicate that Russian grain exports during this period were significantly influenced by international (Liverpool) wheat prices. In particular, a strong positive effect on wheat exports is exhibited by the Liverpool price. Likewise, the results suggest that wheat exports were also significantly affected by domestic prices. Increases in the Odessa price, holding other variables constant, significantly decreased grain exports.

Several authors (see, for example, Timoshenko, 1932; Falkus, 1966) have noted that Russian grain exports during this period were significantly influenced by domestic supplies.[10] The importance of internal production regarding exports is confirmed by the results

Table 8.2. Regression parameter estimates for single-equation models of Tsarist Russian grain exports.

	Parameter estimates[a] (standard error)		
Variable	Model I	Model II	Model III
Intercept	14.5651	−2.1408	−1.8436
	(8.2195)*	(2.0743)	(2.2679)
International (Liverpool) price	3.4809	2.0396	2.0278
	(1.1102)**	(0.6280)**	(0.6452)**
Domestic (Odessa) price	−3.1784	−2.4769	−2.3429
	(0.8827)**	(0.5410)**	(0.6578)**
Internal production	0.7478	0.6404	0.5997
	(0.3864)*	(0.2784)**	(0.3052)*
Railway development (km track)	3.2817	0.5860	0.4350
	(1.6142)**	(0.2087)**	(0.4516)
Population	−7.4953		
	(3.9241)*		
Livestock herd	−2.0217		
	(1.9727)		
Income			0.2896
			(0.7622)
R^2	0.5905	0.5863	0.5900
White's χ^2 specification test	14.7688	10.5989	14.2644
[p-values]	[0.6121]	[0.7172]	[0.8168]

[a] Model I evaluates quantity variables in absolute terms while Models II and III evaluate quantity variables in per capita terms, thus omitting population as a regressor. Domestic production is for the current year in Model I and for the preceding year in Models II and III.

*: statistical significance at the $\alpha = 0.1$ level; **: statistical significance at the 0.05 level.

presented in Table 8.2. Increases in domestic production significantly increased exports. In particular, the results suggest that a doubling of domestic production would have led to 60–75% more exports.

Development of the domestic rail transport infrastructure is revealed to have had an important impact on Russian grain exports. In two of the three models, development of the railway (increases in kilometres of track) significantly increased grain exports. These results confirm contentions (see, for example, Timoshenko, 1932; Falkus, 1966; Metzer, 1974; Morgan, 1979) that the growth of Russian exports was significantly stimulated by developments in the domestic transportation sector that allowed grain to be moved to port areas more easily as well as providing direct overland routes for exports to Western Europe.

Population was allowed to enter one model directly rather than as a factor used to normalize quantity variables by placing them in per capita terms. As expected, increases in the Russian population significantly decreased grain exports, suggesting that domestic demand was stimulated by the increased population. Because significant quantities of grain were (and are) used to feed livestock, one might expect increases in the livestock herd to decrease grain exports. Although a negative effect was revealed for the livestock herd, the effect was not statistically different from zero. Finally, per capita income was included and was not found significantly to influence grain exports.

In all, the results indicate that the Russian agricultural sector was well integrated with the international grain trade. Grain and wheat exports were shown to have been significantly affected by international and domestic prices. Development of the rail system in Tsarist Russia appears to have been an important factor affecting grain exports and shipments of wheat.

4. Implications for Modern Reforms?

The preceding section demonstrated that, during the Tsarist period, Russia possessed a comparative advantage in producing and exporting grain products and, in particular, wheat. With the breakup of the former Soviet Union and the movement to a market-orientated economy, such historical patterns of comparative advantage raise the question of whether modern Russia may someday again be an important wheat exporter. Of course, the pace of reforms following the collapse of the former Soviet Union has been slow and remains incomplete. This is especially true for agriculture, where much of the asset base and production and marketing infrastructure remains state-controlled (Goodwin *et al.*, 1996; USDA–ERS, 1997). Furthermore, inferences regarding possible patterns of comparative advantage in the post-reform period based upon trade patterns 100 years earlier, while interesting, are, at best, very tenuous.

In an attempt to evaluate the modern Russian wheat trade, we estimated a simple fixed-effects model of grain imports in the region for the post-reform period. Production and import figures for wheat, maize, barley, grain sorghum, and oats were collected from US Department of Agriculture (USDA) sources. Corresponding import prices were represented using unit values calculated from US export figures. Data were available for the period 1991–1994 for Armenia, Azerbaijan, Belorussia, Georgia, Kazakhstan, Kirgizia, Moldavia, Russia, Tajikistan, Turkmenistan, Ukraine and Uzbekistan. Gross domestic product indices for each republic were collected from Karasik (1996).

The time-series span of data available for analysis is extremely limited, making inferences fragile. To overcome this limitation, cross-sectional pooling was conducted. Wheat imports from individual sources (i.e. countries of origin) were collected.[11] Such an approach implicitly assumes that former Soviet Union imports from each source country respond to exogenous shocks in an identical manner. Fixed effects (i.e. cross-sectional dummy variables) were included for each cross-sectional unit to allow for fixed differences. For the 4 years of data available for the period following the collapse of the former Soviet Union, the data were pooled across former republics and across individual grain commodities. Again, this approach assumes that price, yield and income responses are identical for the alternative republics and commodities and that any differences among cross-sectional units (i.e. import sources) can be captured by fixed effects.

Table 8.3 contains parameter estimates and summary statistics for the model of the former Soviet Union republics' grain imports. Imports do not appear to respond to prices significantly. However, imports are quite responsive to income shocks. In particular, an income elasticity for grain imports of 0.76 is revealed. The results suggest that yield improvements would be expected to decrease grain imports, although this effect is not statistically significant.

In general, grain imports appear to be significantly more responsive to exogenous shocks in the pre-reform period than in the post-reform period. To examine how this responsiveness may have varied over time, the pre-reform period was divided into seven subperiods and price elasticities were estimated using the cross-sectional data for each subperiod. Figure 8.11 illustrates the estimated elasticities and standard deviations of the estimates. The elasticity estimates were significantly negative and large in magnitude during the 1960s, a period for which Russian imports were small relative to later years. However, as Russian grain imports expanded during the 1970s, elasticity estimates were much closer to zero. This period was characterized by widespread use of insulating trade policies that separated domestic markets from world prices (Grennes *et al.*, 1978).

As noted, both models imply that increases in income and decreases in domestic yields will increase grain imports. To gauge the

Table 8.3. Regression parameter estimates for fixed-effects model of former Soviet Union republics' grain imports.

Variable	Model of post-reform former Soviet Union republics' grain imports (standard error)
Price	−1.0360
	(1.2491)
Income (GNP)	0.7554
	(0.3241)**
Yield	−0.1348
	(0.2225)
R^2	0.6593

GNP: gross national product.
**: statistical significance at the $\alpha = 0.05$ level.

effects of yield and income changes on imports, two simple simulations were considered. In the first, a 2.5% annual growth rate of GDP over the 15 years following 1994 was considered. In the second, steady yield increases (3.2% per year), which would bring Russian wheat yields up to the 1991–1994 US average wheat yield (2.5 tonnes per ha) over this 15-year period, were considered. Other variables were held at their 1994 levels. Figure 8.12 presents the dynamic responses implied by the simulations. The results suggest that modest effects on imports would be likely to be realized from both income and yield changes.

In all, these results suggest that Russian grain trade over the pre- and post-reform periods was responsive to domestic market conditions but was not particularly sensitive to international market prices. A connection between Russian grain trade during the Tsarist period and

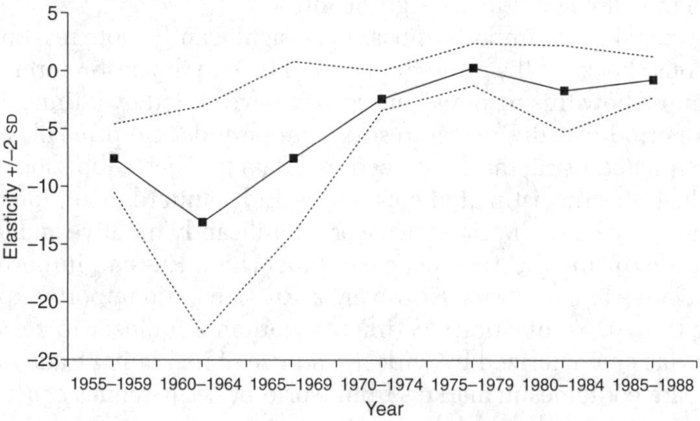

Fig. 8.11. Price elasticity of Russian wheat imports. Source: USDA–ERS, 1997.

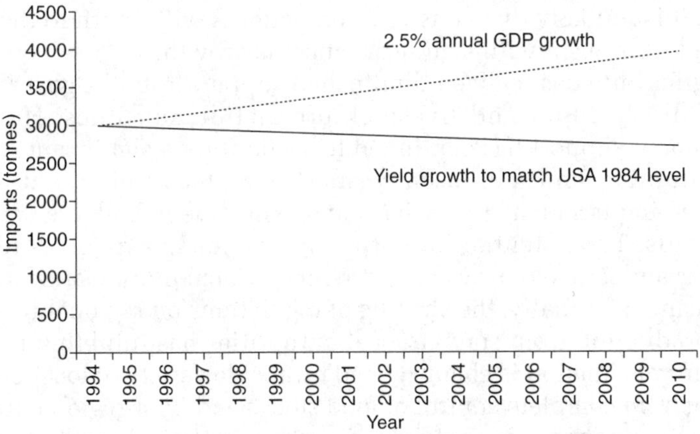

Fig. 8.12. Simulated effects of yield and income growth on Russian wheat imports. Source: USDA–ERS, 1997.

modern patterns of grain imports by Russia is difficult to make. However, one may note that linkages with international market conditions were stronger during the Tsarist period than appears to have been the case in modern times. Models estimated with modern data suggest that it is unlikely that even substantial increases in yields will lead to significant grain exports from countries of the former Soviet Union.

5. Concluding Remarks

This chapter discusses policy reforms and changes in the structure of Russian agriculture that have occurred since the breakup of the former Soviet Union. For the most part, reforms in the agricultural sector have been modest and slow to occur in most regards. The large-scale collective and state farms that characterized Soviet agriculture are, for the most part, still operating much as they did before reforms. These large farms account for the largest share of grain production, although private production is becoming increasingly important for many other commodities. Significant decreases in real income have brought about shifts in consumption patterns, many of which have important implications for grain production and trade. Consumption of most food commodities has fallen, though decreases are especially significant for livestock products. Because the livestock sector was formerly heavily dependent upon imported feed grains, decreases in livestock inventories have corresponded to greatly diminished grain imports. Because consumption of livestock products was kept artificially high through production and consumption policies during the 1970s and

1980s, it is unlikely that consumption patterns will return to their pre-reform levels, even with significant income growth.

Agriculture has realized diminished support from the government, especially in input and livestock production subsidies. However, government support has continued to account for a significant share of agricultural revenues in recent years. The high cost of inputs such as fertilizer and farm machinery has led to a decline in both area cropped and yields. The potential for output and yields to expand as reforms progress and farms to have access to international input markets should be recognized. Finally, the shifting of regulations on regional trade and food production from state to local authorities has inhibited reforms. The current situation is characterized by a wide variety of local policies, ranging from complete control of food stocks and inter-regional trade by oblast authorities to cases of essentially free trade and production.

Recognizing the general dearth of available data on post-reform market conditions, we summarize results from an empirical analysis of wheat trade during the last period of free-market conditions in Russia. Between 1870 and 1913, Russia was the world's largest producer and exporter of wheat. Recent research has presented two competing views of Russian agriculture during the Tsarist period. The first view, summarized by Gerschenkron, stresses the 'backwardness' of Tsarist Russia, especially its agriculture. This literature views Tsarist Russian agriculture as primarily structured around peasant producers who were not integrated with domestic and international commercial agriculture and trade. A second strand acknowledges some differences in Russian institutions, such as post-emancipation restrictions on peasants, but finds that economic agents in Russia responded to market conditions in the same general way as their contemporaries in the West. Our results are consistent with the second view of Russian agriculture. Empirical analysis of grain and wheat trade reveal that exports were very responsive to domestic (Odessa) and international (Liverpool) prices. In addition, grain trade was shown to have been positively stimulated by the development of railways. Finally, grain exports were shown to have been sensitive to domestic yield and production shocks. Large harvests appear to have led to increased exports.

Modern patterns of Russian grain trade are also considered in this analysis. Since 1971, Russia has been a large importer of wheat and other grains. Imports are shown to be only weakly related to international prices. However, the results suggest that income may be an important factor affecting Russian imports. A simple simulation suggests that even large increases in yields would not be likely to lead to significant decreases in wheat imports, much less to a trade reversal whereby Russia again begins to export significant quantities of wheat.

As market reforms in Russia progress, it will be of interest to carefully monitor grain production and trade. Current reforms in the agricultural sector have been modest. Private ownership of agricultural assets remains very limited and current reforms in agriculture cannot be assumed to be reflective of a free-market environment. Whether Russia will be able to regain its role as a prominent wheat exporter in the near future is conditional on more fundamental reform of agriculture. However, results presented in this analysis do not suggest that such an outcome is likely without further policy changes.

Notes

1. Material in this section draws heavily from discussions presented by OECD (1995); Serova and Melyukhina (1995); and von Braun *et al.* (1996).
2. For example, Serova and Melyukhina (1995) note that more that 90% of the annual sales of tractors went to replace existing units written off as unusable on farms.
3. The calculated producer subsidy equivalents (PSE) of Liefert *et al.* (1996) depend heavily upon exchange rate assumptions. In particular, the exchange rate used to convert prices plays an important role in determining the PSE.
4. Prosterman *et al.* (1997) found that, of 213,624 land share owners who had received land share certificates, 190,863 leased their land shares to agricultural enterprises or private farms.
5. An evaluation of the success of privatization efforts by Barberis *et al.* (1996) revealed that those operations that underwent significant changes in management and operating practices have enjoyed considerably more success.
6. Timoshenko (1932, p. 477) noted that Liverpool prices were correlated closely with Russian wheat production during the Tsarist period. This correlation was much stronger than that which existed between Liverpool prices and American wheat production. Britain was the principal market for Russian grain during this period. Between 1871 and 1875, Russian exports accounted for nearly 27% of total British imports of wheat.
7. This is not to say that significant exports of grain from communist Russia did not occur. Timoshenko (1932, pp. 486–487) noted that exceptional crops in 1925/26 and 1926/27 resulted in significant grain exports from Russia, although the levels were significantly below those experienced during the Tsarist period.
8. A detailed discussion of the activities of early grain traders in exporting wheat from Russia is contained in Morgan (1979, pp. 24–41).
9. In the results that follow, the gold dollar prices were not deflated while the local Russian prices and income were deflated using the Russian implicit price deflator of Gregory (1980). Deflating the international prices using Gregory's deflator did not significantly influence the results. Likewise, deflation by the US consumer price index did not significantly alter the results.
10. Falkus (1966) argued that fluctuations in production deriving from yield shocks were the primary factor affecting Russian exports. The results presented here offer a significantly different view in that exports are seen to be equally sensitive to price changes, holding production fixed. Of course, prices and production are closely related and it may be difficult to separate their independent effects.

11. The exporting countries included Argentina, Australia, Austria, Belgium, Britain, Canada, China, Denmark, the Federal Republic of Germany, France, Hungary, Italy, Mongolia, Romania, Spain, Sweden, and the USA. In those cases where imports from a particular country were zero, the observation was not included in the analysis.

References

Barberis, N., Boycko, M., Shleifer, A. and Tsukanova, N. (1996) How does privatization work? Evidence from the Russian shops. *Journal of Political Economy* 104, 764–790.

DeMasi, P. and Koen, V. (1996) Relative price convergence in Russia. *IMF Staff Papers* 43, 97–122.

Dobozi, I. and Pohl, G. (1995) Real output decline in transition economies – forget GDP, try power consumption data. *Transition* 6, 1–2.

Falkus, M.E. (1966) Russia and the international wheat trade, 1861–1914. *Economica* 33, 416–429.

Gatrell, P. (1986) *The Tsarist Economy 1850–1917*. St Martin's, New York, USA.

Gerschenkron, A. (1965) Agrarian policies and industrialization: Russia, 1861–1917. In: *Cambridge Economic History of Europe,* Vol. 6, Part II. Cambridge University Press, Cambridge, UK.

Goodwin, B. and Grennes, T. (1998) Tsarist Russia and the world wheat market. *Explorations in Economic History* 35, 405–430.

Goodwin, B., Grennes, T. and Leetmaa, S. (1996) Agricultural reform in Russia. *Choices*, Third Quarter, 25–28.

Goodwin, B., Grennes, T. and McCurdy, C. (1998) Spatial price dynamics and integration in Russian food markets. *Journal of Policy Reform* 3(2), 157–193.

Gregory, P. (1980) Grain marketings and peasant consumption, Russia 1885–1913. *Explorations in Economic History* 17, 135–164.

Gregory, P. (1982) *Russian National Income: 1885–1913*. Cambridge University Press, Cambridge, UK.

Gregory, P. (1994) *Before Command: An Economic History of Russia From Emancipation to the First Five Year Plan*. Princeton University Press, Princeton, New Jersey, USA.

Grennes, T., Johnson, P. and Thursby, M. (1978) *The Economics of World Grain Trade*. Praeger, New York, USA.

Harley, C.K. (1980) Transportation, world wheat trade, and the Kuznets cycle, 1850–1913. *Explorations in Economic History* 17, 218–250.

Jones, J.R., Li, S.L., Devadoss, S. and Fedane, C.J. (1996) The former Soviet Union and the world wheat economy. *American Journal of Agricultural Economics* 78, 869–878.

Kahan, A. (1973) Note on serfdom in western and eastern Europe. *Journal of Economic History* 33, 86–99.

Karasik, T.W. (1996) *Russia and Eurasia: Facts and Figures Annual*. Academic International Press, Gulf Breeze, Florida, USA.

Latham, A.J. and Neal, L. (1983) The international market in rice and wheat, 1868–1914. *Economic History Review*, second series, 36, 260–280.

Leetmaa, S., Grennes, T. and Goodwin, B. (1997) Effects of market reforms in the former Soviet Union on world grain trade: results from a multi-market wheat trade model. Unpublished manuscript, January, North Carolina State University, Raleigh, North Carolina, USA.

Liefert, W.M., Sedik, D.J., Koopman, R.B., Serova, E. and Melyukhina, O. (1996) Producer subsidy equivalents for Russian agriculture: estimation and interpretation. *American Journal of Agricultural Economics* 78 (August), 792–798.

McCurdy, C., Goodwin, B. and Grennes, T. (1997) Food expenditure in Russia: analysis from the first several years of reform. Unpublished manuscript, March, Department of Agricultural and Resource Economics, North Carolina State University, Raleigh, North Carolina, USA.

Metzer, J. (1974) Railroad development and market integration. *Journal of Economic History* 34, 529–550.

Mitchell, B.R. (1992) *International Historical Statistics: Europe, 1750–1988.* Stockton Press, New York, USA.

Morgan, D. (1979) *Merchants of Grain.* Viking, New York, USA.

OECD (Organization for Economic Cooperation and Development) (1995) *Agricultural Policies, Markets, and Trade in the Central and Eastern European Countries, Selected New Independent States, Mongolia, and China; Monitoring and Outlook, 1995.* OECD, Paris, France.

O'Rourke, K. and Williamson, J.G. (1994) Late nineteenth century Anglo-American factor price convergence: were Heckscher and Ohlin right? *Journal of Economic History* 54, 892–916.

Prosterman, R.L., Mitchell, R.G. and Rorem, B.J. (1997) *Prospects for Peasant Farming in Russia.* Report on Foreign Aid and Development No. 92, Rural Development Institute, University of Washington, Seattle, Washington, USA.

Rothstein, M. (1960) America in the international rivalry for the British wheat market, 1860–1914. *Mississippi Valley Historical Review* 46, 401–418.

Serova, E. and Melyukhina, O. (1995) *Finance Subsidies and Pricing in the Russian Food and Agricultural Sector in Transition.* No. 2 in series on The Russian Food Economy in Transition, Institut für Ernährungswirtschaft and Ernährungspolitik, Kiel, Germany.

Stern, R. (1960) A century of food exports. *Kyklos* 13, 44–61.

Suvorov, A.V. (1997) System of forecasting the structure of the population's expenditures. Problems of forecasting (in Russian). Unpublished manuscript, Moscow, Russia.

tho Seeth, H. and von Braun, J. (1995) Russlands Nahrungsmittelkonsum: kurzfristige Wirkungen der Reformen und langfristige Perspektiven. *Agrarwirtschaft* 44, 305–318.

Timoshenko, V.P. (1932) *Agricultural Russia and the Wheat Problem.* Food Research Institute, Stanford, California, USA.

Tyers, R. (1994) *Economic Reform in Europe and the Former Soviet Union: Implications for International Food Markets.* Research Report 99, International Food Policy Research Institute, Washington DC, USA.

USDA–ERS (US Department of Agriculture, Economic Research Service) (1997) Unpublished data collected from Cornell University Mann Library Internet site: *usda.mannlib.cornell.edu/data-sets.*

USDA–FAS (US Department of Agriculture, Foreign Agricultural Service) (1997) Unpublished data collected from Internet site: *www.fas.usda.gov.*

Veblen, T. (1892) The price of wheat since 1867. *Journal of Political Economy* 1, 68–103.

von Braun, J., Serova, E., tho Seeth, H. and Melyukhina, O. (1996) *Russia's Food Economy in Transition: Current Policy Issues and the Long-Term Outlook.* Discussion Paper No. 18, International Food Policy Research Institute, Washington DC, USA.

Wädekin, K.E. (1993/94) Agrarpolitik in Russland zur Wende. *Osteuropa* 44, 513–530.

III

The GATT Process: Implications for World Wheat Exports

9

Emerging Differences in State Grain Trading: Australia and Canada

Colin A. Carter[1] and William W. Wilson[2]

[1]*Department of Agricultural and Resource Economics, University of California–Davis, USA;*
[2]*Department of Agricultural Economics, North Dakota State University, Fargo, USA*

1. Introduction

The Australian Wheat Board (AWB) and Canadian Wheat Board (CWB) have attracted attention recently because they are two of the largest state trading enterprises (STEs) engaged in agricultural trade (US General Accounting Office, 1995). Over the past 10 years, the AWB and CWB have accounted for 8% and 22% of the world wheat trade respectively,[1] and the CWB is perhaps the world's largest grain merchant. STEs are expected to come under increased scrutiny under the new World Trade Organization (Dixit and Josling, 1997), partly because of the perception in the USA that the AWB and CWB engage in non-transparent pricing practices and 'unfair' trade practices (Chadwick, 1992). The US General Accounting Office (1992) investigated the AWB and CWB and found they were both non-competitive sellers due to unfair pricing, pooling and government underwriting.

The AWB and CWB have traditionally been viewed as nearly sister agencies. Among major STEs in the world market, these two agencies historically had similar characteristics including: price pooling, cost pooling, export sales monopolies, monopoly powers within domestic markets, grain quality control, and government underwriting of initial producer prices and export credit. During the past 6 years, similarities between the AWB and CWB have begun to diminish and the importance of their differences is becoming increasingly apparent. This is particularly true since the early 1990s, though emergence of the dichotomy

All dollars are US dollars, unless otherwise stated.

began in the 1980s. AWB reforms are far ahead of those in Canada and, compared with Canada, the Australian system is now more responsive to changing world market conditions. The AWB is more commercially orientated than the CWB and less dependent on government underwriting.

In addition to the international criticism mentioned above, these agencies have also come under increased public scrutiny within their own countries. In Australia, pressure for reform started outside the AWB during the early 1980s, and this ultimately resulted in a deregulation process (Watson, 1984). Basically, the AWB and organized interests in the wheat industry lost the battle over deregulation. In Canada the level of public inquiry has been half-hearted. This was partly due to generous government subsidies (such as transportation subsidies), which reduced any pressure for change. However, price and income subsidies are coming off now for Canadian farmers and they have become more interested in increasing domestic marketing efficiencies. In addition, implementation of the 1989 Canadian–US free trade agreement (CUSTA) has added domestic pressure for reform of the CWB.

The purpose of this chapter is to identify major emerging differences between the AWB and CWB and to explore potential explanations (hypotheses) for these dissimilarities. We also discuss likely future changes and impacts on the functioning of the world grain market. A major point is that reform of institutional design and legislative changes have given rise to emerging differences in key aspects of the marketing system and performance. Theoretical benefits and costs of state trading are discussed in the following section. Section 3 reviews the empirical evidence on these agencies' performance, whilst the following two sections identify some of the important differences and explore alternative explanations. The final section summarizes the chapter and identifies some possible explanations.[2]

2. Theoretical Benefits/Costs of State Trading Enterprises

Some history

Brenner (1987) argues there are two potential economic explanations for state-owned enterprises: economies of scale and externalities. However, he fails to find empirical support for any causal relationship between economies of scale and state ownership, or between externalities and state ownership. Instead, he finds that *crises* (e.g. wars, economic disasters) often precipitate some form of state ownership. The *crises* theory clearly applies to the establishment of the AWB and CWB: the two world wars and the great depression were crucial events leading to the creation of these two STEs. The CWB was first set up as a 1-year temporary organization in 1919, in response to the British government's cornering of the Winnipeg wheat futures market and the closing of that futures market. During World War II, the demand for grain raised prices, and in 1943 the CWB was made compulsory to help control inflation. The CWB was retained after the war because most of Canada's wheat was exported to Britain under a bilateral agreement, and the CWB made administration of the agreement much simpler (Fowke, 1957). In the case of the AWB, it was originally established as a compulsory wartime pool from 1915 to 1921 (Whitwell and Sydenham, 1991). The AWB was subsequently re-established in 1939, during World War II. After the war, the Australian Wheat Industry Stabilization Act was passed (in 1948). It lasted for 5 years and it established a more permanent AWB. The 1948 Act was succeeded by seven similar acts, each with a 5-year lifespan. The latest Wheat Marketing Act of 1989 does not have a fixed lifespan.

Rotstein (1984) convincingly argues that the rationale for CWB creation was the same as for other Canadian public corporations, a response to major forces from outside the sector that are, to a large extent, uncontrollable. The Liberal government in the late 1930s, and early war years, was committed to terminating the CWB in favour of the open market but external forces – the culmination of the depression effects and the 'extraordinary issues of the war effort' – led to the creation of the Board (Rotstein, 1984).

Benefits and costs

The theoretical rationale that has been offered as justification for the AWB and CWB (i.e. single-desk selling) includes the following (Ryan, 1994; Booz, Allen and Hamilton, 1995; CWB, 1995):

- Exploit market power through price discrimination and thus increase revenue.
- Provide farmers with a form of risk management through price pooling.
- Develop niche markets and new customers through market development.
- Negotiate price premiums with single-desk buyers.
- Exploit economies of scale associated with marketing.

With the exception of the market power argument, most of these potential benefits could be supplied as efficiently by the private grain trade. Therefore, the market power argument is the only point that deserves serious consideration as the others are largely spurious. The market power argument is based on the premise that the international grain market is imperfectly competitive and that markets can be segmented (i.e. there is little or no arbitrage between markets). The AWB and CWB (Ryan, 1994; CWB, 1995) argue that under these conditions they are able to price discriminate by charging relatively higher prices in those markets that are less price-elastic and lower prices in markets that are more price-elastic. If demand responds differently across these (separate) markets, then the alternative demand relationships can be exploited by the STE.

The AWB and CWB have recently argued (e.g. Ryan, 1994) that the US/European Union (EU) wheat trade war has created the perfect price discrimination opportunity for STEs and justifies their continuance. The USA and the EU have been running targeted export subsidy programmes for about 10 years now and these programmes segment the world market into two pieces: the 'subsidized' and 'non-subsidized' markets. The law of one price is violated when comparing subsidized with non-subsidized prices. It is claimed by the AWB and CWB that the trade war has resulted in a whole 'schedule' of prices across importing nations. In essence they argue the law of one price does not even hold for marginal sales within the subsidized markets.

Any additional revenue advantage associated with single-desk selling due to market power has to be weighed against the costs of having a single-desk arrangement in place (Industry Commission, 1991). Lack of competitive discipline within Australia and Canada may mean the costs of marketing grain are higher than would otherwise be the case. In addition, certain practices such as cost pooling and the ideological goal of equity are not conducive to cost minimization.

The current debate over STEs centres on comparing the financial advantages of having a single desk against the costs of having a single desk. With a monopolist in place, the costs typically arise from a general lack of competitive discipline in handling/transport and price distortions due to pooling. Price distortions result in allocative (economic) inefficiency. It is expected that, under a price-pooling arrangement, a farm could remain technically efficient but would be most likely to exhibit allocative inefficiency.

In either Canada or Australia, once the grain gets to the port, the exporting board sells into a competitive market. It is therefore doubtful if the boards overcharge offshore customers as they claim. It is also questionable whether they undercut offshore prices to the degree some critics claim. Most of the economic impact of the STEs is domestic and we expect the domestic welfare costs to be significant.

3. Empirical Evidence on State Trading Performance

Australia: wheat

The theory of the benefits and costs of single-desk selling in wheat has not been confronted with much empirical evidence. This topic has been debated more vigorously in Australia compared with Canada, and thus there has been relatively more work done in Australia on this question. The Australian Industries Assistance Commission (IAC) (now the Industry Commission) reviewed the AWB every 5 years and consistently doubted the ability of the AWB to extract higher prices in world wheat markets than would otherwise be obtainable. The following quotation from the Industries Assistance Commission (1988) illustrates their scepticism of the net benefits of single-desk selling:

> Some wheat markets may provide a premium to Australia, not because of the sole export controller status of the AWB, but rather because they admit only limited quantities of Australian wheat. The Japanese market is widely recognized as such a market which traditionally pays relatively high prices for limited quantities of wheat imported from a variety of sources. Thus, this premium would be available irrespective of the number of sellers of Australian wheat.
>
> Nevertheless, it cannot be denied that, in some circumstances, the AWB may be able to extract price premiums for some (generally smaller) markets by restricting competitive access to them. Although the Commission considers that this ability is limited, it acknowledges that competition from multiple sellers of Australian wheat could result in some erosion of such premiums. However, to some extent, traders may also be able to specialize in servicing certain market niches and extract premiums.
>
> Even if some existing price premium were eroded by allowing competing exporters of Australian wheat, this would not necessarily imply a decrease in growers' returns. Additional competition between sellers could result in a decrease in marketing costs and an increased overall demand for Australian wheat, both of which could enhance growers' returns. More importantly, any potential decrease in premium income needs to be considered in relation to the potential gains that could result from allowing growers and users additional choice and flexibility in marketing wheat and to the impetus which liberalised marketing arrangements could provide in achieving reforms and associated cost savings in grain storage, handling and transport.
>
> (Industries Assistance Commission, 1988, p. 118).

Piggott (1992) agrees with the above IAC findings and he argues that, for the AWB, enhanced gains from any market power in the world wheat market are likely to be very small.

Ryan (1994) disagrees with the IAC and Piggott and suggests there are substantial benefits captured by the AWB due to price discrimination in the world wheat market. Ryan reports the results of an 'internal' AWB analysis of the benefits from price discrimination and he finds the benefits vary from year to year depending on the US Export Enhancement Program (EEP) and the targeting effect. On average, Ryan reports benefits of about $20 per tonne over 1987/88 to 1990/91 – years of very extensive use of EEP, which should have the effect of inflating these values absent of EEP. If market power is so significant, how do we explain why both the AWB and CWB sell a large percentage of their wheat exports to private trading companies and thus do not deal directly with the final importer?

Booz, Allen and Hamilton (1995) conducted a cost–benefit analysis of the single-desk selling of Australian wheat and their findings are somewhat ambivalent towards single-desk selling. Evidence of small benefits was found to be due to differentiated high service strategy, price premiums, market mix and freight advantages. The net benefit of the AWB was found to lie between −$1.31 per tonne and +$5.33 per tonne, or an average of $2.01 per tonne. Gross benefits were estimated at $0.12–$7.96 per tonne and were comprised of a premium price ($0.12–$0.31 per tonne), market mix (0–$3.25 per tonne), and pricing discipline (0–$4.40 per tonne). Estimated costs of the AWB were between $1.43 and $2.63 per tonne, calculated through benchmarking AWB costs against the US and Canadian equivalents. Overall, these results are generally inconclusive, but suggest a very slight advantage of single-desk selling of Australian wheat from a net benefit perspective.

Australia: barley

The EU is the world's largest exporter of barley (about 40% of the market), followed by Canada (25%) and Australia (20%). However, Australia produces a high-quality barley and it has a larger share of the world malting-barley market, compared with Canada and the EU.

South Australia and Victoria together produce approximately 60% of Australia's barley and these two states market their barley through a statutory marketing authority – the Australian Barley Board (ABB). The ABB controls the exportation of all barley from Victoria and all barley and oats from South Australia. The ABB is also permitted to market additional crops such as wheat, sorghum, maize, rye, oilseeds, peas, lupins, lentils and beans. There are three other state-level barley marketing boards in Australia, in addition to the ABB. Barley produced in Queensland is marketed through Grainco; the Grain Pool of Western Australia (WA) markets barley grown in West Australia; and New South Wales barley is channelled through the New South Wales Grains Board.

Boston Consulting Group (1995) analysed barley marketing issues facing Australia. They recommended deregulation of the state-level marketing boards in order to foster competition and introduce competitive discipline into the domestic market. Boston Consulting recommended against the creation of a national single desk for Australian barley.

Canada: barley

In a controversial decision, the CWB monopoly over barley sales into the USA was removed by the Canadian government for a short time in 1993. The Prairie Pools opposed this policy reform and succeeded in having the government order disallowed by a Canadian Court of Law. The Court restored the CWB's single-desk status in barley and the case was never appealed because there was a change in government shortly thereafter. Prior to the 1993 'continental' barley market, Gray *et al.* (1993) argued that a continental market would result in lower barley prices for Canadian farmers due to the elimination of the single desk. Carter (1993) argued the opposite – that barley prices would remain the same under a continental barley market, compared with the situation under the CWB's single desk. Clark (1995) studied the issue ex-post, testing for structural breaks in barley prices before and after the continental market, and his results supported Carter (1993). Clark concluded that CWB arguments suggesting that single-desk selling improves barley revenues need to be subject to greater public scrutiny.

Canada: wheat

A recent study (Kraft *et al.*, 1996) indicated that the CWB has been able to extract a premium of about $C13 per tonne and they attribute this premium to the discriminatory powers of a single seller. However, the price premiums found by the Kraft *et al.* report do not show up at the farm gate for the individual producer (Carter and Loyns, 1996). Furthermore, Kraft *et al.* (1996) fail to distinguish price premiums due to wheat quality or particular services (such as favourable credit terms and technical assistance) accompanying a sale, from those due to the exercise of monopoly power by a single-desk seller.

Carter and Loyns also studied recent developments in barley and oats and found that CWB claims of market power in barley have not been confirmed. The USA has turned out to be an important market for barley and oats, contrary to earlier CWB assertions. They found that the outcome in the oats market is what basic economics would predict about deregulating an over-regulated market.

Carter and Loyns (1996) examined US–Canadian farm gate returns to wheat and barley and found no evidence of any CWB price premium. This is no surprise because Canadian grain must be priced competitively in world markets, and the majority of Canadian wheat sales are into markets where price is more important than quality. Even if the CWB could draw out premiums, would they offset the additional cost to the system? Carter and Loyns found they did not.

The EEP factor and other considerations

As mentioned above, the AWB (Ryan, 1994) and CWB (1995) have recently argued that the US EEP segments world markets and that a single-desk seller can take advantage of this opportunity for further price differentiation. Booz, Allen and Hamilton (1995) suggest that, without EEP, the single-desk status of the AWB would be much more difficult to justify. The EEP argument put forth by the AWB and CWB overlooks the fact that most markets are eligible for EEP, leaving few high-priced 'non-subsidized' markets. Using International Wheat Council data, Booz, Allen and Hamilton (1995) report that over 60% of CWB wheat sales are made into bulk (i.e. low-priced) markets. Both the AWB and CWB sell the majority of their wheat into markets where price is more important than quality. The top ten wheat markets for the AWB and CWB are reported in Table 9.1. The only significant non-EEP markets for wheat are Japan, South Korea, the UK and parts of Latin America. It therefore appears that the AWB and CWB sell (at most) only about 20% of their wheat into non-EEP markets.

Price premiums may also be due to factors other than the existence of market power. For example, Canadian grain quality standards and certification are usually argued to add value to Canadian grain. Such premiums would also be available to private sellers and do not require a monopoly seller in order to be realized (Industries Assistance Commission, 1988; Piggott, 1992).

The theoretical case for single-desk selling is not unlike the 'new trade theory', which suggests the possibility that government intervention in trade may be in the national interest. However, the empirical validity of the 'new trade theory' is questionable because it is virtually impossible to formulate useful interventionist policies given the

Table 9.1. AWB and CWB wheat export by destination (average: 1982/83 to 1991/92).

Australia		Canada	
Importer	Average market share (%)	Importer	Average market share (%)
Egypt	16.1	Former Soviet Union	26.5
China	13.7	China	21.9
Iran	11.8	Japan	7.1
Japan	8.7	Brazil	4.4
Former Soviet Union	8.4	Cuba	4.1
Iraq	7.6	Algeria	2.8
Indonesia	5.8	Iran	2.8
South Korea	4.5	UK	2.8
Pakistan	1.8	Iraq	2.5
Bangladesh	1.3	South Korea	2.3
Other	20.2	Other	22.8

Source: Canada Grains Council, 1994.

empirical difficulties in modelling imperfect markets (Krugman, 1987; Baldwin, 1992). Policy makers cannot estimate import demand elasticities without great uncertainty and, given these empirical difficulties, formulating optimal trade policies could do more harm than good. The Krugman–Baldwin critique of the new trade theory clearly applies to STEs for agricultural products.

As explained above, the AWB and CWB claim there is an entire schedule of prices across markets due to EEP. The non-EEP market is very small and whether or not the law of one price holds within those markets is not worth worrying about. In the EEP markets, it is more plausible to argue that the law of one price holds for marginal sales. This view is contrary to the AWB and CWB but it is supported by two previous studies. In an analysis of the 1980 US grain embargo against the USSR, the US Department of Agriculture (USDA, 1986) found that grain is basically fungible and thus the embargo had little impact on the USSR and little impact on world prices and trade volumes. The embargo study implies that the world grain market is efficiently arbitraged. Goodwin (1992) studied wheat prices in five markets and found that wheat prices in spatially separated markets are closely linked and adhere to the law of one price.

4. Institutional and Legislative Changes Providing Impetus for Emerging Differences

As discussed previously (section 2), the AWB and CWB evolved similarly as a result of the two world wars and the great depression in between the wars. Prior to 1989, the underlying legislation governing these STEs was quite similar, though there were unique aspects of each country's system. Currently, there are several important differences in the governing legislation and institutional organization that have given rise to important changes in strategies and emerging differences in these respective STEs. These differences are described briefly below.

Legislative differences and changes

Sunset clause

One of the unique differences is that the legislative authority for the AWB had always been subject to a sunset clause. The fact that the AWB had to succumb to a 5-year review by the political process and the Industry Commission had an important influence on the organization. This clause was removed in 1989 and the current legislation is open-ended. In contrast, the CWB has rarely been under review, though examination of its operations has escalated in recent years in a less formal way.

Australian grain marketing deregulation

The most important differences emerged with the 1989 Wheat Marketing Act in Australia, which began the process of deregulation and changes that are described below. There were three important features of this legislation: (i) the domestic market was deregulated; (ii) the Wheat Industry Fund (WIF) was introduced; and (iii) the AWB was allowed to trade other grains. Other reforms included a change in the Guaranteed Minimum Price (GMP) scheme from a guaranteed price floor per tonne to a government underwriting on AWB borrowings. The government also changed the AWB's explicit objective to that of maximization of producer (farm gate) returns, as opposed to free-on-board (f.o.b.) values. A subsequent legislative amendment in 1992 allowed the AWB to participate in value-added activities and extended underwriting of AWB borrowing until 1999.

Domestic market deregulation was introduced in Australia to allow for competitive pressures and provide alternatives to growers/end-users in the domestic distribution and pricing of wheat. However, the WIF is unique and was an important by-product of other changes. The elimination of the GMP and the placing of a time limit on the government's willingness to underwrite AWB borrowing meant that the AWB had to establish a capital base. To that end the WIF was established. A 2% (minimum) mandatory levy was established on farm-gate prices and the proceeds are to be used ultimately in making investments to develop a capital base to fund trading activities and finance AWB purchases of wheat.

In contrast, there have been few fundamental changes in the CWB Act since its passage in 1967. In 1974 a 'dual' domestic feed grain market was created in Canada, with open market purchases and sales of feed wheat, oats and barley domestically in competition with the CWB. However, the CWB retained exclusive access to the international market.

Federal government underwriting

An important difference between these two systems is the level of guarantees provided by the governments. The level of guarantee has been greater in Canada than Australia. In fact, in early years the GMP in Australia was as low as 40% of the expected pool returns, and was announced only after the crop was planted (just before harvest). In contrast, the initial payment guarantee provided by the government of Canada has been nearly 90% of the total payment, and was (until recently) normally announced prior to planting.

The existence and level of underwriting by the governments have had very important implications for trading operations. First, underwriting facilitates borrowing at more attractive rates than would otherwise be available.[3] Second, these guarantees have an implicit option value, and therefore an implicit subsidy, which varies with the level of guarantees relative to the market (Wilson, 1995) – results suggest this is much greater for Canada than for Australia. Third, a high guarantee relative to the market precludes the need to be active in pursuing other forward price risk management opportunities (i.e. futures, options and swaps) that have become essential for other firms in the grain business. Finally, the level of the guarantee is critical because of cross-border competition (and competition from alternative domestic feed uses) in the case of Canada. If the guarantee (i.e. initial payment) is much lower than US border (spot) prices, incentives to bypass the CWB and sell direct in the USA escalate, effectively diminishing control of stocks by the CWB.[4]

The effect of this difference was to force the AWB into more overt risk-management strategies encompassing direct hedges, options and swaps. In contrast, the CWB has been involved minimally and only very indirectly in these mechanisms.

Organization structure

A third major difference governing these two STEs is their organizational structure. CWB commissioners are appointed for life without the discipline of a board of directors or accountability to shareholders. It should be noted that the CWB does have a Producer Advisory Committee elected by farmers to represent their views, but this is a committee without authority over CWB operations. This organizational structure continues despite a 1990 review panel recommendation to reorganize the structure of the CWB to be a 'modern corporate structure' with an appointed chair and board of directors, along with a professional president and chief executive officer. The board of directors would represent a broad cross-section of interests and would focus on longer-term planning, and so on.

In contrast, the AWB is organized with a chairman, a board of directors and professional staff to conduct business functions. The composition of the board of directors was changed in the Wheat Marketing Act of 1989 to include a diverse set of individuals with particular expertise. Further, the chairman reports to the board of directors and does not hold a lifetime position.

5. Emerging Differences

The differences described above may appear subtle but have provided much of the impetus to the changes that have occurred between these two STEs. It is also important to recognize that there are some key system differences, which may also contribute to the observed marketing function differences. These include, but are not limited to: market structure and regulatory environment of contiguous marketing functions (transport, handling); controls over the handling system (tariffs in Canada versus bilateral contractual relations in Australia) and rail freight allocation; and the role and function of accredited exporters.

Several emerging differences between the AWB and CWB are discussed below along with their institutional background. These include: grower marketing alternatives, risk management (of forward sales), vertical coordination and control, marketing costs, dual marketing system and trading non-board grains, and vertical integration (value-added).

Grower marketing alternatives

Price pooling with guaranteed initial payments has provided much of the justification for each of these STEs. Indeed, one of the positive benefits experienced with the 'Board of Grain Supervisers' in 1917 (which preceded the formulation of the CWB) was that of price pooling (CWB, undated, p. 2). Though the original purposes in each country were similar, their evolution has differed.

In Australia the mechanism has evolved since 1948. In 1979 the GMP was established as a means of guaranteeing producer returns. Originally, the GMP reflected a 3-year moving average of returns, including those estimated for the current season, the purpose being to provide some degree of temporal stability in growers' incomes. Just prior to harvest, a preliminary GMP was announced for producers (thus precluding signals from affecting production decisions). The GMP was underwritten by the Commonwealth and payouts were only necessary when prices fell sharply within the marketing year. Underwriting allowed an advance payment scheme to develop. An important result was that borrowing costs of the AWB were reduced by the guarantee of the GMP. Without payment guarantees, interest costs would be greater and/or inventories may be valued at a lower level.

The GMP was eliminated in 1989 and this led to numerous subsequent changes in the Australian marketing system. One was pressure to develop alternative grower marketing alternatives. This came from growers themselves, and was probably fostered by increased competitive pressures (offerings) from the newly emerged private grain companies for domestic marketing. As a result, growers were offered numerous alternatives including: pooled prices without GMP; fixed price contracts; minimum price contracts; and direct hedging alternatives using either futures or options in wheat and/or in Australian dollars. Fundamentally, the AWB took the view that 'Growers are themselves demanding more opportunity to make pricing decisions and to manage their own risks ...' (Condon, 1991, p. 3).

In general, the number of alternatives to growers in Canada has been more restricted in contrast to those in Australia. The traditional pricing mechanisms using initial, interim and final payments continue to be the primary alternatives. In recent years other options have been added, including price projections and bonuses paid for contract fulfilment. However, more advanced grower marketing alternatives using options and other risk management techniques have not been offered.

The CWB has also had a system of delivery quotas to regulate grower deliveries, but this has changed. In particular, a system of contracting has been introduced that is now used to regulate flows into the system.

A common theme in both countries is the increase in number of segregations used for marketing, and therefore pooling, purposes. The increase in the number of segregations is being driven by international competitive pressures and buyer demands coinciding with their own increase in sophistication. In Australia, the number of segregations has increased from two for wheat in 1980 to 36 in 1994. The same trend in Canada has occurred, but not as drastically. Ultimately, the increase in the number of segregations will undermine the concept of pooling. At the limit, a separate pool could be introduced for each buyer with unique specifications, resulting in numerous individual pools. The effect of this would be to diminish the validity/ability of providing a unique guarantee for each. Condon (1991, p. 4) conceded that ultimately the effect of increased numbers of segregations will break down the pooling system, and potentially that of a single-seller agency.

Risk management (of forward sales)

As a result of the elimination of the GMP, the AWB became active in futures for hedging purposes, options and swaps.[5] Alternatively, the CWB makes use of futures primarily for facilitating *ex pit* transactions with customers, as opposed to having a maintained hedging strategy that is translated back to individual growers. Interpretation of legislation governing the CWB may preclude their overt involvement in these mechanisms as much as may be necessary to offer growers a full array of alternatives; in contrast, the AWB had the legislation changed.

Vertical coordination and control

There are numerous aspects of vertical control within each marketing system. A common characteristic in recent years is the STEs striving to maintain and increase their control over other aspects of the vertical marketing system. Traditionally, these included variety controls, handling, shipping (goods wagon allocation) and use of accredited exporters. However, there appear to be several salient differences.

Traditionally these STEs have not owned assets, thereby precluding exertion of vertical control through ownership. The CWB has been able to exert tremendous control over other aspects of the system primarily through legislation and rules and regulations. Lacking legislative authority, the AWB pursued other alternatives such as longer-term bilateral contracts for both handling and shipping, and seeking shares of ownership of handling assets. In contrast, the CWB has sought uniform regulations in the form of maximum tariffs for handling, and has been able to depend on WGTA rates for shipping. In a sense, the CWB has sought the benefits of vertical coordination without extensive use of contractual relationships or ownership. Much of this control has been legitimized by appealing to the need for quality control of a single agency. In contrast, the AWB, as a result of loss of much of that control, is now trying to gain vertical market power in a more strategic commercial way. Longer-term contracts with individual handling agencies and shipping companies, and joint ventures (see below) in asset ownership are both components of this commercial strategy. In contrast, the 1990 Review Panel of the CWB recommended not to allow the CWB to become involved in these ventures.

Marketing costs

Both of these STEs suffer from relatively high marketing costs compared with those costs in countries with greater competitive pressures. In the recent Booz, Allen and Hamilton (1995) study they separate trading costs from other handling and shipping costs (pp. 49–55). Results illustrate that both the STEs' trading costs exceed those of US traders, noting that the AWB's were larger, even correcting for economies of scale. Similarly, the costs of moving grain from comparable producing regions to export were \$23, \$28 and \$43 per tonne respectively for the USA, Australia and Canada. Thus, in procuring marketing services, both countries have performed worse than the USA, with Canada experiencing the highest costs. Results also suggest that Australia's costs have declined (in real terms) during the past 4 years, as have those in the USA, but close examination of Canadian data suggests they have not.

Both countries are experiencing higher costs due in part to segregations being maintained within their systems and other regulations, as well as more difficult labour situations *vis à vis* other countries. A particular problem relates to cost pooling within the handling and shipping system, which is under pressure to change in each country. Already, one of the major sources of cost pooling in Canada (St Lawrence Seaway costs) was eliminated in 1995, though it was originally proposed for change in the mid-1980s. Cost pooling is also pervasive in Australian handling and has resulted in numerous inefficiencies. A benchmarking process has been initiated in Australia to compare costs of critical functions with those in competitor countries.

Dual marketing system and trading non-board grains

In 1989 the Australian domestic market became a dual market in which the AWB competes with private traders, handlers and processors. In addition, they were allowed to trade other grains, both domestically and offshore. The AWB remains highly competitive in these markets along with numerous other market channels that have emerged to exploit efficiencies. In addition, there is no evidence that the loss of the control of stocks domestically has hindered their ability to compete offshore.

In Canada, oats was removed from the CWB jurisdiction completely in 1989 and a dual market was not even considered. However, barley operates in a dual marketing system with domestic sales for feeding traded competitively, but offshore sales (including those to the USA) and domestic malting-barley sales are controlled exclusively by the CWB. A proposal was made and accepted to relax that control for trade within North America in 1993, but was subsequently rescinded. In recent debates about liberalizing wheat trade (at least in North America) the CWB has claimed its offshore programme absolutely could not survive without a domestic (including North America) monopoly as well.

An important issue is the control of stocks. In Australia the domestic market comprises a relatively small portion of the crop. Even so, more aggressive pricing and marketing alternatives became necessary for the AWB to secure and control stocks adequate for its export programme. With current trading and risk management practices, concurrently with a more open and transparent US border, the CWB claims it would have difficulty operating an export programme (as traditionally managed). It is significant that under similar situations the AWB has found ways to function without controlling domestic supplies.

Vertical integration (value-added)

The AWB began its involvement in vertical integration and value-added food processing concurrently with deregulation and establishment of the WIF. Apart from this, the general view has been toward closer integration with the processing sector and seeking opportunities for equity participation in these industries (Condon, 1991, p. 4).

To that end, and under the auspices of the WIF, the AWB has invested in several notable operations to exploit economies of vertical integration and develop an asset base. These activities now include milling ventures in Vietnam and China, and a recent investment (30% interest) in an Egyptian flour mill venture.[6] The stated purpose of the latter was 'to shorten the marketing chain and increase the potential for export sales'.

It should be noted that the CWB has recently hired someone for purposes of doing value-added activities, and a study was conducted on value-added opportunities and issues.

6. Summary and Implications

Both countries have operated for years with relatively non-transparent marketing costs. In recent years, and concurrently with deregulation and discussions of such, the levels of marketing costs have come under increased scrutiny. This will probably continue and will create problems for these STEs. This is even more of a problem in Canada, being so geographically close to the USA.

The increased disaggregation of commodities (i.e. increased segregations) traded by the STEs has several important issues. Most important is that at the extreme it will undermine the concept of pooling, which has been the main focus of the origins of these STEs.

As an aside, it is interesting to ask why it is only recently that there has been a demand for increased segregations: have there not always been segments, and have these agencies not served them?

A common theme for each STE is that their existence is important because of their discriminatory powers. Both the AWB and the CWB cite this and claim it is more justified in an EEP environment. In a more commercial situation, such discrimination will be objected to by buyers and will serve to undermine the STE. Thus, this should be viewed as a risky strategy for legitimizing retention of single-seller status.

The AWB, and potentially the CWB, is seeking to integrate vertically. While this is a strategy being exercised in other aspects of the world grain trade, there is one major concern. In doing so, ultimately they will be competing with their existing customers, which will create a major strategic complication.

Notes

1. The AWB only has single-desk authority for wheat exports, whereas the CWB has single-desk authority for wheat and barley exports and domestic sales of wheat and barley for human consumption. In Australia, barley is marketed through four state-level statutory marketing boards. These are the Australian Barley Board in

South Australia and Victoria, the Grain Pool of WA in West Australia, the NSW Grains Board in New South Wales, and Grainco in Queensland.

2. There have been a number of studies on each of these marketing systems in the past decade. Without being exhaustive, these include, in the case of Canada: Loyns and Carter (1984) and Agriculture Canada (1992); and, in the case of Australia, the Australian Bureau of Agricultural Economics (1983) and the Industries Assistance Commission (1988).

3. Concurrently with the recent Alberta plebiscite on the CWB it was pointed out that 'if the board's powers diminish, the government would likely discontinue underwriting $6 billion in loans the board must take to cover the cost of doing business ...' (*Western Producer*, 23 November, 1995, p. 11). The CWB (1995) has estimated the underwriting is worth about $C60 million annually.

4. In fact, this is reflected in much of the current problem on barley.

5. The AWB may be more involved in swaps because of the multi-year time dimension of some transactions.

6. This was along with the Australian Barley Board (5% interest) and Omani, South Arabian and Egyptian business partners (*Financial Times*, Saudi Arabia).

References

Agriculture Canada (1992) *Grains and Oilseeds: Regulatory Review*. Discussion paper, Agriculture Canada, Ottawa.

Australian Bureau of Agricultural Economics (1983) *Wheat Marketing in Australia: an Economic Evaluation*. BAE Occasional Paper No. 86. Australian Government Publishing Service, Canberra, Australia.

Baldwin, R.E. (1992) Are economists' traditional trade policy views still valid? *Journal of Economic Literature* XXX (June), 804–829.

Booz, Allen and Hamilton (1995) *Milling Wheat Project: Consultant's Report to the Australian Grains Council*. Canberra, Australia.

Boston Consulting Group (1995) *Australia's Malting Barley Industry Strategy*. Report prepared for the Grains Council of Australia, Melbourne, Australia.

Brenner, R. (1987) State owned enterprises. In: *Rivalry: In Business, Science, among Nations*. Cambridge University Press, Sydney, Australia.

Canada Grains Council (1994) *Statistical Handbook*. Canada Grains Council, Winnipeg, Canada.

Carter, C.A. (1993) An economic analysis of a single North American barley market. *Canadian Journal of Agricultural Economics* 41, 243–256.

Carter, C.A. and Loyns, R.M.A. (1996) *The Economics of Single Desk Selling of Western Canadian Grain Report*. Prepared for Alberta Agriculture, Food and Rural Development, Edmonton, Alberta, Canada.

Chadwick, A. (1992) *Wheat Boards, Agricultural Subsidies and International Trade Policy*. Report to the US Wheat Associates, Sacramento, California, USA.

Clark, J.S. (1995) Single desk selling by the Canadian wheat board: does it have an impact? *Canadian Journal of Agricultural Economics* 43, 225–236.

Condon, C. (1991) Grain marketing beyond 2000. Speech to the Grains 2000 Conference, Australia.

CWB (Canadian Wheat Board) (1995) *Grain Matters: Special Market Edition.* Canadian Wheat Board, Winnipeg, Canada.

CWB (Canadian Wheat Board) (undated) *The Canadian Wheat Board: the Farmer's Grain Sales Agency.* Undated manuscript, Canadian Wheat Board, Winnipeg, Canada.

Dixit, P.M. and Josling, T. (1997) *State Trading in Agriculture: an Analytical Framework.* International Agricultural Trade Research Consortium Working Paper 4 (July).

Fowke, V.C. (1957) *The World Economy and the Wheat Economy.* University of Toronto Press, Toronto, Canada.

Goodwin, B.K. (1992) Multivariate cointegration tests and the law of one price in international wheat markets. *Review of Agricultural Economics* 1 (January), 117–124.

Gray, R., Ulrich, A. and Schmitz, A. (1993) A continental barley market: where are the gains? *Canadian Journal of Agricultural Economics* 41, 257–270.

Industries Assistance Commission (1988) *The Wheat Industry.* Report No. 411, Australian Government Publishing Service, Canberra, Australia.

Industry Commission (1991) *Statutory Marketing Arrangements for Primary Products.* Report 10, Australian Government Publishing Service, Canberra, Australia.

Kraft, D.F., Furtan,W.H. and Tyrchniewicz, E.W. (1996) *Performance Evaluation of the Canadian Wheat Board.* Canadian Wheat Board, Winnipeg, Canada.

Krugman, P. (1987) Is free trade passé? *Economic Perspectives* 1, 131–144.

Loyns, R.M.A. and Carter, C.A. (1984) *Grains in Western Economic Development to 1990.* Discussion Paper No. 272, Economic Council of Canada, Ottawa, Canada.

Piggott, R.R. (1992) Some old truths revisited. *Australian Journal of Agricultural Economics* 36, 117–140.

Rotstein, A. (1984) The origins of the Canadian Wheat Board. In: *Government Enterprise: Roles and Rationale.* Economic Council of Canada, Ottawa, Canada.

Ryan, T.J. (1994) Marketing Australia's crop: the way ahead. *Review of Marketing and Agricultural Economics* 62, 107–121.

USDA (US Department of Agriculture) (1986) *Embargoes, Surplus Disposal, and US Agriculture.* Ag Econ Report No. 564, Economic Research Service, Washington DC, USA.

US General Accounting Office (GAO) (1992) *International Trade: Canada and Australia Rely Heavily on Wheat Boards to Market Grain.* GAO/NSIAD-92–129, June, Washington DC, USA.

US General Accounting Office (GAO) (1995) *State Trading Enterprises: Compliance with the General Agreement on Tariffs and Trade.* GAO/GGD-95–208, August, Washington DC, USA.

Watson, A.S. (1984) Wheat in 1984. *Review of Marketing and Agricultural Economics* 52, 2.

Whitwell, G. and Sydenham, D. (1991) *A Shared Harvest.* MacMillan Education Australia, Melbourne, Australia.

Wilson, W. (1995) *Pricing to Value.* Special research report prepared for the US/Canada Joint Commission on Grains, February.

10

The European Union Common Agricultural Policy Under the GATT

Anthony Rayner,[1] Robert Hine,[1] Timothy Lloyd,[1] Vincent H. Smith[2] and Robert Ackrill[3]

[1] *Department of Economics, University of Nottingham, UK;* [2] *Department of Agricultural Economics and Economics and Trade Research Center, Montana State University–Bozeman, USA;* [3] *Department of Economics, University of Leicester, UK*

1. Introduction

This chapter reviews the European Union's (EU's) Common Agricultural Policy (CAP) for cereals, with special reference to wheat, in the light of its commitments under the Uruguay Round Agricultural Agreement (UR-AA). The chapter begins (section 2) by drawing attention to the emergence of the EU as a significant exporter of wheat in the 1980s such that by the end of that decade it was responsible for some 20% of world wheat export trade. The growth of exports was characterized by a general expansion of sales to all markets and was supported by heavy subsidization of EU producers. The EU position on wheat was mirrored in several other important commodity markets and was an important factor leading to the crisis in world commodity markets in the 1980s. Section 3 briefly describes the forces leading to agricultural trade reform being made a priority in the Uruguay Round (UR) in the General Agreement on Tariffs and Trade (GATT), which was launched in 1986. It then gives a summary of the EU's position on agricultural trade reform in the period leading up to the start of the negotiations in the Round.

Section 4 presents a brief history of the UR agricultural negotiations and draws attention to the crucial role played by the 1992 MacSharry reform of the CAP in enabling a conclusion to be reached to the negotiations. Section 5 summarizes the commitments made by the signatories to the UR Final Act for reducing agricultural support and

(eds J.M. Antle and V.H. Smith)

protection over the period 1995–2000 under three headings: domestic support, market access and export subsidization. Section 6 then discusses the implementation of these commitments by the EU with reference to cereals. The section concludes by noting that ceiling commitments on the quantities of subsidized exports could be binding on the EU cereals sector and might require adjustments to policy.

Sections 7 and 8 expand on the theme of a possible incompatibility between EU cereals policy and UR-AA commitments on subsidized export volumes. Section 7 reviews the conclusions of models built during and immediately after the conclusion of the Round. Section 8 presents a small stochastic model of the EU wheat sector, based on recent data, which is designed to highlight certain key aspects of the issue. In particular, attention is drawn to: (a) yield trend, set-aside on area planted and consumption growth – all of which determine potential EU wheat exports; and (b) world prices, the relationship between US and EU dollar free-on-board (f.o.b.) prices and the dollar–ecu exchange rate – all of which influence the potential unit export subsidy on EU wheat.

Section 9 points to the likelihood of further CAP reform and examines recent EU Commission policy statements as to the possible direction of reform. Finally, section 10 concludes.

2. The EU and the World Wheat Market

Over the period 1974/75 to 1994/95, world wheat production grew by 80%, from about 350 million tonnes to about 550 million tonnes per annum. During the same period, annual wheat exports increased by 67% from about 60 million tonnes to about 100 million tonnes. The wheat export market has traditionally been dominated by four countries – the USA, Canada, Australia and Argentina – but, as illustrated in Fig. 10.1, the EU has also been a significant net exporter since the early 1980s. In the last decade or so, EU wheat exports have been of the order of 15–20 million tonnes, some two-thirds of US export quantities. Over this period, the EU has accounted for 15–20% of global wheat exports whilst the US share has been around 30–40%. Figure 10.2 illustrates the emergence of the EU as a major player on the world market from the early 1980s and the relative decline of the US market share from this time. At the beginning of the 1980s, the EU and US market shares were about 13% and 45% respectively; by 1990/91, these shares were 20% and 32%. In 1990/91, the export shares of the other major exporters were Canada (23%), Australia (13%) and Argentina (5%).

The destinations of European wheat exports are regionally concentrated, with the former Soviet Union and Africa accounting for more than 60% of exports over the last decade (see Table 10.1). Africa

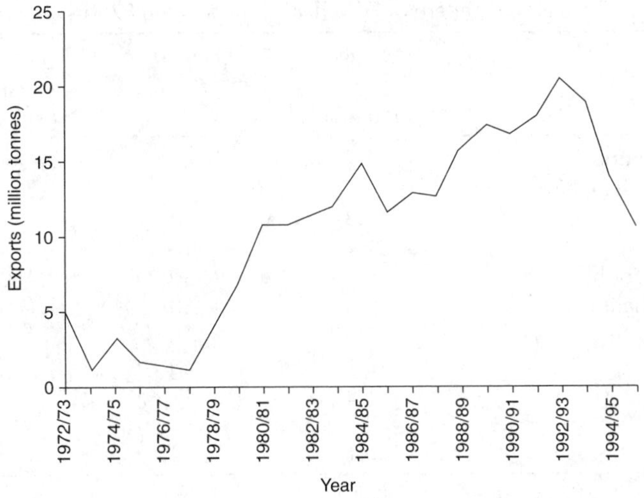

Fig. 10.1. EU wheat net exports.

been the most stable market for EU grain and the area where the EU has consistently achieved the highest market share – over 50% in sub-Saharan Africa. The EU exports to a large number of countries in this region, though often in relatively small amounts. The North African countries – especially Morocco, Tunisia and Algeria – have also been important customers for EU wheat and the EU holds approximately 30% of the market share. In the biggest single market in this region, Egypt, the EU has lost market share to the USA since the early 1980s and the EU's share of this market, despite its

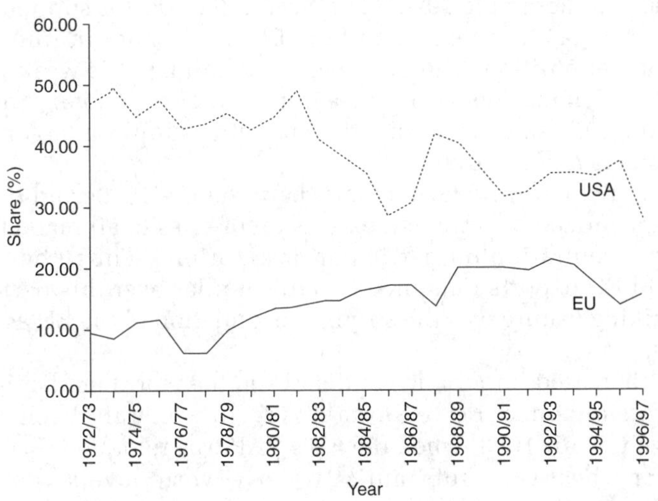

Fig. 10.2. EU and US wheat export shares.

Table 10.1. The regional pattern of EU wheat exports: 1986/87 to 1994/95.

Destination	Average volume (million tonnes)	EU market share (%)	Share of EU exports (%)
Eastern Europe	1.1	45	6
Former Soviet Union	4.2	30	23
Africa	6.8	34	38
Egypt	1.1	18	6
Other North	3.1	30	17
Sub-Saharan	2.6	50	15
Near East	2.0	18	11
Far East	2.1	6	12
Americas	1.2	11	7
Other	0.7	10	3
World	18.1	18	100

Source: International Grains Council, 1996.

geographical proximity, has only been in line with its world market share in recent years.

The former Soviet Union market has taken about a quarter of EU exports over the last decade but the market is volatile and the EU faces strong competition from US and Canadian suppliers. The EU has a large share of the market in the central and eastern European countries, but the trade volumes are relatively small and have been declining in recent years. In the Americas, wheat markets are largely supplied by the USA, Canada and Argentina, and EU exports have only a small presence, apart from in Cuba, where the EU has taken over from Canada as the principal supplier in the 1990s. The Near East market is supplied by the USA, Australia and Canada, and the EU has a share in line with its world market position. The EU's market performance is weakest in the Far East, which represents around a third of the world total. Apart from intermittent EU sales to China, the market is supplied largely by the USA, Canada and Australia.

The growth of EU wheat exports between the 1980s and the 1990s was characterized by a general expansion of sales to all markets rather than a concentration on particular destinations. Thus, the regional pattern of EU exports remained broadly similar over this period. The more striking feature was the strong consolidation of the EU as a major exporter.

The increased importance of the EU on the world market has been controversial since EU exports have, in general, been heavily subsidized. Until 1993, when the EU's CAP was reformed, EU support prices for wheat were substantially above world levels, the average nominal protection rate over the period 1980/81 to 1992/93 being above 50%. However, as shown in Fig. 10.3, the size of the unit refund (subsidy) as a percentage of the EU export price[1] has fluctuated markedly as a result of, first, world market conditions, influenced to a large degree by US production variation, and, second, movements in the dollar–ecu exchange rate. In addition to the use of export subsidies, the EU's influence on the world market was strengthened by its publicly owned stock-holding capacity (intervention stocks). At their peak in 1992/93, EU intervention stocks of wheat exceeded 15 million tonnes, around 15% of annual wheat trade. Figure 10.3 also illustrates the fluctuations in these stocks and their general large size in the 1980s and early 1990s.

3. The EU and the Launch of the Uruguay Round

The expansion and consolidation of the EU's wheat export position in the 1980s took place against the background of increasing world wheat production and stagnant consumption. World prices fell and stocks increased, as illustrated in Fig. 10.4. Other important commodity markets exhibited similar characteristics and the export earnings of the traditional agricultural exporting nations declined quite severely. The deteriorating trade environment led to tensions between the agricultural trading nations and an escalation of trade disputes. Whilst EU trade subsidization was a focal point for complaints about its unfair competition, the USA raised the temperature of trade conflict by introducing an Export Enhancement Program (EEP) in 1985. This policy provided export subsidies to targeted

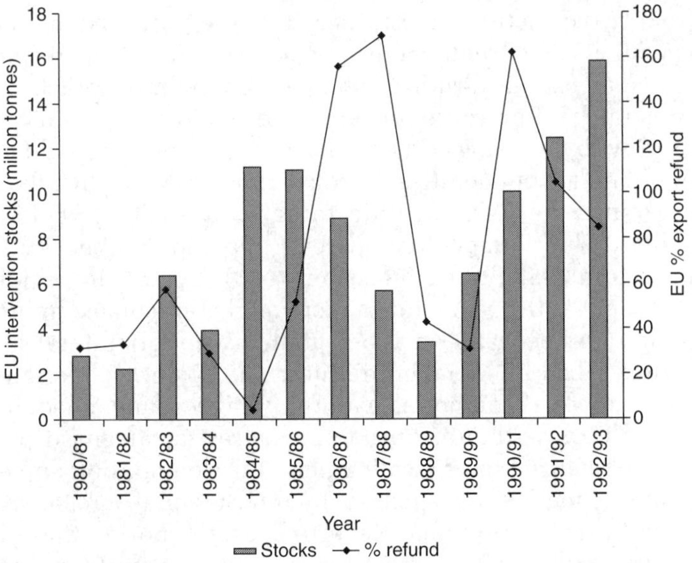

Fig. 10.3. EU percentage export refund and intervention stocks.

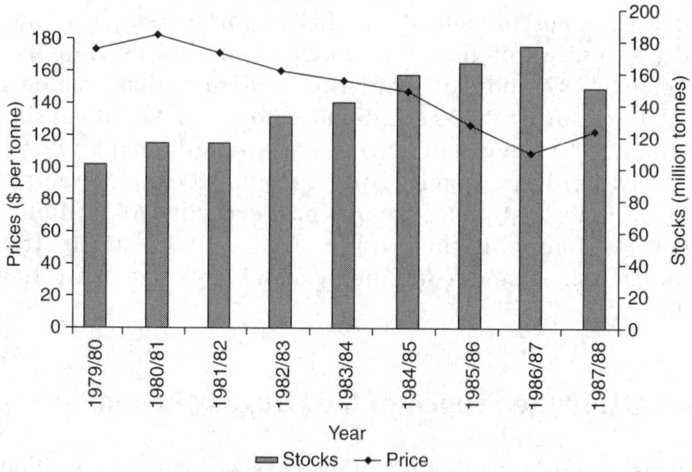

Fig. 10.4. World wheat prices and stocks.

markets as a counter to subsidized exports from competitors. 'The trade tensions created by the emergence of structural surpluses of major commodities by the mid-1980s and the budgetary and political costs of competitive subsidisation, brought agricultural protectionism to the forefront of the international economic policy agenda' (Ingersent *et al.*, 1994, p. 3). The crisis in agricultural trade provided a major incentive for nations to give a priority to reducing agricultural subsidies and liberalizing trade in the UR in the GATT, which was launched in 1986.

At the outset of the Round, the EU was under pressure to reform the CAP from two directions. First, there was pressure from agricultural trading partners who wanted improved access to the EU market for their exports and an end to subsidized competition in third markets. Second, there was internal pressure for reform for mainly budgetary reasons associated with the rising costs of subsidized export disposal for wheat and several other commodities. During the period preceding the launch of the Round, the EU's attitude to agricultural trade reform was ambivalent. The 'Perspectives' Green Paper published by the EU Commission in 1985 (EC Commission, 1985) stressed the inviolability of the CAP, but at the same time a more market-orientated approach to price support levels was seen as essential to keep agricultural spending within prescribed financial guidelines. The objective of aligning EU prices with those of competing exporters was recommended, but only in the long term with appropriate measures to safeguard producer incomes. In referring to price alignment, the Commission appeared to be thinking of market management by international agreement rather than actual price reductions. Nevertheless, the notion that the CAP could not remain insulated from the influence of world markets was quite radical for EU policy makers at that time and laid the basis for subsequent policy adjustments. The 'Perspectives' paper also reiterated the EU's long-standing objective of achieving more balanced protection amongst different commodities, specifically relative to cereals and livestock (highly protected) and oilseeds and non-cereal feed ingredients (very low or zero protection).

The USA was the principal instigator of the UR and its priority in the agricultural negotiations was to regain its market share of world trade in cereals and other commodities by seeking to abolish all forms of protection and support. The USA was supported in this aim by the traditional agricultural exporters. The EU had major misgivings with this focus, suspecting that an unstated aim of the USA was to destroy the CAP. Nevertheless, the EU was committed to the wider aspirations of the Round and in the preparatory meetings for the multilateral trade negotiations it did not block the inclusion of agricultural trade on the agenda. Rather, it attempted to limit the scope of the agricultural negotiations to the modification of existing policies. The Punta del Este Declaration, which launched the Round, stated that the central objective for the reform of agricultural trade was 'to bring all measures affecting import access and export competition under strengthened and more operationally effective GATT rules and disciplines' (OECD, 1995, p. 11). This implied that the EU could not withhold import levies and export refunds, the basic mechanisms of the CAP, from the negotiations. However, the Declaration did not commit any country to the phased abolition of support.

4. The Agricultural Negotiations in the Uruguay Round[1]

The UR of multilateral trade negotiations commenced in 1986 and was concluded on 15 December 1993. Over 100 contracting parties were involved and agriculture was one item on a broad and ambitious agenda, which also addressed tariffs, non-tariff barriers, textiles, tropical products, intellectual property rights, investment measures, services, and GATT disciplines and rules. The scale and complexity of the agenda and the linkages between issues undoubtedly made for protracted and lengthy negotiations. However, the tempo of the Round was largely dictated by the tendentious nature of the agricultural negotiations with a settlement on agriculture being deemed to be crucial to the success of the Round.

At the outset of the Round, there was conflict between the major players – the USA, the EU, the Cairns Group (CG) and Japan – in the agricultural negotiating group over the nature, extent and pace of reform. Broadly speaking, the USA, supported by the CG, pressed for the dismantling of trade-distorting protection whilst the EU, supported by Japan, was unwilling to disengage from traditional measures of farm support and protection. At the mid-term review of the Round, agriculture was identified as a major sticking-point but concessions made by both the USA and the EU in the Geneva Accord (April 1989) led to revised negotiating positions, with all participants displaying a willingness to bring about substantive agricultural trade-policy reform. The abandonment by the USA of its 'zero option' after the Geneva Accord was crucial for the subsequent movement in the talks. The Chairman of the agricultural negotiating group provided a Framework Agreement in July 1990, 6 months before the scheduled date for completion of the Round. The De Zeeuw draft framework 'was based upon the principle of accepting a separate commitment for border protection [tariffication, followed by a substantial reduction of tariffs and a minimum access], internal support [also a substantial reduction of trade distorting support and a strict definition of the allowed support, the so-called "Green Box"] and export competition [effectively more export subsidy reduction, compared with other forms of support and protection]' (De Zeeuw, 1996, p. 112). However, disagreements over the extent and pace of reform, especially as regards import protection and export subsidies, led to the near-breakdown of the talks (Brussels, December 1990) when the EU, other European countries with the exception of Sweden, and Japan rejected the De Zeeuw framework. These countries were not prepared at this point in the negotiations to make the required fundamental changes in their agricultural policies.

An emergency initiative by the GATT Secretary General (Dunkel) revived the negotiations in February 1991 and all participants agreed to renew discussions on the basis of reaching 'specific binding commitments to reduce farm supports in each of three areas: internal assistance, border protection and export assistance'. In December 1991, Dunkel presented the negotiators with a comprehensive draft agreement covering all areas of the Round. As far as agriculture was concerned, the Dunkel draft was based on the De Zeeuw principles but was more detailed and largely foreshadowed the final agreement. However, in 1991, as at the start of the Round, agreement appeared possible only if the EU reformed the CAP in a manner that reduced its trade-distorting impacts. The quite radical CAP reform proposal – the MacSharry plan, first tabled within the EU Commission in February 1991 and finally agreed by the EU Council of Farm Ministers in a revised form in May 1992 – provided the impetus for a resolution of the deadlock on agriculture. The central elements of the MacSharry plan are a phased reduction in support prices towards world market levels, especially for cereals, coupled with set-aside in the arable sector and the supplementation of farmers' incomes by direct payments. The direct payments represent two types of compensation payments: first, for the support price reductions on a fixed production base and, second, for taking arable land out of production. Table 10.2 provides a summary of the 1992 reform measures.

Although the MacSharry Plan would enable the EU to meet commitments in respect of reducing border protection and export subsidies, its enactment into EU law in July 1992 did not lead to an immediate completion of the UR agricultural negotiations. Two issues remained to be resolved. First, the EU regarded the reform as sacrosanct – an agreement had to be compatible with the reform – and, importantly, it demanded that the compensation payments be treated as 'decoupled' from production and not be counted as subsidies in any commitment on reducing internal assistance. Second, a technically separate dispute between the EU and the USA on oilseeds flared up. US oilseed producers had been seeking action in the GATT from the beginning of the Round in respect of what they claimed were the detrimental effects of EU oilseeds subsidies. In particular, they claimed that the EU subsidy impaired the benefits of duty-free access for oilseeds that the EU had agreed in the Dillon Round in 1960/61. In December 1991, the EU revised its oilseeds policy in response to an adverse 1989 GATT panel ruling and introduced acreage-based payments that were a precursor to the MacSharry compensation payments for arable crops. In March 1992, the same panel ruled that the revised oilseeds scheme now linked to the MacSharry reform did not eliminate the damage to US exporters. After bilateral negotiations between the USA and the EU on the oilseeds dispute broke down, Secretary-General Dunkel was given a mandate to act as an intermediary to settle the dispute and to resolve outstanding differences in

Table 10.2. 1992 CAP reform.

Arable sector

1. Reduction of cereal intervention price by one-third over a 3-year period.
2. Integration of support for oilseeds and protein crops into an arable area payments scheme.
3. Introduction of compensation payments to offset price reductions, provided that land is set aside (initial set-aside rate of 15%). Small producers (below 92 tonnes of cereal equivalent) exempt. Compensation payments based on historical regional yields and current areas planted (subject to regional base area limits).

Livestock sector

1. Reduction of beef intervention price by 15% over 3 years.
2. Compensation via direct headage payments subject to maximum stocking rate.
3. Payments subject to individual limits per holding.
4. Limitations on headage payments in sheep sector.

Dairy sector

1. Reduction in intervention price for butter by 5%.
2. No reduction in milk quotas.

the agricultural negotiations. In November 1992 (Blair House I), a bilateral agreement between the USA and the EU was reached on both sets of issues.

The oilseeds component of the agreement specified a maximum EU oilseeds area (equal to the average planted area in 1989/90/91 and identical to the area component of the production base under MacSharry) and that the area would be reduced each year by the rate of set-aside on arable land subject to a minimum rate of 10%.

The Blair House I agreement had five important provisions. First, EU compensation payments were to be excluded from the commitment to reducing internal assistance to producers (the so-called 'blue box' arrangement). Second, the EU was to be allowed to retain a 10% preference margin in respect of commitments to reducing border protection. Third, the EU gained a small but possibly significant concession on the size of commitments to reducing export assistance. In particular, the Dunkel draft agreement had proposed that subsidized export volume be reduced by 24% of base period exports; this was relaxed to 21%. Fourth, if EU imports of non-grain feed imports exceed 1990/92 average imports of these products, then the USA and EU must consult 'with a view to finding a mutually acceptable solution'.[2] Fifth, a so-called 'peace clause' was included, which lays down that domestic support measures and export subsidies are exempt from actions undertaken under Article 16 of the GATT. This peace clause can be interpreted as signalling the granting of outside recognition to and conferring legitimacy on the (reformed) CAP for the first time (Tangermann, 1994, p. 16).

Some further and significant amendments were agreed in last-minute negotiations between the EU and the USA in Geneva in December 1993 as the Round was concluded. This final deal (dubbed 'Blair House II') incorporated two elements of note. First, under the 'front-loading' provision, countries were allowed to choose a different base year from which to start the export subsidy cuts in those cases where exports had increased significantly since the start of the Round. Second, the EU agreed not to apply the full bound tariffs on cereals if that would result in import prices higher than 155% of the EU intervention price (Josling *et al.*, 1996, p. 162).[3] The Final Act was then signed by GATT ministers in Marrakesh in April 1994.

5. Commitments Under the UR-AA

The signatories to the UR Final Act committed themselves to reducing agricultural support and protection over the 6-year period from 1995 to 2000 (1995–2004 for developing countries) under three headings: namely, domestic support, market access and export subsidies. Table

10.3 summarizes the agreed commitments. We comment briefly on each of these commitments.

Domestic support commitments

The required 20% reduction covers the totality of supported commodities and is not commodity-specific, the reductions being based on prices prevailing in 1986–1988. Subsidies taking the form of 'direct payments under production-limiting programmes' are exempt from Aggregate Measurement of Support (AMS) measurement and reduction provided that crop payments are based either upon a fixed area and yield or that they are restricted to 85% of the base area of production and/or that livestock payments are based upon a fixed number of animals. The specification of the AMS commitment in global rather than commodity-specific terms and, especially, the exemption of production-limiting direct payments were crucial adjustments made at Blair House I to the Dunkel draft. These adjustments made compliance with the (already rather weak) domestic support provisions virtually painless for both the EU and the USA.

Market access commitments

The commitment to tariffication was an important achievement since 'tariffication gives a transparency to trade' that was previously missing (Josling, 1993). The agreement requires that all base-period tariffs, including those resulting from the conversion of non-tariff barriers (NTBs), be reduced by an unweighted average of 36% subject to a minimum reduction of 15% in each tariff line. The impact of tariffication is weakened somewhat by world prices for a number of major commodities being rather low in historical terms in the base period. In addition, the specification of the reduction commitment as an unweighted average permits reductions to be spread unevenly across commodities, so allowing rather high protection to be maintained on import-sensitive products.

The problem of import access continuing to be blocked by high tariffs is met to some extent by the minimum access provisions. The *modus operandi* of these provisions is a system of tariff quotas with within-quota tariffs set at a low level. Whether imports enter depends on whether or not the reduced tariffs are prohibitive. With sufficiently low within-quota tariffs, there is the potential for the quotas to be fully utilized.

Tariffication is of significance for countries that have hitherto deployed NTBs to underpin high fixed domestic prices, in that these

Table 10.3. UR-AA reductions in agricultural support and protection (1995–2000).

	Commitments	Qualifications/exemptions
Domestic support	20% reduction in total AMS over 6 years from 1986–1988 base (price support measured against FERPS). Credit for reductions since 1986.	'Green box' instruments exempt (e.g. R&D). Direct payments under production limitation programmes ('blue box' instruments) exempt (e.g. EU compensation payments, US deficiency payments). Special provisions for developing countries.
Market access	All NTBs converted to tariffs. No new NTBs to be created. All base-period tariffs including NTB equivalents to be reduced by an unweighted average of 36% over 6 years from 1986–1988 base (tariffs measured against FERPS). Minimum 15% reduction in each tariff line. All tariffs bound at end of implementation period. Minimum access provision of 3% rising to 5% of base period consumption. Base period imports count toward access requirement. Minimum access provision cannot be cut below actual base period import level.	Country-specific derogations (e.g. Japan and Korea to postpone tariffication of rice imports until 2000). EU 10% Community Preference Margin. Special safeguards. Special provisions for developing countries.
Export subsidy	Agriculture still receives special treatment in that existing export subsidies permitted but capped at base-period (1986–1990) levels in expenditure and volume terms. Subsidized export expenditure to be reduced by 36% and subsidized export volume to be reduced by 21% over 6 years, in each of 22 product categories. Prohibition of export subsidies on commodities not subsidized in base period.	Food aid shipments exempt. Front loading permitted. No restriction on unit export subsidy. Export credits not disciplined. Special treatment for developing countries.

Source: Ingersent *et al.*, 1995.
AMS, Aggregate Measurement of Support; FERPS, Fixed External Reference Prices; NTB, non-tariff barriers.

internal prices are no longer fully insulated from world price movements. However, the special safeguards (SS) provision, which permits 'additional duties' to be imposed when import volumes rise above or import prices fall below base-period-denominated 'triggers', has the potential to cushion domestic prices from the full impact of declines in world prices beyond certain limits.

Export subsidy reduction commitments

Export competition was the most contentious issue confronted during the Round. Under the AA, export subsidies are still 'legal' but are capped at the base-period (1986–1990) level in terms of both the amount of budgetary expenditure and the quantity of exports subsidized, and subject to commodity-specific export subsidy reduction commitments. However, under the so-called 'front-loading' provision, if 1991/92 subsidized exports exceeded the base-period level, then the required cuts can be made from this higher level, provided the same reduced level is still attained by the year 2000. There is no restriction imposed on the size of unit export subsidies so that the export subsidy provisions afford more scope than the market access provisions for continued domestic market insulation (Tangermann, 1994, p. 29). Notwithstanding these qualifications, the export subsidy commitments effectively constrain policy options and have the potential to influence the direction of domestic policy reform.

6. Implementation by the EU with Special Reference to Cereals

Implementation of the UR-AA commitments began in July 1995 and extends over the 6 marketing years 1995/96 to 2000/01. The enlargement of the EU-12 to the EU-15 in January 1995 has required some adjustment of the EU's UR-AA commitments. The new members – Austria, Finland and Sweden – replaced their individual agricultural support systems by CAP mechanisms on joining the EU and aligned their prices with EU levels. The minimum access and export subsidy commitments are adjusted by amalgamating the separate obligations of the new member states with those of the EU-12, netting out base-period trade between the Twelve and the Three. Adjustment of the tariffication provisions has been more complicated and has involved negotiations between the EU and its trading partners over compensation to the trading partners for the impact of the Three adopting the EU's import regime. The outcome of these negotiations is that some third-country suppliers were granted improved access to the EU market under the tariff-quota arrangements; for example, Canada was granted an increase in the import duty rebate for quality cereals and additional tariff-free quotas for durum wheat and processed oats.

Domestic support commitments

The domestic support commitments are binding on a calendar-year basis. The AMS is calculated for each product and product AMSs are aggregated to derive total domestic support. The AMS includes market price support, non-exempt direct payments and input subsidies. It excludes buying-in or storage subsidies. Market price support dominates the measure; this is equal to the gap between the 'applied administered price' (commercial ecu intervention price) and external world reference price (1986–1988 ecu price) multiplied by the quantity of production. A credit is allowed for reductions in support occurring after 1986.

The base-period AMS for the EU-12 is 73.5 billion ecu, of which cereals account for 20.1 billion ecu and beef 18.0 billion ecu. The OECD (1995, p. 41) estimates that the total AMS for the EU in 1993, the first year of implementation of CAP reform, was around 62 billion ecu, a fall of some 11 billion ecu from the base period. This estimated 1993 AMS is close to the final bound level for the EU-12 and the EU 'should not experience any difficulty in meeting its AMS commitment, given the current and planned policy configuration' (OECD, 1995, p. 40). There are a number of reasons why the AMS commitment does not constrain the reformed CAP. First, base-period support was at a high level when ecu-denominated world prices were historically low. Second, support prices for cereals, oilseeds and protein crops were cut by around one-third and the intervention price for beef by 15% under the 1992 MacSharry reform and associated arrangements. Third, compensation payments, introduced as part of the reform and now accounting for some two-thirds of the EU guarantee agricultural budget (FEOGA), are excluded from the AMS calculations. Fourth, the aggregate nature of the AMS allowed the larger cuts in the AMS of some products (e.g. cereals) to be offset by the smaller cuts in other sectors (e.g. sugar). The price cut for cereals (note that cereals account for nearly 30% of base-period total AMS) and the exclusion of compensation payments are sufficient for the EU to deliver on its commitment.

However, the 'due restraint' section of the peace clause constrains the scope for increases in support. This provision is commodity-specific, is actionable over 1995–2004 and effectively constrains support expenditure (including that provided by production-limiting programmes as well as that included in the AMS) to the level decided in the1992/93 marketing year (this covers decisions taken in that year, even if they relate to future years). Thus, existing compensation payments are not in the 'blue box' as far as the peace clause is concerned and can be increased only if, for example, intervention prices are reduced on a proportional basis.

Market access commitments

Base-period tariff equivalents of NTBs were calculated as the difference between average internal and external prices over 1986–1988. For cereals, tariffs have been set at 140 ecu per tonne in 1995/96, falling to 95 ecu per tonne in 2000/01. However, an alternative provision, stemming from Blair House II, prevails for all cereals except oats: under this provision, the duty will be such that the duty-paid cost, insurance, freight (c.i.f.) import price may not exceed 155% of the EU intervention price. This arrangement gives a lower level of protection than the maximum bound tariff; for example, in 1995/96 the duty on low-quality wheat was 60 ecu per tonne as against the bound tariff of 140 ecu per tonne. However, since the arrangement is similar to the 'old' threshold price/variable levy system it creates the possibility that the tariff will, in effect, be variable. The safeguard provisions are optional but can be put in place when world import prices fall to 10% below the trigger (1986–1988) value. However, since the duty-paid price of importing cereals is restricted to 155% of the intervention price, the safeguard tariffs cannot be added to the EU import price limit.

For oats and processed cereal products, fixed tariffs are levied according to the bound schedules. Because base-period tariff equivalents were 'high', these bound tariffs were generally higher in 1995/96 than pre-existing tariffs for 1993/94 and 1994/95. The reduction commitment lowers the tariffs at the end of the implementation period toward these pre-existing tariffs.

The tariffication provisions are unlikely to result in significant increases in imports of cereals in the short term. More immediate impacts may result from the volume commitments under the minimum access provisions. In the first year of the implementation period, market access opportunities must offer the possibility of importing cereals equal to 3% of base-period EU cereals consumption, rising to 5% by 2000/01. Import quotas with a reduced tariff (32% of the basic tariff) are to be implemented when the market access volume is greater than average imports in the base period. The EU is obliged to make further access provisions for wheat by 2000/01. The EU has agreed to import 0.3 million tonnes of quality wheat without tariff starting from 1994/95 to meet this commitment. Other quota obligations for cereals and for non-cereal feed ingredients stem from arrangements existing prior to the UR-AA and subsequently incorporated into the WTO schedules. Effectively, imports of non-cereal feed ingredients are constrained to the quota limits.

Export subsidy reduction commitments

Table 10.4 presents the EU-15 export subsidy ceiling commitments for wheat (including flour) and for coarse grains by both volume and expenditure. The table includes the 'front-loading' element where applicable. Cereals exported without a refund or as food aid and credit-based export sales are not subject to reductions. The Agreement permits any shortfall in subsidized exports during a season compared with the maximum allowed to be carried forward into the following seasons, subject to certain provisos (HGCA, 1996). However, no cumulative shortfall can be carried forward into the final year (2000/01). In a similar fashion, shortfalls in subsidized budgetary expenditures can be carried forward but again the final-year restriction applies.

Potentially, the constraints on the quantities of subsidized exports could be the most binding elements of the UR-AA for the EU cereals sector and require an adjustment to policy. However, there are uncertainties as to the extent to which the 1992 MacSharry reform,

Table 10.4. EU cereals export ceiling commitments.

	Wheat/ wheat flour	Coarse grains
EU-15 maximum volumes (million tonnes)		
1986/87–1990/91 base	18.3	13.7
Start volume for reduction	21.6	14.3
1995/1996	20.4	13.7
1996/97	19.2	13.1
1997/98	18.0	12.6
1998/99	16.8	12.0
1999/2000	15.6	11.4
2000/01	14.4	10.8
EU-15 maximum budgetary expenditures (billion ecu)		
1986/87–1990/91 base	2.015	1.676
Start budget for reduction	2.513	1.719
1995/96	2.309	1.606
1996/97	2.105	1.494
1997/98	1.901	1.382
1998/99	1.697	1.270
1999/2000	1.493	1.159
2000/01	1.290	1.047

Source: HGCA, 1996.

which reduced internal prices and introduced set-aside, will result in supply and consumption adjustments sufficient to meet the export obligations. There are also uncertainties regarding world price developments and the dollar–ecu exchange rate and hence the future requirement for EU export refunds. Here we merely draw attention to Commission and other 'official' statements and projections and defer an extended discussion to sections 7 and 8.

An early assessment by the Commission of Blair House I concluded that 'the most likely outcome is that the exportable (cereals) surplus will remain within the limits authorized in the draft agreement and be compatible with CAP reform' (EC Commission, 1992, p. 8). Certainly, implementation of the 1992 reform has resulted in a decline in production and a rise in domestic utilization of cereals. Export quantities in 1995/96 were well below the ceilings on subsidized exports for that year. In addition, intervention stocks were run down over the period 1992/93 to 1995/96. In the second half of 1995/96, world grain prices were unusually high and the EU did not need to subsidize wheat and barley exports; rather it levied export taxes. The most recent Commission forecasts for 1996/97 (as reported in February 1997, see HGCA, 1997a) indicate that total cereals exports will be a figure close to the aggregate ceiling. However, the EU has a credit to carry forward from 1995/96 in respect of unsubsidized exports. It is also worth noting that the set-aside rate has been set at 5% for plantings in 1996 and 1997 compared with 10% and above for earlier years, reflecting the decline in EU intervention stocks and the strengthening of the world market.

However, the limits on aggregate subsidized exports decline quite substantially between 1995/96 and 2000/01 (see Table 10.4). In documents issued in 1995, both the Organization for Economic Cooperation and Development (OECD) and the EU Commission foresaw possible conflicts between the EU's export potential and the quantities of allowable subsidized exports by the turn of the century. The OECD view is:

> Assuming a slow-down in the growth of crop yields, that the set-aside programme continues to be effective in reducing the area planted and that internal use for animal feed expands strongly, the EU subsidised wheat exports will fall to the levels to which they are constrained by the GATT agreement. However, even if all these conditions are fulfilled there will be some build-up of Community wheat stocks in the medium term suggesting that some further adjustments in cereal policy might need to be considered.
>
> (OECD, 1995, p. 49).

In its Agricultural Strategy Paper, the Commission stated that:

> When the 1992 reform proposals were introduced, ... forecast analyses undertaken by the Commission's services and some external research

> institutions indicated that the expected results of the reform would be, broadly speaking, compatible with the obligations of the Uruguay Round ... In the case of cereals the situation could well deteriorate in the medium term [end of this decade/early next decade], as some of the positive effects of the reform will progressively fade away.
>
> (EU Commission, 1995, pp. 13–14).

The Commission predicts that EU-15 cereals production (with a nominal 15% set-aside rate) in the year 2000 will exceed domestic utilization by some 30 million tonnes. Allowing for cereals imports of around 7 million tonnes, this implies an exportable surplus of some 37 million tonnes compared with the constraint on subsidized exports of around 25 million tonnes for the year 2000. Basically, the Commission projections incorporate a growth in yield, which, with a constant rate of set-aside, leads to an increase in production that is not matched by a continuing increase in utilization.

The constraints on budgetary expenditures for subsidized exports are not expected to be binding. The EU support prices were reduced by some 30% over the period 1992–1995 and world prices have risen since the base period so that the unit export refund has declined substantially in recent years. Indeed, as noted above, the EU imposed an export tax in 1996 and has only recently begun subsidizing exports again. Looking ahead, EU support prices are set to remain unaltered for the next few years so that the value of the unit refund (in ecu) will depend on developments in the world price (as measured in dollars) and movements in the ecu–dollar exchange rate.

7. Cereals Export Commitments and the Reformed CAP: Predictions from Models

Just preceding and following the conclusion of the UR-AA, several models of the impact of CAP reform were used to evaluate the compatibility of projections of EU-12 cereals exports with the mandated constraints on subsidized exports. Here we briefly compare the conclusions reached by the following studies: Guyomard *et al.* (1992: MISS model), Josling and Tangermann (1992), Folmer *et al.* (1993: ECAM model), Helmar *et al.* (1993: CARD model), MAFF (1994) and Rayner *et al.* (1995).[4]

All studies are in agreement that the mandated cutbacks in export subsidy expenditures will not impose constraints on the EU cereals regime. However, the studies reach somewhat different conclusions regarding the compatibility of projected subsidized export volumes with the UR-AA commitments. All models credit CAP reform with leading to a significant cut in production and to increased consumption, but differ in terms of the relative strengths of the twin impacts in projections over the UR-AA implementation period. The ECAM study is the most optimistic, predicting a marked decline in exports by 2002 stemming from the area-induced cut-back in production and productivity increases in the yield of cereals being matched by rising utilization. Josling and Tangermann (1992) predict a rising trend of exports toward 2000 but no incompatibility with the subsidized export commitments. The Ministry of Agriculture, Fisheries and Food (MAFF) model predicts that the volume of exports will be close to the allowable volume by the year 2000 but concludes that the constraint will not be binding unless production growth is toward the upper end of a likely range. The Center for Agricultural and Rural Development (CARD) and MISS models are more pessimistic in their conclusions. The CARD study finds that the roll-back in export volumes mandated by the UR-AA may be expected to lead to a set-aside rate higher than 15% at the end of the implementation period, that is, a higher set-aside rate than that incorporated in the 1992 CAP reform. The conclusions of the MISS model were very dependent on assumptions concerning the strength of induced consumption effects but in a likely scenario found incompatibility between projected export volumes and commitments.

The most pessimistic conclusions regarding the compatibility of the CAP with the UR-AA cereals commitments are probably obtained from the modelling work, detailed in Rayner *et al.* (1995). Subject to the assumption that there are no significant structural changes in the world cereals market over the implementation period, this study finds that: (i) the internal price cuts introduced by CAP reform are highly unlikely to remove the requirement to subsidize exports; (ii) the price cuts have a 'once and for all' constraining impact on exports via supply and demand effects; and (iii) the autonomous growth in production (from a trend increase in the yield of cereals) tends to outstrip any trend increase in consumption stemming from reform of the livestock sector. As such, the study concludes that there is a strong possibility that the volume of subsidized exports will be constrained by the UR-AA mandated volumes. In particular, the study projects a potential export surplus of some 31 million tonnes (mean of projection) by 2000 as against an allowable EU-12 subsidized export volume (excluding wheat flour) of some 22 million tonnes. As a consequence of this incompatibility between internal policy and external constraints, intervention stocks are likely to accumulate and the budgetary costs of the CAP cereals regime are likely to rise. In effect, this study arrives at rather similar conclusions to those of the 1995 EU Commission analysis reported in the preceding section.

8. A Small Stochastic Model of the EU Wheat Sector with Projections to 2000/01

Introduction

The central concern of this section is to ascertain the likely compatibility of projected EU wheat exports with the UR-AA limitations on subsidized exports over the period 1997/98 to 2000/01. Production shocks on the EU and world markets as well as disturbances to the ecu–dollar exchange rate can shift the EU from a position of subsidizing exports to one of exporting without refunds. Here a stochastic model is employed in order to assess the probability that exports require subsidies to be sold on the world market.

The unit refund is approximately equal to the EU support price less the ecu price received for EU exports. The EU export price is linked to world prices in dollars and any predictable movements in the ecu–dollar exchange rate. We use time-series analysis to investigate and represent these relationships.

The analysis presented below excludes durum wheat, the implicit assumption being that EU durum production and consumption roughly balance so that there are no durum exports – recent data suggest that this is not an unreasonable assumption.

Components of the empirical model

EU production

Wheat area is determined by the application of the set-aside instrument to the base arable area (subject to small farm exemptions) with wheat having a lower effective rate of set-aside than other cereals owing to its higher relative yield. The set-aside rate for the arable area is fixed at 5% for 1997/98 (actual value) and is increased to 10% for 1998/99 and 15% by 1999/2000. Wheat yield increases autonomously on a linear trend (confirmed by a Box–Tidwell (Box and Tidwell, 1962) analysis of yield 1973–1996) at a rate of approximately 0.144 tonnes per ha per annum. The variability in yield is represented by a standard deviation of yield around trend of 0.2 tonnes per ha. Yield responds positively to the price ratio of wheat to fertilizer with an elasticity of approximately 0.2.

EU consumption

The animal feed component of wheat consumption responds negatively to the price ratio of wheat to non-cereal feed ingredients (NCFIs) with an elasticity of about −0.15 (note that the prices of other cereals are assumed to move in tandem with wheat prices). Feed consumption also increases autonomously over time under the assumption that pig and poultry numbers increase whilst the stock of beef cattle declines. The remaining uses of wheat show a small positive trend. Total consumption is assumed to increase on trend at a rate of 0.6 million tonnes per annum.

EU exports

Potential exports of wheat are set equal to production plus imports minus food aid minus consumption. Imports are assumed equal to minimum access volumes and food aid is fixed at 1.5 million tonnes per annum. Actual exports are equal to potential either if potential exports are less than the UR-AA ceiling or if exports do not require a subsidy. Otherwise, exports are set equal to the ceiling and the excess over the ceiling is accumulated in public (intervention) stocks. Note that intervention stocks were negligible in 1996/97 – the base period of the model. Random shocks affect production in the EU and in the rest of the world and hence EU exports. Consequently, alternative outcomes for EU exports and the unit export refund can occur within a single year of the projection period depending upon the size and signs of these shocks.[5] Of central importance for policy analysis is the distinction between subsidized and unsubsidized exports. Therefore, the model calculates the probability that a unit refund is required for exports sold to the world market, that is, the probability that exports will be subsidized.

EU export price

The annual (calendar year) real price of US Hard Red Winter (HRW) No. 2 (nominal price deflated by the US wholesale price index) over the period from 1900 to 1995 was represented by an autoregressive integrated moving average (ARIMA) (0,1,2) model in logarithms, and with appropriate dummies (see Newbold *et al.*, 1997). Forecasts from the model suggest that the real price will decline at around 1.5% per annum over the period from 1997 to 2001. Converted to nominal prices, with an assumed 2% rate of wholesale price inflation, the forecasts indicate a price of US HRW of around \$170 per tonne for 2000/01. A cointegration analysis of wheat export prices found two cointegrating vectors relating the prices of US HRW, EU and Argentinian Trigo Pan wheats. One vector – HRW and Trigo Pan weakly exogenous to EU wheat[6] – mirrored the behaviour of the EU's Cereals Management Committee for pricing export refunds at open market export tenders – and the other vector established a simple relationship between the US and the Argentinian wheat prices with neither weakly exogenous (see Lloyd and Rayner, 1997). Solving these relationships suggests that for forecasting purposes the EU net export price could be set at around a \$25 per tonne discount to US HRW. Finally, a change in EU exports from the base-period volume is assumed to have a negative effect on the dollar price of exports, the parameter being −\$0.5 per million tonnes.

A time-series analysis of the logarithm of the monthly dollar–ecu exchange rate[7] over the period January 1980 to March 1987 indicated that the series was best represented by a random walk without drift. The random walk representation was subjected to the variance ratio test developed by Lo and MacKinlay (1989) and the random walk model was not rejected – for details, see Kellard *et al.* (1997). The random walk representation implies that changes in the exchange rate are unpredictable and that the forecast variance increases linearly with the forecast horizon. Whilst the current value of the exchange rate is the 'best' predictor in the short term, the exchange rate itself is essentially unpredictable in the long term. Consequently, whilst the optimum short-run forecast of the dollar–ecu exchange rate is the last value of the sample period (March 1997), it seemed reasonable to assess the implications of alternative exchange-rate values for the years 1997/98 to 2000/01. In the projection model, we use three alternative exchange rates, which are of potential policy interest in that they all lie within the band of values encompassed by the time-series history of the series. Specifically, the following alternative values of the ecu–dollar exchange rate are used in the projections: 0.88, which is the March 1997 rate; 0.82, which is the mean annual rate over the period 1987/98 to 1995/96; and 0.76, which is toward the lower band of the values taken over the 1990s. These rates convert the projected EU net export price of $145 per tonne into 128 ecu per tonne, 119 ecu per tonne and 110 ecu per tonne respectively.

Projections

Table 10.5 presents projections for EU-15 wheat (excluding durum) yield, area, production, consumption, potential exports and intervention stocks, with EU support prices and the prices of fertilizer and NCFIs held constant. The UR-AA ceiling commitments on subsidized wheat exports are also shown and the last row presents estimates of the probability that potential exports exceed the ceiling on subsidized exports. Table 10.6 presents the estimated probability that the unit refund will be positive in 2000/01 at each exchange rate, that is, the probability that subsidies will be required on EU exports in that year. The results from Tables 10.5 and 10.6 suggest a 90% probability that the EU's export quantity limit will be exceeded but only a 50% probability, for the central exchange rate, that export subsidies will be required in 2000/01.

Taken together, the projections for potential exports and the probability of export subsidization suggest that the EU will be on a knife-edge in respect of meeting its commitments on subsidized exports by 2000/01 without further policy adjustments. However, it is rather

Table 10.5. EU-15 wheat projections (excluding durum).

	1997/98	1998/99	1999/2000	2000/01
Yield (tonnes per ha)[a]	6.52	6.67	6.81	6.96
Area (million ha)	13.96	13.80	13.04	13.04
Production (million tonnes)[a]	91.07	92.02	88.85	90.73
Consumption (million tonnes)	72.6	73.2	73.8	74.4
Potential exports (million tonnes)[a]	18.87	19.62	16.25	17.82
UR-AA ceiling (million tonnes)	18.0	16.81	15.6	14.4
Intervention stocks (million tonnes)[a, b]	0.9	3.7	4.3	7.8
Probability that exports exceed UR-AA ceiling	0.62	0.84	0.58	0.90

[a] Mean value of random variable. [b] Assuming exports constrained to UR-AA ceiling.
Assumed set-aside rates: 1997/98, 5% arable (1% wheat); 1998/99, 10% arable (2.2% wheat); 1999/2000 and 2000/01, 15% arable (7.5% wheat).

Table10.6. EU-15 wheat: probability of export subsidy.

Dollar–ecu exchange rate	Probability of positive export refund
0.88	0.16
0.82	0.50
0.76	0.84

striking that there is an estimated 50% probability that export subsidies will not be required using the central exchange rate: this is a major change from the experience of the 1980s and early 1990s when subsidization was the norm. The reduction in the intervention price brought in by the 1992 reform package would appear to be the critical factor in bringing about this change. These conclusions are, of course, subject to the caveat that the results are dependent upon the model structure and parameters; of critical importance is the forecast for the EU export price, this being determined by the forecast for the price of US HRW wheat and the premium obtained by this wheat over EU wheat on the world market. Antle *et al.* discuss the issues involved in forecasting the price of wheat in Chapter 3 of this volume.

9. Further CAP Reform?

As has been documented elsewhere,[8] there are strong pressures for a continuation of the process of CAP reform: political and economic realities will require the development of and adjustments to the 1992 policy reform. The existence of the UR-AA disciplines and the prospect of the 1999 'mini-round' of agricultural negotiations are two such realities that impact on the agricultural policy process in the EU, as revealed in the Commission's 'agricultural strategy' paper published in November 1995 (EU Commission, 1995) and reiterated in the Commission's *Agenda 2000* paper published in July 1997 (EU Commission, 1997). Both papers deal with agricultural policy reform within a wider context: in the former, the major concern is the agricultural policy implications of enlargement of the Union to the east, whilst the latter presents proposals for the development of the EU and its policies into the next century, including its future financial framework and the impact of enlargement. Nevertheless, both papers incorporate a strategy for further CAP reform, in outline in the 'strategy' paper and in detail in the *Agenda 2000* paper. In essence, the Commission advocates a deepening and an extension of the 1992 reform through a further shift from price support to direct payments accompanied by the development of a coherent rural policy and enhanced agri-environmental payments.

Both papers stress the positive results of the 1992 reform in that market imbalances have declined and public stocks have been reduced. So, for example, 'In the case of cereals, set-aside has helped to keep production under control, while the increased price competitiveness has allowed significant additional quantities to be used on the domestic market, mainly for animal feed' (EU Commission, 1997, p. 27). It is noted that the CAP has been going through a period of relative stability since 1992, with the progressive implementation of the UR-AA commitments charting the way until the year 2000 (see, for example, EU Commission, 1995, p. 36). However, new challenges are foreseen that will determine the shape of the CAP at least until the end of the first decade of the 21st century. These include: (i) increasing market imbalances leading to non-exportable surpluses after 2000, taking into account UR-AA constraints for commodities such as cereals, beef, dairy products and sugar; (ii) the agenda for the 1999 WTO mini-round, in which the Commission expects to include further reductions in border protection and export subsidies and a reshaping of internal support toward more 'decoupled' payments; (iii) eastward enlargement expanding the agricultural area of the Union by 50% and the agricultural labour force by 100%; (iv) increased demands for the integration of environmental concerns into the CAP, including the provision of payment to farmers for the supply of environmental services; and (v) an increasing requirement that public support for agriculture be deemed to be economically sound and socially acceptable.

As far as the cereals sector is concerned, the Commission predicts that, without further reform, there will be a rising market imbalance which will be incompatible with the UR-AA commitments on subsidized export volumes from 2000/01 onwards. Specifically, with set-aside at 5% for 1996/97 and 1997/98 and then returned to its reference level of 17.5% for subsequent years, crop areas are expected to be stable from 1998/99 onwards but yields are predicted to increase at a faster rate than consumption. Tables 10.7 and 10.8 present the Commission projections for wheat and for total cereals respectively. After 2000, the current GATT commitments on subsidized exports are expected to constrain exports of both wheat and coarse grains, leading to a rapid rise in intervention stocks (some 58 million tonnes by 2005, of which wheat equals 45 million tonnes). The Commission considers the possibility of trying to contain this predicted rising surplus by increasing the set-aside rate gradually to over 20%. However, this option is rejected in favour of a bolder strategy of reducing internal prices to a 'safety-net' level, whereby the EU would hope to avoid the routine use of export subsidies. It would, thereby, be able to export in most years without reference to the UR-AA subsidized export volume constraint. In this context, it is noteworthy that the Commission puts its faith in analysts expecting that 'strong' world prices will prevail for cereals up to 2006 and even beyond (see EU Commission, 1997, p. 28). The specific Commission proposals contained in the *Agenda 2000* paper (EU Commission, 1997, p. 33) are:

- To reduce the cereals intervention price in one step in 2000 from 119.19 ecu per tonne to 95.35 ecu per tonne, that is, a price reduction of up to 23.84 ecu per tonne if world prices are below the intervention price.
- To increase compensation payments from 54 ecu per tonne to 66 ecu per tonne (multiplied by the regional cereals reference yields of the 1992 reform). This payment is to be lowered if market prices are higher than currently anticipated. Thus the maximum compensation is 12 ecu per tonne for the reduction in the intervention price so that producers could lose considerably if world prices are weak and the EU internal price falls to the new intervention price.
- To abolish compulsory set-aside by fixing the reference level at 0% whilst still permitting voluntary set-aside.

In addition, the Commission is to table a proposal 'enabling Member States to make the granting of direct payments for arable crops and set-aside conditional on the respect of environmental provisions, allowing them to be increasingly used to pursue environmental objectives' (EU Commission, 1997, p. 33).

At the time of writing, July 1997, the fate of the *Agenda 2000* proposals for CAP reform is unknown; they remain to be discussed by the Member States, the Council of Farm Ministers and the European Parliament. It is quite probable that the proposals will be 'watered down' but it is clear that reforms of this nature will have to be undertaken if the EU is to deal with current and prospective export subsidy volume constraints and enlargement to the east.

Table 10.7. EU Commission's forecast of EU-15 wheat market balances (million tonnes, including durum).

	1996/97	1997/98	1998/99	1999/2000	2000/01	2001/02	2002/03	2003/04	2004/05	2005/06
Production	98	100	99	102	104	107	109	111	113	116
Consumption	81	83	83	84	85	87	88	89	90	91
Imports	1	2	2	2	2	2	2	2	2	2
Exports	19	20	18	17	16	16	16	16	16	16
Closing stocks	9	8	8	10	15	21	28	36	46	56
Intervention stocks	0	0	0	0	5	11	17	25	35	46

All figures rounded to nearest million tonnes.
Source: HGCA, 1997b.

Table 10.8. EU Commission's forecast of EU-15 cereals market balances (million tonnes).

	1996/97	1997/98	1998/99	1999/2000	2000/01	2001/02	2002/03	2003/04	2004/05	2005/06
Production	201	201	192	195	198	201	204	207	210	213
Consumption	170	171	172	172	173	174	175	176	177	178
Imports	4	5	5	5	5	5	5	5	5	5
Exports	31	32	30	28	26	26	26	26	26	26
Closing stocks	27	30	25	25	29	35	43	53	65	79
Intervention stocks	5	11	7	5	8	14	22	32	44	58

All figures rounded to nearest million tonnes.
Source: HGCA, 1997b.

It is of interest to note the parallels in recent policy reform in the USA under the 1996 Federal Agricultural Improvement and Reform (FAIR) Act. This Act sets the course of agricultural policy for 1996 to 2002. Its main feature is the:

> removal of the link between income support payments and farm prices by providing for seven annual fixed but declining production flexibility contract payments whereby participating producers may receive government payments largely independent of farm prices, in contrast to the past when deficiency payments were dependent on farm prices.
> (USDA, 1996, p. 1).

These contract payments are similar to the EU compensation payments in that they are related to a fixed base acreage and to historic yield, but US producers, unlike EU producers, do not have to plant anything in the current period to qualify for payments. Thus US payments are completely decoupled from production whilst EU payments are only partially decoupled. The Act also eliminated the annual acreage idling programmes that are akin to set-aside in the EU. Finally, the Act retains non-recourse commodity loans, which provide 'safety-net' price floors; loan rates are set at 85% of the preceding 5-year average, excluding high- and low-price years. Maximum loan rates are set at 1995 levels of $2.58 per bushel for wheat and $1.89 per bushel for maize – equivalent to $95 per tonne and $74 per tonne, respectively. These US safety-net prices are somewhat lower than the proposed EU price of 95 ecu per tonne for all cereals when viewed in the context of an ecu–dollar exchange rate that has varied between 0.7 and 0.9 ecu per dollar in the past 10 years.

10. Conclusion

The EU emerged as a major wheat exporter in the 1980s, a position it secured by heavy export subsidization and a costly stock-holding policy. Although the CAP was operated without regard to the rest of the world, both external and internal forces were exerting pressures for reform in this period. There was pressure from third-country exporters who wanted an end to subsidized competition on third markets and improved import access. There was also pressure from within to contain the mounting budgetary costs of support for cereals production. In the 1985 *Perspectives* paper, the EU Commission recognized that the CAP could not remain insulated for ever from world market forces. However, reform was a long time coming and it was only under the pressures of the UR negotiations that changes were made to the CAP in order that a deal on agriculture could be reached between the EU and competing exporters, principally the USA.

The 1992 CAP reform instigated a limited shift from price support to direct payments only partially decoupled from production and only for a restricted range of commodities, principally cereals. Nevertheless, it allowed the EU to sign up to and abide by the new international trading rules established by the UR Agreement. As a result, the EU became a more responsible and less aggressive wheat exporter, a position helped by the strengthening of the world market in recent years.

While the 1992 reform to the EU's cereals policy was instrumental in securing a UR Agreement on agriculture, it is clear that further reform is required if the EU is to cope with new challenges. These include the inevitability of further international disciplines on export subsidies, enlargement to the east, and possible opposition in the forthcoming WTO mini-round to the exclusion of its compensation payments from obligations on domestic support reduction. The recent proposals made in the *Agenda 2000* paper represent a significant, if partial, policy response to these challenges. If the proposals are enacted then the EU will take another step along the road toward a liberal market policy for wheat and other cereals.

Notes

1. This section and the following two sections draw on Ingersent *et al.* (1994, 1995), OECD (1995), Swinbank (1996), Tangermann (1996, 1998) and Thomson (1998).
2. The EU had sought from the outset of the Round to obtain agreement to raise import barriers for oilseeds and 'cereal substitutes' as a quid pro quo for reducing protection on other commodities, especially cereals. The demand for 'rebalancing' protection was opposed by exporting countries and was finally dropped from the negotiations in the final stages of the Round. Blair House I merely allows the issue to be reconsidered if imports of non-grain feeds into the EU rise appreciably.
3. Another exemption to the 'bound tariff' principle was added at the insistence of Japan and Korea under the so-called 'rice clause', whereby these countries were allowed to postpone the tariffication of rice imports until the end of the implementation period.
4. A direct quantitative comparison is not presented since the models do not all have the same coverage: the models differ in terms of the inclusion/exclusion of the former East Germany and in the inclusion/exclusion of intervention stocks. A comparison of CAP reform models is also contained in Meyers *et al.* (1998), but this study does not evaluate the compatibility of CAP reform with the UR-AA commitments.
5. The variance of EU exports is equal to the variance of yield multiplied by area squared. The variance of rest-of-the-world imports is set at 20 times the variance of EU exports; this figure is based upon an analysis by Willis (1994) of yield variances and harvested areas in various regions of the world.

6. This analysis also found the price of US Soft Red Winter (SRW) to be cointegrated with the price of US Hard Red Winter (HRW) in a bivariate relationship with US HRW price weakly exogenous to the SRW price.
7. Close-of-day price on the 15th of each month.
8. See, for example, various chapters in Ingersent *et al.* (1998).

References

Box, G.E.P. and Tidwell, P. (1962) Transformation of the independent variables. *Technometrics* 2, 531–550.

De Zeeuw, A. (1996) *International Trade Negotiations under GATT/WTO Experiences: Future Challenges and Possible Outcomes.* The European Association of Agricultural Economists, VIII Triennial Congress, Edinburgh, UK.

EC Commission (1985) *Perspectives for the Common Agricultural Policy.* COM (85)333, EC Commission, Brussels, Belgium.

EC Commission (1992) *Agriculture in the GATT Negotiations and the Reform of the CAP.* SEC (1992) 2267 final, EC Commission, Brussels, Belgium.

EU Commission (1995) *Study on Alternative Strategies for the Development of Relations in the Field of Agriculture between the EU and the Associated Countries with a View to Future Accession of these Countries.* EU Commission, Brussels, Belgium.

EU Commission (1997) *Agenda 2000 – Volume 1 – Communication: For a Stronger and Wider Union.* Doc/97/6, EU Commission, Strasbourg, France.

Folmer, C., Keyser, M.A., Merbis, M.D., Stolwijk, H.J.J. and Veenedaal, P.J.J. (1993) *CAP Reform and Its Differential Impact on Member States.* Research Memo No. 105, Central Planning Bureau, The Hague, The Netherlands.

Guyomard, H., Mahé, L.P. and Roe, T. (1992) *The EC and US Agricultural Conflict and the GATT Round: Petty Multilateralism?* European Association of Agricultural Economists, 31st European Seminar, Frankfurt, Germany.

Helmar, M.D., Meyers, W.H. and Hayes, D.D. (1993) *GATT and CAP Reform: Different, Similar or Redundant?* Center for Agricultural and Rural Development (CARD), Iowa State University, Ames, Iowa, USA.

HGCA (Home Grown Cereals Authority) (1996) GATT provisions for the EU cereal market. *Market Information Supplement* 31, issue 22 (4).

HGCA (Home Grown Cereals Authority) (1997a) EU cereal supply and demand. *Weekly Digest* 23, issue 33.

HGCA (Home Grown Cereals Authority) (1997b) Summary of Commission's 'Long-term Prospects' paper. *Weekly Digest* 23, issue 43.

Ingersent, K.A., Rayner, A.J. and Hine, R.C. (eds) (1994) *Agriculture in the Uruguay Round.* Macmillan, London, UK.

Ingersent, K.A., Rayner, A.J. and Hine, R.C. (1995) Ex-post evaluation of the Uruguay Round Agricultural Agreement. *The World Economy* 18, 707–728.

Ingersent, K.A., Rayner, A.J. and Hine, R.C. (eds) (1998) *The Reform of the Common Agricultural Policy.* Macmillan, London, UK.

International Grains Council (IGC) (1996) *World Grain Statistics 1995/6.* IGC, London, UK.

Josling, T.E. (1993) Agricultural trade issues in transatlantic trade relations. *The World Economy* 13, 553–574.

Josling, T.E. and Tangermann, S. (1992) *MacSharry or Dunkel: Which Plan will Reform the GATT?* IATRC Working Paper No. 92–10, Food Research Institute, Stanford University, Stanford, California, USA.

Josling, T.E., Tangermann, S. and Warley, T.K. (eds) (1996) *Agriculture in the GATT.* Macmillan, London, UK.

Kellard, N., Newbold, P., Rayner, A.J. and Ennew, C.T. (1997) *The $/ECU Rate as Random Walk.* Discussion Paper No. 97/8, Department of Economics, University of Nottingham, Nottingham, UK.

Lloyd, T.E. and Rayner, A.J. (1997) *A Cointegration Analysis of Price Relationships on the World Wheat Market.* Discussion Paper No. 97/9, Department of Economics, University of Nottingham, Nottingham, UK.

Lo, A.W. and MacKinlay, A.C. (1989) Variance ratio tests in finite samples. *Journal of Econometrics* 40, 203–238.

MAFF (Ministry of Agriculture, Fisheries and Food) (1994) *The GATT Uruguay Round Agreement for Agriculture and the Implications for EU Agriculture.* Ministry of Agriculture, Fisheries and Food, London, UK.

Meyers, W.H., Helmar, M.D. and Hart, C.E. (1998) Modelling the outcomes of Common Agricultural Policy reform. In: Ingersent, K.A., Rayner, A.J. and Hine, R.C. (eds) *The Reform of the Common Agricultural Policy.* Macmillan, London, UK.

Newbold, P., Rayner, A.J., Kellard, N. and Ennew, C.T. (1997) *Long-run Price Behaviour of Wheat and Maize: Trend Stationarity or Difference Stationarity?* Discussion Paper No. 97/7, Department of Economics, University of Nottingham, Nottingham, UK.

OECD (Organization for Economic Cooperation and Development) (1995) *The Uruguay Round: A Preliminary Evaluation of the Impacts of the Agreement on Agriculture in the OECD Countries.* OECD, Paris, France.

Rayner, A.J., Ingersent, K.A., Hine, R.C. and Ackrill, R.W. (1995) Does the CAP fit the GATT? Cereals and the Uruguay Round. *Oxford Agrarian Studies* 23, 117–132.

Swinbank, A. (1996) Capping the CAP? *Food Policy* 21, 393–407.

Tangermann, S. (1994) *An Assessment of the Uruguay Round Agreement on Agriculture.* Paper prepared for the OECD, Stanford University, Stanford, California, USA.

Tangermann, S. (1996) Implementation of the Uruguay Round Agricultural Agreement: issues and prospects. *Journal of Agricultural Economics* 47, 315–337.

Tangermann, S. (1998) An ex-post review of the 1992 MacSharry Reform. In: Ingersent, K.A., Rayner, A.J. and Hine, R.C. (eds) *The Reform of the Common Agricultural Policy.* Macmillan, London, UK.

Thomson, K. (1998) The Common Agricultural Policy and the World Trade Organisation after the Uruguay Round Agricultural Agreement. In: Ingersent, K.A., Rayner, A.J. and Hine, R.C. (eds) *The Reform of the Common Agricultural Policy.* Macmillan, London, UK.

USDA (US Department of Agriculture) (1996) *Provisions of the 1996 Farm Bill.* Agricultural Outlook, Special Supplement, USDA/Economic Research Service, US Government Printing Office, Washington DC, USA.

Willis, R.M. (1994) Agriculture in the 1990s: implications for international trade in grains. Unpublished MPhil thesis, University of Nottingham.

11

State Trading Companies, Time Inconsistency, Imperfect Enforceability and Reputation

Tigran A. Melkonian[1] and Stanley R. Johnson[2]

[1]*Center for Agricultural and Rural Development (CARD), Department of Economics, Iowa State University, Ames, USA;* [2]*Extension Administration, Department of Economics, Iowa State University, Ames, USA*

1. Introduction

Strategic trade in international markets is important for agricultural and other basic commodities. Distribution systems for these commodities are dominated by agents that have the potential for exclusive monopoly power. State trading companies (STCs) and large private firms control most of the trade volume. For agriculture in particular, the seasonal nature of the production process compared with a relatively constant demand for the commodities also brings into play concepts of timing in trade contracting, and time-inconsistent behaviour.

Melkonian and Johnson (1996) have explored a model in which an STC, which has a monopsony power, cannot credibly commit to a particular policy or contract. An annual trading cycle was considered. In the sequence of economic decisions, the STC moves first and announces a planned level of import. Producers in the exporting countries make their decisions on the allocation of the more fixed inputs (e.g. land) based on related price expectations. However, before decisions on the allocation of the more variable inputs (e.g. labour or fertilizer) by the producers in foreign countries are made, the STC has the opportunity to revise the announced level of imports. Then, the labour or variable-input allocation decisions of the producers in the exporting countries are made, given the revised (and predetermined) level of imports and the previous allocation of the more fixed inputs (e.g. land). Finally, trade takes place.

A standard monopsony argument can be used to obtain the optimal level of import, if the STC can commit itself to the announced import level. But, when the STC cannot be held to the precommitted or the *ex ante* optimal level of import, it has an incentive to set a lower *ex post* level, once the land allocation decision has been made (the STC will face an *ex post* supply that is less elastic than the *ex ante* supply). In standard terminology, the *ex ante* optimal level of import is not time consistent. If foreign producers are assumed to know the rule used in setting *ex post* level of import, they will use this information when making their land allocation decisions. We showed that both the importer (STC) and the exporting countries are worse off as a result of inability of the importer to precommit to the optimal level of import. We also showed that if forward contracts are introduced, then the *ex ante* optimal level of import can be supported as a time-consistent equilibrium.

In this chapter, we use a standard game-theoretic formulation to model the strategic behaviour described above and to explain apparent anomalies in trade performance. The same game-theoretic formulations can be used to examine the impact of mechanisms that have potential for dealing with time inconsistency. In particular, precommitment penalties that might be enforced by bonding or other types of trade management systems are evaluated. These mechanisms can result in Pareto superior trade (and investment) patterns. An alternative is to consider the trading strategies in a sequential game context. The implications of signalling and reputation effects are at issue in this sequential or multi-stage trading context. This formulation opens the possibility of behaviour that avoids the suboptimal elements of the single-period game. Also, the strategies that emerge suggest alternative mechanisms that dominate the unregulated outcomes for the simple sequential game, even if they involve contracts that are imperfectly enforceable.

2. The Perfect Information Game

We consider a sequential game between two players. The game has three periods. In the first period, player 1 (the STC) announces the policy she intends to implement in the third period. That is, player 1 makes one of two announcements: 'benevolent' or 'non-benevolent'. This announcement becomes known to player 2 (the STC's trading partner). After either of the two announcements is made, players 1 and 2 play the game depicted in Fig. 11.1 (numbers at the decision nodes in the game tree represent the player whose turn it is to move; the first of the pair of numbers at terminal nodes represents pay-off of player 1, and the second the pay-off of player 2). As will be clear, the 'cheap talk' of player 1 does not affect the future strategic interaction between the players.

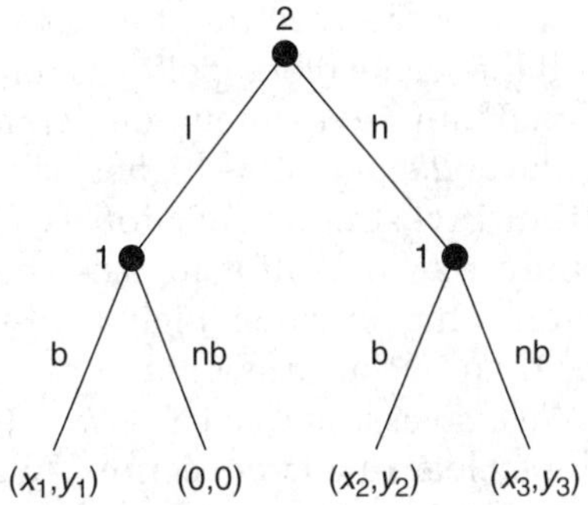

Fig. 11.1. Investment choice – policy implementation sequence.

Specifically, in the subgame following player 1's initial announcement, player 2 moves and chooses one of two levels of investment, 'high' or 'low' (in Fig. 11.1, h and l respectively). After observing the level of investment, player 1 makes her choice of policy to be implemented: 'benevolent' or 'non-benevolent' (b and nb respectively, in Fig. 11.1). The complete (with the policy announcement) game form and the pay-offs to the players, depending on the history of the game, are shown in Fig. 11.2. Note that the two proper subgames starting at the nodes where it is player 2's turn to move are equivalent (the game forms and the pay-offs are the same). This reflects the non-credible cheap talk announcement of player 1.

Now, consider in more detail pay-offs to the players for different strategy profiles. For both of the possible levels of investment selected by player 2, player 1's pay-off is higher if she chooses to implement 'non-benevolent' compared with the 'benevolent' policy; $x_1 < 0$ and $x_2 < x_3$.

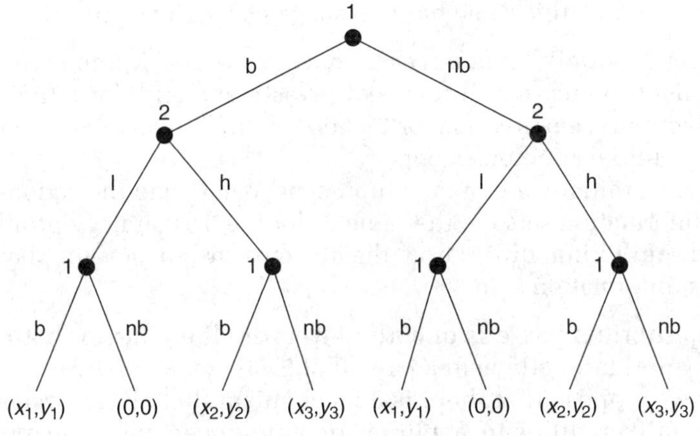

Fig. 11.2. The basic model.

In contrast, player 2's pay-off, given that the investment decision has been made, is higher if the 'benevolent' policy is implemented by player 1; $y_1 > 0$ and $y_2 > y_3$. If an investment decision is followed by a 'benevolent' policy, player 2's pay-off is higher when he chooses 'high'; $y_2 > y_1$. However, if an investment decision is followed by a 'non-benevolent' policy, player 2's pay-off is higher when he chooses 'low'; $y_3 < 0$. Player 1's pay-off is higher when 'high' investment is followed by a 'benevolent' policy than in the case when 'low' is followed by 'non-benevolent'; $x_2 > 0$. We also assume that $x_3 + x_1 > 0$ (the importance of this assumption will be clear in a later section). With this assumption, the sign restrictions on the pay-offs can be easily summarized: $x_1 < 0$, $0 < x_2 < x_3$, and $x_3 + x_1 > 0$; $y_3 < 0$ and $0 < y_1 < y_2$.

Consider either of the two proper subgames following the initial policy announcement, i.e. the game depicted in Fig. 11.1. If player 2 chooses 'low', player 1 chooses between x_1 if she plays 'benevolent' and 0 if she plays 'non-benevolent'. Thus, obviously player 1 will play 'non-benevolent'. The same reasoning leads us to conclude that when 'high' investment is chosen by player 2, 'non-benevolent' policy will be implemented (in that case, player 1 chooses between x_2 and x_3). That is, 'non-benevolent' is the *ex post* (after the investment decision) optimal policy. Anticipating that either level of investment will be followed by implementation of 'non-benevolent' policy, player 2, when making his investment decision, chooses between 0 if he plays 'low' and y_3 if he plays 'high'. Obviously, he will choose the 'low' investment. When making her initial announcement, player 1, anticipating that she and her opponent will play optimally at later nodes, chooses between 0 if she announces 'benevolent' and 0 if 'non-benevolent', and she is indifferent between the two.

The argument presented is just a simple application of backward induction to the solution of a game of perfect information.[1, 2] Thus, we have shown that this game has two subgame perfect equilibria:

1. Player 1 initially announces 'benevolence' and implements 'non-benevolent' policy for all levels of investment, and, for either of the initial announcements, player 2 chooses 'low' investment no matter what the initial announcement.
2. Player 1 initially announces 'non-benevolent', and the actions at all other information sets are the same as for the first strategy profile (the second equilibrium differs from the first only by the move of player 1 at her first information set).

The equilibrium pay-offs of both players are the same for both of the strategy profiles. Both yield a pay-off of 0.

Now, suppose that there is a mechanism that allows player 1 to precommit credibly to a policy or announcement. One possible mechanism can be described as follows: suppose that before the game is played player 1 signs a perfectly enforceable (binding) agreement saying that she is going to burn c ($c > x_3$) units of money if she does not implement the announced policy. The tree for this game is presented in Fig. 11.3. Note that the game form is unchanged and only the pay-offs to player 1 at the terminal nodes, corresponding to histories where the announced and implemented policies differ, have been modified. There is also another interpretation of the extensive-form game presented in Fig. 11.3. Suppose that player 1 is known for sure to be a 'commitment' (or an 'honest') type, that is, a player who gets a very high negative pay-off (c) from reneging on her announcement in the first period. In other words, player 1 incurs a very high cost for being inconsistent.

Now, we solve the game with this commitment mechanism. Consider the proper subgame starting with the node following player 1's initial announcement of 'benevolence'. If player 2 chooses 'low', player 1 chooses between x_1 if she plays 'benevolent' and $(0 - c)$ if she plays 'non-benevolent'. Thus, obviously player 1 will choose 'benevolent'. The same reasoning leads us to conclude that 'benevolent' policy will be implemented by player 1 when 'high' investment is chosen by player 2 (in this case, player 1 would choose between x_2 and $(x_3 - c)$). Hence, when player 2 makes his investment decision after the announcement of 'benevolence' and anticipates the above-characterized response (implementation of the 'benevolent' policy), he chooses between y_1 if he chooses 'low' and y_2 if he chooses 'high'. Surely, he will choose 'high' investment.

Applying the same reasoning (backward induction) to the proper subgame starting with the node following a 'non-benevolent' announcement, we find that in the subgame either investment decision will be followed by the implementation of the 'non-benevolent' policy and

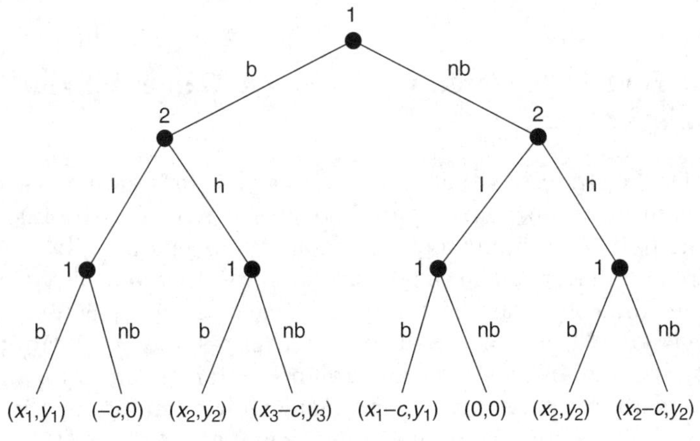

Fig. 11.3. The game with a perfectly enforceable commitment mechanism.

player 1 (anticipating a 'non-benevolent' response) will choose 'low' investment. Thus, rolling back the pay-offs of the players (when the strategies obtained by backward induction are followed) to the nodes that follow initial announcement, we see that player 1 chooses between x_2 if she chooses a 'benevolent' announcement and 0 if she chooses 'non-benevolent', and hence she will choose 'benevolent'. Thus, we have shown that this game has a unique subgame perfect equilibrium where player 1 announces 'benevolent' in period 1, and at the node following a particular announcement she implements the policy that was announced, and player 2 chooses 'high' if 'benevolent' was announced and 'low' if 'non-benevolent'. The subgame perfect equilibrium pay-offs to the players are (x_2, y_2).

We could consider a yet larger game where player 1 chooses in period 0 whether to play the game described in Fig. 11.2 or the game of Fig. 11.3 (the first interpretation (burning money) will be chosen for Fig. 11.2, since it is not sensible to assume that players choose to be honest or not) and that decision is made known to player 1. In this game player 1 will choose the game with the precommitment mechanism. There are two subgame perfect equilibria of this game: player 1 in period 0 chooses to play the game with the commitment mechanism and the choices of both players after the choice in period 0 are exactly the same as the equilibrium strategy profiles of players 1 and 2 for the games presented in Figs 11.2 and 11.3.

The multiplicity of equilibria arises from the fact that the proper subgame following the choice of player 1 not to choose the commitment mechanism has two subgame perfect equilibria (as described above). The pay-offs for both the equilibria described are (x_2, y_2). Thus, if player 1 has an option of a commitment mechanism, she will use that option and the pay-offs of both players are higher in the game when this option is available ($x_2 > 0$, $y_2 > 0$) as compared to the case when it is not.

3. The Finitely Repeated Version of the Game Without Commitment

Consider the strategic situation when player 1 does not have access to the commitment mechanism and there are finitely many trading cycles after the policy announcement is made. Again, there are two players: player 1 and player 2. The game has N+1 stages (N is a positive integer). We index time backwards, i.e. the first stage of the game is N+1, second N, and so on. At the stage N+1, player 1 makes one of two announcements; 'benevolent' or 'non-benevolent'. After the announcement is made and observed by player 2, the game depicted in Fig. 11.1 is played N times. We assume that the announcement in stage N+1 is noncredible in the sense that it does not affect the moves available to the players and the pay-offs for each strategy profile (the two proper subgames, following the announcement, are exactly the same).

The sign restrictions for different strategy profiles are the same as in the previous section.[3] The pay-offs of players 1 and 2 are the sums (undiscounted) of their respective pay-offs in the stages of the game. This is a finite game with perfect information, which again can be solved by application of backward induction. First, let us conjecture how the game might progress. We might expect that player 1 will announce 'benevolent' in stage $N+1$, and then will implement 'benevolent' policy no matter what the level of investment, to convince player 2 that she is honest (committed to her announcement) and that she will continue to implement the announced policy. In other words, player 1 will try to establish a reputation for being a 'commitment' type. Observing this kind of choice by player 1, player 2 will become convinced that player 1 will keep to the announced policy ('benevolent') and will choose 'high' investment level. Thus, we would expect 'benevolent' policy to be implemented and 'high' investment for player 2 in the first stages of the game. However, we also expect that this kind of behaviour will not be observable at very late stages in the game, since later in the game there is not much benefit from demonstrating commitment (the reputation value is low). That is, we would expect 'non-benevolent' policies to be implemented at later stages of the game. Though the behaviour we have just described seems likely to develop and is very intuitive, the game-theoretic prediction discards it.

To solve for the subgame perfect equilibrium, consider a proper subgame starting with the node following either of the two announcements. Within that subgame consider the last stage. In this stage, player 1 will implement the 'non-benevolent' policy for both levels of investment by player 2, since there are no gains left to maintaining her reputation. Anticipating this response, player 2 will choose 'low' investment. In the next to the last stage, player 1 will implement a 'non-benevolent' policy whatever the level of investment, since it is more beneficial in the short run and does not affect the play in the last stage. Anticipating this, player 2 will choose 'low' investment in the next to last stage. Carrying this argument to the beginning of the subgame, we find that player 2 chooses 'low' investment in all stages, and player 1 always implements the 'non-benevolent' policy. Again, as in section 2, the game has two subgame perfect equilibria, which differ only by the initial announcement and have 'low' investment and 'non-benevolent' policy implementation for each possible history. The outcomes for both equilibrium strategy profiles are (0,0).

Now, suppose we consider the game that consists of K stages (K is a finite positive integer), where each stage is exactly the game described above (announcement of a policy followed by N repetitions of the game in Fig. 11.1). Again, we reach the conclusion that the subgame perfect equilibria will have 'low' investment and 'non-benevolent' policies implemented for all information sets (recall that all information sets are singletons in this game). Thus, even in the case when there are multiple (and finite) subperiods of announcements followed by investment choice-implementation sequences, the reputation effect does not 'come alive'.

In summary, we showed that, although it is intuitive and plausible for player 1 to try to maintain a reputation for being a 'commitment' type by implementing the policy announced to persuade player 2 to make a 'high' investment, in none of the subgame perfect equilibria is this an optimal strategy.

4. Imperfect Enforceability, Pooling and Reputation Effects

In section 2 it has been shown that, for the basic game, if there is an option of a commitment mechanism that is also perfectly enforceable then 'high' investment is chosen and the *ex ante* optimal policy is implemented. This results in pay-off increase for both players. In section 3, we turned to the case when the trading game is repeated finitely many times, but with the commitment mechanism absent. We showed that, no matter how many (finite) times the game is to be played, reputation effects do not come alive and the pay-offs to the players are the same as in the one-period version of the game (0,0).

In this section we investigate a model with an imperfectly enforceable commitment mechanism. As before, the commitment mechanism obliges the party (player 1) reneging on the announcement to pay a penalty of c.

First, consider the game where announcement of the policy is made followed by N repetitions of the investment choice-implementation sequence. As previously, we assume that the game has two players. Before the game is played, player 1 makes a contract with the third party that obliges her to implement the announced policy. The information on whether the commitment contract is going to be honoured is, however, the private information of player 1. That is, the commitment contract with the third party is 'imperfectly enforceable'. We assume that player 2 has a prior probability belief ρ that player 1's pay-offs are the same as in Fig. 11.3 each time she reneges on her announcement. That is, ρ is the probability of player 1's being a 'commitment' type. With probability $(1 - \rho)$ player 1's pay-offs are as in Fig. 11.2. That is, $(1 - \rho)$ is the probability of player 1 being a 'non-commitment' type, for whom the policy announcement is cheap talk (for a 'non-commitment' type it does not cost anything to renege on the announced policy). In other words, player 2 is uncertain about player 1's cost of reneging on her announcement. This is a game of incomplete information (Harsanyi, 1967–1968), which can be transformed into a game of imperfect information where nature moves first and chooses player 1's pay-off structure, player 1 observes nature's move but player 2 does not. The game when there is only one investment choice-policy implementation stage is depicted in Fig. 11.4. We denote by θ_c the 'commitment'-type player 1, and by θ_N the 'non-commitment' type.

We first analyse the game depicted in Fig. 11.4 and then move on to solve the case of an arbitrary number (finite) of investment choice-policy implementation stages. Note that for the 'commitment' type it is a strictly dominated strategy to renege on the announcement made in the first stage. Thus, we can eliminate the strategies where the 'commitment' type implements policy different from the one announced as possibilities for equilibrium behaviour. Given an initial announcement and either investment level, implementation of the 'non-benevolent' policy is optimal for the 'non-commitment' type (by application of backward induction). In other words, it is a strictly dominated strategy for the non-commitment type to implement a 'benevolent' policy at any information set. Eliminating the strictly dominated strategies for different player 1 types, it is easy to show that the best response for player 2 at the information set following a 'non-benevolent' announcement is to choose 'low' investment for any beliefs about the type of player 1 (the 'commitment' type implements the policy announced, and the 'non-commitment' type always implements 'non-benevolent' policy).

Thus, the choice of the 'low' investment after the announcement of the 'non-benevolent' policy is justified. Given these rounds of elimination of the strictly dominated strategies, the strategies in which the 'non-commitment' type of player 1 announces the 'non-benevolent' policy are weakly dominated by the strategy where she announces the

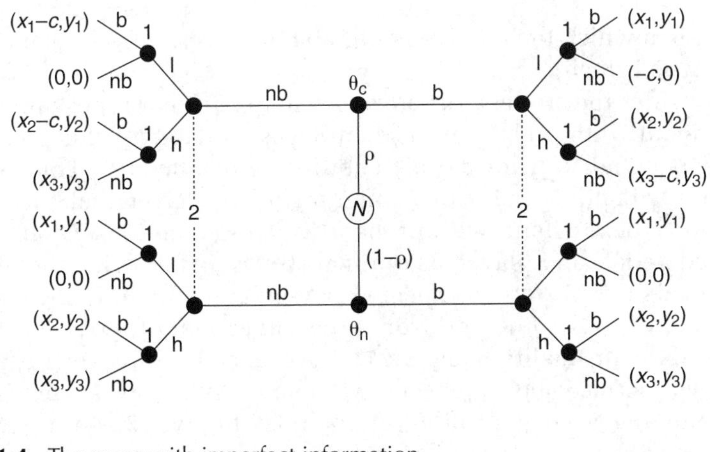

Fig. 11.4. The game with imperfect information.

'benevolent' and implements the 'non-benevolent' policy for either investment level. To eliminate weakly dominated strategies, we invoke Kohlberg and Mertens' (1986) requirement that the equilibria set be stable. Elimination of weakly dominated strategies corresponds to setting their admissibility condition. The above-described elimination of dominated strategies has allowed us to reduce the set of possible modes of behaviour for the two players. Now, we can move on to finding the Nash equilibria of the game in Fig. 11.4.

Note that, no matter what the value of ρ in the interval (0,1), the following strategy profile is a Nash equilibrium of the game in Fig. 11.4:

1. The 'commitment' type of player 1 announces 'non-benevolent' policy and at the information sets following a particular announcement implements that promise; the 'non-commitment' type announces 'benevolent' policy and implements 'non-benevolent' policy given either level of investment and either announcement.
2. Player 2 chooses 'low' investment following either announcement by player 1.

It is easy to note that the equilibrium just described is sequential if we specify beliefs at the two information sets of player 2 using Bayes' law to update prior beliefs, given player 1's equilibrium strategy. We denote this equilibrium by (*). Using the terminology of signalling games, this equilibrium is separating in the sense that the signal (the announcement) sent by player 1 in the first stage reveals her type. This equilibrium set (singleton) is also stable. To find all possible equilibria, we consider two possible cases differentiated by the magnitude of ρ and relative values of player 2's pay-offs for different strategy profiles:

$$\rho \geq \frac{-y_3}{y_2 - y_1 - y_3} \tag{11.1}$$

(the case in which the relative likelihood of player 1's being a 'commitment' type is high).

Consider the strategy of player 1 where both her types announce 'benevolent' with probability 1: then Bayes' updating yields posterior, which is equal to prior beliefs about type of player 1. That is, the probability that player 1 is of 'commitment' type, given that both types announce 'benevolent' with probability 1, is equal to ρ. Then, given updated beliefs and player 1's optimal strategies following the investment decision, player 2's expected pay-off from 'high' investment is equal to $\rho y_2 + (1 - \rho)y_3$ and from 'low' investment to $\rho y_1 + (1 - \rho)0$. Hence, if the inequality Equation 11.1 is satisfied and player 1 uses the strategy described above, player 2 will choose 'high' investment. Thus, the following strategy profiles and beliefs of player 2 about player 1 constitute a sequential equilibrium (also stable as a set):

1. Both player 1 types announce 'benevolent' policy in the first stage: at the information sets following a particular announcement the 'commitment' type of player 1 implements the announced policy (implementation of 'benevolent' policy after announcement of 'benevolence', and similarly for 'non-benevolent' policy); the 'non-commitment' type chooses to implement 'non-benevolent' strategy at all of her information sets.
2. Player 2 chooses 'low' investment at the information set following a 'non-benevolent' announcement, and chooses 'high' investment at the information set following a 'benevolent' announcement.
3. At the information set following the 'benevolent' announcement, the probability (posterior) that player 1 is of 'commitment' type is equal to the prior ρ (Bayesian updating is invoked using the equilibrium strategy of player 1); at the information set following the 'non-benevolent' announcement the posterior probability that player 1 is of 'commitment' type is equal to q, where q is any real number in the segment [0,1].

It is easy to observe that the (strategy profile, beliefs) pair is consistent and sequentially rational (requirements of a sequential equilibrium). This is a pooling equilibrium in the sense that both player 1 types choose to send the same signal (announcement of 'benevolence'). The equilibrium pay-offs of the 'non-commitment' type of player 1 and of player 2 are x_3 and $\rho y_2 + (1 - \rho)y_3$ respectively. Pay-offs of both players are higher than in the case when player 1 does not have a reputation for being a 'commitment' type (that is, when $\rho = 0$).

Recall that for the values of ρ satisfying inequality Equation 11.1 the (strategy profile, beliefs) pair (*) also represents a sequential equilibrium, but the outcome pay-offs of both players for this equilibrium are Pareto-dominated by the equilibrium pay-offs for the just-described pooling equilibrium. We use the coalition-proof Nash equilibrium[4] concept of Bernheim *et al.* (1987) to discard the equilibrium (*). We argue that the pooling equilibrium is more likely to be played than the separating one, because if preplay communication were possible then both players would have an incentive to agree to play the pooling equilibrium (which is a self-enforcing mode of behaviour).

When the initial reputation for credibility is low:

$$\rho < \frac{-y_3}{y_2 - y_1 - y_3} \qquad 11.2$$

The only sequential equilibrium, which also survives the elimination of dominated (strictly as well as weakly) strategies, is separating where the 'non-commitment' type chooses the 'benevolent' announcement and the 'commitment' type chooses the 'non-benevolent' announcement (that is, equilibrium (*)). The equilibrium pay-offs of both player 1 types and player 2 are equal to zero, i.e. they are the same as in the case when player does not have a reputation for being a 'commitment' type.

Our conclusions can be easily summarized: for the game where there is only one investment choice-policy implementation stage after the policy announcement, and if the prior probability of player 1 being a 'commitment' type is not sufficiently large, the resulting equilibrium is the one where the different player 1 types separate in the first stage (announcing different policies) and the equilibrium pay-offs of both players are equal to zero (the same as when there is no reputation for being a 'commitment' type). When the reputation of being a 'commitment' type is sufficiently large, the pooling equilibrium is the only one that survives all the criteria that we have imposed and the pay-offs of both players are higher than in the case where reputation is absent.

Now, we consider a more general game in that we allow the announcement stage to be followed by an arbitrary but finite number of investment choice-policy implementation stages. Again, there are two players in the game: player 1 and player 2. The game has $N+1$ stages (N is a positive integer). As previously, we index time backwards. Again, the first stage of the game is $N+1$, the second N, etc. At the stage $N+1$ player 1 makes one of two announcements: 'benevolent' or 'non-benevolent'. After the announcement is made and observed by player 2, the investment choice-policy implementation game form is played N times. But, in contrast to the game described in the third section, player 2 is uncertain about the pay-offs of player 1, and holds a prior probability ρ that player 1 incurs a cost each time she (player 1) reneges on the announcement (her pay-offs are as in Fig. 11.3). With probability $(1 - \rho)$ the pay-offs of player 1 for each stage of the game are those given in Fig. 11.2. That is, $(1 - \rho)$ is the probability of player 1 being a 'non-commitment' type. The pay-offs of players 1 and 2 are the expected sums (undiscounted) of their respective pay-offs in the stages of the game. In the following we will be interested in the pay-offs for the 'non-commitment' type of player 1 and the pay-offs of player 2.

Before trying to determine how this game will be played, note that the 'commitment' type of player 1 will implement the announced policy along each equilibrium path of this game. That is, there are two possibilities for the 'commitment' type's behaviour in equilibrium: announce and then in all stages implement 'benevolent' policy, or announce and then in all stages execute 'non-benevolent' policy. Note that our model differs from other reputation models since we allow the type, whose reputation is to be maintained, to be strategic, i.e. that player type is not restricted to a single strategy along the equilibrium path. Let h_j denote the history of the game up to stage j. Player 2 will update his beliefs about the player 1 type conditional on the previous moves of both players (h_j). We denote these beliefs at the beginning of stage j by p_j. As indicated above, p_j is a function of h_j. For any value of ρ (the initial reputation for being the 'commitment' type) between 0 and 1, the following strategy profile and belief structure constitute a sequential equilibrium:

1. The 'commitment'-type player 1 announces a 'non-benevolent' policy and at the information sets following a particular announcement implements the promised policy; the 'non-commitment' type announces a 'benevolent' policy and implements 'non-benevolent' at all of her information sets.
2. Player 2 chooses 'low' at all of his information sets.
3. At all information sets following the announcement of the 'non-benevolent' policy, player 2's belief that player 1 is a 'commitment' type is equal to 1; at all information sets following the announcement of the 'benevolent' strategy, player 2's belief that player 1 is a 'commitment' type is equal to 0.

It is possible to show that the equilibrium set (a singleton) just described is stable. Using the terminology of signalling games, this is a separating equilibrium, because the signal (in this case, the signal is an announcement of policy) sent in the first stage of the game reveals the sender's type. Subsequently, we term this a separating equilibrium.

This game also has another sequential equilibrium for a large enough ρ and/or N. To solve for this equilibrium of the finite game of imperfect information, we first find the sequential equilibrium when there is only one investment choice-policy implementation stage after the announcement. Then we solve when there are two stages, and then invoke mathematical induction to find the solution for an arbitrary (finite) number of stages. The following strategies and beliefs constitute a sequential equilibrium[5] if:

$$\rho \geq \left(\frac{-y_3}{y_2 - y_1 - y_3} \right)^N \qquad 11.3$$

Beliefs

1. $p_{N+1} = \rho$.
2. For any $j \leq N$, the probability that player 1 is of the 'commitment' type at each information set of player 2 following the announcement of a 'non-benevolent' policy is equal to 1.
3. $p_N = \rho$ at the information set following a 'benevolent' announcement.
4. If the history of the game up to stage $j < N$ includes a 'benevolent' announcement and any instance of implementation of a 'non-benevolent' policy, then $p_j = 0$.[6]
5. If $p_{j+1} = 0$, then $p_j = 0$.

6. If $j > 1$, $p_j < \left(\frac{-y_3}{y_2 - y_1 - y_3}\right)^{j-1}$ and the investment decision is followed by implementation of the 'benevolent' policy, then $p_{j-1} = \left(\frac{-y_3}{y_2 - y_1 - y_3}\right)^{j-1}$.

The strategy of player 1 is described as follows:

1. The 'commitment' type announces 'benevolent' policy in stage N+1; at information sets following an announcement of 'benevolence' she implements 'benevolent' and at information sets following 'non-benevolent' she implements 'non-benevolent'.

2. The 'non-commitment' type announces a 'benevolent' policy in stage N+1; at all information sets following a 'non-benevolent' announcement she implements a 'non-benevolent' policy; the choice of the 'non-commitment' type at the information sets following the 'benevolent' announcement (nodes following both 'high' and 'low' investment) depends on p_j and j:

If $j = 1$ then she implements the 'non-benevolent' policy, given any investment choice;

If $j > 1$ and $p_j \geq \left(\frac{-y_3}{y_2 - y_1 - y_3}\right)^{j-1}$ then she implements the 'benevolent' policy.

If $j > 1$ and $p_j < \left(\frac{-y_3}{y_2 - y_1 - y_3}\right)^{j-1}$ then she implements the 'benevolent' policy with probability $\frac{p_j(1 - A^{j-1})}{(1 - p_j)\,A^{j-1}}$ (where $A = \frac{-y_3}{y_2 - y_1 - y_3}$) and the 'non-benevolent' with complementary probability.

The strategy of player 2 can be described using related conditions:

Player 2 chooses 'high' investment in stage j if $p_j > \left(\frac{-y_3}{y_2 - y_1 - y_3}\right)^{j=1}$, he chooses 'low' investment if $p_j < \left(\frac{-y_3}{y_2 - y_1 - y_3}\right)^{j}$. If $p_j = \left(\frac{-y_3}{y_2 - y_1 - y_3}\right)^{j}$, then player 2 randomizes between his choices, playing 'high' with probability $\frac{x_3 - x_2}{x_3}$ in a case when 'high' investment was chosen in the previous stage and with probability $\frac{-x_1}{x_3}$ if 'low' investment was chosen in the previous stage.

The nature of the equilibrium is the following: for every $\rho > 0$ there is a number $n(\rho)$ such that, if there are more than $n(\rho)$ investment choice-policy implementation sequences remaining to be played, the 'non-commitment' type will implement the 'benevolent' policy and player 2 will choose 'high' investment. The 'non-commitment' type chooses 'non-benevolent' in the last stage and mixes between 'benevolent' and 'non-benevolent' in stages $n(\rho)$, ..., 2. Accordingly, player 2 mixes between 'high' and 'low' or chooses 'high' with a probability which depends on the relative magnitudes of ρ and the players' pay-offs. Thus, in each of the stages $n(\rho)$, ..., 1, reputation breaks down with a positive probability.[7] Reputation breaks down in the later stages, since long-run value from having reputation for 'commitment' is outweighed by the (opportunity) cost of pretending to be a 'commitment' type. Note that, for large enough N, pay-offs of both players converge to 3. For large enough $\rho\delta$ and/or N, this equilibrium outcome dominates the separating outcome. Hence, applying the coalition-proof Nash equilibrium concept, we discard the separating equilibrium.

If we consider a larger game consisting of K stages, where each stage is the game just described, then the equilibrium (that survives the refinements we pose) will have the following properties: in $K-1$ first stages, both types of player 1 announce the 'benevolent' policy and subsequently implement 'benevolent' in all periods of the stage; player 2 chooses 'high' investment in all periods of the first $K-1$ stages; the play in the last stage is the same as for the single-stage game described above (that is, the game with the announcement followed by N repetitions of investment choice-policy implementation sequence).

5. The Canadian Wheat Board As an Illustrative Example

The results developed can be directly applied to modern issues on the performance and welfare impacts of STCs. We select the Canadian Wheat Board (CWB) as an illustration. The CWB makes to farmers 'an initial or partial payment upon delivery, which is guaranteed by the Government of Canada' (CWB website 1997). This initial payment, which is announced prior to planting, has been historically at about 80–90% of the total payment. It has been argued by many authors that the presence and the level of the guaranteed initial payment have a considerable impact on farmers' planting decisions and on the trading practices of the CWB. Various explanations for the effects of these policies and Board management have been provided (Clark, 1995; Carter and Wilson, 1997). We recapitulate the essentials of these arguments.

First, the initial payment is a clue to the farmers on what the final price is likely to be. But producers are unaware of the exact level of final price that will be realized with the final payment. This uncertainty for the farmer arises due to a lack of information on the share of the crop that will be sold at different grades, and on the decisions of the CWB on levels of exports in the various segments of the international market. Thus, this initial signal to producers might not reflect the real intentions of the CWB, or the CWB may not be able to fulfil the plan that led to the initial payment, i.e. the payment scheme is time-inconsistent. This will probably distort the resource allocation decision of farmers, and in turn lead to a decrease in their welfare.

Second, a high initial payment announcement (even compared with US border prices) diminishes the incentive of the Canadian farmers to bypass the CWB, and secures a larger and more predictable supply. This, in turn, increases the control of the CWB in marketing domestic stocks. Countries in which the highest priority is food security will be more likely to contract with the CWB than with other grain traders. This will occur because dealing with the CWB assures the country of a consistent grain supply. Thus, we can view a high guarantee as a credible commitment of the CWB to honour agreements with its trading partners. If this commitment mechanism really works, then it will probably result in welfare increases for Canadian producers. The latter follows due to the simple fact that the CWB is presumed to be optimizing in trade and that a mechanism is in place to assure honouring of *ex ante* commitments (which, since they are optimizing, contribute to the welfare of Canadian farmers).

The orders of magnitudes of these two effects are questions for empirical analysis. The value of the game-theoretic framework is to show that the welfare trade-offs are much more subtle than they may at first appear. Clearly, simply taking averages over time of export prices is at best a most crude approximation of the impact of the CWB. Perhaps this is the reason for the different conclusions of available analyses. Added structure will be necessary if there is to be an analysis of the STCs that can stand the light of day in terms of modern economic theory.

6. Concluding Comments

We have used concepts of modern game theory to treat time-inconsistency issues associated with strategic trade. The results are particularly applicable to trade in commodities with production periods that are lengthy, as in agriculture. A game with a sequence of decisions is envisioned, in which an importing firm or country might announce its planned level of import. The producer or suppliers then 'invest' by perhaps allocating land to the commodity to be exported. The importer may then change the first decision or be credible and follow through as planned. Clearly, the investment decision of the exporter will be different depending on whether or not the importer's announcement is believed (high or low in our stylized model). From the results on time consistency, we know that revision or non-commitment can lead to an outcome that is suboptimal compared with the initial (*ex ante*) decision on the announcement. Mechanisms are then explored that impose a 'cost' for the failure to honour the initial commitment. An example of such a mechanism in actual trade might be the posting of a bond by one of the parties. Both parties (the STC and its trading partner) gain if these mechanisms are perfectly enforceable.

We investigated the game in which the parties are assumed to trade for more than one period, and where enforcement mechanisms are absent. Results show that the optimality problems are similar to those for the single-stage game, in terms of their time-inconsistency implications. Then the sequence of trading decisions or games is examined in which the commitment mechanism is present, but imperfectly enforceable (we represent this by assuming that information on whether a commitment contract will be honoured is the private information of the STC). This opens the signalling possibilities and the use of experience with previous trading actions to establish reputations. We show that if the parties trade for a sufficient number of periods, and/or their initial reputation for being a commitment type is sufficiently high, then reputation effects dominate the play of the game. Both players gain compared with the case in which the commitment mechanisms are absent. The major applied implication is for a role of some type of authority that could 'enforce' announced intentions.

The concepts developed for understanding STC behaviour and strategic trade were applied to a stylized version of the CWB policies. Even this cursory application suggests areas of major concern relative to the available assessments of the welfare impacts of the CWB and other STCs. There are two clear welfare impacts, and of opposite sign. The obvious conclusion is that much more sophisticated economic analysis will be required, compared with that available, to determine the natural benefits of STCs. Current results simply do not take advantage of the available theory on strategic trade and time inconsistency.

Finally, we observe that the model of strategic trade has required innovations in the game-theoretic formulation. The most important of these follow from the 'personality' of the 'commitment' type.

The model provides an important context for exploring impacts of signalling, reputation and third-party interventions that approximate the institutions and authorities governing international trade.

Notes

1. In a game of perfect information, players move sequentially and each player knows all previous moves when making his decision; that is, all information sets are singletons.
2. The backward induction argument is the following: solve for the optimal choice of the last player depending on each possible history of the game, and

then solve for the optimal choice of the next to the last mover, given that the last mover, will make his/her optimal choice.
3. When $N = 1$, this game coincides with that depicted in Fig. 11.2.
4. Note that, for two-player games, the sets of coalition-proof and Pareto-undominated equilibria coincide.
5. We do not present an algorithm for finding sequential equilibria of the game since it is similar to the one used to find equilibria of multiple versions of the 'chain-store' game (Kreps and Wilson, 1982b; Milgrom and Roberts, 1982).
6. Note that the beliefs of player 2 about player 1 are such that any failure to implement the policy announced is perceived as a sure sign of 'non-commitment'.
7. Compare our findings with conjectures about what would be the intuitive outcome of the game.

References

Bernheim, D., Peleg, D. and Whinston, M. (1987) Coalition-proof Nash equilibria. I: Concepts. *Journal of Economic Theory* 42, 1–12.

Carter, C.A. and Wilson, W.W. (1997) *Emerging differences in state grain trading: Australia and Canada*, paper presented at a Conference on: The Economics of World Wheat Markets: Implications for the Northern Rockies and the Great Plains, Trade Research Center, Montana State University.

Clark (1995) Single desk selling by the Canadian Wheat Board: does it have an impact? *Canadian Journal of Agricultural Economics* 43(2), 225–236.

CWB website 1997, *www.cwb.ca/aboutcwb.*

Harsanyi, J. (1967–1968) Games with incomplete information played by Bayesian players. *Management Science* 14, 159–182, 320–334, 486–502.

Kohlberg, E. and Mertens, J.-F. (1986) On the strategic stability of equilibria. *Econometrica* 54, 1003–1038.

Kreps, D. and Wilson, R. (1982a) Sequential equilibrium. *Econometrica* 50, 863–894.

Kreps, D. and Wilson, R. (1982b) Reputation and imperfect information. *Journal of Economic Theory* 27, 253–279.

Melkonian, T. and Johnson, S. (1996) *State Trading and Importing of Grains in the Former Soviet Union (FSU).* Working paper, Iowa State University, Ames, Iowa, USA.

Milgrom, P. and Roberts, J. (1982) Predation, reputation and entry deterrence. *Journal of Economic Theory* 27, 280–312.

IV

Western Hemisphere Integration

12

Canadian/US Farm Policies and the Creation of a Single North American Grain Market

Bruce L. Gardner

Department of Agricultural and Resource Economics, University of Maryland, University Park, USA

1. Introduction

Despite cultural similarities and a lack of overt hostilities between the two countries, the border between Canada and the USA remains an economically significant barrier in key agricultural product markets. How far are we from a single North American market in farm commodities? What obstacles impede the development of such markets? This chapter addresses these and related questions, in the case of wheat.

The existence of the North American Free Trade Agreement (NAFTA) and generally low barriers to the movement of goods and people across the border indicates at least a near-integrated market, in which the existence of a political boundary means as little as one could ever expect between two independent nations. Yet, attending to what farmers and others in the grain trade say on either side of the border, and to what their political representatives say and do in Bismark and Saskatoon or Ottawa and Washington DC, national differences loom large. It seems almost that every significant cross-border shipment of goods or potential new opening of trade is resented, and where possible contested. The USA and Canada have both enacted domestic market-orientated reforms in grains, but this seems in matters of trade only an occasion to revise tactics that are expressed in ongoing regulation and repression of international market forces. This chapter reviews the evidence on wheat policies and their consequences as follows. First, the evolution of domestic and trade policies in both countries is outlined. The general story is that the USA had a substantially more regulated wheat market than Canada's in the 1950s and 1960s. Canada increased its intervention in wheat in the 1970s, however. Since 1980 both countries have scaled back their regulatory regimes, and both countries have had about the same (still substantial) level of economic support for wheat producers in the 1990s. Both countries have been moving toward non-distorting transfers as a means of support. Canada has recently sealed back its long-standing grain transportation subsidies but state regulation of export market through the Canadian Wheat Board (CWB) remains largely in place. Trade policy took a step toward integration between Canada and the USA with the Canadian–US Free Trade Agreement (CUSTA) in 1989 and NAFTA in 1994. US wheat imports from Canada have none the less not moved to a free-trade basis.

The second section of the chapter considers the economic consequences of wheat policy changes on market integration. The analysis is carried out mostly by econometric investigation of wheat price movements in the two countries. The effects of two policies are emphasized: the US Export Enhancement Program (EEP), and the CWB's price discrimination in wheat marketing. Other policies – such as US deficiency payments and area set-asides, and Canada's transportation subsidies and revenue insurance – have made a difference in producers' behaviour, but the former two policies are the ones that most directly influence the relative prices of wheat in the two countries.

The third section of the chapter briefly discusses the farm-level situation in the USA and Canada, considering integration of the wheat industry in matters other than price – technology, farm specialization, and farmers' returns from wheat growing.

The final section draws the overall conclusions that appear warranted.

2. Farm Policies and Policy Changes

There are two related but distinct issues in assessing the agricultural policies of Canada and the USA in the context of their international commodity markets: the extent to which each country intervenes in farm commodity markets, and the extent to which the countries' interventions are detrimental to the emergence of a single North American market.

The first issue is easiest to address empirically. Of the several ways of attempting to quantify intervention, perhaps the best starting-point is the 'producer subsidy equivalent' (PSE), which expresses assistance to agriculture through price support, output and input subsidy payments, and other measures as a percentage of commodity receipts. The estimate of Nelson *et al.* (1995) for each country's main agricultural commodities in aggregate in the period 1982–1992 is 34.8% for Canada and 23% for the USA. However, the difference is smaller for crops: 34.3% for Canada and 27% for the USA. And for the commodity of interest in this book, wheat, Canada's PSE was 36.9% and that of the USA 39.8%. Table 12.1 shows more detail of support by commodity and of the instrumentalities of support. Table 12.2 shows the evolution of the wheat PSE over time in recent years.

Although the Uruguay Round (UR) negotiations on agriculture helped generate an internationally agreed approach for measuring PSEs, serious questions remain about the accuracy and meaning of these calculated indicators of support. The US 'economy-wide' policies consist of tax provision and transport subsidies, whose value to farmers is not possible to quantify with confidence – similarly for research spending, under the infrastructure heading, and marketing and inspection services, under marketing assistance.

Table 12.1. Producer subsidy equivalents (percentage of product's market value), 1982–1992.

Commodity	Canada	USA
Wheat	36.9	39.8
Maize	22.1	27.2
Barley	42.4	36.4
Oats	30.8	9.9
Rapeseed	30.2	—
Rice	—	95.3
Soybeans	14.8	7.7
Sugar	29.0	59.0
Beef	12.6	8.0
Dairy	69.3	48.4
Pork	12.7	5.7
Poultry	23.4	8.7
Crops	34.3	27.0
Livestock	35.2	19.9
Crop–livestock aggregate	34.8	23.0
Method of support	(9 main crops)	(8 main crops)
Income support	15.3	15.5
Price support	12.3	3.7
Input subsidy	0.5	3.3
Marketing assistance	0.7	1.0
Infrastructure and regional	5.5	2.6
Economy-wide policies	0.0	1.0
Total	34.3	27.0

Source: Nelson *et al.*, 1995, Appendix tables.

Table 12.2. Producer subsidy equivalents for wheat.

Year	Canada	USA
1982	18.8	16.1
1983	22.5	38.8
1984	32.8	28.6
1985	38.5	38.2
1986	49.6	60.5
1987	54.2	61.8
1988	35.6	37.7
1989	31.6	24.5
1990	44.7	43.7
1991	43.5	52.4
1992	34.0	35.2
Average	36.9	39.8

Source: Nelson *et al.*, 1995.

For a more partial but more recent comparison based on each country's own summary data, Table 12.3 shows government payments as a percentage of the gross value of farm commodity receipts, 1985–1995. This comparison indicates more support of agriculture by the USA, but in both comparisons the orders of magnitude are similar in the two countries. Table 12.4 shows spending by type of programme in 1995.

Table 12.3. Government payments to farmers.

	Canada government payments		USA government payments	
Calendar year	($C billion)	(% of farmers' receipts)	(US$ billion)	(% of farmers' receipts)
1985	1.9	9.42	7.7	18.70
1986	2.5	7.24	11.8	11.95
1987	3.3	5.45	16.7	8.86
1988	3.4	5.59	14.5	10.97
1989	3.2	6.13	10.9	15.50
1990	1.8	11.17	9.3	19.14
1991	2.3	8.52	8.2	21.46
1992	3.8	5.24	9.2	19.57
1993	2.9	7.34	13.4	13.96
1994	1.8	13.33	7.9	24.05
1995	1.2	21.25	7.3	26.99
1996	—	—	8.6	24.53

Sources: Agriculture Canada, 1996; USDA, 1996.

Table 12.4. Composition of Canadian and US government commodity programme outlays in 1995.

Canada		USA	
Programme or activities	$C (million)[a]	Programme or activities	US$ (million)
Western Grain Stabilization Act	−1	CCC Loan and Purchase Programs	−170
Crop insurance indemnities	310	Deficiency payments	4096
Dairy	214	Disaster and other payments	689
Transportation subsidies	22	Export programmes	1361
Gross Revenue Insurance Program	178	Other	54
Net Income Stabilization Act	90		
Input rebates	267		
Other payments	371		
Producer premiums	507		
Total	1958	Total	6030

[a] Note that Canadian data are in Canadian dollars and US data in US dollars. To make a direct comparison the 1995 exchange rate was 1.366 $C per US$ on average for the year (US Federal Reserve Board).
Sources: Agriculture Canada, 1996; USDA, 1996. US data omit crop insurance and Conservation Reserve Program. Canadian data omit export activities and government administrative costs.

The second question that began this discussion is more difficult, because it requires analytical distinctions among the policy mechanisms used. A government may spend a lot on supporting farms and yet still permit markets to allocate goods and productive activities. Most notably, in neither country do the data show a trend toward less government activity, overall or in the wheat market. Yet recent policy actions and discussion indicate an increase in market orientation in both countries. In this respect the data on government spending are misleading. In the USA the successive reforms of the omnibus 1985, 1990 and 1996 farm legislation moved government spending increasingly toward non-distorting transfers to farmers. The 1996 Federal Agricultural Improvement Reform (FAIR) Act reforms decouple the wheat programme payments almost completely from market prices and largely from production decisions.

A longer-term perspective can be obtained from the assessment of Floyd (1965) of the period immediately following World War II, 1945–1957. He compared policies and factor incomes in the Northern Great Plains (Manitoba, Saskatchewan, Alberta, Montana, and North Dakota). He found Canadian policies focused on stabilization, 'with little attempt to raise prices above the underlying free market level. In contrast, higher farm prices and incomes have been the overriding goals of the United States program' (Floyd, 1965, p. 140). Using the free-market 1926–1929 period as a basis for comparison, Floyd (1965) estimated that policy differences raised field crop prices 8–26% in the US Plains States as compared with the Canadian Prairie Provinces. His equivalent measure to the PSE was 13.6% for the USA and 7.6% for Canada (in the Plains regions).

US grain price support policies have required border controls. Floyd estimated wheat prices in the USA at $26 to $29 per tonne higher than in Canada in 1953–1957 (when the average US farm price was $74). Now, with the CUSTA and its successor NAFTA in effect, and policies more orientated to non-distorting domestic support, we should expect to see a better approximation to a single North American grain market than in the 1950s or 1960s.

CUSTA went into effect at the beginning of 1989 and NAFTA at the beginning of 1994. The agricultural provisions of NAFTA, incorporating the provisions of CUSTA, relax certain quantitative import restrictions, but leave in place some of the most important ones for each country. More broadly, the agreements reduce tariffs on practically every product where they exist (see USDA, 1995, pp. 9–10 for a useful summary list). Typical are reductions in Canada's tariff's on tomatoes, onions, lettuce, cucumbers, grapes and several important fruits from 10–21% in the pre-1989 base period to 3–4.5% in 1995. However, quantitative restrictions needed to protect programme-supported commodities remain in place in both countries. Canada agreed to increase its (global) import quotas by about 1.5% of Canadian production for chicken, turkey and shell eggs, but very restrictive levels remain in place. The USA retained its rights to restrict imports to protect its price support programme in the area of interest in this volume, for grain, and this resulted in a series of disputes and negotiations on limiting Canadian wheat, especially durum, exports to the USA. A question for the future of the grain trade between the two countries is how far the US adoption of the FAIR Act of 1996, which took effect with the 1996 crops and extends to 2002, will go toward making genuine free trade in grains possible.

To obtain a consistent indicator over time of the overall market price effects of the two countries' policies in wheat, Fig. 12.1 shows time-series prices of wheat received by farmers in Canada and the USA. The difference between these prices is intended to be comparable to the $26 to $29 per tonne price difference Floyd (1965) estimated for 1953–1957. At the midpoint, the 1953–1957 price difference is $27.50 per tonne. Unfortunately, I do not have a consistent time series of Canadian and US farm prices for Plains wheat from 1953 to the present. Figure 12.1 shows the CWB's final price to farmers and the US season-average farm price for all wheat from 1962 to the present, placed in real terms (1992 US$) by converting Canadian to US dollars at the annual average exchange rate (from the US Council of Economic Advisers) and

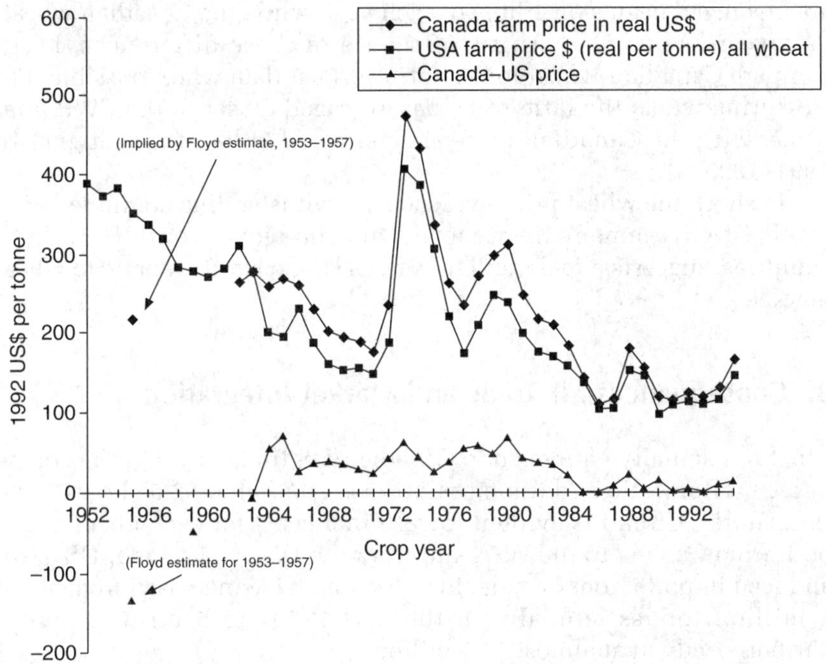

Fig. 12.1. Farm price of wheat and Canada–US difference.

deflated by the US gross domestic product (GDP) deflator. That deflator, 20.9 in 1953–1957, means Floyd's (1965) $27.50 per tonne is $132 per tonne in 1992 dollars. In 1962 the difference is $45 (1992 US$). But in the mid-1960s the picture is reversed, with the Canadian prices substantially exceeding the US price. This may be attributable in part to increasing effectiveness of the CWB in marketing wheat (e.g. extracting more from domestic Canadian millers relative to foreign buyers) or other Canadian policies. But the big change was in US policy, where a wheat growers' referendum generated a move away from a high-market-price policy to less area control, lower market prices, and higher direct payments to producers. The Canadian and US prices gradually move closer together until 1985, and since 1989 move quite closely together, with an average difference of $13 per tonne.

An issue that complicates Canadian and US price comparisons is differences in wheat grown in the two countries. Canada produces spring wheat almost entirely, but the US wheat crop is predominantly winter wheat, which has somewhat different characteristics and typically sells for a slightly lower price. In addition, because of winter wheat's predominance and its earlier harvest dates – beginning in May in Texas – the US wheat marketing year according to which annual data are organized begins on 1 June of each year, while the Canadian wheat-data year begins on 1 August. Because of these differences, I will compare Canadian wheat to US spring wheat data when possible. For US spring wheat the farm price has averaged closer to the CWB final price, with the Canadian price an average of $6 per tonne higher in 1991–1995.

In short, the wheat price evidence, notwithstanding continued high levels of government involvement and budgetary outlays in both countries, suggests a real trend towards a single North American wheat market.

3. Consequences for Trade and Market Integration

What has actually happened to Canadian/US trade flows in the course of recent domestic and trade policy changes? Table 12.5 shows some indicators. A trend is evident toward increased movements of goods both from Canada to the USA and from the USA to Canada. US grain and feed imports from Canada, in particular, have increased from about 1 million tonnes annually in the mid-1980s to 5 million tonnes currently, valued at almost $1.5 billion.

Role of NAFTA/CUSTA

Would these increases have occurred even without CUSTA and NAFTA? The plot of Fig. 12.2 suggests a substantial boost in both exports and imports coinciding with the introduction of CUSTA in 1989. To test for the significance of trade agreement effects, the regressions shown in Table 12.6 were estimated on the 15 years of data, 1982–1996. The joint effect of the free-trade agreement variables is significant (F test on residuals at a 5% level). The point estimate is that on average, over 1989–1996, the CUSTA and NAFTA increased US imports from Canada by $1.3 billion and exports by $2.9 billion over what they would have been in the absence of the agreements. The estimated effect on exports is larger because, as Fig. 12.1 suggests, there is no significant upward trend in exports between 1982 and 1988. Therefore, CUSTA and NAFTA get essentially all the credit, in the regression, for the post-1989 increase.

Very similar estimates were obtained by Tweeten *et al.* (1997, p. 16). These results are preferable because they use Canadian data on imports from the USA rather than US data on exports to Canada. US counting of exports was incomplete in the late 1980s (evident in the larger quantities in Canadian data imports from the USA compared with US data on exports to Canada). Since 1990 each country has agreed to use the other's import data to reckon its own exports.

Table 12.5. US imports from and exports to Canada.

	Agricultural imports				Agricultural exports
	Value (million US$)		Quantity (million tonnes)		
	Total	Grain & feed	Grain & feed	Wheat	Total value (million US$)
Calendar year					
1982	1396	221	1.0	0.05	1820
1983	1506	239	1.2	0.05	1844
1984	1850	262	1.2	0.10	1963
1985	1894	257	1.1	0.27	1622
1986	2086	294	1.5	0.25	1542
1987	2214	332	1.7	0.80	1807
1988	2443	424	2.2	0.40	2019
1989	2915	560	2.3	0.30	2220
1990	3152	539	2.4	0.60	4197
1991	3306	566	2.5	0.60	4554
1992	4102	778	5.4	1.50	4902
1993	4620	944	6.4	1.80	5271
1994	5231	1275	9.5	2.50	5504
1995	5559	1292	7.1	1.50	5738
1996	6798			1.30	
Fiscal year					
94/95	5429	1231	5.9	1.60	5911
95/96	6485	1445	5.2	1.00	6000

Source: USDA, various issues.

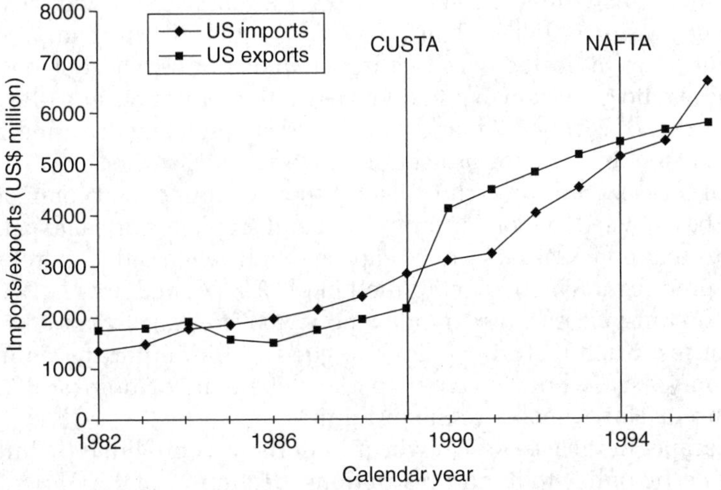

Fig. 12.2. US agricultural imports and exports from Canada. Source: USDA, various issues; 1996 is estimated from change in the fiscal year (FY) 1995 to FY 1996 levels.

Table 12.6. Regressions estimated on US imports from and exports to Canada, 1982–1996.

	Dependent variable			
	US imports from Canada		US exports to Canada	
Independent variables	Coefficient	*t* statistics	Coefficient	*t* statistics
Intercept	1228	7.0	1788	5.2
Time (trend)	169	4.3	3.6	0.1
CUSTA	−2470	3.9	−3549	2.9
NAFTA	268	0.9	−916	1.7
CUSTA × time	72	4.4	595	4.3
R^2	0.98		0.98	

National policies and market integration: the case of wheat

Turning more narrowly to wheat, US imports from Canada increased from essentially nothing in the early 1980s to about 0.5 tonnes annually at the beginning of the 1990s. At that level, imports amount to less than 1% of annual US production. In 1992, market conditions encouraged a substantial increase in US demand for durum wheat, and in 1993 supply conditions in Canada resulted in a further increase in both durum and other wheat to 3 million tonnes (109 million bushels) in the 1992/93 crop year. This quantity is 4.5% of that year's US production, an amount that cannot be assumed to have trivial economic effects. This episode thus provided a test of how well accepted free-trade ideas had become under CUSTA. The answer, as other US/Canadian trade disputes also indicated, was that free trade is not well accepted except by those who gain from exports. Voices on the importing side (the USA) supportive of letting the market work were completely drowned out, if they existed, by calls for protection of US wheat growers.

Of course, producers who must compete with imported commodities must be expected to look for protection, and ample historical experience tells us that policymakers can be expected to listen to calls for protection from producers. The practical function of CUSTA, and now NAFTA, in such circumstances is to restrain the policymakers' reflexive protectionist responses. Such restraint is for the good of the importing country's economy as a whole, even if to the detriment of domestic wheat producers. How effective is the restraint?

Escape, in the case of US wheat imports, was provided by linkages of domestic policy to import restrictions. Section 22 of the Agricultural Adjustment Act of 1933 (as amended) calls for limitations on imports when such imports materially interfere with a US price and income support programme (US Code, Section 624). In November 1993 President Clinton, on the advice of the Secretary of Agriculture, wrote to the US International Trade Commission (ITC) stating his belief that wheat was being imported 'under such conditions or in such quantities as to render or tend to render ineffective, or materially interfere with the price support, payment, and production adjustment program for wheat' (US International Trade Commission, 1994, p. A-3). He therefore directed the ITC to investigate the truth of this claim. In July 1994 the six ITC commissioners, after hearing a quite interesting array of evidence, split three to three on the key issue of material interference. Three concluded that material interference occurred and three that the evidence 'could support the President finding either material interference or no material interference' (US International Trade Commission, 1994, p. 3). All six recommended the President impose some additional barriers to US imports of wheat from Canada.

CUSTA requires that a Section 22 import restriction must be a response to imports caused by a substantial change in either US or Canadian policy. In addition, the UR General Agreement on Tariffs and Trade (GATT) agreement on agriculture prohibits imposition of new quantitative restrictions on agricultural imports, limiting the President's options during the 1995–2000 implementation period. However, the GATT allows for countries to raise tariffs unilaterally (for which other countries may demand compensation) under certain notification procedures. In April 1994 the USA notified the GATT that it intended to modify wheat tariffs under these provisions (GATT article 28). The provisions require consultations with affected countries. In August 1994 the USA and Canada announced an agreement that US imports of wheat from Canada would be limited through tariff-rate quotas (tariffs that sharply increase for imports above the quota level) to 1.5 million tonnes for the next year (ending 11 September 1995). The 1.5 million tonne restriction was divided between durum and other wheat, 0.45 million tonnes of durum and 1.05 of other wheat, with an intermediate step of a $23 per tonne levy on durum imports between 0.30 and 0.45 million tonnes (Babula *et al.*, 1996, p. 134). In September 1995 the agreement lapsed and there have been no further restrictions. Supply–demand forces in 1995–1997 have kept Canadian exports of wheat to the USA below the 1.5 million tonne level.

When economic forces again generate substantial US durum or other wheat imports from Canada, as is practically certain to occur at some point, will the result be less protectionist? One reason for believing so is the US FAIR Act. Under the FAIR Act, wheat imports cannot affect government payments to farmers in the wheat programme, because these payments ('production flexibility contract payments') are fixed in advance in dollar terms until 2002. In order to affect the Commodity Credit Corporation (CCC) loan programme or loan deficiency payments, US wheat prices would have to be driven down to $95 per tonne since that level (the 1995 loan rate) is the maximum loan rate under the FAIR Act. Since 1990 the farm price of wheat has been below $95 for only a few months (in several states early in the marketing year 1991/92) and the lowest US season-average farm price has been $110, in 1991/92. Thus, there is little chance of Canadian imports being seen as materially interfering with the wheat programme.

None the less, future increases in US wheat imports from Canada are certain to generate political pressure to protect US wheat growers. One reason such imports are likely to occur on a continuing basis is the economics of marketing Canadian grain through the US transportation system. Using US ports and transportation infrastructure to export Canadian grain may be seen as different from consumption of Canadian grain in the USA, but, once a load of wheat from Saskatchewan, say, is delivered to an elevator in Montana, the effect on the US market should be the same regardless of the purpose of the delivery. The argument for a smaller, or negligible, US price effect of wheat for re-export being imported from Canada is that each tonne of grain imported for this purpose, and thus added to the US supply of wheat, is accompanied by a tonne of additional demand for wheat exported from the USA.

In any case, political pressure to restrain surges in US wheat imports will be felt under the FAIR Act, and felt even more intensely than before 1996. The reason is that a 1-cent decline in the US price of wheat is more costly to wheat growers under the FAIR Act than was the case under the pre-1996 deficiency payment programme. In 1991–1995, deficiency payments were made on an average of about 49 million tonnes (the amount varying from year to year because of varying aggregate area eligibility and area reduction programme percentages), or 70–75% of production. Therefore, about 70–75 cents lost through lower market price was offset by a higher deficiency payment.[1] Under the FAIR Act, however, each dollar lost through lower market prices is lost, so growers' interest in maintaining higher market prices through any available means is intensified.

Characteristics of the international wheat market

While the FAIR Act substantially altered the domestic US wheat programme, the structure of export promotion programmes remains largely intact. The role of the programmes in the relationship between the Canadian and US wheat markets will remain important. A complicating factor is that the policies of the two countries are interdependent. At the same time, the CWB continues to manage the international marketing of Canada's wheat, and its pricing strategies necessarily take into consideration US export promotion policies. Simultaneously, US export promotion efforts respond to emerging market conditions, including Canada's export pricing.

It is unclear exactly how the US and Canadian markets and policies interact, and the question is further complicated by the policies of other wheat-exporting and -importing nations. Many authors have attempted to explain the nature of competition and the resulting prices and trade flows in the international wheat market. Kolstad and Burris (1986), for example, simulate wheat trade flows that would result under perfect competition with free trade (using underlying excess demand and transportation cost information developed in Shei and Thompson, 1977), and compare the trade flows resulting from models of a USA–Canada duopoly, a USA–Canada–Australia triopoly and a Japan–EC duopsony. They find actual trade flows best explained by the USA–Canada duopoly, which predicts more diversified shipments of each country to different importing countries than the competitive model predicts. However, Kolstad and Burris (1986) do not account for differences in seasonal production patterns and consequent seasonal variation in delivered prices to different import locations (e.g. it might pay to ship Australian wheat to all Asian locations in March–May, and to none in September–December, while the Kolstad–Burris competitive model says Australian wheat should all go to the closest Asian markets (which can absorb it all over the course of a year). Also, Kolstad and Burris's oligopoly model predicts higher than competitive prices and restricted export volume for all import locations outside Europe, and so cannot account for the predominant use of export subsidies to increase trade levels in US and EC policy.

A further complication is qualitative differences in wheat from different countries. Product differentiation by country yields different trade patterns, as compared with a homogeneous-product model, even under perfect competition, and opens further possibilities for market power and imperfect competition. Haley (1995) reviews the literature on wheat as a differentiated product in trade and simulates the effects of the US EEP in this context, but he does not incorporate oligopoly behaviour in the sense of exporters attempting to exploit downward-sloping demand functions for their countries' wheat(s). The reason is probably that this behaviour by exporters would involve taxing or otherwise restricting wheat exports, whereas the topic Haley (1995) considers is export subsidies.

Differentiated wheats increase the opportunities for price discrimination among wheat buyers by exporters. The possibilities of price discrimination are a major rationale for the CWB as the monopoly seller of Western Canada's wheat in foreign markets. If these were many competing Canadian export firms, competition among them would tend to drive prices down in the most lucrative markets. Pick and Carter (1994) use evidence on prices at which wheat from both Canada and the USA is sold in several importing markets, and how these prices change when the US/Canadian real exchange rate changes, to argue that price discrimination (or 'pricing to market') is in fact important in the international wheat trade. Price discrimination offers an explanation of why limited export subsidies exist in the sense of selling at a loss in some markets. With free entry and competition in wheat production, a country's marginal cost of producing (each type of) wheat is expected to equal the expected average price. Then, if price discrimination by an unsubsidized marketing agency results in wheat prices above the average price for sales to some countries, the price of wheat sold to at least one other country must be below the average price and hence below marginal cost. So there is an (industry-financed) export subsidy in this limited sense.

An oligopoly in wheat marketing could even generate an average export price below the domestic consumer price if the export authority (such as the CWB) has sufficient control to permit the domestic market to be a high-price market in the price discrimination scheme. However, if domestic market competition forces the domestic price of wheat for export and for domestic consumption to be the same, there is no scope for overall export subsidy by a self-financed oligopoly exporter. An outside, i.e. governmental, subsidy is required for an overall export subsidy to make sense for the industry, and then it becomes an issue why an export subsidy is a sensible policy for the government.

US export promotion

In 1990–1995, US wheat exports averaged 32 million tonnes, of which 75% was assisted by export programmes. The most important programme is the EEP, which in 1990–1993 paid an average subsidy (or 'bonus') to wheat exporters averaging about $32 per tonne on 18 million tonnes (a little over half of all wheat exported). In addition, the US Department of Agriculture (USDA), through its CCC, offers credit guarantees, under which the CCC will compensate private-sector lenders in case of default on loans made to USDA-approved foreign buyers for purchasing US grain on credit. Such guarantees enable US lenders to offer more favourable credit terms to foreign buyers. USDA estimates an average of 9.5 million tonnes of wheat annually was exported under CCC credit programmes in 1990–1993. Finally, US food-aid programmes (known as 'P.L. 480' and 'section 416' after their authorizing legislation) have generated substantial wheat exports throughout the period following World War II. P.L. 480 exports reached a peak of 13.4 million tonnes in 1965. During 1990–1993, an average of 3 million tonnes was shipped under P.L. 480 and section 416 authorities (Hoffman *et al.*, 1995, p. 44). For a historical perspective on these programmes, see Table 12.7.

The EEP has recently been in abeyance, with no export bonuses paid since August 1995. Export credit and food-aid shipments continue but at a significantly reduced level of activity. However, all these programmes will resume as soon as international wheat demand weakens sufficiently

Table 12.7. US wheat exports under promotion programmes.

Fiscal year[a]	Foreign food aid (million tonnes)	CCC export credit (million tonnes)	EEP (million tonnes)	Export under programme as percentage of of total wheat exports
1980	2.8	1.9	0	13
1981	2.5	3.3	0	14
1982	3.0	3.7	0	15
1983	3.5	8.6	0	33
1984	3.4	11.4	0	36
1985	4.5	8.2	0	44
1986	5.3	7.8	4.9	59
1987	4.3	8.1	12.2	67
1988	4.8	9.3	26.7	80
1989	4.0	8.9	17.9	68
1990	3.1	7.6	12.8	70
1991	3.2	8.3	15.1	78
1992	2.4	13.3	21.1	76
1993	4.0	8.5	21.8	79
1994	3.5	5.9	18.2	75
1995	1.9	4.2	18.1	68

[a] The calendar year shown is by convention the one in which the fiscal year ends: for example, fiscal year 1980 runs from 1 October 1979 to 30 September 1980.
CCC, Commodity Credit Corporation; EEP, Export Enhancement Program.
Source: USDA, 1997, p. 93.

to cause a significant reduction in US wheat exports. The GATT agreement limits both expenditures and quantities shipped under EEP to a level of $500 million or so annually, enough to mount an export subsidy programme half as large as the EEP became in 1986–1993.

How have and will export programmes affect the emergence of a single North American grain market? The question is difficult because the answer depends on the interacting effects of both US and Canadian grain export programmes, neither of which is straightforward analytically. Analysis of the EEP as an export subsidy is in principle straightforward enough: the policy places a wedge between US domestic and foreign grain prices equal to the amount of the subsidy. But there are problems of both the theory and the practice of interpreting the EEP as such a subsidy. The problems in applying the theory are that: (a) the EEP (as well as export credit guarantees and food aid) is limited to particular quantities, and (b) it was paid in kind, in grain from CCC stocks, during much of its history (until December 1991).

The first problem, of limited quantities, means that the subsidy may be inframarginal – paid only on grain that would be exported even without subsidy – and thus have little or no effect on sales at the margin. This of course is not the intent of EEP. Indeed the intent, as articulated by USDA officials (see quotations in Gardner, 1996) is rather to pay subsidies only on sales that otherwise would not be made. There has been no imminent threat of loss of US wheat sales to Japan, for example, so no EEP subsidies have been paid on those sales. At least one-third of US wheat exports were sold without EEP bonuses even in the peak years of EEP programming (1988/89 and 1991/93). One can reasonably wonder whether observed prices in countries receiving EEP wheat reflect non-EEP or EEP sales prices, or whether EEP sales were large enough to increase grain world consumption appreciably and thus affect the non-EEP price.

The second problem, of EEP payment in kind, can be taken to mean that every EEP bonus of, say, one-third of the price of wheat, caused the release of one-third of a tonne of grain (not necessarily wheat, because the in-kind subsidies were generic) from CCC stocks. This scenario could easily result in the EEP causing a decline in both foreign and domestic wheat prices (see Chambers and Paarlberg, 1991). However, CCC stock disposal was not tied solely to EEP. By the end of the 1980s the CCC was directly auctioning off its stocks, so that if the CCC's wheat had not been released as EEP bonuses that wheat would have been placed on the market anyway by other means. Therefore, we cannot attribute the increase in marketed supply to EEP, but rather to the USDA's general stock-disposal policy.

The practical problems of analysing the EEP as a standard export subsidy stem from the bonus levels varying by country receiving the grain and by type of wheat, and most importantly the fact that none of the widely quoted market prices of wheat available are internal prices in EEP-receiving countries. Rather, prices are quoted at international export or import transit or storage locations (Rotterdam, St Lawrence River, Buenos Aires). It is not obvious how these prices are affected by EEP. Suppose there were free trade between these locations and EEP-receiving locations – for example in North Africa – and that EEP drove down wheat prices in EEP-receiving countries. Then these international prices should fall, too, and by roughly the same amount. However, if there is free trade between the international price-quote locations and the USA, then these international prices should follow US prices, and thus rise if EEP has a price-increasing effect in the USA.

Now consider the situation of Canada and the North American grain market, as affected by EEP and other US export promotion programmes. To the extent that EEP sales are sales at the margin, grain prices in competing export markets are expected to adjust to world market prices including EEP bonuses, that is, lower prices, in order to compete with EEP sales. On the other hand, prices in Canada should adjust to US domestic prices to the extent that the US and Canadian markets are integrated. But, if the EEP is effective, market prices in EEP-receiving countries fall and in the USA rise. So which way do Canadian prices go? In a frictionless (zero transportation cost) world with Canada a price-taking, free-trading nation, EEP subsidies would replace Canadian sales in EEP-receiving countries. The Canadian grain would instead go to the next-best market. As Canada and other exporters adjust, prices would fall in all importing countries and in Canada too as more grain remains there until the Canadian price falls to the level of lower foreign prices plus transportation costs. This, however, creates a wedge between the lower Canadian price and higher US price. In a competitive market, as soon as the wedge becomes large enough to cover Canada–USA transportation costs, Canadian grain would be imported into the USA, until US prices are driven down to the lower EEP-reduced level plus transportation. That is, if the USA maintains an open border with Canada, US export subsidies can only achieve a wedge between US and foreign prices equal to or less than Canada–USA transportation costs. This is in fact the theory endorsed by Sumner *et al.* (1994) and in part by the US ITC (1990), in their analyses of durum wheat imports, to explain why Canadian wheat imports to the USA increased since the mid-1980s.

The preceding theory does not necessarily imply that observed wheat prices in the USA or Canada will go up or down with EEP, but it does imply that the difference between US and Canadian prices will increase with EEP (otherwise no shipments would be induced).

Canadian wheat export policy

The main complicating factor omitted from the preceding discussion is Canadian grain policy. Canada is, of course, not simply a price taker in the international wheat market. Through the CWB, 'Canada's 110,000 wheat and barley farmers sell as one and therefore can command a higher price for their product,' as the CWB hopefully states (CWB, 1997). Receipts from all export sales of wheat during a crop year are pooled (except durum, pooled separately), so that 'all farmers delivering the same grade of wheat or barley will receive the same return at the end of the crop year' (CWB, 1997). The CWB sells in each export market, and in western Canada for domestic human consumption, at prices the CWB or its selling agents find most remunerative. It is apparently possible for the CWB to price-discriminate – to charge higher prices in some markets without competitive pressures from the USA, the EU or other exporters forcing a common price level.[2] It is believed by many Canadian producers that the CWB could sell more grain at more advantageous prices in the USA if the CWB tried to do so, and producers would like the opportunity widened to sell on their own in the US market (see Schmitz *et al.*, 1997).

Given the CWB as monopoly seller of exported Canadian wheat, the effect of EEP on Canadian relative to US prices depends on the CWB's reaction to a loss of overseas markets due to EEP sales. The CWB could choose not to sell wheat to the US market in response to a rise in the US price relative to overseas prices (assuming this price change occurred). In this case, the EEP would cause an increase in the US relative to Canadian prices, even a price wedge larger than transportation costs. But there would be an incentive for the CWB to make such sales, and a larger incentive the more Canadian wheat is displaced from overseas markets by EEP sales. And of course we know that Canadian exports of wheat to the USA have increased in some large-EEP years. So we would expect under the CWB to see the same kind of price effect on Canadian relative to US wheat prices as if Canada were a price taker. But the connection would be less predictable. The Canadian and US wheat markets would be integrated, in the sense of prices moving in parallel, only to the extent the CWB wanted this to occur.

More importantly for research on wheat markets, CWB operations create practical difficulties in using observed prices as indicators of market integration. What Canadian prices does one compare with those of, say, the Minneapolis Grain Exchange or with the US National Agricultural Statistics Service (NASS) monthly survey of the price of wheat received by farmers in North Dakota? One cannot observe a comparable monthly price received by farmers in Alberta, say, because the whole year's wheat for export and human consumption is pooled, with the common price received only at the end of the marketing year. The most-used international comparisons, in studies like Goodwin and Smith (1995) or Smith *et al.* (undated), are with Canadian export location price quotes from the International Wheat Council's *World Wheat Statistics* or USDA *Wheat Yearbook*. These are not, however, prices at which market transactions are known to have been made. They are 'asking' prices, which are quotations from the CWB. Some customers, perhaps the ones who buy US wheat without EEP bonuses, may buy at those prices, but this does not happen every day or every week, and may happen quite rarely.

As an alternative to the export asking price, the 'St Lawrence' and 'Vancouver' prices (the former of which is the representative monthly Canadian price in USDA's *Wheat Yearbook* (1997) series of 'foreign prices'), one could use the 'Thunder Bay' quotation.[3] This last price is asked of domestic Canadian mills that make flour or other wheat products for human consumption. There are likely to be more actual transactions at these prices (but, to repeat, we have no actual transactions data). So the Thunder Bay price may give a better indication of the extent to which the US and Canadian markets are integrated.

The main source of prices in actual purchases and sales of Canadian wheat are price quotations on the Winnipeg Grain Exchange. However, wheat traded can legally be used only for domestic feeding of livestock. So the price quotes may be for a commodity qualitatively different from wheat represented by CWB quotes. None the less, feed wheat is to a first approximation, given its grade, the same commodity as milling and export wheat. So if the US and Canadian markets are truly integrated we ought to see Winnipeg and Minneapolis prices changing in parallel to roughly the same degree as Minneapolis and Kansas City or Chicago wheat prices.

Econometric evidence on wheat policies and market integration

I will pursue two possibilities for econometric estimation of policy effects on the wheat market in Canada as compared with the USA. The first uses annual farm price received data, the same data plotted in Fig. 12.1 above. These data should reveal the extent to which US export programmes and/or the CWB have been able to influence their farmers' prices. The extent to which either party has been able to do so is an indicator of the extent to which policies impeded market integration. Table 12.8 shows regression results explaining 33 years of price data (1963–1995). The dependent variables are the three series as plotted in Fig. 12.1.

Table 12.8. Regression coefficients (*t* statistics) explaining farm prices of wheat, 1963–1995.

	Dependent variable (1992 US$ per tonne)				
Independent variables	US price	Canadian price	Canadian–US price difference		
Intercept	349	404	55	44	39
	(6.1)	(6.8)	(3.3)	(2.7)	(2.1)
EEP bonus	0.29	−0.15	−0.44	−0.83	
	(0.3)	(0.1)	(1.4)	(3.3)	
EEP tonnage	—	—	—	—	−1.64
					(2.9)
CCC stock change	2.79	3.25	0.46	−0.005	−0.82
	(1.0)	(1.1)	(0.6)	(0.01)	(1.0)
World supply	−0.55	−0.63	−0.08	−0.006	0.006
(million tonnes)	(2.4)	(2.7)	(1.2)	(0.2)	(0.1)
Canadian exports	−7.16	−8.34	−1.18		
(million tonnes)	(1.9)	(2.1)	(1.1)		
US exports	6.16	7.30	1.14		
(million tonnes)	(3.2)	(3.6)	(2.0)		
R^2	0.55	0.64	0.52	0.45	0.44

Note: The US price is the season-average farm price received for all wheat (USDA, 1997); the Canadian price is the CWB final price paid to producers, basis St Lawrence (Canadian Grains Council, 1992).
EEP, Export Enhancement Program; CCC, Commodity Credit Corporation.

These regressions are intended to identify the effects of EEP and, if possible, Canadian export policies. To accomplish this one would like to hold underlying supply–demand conditions constant. On the supply side, world supply (production plus carry-in stocks) at the beginning of each crop year is used as an independent variable. The demand side poses greater problems. World real GDP or another aggregate income variable might be considered, but no consistent time series for it was available. The other right-hand-side variables are arguably not exogenous, but I see no good alternative to them. The argument for using the EEP bonus, CCC stock release and Canadian exports as independent variables is that they are predominantly policy variables. This approach is in the spirit of Bresnahan (1989), which reviews models in which quantities sold by oligopolists are used as independent variables in empirical tests of market power. The regressions in columns 4 and 5 of Table 12.8 omit the US and Canadian export levels, in order to test whether their inclusion influences the estimated EEP effect.

The Table 12.8 estimates of a 44-cent to 83-cent per tonne effect on the Canadian–US price difference for each US$1 of EEP bonus gives some support to Canadian arguments that the EEP has been harmful to them. However, there appears to be no significant effect of EEP on the absolute real level of either the Canadian or US price – an inconsistency that blunts the argument. On the other hand, world supply significantly reduces both the US and the Canadian price, but not the difference between them.[4] The coefficient on the net change in US CCC stocks (negative values meaning stocks released to the market) has a larger estimated impact, of the expected sign, but is not statistically significant. The regression (column 5) of Table 12.8 uses tonnage shipped under EEP rather than the average EEP bonus as the indicator of the size of EEP. The tonnage variable gives the same results as the EEP bonus level qualitatively, but with slightly less statistical significance.[5]

The most problematic variables are the levels of Canadian and US wheat exports. The Canadian export level can be taken as a policy variable, since it measures CWB decisions to place wheat on the world market. The negative coefficient indicates that increased CWB exports drive down both Canadian and US wheat prices, and possibly (because, while the sign is right, the negative effect on the price difference is not significantly different from zero at the 5% level) drives down the Canadian price by more than the US price. On the other hand, it is possible that causality runs from wheat price to exports. The CWB is in this latter interpretation essentially passive (Canada is a price taker) and ships whatever is ordered at each year's world price. Under this interpretation the coefficient on Canadian exports just measures the elasticity of demand for Canada's wheat in international trade. With Canada's exports averaging about 15 million tonnes in the data period, the coefficient of −8.3 on the Canadian farm price would mean that a

5% price increase would generate an 8% decrease in exports. Or, in terms of world quantities, Canada's additional export of 0.2% of the world supply would drive down the world price by 6%. Taken either way, the price effects are too large to be consistent with Canada's being a passive price taker in world markets.

US exports are equally unlikely to reflect price-taking behaviour, but the active policy element in US exports is supposed to be measured by the EEP variable. My interpretation of the significant positive sign on US exports is that the variable is an indicator of strength of demand. Other variables in the regressions hold constant the world supply of wheat and US and Canadian export policy decisions. In the absence of a variable that measures shifts in world demand, the level of US exports serves as a proxy for demand; hence the positive sign. This interpretation is supported by the fact that this variable has a significant positive sign in the equation explaining the difference between the Canadian and US wheat price. Figure 12.1 shows this difference as being especially notable in 1972/73 and 1979/80, which were strong-demand years. Why should the Canadian price rise relative to the US price in high-demand years? Because in such years Canada's opportunities for sales in high-price markets increase under the CWB's price-discriminating marketing strategy, while US export policy, by this interpretation, is essentially passive apart from EEP, which is already accounted for by the EEP variable.

The second econometric approach to investigating policy and market integration is to use monthly data on market prices. The number of observations of monthly prices is large enough for an econometric analysis considering their time-series properties to be helpful. A substantial literature has developed over the past decade on the use of 'cointegration' tests to estimate whether observed time series of prices in two different markets indicate economic integration of the two markets. Economic integration in econometric practice means price in one market is a linear function of price in the other. If prices move together in this sense, it is presumed that an underlying arbitrage mechanism is at work.

A problem with this approach is that prices in two markets may move together for reasons other than market equilibration – for example, a common rate of inflation swamping changes in relative prices. Much of the recent applied econometric literature is aimed at detecting and removing such spurious co-movements. Unfortunately, it is not easy to apply these methods with confidence. Price series may have either a deterministic trend or follow a random-walk process with drift, both of which cause problems that require different approaches to correct but are difficult to distinguish in actual price data. Unit root tests can accept or reject a null hypothesis of a random walk, but the tests are often inclusive. Mills (1993) provides a lucid exposition.

Figure 12.3 plots the monthly prices of Canadian Western Red Spring (WRS) Wheat, St Lawrence, 13.5% protein and Minneapolis No. 1 Dark Northern Spring Wheat, 13% protein, from June 1982 to January 1997, all in US$ per tonne from USDA, *Wheat Yearbook* (1997). Both series appear almost trendless, but fitting a linear trend to the data indicates a positive trend of $0.228 per month for the US price and $0.313 per month (US$) for the Canadian price. The '*t*' statistics are 5.8 and 7.7 respectively, rejecting the null hypothesis of no trend. The coefficients imply an average annual rate of increase of 1.8% in the US price and 2.1% in the Canadian price. In both cases, the rate of price increase is about 1% less than the inflation rate, indicating a rate of real wheat price decline of about 1%, roughly the same as the long-term rate of wheat price decline in the 20th century.

Both the Canadian and US time series were tested for unit roots using the equation:

$$\Delta P_t = \alpha + \gamma P_{t-1} + \sum_{j=1}^{T} B_j \Delta P_{t-j}.$$

Following the discussion in Mills (1993, pp. 53–55), a value of $T = 4$ (four lagged monthly price changes) is used, although only the first lag turns out to be significant. The estimated γ is -0.058, for the Canadian data (June 1982 to January 1997). This implies an estimate of 0.942 for the autoregressive coefficient, ρ in $P_t = \alpha + \rho P_{t-1}$. The standard error of the estimated γ is 0.024, so $t = -0.058/0.024 = -2.41$, a level which the Dickey–Fuller test indicates cannot reject the hypothesis that

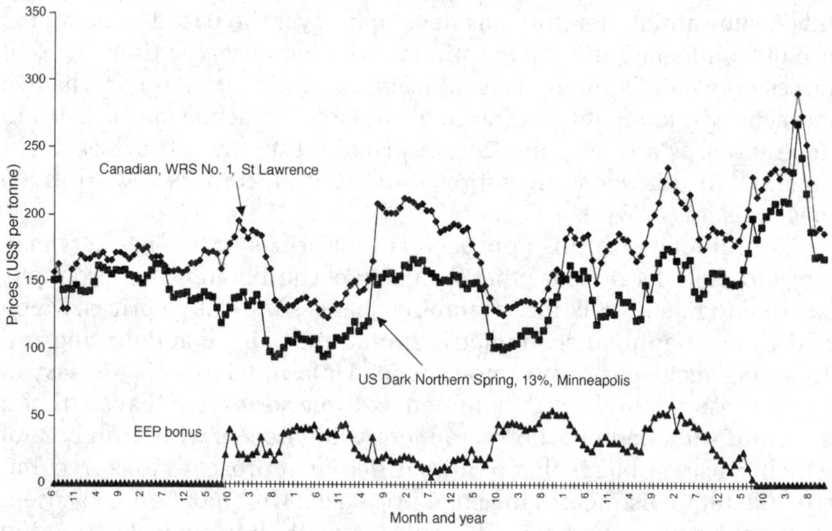

Fig. 12.3. Canadian and US wheat prices. Source: USDA, 1997.

a unit root exists ($\rho = 1$, or random walk) at the 5% level, but which is just about at the critical value for the 10% confidence level for 175 observations. The US price series yields an estimated $\rho = 0.939$ and a Dickey–Fuller test that cannot reject a unit root at the 5% level but can reject it at the 10% level. Thus, the results are qualitatively ambiguous. It is most likely that there is no unit root, i.e. prices do not follow a random walk; but we cannot reject the null hypothesis of a random walk with 95% confidence of being correct.

The substantive results are: (a) a significant but slowly growing trend exists in both prices (after converting to US dollars), and (b) a persistence in price innovations exists, but we cannot determine conclusively whether these series follow a random walk or not.

An alternative test for the random-walk hypothesis as opposed to mean reversion is an examination of the variances of price differences, var $(p_t - p_{t-k})$, with prices at increasingly long lags (k). With a random walk these variances become larger with longer lags, but under mean reversion the variances approach a constant as k increases. Moreover, the 'k-differences' (Cochrane, 1988) grow linearly with k under a random walk. Therefore, $\frac{1}{k}$ times the k differences should be a constant for a random walk, but should decline to zero as k increases if price are random fluctuations around a deterministic trend (mean reverting).

Results for the Minneapolis and St Lawrence monthly prices are shown in Fig. 12.4. Figure 12.4 plots the statistic $\frac{1}{k}$ (var $(p_t - p_{t-k})$). The above linearity in k implies that the graph should be a horizontal line at the level of 80 or 100 (the level of var $(p_t - p_{t-1})$, with $k = 1$) if prices follow a random walk but approach zero if prices follow random fluctuations around a determinate trend. In the 175 monthly 1982–1997 data series, $\frac{1}{k}$ var $(p_t - p_{t-k})$ levels out at about half of the $k = 1$ value at $k = 48$ to 60 months for both the Canadian and US wheat prices. The asymptotic standard error of $\frac{1}{k}$ var $(p_t - p_{t-k})$ is its estimated value times $(\frac{4k}{3T})^{\frac{1}{2}}$, where $T = 175$ in this case. At $k = 48$, this implies a standard error of about 25 for both the US and the Canadian data. Although the normality of the distribution is in doubt, the results make it quite unlikely that the prices follow either a pure random walk (horizontal line in Fig. 12.4) or deterministic trend (graph approaches zero at large k) but instead has components of each.

Because of the likelihood of Canadian and US wheat prices having a common deterministic trend, or a random walk with drift, which could cause spurious regression results, it is worth considering cointegration tests rather than simple regression as used above in the annual data. Instead of regressing the US price on the Canadian price or subtracting one from the other, we estimate the cointegrating equation, which in the monthly Canadian/US wheat price data is:

$$P_{\text{CANADA}} = \underset{(5.5)}{35.0} + \underset{(0.037)}{0.975}\ P_{\text{USA}},\ R^2 = 0.80 \qquad 12.1$$

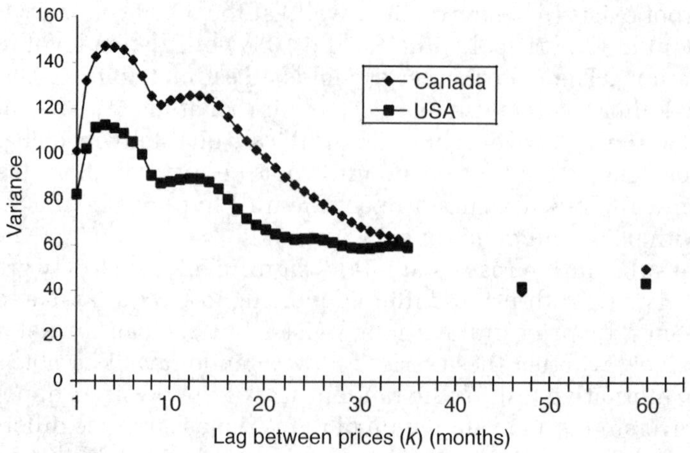

Fig. 12.4. Variance of *k*-period price differences times $\frac{1}{k}$.

Standard errors are in parentheses. The intercept is roughly the spread between the two prices. If the cointegrating relationship were perfect, the coefficient on P_{USA} would be 1 and the intercept would measure the spread exactly. With a standard error of 0.037 on the coefficient of 0.975, the coefficient is not significantly different from 1. A test for cointegration is whether the residuals, u_t, from the above equation have a unit root or not. Using the same unit-root test equation as above, but with only one lag on the change in residual, $u_t - u_{t-1}$, the test equation as estimated is:

$$\underset{}{(u_t - u_{t-1})} = \underset{(0.568)}{0.096} - \underset{(0.042)}{0.138}\, u_{t-1} - \underset{(0.075)}{0.174}\, (u_{t-1} - u_{t-2}),\ R^2 = 0.113 \qquad 12.2$$

Standard errors are in parentheses. The coefficient of u_{t-1} is significantly different from zero, using the Dickey–Fuller criteria, indicating we can reject a unit root and the US and Canadian price series are cointegrated. This is the same result obtained by Smith *et al.* (undated) for both durum and spring wheat prices, 1978 to 1993 monthly data. They analysed monthly US Gulf prices for Dark Northern Spring and Canadian Pacific Western Red Spring wheat prices, January 1978 to June 1993. They found the US and Canadian price series to be cointegrated for both the pre-EEP and EEP periods. It is notable also that US/Canadian wheat is one of the few cases in which Ardeni (1989) could not reject cointegration. Indeed, on 1967–1983 monthly data that only overlap the Equation 12.1 data set in 12 of 175 months, Ardeni (1989) estimated a cointegrating coefficient of 0.975, the same as in Equation 12.1 above.

Finding cointegration may not be surprising in view of the fact that the Canadian price is a 'posted' or 'asking' price of the CWB, and CWB officials state that they base their asking price largely on what happens in the most comparable US markets. Earlier it was suggested that Winnipeg Commodity Exchange feed wheat prices might be a better indicator of market integration, despite the specialized nature of this market. Figure 12.5 shows annual data on Winnipeg cash market prices (from the Canadian Grains Council, 1992) along with US prices for wheat at Chicago, which is generally a lower-priced US wheat, and the US average farm price for all wheat. The US and Canadian prices have obvious co-movements, but with substantial-looking divergences, especially in the 1990s.

Returning to the St Lawrence price, while their being asking rather than transactions prices changes the interpretation of what cointegration means in economic terms, we would not expect to see the CWB postings that are just a mechanical mark-up from the Minneapolis Exchange price. This is true especially if the price leadership role attributed to the CWB in Smith *et al.* (undated) as well as Goodwin and Smith (1995) and others is correct. In particular, the EEP would be expected to bring down the CWB price relative to the US price (unless the CWB simply offers bigger discounts from their asking price in response to EEP).

The spread between the series as plotted in Fig. 12.3 changes over time. The surprising aspect of these changes is that they appear to be the opposite of what the EEP is expected to generate. That is, the Canadian price tends to be *higher* relative to the US price when the EEP is in effect.

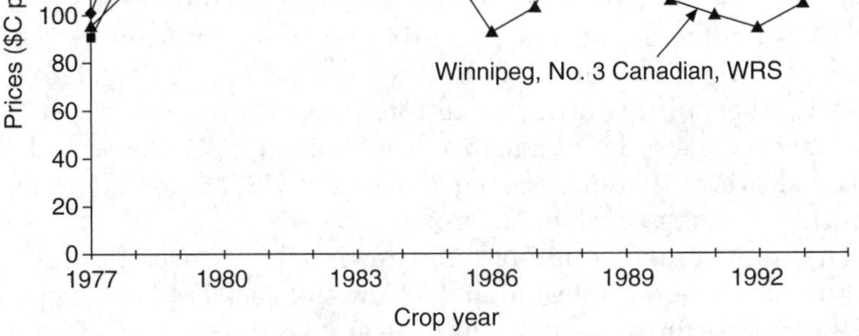

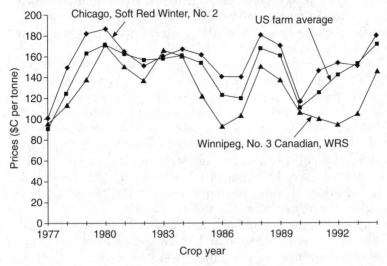

Fig. 12.5. US and Canadian wheat prices. Source: Winnipeg price – Canadian Grains Council, 1992; US prices – USDA, 1997.

Looking separately at the 118 months during which the EEP was in effect, the cointegrating equation corresponding to Equation 12.1 is:

$$P_{\text{CANADA}} = \underset{(6.2)}{15.2} + \underset{(0.045)}{1.16}\ P_{\text{USA}},\ R^2 = 0.85 \qquad 12.3$$

The basis spread is smaller, which is consistent with observation of the plotted data, and more surprisingly the Canadian reaction to the US price has a coefficient significantly larger than 1. The unit-root test for the EEP period is based on the equation:

$$(u_t - u_{t-1}) = \underset{(0.733)}{-0.268} - \underset{(0.072)}{0.236}\ u_{t-1} - \underset{(0.092)}{0.226}\ (u_{t-1} - u_{t-2}),\ R^2 = 0.194 \qquad 12.4$$

The coefficient on u_{t-1} is even further less than zero than above, but the standard error is sufficiently higher for us to reject a unit root with the same confidence. Thus, we conclude the price series are just as integrated in the EEP period as in the whole data set, although the cointegrating equation is different.

The econometric time-series analyses of these price data leave one with an unsatisfying lack of understanding of what is generating either the US or the Canadian prices, or the relationship between them. There is clearly a relationship between the series of the general kind one would expect in an integrated North American grain market, namely the prices move together. The econometric results indicate this relationship is indeed statistically significant, and is not just attributable to the two series sharing a common trend, and that it is likely both countries' monthly price series are characterized by mean reversion as opposed to being random walks. However, we do not know enough to be either impressed or unimpressed by the extent of integration, nor do we know what causes observed departures from perfect integration, or how integration is related to EEP or to Canadian policies.

Departures from perfect integration are indicated by the data plotted in Fig. 12.6, which show both actual Canadian–US price differences and the residuals from Equation 12.1 above. The easily observable parallel movements of the two series are the essential evidence that the two markets are integrated (the Appendix provides a relevant example of failure of integration). But if the series were perfectly integrated, in the sense of the cointegrating equation providing a perfect fit with parameters of the order of magnitude estimated, Fig. 12.6 would show the actual price differences being constant at US$35 (for example) and the residuals being constant at zero.

The interesting economic question is what causes the observed departure from perfect integration. McNew and Fackler (1997) emphasize that these departures need not indicate any kind of imperfection in the functioning of grain pricing or marketing. Price differences in fully integrated markets should not exceed transportation costs but they can be

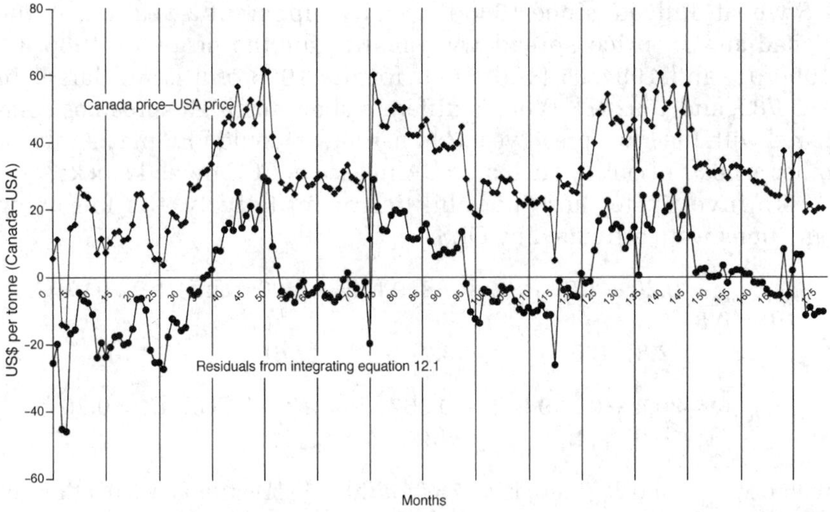

Fig. 12.6. Actual price differences and integrating equation residuals. The price differences are calculated from data shown in Fig. 12.4. Vertical grid lines are 1 year apart. The first starts in June 1982 and the series ends with January 1997.

less than transportation costs, and transportation costs themselves can change over time. And, as Goodwin *et al.* (1990) emphasize, when transportation takes time and random supply or demand shocks occur at different times in different countries, the propagation of price shocks between markets can have lags and still not indicate market imperfection in any economically relevant sense.

So what explains the variations in the Canadian–US price difference? The first candidate must be seasonal difference in crop production. The US wheat harvest, and marketing year, starts about 2 months earlier in the USA than in Canada. By each country's statistical convention, the US marketing year begins on 1 June and the Canadian on 1 August. (The International Wheat Council, in Solomonic UN mode, starts the international wheat marketing year on 1 July.) One would therefore expect average wheat prices in the USA to be seasonally low relative to Canada in June and July of each year. However, the comparison in the monthly econometrics is between US spring wheat at Minneapolis and Canadian wheat, where the lower US price ought to be observed only in late July or early August at most. None the less, the mean Canadian–US price difference in the 1982–1996 period is no different in July or August from other months. The mean difference in all months is a US$31.48 per tonne higher Canadian price. The mean July price difference is US$31.79 and the mean August price difference US$30.27.[6] Generally, there is no significant seasonal price-difference pattern.

What looks more likely from the Fig. 12.5 graph is that in some year-long periods Canadian wheat sells at a higher or lower price relative to

US wheat. Indeed, since 1986 there is an apparent 2-year cycle: the Canadian–US price spread was smaller for the crops of 1986/87, 1990/91, and 1994/95 (and so far for the 1996 crop); and larger in 1988/89, and 1992/93. What is different about the high-spread as compared with the low-spread years? In particular, could EEP play a role, or other aspects of policy such a USDA release of CCC-owned stocks?

To investigate these possibilities quantitatively, the following equations were estimated by OLS:

$$P_{\text{Canada}} = \underset{(2.8)}{0.20} + \underset{(20.3)}{1.00}\, P_{\text{USA}} + \underset{(3.2)}{0.239}\ \text{EEP} + \underset{(2.6)}{0.066}\ \text{Time} + \underset{(1.5)}{0.79}\ \text{CCC},\quad R^2 = 0.84$$

$$P_{\text{Spread}} = \underset{(10.0)}{20.4} + \underset{(4.3)}{0.239}\ \text{EEP} + \underset{(34)}{0.067}\ \text{Time} + \underset{(1.5)}{0.79}\ \text{CCC},\quad R^2 = 0.20$$

where P_{Canada} and P_{USA} are the 176 monthly observations of wheat prices described above, and P_{Spread} is the difference between the Canadian and US price. EEP is the average EEP subsidy in each month, and zero when no subsidies were paid. The figures in parentheses are *t*-statistics of the estimated coefficients. The estimated EEP effect is to increase the Canadian price relative to the US price. For example, a monthly-average EEP bonus at the typical level of US\$30 per tonne is estimated to increase the Canadian price US\$7 per tonne relative to the US price. The CCC variable is net acquisition of US government stocks in the quarter in which the price is observed. The variable has no significant effect on the price spread. The trend variable implies that over the 1982 to 1996 period the spread between the Canadian and US price would have increased about US\$11.5 per tonne in the absence of other influences.

Thus, the unexpected positive effect of EEP on the Canadian–US price spread remains a puzzle. It could be caused by a number of factors: (i) non-EEP variables left out of the model might explain the higher spread in the EEP period; (ii) the 43 pre-EEP months and 16 post-EEP months in the sample, as shown in Fig. 12.3, may have an unusually narrow spread (this is really a variant of the first point); (iii) EEP bonuses were accompanied by other policy moves, notably US CCC stock release, that caused the price spread to increase; and (iv) the EEP really did cause the price spread to increase, despite the prediction of economic theory. For example, recalling that the Canadian price is a CWB asking price and the US price is an indicator price for actual transactions on the Minneapolis Exchange, it is possible that the CWB increases its asking price as EEP bonuses rise as a strategic move so they can offer nominally larger discounts to compete with EEP while not cutting their actual selling prices as much as the discounts would indicate.

What is the plausibility of, and evidence for, these possibilities? With respect to items (i) and (ii), the annual model whose results were reported in Table 12.8 included some relevant supply–demand variables, and considered a longer time series. It did find a marginally significant effect of EEP in reducing the Canadian–US price spread. Using crop-year (CY) annual data for the longer period 1971–1996, it does appear that the Canadian–US margin was unusually small in CY 1983/84 and 1984/85, immediately preceding the EEP, and in 1996, which followed EEP. However, re-estimating the regressions of Table 12.8 for shorter time periods, and with right-hand side variables other than EEP omitted, the annual data still generate a negative effect of EEP on the Canadian–US price spread, and indeed the significance level increases. The estimated EEP effect is robust to inclusion or exclusion of any of the non-EEP supply–demand variables of Table 12.8, as well as to time period analysed.

With respect to possibility (iii), inclusion of the change in quarterly CCC stocks leaves the estimated results of EEP unchanged.

The key difference between the unexpected monthly result and the Table 12.8 result using annual data is the use of the CWB's final price in the annual regressions but the St Lawrence posted price in the monthly ones. When regressions are estimated using annual averages of the St Lawrence price, the results of the monthly regression are replicated – the EEP does not reduce the premium of the Canadian over the US price, and if anything increases the spread. What is going on can be seen in Fig. 12.7, namely, introduction of the EEP increases the spread between the St Lawrence posted price and the final price that Canadian farmers receive. This is how the EEP can have no apparent effect on the St Lawrence price and yet a significant negative effect on the farm price in Canada. Recalling that the price generally used in time-series econometrics of the Canadian wheat market is the St Lawrence price or another posted price closely related to it (because the posted prices can be observed daily, weekly or monthly while the final farm price can only be observed annually), studies using the higher-frequency data are inevitably going to miss the story of EEP effects on Canadian agriculture.

These results indicate that the puzzling results in the monthly posted-price regressions are to be explained by item (iv) in the earlier list, or some variant of it. That is, CWB pricing strategy in the face of EEP is what drives the effects of EEP on Canada.[7] This means it is time, in our discussion of US and Canadian policies in the emergence of an integrated North American grain market, to turn our attention to the Canadian side, in particular to CWB marketing policies.

While the production and government payment policies of Canada, as in the USA, have moved in the direction of non-distorting transfers and income insurance schemes, the CWB marketing monopoly for wheat in foreign trade and domestic milling remains largely in place (like the US export promotion programmes). However, the CWB policies are under criticism from Canadian farmers in a way US export

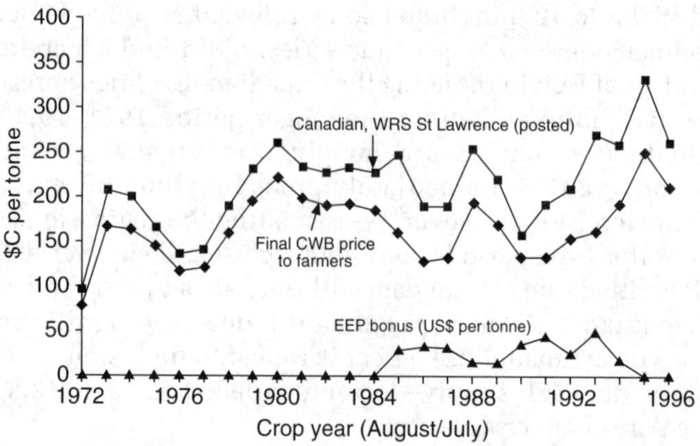

Fig. 12.7. Canadian wheat prices and EEP. Note: 1996 prices are estimated from data up to January 1997. The CWB final price estimate is from the Saskatchewan Wheat Pool's website.

programmes are not from US farmers. In part this political difference is probably attributable to the fact that the US programmes are financed mainly by US non-farm taxpayers, while the CWB draws on the public treasury only to the modest extent necessary to guarantee its initial price when this creates a deficit in the pool account.[8] Beyond this, many Canadian wheat growers believe they could sell directly to the US market for a return higher than they will obtain from the CWB. The issue is lucidly discussed in Schmitz *et al.* (1997).

Schmitz *et al.* (1997) also review evidence as to how well the CWB has performed its mission to increase farmers' returns from exported wheat by strategic selling, mostly by selling at high prices where market conditions permit (certain Far Eastern markets, particularly) and at low prices where competition with the USA and EU is especially fierce (e.g. North Africa). The evidence on this matter has to be indirectly adduced because the actual transactions prices for CWB exports are kept confidential. Various studies have estimated that the CWB is able to sell an average tonne of exported wheat for US$15–35 more than would be obtained if wheat export was open to all and conducted by competitive grain traders. However, the studies also estimate that the CWB involves extra costs that may offset much of the price gain (Schmitz *et al.*, 1997, p. 38). Farm-level prices suggest that the biggest premium the CWB has been able to achieve for Canadian Prairie wheat producers over their US Northern Plains counterparts was about US$25 per tonne, in 1977–1980, and that since 1985 (i.e. since EEP) they have been able to generate no significant premium. Indeed,

Saskatchewan pool prices, Saskatoon basis, have averaged about $C20 per tonne less than the CWB final price, basis St Lawrence. Hence the Canadian farmers' belief they could sell more profitably in the US market on their own.

If the CWB let Canadian farmers ship to the USA on their own, the resulting US wheat imports would be a real test of NAFTA as a liberalizing agreement. It is a fairly safe bet that the USA would act to stop such imports. Such a protectionist act could be justified under NAFTA because it could reasonably be argued to constitute an import surge caused by a significant change in Canadian policy. Import barriers have been erected under CUSTA and NAFTA on flimsier rationales than this, and US wheat growers are particularly vigilant on such matters. So the CWB has a political as well as economic strategic element in its marketing of wheat in the USA, which Canadian farmers should probably take more notice of than Canadian critics of the CWB appear to recognize.

4. Integration at the Farm Level

While studies of market integration typically focus on price behaviour, there are other indicators that ought to be considered in assessing the extent to which one can speak of a single North American grain market. In particular, what are the connections and similarities in input markets, technology and economic organization of farms? Floyd (1965) and MacKenzie (1965) both found basic similarities in the Canadian and US farm economies in 1945–1960, with Canada having overall slightly lower crop prices (Floyd, 1965) and technical efficiency (MacKenzie, 1965) but with productivity and income per worker rising faster in Canada. Generally, though, the differences are no larger than between states of the USA.

Grimard (1996) presents more detailed comparisons of Canadian and US farm operations. For purposes of this chapter, her comparison of grain producers in the Prairie Provinces of Canada with those of the US Northern Plains states (Montana, Minnesota, North and South Dakota) are of particular interest. Table 12.9 shows some key data for 1993. The most striking feature of these data is how similar the farms are in financial terms, in income generated, net worth, debt/assets, and importance of government payments. The average size of US farms, as measured by value of sales, is larger by about 50%, however, and the amount of off-farm income is about twice as large.

Indications of the similar technological and economic evolution of wheat farming over time are evident in wheat yield trends. Both Canadian and US spring wheat have had similarly variable yields, and rates of yield increase over time. During 1962–1996, Canada's yields

Table 12.9. Economic characteristics of prairie grain farms (per farm), 1993 (in $C).

	Canada	USA
Farm sales	71,599	113,840
Government payments	18,190	27,977
Total revenue	89,789	141,817
Total expenses	61,371	113,509
Net cash income	28,418	28,308
(Per family)	23,681	25,569
Off-farm income	21,142	30,629
Total income per family	44,823	56,198
Total farm assets	529,482	683,733
Total debt	79,141	137,651
Net worth	450,341	546,083
Debt: asset ratio	0.15	0.20
Rate of return on assets	6.5%	5.7%
Government payments/revenue	20.3%	19.7%
Percentage of family income from farm	52.8%	45.5%
Number of farms	60,000	

Source: Grimard, 1996, Table 9.1. The Canadian definition of a farm requires $2000 in sales of farm products. The US data were obtained from USDA's Costs and Returns Survey, applying the Canadian farm definition.

increased annually by 31 kg per ha, and the USA's 25 kg per ha. So Canada's yield is growing slightly faster. But consider also the percentage rates of growth, as indicated by the linear trend line in the natural log of yield. Canada's yield grows at 1.04% per year, US yield at 1.26%. So in terms of growth rates the USA is ahead.

With respect to wheat area, both countries have expanded harvested area, but the USA has expanded more. The USA added 8 million harvested hectares since 1962 (and 5 million even after adjustment to the mid-1960s shift away from production controls in wheat). Canada has added about 2 million hectares since 1962 (about an 18% increase). A more notable difference between the countries is the larger year-to-year change in US wheat area (except in 1970 when the Canadian harvested area fell by half).

5. Summary and Conclusions

In many respects, the Canadian and US grain sectors are well integrated. Farms generally, and those that specialize in wheat in particular, are organized similarly, use similar technology and information sources and earn similar incomes for their owners in both countries. Pricing and marketing institutions, however, particularly as related to international grain marketing, have evolved quite differently. Producers in both countries have sought, on occasions when it appeared economically necessary, to erect trade barriers to shield themselves from the other country's competing producers. Since in wheat the more usual flow of unrestricted trade would result in US imports from Canada, the main illiberal acts have been instigated from the US side.

Since 1989, CUSTA and NAFTA have been the formal political context for a weakening of protection and a substantial increase in bilateral agricultural trade. Outcries from injured parties have slowed but not stopped the liberalization. In domestic policy, both countries have also taken significant steps toward less governmental regulation of markets, in grain particularly. Canada has moved quite thoroughly toward income stabilization through insurance schemes that are partly producer-financed, rather than legislated support prices, and long-standing transportation subsidies are being abandoned.

Most of this chapter has been devoted to an attempt to quantify the extent to which policy changes have reduced each country's protection of wheat, and the extent to which prices in the two countries are indicative of an integrated bi-national wheat market. A review of estimated producer subsidy equivalents, which represent wheat support activities by governments as an aggregate dollar value, indicates about the same level of support in Canada and the USA. Annual government benefits to wheat producers add up to 35–40% of the value of wheat production in both countries. However, the market-distorting policies that implement this support are very different in the two countries: area idling and export subsidies in the USA, and transportation subsidies and centralized export marketing in Canada. In addition, both countries are moving toward non-distorting means of support, most recently the US FAIR Act of 1996, and Canada's phase-out of rail transportation subsidies. CUSTA and NAFTA are supposed to remove barriers to international trade and so establish market integration, but in wheat both countries' export programmes remain in place, and the USA has restrained wheat imports from Canada.

Because policy reforms have been incomplete, the question of whether there has been movement towards an integrated North American wheat market can only be settled by empirical evidence. The findings of the chapter are:

- Agricultural trade between the countries, and wheat trade in particular, has increased in the 1990s, and CUSTA/NAFTA and other policies are in part responsible.
- The wheat markets in the two countries are not, however, integrated in the sense of wheat prices differing only by market-driven factors like transportation costs.

The evidence for the latter conclusion is derived from the co-movements of wheat prices in the two countries. Some quoted prices move very closely together, but on the Canadian side these are asking prices posted by the CWB, in part in response to US market prices of wheat traded at the Minneapolis Grain Exchange and other locations. Prices that reflect market transactions directly, notably prices at the Winnipeg Grain Exchange, do not move so closely with US prices. More direct evidence of non-integration is that there is a significant effect of US export subsidy levels on the differences between annual prices received by Canadian and US farmers.

Further liberalization is possible as budgetary outlays remain substantial; about 4 million ha formerly in wheat remain idled in the US Conservation Reserve Program and the CWB's marketing monopoly powers are under fire from producers. The US FAIR Act ends area control through annual set-asides, governmental attempts to stabilize markets by regulation of commodity stockholding, and price guarantees to producers through deficiency payments. Further liberalization in the USA would mean principally extending the FAIR Act beyond its 2002 expiration while eliminating or greatly reducing the schedule of payments to producers that bought farmers' acceptance of the FAIR Act in 1996, and elimination of the supply management role of the Conservation Reserve Program.

Whether further liberalization will occur in either trade or domestic grain policy, in either country, is quite uncertain. But the trend is in the direction of liberalization and, as the data on bilateral trade indicate, liberalization has been significant in fact and not only in statements of policy.

Appendix: Cointegration Results with Independent Random Walks

The Fig. 12.5 parallels between actual Canadian–US price differences and residuals from the cointegrating Equation 12.1 look so easy to obtain that one may question whether the plots would look much the same even if the two price series were independent random walks with drift (and so not cointegrated). I constructed random-walk price series for countries which, to avoid confusion, I will call 'Canada' and 'USA'. Prices in 'Canada' evolve according to:

$$P^{C}_{t+1} = P^{C}_{t} + \delta^{C} + v_t,\ v_t \sim N(0, 20) \qquad 12.5$$

and

$$P^{US}_{t+1} = P^{US}_{t} + \delta^{US} + u_t,\ w_t \sim N(0, 20) \qquad 12.6$$

P_t^c starts at \$160 in June 1982 and is moved by v_t, whose standard deviation of \$20 is roughly the actual standard deviation of monthly price changes in 1982–1997, and drift δ^c, which is \$0.25 per month, comparable to actual-trend monthly growth of wheat prices in Canada. P_t^{US} starts at \$150 in June 1982 and is moved by drift of δ^{US} = \$0.22 and random variable w_t, which is independently normally distributed. Random sequences of v_t and w_t were then drawn (using the normal random variate generator in the spreadsheet program Excel) and a 175-month price series generated for each country. The resulting price differences are plotted in Fig. 12.8, along with residuals from the estimated cointegrating equation, which is:

$$P_t^c = \underset{(10.1)}{162} - \underset{(2.11)}{0.137}\, P_t^{US},\ R^2 = 0.025 \qquad 12.7$$

(t-ratios in parentheses). The coefficient of u_{t-1} on Δu_t, where u_t are the residuals from Equation 12.7, is −0.056 with a t statistic of −1.93. The Dickey–Fuller test does not reject the existence of a unit root at either the 5% or 10% level (which is good, because a unit root exists by construction, and moreover this shows the importance of using the Dickey–Fuller tests rather than the usual significance values for t-tests in OLS regressions). In short, drift in independent random walks does not automatically generate prices that move together in the way Canadian and US wheat prices do.

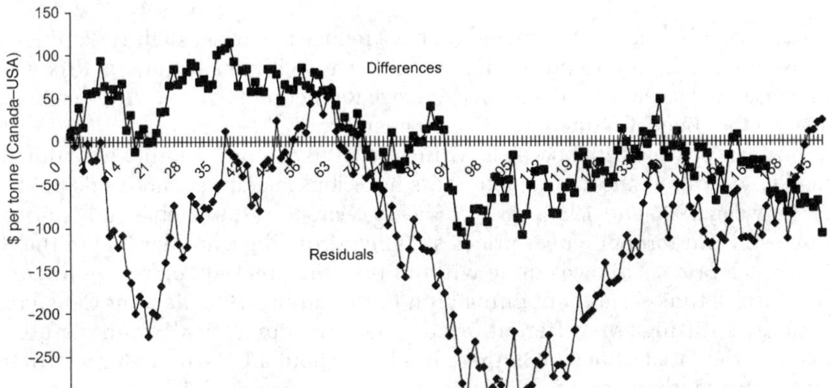

Fig. 12.8. Price differences and integrating residuals with random walk and drift. USA follows $P(t) = P(t-1) + 0.22 + e(t)$ is $N(0,20)$; Canada follows $P(t) = (Pt-1) + 0.23 + e(t)$, $e(t)$ is independently $N(0,20)$. Initial values are $P(US) = 150$, $P(CAN) = 160$.

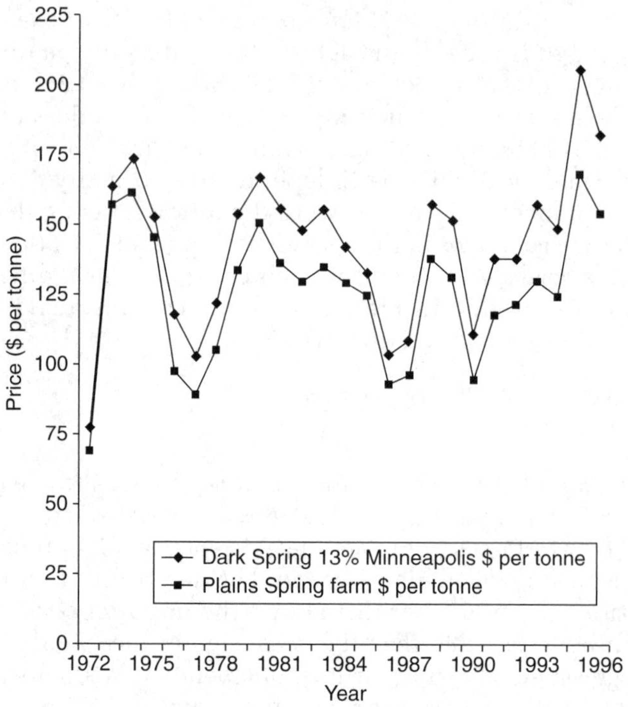

Fig. 12.9. Minneapolis and farm price of spring wheat.

Notes

1. A full analytical assessment would have reduce this offset slightly. Producers were not cushioned to quite this extent because higher payments this year increase the probability of a higher Average Reduction Program (ARP) percentage or other budget-reducing measures next year.
2. 'Apparently' possible because, while the CWB claims an ability to maintain market separation, the transaction prices in various markets are not made public.
3. Between 1985 and 1987, USDA's *Wheat Yearbook* (1997) table on historical domestic and foreign wheat prices switched from the Thunder Bay to the St Lawrence price. This was done without revising pre-1985 prices, so anyone who uses a time series containing both post- and pre-1985 data for Canada is actually splitting two different price series, one domestically and the other export-orientated. Since 1989 there has been about a US$10 per tonne difference between them, and the difference is not a constant, reflecting changes in the CWB's uses of the two different quotations and how each is related to Minneapolis prices.
4. A world supply of 1 million tonnes (0.2% of average supply in the data period) reduces price by about 60 cents per tonne (0.4% of average price) according to the point estimate, implying an elasticity of world wheat demand, including demand for stocks of about −0.5.

5. Regressions were also estimated using the product of the average EEP bonus and EEP tonnage, i.e. the level of EEP spending, and including both the bonus level and tonnage in the same equation. All experiments indicated that the EEP bonus level best captures the negative effect of EEP on the Canadian–US wheat price difference.
6. The Canadian–US farm-level difference in price of spring wheat is less than US$10 per tonne during this period. Why then is the St Lawrence–Minneapolis spread $31? The difference probably reflects either the CWB's effectiveness in price discrimination (with St Lawrence postings being the highest prices) or higher marketing costs in Canada, or both.
7. It might be argued that marketing costs were generally higher in the EEP period, so the margin between prices at port or central locations and farmers' price received would be larger in these years regardless of CWB strategy. However, as Fig. 12.9 shows, the US marketing spread did not widen. The gap between the Minneapolis Dark Northern Spring price and the US average price received by farmers for spring wheat appears instead to have narrowed in the EEP years.
8. Since 1980 the total deficits in the wheat and durum pools have amounted to $C770 million. On total sales of 300 million tonnes this amounts to a producer subsidy equivalent of about $C2.50 per tonne (Gray and Gardner, 1995, p. 23; Loyns and Kraut, 1995, p. 25).

References

Agriculture Canada (1996) *Farm Data Book*, September. Ottawa.

Ardeni, P.G. (1989) Does the law of one price really hold for commodity prices? *American Journal of Agricultural Economics* 71, 661–669.

Babula, R.A., Jabara, C.L. and Reeder, J. (1996) Role of empirical evidence in US/Canadian dispute on US imports of wheat, wheat flour, and semolina. *Agribusiness* 12, 183–199.

Bresnahan, T.F. (1989) Empirical studies of industries with market power. In: Schmalensee, R. and Willig, R.D. (eds) *Handbook of Industrial Organization*, Vol. II. Elsevier Science Publishers, New York, pp. 1011–1058.

Canada Grains Council (1992) *Statistical Handbook*. Canadian Grains Council, Winnipeg, Manitoba.

CWB (Canadian Wheat Board) (1997) Website Description of CWB, *www.cwb.ca/aboutcwb*, 12 March.

Chambers, R.G. and Paarlberg, P.L. (1991) Are more exports always better? Comparing cash and in-kind export subsidies. *American Journal of Agricultural Economics* 73, 142–154.

Cochrane, J.H. (1988) How big is the random walk in GNP? *Journal of Political Economy* 96, 893–920.

Floyd, J.E. (1965) The costs of and returns to farm policy: a United States–Canadian comparison. *Journal of Farm Economics* 47, 1140–1151.

Gardner, B.L. (1996) The political economy of US export subsidies for wheat. In: Krueger, A. (ed.) *The Political Economy of American Trade Policy*. University of Chicago Press, Chicago, Illinois, USA, pp. 291–331.

Goodwin, B.K. and Smith, V.H. (1995) *Price Discrimination in International Wheat Markets.* Wheat Export Trade Education Committee Report, March.

Goodwin, B.K., Grennes, T. and Wohlgenant, M. (1990) Testing the law of one price when trade takes times. *Journal of International Money and Finance* 9, 21–40.

Gray, R. and Gardner, B. (1995) *The Impact of Canadian and US Farm Policies on Grain Production and Trade.* Prepared for the Canada/US Joint Commission on Grains, February, New Orleans, USA.

Grimard, J. (1996) *Financial Characteristics of Canadian and US Farms, 1991 and 1993.* Policy Branch, Agriculture and Agri-Food Canada, November, Ottawa.

Haley, S.L. (1995) *Product Differentiation in Wheat Trade Modeling.* Technical Bulletin No. 1838, June, Economic Research Services, USDA, Washington DC, USA.

Hoffman, L.A., Schwartz, S. and Chomo, G.V. (1995) *Wheat: Background for 1995 Farm Legislation.* Agricultural Economics Report No. 712, April, Economic Research Service, USDA, Washington DC, USA.

Kolstad, C.D. and Burris, A.E. (1986) Imperfectly competitive equilibria in international commodity markets. *American Journal of Agricultural Economics* 68 (February), 27–36.

Loyns, R.M.A. and Kraut, M. (1995) *Pricing to Value.* Prepared for the Canada/US Joint Commission on Grains, February, New Orleans, USA.

MacKenzie, W. (1965) Comparative resource, productivity and income effects of Canadian and US farm policies. *Journal of Farm Economics* 14, 1130–1139.

McNew, K.P. and Fackler, P.L. (1997) Testing market equilibrium: is cointegration informative? *Journal of Agricultural and Resource Economics* (December), 191–207.

Mills, T.C. (1993) *The Econometric Modeling of Financial Time Series.* Cambridge University Press, New York, USA.

Nelson, F.J., Simone, M.V. and Valdes, C.M. (1995) *A Comparison of Agricultural Support in Canada, Mexico, and the United States.* Agriculture Information Bulletin No. 719, September, Economic Research Service, USDA, Washington DC, USA.

Pick, D.H. and Carter, C.A. (1994) Pricing to market with transactions denominated in a common currency. *American Journal of Agricultural Economics* 76, 55–60.

Schmitz, A., Furtan, H., Brooks, H. and Gray, R. (1997) The Canadian Wheat Board: how has it performed? *Choices*, 1st quarter, 36–42.

Shei, Shun-yi and Thompson, R.L. (1997) The impact of trade restrictions on price stability in the world wheat market. *American Journal of Agricultural Economics* 59, 628–638.

Smith, D.B., Mohanty, S. and Peterson, E.W. (undated) *Time Series Evidence on Price Relationships between the US and Canadian Wheat Prices.* CARD Working Paper, Iowa State University, Ames, Iowa, USA.

Sumner, D.A., Alston, J.M. and Gray, R. (1994) *A Quantitative Analysis of the Effects of Wheat Imports on the US Market for Wheat.* Report to the Canadian Wheat Board, Winnipeg, Canada.

Tweeten, L., Sharples, J. and Evers-Smith, L. (1997) *The Impact of CFTA/NAFTA on US and Canadian Agriculture.* Working Paper 97–3, International Agricultural Trade Research Consortium, March.

USDA (US Department of Agriculture) (1995) *Wheat: Situation and Outlook Yearbook.* Economic Research Service, Washington DC, USA.

USDA (US Department of Agriculture) (1996) *Agricultural Outlook.* Economic Research Service, Washington DC, USA.

USDA (US Department of Agriculture) (1997) *Wheat: Situation and Outlook Yearbook.* Economic Research Service, WHS-1997, Washington DC, USA.

USDA (US Department of Agriculture) (various issues) *Foreign Agricultural Trade of the USA (FATUS).* Economic Research Service, Washington DC, USA.

US International Trade Commission (1990) *Durum Wheat: Conditions of Competition Between the US and Canadian Industries.* USITC Publication 2274, June, Washington DC, USA.

US International Trade Commission (1994) *Wheat, Wheat Flour, and Semolina.* Investigation No. 22–54, USITC Publication 2794, July, Washington DC, USA.

13 South American Wheat Markets and MERCOSUR

Eugenio Diaz-Bonilla

International Food Policy Research Institute (IFPRI), Washington DC, USA

1. Introduction

The objective of this chapter is to provide an overview of recent major changes in wheat markets in South America, and particularly in MERCOSUR, and to discuss some possible scenarios for wheat production and trade in light of the continuation and deepening of trade integration in the Americas. As a background, the next section briefly reviews macroeconomic and trade developments in the region. The third section examines overall production and consumption patterns. The fourth and fifth sections focus on Argentina's and Brazil's policies affecting wheat production, consumption and trade, including the MERCOSUR agreement. Section 6 summarizes different quantitative studies of wheat trade issues and projections. The chapter closes with some comments and conclusions.

2. Macroeconomic and Agricultural Background[1]

The world macroeconomic and agricultural cycles of the last three decades

Changes in the agricultural sector and food markets of Latin America and Caribbean (LAC) countries over the last 20 years, and in fact in their economies in general, have been heavily influenced by major world macroeconomic developments, particularly by the cycle that has been labelled as the 'rise and fall of inflation' (International Monetary Fund,

World Economic Outlook, 1996). Stimulative macroeconomic policies during the 1960s and 1970s led to higher rates of economic growth and eventually to higher inflation by the second half of the 1970s. The macroeconomic environment changed radically during the 1980s, when tight monetary policies lowered growth and inflation rates and turned real interest rates strongly positive during the whole decade. By the mid-1990s inflation had been brought down to levels similar to 30 years previously, but the average annual growth rate for the world in the first half of the 1990s stayed below the average for the 1960s (Table 13.1).

LAC countries were very vulnerable to the radical change in world macroeconomic conditions after the second oil crisis at the end of the 1970s because of policies that left the region with a comparatively small export base, heavily dependent on primary commodities and holding greatly expanded external debt. At the beginning of the 1980s, the need to absorb the triple shock of declining terms of trade, declining export volumes and sky-rocketing interest rates led to a painful process of economic restructuring in LAC countries (see references in Diaz-Bonilla, 1991a).

The region suffered another trade shock in 1986 when commodity prices collapsed worldwide, erasing some of the gains of the adjustment efforts of the first half of the decade. Nevertheless, governments in the region persevered with the process of fiscal consolidation and monetary stabilization and at the same time domestic markets and international trade were progressively liberalized. Helped in the period following 1989 by the implementation of the Brady Plan, external indicators improved for several LAC countries, although prices of LAC's export commodities continued to be soft.

During this period of adjustment the performance of the region's agricultural sector reflected the convergence of conflicting influences. On the one hand, exchange rate devaluations and trade liberalization removed at least part of the existent policy bias against agriculture. As a result, the real exchange rate (defined as the price of tradables over non-tradables) increased in many countries, favouring agricultural exports and import-substitution agricultural production. On the other hand, however, the positive impact of the reduction of the policy bias against agriculture was, to some extent, offset by several factors such as: (i) decreases in world prices; (ii) slowdowns of domestic demand; (iii) problems in the industrial sector (which reduced demand for agricultural raw materials); (iv) lack of infrastructure and credit, because of fiscal and monetary adjustment; (v) higher prices of imported inputs and machinery, due to devaluations; and (vi) the fact that LAC governments, as a consequence of fiscal constraints and low world prices, terminated the support programmes to non-trivial segment of import substitution crops, which, until then, and inspite of the overall bias against agriculture, received net assistance (Diaz-Bonilla, 1990).

Table 13.1. World macroeconomic indicators.

	1961–1965	1966–1970	1971–1975	1976–1980	1981–1985	1986–1990	1991–1995	1996–1997
Growth of GDP	4.9	4.6	3.5	3.7	2.3	3.3	3.0	4.1
Growth of trade (volume)	8.5	8.5	5.7	5.7	4.5	4.5	6.3	8.0
Inflation (CPI)[a]	2.5	4.1	8.6	9.4	6.5	3.8	3.3	2.3
Interest rates[b]	4.0	5.9	6.95	8.9	12.2	8.1	7.4	6.1
Real interest rate[c]	1.5	1.7	−1.5	−0.5	5.35	4.1	4.0	3.7

CPI, Consumer Price Index.

[a] Industrial countries.

[b] Industrial countries; nominal long-term rates.

[c] (((1 + interest rate in 1/100th)/(1 + inflation rate in 1/100th)) − 1) × 100.

Source: International Monetary Fund (*International Financial Statistics*, several issues; *World Economic Outlook*, several issues).

All in all, during the harsh decade of the 1980s, agriculture performed better than the rest of the economy, growing above the average for the economy and far more than the industrial sector (Table 13.2). Still, the growth rate of the agricultural sector in the 1980s was clearly below the levels achieved during the previous decades. Agricultural production per capita, which was growing during the 1960s and 1970s, stagnated or declined in the 1980s.

Following the deceleration of the world growth at the beginning of the 1990s, macroeconomic conditions changed again, when the Federal Reserve embarked on an expansionary monetary policy to kick-start the US economy out of the 1990/91 recession. This, coupled with an improved policy environment in LAC, has led to an important surge in capital flows to the region since 1991, only briefly interrupted after the 1994 Mexican devaluation. Capital flows to the region lifted the external constraints under which the region had been operating during the 1980s and led to the resumption of growth in many LAC countries.

The process of trade liberalization that began in the 1980s accelerated during the 1990s as a result of different causes. Regional trade integration progressed through the creation of new trade agreements (such as the North American Free Trade Agreement (NAFTA) and MERCOSUR), the revitalization of older ones (such as the Central America Common Market, the Andean Pact and the Caribbean Common Market (CARICOM)) and the proliferation of smaller trade pacts (such as G-3, and the active presence of Chile in the signing of bilateral agreements). Moreover, several countries in Latin America liberalized their trade regimes in the 1990s either because they joined

Table 13.2. Latin America and the Caribbean: economic indicators and population.

	1970–1980	1980–1990	1990–1997
GDP growth (annual %)			
Total	5.90	1.00	3.70
Industry	5.70	0.40	3.50[a]
Agriculture[b]	3.50	2.00	2.90[a]
Inflation (annual %)[c]	45.2	186.4	141.7[d]
Population growth (annual %)	2.4	2.1	1.7

[a] 1990–1996.
[b] Including Forestry and Fishery.
[c] Consumer Price Index.
[d] It should be noticed that since 1995 inflation has declined significantly, dropping to an annual average for the region of 12.3% in 1997.
Source: Reca and Diaz-Bonilla, 1997.

the General Agreement on Tariffs and Trade (GATT) (for example, Mexico in 1986 and Venezuela in 1990), or because they unilaterally pursued policies of greater openness (for example, Chile earlier in the 1980s, and Colombia during the 1990s, although in the latter case there has been some reversal of policies). Finally, the culmination of the Uruguay Round led to the phased implementation of the negotiated agreements.

For the agricultural sector of LAC the decade of the 1990s started slowly due to low growth at both world and regional levels and the continuous softness in agricultural world prices. But, by the mid-1990s, LAC's agricultural production seemed to have picked up again (see Table 13.2), as well as exports and imports of agricultural goods. Since the second half of 1997, however, the Asian crisis appeared to have slowed down the rate of growth in Latin America at the aggregate and sectoral levels.

3. Changes in Wheat Markets

Overall view

South America as a whole, has been traditionally a net importer of wheat. On average, during the 1990s, South America produced a little less than 16 million tonnes of wheat while it consumed more than 19 million tonnes, with net imports of over 3 million tonnes during that period (Table 13.3). This aggregate, however, disguises the fact that Argentina is a net exporter of wheat, with average net exports of about 6.5 million tonnes during the 1990s. The rest of the countries in the region are basically net importers, with an average of about 9.9 million tonnes of wheat imports per year for the same period (Table 13.4).

In the 1990s, Argentina accounted for about 68% of total production in the region and some 99% of total exports (Table 13.4). Brazil produced about 16% of total wheat output and the balance was divided among the rest of the countries in South America, where Chile, Paraguay and Uruguay are the main producers. Brazil, which consumes almost 8 million tonnes of wheat, accounts for more than 40% of total use in South America. Argentina consumes 4.4 million tonnes (about 23%). Other countries with important levels of consumption are Chile (almost 2 million tonnes), Peru (1.2 million tonnes), and Colombia and Venezuela (about 1 million tonnes each). Brazil is the main importer, with an average of more than 5 million tonnes during the 1990s. The next two most important importers are Peru (1.1 million tonnes) and Venezuela (1 million tonnes), followed by Colombia and Chile (Table 13.4). Except for Uruguay and Paraguay (which each import about 15% of their consumption) and Chile (which imports about 30%), the rest of

Table 13.3. Wheat production, consumption and trade in South America (000 tonnes).

	Production	Consumption	Imports	Exports	Net trade
1960–1964	9,034.2	9,077.0	3,635.6	3,103.8	−531.8
1965–1969	9,014.8	11,194.8	4,665.0	3,015.0	−1,050.0
1970–1974	9,565.0	12,936.2	5,107.2	1,871.4	−3,235.8
1975–1979	12,471.6	15,684.8	7,220.6	3,960.2	−3,260.4
1980–1984	15,171.6	16,479.0	8,273.0	6,989.2	−1,283.8
1985–1989	17,076.8	18,049.0	5,365.6	4,597.2	−768.4
1990–1994	15,383.6	18,964.6	9,837.0	5,975.0	−3,862.0
1995–1998	17,687.3	20,570.3	10,832.3	8,019.5	−2,812.8
1990–1998	16,407.4	19,678.2	10,279.3	6,883.7	−3,397.6

Source: USDA/ERS PSDVIEW, 1997.

the countries in the region import more than two-thirds of their consumption, with several countries showing import ratios of 90% of consumption or more.

South America in a world context

South America has reduced its participation in world production and consumption of wheat from 3.8% in consumption and around 3.4% in production during the 1960s to about 3.5% (consumption) and 2.9% (production) during the 1990s. Exports as a ratio of world exports, which declined sharply during the 1970s, rebounded strongly and by the 1990s the average ratio was above that of the 1960s (5.9% against 5.65%) (see Table 13.5). This increase has been influenced by the large Argentine harvests of 1996–1997, which pushed that ratio close to the highest point, achieved in the mid-1960s.

The ratio of regional to world imports, which was increasing steadily during the 1960s and 1970s, dropped during the difficult decade of the 1980s (where the debt crisis in the region determined the financeable level of imports) but recovered significantly with the resumption of growth in the region and the availability of external financing (Table 13.5).

Production patterns

Over the last 30 years, the main characteristics of wheat production in the region have been the increase in Argentina's production, although with great volatility (Table 13.6) and two Brazilian campaigns to increase wheat production. The first Brazilian campaign round during the 1960s and first half of the 1970s (increased production from less

Table 13.4. Production, consumption and trade by country ('000 tonnes; average during the 1990s).

	Production	Production/ total	Consumption	Consumption/ total	Exports	Exports/ total	Imports	Imports/ total	Imports/ consumption	Exports/ production
Argentina	10,897.1	0.69	4,386.0	0.23	6,495.4	0.99	0.0	0.00	0.00	0.51
Brazil	2,592.7	0.16	7,879.9	0.41	0.0	0.00	5,362.0	0.54	0.68	0.00
Rest of SA	2,420.6	0.15	6,827.3	0.36	77.9	0.01	4,525.4	0.45	0.66	0.01
Bolivia	101.4	0.01	492.3	0.03	0.0	0.00	392.3	0.03	0.79	0.00
Chile	1,364.6	0.08	1,941.6	0.10	0.0	0.00	579.4	0.05	0.29	0.00
Colombia	95.6	0.00	931.9	0.05	0.0	0.00	839.1	0.08	0.90	0.00
Ecuador	21.0	0.00	364.9	0.02	48.6	0.01	395.9	0.03	1.08	0.01
Paraguay	348.6	0.02	345.1	0.02	17.9	nil	44.9	0.00	0.13	0.05
Peru	112.4	0.01	1,219.0	0.06	0.0	0.00	1,113.4	0.11	0.91	0.00
Uruguay	377.0	0.02	433.9	0.02	11.4	nil	68.3	0.01	0.16	0.03
Venezuela	0.0	0.00	1,098.6	0.06	0.0	0.00	1,092.1	0.11	0.99	0.00
Total	15,910.4	1.00	19,093.2	1.00	6,573.3	1.00	9,887.4	1.00	0.52	0.41

Note: There are some minor statistical differences because of changes in stocks and rounding. SA, South America.
Source: USDA/ERS PSDVIEW, 1997.

Table 13.5. South American production, consumption and trade as percentage of world variables.

	Production	Consumption	Exports	Imports
1960s	3.40	3.81	5.65	8.20
1970s	2.95	3.87	3.92	8.71
1980s	2.76	3.57	4.13	7.99
1990s	2.85	3.46	5.91	9.13
1960–1990	3.14	3.68	5.11	8.00

Source: USDA/ERS PSDVIEW, 1997.

than 0.5 million tonnes per year to about 2 million tonnes per year). The second took place during the mid-1980s (when production increased to about 5.5 million tonnes). The second campaign sustained production well over trend for about 5 years (from 1985 to 1989), through several incentives (Fig. 13.1). Producer Subsidy Equivalents in Brazil calculated by the US Department of Agriculture, Economic Research Service (USDA/ERS) for 1982–1987 indicated that farmers received an average of 51% over the market price during that period (see USDA/ERS, 1994). Those incentives were significantly reduced since 1990 and production reverted to the 2–3 million tonnes achieved during the first production push.

Chile had stagnant or declining production during the 1960s and 1970s, but increased its production during the 1980s, achieving self-sufficiency briefly in 1986. As a result, aggregate production for the rest of South America peaked at about 2.6 million tonnes during 1985–1989, but declined to an average of some 2.4 million tonnes per year in the 1990s. From that high level, however, production began to decline again. Among the other two important producing countries, the rapid increase in production in Paraguay contrasts with the stagnant production in Uruguay.

Growing wheat production in Argentina is the result of increases in both area and yield, which are both trending upwards, but with some volatility. The area planted with wheat oscillated between 3.5 million ha and 7 million ha at the beginning of the 1980s. While for most of the rest of the 1980s and 1990s cultivated area in Argentina stayed within the range of 4.5–5.5 million ha, by 1996 it had climbed back to almost 7 million ha. Yields have been increasing at a rate of 1.6% per year over the last three decades, and are now at about 2.0–2.3 tonnes per ha.

Argentina's yields during the 1960s did not exceed 60% of US levels. Over time, the gap between wheat yields in both countries has been getting smaller, and by the mid-1990s Argentina's levels were about 90% of the US average (Fig. 13.2). Yields have also been increasing in Brazil and the rest of South America, but the area has trended downward, in

Table 13.6. Production, consumption and trade by main country and period ('000 tonnes).

	Argentina			Brazil			Rest of South America			
	Production	Consumption	Exports	Production	Consumption	Imports	Production	Consumption	Imports	Exports
1960–64	7,117.0	3,616.6	3,070.8	236.4	2,355.4	2,147.6	1,680.8	3,105.0	1,488.0	33.0
1965–69	6,481.2	4,138.2	2,966.8	545.2	2,845.6	2,345.6	1,988.4	4,211.0	2,319.4	48.2
1970–74	6,006.0	4,286.4	1,831.4	1,870.4	4,088.6	2,194.8	1,688.6	4,561.2	2,912.4	40.0
1975–79	8,294.0	4,416.8	3,934.4	2,528.0	6,253.0	3,762.6	1,649.6	5,015.0	3,458.0	25.8
1980–84	11,406.0	4,479.8	6,921.6	2,174.4	6,406.0	4,235.6	1,591.2	5,593.2	4,037.4	67.6
1985–89	8,956.0	4,535.8	4,506.8	5,470.0	7,420.0	854.0	2,650.8	6,093.2	3,511.6	90.4
1990–94	10,316.0	4,398.4	5,903.6	2,681.8	7,791.8	5,346.8	2,418.8	6,764.2	4,479.8	89.0
1995–96	12,350.0	4,355.0	7,975.0	2,370.0	8,100.0	5,400.0	2,425.0	7,167.5	4,822.5	50.0
Growth ratio										
1965–69:1960–64	0.910	1.144	0.966	2.306	1.208	1.092	1.183	1.356	1.558	1.460
1970–74:1965–69	0.926	1.035	0.617	3.431	1.437	0.936	0.849	1.083	1.256	0.830
1975–79:1970–74	1.381	1.030	2.148	1.352	1.529	1.714	0.977	1.099	1.187	0.645
1980–84:1975–79	1.375	1.014	1.759	0.860	1.024	1.126	0.965	1.115	1.168	0.620
1985–89:1980–84	0.785	1.012	0.651	2.516	1.158	0.438	1.666	1.089	0.870	1.337
1990–94:1985–89	1.152	0.970	1.310	0.490	1.050	2.884	0.912	1.110	1.276	0.984
1995–96:1990–94	1.197	0.990	1.351	0.884	1.040	1.010	1.003	1.060	1.076	0.562

Growth ratio: ratio of the average production in any 5-year period divided by the previous period.
Source: USDA/ERS PSDVIEW, 1997.

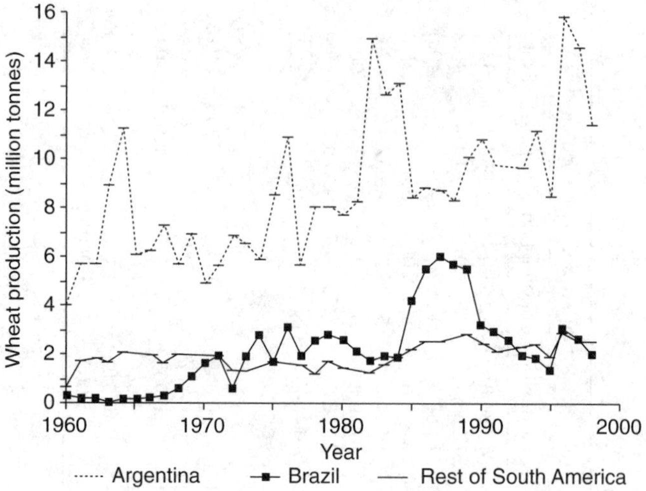

Fig. 13.1. Wheat production in South America: 1960–1997.

Brazil since the end of the incentives of the second half of the 1980s and in the rest of South America since the 1960s (see Figs 13.3, 13.4 and 13.5).

Table 13.7 shows an index of variability (standard deviation/mean) for Argentina, the USA, Brazil and the rest of South America. Volatility in yields and area in the rest of South America and, particularly, in Brazil are higher than in Argentina and the USA.

Consumption trends

There was a rapid increase in total consumption in Brazil and in the rest of South America during the 1960s and 1970s, followed by a slow-down

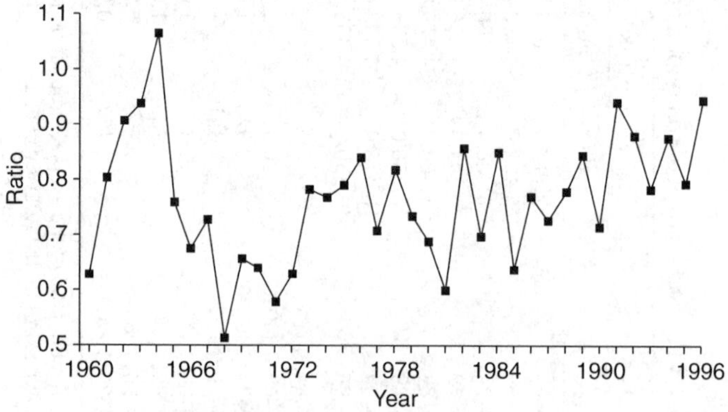

Fig. 13.2. The ratio of Argentina's wheat yields to US wheat yields: 1960–1996.

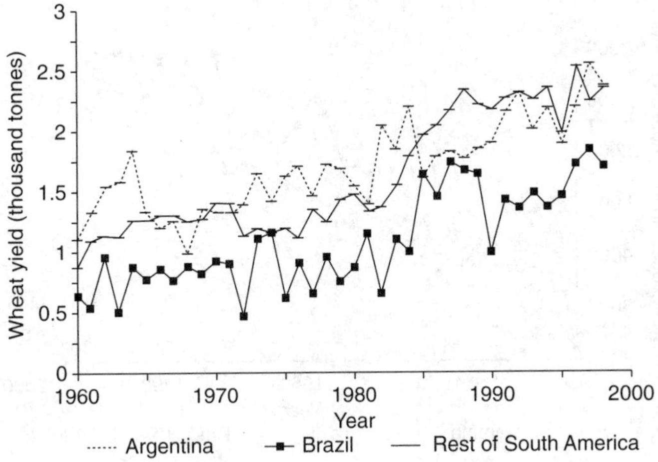

Fig. 13.3. Wheat yields in South America: 1960–1997.

or decline during part of the 1980s (linked to the difficult economic conditions in LAC during that decade) and the resumption of growth in the 1990s, although at lower rates (Fig. 13.5). In constrast, Argentina's total consumption of wheat has decreased since the mid-1970s (Fig. 13.5). There has been a continuous upward trend in total consumption in the rest of South America, which appears to have accelerated in the 1990s (Fig. 13.5). However, per capita consumption has constantly declined since the mid-1960s in Argentina and the rest of South

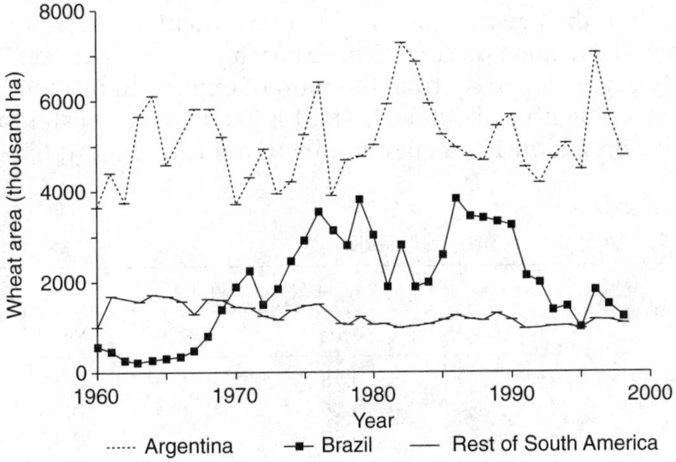

Fig. 13.4. Wheat area in South America: 1960–1997.

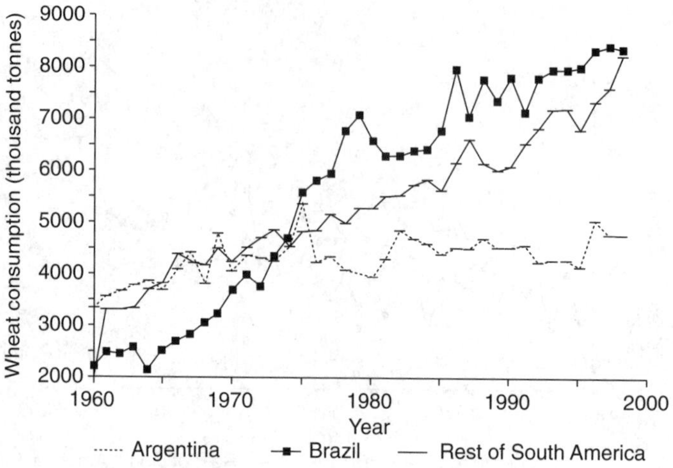

Fig. 13.5. Wheat consumption in South America: 1960–1997.

America, and, in the case of Brazil, since the late 1970s (Table 13.8). Thus, currently, Argentina consumes about 125 kg per person per year compared with about 50 kg per person per year in Brazil and almost 58 kg per person per year in the rest of South America. Consumption shows smaller year-to-year variability than production or exports (see Table 13.9), and Brazil displays larger volatility than Argentina or the rest of South America.

Importance of trade

As a result of the production/consumption equation, domestic wheat markets in the region appeared to have become more 'globalized' during the last decades. In Argentina, the ratio of exports to production has increased, rising from about 0.4 in the 1960s and 1970s to almost 0.6 in the 1990s. Brazil, during its first production push, reduced the ratio of

Table 13.7. Variability in area and yields.

	SD/mean	
	Area	Yield
Argentina	0.18	0.21
USA	0.16	0.15
Brazil	0.58	0.37
Rest of South America	0.18	0.30

Source: Based on USDA/ERS (1960–1996) data.

Table 13.8. Consumption per capita.

	Argentina	Brazil	Rest of South America
1960–1964	169.78	30.57	53.97
1965–1969	180.26	31.94	63.94
1970–1974	172.97	40.55	60.95
1975–1979	164.76	55.10	59.43
1980–1984	154.42	50.58	58.97
1985–1989	145.28	52.84	57.77
1990–1994	131.89	50.65	57.94
1995–1996	125.16	49.65	57.52

Source: USDA/ERS PSDVIEW, 1997.

imports to consumption from close to 1 to about 0.5, but the ratio began to increase again to more than 0.6 until the second push dropped the ratio to below 0.2. With the abandonment of the self-sufficiency programme, this ratio climbed back to about 0.7 during the 1990s. The rest of South America shows a continuous increase in the import/consumption ratio from below 0.5 to over 0.7, except during part of the 1980s where the support given to production in Chile coincided with balance-of-payments difficulties in several countries as a result of the debt crisis, which reduced growth and imports.

In summary, over the last years Argentina (with growing production and stagnant consumption) has consolidated its position as a net exporter, while Brazil and the rest of South America (with opposite trends for total production and consumption) are increasing their net imports of wheat. These changes, in turn, are reshaping trade patterns in the region, as shown in the next section.

4. Wheat Trade in South America

Wheat trade patterns in the region have changed significantly in the last 10 years, with a growing presence of Argentina as supplier of Brazil and

Table 13.9. Variability of production consumption and trade.

	SD/mean			
	Production	Consumption	Imports	Exports
Argentina	0.3177	0.0954	—	0.5654
Brazil	0.7417	0.3911	0.4393	—
Rest of South America	0.2410	0.2457	0.3267	1.0417
South America (total)	0.3023	0.2409	0.3580	0.5620

Source: Based on USDA/ERS (1960–1996) data.

the rest of South America. Tables 13.10 and 13.11 show the size of the shift. While in 1985 Argentina's exports to Brazil represented less than 10% of Argentina's total exports, that percentage kept on growing to about 24% during the end of that decade, reached 50% at the beginning of the 1990s and jumped to about 60–79% during 1993–1996. The decline in 1997 is a function of the large 1996/97 harvest, which was aggressively sold in different markets (Table 13.10).

In 1985, Argentina and Canada individually, and the USA and the European Union (EU) together, had about one-third each of the Brazilian wheat import market. Argentina's participation jumped to more than 90% during the drought years at the end of the decade, and then stabilized at about 60–70% of Brazilian imports, on average, in the 1990s. Canadian participation from 1990 to 1996 averaged about 25% of total Brazilian imports, with the EU and the USA supplying the rest. US participation had been increasing, reaching almost 15% in 1996/97 without the utilization of the Export Enhancement Program (EEP) (Table 13.11). However, after September 1996, the USA was excluded from the Brazilian market because of phytosanitary issues.[2]

In general for Argentina, Table 13.10 shows the same shift toward a greater importance of South America as a market for exports of cereals. Besides Brazil, other important markets for Argentina are Peru, Chile and Colombia. Those three markets represented on average about 9% of Argentina's total annual exports of wheat during 1993–1997. In value terms, exports of cereals to South America almost quadrupled from about US$300 million in 1986 to almost US$1200 million by the mid-1990s (although part of this increase reflects price variations).

This change in trade flows for wheat is part of a larger trend toward more intra-regional trade, in total and for agricultural products for different countries in the region.[3] The trend is clearly exhibited in Argentina's agricultural exports: considering both primary agricultural and agroindustrial products, the participation of the region moved from about 20% of exports at the beginning of the 1980s to more than 30% by the mid-1990s. Overall, however, after the collapse of the former Soviet Union, the EU has been the main destination of Argentina's agricultural exports (with about 35–38% of total exports of primary products plus manufactures of agricultural origin during the first half of the 1990s).

On the trade creation side, the most important cause of this reorientation of trade flows has been the process of economic integration with Brazil, as part of the creation of MERCOSUR. Brazil has become Argentina's main trading partner (26% of total trade in 1997, followed by the EU with 22% and the USA with 14%). Also, as mentioned before, several countries in Latin America liberalized their trade regimes, old regional trade agreements have been revitalized and new ones have been created, all of which have fuelled the expansion of intra-regional trade.

Table 13.10. Argentine exports by destination ('000 tonnes).

	1985	%	1990	%	1993	%	1994	%	1995	%	1996	%	1997	%
Bolivia	89.1	0.9	1.5	0.0	65.0	1.2	53.3	1.0		0.0	19.7	0.3		0.0
Brazil	847.0	8.8	1810.3	31.0	3475.5	61.9	3761.0	71.3	4379.6	64.4	3861.3	66.2	3965.2	45.7
Chile	14.9	0.2	0.0	0.0	126.5	2.3	259.5	4.9	167.7	2.5	38.9	0.7	21.9	0.3
China	877.3	9.1	749.8	12.8	32.6	0.6		0.0	231.6	3.4	11.3	0.2	31.5	0.4
Colombia	n/a	0.0	n/a	0.0	92.0	1.6	23.4	0.4	77.8	1.1	63.2	1.1	30.6	0.4
Indonesia	187.6	2.0	308.2	5.3	292.5	5.2	514.7	9.8	439.6	6.5	129.4	2.2	266.2	3.1
Iran	548.2	5.7	1469.8	25.1	95.7	1.7		0.0	214.0	3.1		0.0	504.0	5.8
Paraguay	0.0	0.0	0.0	0.0	40.9	0.7	7.2	0.1	62.4	0.9	65.5	1.1	4.7	0.1
Peru	662.2	6.9	307.1	5.3	495.5	8.8	472.0	9.0	443.1	6.5	96.1	1.6	333.7	3.8
USSR/Russia	4612.7	48.0	466.0	8.0		0.0		0.0		0.0		0.0	21.6	0.0
Turkey	n/a	0.0	n/a	0.0	405.2	7.2		0.0	55.8	0.8	232.6	4.0	642.9	7.4
Venezuela	0.0	0.0	0.0	0.0	28.6	0.5	30.4	0.6	43.4	0.6		0.0	79.4	0.9
Other	1764.7	18.4	734.7	12.6	463.2	8.3	150.8	2.9	683.6	10.1	1314.7	22.5	2798.4	32.2
Total	9603.7	100.0	5847.4	100.0	5613.2	100.0	5272.4	100.0	6798.8	100.0	5832.7	100.0	8678.6	100.0

Source: SAPyA, 1996b, c.

Table 13.11. Brazilian imports by country of origin ('000 tonnes).

	Argentina		Canada		EU		USA		
	Volume	%	Volume	%	Volume	%	Volume	%	Total
1985/86	873.0	34.6	829.0	32.9	51.0	2.0	767.0	30.4	2520.0
1986/87	973.0	34.5	885.0	31.3	388.0	13.7	577.0	20.4	2823.0
1987/88	986.3	48.8	632.8	31.3	334.4	16.5	69.3	3.4	2022.8
1988/89	757.4	98.1	14.3	1.9	0.0	0.0	0.0	0.0	771.7
1989/90	1163.6	76.9	216.4	14.3	0.0	0.0	133.2	8.8	1513.2
1990/91	2175.0	100.0	0.3	0.0	0.1	0.0	0.0	0.0	2175.4
1991/92	2539.0	52.5	1595.0	33.0	0.0	0.0	700.0	14.5	4834.0
1992/93	4477.5	77.5	1147.2	19.9	1.0	0.0	150.6	2.6	5776.3
1993/94	3043.0	55.1	1937.1	35.1	400	7.2	145.9	2.6	5526.0
1994/95	4927.0	77.2	1076.0	16.9	377.0	5.9	0.3	0.0	6380.3
1995/96	3775.0	69.6	1013.0	18.7	101.0	1.9	533.0	9.8	5422.0
1996/97	3765.2	66.7	749.0	13.3	n/a	n/a	852.0	15.1	5646.0

Source: SaGyP, 1995a; SaPyA, 1996c; USDA/FAS, 1996.

Besides the pull of expanded regional trade, recent changes in wheat trade flows have also been influenced by the reduction of market opportunities elsewhere for Argentina. First, there was the impact of the deep economic problems experienced by the former Soviet Union in the second half of the 1980s and, later, its disappearance as a political entity in 1991. As recently as the first half of the 1980s the former Soviet Union still accounted for over 20% of Argentina's total exports (and more than one-third of agricultural sales), while by the mid-1990s the successor republics of the former Soviet Union represented less than 1% of total exports. The export subsidy war in agricultural products between the EU and the USA since the mid-1980s (especially in cereals and oilseeds) also depressed Argentine free-on-board (f.o.b.) prices and/or eliminated export opportunities. Together, these events contributed to the shift in wheat trade flows in South America.

5. Argentina, Brazil and MERCOSUR

Macroeconomic and agricultural policies

The policy environment for the agricultural sector changed significantly during the 1990s in both Argentina and Brazil.

In Argentina the main policy changes were as follows. The Convertibility Law (CL), approved in 1991, fixed the exchange rate at a one-to-one ratio with the dollar, where it has remained since then. Also, the CL did not allow financing of the government by the Central Bank and the monetary base had to be covered fully by international reserves (although a small percentage of government bonds denominated in foreign currencies was allowed). Indexation in contracts was prohibited. In fact, the CL transformed the Central Bank into a currency board, working under the dollar equivalent of a gold standard for the monetary base.[4] The monetary base would expand or contract depending on whether dollars (or foreign currencies in general) were being bought or sold by the Central Bank, depending on the size of the current and capital accounts. After fixing the exchange rate, a consumption boom ensued, and due to changes in domestic and international conditions, the economy received an important inflow of capital.[5] In addition, the Central Bank reduced somewhat its banking reserve requirements, which contributed to the expansion of broader monetary aggregates. The convergence of a consumption boom, inflows of capital and expansionary monetary and fiscal policies led to an important appreciation of the Real Exchange Rate (RER) which began to correct itself through the deflation of the 1995/96 recession (Table 13.12) (see Diaz-Bonilla, 1996b).

The Argentine National Grain Board was eliminated in November 1991, and all marketing activities were transferred to the private sector, as part of a broader effort to deregulate and liberalize the economy. Government-owned inland and terminal elevators were privatized. Exports taxes were eliminated for almost all agricultural products (with the exception of some oilseeds and hides), and import tariffs for fertilizers, agrochemicals and agricultural machinery and equipment were reduced, in line with the broader policy of trade liberalization. Special programmes of agricultural credit were eliminated and the Central Bank, because of the CL, could not use, as in the past, rediscounts to offer credit on favourable terms to selected sectors or products. The Banco Nacion (a public financial institution and the largest bank in Argentina) continued to be the main provider of credit for the agricultural sector, although on a commercial basis.

Argentine ports were privatized starting in 1990, and investments in storage capacity and loading facilities in the four main ports increased from a little more than 1.135 million tonnes in 1980 to about 3.9 million tonnes by the mid-1990s. The combined loading rate is 40,000 tonnes per hour. Total storage in the country moved from about 30 million tonnes in the mid-1980s to about 46 million tonnes in the mid-1990s. River waterways have been improved, railways were privatized and their productivity improved, while the truck fleet has been modernized and enlarged. As a result of these changes Argentina can handle larger volumes of production, and at lower costs, than in the recent past (see SAPyA, 1996a). Finally, trade negotiations with Brazil, which began in 1986, gained a further impetus through the creation of MERCOSUR, beginning in 1991.

Table 13.12. Macroeconomic indicators in Argentina and Brazil.

	1993	1994	1995	1996	1997
GDP (annual % growth)					
Argentina	5.3	6.7	−4.6	4.3	8.4
Brazil	4.4	5.7	3.9	3.0	3.5
Trade balance (billion US$)					
Argentina	−3.7	−5.9	0.8	0.05	−4.8
Brazil	9.5	6.2	−9.5	−12.5	−17.7
Bilateral trade					
Argentina trade balance with Brazil (billion US$)	−0.75	−0.67	1.29	1.59	0.9
Money supply (M1) (annual % change)					
Argentina	33.0	15.7	1.3	11.2	8.6
Brazil	2568	1796	28.9	43.1	27.6
Inflation (CPI) (annual % change)					
Argentina	7.4	3.9	1.6	0.1	0.3
Brazil	2489.1	929.3	22.0	9.1	4.3
Fiscal deficit (% GDP)					
Argentina	1.4	−0.2	−0.5	−1.8	−1.4
Brazil[a]	−0.7	1.1	−4.8	−4.5	−4.6
Real exchange rate (1990 = 100)					
Argentina	59.9	63.6	71.1	73.1	71.3
Brazil	119.8	94.9	72.0	66.1	64.5

Source: CEPAL, 1996; International Monetary Fund (*International Financial Statistics*, several issues).

[a] The Brazilian deficit is published adjusting for the inflationary component of the payments of interests on public debt; without that adjustment the deficit is larger, around 5–7% over the last 3 years.

CPI, Consumer Price Index; M1: monetary aggregate.

These policy innovations put in motion a complex process characterized by increases in the scale of the operations, greater adoption of technology and innovations in financing and marketing techniques, all of which, when prices began to improve toward the mid-1990s, led to increases in investments, cultivated areas and production. Macroeconomic stability allowed medium-term planning while the reduction in export taxes for products and import tariffs for inputs, along with trade expansion in MERCOSUR, compensated in part for the softness of world markets in the first part of the 1990s. Reduced transportation costs also helped to improve the cost equation. At the same time, however, the decline in the ratio between the price of tradables and non-tradables generated an 'income squeeze' for family farms: with soft world prices and a fixed exchange rate (and notwithstanding the reduction in production costs mentioned before), the income obtained from an average family farm appears to have been severely eroded by the increase in cost of living. Table 13.13 shows the ratio of a price index of agricultural products and the price index of services, and the same ratio for agricultural and industrial goods. The substantial relative deterioration of agricultural and service prices provides an indication of the decline in buying power of agricultural incomes. The ratio of industrial and agricultural prices, although above the 1983 base, does not show an imbalance comparable to the one existing between agriculture and services. In fact, and as another manifestation of the decline in the RER, the prices of both agricultural and industrial goods (mainly tradables) have deteriorated with respect to services (mainly non-tradables) (Table 13.13).

Producers reacted to the new environment by improving technology, expanding investments and increasing scale. Technological changes have led to greater use of fertilizers, which in the case of wheat has increased from 25% of the area in 1991 to about 64% in 1996 (SAPyA, 1996a). Table 13.14 shows the important increases in the use of different inputs, machinery and equipment, in general (not only for wheat). As indicated, macroeconomic stability, reduced prices of inputs (see Table 13.15 for fertilizers) and the impact of MERCOSUR contributed to the adoption of technology. The increase in scale seems to have had the traditional form of selling and consolidation of small farms that were squeezed out of production (although there do not seem to be hard data on this yet), but also the non-traditional form of expansion of new forms of production, such as 'planting pools'. The 'pools' are groups of producers, or, perhaps more frequently, investors, who pool together land

Table 13.13. Relative prices (index base 1983 = 100).

	Industrial price/ services	Agricultural price/ services	Industrial price/ agricultural price
1986	67.6	60.8	114.4
1987	62.3	63.9	97.5
1988	76.2	72.9	104.4
1989	90.7	84.2	107.6
1990	57.4	43.7	131.1
1991	36.0	28.8	125.0
1992	28.1	25.4	110.2
1993	24.9	21.6	115.1
1994	23.8	20.2	117.3
1995	24.5	21.2	115.2

Source: CEPAL (various issues).

Table 13.14. Productive inputs.

	1990	1991	1992	1993	1994	1995	1996
Fertilizers ('000 tonnes)	165.5	185.1	242.8	297.1	464.2	601.7	840.0
Tractors (units sold)	—	3400	4871	5192	6393	4615	7720
Harvesters (units sold)	1120	760	415	344	1011	662	1276
Agrochemicals (million US$)	—	—	—	—	522	626	720

Source: Fertilizers: FAOSTAT, 1997; rest: SAPyA, 1996a, b.

and resources to be managed in a more unified way, for a single campaign. In this way, they diversify production, geographical regions and, therefore, risks. In its most 'Ricardian' form, a group of investors put together an investment fund (typically in the $0.5–2 million range) for the planting pool, rent land in different areas and manage the production process through a professional team of agricultural engineers and contractors. At the end of the growing year the grain and oilseeds are sold, expenses are paid out (including the administration fees of the professional team) and profits distributed among investors. The cycle usually repeats itself during the next growing year.

The fate of smaller producers depends on whether they have been able to adopt better technology and/or to participate in the economies of scale of the planting pools, directly as part of the group of producers, or more indirectly, by renting land, operating as contractors of machinery and equipment and/or working as paid labour. The possible social cost of Argentina's technological jump (in terms of higher unemployment because of displaced family farms and labour-saving investments) is not fully understood. However, these organizational and technological changes, coupled with higher world prices, led to a record harvest in 1996/97.

In Brazil, the main policy changes in the 1990s have been as follows. The Brazilian government began the deregulation of the flour milling industry in September 1990, when the wheat office of the Banco de Brazil ceased to be the only importer of wheat and main buyer of the

Table 13.15. Price of fertilizers in wheat production, Argentina (kg of grain per kg of fertilizer).

	Urea	Phosphate
1980–1984	2.54	3.08
1985–1990	2.36	3.41
1990	2.25	3.20
1991–1992	2.89	3.44
1993–1994	2.11	2.68

Source: SAPyA, 1996a.

domestic product, and the prohibition of wheat flour imports was eliminated. Deregulation and opening up of the wheat-flour market led to concentration at the milling and bakery levels, and to increased imports, especially from Argentina.[6]

Several agricultural support programmes were scaled down, beginning in 1990. The Real Plan of mid-1994 accelerated the process toward greater market liberalization and less government intervention in the agricultural sector. However, the government still administers instruments of support such as production credit (although subsidies, mainly in the form of negative interest rates, have been reduced or eliminated) and a system of crop insurance and support prices, and, most recently, some subsidies have been extended to millers to buy low-quality wheat. However, the level of production in support programmes was estimated at less than US$7 billion in the mid-1990s, as compared with US$38 billion in 1979/80. This reflects the reduced level of government involvement and declining support prices (which have been cut by about 40–50% in nominal terms from a high of $260 in the mid-1980s to about $110–140 in 1996/97, depending on the type and quality of wheat). The reduced level of support for grain production, coupled with the reduction in inflation brought about by the Real Plan, revealed the extent of the problem of indebted farmers, who, previously, had been subsidized through the erosion of the real value of debt by inflation (see USDA/FAS, 1996).

At the macroeconomic level, the Real Plan in mid-1994 resulted in an important decrease in inflation from about 2500% in 1993 to 4% in 1997 (Table 13.12). The stabilization programme utilized the exchange rate as an anchor, and, as has been documented in other instances, this led to a consumption boom, and a deterioration of the trade balance. A trade deficit emerged in 1995, the first since the oil crisis of the mid-1970s (Table 13.12). This macroeconomic context stimulated consumption and imports in general, including wheat, at least up to the end of 1997. At the same time, there seems to be a growing trend toward greater utilization of wheat, linked to the expansion of pasta consumption and fast-food operations (see USDA/FAS, 1996).

More recently, the government has tightened its monetary policy, which has kept interest rates high, and has contributed to some deceleration of consumption and increases in the fiscal deficit (Table 13.12). Also, as a result of the 1997 Asian crisis, the government announced a programme of fiscal adjustment, which was followed more recently in 1998 by further tightening of public accounts. Both high interest rates and the lack of public funds have affected the level of support that the government can offer to the agricultural sector. At a more general level, the monetary and fiscal policy mix has slowed economic growth, with broader repercussion on consumption, production and trade.

Generally, all those macroeconomic and sectoral policies have reduced wheat production to the levels previous to the big production push of the mid-1980s while at the same time they have expanded consumption of wheat. In the future, the current policy framework seems to indicate that macroeconomic and trade policies, such as the fate of the Real Plan and the full implementation of MERCOSUR, rather than sectoral policies, will be the main drivers of wheat production, consumption and trade patterns in Brazil.

Trade policies and MERCOSUR

Trade between Argentina and Brazil has increased with the progressive economic integration between both countries, beginning with the 1986 and 1988 agreements, later superseded by the Buenos Aires Charter of July 1990 and the creation of MERCOSUR. The MERCOSUR agreement was signed in March 1991 when the Presidents of Paraguay and Uruguay joined the Presidents of Brazil and Argentina to form a common market by 1 January, 1995. Under this agreement, the four countries agreed to: (i) free trade (0% tariffs) among themselves by 31 December, 1994; (ii) elimination of non-trade barriers; (iii) establishment of a Common External Tariff (CET) by 31 December, 1994; (iv) redefinition of the Rule of Origin; and (v) implementation of a mechanism for settlement of disputes. MERCOSUR countries also agreed to work towards the coordination of macroeconomic and sectoral policies of MERCOSUR, and to achieve free circulation of goods, services, financial and human resources between MERCOSUR participants.

The Treaty of Asunción established the creation of Working Groups to coordinate macroeconomic and sectoral policies. Working Group 8 (WG8) deals with agricultural policy and has held several meetings since the treaty was signed. The main issues analysed by the WG8 included analysis of asymmetries in domestic agricultural policies (price, marketing, financing, insurance and tax policies), harmonization of sanitary and phytosanitary measures, technological policies and programmes, external competitiveness, small farmers and sustainability, and the existence of other trade barriers. In parallel, a series of seminars and meetings have been held by the private sector since 1991 (see SAGyP DEAyAI, 1995b).

After the meeting at Ouro Preto (December 1994) the Custom Union was established, with a CET and free trade (FT) among the members (0% tariff), although in an imperfect form because of exceptions to both the CET and the FT area. The exceptions, however, were less than 15% of total trade in 1995, and most of them (but not all) had a specific schedule for their elimination over time (SAGyP DEAyAI, 1995b).

Trade, production and consumption within MERCOSUR are influenced by the complex interaction of the different components of this structure of import and export taxes and rebates: the CET and the exceptions; the 0% internal import tax and its exceptions; and the use of export rebates and restitutions and the exceptions.

In addition, other factors will also affect the patterns of production and trade, such as: (i) the degree of synchronization in the economic business cycles of Argentina and Brazil; and (ii) the presence of asymmetries in macroeconomic policies (particularly exchange rates) and in sectoral policies (especially agricultural policies). Also, for wheat trade in MERCOSUR, the behaviour of other exporting countries to the Brazilian market matters in terms of the use of export subsidies and the pricing strategies of state trading companies.

Wheat agreements in MERCOSUR

In 1987, the governments of Argentina and Brazil agreed on a minimum import quota for Brazil of 1.2 million tonnes per year of Argentine wheat. In 1990, a new agreement committed Brazil to buy a minimum of 2 million tonnes of wheat per year, which was later extended, and a quota of wheat flour of 320,000 tonnes per year was included. With the implementation of MERCOSUR since 1991, tariffs faced by Argentina's exports have been reduced according to a predetermined schedule (they have been 0% since December 1994), and quotas have been phased out. The CET for wheat and wheat flour are, respectively, 10% and 12% (but they were increased at the end of 1997 to 13% and 15%, as part of a joint programme with other MERCOSUR members to counter the impact of the Asian crisis).

On the other hand, after 1994 Argentina had to progressively reduce, until its elimination, the utilization of indirect tax rebates (other than VAT) to exporters within MERCOSUR. Brazil charges a Merchant Marine Tax of 25% to ocean freight costs, but MERCOSUR countries have the alternative of land transportation. In January 1997 the Brazilian government exempted the North and North East regions from this tax, which has improved the competitiveness of wheat exports from the USA and Canada.

6. Quantitative Estimations of Macroeconomic and Trade Issues

Export subsidies and other trade practices in regional wheat markets

Since the creation of MERCOSUR, the use of export subsidies and the operation of state trading enterprises from countries outside the trade agreement have been recurrent issues in the Brazilian market. Different LAC countries were, in the past, the destination of subsidized exports of wheat and other products. Table 13.16 shows the operations of the USA's EEP for wheat in Latin America and the Caribbean. From the fiscal years 1987 to 1995, the USA exported around 5,100,000 tonnes of subsidized wheat, with Mexico as the main destination (about 1.9 million tonnes) followed by Colombia (almost 1.2 million tonnes) and Brazil (about 0.9 million tonnes). However, since 1996 US wheat exports have not been subsidized through the EEP. The participation of the EU in the Brazilian market has been relatively modest (see Table 13.11). The criticisms about Canadian unfair trade practices have focused on the possibility of dumping activities by the Canadian Wheat Board (CWB) and, in the past, on whether transportation subsidies have been utilized for some Canadian regions.

Diaz-Bonilla *et al.* (1994) examined the possible impact of export subsidies by considering the ratio of the f.o.b. price of Argentine wheat to US wheat price (f.o.b. Gulf : 2 Hard Red Winter). That ratio should have been more or less constant, correcting for transport costs, quality differentials and relative world and local supply and demand conditions.[7] It was found, however, that export subsidies (defined as the net exports of wheat by the EU plus the volume of executed operations under the EEP) had a statistically significant negative impact on such a price ratio.[8] It was estimated that the f.o.b. price for Argentine wheat would have been about 5% higher during the first half of the 1980s had it not been for the expansion of subsidized European exports. Since 1986, the interaction of the EEP (created by the 1985 Farm Bill) and mounting European surpluses of wheat that were sold on world markets affected Argentina even further. Without those subsidies, the f.o.b. price in Buenos Aires would have been almost 21% larger than the baseline. For the period 1980–1992, total income losses of producers were calculated at a little more than US$2100 million, of which almost 60% have been associated with the larger amount of European subsidized

Table 13.16. US wheat exports to Latin America under EEP ('000 tonnes).

Country	1987	1988	1989	1990	1991	1992	1993	1994	1995	1996
Brazil	66				700	25	106.4			
Colombia		300	155	230	512.9					
Mexico		800.4	391.7	207.3			214.7	266.1		
Nicaragua								35.8	42.4	
Honduras								10.3	28.2	
Trinidad and Tobago					129.3	134	93.3	71.4	75.9	
Venezuela						331	134.6			
Total	66	1100.4	546.7	437.3	1342.2	490	549.0	383.6	146.5	

exports and the rest (about US$810 million) with EEP operations in wheat. The greater accumulated impact of the European subsidized exports is due to the fact that the EU subsidies were initiated earlier in the decade. However, once the EEP began to operate, annual losses appeared to be explained almost equally by American and European subsidies.

Within MERCOSUR, the main issue is that Argentina, generally, does not produce enough to supply both its internal demand and Brazil's import needs. Therefore, Brazil also has to buy wheat from other sources. In this context, the pricing of Brazil's wheat imports from sources other than Argentina became an issue within MERCOSUR. From Argentina's point of view, wheat imports from other sources priced low because of subsidies or other trade practices depress the price structure in the region, negating the value of preferences granted in MERCOSUR and violating the agreements reached, particularly Article 4 of that Treaty.[9] The Brazilian milling industry, however, wanted to have access to the cheapest source of raw material available.

When this discussion first began in 1991, with an important sale of subsidized wheat from the USA, the government of Argentina tried to defend the Brazilian export market through a two-pronged approach: representations to the Brazilian government requesting measures to counter subsidized exports and dumping (as indicated in Article 4 of the Treaty of Asunción) and petitions to Canada, the USA and the EU to refrain from utilizing those practices to sell to the Brazilian market. Eventually, subsidized exports from the USA were countervailed, although the countervailing duties (CVDs) were eventually eliminated. Also, the Argentine government proposed the idea of declaring the American continent as a subsidy- and dumping-free zone, expanding to agricultural products the full disciplines of GATT/World Trade Organization (WTO). This proposal is being considered within the process initiated with the Presidential Summit of the Americas in December 1994.

During the second half of 1995 and 1996, the tight situation of wheat stocks caused temporary suspension of export subsidies by the EU and the USA and, therefore, the issue of subsidized exports to the Brazilian market has been dormant since then. The resumption of EU wheat subsidies may bring the issue back to the table, as well as the possibility of US wheat sales with the special lines of credit (GSM) administered by the US Department of Agriculture (USDA).

Modelling the impact of trade and macroeconomic policies

The implementation of different types of trade and macroeconomic policies and the various combinations in which they can be applied require the use of more complex models to analyse their possible impacts. A brief summary is presented of some results from four trade models focusing on MERCOSUR and agriculture. Two are multi-market models (Diaz-Bonilla *et al.*, 1994; Diaz-Bonilla, 1995), based on the Static World Policy Simulation (SWOPSIM) framework developed at the USDA.[10] Those models differ from the basic SWOPSIM approach in that they include bilateral trade flows modelled through the Armington specification.

The first of those multi-market (MM) models includes seven countries/regions (Canada, USA, Mexico, Brazil, Argentina, rest of Latin America, rest of the world (ROW)) and four groups of products (food grains, feed grains, oilseeds and oilseed products, and livestock). The other MM model includes three countries/regions (Brazil, Argentina, and ROW) and 18 products (beef, pork, poultry, fluid milk, dairy products, wheat, maize, coarse grains, rice, soybeans, soybean meals, soybean oils, other oilseeds, other oilseed meals, other oilseed oil, cotton, sugar and tobacco).

Those models are based on supply-and-demand equations for the different individual products or groups of products in the respective countries/regions. World prices move to clear world markets for the products considered and domestic prices (consumer and producer prices) clear the domestic markets of those products. There are no macroeconomic aggregates for the economy as a whole, and the behaviour of the rest of the economy, in this type of model, is exogenous.

The third model (Burfisher *et al.*, 1998) is a linked set of Computable General Equilibrium (CGE) trade models for four countries (Brazil, Argentina, USA and Mexico) plus ROW.[11] The models incorporate the whole economy (divided into 11 sectors, four of which are agricultural), factor markets and the basic macroeconomic aggregates for each country, including the government accounts, the balance of trade and the savings/investment balance. The ROW is represented by export demand and import supply for the tradable goods of the countries specifically considered in the model.

The model database consists of social accounting matrices (SAMs) for each country, including their trade flows. SAMs start from multisectoral input–output data, which are expanded to provide information on the circular flow of income from producers to factors to 'institutions', which include households, enterprises, government, a capital account, and trade accounts for each partner country, and for the ROW. For each production sector, the model specifies output-supply and input-demand equations. Output is produced according to the constant elasticity of substitution (CES) production function of the primary factors, with intermediate inputs demanded in fixed proportions. Sectoral output is a CET (constant elasticity of transformation) aggregation of total supply to all export markets and supply to the domestic market.

The single aggregate household in each economy has a Cobb–Douglas expenditure function, from which demand for specific goods is obtained. Composite demand is for a CES aggregation of sectoral imports and domestic goods supplied to the domestic market. Burfisher *et al.* (1998) utilize the Almost Ideal Demand System to model import demands.

The parameter estimates for the sectoral production functions, consumer expenditure functions, import aggregation functions and export transformation functions were drawn from a variety of econometric and less formal sources. The model is calibrated to the baseline year (1993) so it replicates the data for that period.

In common with the Walrasian tradition embedded in CGE models, the model only determines relative prices and the absolute level must be set exogenously. Simulations are run with full employment and constant aggregate factor supplies. Capital and land are sectorally mobile. There are four types of labour and they are mobile across sectors within labour categories. Government expenditures are fixed exogenously, but government revenues, and therefore public-sector deficits, are endogenous. Aggregate investment in each country is assumed to be a fixed percentage of the gross domestic product (GDP) and aggregate savings are assumed to adjust to equate savings and investments. The model does not include money or other assets. The currency of the rest of the world defines the international numeraire.

The fourth model (Diaz-Bonilla and Robinson, 1997) is a CGE-like structure of a multicountry world model, where the supply and demand functions are estimated based on flexible forms of profit and cost functions, utilizing cointegrating techniques. This is a step beyond the usual empirical implementation of CGE models based on calibration of the values of elasticities and coefficients.

The model includes five countries or separate regions (Argentina, Brazil, the EU, Japan and the USA) and the ROW. Except the ROW, which is modelled by simple export and import functions, the economies of the other five countries or regions are disaggregated into an exportable, an importable and a non-tradable good. The economies produce two goods: a domestic good (DS), which is only sold domestically, and an export good (EX), which is sold to other countries. They are produced as a combination of value added (generated by two factors of production, capital and labour) and intermediate inputs. In a generalized Armington specification, the domestically produced goods can be differentiated from the exportable goods (on the production side), and there is some degree of substitutability in production between the domestic and the exportable goods.

For consumption, investment, government, and intermediate uses, the country utilizes a composite good (Q) of domestically produced (DS) and imported goods (IM). Domestically produced goods can be differentiated from imported goods (on the demand side), and there is some degree of substitutability in their utilization by domestic agents between both goods.

There are only three types of agents in the economy: Households, Firms and the Government. Each country sells exports and buys imports from the other countries at world prices and lends to (or perhaps borrows from) world capital markets at the world rate of interest. There are two assets in the economy: physical capital and an external financial asset/liability. Both consumption and investment decisions are based on an intertemporal optimizing framework, which, given the form assumed for the utility and production functions, can be separated into a two-stage budgeting problem, differentiating an intertemporal and an intratemporal problem for the economic agents.[12] In the simulations, however, only the intratemporal component is implemented.

Money is introduced through a 'cash-in-advance' constraint, as in Dornbusch *et al.* (1977). The macro aggregates include the government accounts, the balance of payment and the overall savings/investment balance. The model is solved only for the temporary equilibrium (see Grandmont, 1977, 1988), with predetermined levels of capital, labour and non-monetary assets/liabilities.

The model is implemented empirically by estimating flexible functional forms of the supply and demand sides of the economy. For the profit functions, the Fuss Quadratic Restricted Profit Function with constant returns to scale is utilized (see Diewert and Ostensoe, 1988); the expenditure functions are based on the Generalized McFadden Cost Function (see Diewert and Wales, 1987).

They are estimated by cointegration techniques in several steps. First, the variables included in the system of equations derived from the profit and cost functions are tested in levels for non-stationarity. If the variables are characterized as non-stationary, then the second step is to estimate the system of related supply and demand equations for every country in levels by seemingly unrelated regressions (SURE). This would yield superconsistent estimates of the coefficients if: (a) the individual variables are non-stationary, but (b) they appear to be cointegrated as a group. This is the simultaneous-equation equivalent of the ordinary least squares (OLS) approach postulated by Engle and Granger (1987) (see also Barr and Cuthbertson, 1991; Allen, 1994). Third, the residuals of the simultaneous-equation estimations are checked for stationarity. The superconsistency of the OLS/SURE procedure is valid only if the variables are cointegrated, which requires that the residuals be stationary. Fourth, although SURE produces superconsistent estimates of the long-run coefficients, they may be inefficient and biased, and the *t*- and F-tests of the significance of the estimates do not have limiting normal distributions. Several procedures have been suggested to estimate the coefficients of the long-run equations in a manner that is not only consistent, but also efficient and unbiased, and that allows tests on the significance of the estimates (see, for instance,

Johansen, 1988, 1991, 1994; Engle and Yoo, 1991; Park, 1992; Stock and Watson, 1993).

In the Diaz-Bonilla and Robinson (1997) paper a variation of the procedure followed by Engle and Yoo (1991) is utilized, which itself is an extension of the two-step approach suggested by Engle and Granger (1987). The estimated model is utilized to evaluate the intratemporal impact of the creation of MERCOSUR in terms of trade flows, taking 1993 as the baseline. The simulations are run with fixed exchange rates for Argentina (which pegged its currency to the dollar in 1991) and Brazil (which did the same in the first half of 1994, although subsequently, in March 1995, entered in a managed crawl within established bands). Europe's and Japan's currencies float against the US dollar, which is the numeraire (and normalized to 1), with all exchange rates expressed in domestic currency per dollar and world prices expressed in dollars.

The simulations determine the intratemporal impact of changes in relative prices with respect to the baseline year, keeping the level of employment, the stock of physical capital, and financial flows all fixed at baseline values. The equilibrating mechanism is the behaviour of the real exchange rate (defined as the price of tradables over non-tradables).

The main results from those models can be summarized as follows:

- For the agricultural sector in MERCOSUR, and particularly for Argentina, the implementation of the Uruguay Round (UR) agreement is more important than MERCOSUR or a Free Trade Area of the Americas (Diaz-Bonilla *et al.*, 1994).
- In the simulations, the MERCOSUR agreement leads to the expansion of the agricultural sector in Argentina, but it produces a small contraction in that sector in Brazil. The opposite result occurs in the industrial sector, except for the food manufacturing activities in Argentina, which show some gains (Burfisher *et al.*, 1998).
- Unsurprisingly, Argentina's wheat production and exports to Brazil increase with MERCOSUR (Diaz-Bonilla *et al.*, 1994).
- MERCOSUR appears to be trade-creating (Diaz-Bonilla and Robinson, 1997; Burfisher *et al.*, 1998), but the issue of trade-creation and trade diversion may have some additional wrinkles. For instance, in Diaz-Bonilla and Robinson (1997), the direct MERCOSUR effect is trade-creating, as the net result of an increase in trade between MERCOSUR members turns out to be larger than the reduction in trade with non-members. But there is also a very small increase in trade among the EU, Japan, the USA and the rest of the world themselves, without including MERCOSUR countries. Besides the two dimensions usually considered in the trade creation/trade diversion calculations (i.e. trade between members of a trade agreement only, and trade between members and non-members of a trade agreement), this analysis highlights a third dimension of trade (trade between only non-

members of a trade agreement) that is not usually considered, and which requires a general equilibrium approach to be estimated.

Also in Diaz-Bonilla *et al.* (1994) (which also analyses scenarios for the interaction of the UR agreement, NAFTA and MERCOSUR) it is found that, although Argentina suffers some trade diversion in agricultural products in Mexico because of NAFTA, it ends up exporting a larger value of agricultural products under the NAFTA scenario, because the implementation of this agreement leads to small increases in world prices and total Argentine exports.[13]

- Other policies, such as devaluation of the exchange rate (Burfisher *et al.*, 1998), or changes in the money supply (Diaz-Bonilla and Robinson, 1997), may have larger impacts on production, consumption and trade than the specific trade policies, and they may change the final impact of such trade policies. For instance, in Diaz-Bonilla and Robinson (1997) the implementation of MERCOSUR alone leads, obviously, to increases in bilateral trade. However, the effect seems bigger in the case of Argentina's imports from Brazil (which jump about 12.7% in real terms) than in Argentina's exports to Brazil (which increase by almost 4.2%). This result only indicates the magnitude of the price effect within the temporary equilibrium considered, given fixed endowments of factors of production and the fixed cash-in-advance constraint.

As an illustration of the impact of other macroeconomic policies on trade, the same trade policy settings as in the first MERCOSUR scenario were run with an increase in Brazil's money supply, keeping the rest of the money supplies fixed. Obviously, with a change in only one of the money supplies, the model did not dichotomize, and Brazil's monetary policy influenced real variables. In particular, under this simulation Argentina's exports to Brazil increase about 13% (instead of 4.8%), and Brazil's exports move up 10% (instead of 12.6%). These results (and the different outcomes obtained in Burfisher *et al.* (1998) for different devaluation scenarios in the USA and Brazil) underscore the importance of other macroeconomic policies in trade flows.

One conclusion of these studies is that macroeconomic changes tend to dominate the effect of trade policies. In consequence, the evaluation of the different trade and macroeconomic issues posed by the integration in MERCOSUR and the continent would require a more general framework that includes CGE and macroeconomic components, and that is implemented through econometric techniques rather than calibration.[14]

7. Conclusion

Wheat markets in South America have undergone significant changes over the last decade, driven by the world macroeconomic and agricultural cycle of the last quarter of the century, as well as specific economic and sectoral policies in the region.

Latin America's economic environment is now characterized by fiscal constraints and greater price stability, market liberalization and trade openness. In this new setting, Argentina has consolidated its position as a net exporter, due to both increased production and stagnant or even declining domestic consumption, while Brazil and the rest of South America, with opposite trends in production and consumption, are increasing their net imports of wheat. MERCOSUR in general, and Brazil particularly, has become an important and growing market for Argentina's agricultural products, which has helped to limit the impact of weaker demand from other traditional buyers.

These supply and demand changes, along with greater trade liberalization, are reshaping trade patterns in the region, increasing Argentina's exports to Brazil and the rest of South America. This trade environment will continue to change due to the phasing in of WTO disciplines and the possible expansion of regional trade agreements. Wheat trade issues that in the past focused prominently on export subsidies and trade practices of state trading enterprises may, in the future, be more related to sanitary and phytosanitary practices (for instance the problem with the *Tilletia controversa* (TCK) fungus in Brazil and Chile's ban on imports from the USA between March 1996 and October 1997 after the discovery of 'Karnal bunt' in some growing areas in the US Southwest) or to controversies linked to wheat flour and wheat-based manufactured goods, rather than to the primary product.

Simple projections of production and consumption in Argentina, Brazil and the rest of South America, suggest that by the year 2000 those countries as a whole will still be net importers of about 1–2 million tonnes. These figures, however, would indicate a declining trend in net imports from the 1990–1996 average of about 3.4 million tonnes.

At the microeconomic level, the evolution of the milling industry and the bakery, pasta and related industries in Brazil and Argentina (which will depend on other aspects of economic policy and business strategies rather than the more circumscribed agricultural sectoral policies) will probably have important consequences for trade and production patterns in wheat and wheat products in the region. An issue in this context is whether Argentina will specialize in supplying the raw material while the Brazilian industry processes it, or whether Argentina's agroindustry will be able to manufacture the raw material itself and export products with greater value added to Brazil and other world markets. Here, an indicator would be how the issue of increasing exports of wheat flour from Argentina to Brazil develops, at the level of both business strategies and public policies.

Also the continuation of the process of trade expansion within MERCOSUR, and indeed in the whole continent, would require a careful consideration of the macroeconomic asymmetries, including the type of exchange rate regimes.[15] The analysis of complex macroeconomic and trade scenarios would also require a more developed modelling framework, combining CGE and macroeconomic features, and implemented empirically through econometric techniques rather than calibration.

Notes

1. For further discussion, see Diaz-Bonilla (1991a, b) and Reca and Diaz-Bonilla (1997).
2. Brazilian sanitary and phytosanitary (SPS) authorities based their decision on the presence of the fungus TCK in US wheat, a ruling that has been considered excessively strict by the US government and exporters. At the moment of writing, the issue was still being discussed between both countries.
3. Lee (1995) shows that intraregional exports of agricultural products in the Americas (including the USA and Canada) moved from 26% of total agricultural exports of the continent in 1981–1983 to 36% in 1991–1993. This pattern holds true for the majority of countries in the American continent during that period, except for Brazil and the Caribbean (see Lee, 1995).
4. The Central Bank can still modify bank reserves ratios, which weakens the link between reserves and broader monetary aggregates.
5. The expansion in consumption is a well-documented stylized fact of exchange-rate-based stabilization programmes that has been explained by slowly adjusting nominal prices (as in Rodriguez, 1982) or by credibility problems (as in Calvo and Végh, 1993). In addition, lower interest rates in the USA led to capital outflows, part of which were directed to Latin America, lifting credit constraints and giving further impulse to the consumption boom (on capital flows see Schadler *et al.*, 1993). The policy recommendations to avoid unsustainable consumption expansions associated both to exchange-rate-based stabilization programmes and large capital inflows have usually been a tightening of monetary and fiscal policies. Contrary to that recommendation, monetary, financial and fiscal policies in Argentina were expansionary, which added further impetus to the consumption boom (see Diaz-Bonilla, 1996b). The boom–bust nature of the exchange-rate-based stabilization programmes is also a documented fact: while they usually begin with a consumption boom, they normally end up with a recession. Therefore for countries suffering from high inflation it is a matter of 'recession now or recession later' (see, for instance, Kiguel and Liviatan, 1992; Hoffmaister and Végh, 1996).
6. Wheat flour production in Argentina has been traditionally sold to the internal market. There was a small surplus exported, mainly towards Bolivia, which by mid-1980 absorbed about 65% of total exports of wheat flour. Over the last years, the percentage of exported wheat flour over total production began to increase (from 2% in 1989 to about 9% in 1996, reaching about 300,000–400,000 tonnes) and the destination has been now mainly Brazil, with more than 50% of the exports, followed by Bolivia. This increase in exports to Brazil is creating some tensions with the Brazilian milling industry.

7. In fact, except for some exceptional years, the Argentina:US price ratio stood at around 0.95 during the 1960s and 1970s. At the beginning of the 1980s it jumped above 1 as a result of Soviet demand for Argentine wheat while the grain embargo was in effect, then it fell below 0.9 in 1984/85 and it dropped further under 0.8 during 1985–1987. Afterwards, the ratio recovered somewhat because of the impact of the 1988/89 drought. It dropped again below 0.8 once the effect of the drought disappeared and export subsidies from the USA targeted Brazil (which by then was becoming the main buyer of Argentine wheat). If, instead of the annual price average, the December–February price is utilized (those months being the period of larger sales and exports from Argentina) the decline of the price ratio was even more significant. After 1991, with the implementation of MERCOSUR and the decline in subsidized exports to Brazil, the ratio began to climb back up, and in 1996 (a year without wheat subsidies at the world level by the USA or the EU), it went over 1 for the first time since the Soviet grain embargo.

8. The estimated equation also includes a variable trying to capture the relative supply and demand conditions that may affect the price differential, and dummy variables for the Soviet grain embargo and the drought in the second half of the 1980s (all of them are significant). The equation seems satisfactory in terms of R-square and stability and determination of the coefficients, and the residuals pass other tests (normality, homoskedasticity, non-serial correlation).

9. The issue of unfair commercial practices is covered in Article 4 of the Treaty of Asunción (which created MERCOSUR). That article indicates that 'in their relations with third countries the Member Countries will ensure equitable trade conditions'. Then it adds that 'to this effect they will use their local legislation to inhibit imports whose prices are influenced by subsidies, dumping or any other unfair trade practice'.

10. A detailed discussion of the structure and construction of multimarket models can be found in Braverman and Hammer (1986) and Quizon and Binswanger (1986). Also Sadoulet and de Janvry (1995) have a very useful discussion of this type of model, along with other modelling frameworks. For a full description of the SWOPSIM framework see Roningen *et al.* (1991).

11. The classical work on CGE models is Dervis *et al.* (1982). A complete review of this category of models can be found in Robinson (1989). In Lewis *et al.* (1995) there is a more detailed description of the specific model utilized in the simulations. The main differences between multimarket and CGE models are that, while the former usually have a greater disaggregation of the agricultural sector (with supply and demand functions defined in terms of quantity and price variables), they model only links between the markets considered but do not include interactions with the rest of the economy. They are a step beyond partial equilibrium analysis of individual products and markets, but are short of a general equilibrium representation of the whole economy. CGE models, on the other hand, represent a general equilibrium view of the real economy, although they normally do not consider the monetary and financial aspects needed to have a full CGE macroeconometric model.

12. Frenkel and Razin (1996), among others, utilize the two-stage decision process in a theoretical model of intertemporally optimizing agents. Jorgenson and Wilcoxen (1993) and Go (1996) constructed CGE models with the intertemporal and intratemporal separation. The optimization frameworks for Firms

and Households in the type of model utilized in this chapter are discussed in greater detail in Diaz-Bonilla (1996a, b).

13. The mechanism seems to be as follows: the elimination of protection for the products considered in Mexico reduces domestic producer and consumer prices, leading to less production and more consumption internally. This in turn generates more demand for imports, which is supplied mainly by the USA. Although in the simulation Argentina suffers some trade diversion in the Mexican market, supply and demand conditions are such that world prices for the products considered increase slightly and Argentina ends up exporting to other destinations left undersupplied by the redirection of US exports towards Mexico at higher prices. It must be emphasized that the overall impact is very small.

14. The estimation of the full multicountry CGE macroeconomic model is an ongoing project, following the approach utilized in Diaz-Bonilla (1996a, b) and Diaz-Bonilla and Robinson (1997).

15. See Diaz Bonilla *et al.* (1994) for a discussion of the macroeconomic asymmetries in MERCOSUR.

References

Allen, C. (1994) *A Supply Side Model of the UK Economy: an Application of Non-Linear Cointegration.* August Discussion Paper No. DP 19–94, Centre for Economic Forecasting, London Business School, London, UK.

Barr, D.G. and Cuthbertson, K. (1991) Neoclassical consumer demand theory and the demand for money. *The Economic Journal* 101, 855–876.

Braverman, A. and Hammer, J. (1986) Multimarket analysis of agricultural pricing policies in Senegal. In: Singh, I., Squire, L. and Strauss, J. (eds) *Agricultural Household Models: Extensions, Applications and Policy.* Johns Hopkins University Press, Baltimore, Ohio, USA.

Burfisher, M., Robinson, S. and Thierfelder, K. (1998) Agricultura, comercio y tasa de cambio en MERCOSUR. In: Reca, L. and Echeverria, R. (eds) *Agricultura, Medio Ambiente y Pobreza Rural en Amèrica Latina.* International Food Policy Research Institute, Banco Interanne nicanode Desarrollo, Washington DC, USA.

Calvo, G. and Végh, C. (1993) Exchange-rate-based stabilization under imperfect credibility. In: Frisch, H. and Wargotter, A. (eds) *Open Economy Macroeconomics.* International Monetary Fund, Macmillan Press, London, pp. 3–28.

CEPAL (various issues) *Panorama Económico de América Latina.* Naciones Unidas, Santiago de Chile, Chile.

Dervis, K., de Melo, J. and Robinson, S. (1982) *General Equilibrium Models for Development Policy.* Cambridge University Press, Baltimore, Maryland, USA.

Diaz-Bonilla, E. (1990) Politicas macroeconomicas y sectoriales y las estrategias de desarrollo rural. In: Alex Barril (ed.) *Politicas Diferenciadas para el Desarrollo Rural.* IICA-Ministerio de Agricultura, Santiago de Chile, Chile.

Diaz-Bonilla, E. (1991a) *Ajuste con crecimiento y finanzas públicas en América Latina.* EDI Policy Seminar Report No. 27, World Bank, Washington DC, USA.

Diaz-Bonilla, E. (1991b) *Global Grain Wars and Argentina*. Canada Grains Council, 22nd Semi-Annual Meeting, 23 October, Toronto, Canada.

Diaz-Bonilla, E. (1995) Argentina's agricultural trade and Mercosur. IFPRI (mimeo), Washington DC, USA.

Diaz-Bonilla, E. (1996a) *The Interaction of the Real Exchange Rate and Real Wages in the Convertibility Plan of Argentina (1991–1994)*. IFPRI/Fundacion Andina (draft), Washington DC, USA.

Diaz-Bonilla, E. (1996b) *Argentina, the Washington Consensus and the Myth of the Tequila Effect*. Discussion Paper, Fundacion Andina, Washington DC, USA.

Diaz-Bonilla, E. and Robinson, S. (1997) The temporary equilibrium in a multi-country trade model: estimation and simulations with a focus on MERCOSUR. IFPRI (mimeo), Washington DC, USA.

Diaz-Bonilla, E., Molina, J., Casas, S., Fidel, G. and Ripari, M. (1994) *Argentina and Agricultural Trade in the American Continent*. IDB-ECLAC Working Papers on Trade in the Western Hemisphere, Washington DC, USA.

Diewert, W.E. and Ostensoe, L. (1988) Flexible functional forms for profit functions and global curvature conditions. In: Barnett, W.A., Berndt, E.R. and White, H. (eds) Dynamic econometric modeling. IFPRI (mimeo), Washington DC, USA.

Diewert, W.E. and Wales, T.J. (1987) Flexible functional forms and global curvature conditions. *Econometrica* 55(1), p. 46.

Dornbusch, R., Fischer, S. and Samuelson, P.A. (1977) Comparative advantage, trade and payments in a Ricardian model with a continuum of goods. *American Economic Review*, December, 823–839.

Engle, R.F. and Granger, C.W.J. (1987) Cointegration and error correction: representation, estimation and testing. *Econometrica* 55(2), p. 68.

Engle, R.F. and Yoo, B.S. (1991) Cointegrated economic time series: an overview with new results. In: Engle, R.F. and Granger, C.W.J. (eds) *Long-run Economic Relationships. Readings in Cointegration*. Oxford University Press, Canada.

FAOSTAT (1997) *FAOSTAT Statistics Database*. Food and Agriculture Organization (FAO), United Nations, Internet Web Page, Rome, Italy.

Frenkel, J.A. and Razin, A. (with Yuen, C.W.) (1996) *Fiscal Policies and Growth in the World Economy*, 3rd edn, MIT Press, Cambridge, Massachusetts, USA.

Go, D.S. (1996) External shocks, adjustment policies and investment in a developing economy: illustrations from a forward looking CGE model of the Philippines. *Journal of Development Economics* 44, 229–262.

Grandmont, J.M. (1977) Temporary general equilibrium. *Econometrica*, April, 45(3), 535–573.

Grandmont, J.M. (1988) *Temporary Equilibrium: Money, Expectations and Dynamics*. Seminar Paper No. 422, Institute for International Studies, Stockholm, Sweden.

Hoffmaister, A. and Végh, C. (1996) *Disinflation and the Recession-Now-Versus-Recession-Later Hypothesis: Evidence from Uruguay*. IMF Staff Papers, International Monetary Fund, USA.

International Monetary Fund (several issues) *International Financial Statistics (IFS)*. Washington DC, USA.

International Monetary Fund (several issues) *World Economic Outlook.* Washington DC, USA.
Johansen, S. (1988) Statistical analysis of cointegration vectors. *Journal of Economic Dynamics and Control* 12, 231–254.
Johansen, S. (1991) Estimation and hypothesis testing of cointegration vectors in Gaussian vector autoregressive models. *Econometrica* 59, 1551–1580.
Johansen, S. (1994) Estimating systems of trending variables. *Econometric Reviews* 13(3), 351–386.
Jorgenson, D.W. and Wilcoxen, P.J. (1993) *Energy, the Environment, and Economic Growth.* Handbook of Natural Resource and Energy Economics, Vol. III, Internet Web Page, FAO.
Kiguel, M. and Liviatan, N. (1992) The business cycle associated with exchange rate-based stabilization. *World Bank Economic Review*, May.
Lee, D.R. (1995) Western hemisphere economic integration: implications and prospects for agricultural trade. *American Journal of Agricultural Economics* 77, 1274–1282.
Lewis, J.D., Robinson, S. and Wang, Z. (1995) Beyond the Uruguay Round: the implications of an Asian free trade area. *China Economic Review* 6, 35–90.
Park, J.Y. (1992) Canonical cointegration regressions. *Econometrica* 60, 119–143.
Quizon, J. and Binswanger, H. (1986) Modeling the impact of agricultural growth and government policy on income distribution in India. *World Bank Economic Review* 1, 101–148.
Reca, L. and Diaz-Bonilla, E. (1997) Changes in Latin-American agricultural markets. Paper presented at the 19th International Policy Council, Plenary Meeting, May, Belo Horizonte, Brazil.
Robinson, S. (1989) Multisectoral models. In: Chenery, H. and Srinivasan, T.N. (eds) *Handbook of Development Economics*, Vol. 2. Elsevier Science Publishers, North Holland.
Rodriguez, C.A. (1982) The Argentine stabilization program of December 20th. *World Development* 10(9), pp. 801–811.
Roningen, V., Sullivan, J. and Dixit, P.M. (1991) Documentation of the Static World Policy Simulation (SWOPSIM) modeling framework. *Staff Report – Economic Research Service, United States Department of Agriculture*, p. 198.
Sadoulet, E. and de Janvry, A. (1995) *Quantitative Development Policy Analysis.* Johns Hopkins University Press, Baltimore, Maryland, USA.
SAGyP (Secretaria de Agricultura, Ganaderia y Pesca) (now SAPyA) DEAyAI (1995a) *MERCOSUR Agropecuario. Actualidad y Perspectivas.* Año 1 No. 1, Enero.
SAGyP (Secretaria de Agricultura, Ganaderia y Pesca) DEAyAI (1995b) *MERCOSUR Agropecuario. Actualidad y Perspectivas.* Año 1 No. 2, Febrero.
SAPyA (Secretaria de Agricultura Pesca y Alimentacion) (1996a) *Trigo Argentino.* Argentina.
SAPyA (Secretaria de Agricultura Pesca y Alimentacion) (1996b) *Analisis y Perspectivas de la Comercializacion de Trigo.* Argentina.
SAPyA (Secretaria de Agricultura Pesca y Alimentacion) (1996c) Data from website: *www.mecon.ar/agricultura.*
Schadler, S., Carkovic, M., Bennett, A. and Kahn, R. (1993) *Recent Experiences with Surges in Capital Inflows.* Occasional Paper 108, IMF, Washington DC, USA.

Stock, J.H. and Watson, M.W. (1993) A simple estimator of cointegrating vectors in higher order integrated systems. *Econometrica* 61, 783–820.
USDA/ERS (US Department of Agriculture, Economic Research Service) (1994) *Estimates of Producer and Consumer Subsidy Equivalents. Government Intervention in Agriculture, 1982–92.* Economic Resource Service, US Department of Agriculture, Washington DC, USA.
USDA/ERS (US Department of Agriculture, Economic Research Service) PSDVIEW (1997) *PS&D (Production, Supply & Distribution) View Database.* Economic Resource Service, US Department of Agriculture, Washington DC, USA.
USDA/FAS (US Department of Agriculture, Foreign Agricultural Service) (1996) *Attache Reports. Grain and Feed Annual Report Brazil.* Foreign Agricultural Service, US Department of Agriculture, Washington DC, USA.

V

Implications of Domestic International Trade Policies and Markets for Wheat Producers in the USA

14

The Provision of Rail Service: the Impact of Competition

Murray Fulton[1] and Richard S. Gray[2]

[1]*Centre for the Study of Cooperatives, Department of Economics, University of Saskatchewan, Saskatoon, Canada;* [2]*Department of Agricultural Economics, University of Saskatchewan, Saskatoon, Canada*

1. Introduction

Grain transportation is one of the most important economic issues for grain producers in the Northern Plains. The reliance on export markets and the long distances to port position mean that transportation costs have a significant effect on the price received by farmers.

In the prairie region of Canada, rail transportation is undergoing a major transformation that will affect the competitive positions of agriculture in both the USA and Canada and influence the direction of grain flows between the two countries. Rail rates are no longer legislated (although a cap is still in place), restrictions on branch line abandonment have been lifted, and further deregulation of price and car allocation is being considered. Some parties, including the railways, argue that a completely deregulated system, similar to the US system, is the only way to achieve transportation efficiencies. Other groups, supporting the status quo, argue that the regulation of rates is essential to control the monopoly power of the railways. There has been very little discussion of other policy options, with the exception of a limited discussion of nationalized railbeds.

The purpose of this chapter is to explore some policy options for providing competition in the rail industry. The chapter begins with a description of the rail industry in Canada and the USA. An analysis of the market structure of the industry indicates that lack of competition is a concern in rail transportation in certain geographical locations. At the same time, it is shown that regulation results in inefficiencies. The result is a policy dilemma: although some sort of regulation is required, regulation also has costs.

The solution proposed in this chapter is to examine types of regulation other than those traditionally used. The option examined here is to require railways to make their track and switching equipment available to anyone who wishes to run a train service on a line. This encouragement of entry into rail service provision follows similar efforts in the telecommunications and electrical generation industries. The chapter examines the case of the British rail system, where the ownership of the track has been separated from the operation of the rail equipment and the provision of service, and explores the applicability of this model to grain transportation on the Great Plains.

2. The Rail Industry in Canada

Regulation of grain transportation in western Canada began in 1897 when Canadian Pacific Railways agreed to move western grain at the predetermined statutory 'Crowsnest Pass Rates' in exchange for a number of important concessions. These statutory rates were extended to all railways in 1925. By the 1970s, Canadian Pacific (CP) and Canadian National (CN) were losing substantial amounts of money hauling western grain at the statutory rate and were no longer investing in transportation infrastructure (see Vercammen, 1996, for more detail on the material in this section).

In response to this lack of infrastructure, the federal government purchased hopper cars (provincial governments in the Prairies also participated in this purchase), rehabilitated branch lines, and helped finance construction of a grain terminal at Prince Rupert. In addition, the federal government passed the Western Grain Transportation Act (WGTA) effective from 1 August, 1984. The main goals of the WGTA were to preserve the basic features of the Crowsnest Rates (distance-based and equitable freight rates), to ensure that the railways would earn a fair return for hauling western grain, and to provide a mechanism whereby producers and the federal government would share the total freight cost.

Under the WGTA, the federal government paid a share of the annual total freight cost directly to the railways; the remainder was paid by farmers. The annual Crow Benefit – or the amount paid by the federal government – was initially set at $658.6 million. This value changed over time. In 1988/89, the government payment to the railways was $695.1 million (72.3% of the total freight charge); in 1994/95, the government's contribution was $528.5 million (51.5%); and in 1995/96, the government's share declined to 48.3% of the total freight charge.

The WGTA was eliminated effective from 1 August, 1995. The removal of the WGTA was due to at least two reasons. First, under the recent General Agreement on Tariffs and Trade (GATT), the WGTA was viewed as an export subsidy and was subject to volume restrictions. Second, the transportation subsidy represented a sizeable financial commitment for a cash-strapped federal government that, during the latter part of the WGTA era, was no longer able or willing to maintain its financial commitment to grain producers.

After the removal of the WGTA, the Canadian Transportation Act (CTA) was passed and it contains all the relevant legislation concerning the transportation of western grain. An important element of the CTA is the introduction of a Maximum Rate Scale, which effectively caps the level of freight rates for the transportation of western grain. The CTA also contains provisions for a review of the legislation in 1999 to 'determine the efficiency of the grain transportation system and [review] the sharing of efficiency gains between shippers and railway companies' (CTA, section 155).

A final element of the grain transportation system in western Canada is the allocation of cars to various shippers. The Car Allocation Policy Group is responsible for allocating on a weekly basis the railcar fleet between Canadian Wheat Board (CWB) shipments and open-market shipments and for specifying the precise allocation of cars by elevator company and location.

3. The Rail Industry in the USA

Regulation of US railways began in 1887 with the formation of the Interstate Commerce Commission (ICC). A major factor in the regulation of the rail industry in the USA was a concern about monopoly practices. The formation of the ICC was primarily a reaction against price discrimination that targeted specific people, companies and geographical areas. Interestingly, however, the ICC sanctioned commodity price discrimination in its acceptance of value-of-service pricing (Friedlaender, 1969).

By the early 1970s, the US railways were experiencing financial problems as a result of business lost to the trucking industry and because the regulatory environment prevented the railways from introducing pricing flexibility and from abandoning unprofitable rail lines (see Wilson, 1994, and the references therein). These financial problems led to the passage of the Staggers Rail Act in 1980, which reduced the degree of regulation in the system. The impact of deregulation for the period up through the mid-1980s has been estimated using a number of different approaches (see Fuller *et al.*, 1987; MacDonald, 1989; Wilson, 1994). The conclusion is that deregulation reduced freight rates in the Great Plains region of the USA where intermodal competition was limited; deregulation appeared to have little effect on rates in eastern Corn Belt areas, where barges provided competition.

The general conclusion is that prior to the Staggers Rail Act the railways were able to use regulations to form an effective monopoly and to raise prices to the level the market would bear.

The passage of the Staggers Rail Act resulted in a significant change in the US railway system. The system became much more market-based for many aspects of railway operations including rate setting, line abandonment and car allocation. The ICC was also given the responsibility to protect captive shippers from excessively high freight rates (see Wilson, 1994, and the references therein). On 1 January, 1996, the ICC was removed and replaced with the National Transportation Agency and the Surface Transportation Board.

Prior to the Staggers Rail Act, cars were allocated under 'common carrier obligations' (i.e. cars were essentially allocated on a 'first come, first served' basis), and shippers were not assessed penalties if they cancelled the cars. At the current time, railcar allocation is predominantly controlled by the railways, with shippers having some input. Approximately half the hopper car fleet is railway-owned. The railways also control up to 40% of the privately owned fleet, giving them control of the placement of 65–70% of the total available fleet. Railroads use various approaches to allocate cars to individual shippers. Burlington Northern, Union Pacific, and Canadian Pacific-Soo Line use a market-based approach for the allocation of their cars. This approach involves the shippers bidding on cars to secure guaranteed placement at some future date.

As an example, Burlington Northern (BN) uses three different approaches to allocate their cars. The first method uses Certificates of Transportation (COTs), which guarantee grain cars. Shippers bid for COTs in an auction-type setting. Shippers who do not buy COTs at auction have the opportunity to purchase them in a secondary market, which allows those who previously ordered but no longer need COT cars to dispose of them. Usually 30% of BN's fleet is allocated to this use.

The second method allows shippers to place their own cars into BN's Guaranteed Car Pool (GCP) programme. This programme guarantees them a claim on an equal number of cars in the future. During periods of low demand for railcars, BN may refuse to allow shippers to use these private cars on their tracks in order to increase demand for their own cars. Users of the GCP have no guarantee on the rate (as they would with the COT programme). GCP users also carry a car cancellation fee of $200 per car. The GCP programme accounts for approximately 25–30% of BN's total fleet.

Finally, shippers may place orders for railcars under the ordinary tariff system called the General Car Order (GCO) programme. Cars are assigned to various corridors based on historical usage and are awarded to individual shippers according to demand; when the number of car orders exceeds the supply, a lottery is used for allocation. This programme accounts for approximately 40% of BN's fleet.

4. Market Structure of the Rail Industry

The rail industry in the Northern Plains region of North America is highly concentrated. In Montana and the western portion of North Dakota, BN has a monopoly. In Canada, the Prairie provinces of Manitoba, Saskatchewan and Alberta are served by a duopoly – the two railways are CN and CP. However, the areas served by CN and CP are often geographically distinct so that in many areas the market structure is a monopoly. Figure 14.1 shows the rail network in Saskatchewan in 1998. Although there is a corridor running from the southeast to the northwest in which farmers have reasonable access to both CN and CP, outside this corridor most farmers have reasonable access to only one railway.

In addition to facing a highly concentrated industry, grain shippers have few other options available when it comes to shipping grain for export. West Coast ports are 600–1600 miles from grain production on the Canadian Prairies, making trucking a very expensive option. Exporting grain via the East Coast or Gulf ports requires trucking several hundred miles plus significant waterway costs.

The presence of a duopoly, and in some cases a monopoly, raises concerns about monopoly pricing should the Canadian rail industry be completely deregulated. There are empirical and theoretical reasons to suggest these concerns are valid. From a theoretical perspective, high levels of concentration are a problem in an industry if the threat of entry is low (an industry is highly concentrated if the largest four firms have more than 70–75% of the market). Without the threat of entry, existing firms can raise prices without fear of losing market share to new entrants. To be a real threat, however, potential entrants must be able to enter and exit an industry without much cost.

Although new firms can and do enter industries such as the grain handling business, this ease of entry is not present in the rail industry. Indeed, the cost to a new firm of entering the rail industry and building new rail lines is likely to be prohibitive. The need to meet environmental regulations and the expenditures required to acquire land are two reasons for this prohibitive cost.

The CTA includes provisions that are designed to stimulate competition such as confidential contracts, interswitching, competitive line rates and final-offer arbitration (Vercammen, 1996). However, the high concentration in the industry and the geographical location of the rail lines reduce the effectiveness of these provisions. Simply put, the CTA provisions will lead to competitive prices if the railways are

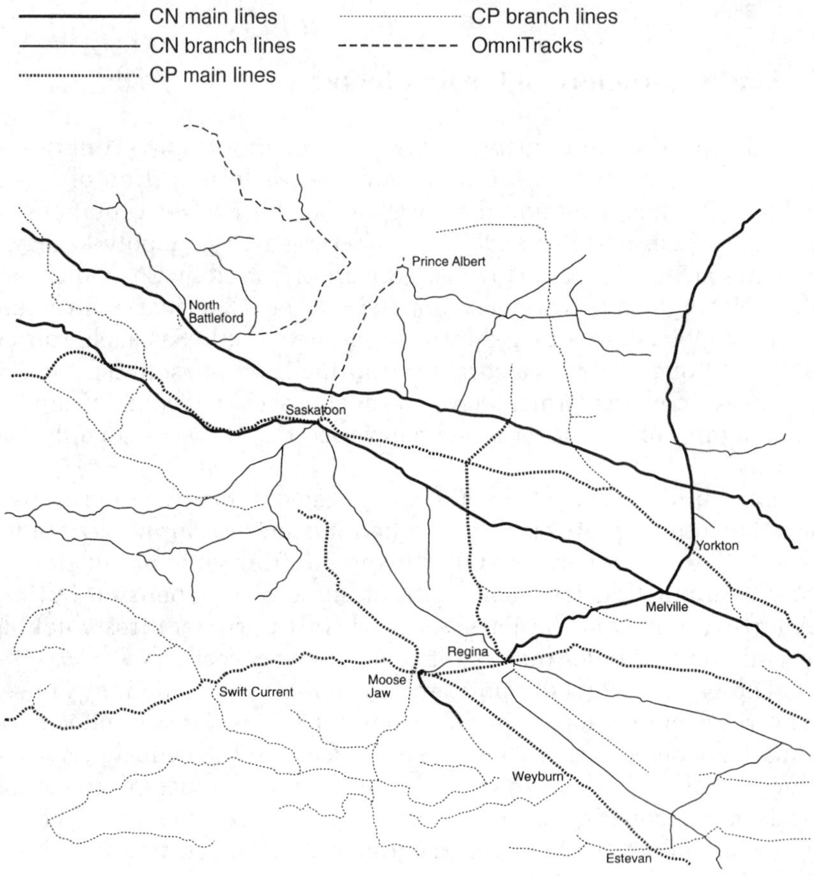

Fig. 14.1. Saskatchewan rail network, 1998.

willing actively to compete with each other. If the railways are aware of the market influence they possess and act accordingly, the effectiveness of the CTA provisions will be limited.

The empirical evidence also suggests that monopoly pricing is a concern. Figure 14.2 shows the freight rates from four different delivery points in the USA and Canada to the closest port. Three of these delivery points are in the USA, and one is in Canada. The delivery points were chosen based on the level of competition among railways and between railways and other modes of transportation, the ability to handle a 52-car spot, and the types of crops handled by the elevators

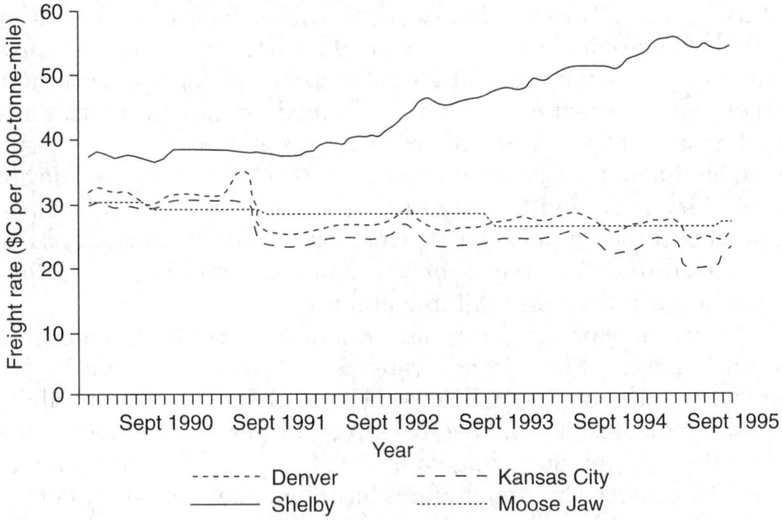

Fig. 14.2. Freight rates for wheat, selected US and Canada points, 1990–1995.

and produced in the local area. Where possible, delivery points were chosen with similar distances to port. However, since the analysis is based on a per 1000-tonne-mile basis, the distance to port is not a critical factor. The values in Fig. 14.2 are in Canadian dollars per 1000-tonne-mile. Since the points selected for comparison are roughly 1000 miles from their respective ports, the values represent the total amount paid per tonne for grain shipment (see Government of Saskatchewan, 1997, for more detail on the material in this section).

The Canadian point is Moose Jaw, Saskatchewan. Moose Jaw is approximately 1190 miles from Vancouver and was chosen because of the presence of a large inland terminal and its location on the CP mainline. The rate shown in Fig. 14.2 reflects average railway costs. The rate does not include an ownership charge for the government-owned hopper cars and thus probably understates the actual costs.

The three points chosen in the USA are Shelby, Montana; Denver/Commerce City, Colorado; and Kansas City, Kansas. These points were chosen because of their differing levels of competition between railways and other modes of transportation. The destination ports (that is, the ports served by the three originating stations) were chosen because of the direct connections on BN lines from the originating station to the port.

Shelby, Montana, to Portland, Oregon, is approximately 782 miles and is served by only one railway, BN. Portland was chosen as the destination point because the majority of the grain from the Shelby area is exported via ports in the Pacific Northwest. Denver/Commerce City, Colorado, to Galveston, Texas, is approximately 961 miles and is served by three major Class 1 railways (BN, Union Pacific and Southern Pacific) and one small carrier (Denver and Rio Grande Western Railway Company). Galveston was chosen as the destination point because it is a major port for wheat from this area destined for the Gulf ports. Kansas City, Kansas, to Galveston, Texas, is approximately 861 miles and is served by numerous Class 1 and small railway companies. In addition, Kansas City is served by barge on the Missouri River system. The common destination point for Denver/Commerce City and Kansas City can be used to determine if the presence of barge transportation at Kansas City is reflected in rail freight rates.

At least three observations and conclusions can be made from the data in Fig. 14.2. First, freight rates from Kansas City and Denver/Commerce City are significantly lower than rates from Shelby, suggesting the presence of effective rail and/or barge competition has a direct effect on the rates charged by BN. Second, the Kansas City and Denver/Commerce City freight rates have remained relatively constant over time, although there have been some relatively small changes from month to month. This price pattern suggests a relatively competitive market in which the price is determined by the cost of providing the service. Third, the Shelby freight rate has changed considerably over time, rising from just under $C40 dollars per 1000-tonne-mile in 1990/91 to about $C55 dollars per 1000-tonne-mile in late 1995, a value that closely reflects the cost of trucking. This freight rate pattern suggests that in Montana BN is operating in a market where considerable latitude is available for setting prices.

5. The Policy Dilemma in the Rail Industry

The concern about monopoly pricing in the rail industry is mirrored in other areas such as power distribution, telephone systems, pipelines and rail service. These activities are often described as natural monopolies and have been either allowed to operate as regulated monopolies or operated as monopoly enterprises owned by government. Transportation corridors such as waterways, ports, roadways and railways have also been largely claimed for operation as monopolies through the public domain.

Government creation and regulation of these monopolies has been based on the argument that these industries have economies of scale; one firm can provide the good or service at lower cost than can two or more firms. Although there are undoubtedly some economies of scale in the provision of these services, these industries have had another more important characteristic in common: the need to secure the right of access to a continuous corridor to provide these services. The necessity of acquiring an uninterrupted corridor meant landowners along the route could hold out for a share of the potential profits, resulting in land acquisition costs outweighing the returns that could be earned by a company wishing to provide the service.

The historical use by governments of their power of eminent domain to acquire land (including expropriation when necessary) suggests this entry barrier is very large and that government action is required to facilitate the entry of even a single firm. Providing entry to one player, however, creates another problem: The monopoly that has been created is now free to raise prices. Governments have historically reacted to this threat by instituting public ownership and regulation of these industries.

The history of the rail industry in both Canada and the USA is a good example of this pattern of government interest and involvement. For example, in Canada, the railways were initially established through government land grants. The rail industries in both countries have been heavily regulated since the last decade or two of the 1800s. The evidence on railway pricing presented earlier also suggests that concerns about monopoly pricing are real and need to be addressed.

The traditional form of regulation focuses on controlling price. Price regulation, however, has its own costs. In both the USA and Canada, regulation of the rail industry resulted in financial problems, lack of investment, and poor maintenance of infrastructure (e.g. some branch lines) that was no longer cost-effective. More generally, the lack of price signals inherent in regulatory environments reduces the incentive for industry participants to perform. Rail companies may also disrupt the system – as a form of bargaining – to create pressure for deregulation. Finally, the uncertainty created by the possibility of switching to a deregulated system discourages industry participants from making investments that rely on regulated freight rates.

The unique structural characteristics of industries such as rail transportation create a dilemma for policymakers. The prohibitive cost of entry means monopoly pricing is a real concern and regulation is required. At the same time, traditional price regulation is costly and creates inefficiencies.

The solution is to examine types of regulation other than those traditionally used. One option is to use regulations to encourage entry into rail service provision. Traditionally, entry into an industry has been thought to require investment in new facilities and infrastructure. Since this route is effectively blocked in the rail industry, attention needs to be focused on encouraging entry into the provision of service.

Entry regulation has been introduced in industries outside transportation. For instance, in the field of telecommunications, regulations have been introduced to force local companies to carry long-distance services from other companies. This has resulted in a dramatic reduction in the cost of long-distance services. Similarly, electrical utilities are being forced to carry current from other suppliers to their customers, which has eliminated their monopoly over their customers and has given them an incentive to find lower-cost technologies (Joskow, 1997).

These options are available for the rail industry. Just as telecommunication companies are required to allow competitors to use their phone lines, existing railways could be required to make their track and switching equipment available to rail operators who wish to run train services on a line, on the condition that the access price covers the infrastructure cost. The next section examines the case of the British rail system, in which the track ownership has been separated from the ownership and operation of the rail equipment, and hence the provision of rail service. The applicability of this model to grain transportation on the Great Plains is also explored.

6. Rail Service Provision Entry – the British Rail System

The British rail system has historically been operated by British Rail, a government-owned enterprise. In 1993, the British Railway Act was introduced: its objective was to create a system that operates in the public interest by enhancing the competitive forces in the British railway system. A government agency called the Office of the Rail Regulator (ORR) supervised the transition from the previously government-owned and controlled system to the new system. The ORR is now the main regulatory body in the system (Office of the Rail Regulator, 1998). Figure 14.3 contains a schematic representation of the set of public and private organizations involved in the current British railway system.

A key feature of the British system is that ownership of the rail infrastructure is separated from the provision of train service. The rail infrastructure (signalling equipment, rail lines, and stations) is owned by a company called Railtrack, which leases access to 30 independent rail operators, which provide passenger and freight service for the public. Originally owned by the government, Railtrack is now privately owned. Railtrack covers the costs of infrastructure maintenance and investment largely from access charges paid by the rail operators. The government in certain circumstances may also provide direct capital grants. The ORR must approve the access agreements between Railtrack and the rail operators. Railtrack is responsible for central timetabling and coordination of all train movements, signalling, and planning and undertaking infrastructure investment (Glaister, 1997; Railtrack, 1998).

The train operators provide train service on routes for which the Office of Passenger Rail Franchising (OPRF) has awarded them a franchise. Rail operators with a franchise then receive exclusive rights

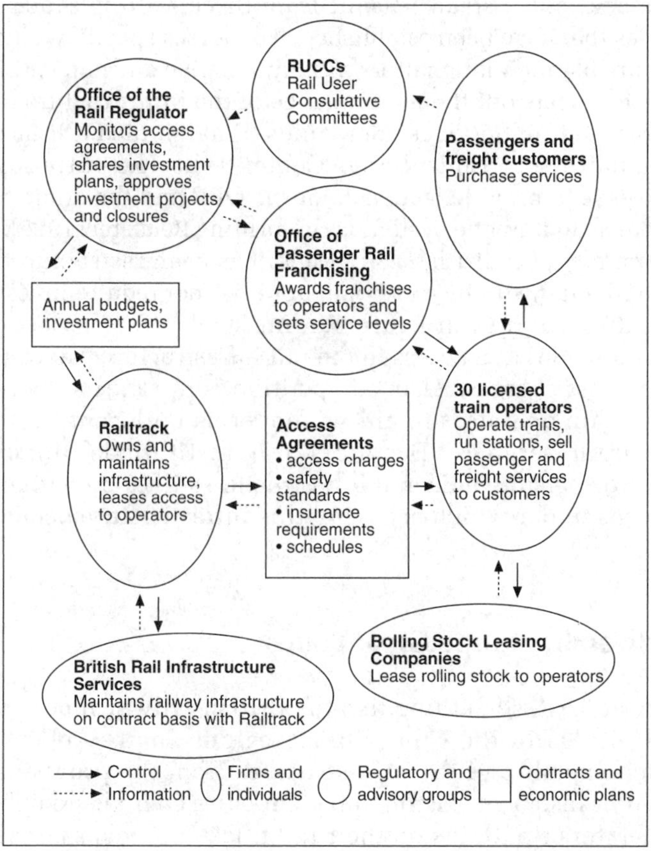

Fig. 14.3. The operation and control of the British railway system.

to that route for the duration of the franchise. Franchises are awarded to operators using a competitive tendering process. Rail operators bid on a franchise by specifying the level of service they will provide (e.g. number and time of the trains each day), ticket prices and any subsidy required to provide the specified service at the specified ticket prices. For a passenger service, it is generally anticipated that costs will exceed revenues and a subsidy will be required. The subsidy is provided for the OPRF by the government. Prior to the bidding, the OPRF establishes a minimum level of service that must be provided. Franchise bidders must meet this minimum level of service and are expected to offer services over and above this minimum (Glaister, 1997; Office of Passenger Rail Franchising, 1998).

Other organizations are also involved in the system in addition to those specified above. The train operating companies do not own the rolling stock, but instead lease it from three Rolling Stock Leasing Companies that have been established. The leases specify which parties are responsible for such matters as maintenance and safety. Likewise, Railtrack contracts out the maintenance of the infrastructure to British Rail Infrastructure Services companies. Finally, the ORR has helped establish Rail Users' Consultative Committees. The purpose of these committees is to provide feedback for the ORR and the other parties in the system as to how the system is performing (Glaister, 1997).

In summary, the British rail system has been restructured so that entry into the industry by a rail operator does not require investment in new facilities and infrastructure. Rolling stock can be leased from the leasing companies and access to the rail infrastructure can be obtained through access charges. Also, competition is introduced by requiring potential train operators to bid on the terms under which they will provide train services. Despite these institutional innovations, monopoly ownership of the rail infrastructure still exists and regulation of the terms under which access to this infrastructure occurs is still required.

7. Applicability to the Great Plains

In theory at least, something like the British railway model could be adapted for use in the Great Plains region. The key element is to separate ownership of the infrastructure from the provision of rail services. For instance, existing rail companies could be required to let other operators run trains on their rail track at predetermined access rates. This would effectively introduce competition into the industry, with the result that freight rates would drop to competitive levels. Railway companies would probably specialize, with some concentrating on the provision of railway infrastructure and others concentrating on train operations. If both Canada and the USA adopted such a model, train operators would most probably operate in both countries and freight rates would equalize. If only one country adopted this policy, competition in that country could be expected to increase, resulting in relatively lower freight rates. Train operators from both countries would probably enter the more competitive market, whereas the restricted market would continue to have railway service and rail infrastructure provided by the same company.

Major shifts in the rail industry would be required for this policy change to be implemented. At the operational level, switching devices would need to become much more automated and train location determination would need to be improved. As is the case in the electrical industry, where electricity generation and transmission are being separated, train operation logistics would probably have to be turned over to independent system operators who would coordinate train movement. These system operators would require a unique ownership structure that provides both infrastructure owners and rail operators a say in the operations. Although most rail infrastructure investment decisions could be left with the infrastructure owners, some investment decisions may have to be made on an industry-wide basis. Electronic 'markets' may have to be created to allocate demand across the various train operators (see Joskow, 1997, for an excellent discussion of the organizational changes required in the electrical industry). Finally, an organization something like the ORR would have to be formed to establish access terms and rates.

Since railways operating in the Great Plains region of the USA and Canada haul much more than grain, this new regulatory environment would have to apply to all the commodities handled by the railways. Also, because the impact of a regulatory change would affect other carriers, such as trucking, changes to other transportation systems would be required and would have to be coordinated.

Although this new regulatory model would generally improve the economic performance of the rail system, some problems would emerge. One of the most important is likely to be the impact of low-demand volume on certain railway lines. The ability to provide rail service to low-demand areas may hinge on the ability of producers and shippers in these areas to provide rail infrastructure at rates that make rail operation profitable. Thus, mechanisms that allow effective local ownership also need to be developed.

Although these changes are substantial, changes of this magnitude are occurring in the electrical industry. If anything, the separation of electricity generation and transmission is much more difficult than the separation of rail infrastructure provision and railway service provision. Nevertheless, a great deal of thought and research needs to take place before this type of regulatory reform could occur in the rail industry.

8. Summary and Conclusions

The unique structural characteristics of industries such as rail transportation create a dilemma for policymakers. The prohibitive cost of entry means monopoly pricing is a real concern and regulation is required. At the same time, traditional price regulation is costly and creates inefficiencies. The solution is to examine types of regulation other than those traditionally used.

One option is to use regulations to encourage entry into rail service provision. Traditionally, entry into an industry has been thought to require investment in new facilities and infrastructure. Since this route is effectively blocked in the rail industry, attention is focused on encouraging entry into the provision of service. Regulations that facilitate entry have been introduced in industries outside transportation. For instance, in the field of telecommunications, regulations have been introduced to force local companies to carry long-distance services from other companies. This has resulted in a dramatic reduction in the cost of long-distance services. Similarly, electrical utilities are being forced to carry current from other suppliers to their customers, which has eliminated their monopoly over their customers and has given them an incentive to find lower-cost technologies.

These options are available to the rail industry. One example is the British railway system. In Britain, the ownership of the track has been separated from the operation of the rail equipment and the provision of service. Ownership of the track rests with a company called Railtrack. Railtrack leases access to 30 train operators for fees that are regulated by the Office of the Rail Regulator to cover maintenance costs and provide a return on investment. The 30 rail operators then compete to provide services for customers.

This model and others similar to it need to be developed and articulated before they can be considered in the public policymaking framework. Nevertheless, given the importance of rail transportation to the grain industry in the Northern Plains, it is imperative that options such as these be investigated to address the very thorny issue of freight rate and entry regulation.

References

Friedlaender, A. (1969) *The Dilemma of Freight Transport Regulations.* Brookings Institute, Washington DC, USA.

Fuller, S., Bessler, D., MacDonald, J. and Wohlgenant, M. (1987) Effect of deregulation on export-grain rail rates in the Plains and Corn Belt. *Journal of the Transportation Research Forum* 28, 160–167.

Glaister, S. (1997) Deregulation and privatisation: British experience. In: de Rus, G. and Nash, C. (eds) *Recent Developments in Transport Economics*, Ashgate Publishing, Aldershot, UK.

Government of Saskatchewan (1997) *Grain Freight Rates Under Competition and Regulation: A Case Study.* Saskatchewan Agriculture and Food, Regina, Canada.

Joskow, P.L. (1997) Restructuring, competition and regulatory reform in the US electricity sector. *Journal of Economic Perspectives* 11, 119–138.

MacDonald, J.M. (1989) Railroad deregulation, innovation, and competition: effects of the Staggers Act on grain transportation. *Journal of Law and Economics* 32, 63–95.

Office of Passenger Rail Franchising (1998) *http://www.opraf.gov.uk.* 2 December.

Office of the Rail Regulator (1998) *http://www.rail-reg.gov.uk.* 2 December.

Railtrack (1998) *http://www.railtrack.co.uk.* 2 December.

Vercammen, J. (1996) Description of regulatory change. In: Vercammen, J., Fulton, M. and Gray, R. (eds) *The Economics of Western Grain Transportation and Handling* Vol. Module B-1. Van Vliet Research Endowment, Saskatoon, Saskatchewan, Canada.
Wilson, W.W. (1994) Market-specific effects of rail deregulation. *Journal of Industrial Economics* 42, 1–22.

15

Grain Quality and North American Hard Wheat Exports

William W. Wilson and Bruce L. Dahl

Department of Agricultural Economics, North Dakota State University, Fargo, USA

1. Introduction

Much of the past analysis and debate on wheat quality has focused on class (Hard Red Spring, Hard Red Winter, etc.) and country of origin (e.g. USA and Canada) as salient sources of differentiation. In that context, the USA and Canada are the principal competitors in the hard wheat market. Both countries are dominant producers of Hard Red Spring Wheat (HRS in the USA and Canadian Western Red Spring (CWRS) in Canada); the USA is the dominant producer of Hard Red Winter (HRW); and both countries are large producers of durum (Hard Amber Durum (HAD) in the USA and Canadian Western Amber Durum (CWAD) in Canada). Due to the indigenous similarities among these wheats, the competitive environment is particularly acute.

Distinct differences exist between the US and Canadian grading systems, which in turn have an impact on trade (McLaughlin, 1994; Canada–USA Joint Commission on Grains, 1995). Other studies have noted the effects of the differences, mostly in terms of the results of surveys of importers (Hyberg *et al.*, 1993; Mercier, 1993) and hedonic values (e.g. Veeman, 1987; Wilson, 1994). The principal difference is that the US system, in general, relies upon specifications of characteristic limits in contracts between buyers and sellers with reference to grade-determining factors and measurement standards. As such, it is incumbent upon buyers, through negotiations with suppliers subject to competition from other buyers, to determine the optimal level of a particular characteristic. In contrast, the Canadian system has relied more upon a regulatory approach of grading and standards with less use of individual specifications than in the USA. However, pressure is emerging for less homogeneity in order to meet conformance demands.

Besides the differences in the grading systems, there are two particularly important phenomena that contribute to competition. One is that the USA has a relatively large domestic market and, in recent years, has purchased up to 57% of the domestic wheat crop. Traditionally, the US domestic milling industry has purchased primarily No. 1 and No. 2 grades for processing. Given that about 75% of the HRS and 85% of the HRW wheat crops typically grade as No. 2 or better, a large percentage of the higher-quality wheat is consumed domestically, leaving lesser amounts for the offshore market. In contrast, Canada consumes about 20–35% of its wheat crop domestically. The proportions of the crops in each country graded as desirable quality for the hard wheat milling industries are similar. Thus, in general, Canada has a greater proportion of exportable excess supply of higher grades than the USA.

The second major factor affecting the dynamic changes in grades of wheat purchased is the shift toward privatization of wheat imports (Wilson, 1995). One of the important implications of privatization is a tendency for greater specificity in purchase contracts. Generally, private buyers have a greater ability to evaluate higher quality and are more willing to pay premiums (or discounts) if that greater (lower) quality enhances (reduces) their profits. Importer procurement strategies, that is, the combinations of price and quality specificity, are critical factors in the HRS market. Some importers use more stringent contract specifications than US domestic millers. The latter are accustomed to mixing and blending and can target specific producing regions for their wheat procurement. Contract specifications have considerable strategic importance, particularly in view of competition among buyers (Johnson *et al.*, 1995).

This study analyses the market segments and growth rates of exports of hard wheat from the USA with comparisons with Canada when data are available. The study focuses on hard wheats, which are defined to include HRS, HRW and CWRS; durum wheats are also included in the analysis. Other wheat classes (US soft wheat, a combined group including Soft Red Winter and white wheat classes, and Canadian Other, a class representing largely feed wheats) are included for completeness but are not the focus of this chapter. Shift–share analysis is used to compare the observed changes over time for class and grade comparisons. Then high-quality importing segments are analysed using two measures. First, importing segments are examined using an existing definition of high-quality importers. Second, cluster analysis is used to identify segments of buyers for US hard wheats according to the grade factor specifications, and comparisons are made through time.

2. Previous Studies and Policy Issues

There have been two major studies addressing these issues in the USA. The first was undertaken by the US Congress Office of Technology Assessment (OTA) (1989); the second was a US Department of Agriculture (USDA) study and is summarized in Mercier (1993) and in Hyberg *et al.* (1993). Since each country has a multitude of institutions and mechanisms that influence quality, OTA suggested a paradigm for evaluating issues related to grain quality. The concept was that a highly interdependent 'system' has an impact on the quality of grain offered for export. This includes variety development and release mechanisms, agronomic conditions, trading practices, grades and standards, and farm policies. The important point of the paradigm is that the institutions and policies that have an impact on the quality of grain exported are very complex and involve more than issues related to grades and standards. This, of course, has been the traditional area of debate in the USA.

The purpose of variety release and control mechanisms is to provide a means to regulate quality for characteristics not capable of being easily measured in the market system (Dahl and Wilson, 1997). A prerequisite for market regulation (premiums and discounts) is the ability to measure the characteristic easily. Another implicit effect of these mechanisms is that they provide a means to increase uniformity in end-use products, an increasing demand of domestic and export millers.

The US grading system typically measures only physical (not chemical) characteristics, and these are the mechanisms upon which the establishment of quality measures for premiums and discounts rely. Trading practices cover a range of issues but are crucial in making cross-country comparisons. These include the mechanisms by which premiums and discounts develop, whether by marketing boards or through a market system; local competitive environment; trading practices with respect to indigenous and extraneous quality characteristics; regulations regarding cleanliness and hygiene (e.g. infestation); and the extent to which variety is used in the marketing system.

The US system with respect to wheat cleaning, which was the primary focus of these analyses, operates differently from systems in other countries. Both Canada and Australia include wheat cleaning, either in terms of restrictive factor limits or as a regulation to induce cleaning, on a large portion of wheat entering the market system. In contrast, this is not a grade-determining factor in the USA. It is a contractual term, the level of which is determined through negotiation and buyer–seller competition. The upshot is that wheat is cleaned extensively in the USA but only for those competitive conditions in which buyers and sellers specify the limit contractually.

Other countries are going through related debates and policy analysis. The Grains Council of Australia conducted a series of studies on the international market and implications for organization of the domestic market (Grains Council of Australia, 1995). One of the more interesting conclusions indicated that a large portion of the variability in prices received by the Australian Wheat Board (AWB) was due to variability in quality characteristics. Further, it suggested that Canada and Australia are thought to be 'quality suppliers' and that the USA, along with the European Union (EU), Saudi Arabia and Argentina, is a price supplier.

Interesting and important debate is evolving in Canada. Although it has always been claimed that Canadian wheat has certain characteristics preferred by importers, mostly related to cleanliness and uniformity, the value of these in terms of higher sales prices has always been a mystery. The recent study by Kraft *et al.* (1996) analyses prices and differentials for sales of Canadian wheat from 1980 to 1994. Results indicate that the average premium received for Canadian wheat relative to its benchmark was $C13.35 per tonne. However, as Carter and Loyns (1996) indicate, the additional costs imposed on the Canadian system necessary to achieve this premium were about $C21–28 per per tonne.

3. Data

The data used in this study include aggregate exports of US and Canadian wheats by class and exports by class and grade for US HRS, HRW, HAD and soft and Canadian CWAD, CWRS and Canadian Other. Data on aggregate US wheat export volumes by class were obtained from the USDA, *Wheat Situation and Outlook* (various issues). Aggregate Canadian exports by class were obtained from a number of sources (Canada Grains Council, various years; Canadian Wheat Board (CWB), various issues).

Data on exports by class and grade were obtained from two sources. Data for US exports were obtained from the *Export Grain Inspection System* (EGIS) wheat database (USDA, 1995). These data (by shipment) include information on wheat class, grade, quantity, importer, and characteristics for most grade parameters, protein, and dockage from January 1986 to August 1995. Similar information does not exist for Canadian exports. Data on grade and class of Canadian exports were obtained from the Canada Grains Council's *GRAINBASE Database* (1995). Information includes import grades and quantities of classes of Canadian wheat and durum for each importer during the period 1977–1991. Canadian data are aggregated by crop marketing year, class and grade for respective countries. To allow for cross-comparisons, US data are aggregated by crop marketing years (1 June to 31 May) for class and grade by country. Data on aggregate Canadian wheat exports by class and grade after 1991 are not available.

Using these data, two sets of results were derived. In the first analysis, shifts in market shares among these classes and grades of hard wheats were estimated using 'shift–share analysis'. These results provide a summary measure of the growth of individual classes/grades in comparison with the average growth for the market. Then cluster analysis is used to define market segments based on the quality characteristics purchased by importing countries. This was done only for US exports since similar data are not available for Canadian exports.

4. Changes in the Distribution of Exports: Shift–Share Analysis

Identification of growth or decline within a market can be analysed by comparing market shares over time. Comparisons of changes in the composition of exports are conventionally measured with actual or percentage changes over time. However, a percentage change tends to overestimate effects of smaller market segments, and an actual change tends to overestimate effects of larger market segments. An alternative is shift–share analysis, which can be used to identify differences in growth and overcomes problems associated with actual and percentage measures (Huff and Sherr, 1967; Green and Allaway, 1985). It evaluates the rate of growth for each class and grade in relation to the market as a whole and is a more appropriate method of comparing relative growth rates among classes. The summary statistic from this method is the net per cent shift, which is an estimate of the per cent deviations from the average growth rate captured by each class and grade.

The data are analysed using shift–share analysis to evaluate changes in the distribution of classes and grades over time. Time periods used to evaluate the changes vary according to the availability of data. The net per cent shift is used for interpretation purposes because it more appropriately captures the changes in distribution of shares over time. However, for reference, changes in trade volumes of each class and grade are shown in Tables 15.1–15.3. It is important to note that these are changes in equilibrium trade shares and cannot necessarily be ascribed to changes in importers' demands or in exporters' supply. In fact, observed changes in shares are probably a result of both forces.

Analytical model: calculation of per cent net shift

The actual change in market segment i from time period $t-1$ to t is measured as:

Table 15.1. Average exports and measures of changes in exports, for hard wheat classes, 1980–1983 to 1990–1993.

	Exports (thousand tonnes)			Measures of change	
Grade	1980–83	1990–93	Change	%	Net % shift
US HAD	1,783	1,327	−456	−25.6	−3.3
US HRW	19,309	12,682	−6,627	−34.3	−58.1
US HRS	5,796	8,804	3,008	51.9	49.6
US soft wheat	15,431	10,709	−4,722	−30.6	−38.7
CWAD	2,405	2,839	435	18.1	9.7
CWRS	14,593	14,332	−261	−1.8	19.8
Canadian Other wheat	787	2,251	1,463	185.8	20.9
Total	60,105	52,945	−7,160	−11.9	n/a

HAD, Hard Amber Durum; HRW, Hard Red Winter; HRS, Hard Red Spring; CWAD, Canadian Western Amber Durum; CWRS, Canadian Western Red Spring.

$$\Delta V_i = V_{i,t} - V_{i,t-1}$$

Total growth rate for the market composed of m segments is equal to the ratio of the total value in the terminal period to the corresponding value in the initial period:

$$k = \sum_{i=1}^{m} V_{i,t} / \sum_{i=1}^{m} V_{i,t-1}$$

To calculate net shift, an expected change is calculated for each market segment (i) where

$$E(\Delta V_{i,t}) = V_{i,t-1} \times (k - 1)$$

Net shift is estimated as the difference between the actual change and the expected change for a given market segment:

$$N_i = \Delta V_i - E(\Delta V_i)$$

A total absolute net shift is calculated as the sum of all positive net shifts or the sum of all negative net shifts or alternatively:

$$S = [\sum_{i=1}^{m} | \Delta V_i - E(\Delta V_i) |]/2$$

The per cent net shift for each market segment (P_i) is the net shift (N_i) divided by the absolute net shift (S) multiplied by 100.

$$P_i = N_i / S \times 100$$

Table 15.2. Average exports and measures of changes in exports, for US HAD, HRS and HRW, by grade, 1986/87, 1993/94.

	Exports (thousand tonnes)			Measures of change	
Grade	1986/87	1993/94	Change	%	Net % shift
HAD					
US No. 1	44.7	121.3	76.6	171	38
US No. 2 OB[a]	547.2	473.2	−73.9	−14	61
US No. 2	5.7	5.0	−0.6	−11	1
US No. 3 OB	1,303.3	514.0	−789.3	−61	−100
US No. 3	1.6	0.0	−1.6	−100	0
US No. 4 OB	0.0	1.8	1.8	>100	1
US No. 4	0.3	0.0	−0.3	−100	0
Total HAD	1,902.7	1,115.4	−787.2	−41	n/a
HRS					
US No. 1	349.7	963.5	613.9	176	99
US No. 2 OB[a]	5,747.3	6,511.9	764.5	13	−99
US No. 2	5.7	4.5	−1.3	−22	0
US No. 3 OB	28.3	29.4	1.1	4	−1
US No. 3	0.3	3.2	2.9	1,020	1
US No. 4 OB	0.0	1.7	1.7	>100	0
Total HRS	6,131.4	7,514.2	1,382.8	23	n/a
HRW					
US No. 1	355.5	812.3	456.8	129	91
US No. 2 OB[a]	16,785.3	11,074.9	−5,710.4	−34	−94
US No. 2	108.7	41.8	−66.8	−62	−5
US No. 3 OB	10.3	23.4	13.1	128	3
US No. 3	3.4	0.1	−3.4	−99	0
US No. 4	0.0	0.4	0.4	>100	0
US No. 5	0.0	4.5	4.5	>100	1
SG	0.0	37.2	37.2	>100	6
Total HRW	17,263.2	11,994.6	−5,268.6	−31	n/a

HAD, Hard Amber Durum; HRS, Hard Red Spring; HRW, Hard Red Winter; SG, US Sample Grade.

Note: Numbers may not sum due to rounding.

[a] OB refers to shipper's preference. For example, US No. 2 OB allows for shipment of grain equivalent to either US No. 2 or US No. 1.

Shift–share analysis: hard wheat exports by class

Comparison across two periods (1980–1983 and 1990–1993) was made to quantify shifts in exports of wheat classes. HRS is the class with the highest growth, capturing 50% of the variability in growth from 1980–1983 to 1990–1993 (Fig. 15.1). The level of CWRS exports declined over this period but captured 20% of the variability in growth between the two periods. Comparison of results shows that the classes

Table 15.3. Average exports and measures of changes in exports, for CWAD and CWRS, by grade, 1986/87 to 1990/91 and 1992/93.

	Exports (thousand tonnes)			Measures of change	
Grade	1986/87	1990/91	Change	%	Net % shift
CWAD					
CWAD No. 1	309.2	960.0	650.8	210	74
CWAD No. 2	524.3	769.9	245.6	47	27
CWAD No. 3	1,006.3	432.7	−573.6	−56	−68
CWAD No. 4	263.4	33.7	−229.7	−87	−27
Other CWAD	52.7	7.9	−44.8	−85	−5
Total CWAD	2,155.7	2,204.2	48.5	2	n/a
CWRS	1986/87	1992/93			
CWRS No. 1	5,471.8	6,451.1	979.3	18	95
CWRS No. 2	4,822.7	2,214.7	−2,607.0	−54	−100
CWRS No. 3	4,527.5	3,935.6	−591.9	−13	5
Other CWRS	0.0	0.0	0.0	0	0
Total CWRS	14,822.0	12,601.5	−2,220.5	−15	n/a

CWAD, Canadian Western Amber Durum; CWRS, Canadian Western Red Spring.

with the greatest loss were HRW, US soft and HAD. These comparisons indicate strong growth in trade in HRS, CWAD and Canadian Other.

Growth in Canadian Other appears to be largely a function of exceptionally large exports of Canadian feed wheat in 1993 (4.6 million tonnes), which is probably a 1-year phenomenon. Strong growth in both

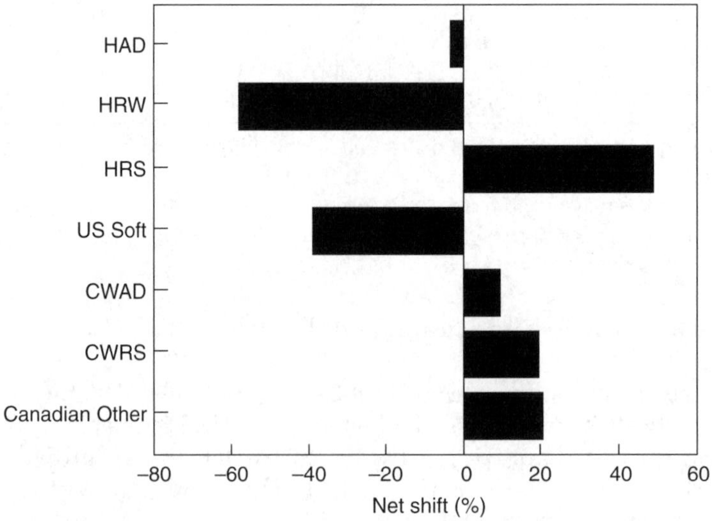

Fig. 15.1. Per cent net shift in exports, by class, 1980–1983 to 1990–1993.

HRS and CWAD are longer-term trends. Another notable result is the decline in HRW exports, which appears to be a longer-term trend.

It is interesting to note that CWAD exports increased from the earlier period to the later period while CWRS exports declined (Table 15.1). Actual and percentage changes indicate that CWAD increased while CWRS decreased, suggesting that CWAD had gained export shares while CWRS had lost export shares. Comparison of net per cent shifts, however, indicates that the decline in CWRS exports was at a slower rate than the market as a whole. Thus, even though exports of CWAD increased, the larger size of the market for CWRS compared with CWAD allowed CWRS to capture more of the market shares that were lost by other classes of wheat exports than did CWAD. Using a net per cent shift measure, CWRS fared better than CWAD over this period. These results are contrary to those indicated by the other measures (actual and percentage changes).

Shift–share analysis: hard wheat exports by grades

The analysis was also conducted for each grade of wheat over the period 1986/87 to 1993/94 and results are shown in Tables 15.2 and 15.3. Over this period, exports of HRS No. 1 and No. 2 increased, with most of the increases (on a percentage basis) accruing to No. 1. Comparison of net per cent shifts indicated that exports of HRS No. 1 grew faster than exports of HRS No. 2 OB (see footnote, Table 15.2) and captured all of the growth in market shares (99%) lost by the slower growth of the HRS No. 2 OB segment (−99%). This indicates a shift in the exports of HRS toward higher grades in the more recent time period.

During the same period, exports of HRW No. 1 increased while exports of HRW No. 2 OB declined. Exports of HRW No. 2 and HRW No. 3 also declined, while exports of HRW No. 3 OB and HRW US Sample Grade (SG) showed increases. These changes suggest a shift away from conventional grades toward higher grades (No. 1) and an increase in exports to nominal amounts of lower-quality HRW in 1993/94. Comparisons of net per cent shifts for HRW show the same pattern as for HRS, with growth in exports of higher grades at the expense of lower grades. Deviations from average market growth rates captured by No. 1 segments (91%) were lost by lower grades (primarily No 2. OB for HRW (−94%)).

Analysis of CWRS exports indicates an increase in exports of No. 1 from 1986/87 to 1992/93. The net per cent shift method indicates that CWRS No. 1 captured 95% and No. 3 captured 5% of the variability in growth while No. 2 incurred all of the loss. Thus, there has been a shift toward exports of higher grades of CWRS wheats, with most of the declines coming from reduced exports of CWRS No. 2.

Analysis of CWAD exports indicates that No. 1 and No. 2 gained while other grades declined. CWAD No. 3 was the class that lost the most exports in both net per cent shift and volume. CWAD No. 4 and Other CWAD had the highest percentage declines in exports across the time periods. These measures of changes in exports are consistent with other results indicating that exports of Canadian durum are increasing for higher-quality durum.

5. Comparison of Exports of Hard Red Wheats by Grade into High-quality Markets

An important element of market strategy is the identification of market segments. In this case, the higher-quality hard wheat market segment is of particular interest. Kraft *et al.* (1996) identified countries within the high-quality commercial export market. Analyses are conducted in this study to evaluate the penetration by the USA and Canada into these higher-quality hard wheats in these markets. Exports by grade are compared for exports of No. 1 to all countries and total exports of CWRS, HRS and HRW to these high-quality wheat importing countries.

Exports of CWRS No. 1 to markets designated as high-quality averaged 2.5 million tonnes per year from 1986 to 1991 (Table 15.4). This represented 29% of the total CWRS No. 1 exported to all markets. For the USA, exports of No. 1 HRS and HRW to these high-quality markets were 98% and 100% of total US exports of HRS and HRW No. 1 respectively. Therefore, these markets imported almost all the US No.1 but imported less than 30% of the Canadian No. 1. A complementary interpretation is that US exporters do a better job at assuring that the higher-quality wheat that is exported goes to those higher-quality markets.

The distribution of exports to these markets from Canada is largely No. 1 (84%). However, even though these markets import almost all of the No 1. HRS and HRW, imports of US No. 1 are still a small portion of US hard red wheat imports to these markets (18.9% and 15.4% of HRS and HRW imports respectively).

6. Cluster Analysis of Quality Characteristics of US Shipments

Cluster analysis is an alternative analytical method to identify market segments. Clustering markets into like groups can be used to identify segments of buyers and characteristics of segments. In traditional market strategy these results can be used for standardizing products desired by each market segment, evaluating market promotion strategies and competition within segments, and targeting groups that have the greatest potential, thereby reducing costs.

Table 15.4. Comparison of hard wheat exports to high-quality markets.

	No. 1	No. 2	No. 3	No. 2 OB	No. 3 OB
Average exports to all markets (thousand tonnes)					
CWRS[a]	8,740	2,996	2,565		
HRS[b]	608	3	2	6,882	16
HRW[b]	540	60	1	12,895	7
Average exports to high-quality markets (thousand tonnes)					
CWRS[a]	2,545	369	106		
HRS[b]	594	2	1	2,543	3
HRW[b]	537	36	1	2,909	2
Per cent of total exports shipped to high-quality markets by grade (%)					
CWRS	29	12	4		
HRS	98	53	7	37	21
HRW	100	61	10	23	30
Grade distribution for exports to high-quality markets (%)					
CWRS	84	12	4		
HRS	19	0	0	81	0
HRW	15	1	0	84	0

CWRS, Canadian Western Red Spring; HRS, Hard Red Spring; HRW, Hard Red Winter.
Note: 'High-quality' is defined as in Kraft *et al.* (1996) to include Australia, Colombia, Dominican Republic, Ecuador, the EU, Finland, Hong Kong, Israel, Jamaica, Japan, Malaysia, Mexico, New Zealand, Norway, Panama, Portugal, Singapore, South Africa, South Korea, Taiwan, Thailand and the USA.
[a] Average of 1986–1991.
[b] Average of 1986–1994.

Clustering algorithms are a method of identifying observations with similar characteristics. Quality characteristics of shipments of US HAD, HRS and HRW are compared to identify countries with similar purchasing patterns. Similar detailed data do not exist for Canadian exports, and thus the analysis is applied only to US wheat imports. Four grade and non-grade parameters are used to derive market segments; these include dockage, test weight, protein, and total defects. The analysis is conducted over two time periods to determine the extent of changes in both the number and composition of segments over time (1986–1989 and 1991–1994).

HAD cluster analysis

Three distinct market segments existed in the period 1986–1989 for countries that imported HAD (Table 15.5). Two of the market segments

Table 15.5. Segment means for grade and non-grade parameters for HAD, 1986–1989 and 1991–1994.

Segment	1	2	3	4
Segment means 1986–1989				
Dockage (%)	0.90	1.11	0.77	
Test weight (kg per hl)	79.2	77.4	80.2	
Total defects (%)	4.0	5.8	1.8	
Average protein (%)	14.2	13.3	14.4	
Specify protein (%)	11.0	2.0	98.0	
Share of exports (%)	50.8	41.9	7.2	
Countries (number)	22	18	4	
Segment means 1991–1994				
Dockage (%)	0.82	0.60	0.70	0.55
Test weight (kg per hl)	77.9	79.3	78.9	80.3
Total defects (%)	4.5	2.7	3.5	2.1
Average protein (%)	13.2	13.8	13.5	13.4
Specify protein (%)	2.0	91.0	4.0	3.0
Share of exports (%)	48.1	16.6	18.0	17.3
Countries (number)	15	11	10	8

tended not to specify protein and imported lower-quality HAD. Segments 1 and 2 had average total defects of 4% and 5.8%. Segment 3 tended to specify protein and had the lowest average total defects (1.8%). Test weight and dockage followed the same pattern, with the worst averages belonging to group 2 and the best to group 3. Exports in this earlier time period went largely to the segments representing the lower-quality exports (Segments 1 and 2). Thus, in this earlier time period, three distinct groupings emerge, generally coinciding with grades 1–3, where protein levels tended to be specified only for US No. 1.

From 1991 to 1994, four distinct market segments were identified. Three of the segments resemble the three groups indicated in the earlier period. However, in this later time period, it appears that the segment importing the highest-quality HAD in the prior time period split into two groups: one that tended to specify protein and one that did not. Shares of exports went largely to the lowest-quality segment (Segment 1 with 48.1% of exports) with the remainder split about equally between the other three higher-quality segments.

Segments representing countries importing higher-quality HAD wheat are Segment 3 for 1986–1989 and Segments 2 and 4 for 1991–1994. Two segments are identified for the latter time period because both have average total defects less than grade 1 specifications; however, one tends to specify protein, while the other does not. This is interesting because Italy, one of the dominant importers of HAD, did not specify protein. In the 1986–1989 period, Italy was grouped into a segment of lesser quality that did not specify protein. Further, both segments that did not specify protein in the later time periods had higher average test weights than the segments that did specify protein, and the segment for 1991–1994 has lower average total defects than its counterpart. This suggests that factors other than protein may have large impacts on purchases of high-quality HAD wheat, such as total defects and test weight. Another interesting aspect is that the number of countries classified into higher-quality importer segments increased from the earlier time period to the later time periods.

HRS cluster analysis

When HRS is examined across time periods, an increase in differentiation similar to that for HAD is indicated (Table 15.6). In 1986–1989, there are two distinct segments of importing countries. Each segment tends to specify protein; however, differences in average total defects indicate a larger group that buys lower-quality wheat (average total defects 3.9%, test weight 78.4 kg per hl, dockage 0.9%, and protein 14%) and a smaller group that buys higher-quality wheat (average total defects 2.2%, test weight 81.1 kg per hl, dockage 0.8%, and protein 14.4%). The larger group consisted of 51 countries and imported more than 81% of HRS exports. The smaller group consisted of 16 countries and imported more than 18% of the HRS.

Table 15.6. Segment means for grade and non-grade parameters for HRS, 1986–1989 and 1991–1994.

Segment	1	2	3	4	5
Segment means 1986–1989					
Dockage (%)	0.88	0.77			
Test weight (kg per hl)	78.4	81.1			
Total defects (%)	3.9	2.2			
Average protein (%)	14.0	14.4			
Specify protein (%)	71.0	99.0			
Share of exports (%)	81.7	18.3			
Countries (number)	51	16			
Segment means 1991–1994					
Dockage (%)	0.84	0.79	0.96	0.65	0.79
Test weight (kg per hl)	79.2	79.8	78.8	80.5	78.4
Total defects (%)	3.5	3.0	3.4	2.4	4.1
Average protein (%)	13.4	13.9	14.1	14.3	13.7
Specify protein (%)	11.0	96.0	85.0	89.0	91.0
Share of exports (%)	24.7	22.5	15.0	16.5	21.3
Countries (number)	22	36	31	30	41

In the later time period (1991–1994), five segments are identified. Two pairs of segments (1 and 3, and 2 and 5) are similar, with the fifth segment (Segment 4) importing the highest-quality HRS. Segments 1 and 3 are similar in that they both have high levels of dockage and average total defects of 3.4% to 3.5%. They differ in that Segment 1 tended not to specify protein and had slightly higher test weights and lower protein, while Segment 3 tended to specify protein and had slightly lower test weights and higher protein. Segments 2 and 5 have similar protein and dockage; however, Segment 2 has lower defects and higher test weights while Segment 5 has higher defects and lower test weights. The number of countries in each cluster ranged from a low of 22 in Segment 1 to a high of 41 in Segment 5. Shares of exports were spread more equally across all segments, with the smallest segment (3) representing 15% of HRS exports. These clusters suggest that importers are increasing their specificity over earlier time periods.

Countries in the high-quality HRS segment across the two time periods are largely East Asian countries (Table 15.7). The number and composition of countries are different in the earlier period, 1986–1989, from in the later period. The 1991–1994 segment has twice as many countries as the earlier time period. Most of these new importing countries appear only once. Further, not all of the traditional high-quality HRS importers are included in every year of this later clustering. Dahl and Wilson (1996) show similar information for HRW and durum.

Table 15.7. Composition of importing countries within high-quality HRS segments and years in segment for two time periods: 1986–1989 and 1991–1994.

Segment 2 1986–1989	Years in segment	Segment 4 1991–1994	Years in segment	Segment 4 (cont.) 1991–1994	Years in segment
Hong Kong	4	Taiwan	4	South Korea	4
Japan	4	Belgium	2	Malaysia	3
Malaysia	4	Barbados	1	New Zealand	3
Singapore	4	Benin	1	Singapore	3
South Korea	4	Burkina Faso	1	Japan	2
Taiwan	4	Canary Islands	1	Norway	2
Thailand	4	Colombia	1	Philippines	2
Philippines	3	Cyprus	1	Thailand	2
Indonesia	2	Finland	1	Mali	1
Sri Lanka	2	Gabon	1	Malta	1
Benin	1	Hong Kong	1	Martinique	1
Netherlands	1	Iceland	1	Mexico	1
Nigeria	1	Israel	1	Netherlands	1
UK	1	Ivory Coast	1	Senegal	1
USSR	1	Jamaica	1	Sri Lanka	1

HRW clusters

Clustering of HRW identified two segments of importing countries in the period 1986–1989 (Table 15.8). Groupings are similar to those of this period for HRS. Segment 1 is a large segment with more dockage, lower test weight, higher total defects, and a lower tendency to specify protein than Segment 2. Segment 2 is a small higher-quality segment: it consists of 26 countries and imported 17.6% of HRW exports. Clustering for 1991–1994 appears to be more distinct. It clustered into four segments. Segment 3 is a high-quality segment. It has the highest test weight and protein and lowest dockage and total defects. Segments 1 and 2 are similar. Both have average total defects that would meet grade specifications for US No. 2. Dockage, test weight, and protein are similar. The major difference between these two segments is that one specifies protein (Segment 1) and the other does not (Segment 2). The fourth segment (Segment 4) is the lowest-quality segment. It has the lowest test weight and protein and highest dockage and total defects. The average total defects would meet grade specifications for US No. 3.

Countries in the highest-quality segments for each of the time periods are predominantly the East Asian countries, and Norway and Finland. A larger number of countries are included in the 1986–1989 clustering; however, a higher number of countries have more years in the segment for the 1991–1994 clustering. Shifts in composition of the highest-quality importing segments appear minimal.

Table 15.8. Segment means for grade and non-grade parameters for HRW, 1986–1989 and 1991–1994.

Segment	1	2	3	4
Segment means 1986–1989				
Dockage (%)	0.72	0.58		
Test weight (kg per hl)	79.8	81.7		
Total defects (%)	3.9	2.6		
Average protein (%)	12.1	12.3		
Specify protein (%)	43.0	92.0		
Share of exports (%)	82.4	17.6		
Countries (number)	67	26		
Segment means 1991–1994				
Dockage (%)	0.67	0.69	0.55	1.24
Test weight (kg per hl)	79.3	79.7	81.1	78.8
Total defects (%)	3.7	3.6	2.1	5.5
Average protein (%)	12.0	11.8	12.3	11.6
Specify protein (%)	94.0	20.0	89.0	79.0
Share of exports (%)	43.5	41.3	12.3	2.9
Countries (number)	44	41	21	7

An interesting result of these clustering analyses for both HRS and HRW is revealed when countries grouped in the high-quality market segments are compared with those countries identified as 'high-quality' markets by Kraft *et al.* (1996). Most of the East Asian countries that were grouped into the highest-quality segments were also identified as 'high-quality' markets by Kraft *et al.* (1996). However, there is a large subset of countries identified by Kraft *et al.* (1996) composed of Caribbean, some South American and EU countries and Israel and South Africa that is not consistently in the highest-quality segments identified here. Further, a few Asian countries, such as the Philippines, Indonesia, and Bangladesh, are identified as being high-quality importers but were not identified as such by Kraft *et al.* (1996).

7. Summary and Conclusions

An important aspect of competition and demand in the international wheat market in recent years is related to quality differences among exporters. Of particular interest are the differences in exports by grade and class. Maturing of the international market has the effect of increasing the importance of differentiation as a source of competitive advantage among exporters. The importance of quality as an element of competition is further enhanced as countries privatize their importing functions, a major trend in the world market. This shift toward greater quality differentiation is particularly apparent in the competition among hard wheats, notably HRS, HRW and durum. The USA and Canada are the dominant producers of these types of wheat. However, these countries' marketing systems differ with respect to quality, as does the distribution among grades of their excess exportable quantities.

This study analyses the composition of exports in hard wheat from the USA, with comparisons with Canada. The scope of the study is limited to hard wheats.

There have been some dramatic changes in the distribution among exports by grade and class that have important implications for demand and competition. Generally, results from this study indicate the following:

HRS has been the class that has increased the fastest relative to other classes

From the early 1980s to the mid-1990s, wheat classes whose exports increased the fastest (measured as *net shift* from a shift–share analysis and listed in rank order) were HRS, followed by Canada Other, CWRS and CWAD. Those classes experiencing negative growth included HAD, US soft and HRW (listed from least to greatest negative growth). The growth in Canadian Other is probably attributable to a 1-year increase in feed wheat experienced during 1993 and probably related to crop quality problems in that year.

Exports of higher grades of wheat increased faster than lower grades

There have also been some notable changes in the composition of exports among grades from each country. Over the period 1986/87 to 1993/94, there was a notable shift in quality of exports of HRW, HRS and HAD, in all cases from lesser amounts of lower-grade wheat to greater proportions of higher-grade wheat. Most notable (in per cent net shift) is the growth in No. 1 exports of HRS, followed by No. 1 HRW. In both cases, the change represents a shift from lower grades. Similar growth has occurred in No. 1 HAD, but it has not been as dramatic, although the reduction in No. 3 is notable.

There have been important changes in the composition of market segments

Cluster analysis is used to identify countries importing similar quality. However, this analysis could only be applied to US hard wheat exports as comparable data are not available for Canadian exports. Countries importing wheat with similar characteristics are referred to as segments, and their behaviour and composition have important marketing implications. Market segments were distinguished by the levels of dockage, test weight, defects and protein level. Results from this analysis indicate the following:

- There were notable changes in the definition and composition of segments. The number of segments in the HAD market increased from three to four, HRS increased from two to five segments and HRW increased from two to four segments. These changes probably reflect the emergence of shifts in the composition of demand, as well as supply shifts, induced by the effect of interfirm and intercountry competition.
- Countries in the higher-quality segment. Countries included in what is defined as the higher-quality segments varied and, in some cases, they jumped in and out of segments. Those countries that were in the higher-quality HAD segment more than 50% of the time in more recent years were Italy, Costa Rica, Japan and Kuwait. Those in the higher-quality HRS segment at least 50% of the time were Taiwan, South Korea, Malaysia, New Zealand and Singapore. Those in the higher-quality HRW segment at least 50% of the time include Japan, South Korea, Taiwan, Thailand, Bangladesh, Hong Kong, Malaysia and Norway. Other countries were also categorized as being part of these segments but were there only periodically.

A number of implications can be discerned from these results that are important for both the public and private sectors. First, it is notable that the fastest growth market has been HRS, while HRW has fallen sharply, suggesting a significant shift in the composition of demand over the past decade. Second, these results probably have important market development implications. Past efforts to encourage buyers to specify tighter quality specifications are having an effect (Dahl and Wilson, 1996).

A number of implications for the private sector can also be identified from these results. First, the shift in US exports toward greater specificity and generally toward higher-quality wheats has implications for the domestic processing sector. Traditionally, the processing sector dominated the consumption of higher-quality hard wheats, leaving the remainder for the export market. The shifts identified in this analysis suggest that, in the future, the domestic market will have less dominance over the higher-quality wheat supply, having the effect of raising premiums (Johnson *et al.*, 1995). A second notable implication relates to the apparent increase in differentiation and number of segments in the international wheat market. It demonstrates the extent to which the private trading/handling sector has been responsive to changes in demand. It should also be viewed positively by traders and others in the supply chain in that the increased differentiation of the market allows them to compete in segments less characteristic of 'commoditization', as defined by Rangan and Bowman (1992) and developed in the context of the international wheat market by Wilson (1995). However, doing so may very well require the ability to create segregations that are maintained throughout the supply chain through the use of increasingly more sophisticated premium/discount schedules and/or through other vertical coordination mechanisms.

Definitions

Class: Wheat is divided into eight classes based on colour and kernel and varietal characteristics. There are eight classes of US wheats: durum, Hard Red Spring, Hard Red Winter, Soft Red Winter, Hard White, Soft White, unclassed and mixed wheat. Classes can be subdivided into subclasses.

Grade: A numerical grade is established based on a characteristic's position within factor limits. Characteristics utilized for grade determination include test weight, moisture, damaged kernels, foreign material, shrunken and broken kernels, total defects, etc.

Non-grade parameters: These are wheat characteristics not utilized for grade determination. These include protein, falling number, dockage, etc.

Dockage: All matter other than wheat that can be readily removed. It is defined as:

> all matter other than wheat that can be removed from the original sample by use of an approved device according to procedures prescribed in FGIS

instructions. Also, underdeveloped, shrivelled, and small pieces of wheat kernels removed in properly separating the material other than wheat and that cannot be recovered by properly rescreening or recleaning.

(USDA–GIPSA, 1997).

Test weight: The determined bushel weight (metric) of a 1 g sample of wheat.

Total defects: Total of damaged kernels, foreign material and shrunken and broken kernels. The sum of these three factors may not exceed the limit for the factor defects for each numerical grade.

References

Canada Grains Council (various years) *Statistical Handbook*. Winnipeg, Manitoba, Canada.

Canada Grains Council (1995) *GRAINBASE Database*. Winnipeg, Manitoba, Canada.

Canada–USA Joint Commission on Grains (1995) *Canada–United States Joint Commission on Grains Final Report*, Vol. 1. Canada–United States Joint Commission on Grains, Washington DC, USA.

Canadian Wheat Board (CWB) (various issues) *The Canadian Wheat Board Annual Report*. Canadian Wheat Board, Winnipeg, Manitoba, Canada.

Carter, C. and Loyns, A. (1996) *A Report on Single Desk Selling of Canadian Grain*. Paper prepared for the Alberta Ministry of Agriculture, Edmonton, Alberta, Canada.

Dahl, B.L. and Wilson, W.W. (1996) *Grades/Classes of Hard Wheats Exported from North America: Analysis of Demand and Trends*. Agricultural Economics Report No. 348, Department of Agricultural Economics, North Dakota State University, Fargo, North Dakota, USA.

Dahl, B.L. and Wilson, W.W. (1997) *Factors Affecting the Supply of High-Quality Spring Wheats: Comparisons Between the USA and Canada*. Agricultural Economics Report No. 374, Department of Agricultural Economics, North Dakota State University, Fargo, North Dakota, USA.

Grains Council of Australia (1995) *Milling Wheat Project: Consultant's Report*. Grain Research and Development Corporation, Australia.

Green, R.T. and Allaway, A.W. (1985) Identification of export opportunities: a shift–share approach. *Journal of Marketing* 49 (Winter), 83–88.

Huff, D.L. and Sherr, L.A. (1967) Measure for determining differential growth rates of markets. *Journal of Marketing Research* 4 (November), 391–339.

Hyberg, B., Ash, M., Lin, W., Lin, C., Aldrich, L. and Pace, D. (1993) *Economic Implications of Cleaning Wheat in the United States*. Agricultural Economics Report No. 669, Commodity Economics Division, Economic Research Service, USDA, Washington DC, USA.

Johnson, D., Wilson, W. and Diersen, M. (1995) *Quality Risks, Procurement Strategies, and Wheat Trading*. Agricultural Economics Report No. 333, Department of Agricultural Economics, North Dakota State University, Fargo, North Dakota, USA.

Kraft, D., Furtan, H. and Tyrchniewicz, E. (1996) *Performance Evaluation of the Canadian Wheat Board.* Winnipeg, Manitoba, Canada.

McLaughlin, G. (1994) Quality assurance and the grading system in Canada. Paper prepared for the Analytical Group on North American Agricultural Trade, 18 October, at Crookston, Minnesota, and Policy Branch, Agriculture and Agri-Food Canada, Winnipeg, Manitoba, Canada.

Mercier, S. (1993) *The Role of Quality in Wheat Import Decision Making.* Agricultural Economics Report No. 670, Commodity Economics Division, Economic Research Service, USDA, Washington DC, USA.

Rangan, V. and Bowman, G. (1992) Beating the commodity magnet. *Industrial Marketing Management* 21, 215–224.

US Congress Office of Technology Assessment (OTA) (1989) *Grain Quality in International Trade: a Comparison of Major US Competitors.* F-402, Office of Technology Assessment, Washington DC, USA.

USDA (US Department of Agriculture) (various issues) *Wheat Situation and Outlook.* Economic Research Service, Washington DC, USA.

USDA (US Department of Agriculture) (1995) *Export Grain Inspection System (EGIS) Wheat Data.* Federal Grain Inspection Service, Washington DC, USA.

USDA–GIPSA (1997) *Official United States Standards for Grain: Subpart M – United States Standards for Wheat.* 7 CFR Part 810, Grain Inspection Packers and Stockyards Administration, USDA, Washington DC, USA.

Veeman, M. (1987) Hedonic price function for wheat in the world market: implications for Canadian wheat export strategy. *Canadian Journal of Agricultural Economics* 35 (November), 535–552.

Wilson, W. (1994) Demand for wheat classes by Pacific Rim countries. *Journal of Agricultural and Resource Economics* 19(1), 197–209.

Wilson, W. (1995) *Decentralization of International Grain Trading: Trends and Implications.* Australian Wheat Board Address to the Australian Agricultural Economics Association Annual Meeting, Perth, Australia.

16

Impacts of Agricultural and Trade Policies on Northern Plains Agriculture: a Case Study of North Dakota Representative Farms

Won W. Koo

Department of Agricultural Economics, North Dakota State University, Fargo, USA

1. Introduction

Farm programmes and trade policies in the USA and other countries change in response to market developments and political initiatives. Impacts of these policy changes can differ substantially across regions in the USA because each region has its own unique soils, climate, crop mix, marketing conditions, and economic base. Even within regions, such as the Northern Plains, there is substantial variability in these features, which leads to different farm-level impacts. Evaluating the regional effects of national and international policies is of vital concern to decision makers at the national, state and local levels.

The overall objective of this study is to discuss methods for evaluating farm-level impacts of national and international policy changes. Special attention is given to changes in net farm incomes, land prices, cash rents, and debt-to-asset ratios for representative farms in North Dakota under the 1996 Federal and Agricultural Improvement and Reform (FAIR) Act (Conference Report, 1996), the Uruguay Round (UR) Agreement, the Canadian–US Free Trade Agreement (CUSTA) and the North American Free Trade Agreement (NAFTA).

The Northern Plains states represent a major agricultural area with a distinctive climate and crop mix. The region is also uniquely situated in terms of marketing and logistics within the USA in terms of sharing a border with its largest trading partner, Canada. Changes in government policies through the 1996 FAIR Act and the UR Agreement have affected the region's economy more than any other US region. CUSTA has also affected the region more than any other region in the USA.

2. Modelling Approaches and Issues

Several analytical tools were developed to evaluate impacts of national and international policy changes on national and regional agricultural economies of the USA. These are the large-scale policy simulation models and farm-sector models.

Large-scale policy simulation models are typically non-spatial, partial, dynamic simulation models. The models are non-spatial because they do not identify trade flows of agricultural commodities and are partial because they deal with only the agricultural sector. Most of these models are behavioural models based on econometric techniques rather than optimization models. Some models deal with major agricultural commodities and livestock produced, consumed and traded in major exporting and importing countries (e.g. the Food and Agricultural Policy Research Institute (FAPRI) model). Others deal with a single commodity (North Dakota global wheat model (Benirschka and Koo, 1995), North Dakota global sugar model (Benirschka *et al.*, 1996), and Arkansas global rice model (Wailes and Cramer, 1993)). Some single-commodity models, such as the North Dakota global wheat model, divide the commodity into different classes to evaluate impacts of policy changes on different classes of the commodity and to avoid aggregation bias (Yang and Koo, 1996). However, a major problem associated with the single-commodity model is that the prices of other commodities are exogenous in the model. Therefore, it cannot incorporate substitution and complement relationships with the other crops unless it is linked to other commodity models.

North Dakota State University developed a single-commodity simulation model focusing on wheat. In the model, wheat is divided into five classes (Hard Red Winter (HRW), Hard Red Spring (HRS), Soft Red Winter (SRW), white and durum) in production and two classes (common and durum) in consumption to avoid aggregation bias. Since the wheat classes except durum wheat are highly substitutable in consumption, these wheats are aggregated into common wheat on the consumption side. But the model maintains the five wheat classes in production to capture substitution in production among the wheat classes even though substitution is limited, due mainly to differences in weather conditions and soil types among regions. This model interacts with the FAPRI model to capture substitution and complement relationships with the other crops. It can provide the impacts of national and international policies on different types of wheat and regions or countries where the wheats are produced and/or consumed.

Farm-sector models focus on the impacts of policy changes on farms in a region. Since these models focus on small subregions, they are not capable of determining equilibrium conditions. Therefore, development of the model is based on the equilibrium conditions developed by national models. Texas A&M University and North Dakota State University developed representative farm models to analyse the impacts of national and international policy changes on representative farms in the USA and North Dakota respectively. The Texas A&M farm model is linked to the FAPRI model and uses the FAPRI prices as an input, while the North Dakota farm model is linked to both the FAPRI and the North Dakota global wheat models. The Texas farm models predict farm income of different types of farms in different regions, of which characteristics are arbitrarily determined, under the given agricultural economic conditions provided by the national/ international models. However, the North Dakota farm model uses actual farm survey data obtained from the Farm and Ranch Management Association.

3. North Dakota Representative Farm Model

The North Dakota Representative Farm Model is a deterministic simulation model that analyses the impacts of policy changes on farm income. The model projects average net farm incomes, debt-to-asset ratios, cash rents and cropland prices for representative farms producing five major crops: wheat, barley, maize, soybeans and sunflowers. The model is linked to the FAPRI and North Dakota global wheat models and uses the prices of the crops generated from the models (Fig. 16.1). In addition, macro policies and assumptions, trade policies and agricultural policies are incorporated into the model directly or indirectly.

Alternative farm policies affect net farm income for the representative farms. Changes in return to cropland, given the market-determined capitalization rate, result in changes in land prices. Changes in land prices affect cash rental rates farmers are willing to pay on land used to produce crops. Changes in land price and cash rental in turn affect net farm income through adjustments in farm expenses. These changes affect the debt-to-asset ratios of the representative farms.

The North Dakota representative farm

The model has 12 representative farms, three farms in each of four regions of North Dakota. These regions are the Red River Valley (RRV), North Central (NC), South Central (SC) and Western (West) (Fig. 16.2). Farms in each region are representative of small, medium and large-sized farms enrolled in the North Dakota Farm and Ranch Business Management Association.

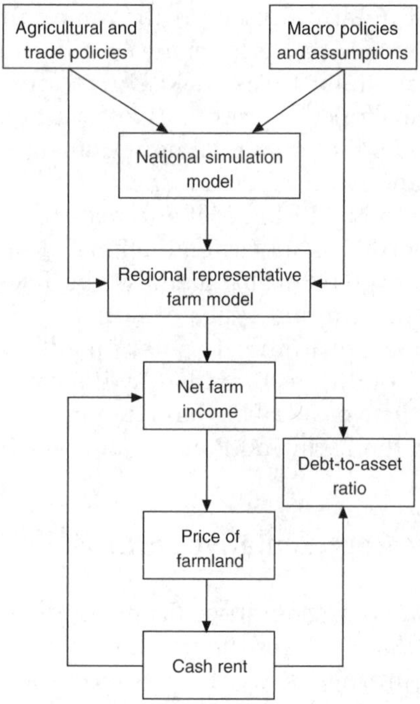

Fig. 16.1. Structure of North Dakota representative farm model.

The large farm is the average of the largest 25% of farms in cropland hectares for each producing region. The small representative farm is the average of the smallest 25% of the farms for each producing region. The medium-sized farm is the average of the remaining 50% of the farms. The average farm sizes are 954 cropland ha for the large-sized farm, 478 cropland ha for the medium-sized farm, and 192 cropland ha for the small-sized farm (Table 16.1).

Structure of the representative farm model

The model consists of four components: net farm income, debt-to-asset ratio, land price and cash rent. The following section discusses the definition of each component and the formula used to calculate the components.

Net farm income

Net farm income is calculated by subtracting total crop and livestock expenses from total farm income. The cost components include all expenses incurred in producing the crop and livestock. The expenses

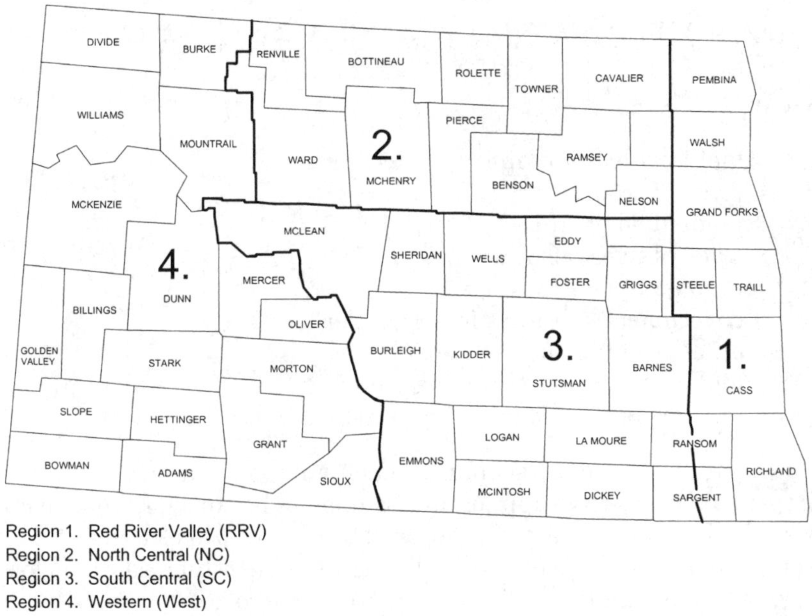

Fig. 16.2. North Dakota farm and ranch business management regions.

consist of direct costs – including seed, fertilizer, fuel, repairs, feed, supplies, feeder livestock purchases and hired labour – and indirect costs, which include machinery depreciation and overheads, such as insurance and licences, land taxes, and land rent or interest on real-estate debt. The revenue component represents the total income from the farm operation, including farm programme payments from the federal government. Total farm income is the sum of cash receipts from crop and livestock enterprises, government payments, Conservation Reserve Program (CRP) payments, custom work, patronage dividends, insurance income and miscellaneous income. Net farm income is calculated as:

Table 16.1. Characteristics of North Dakota representative farms, 1994 (ha).

	Size		
	Large	Medium	Small
Total cropland	954	478	192
Spring wheat	422	198	81
Durum wheat	142	74	36
Barley	99	62	23
Maize	20	18	10
Sunflowers	78	37	11
Soybeans	48	25	5

$$NFI = \sum_{j=1}^{n} Y_j P_j A_j + \sum_{h=1}^{m} P_h L_h + \sum_{j=1}^{n} S_j A_j + I^o - \sum_{h=1}^{m} EX_h^L - \sum_{j=1}^{n} EX_j^C \qquad 16.1$$

where

Y_j = yield per ha for crop j
P_j = price of crop j
A_j = planted ha of crop j
P_h = price of livestock h
L_h = number of livestock h sold
S_j = government subsidies for crop j per ha
I^o = other farm income
EX_j^C = total expenses in producing crop j
EX_h^L = total expenses in producing livestock h

Inventory changes, accounts receivable, accounts payable and prepaid expenses and supplies are assumed to be constant from year to year. Cash receipts are based on predicted cash prices and yields in North Dakota. Cash prices received by farmers are estimated from North Dakota price equations, which were estimated on the basis of the historical relationships between North Dakota prices and US farm prices of the commodities. Regional North Dakota yield equations were used to forecast crop yield trends.

Cropland prices

Land prices are estimated on the basis of the implicit discount rate the farms have previously used and the expected return on land. Therefore, the land prices are defined as the amount that farmers can afford to pay for farmland and are not prevailing market prices. Financial data from average representative farms for each region are used to calculate a dollar return to land. To do this, all production expenses for the crops, including depreciation, land taxes, a labour charge for unpaid family labour, net return from a livestock enterprise and a management fee equivalent to that charged by bank trust departments for management of share-rented farms, are subtracted from gross farm income. To the remaining balance, interest on real estate debt is added back because the return to land is not affected by ownership of the land. This figure is used as the return allocated to cropland.

The average return allocated to each area of cropland per year is divided by the average cropland price to determine the long-run capitalization rate used by farmers as follows:

$$R_g = \frac{M_g}{PL_g} \qquad 16.2$$

where

R_g = long-run capitalization rate in region g
M_g = average net return allocated to cropland in region g
PL_g = average observed price of cropland in region g

This capitalization rate is applied to an n-year weighted moving average of income per area to determine cropland value utilized to produce wheat, maize, soybeans, barley and sunflowers. Cropland price is calculated as follows:

$$PL_{gT} = \frac{1}{R_g} \sum_{t=T-n}^{T} W_t M_{tg} \qquad 16.3$$

where

PL_{gT} = cropland price in region g in time T
W_t = weighting factor for year t
M_{tg} = net return allocated to cropland in region g and year t

The price of cropland calculated in Equation 16.3 can be defined as the amount farmers are willing to pay for the cropland to produce wheat, barley, maize, soybeans and sunflowers.

Cash rent

Cash rent for cropland is calculated by multiplying a k-year moving average of farmland price by the long-run capitalization rate plus taxes on land. Cash rents are calculated as:

$$CR_{gT} = \sum_{t=T-k}^{T} EM_{gt} R_g + TX_T \qquad 16.4$$

where

CR_{gT} = cropland cash rent in region g in time T
EM_{gt} = estimated net return to cropland in region g and year t
TX_T = taxes on land in time T

This cash rent is defined as the amount that farmers are willing to pay for the rented cropland to produce crops such as wheat, barley, maize, soybeans and sunflowers.

Data used for the representative farm

The prices of crops obtained from FAPRI and North Dakota global wheat models are average farm prices of the crops in the USA (FAPRI Baseline Projections, 1996). The national average farm prices are converted to the prices received by North Dakota representative farms by using the North Dakota price equation, which was estimated by regressing average farm price of each crop produced in North Dakota against the national average farm price of the same crop. The price equation used for this study is specified in a dynamic framework on the basis of the Nerlove's partial adjustment hypothesis as follows:

$$P_{it} = a_0 + a_1 P_t + a_2 P_{it-1} + e_{it} \qquad 16.5$$

where

P_{it} = average farm price of a crop in region i in time t
P_t = national average farm price of a crop in time t

The price equation is estimated for each crop produced in North Dakota using the time series data from 1975 to 1996 (North Dakota Agricultural Statistics, various issues). The estimated equations are used to predict average prices received by farmers in each region in North Dakota from the national average prices from the FAPRI and North Dakota global wheat models.

Crop yields in each region are also predicted by using the estimated yield equations for crops produced in each region. The yield equation for each crop in each region is specified in the same dynamic framework as that in the price equation, as follows:

$$y_{it} = b_0 + b_1 \text{ trend} + b_2 y_{it-1} + e_{it} \qquad 16.6$$

where y_{it} represents yield of a crop in region i in time t and e_{it} is a random-error term. The trend variable is included to capture changes in technology in producing the crops.

This equation is estimated for each crop in each region using the time series data from 1976 to 1996. The estimated equations are used to predict crop yields in each region.

The crop mix changes over time as a function of prices of the crops produced in each region. A dynamic area equation for each crop is specified on the basis of the Nerlove's partial adjustment hypothesis as follows:

$$A_{jit} = C_0 + \sum_{j=1}^{n} c_j P_{jit} + c_{n+1} A_{jit-1} + c_{n+2} G_{it} + e_{jit} \qquad 16.7$$

where

A_{jit} is the total ha of the jth crop in region i in time t
P_{jit} is the price of the jth crop in region i in time t
G_{it} is government policy variables applied to the jth crop in time t
e_{jit} is a random-error term

The equations are estimated using time series data from 1976 to 1996. The estimated equations are used to predict the total areas of each crop produced in each region. The predicted prices from Equation 16.5

are used in the area equations. The *j*th crop share of cropland areas in region *i* in time *t* is then calculated as follows:

$$S_{jit} = A_{jit} / \sum_{j} A_{jit} \qquad 16.8$$

where S_{jit} is an area share of the *j*th crop in region *i* in time *t*.

The estimated area share of a crop in a region is used to calculate the total areas of the crop produced in the region by multiplying the total areas in the region by the share.

Other data needed for the model are obtained from the North Dakota Farm and Ranch Business Management Association *Annual Reports* (1993–1994).

4. North Dakota Agricultural Outlook

The North Dakota agricultural outlook for the 1998–2007 period is based on the baseline results produced by the FAPRI and North Dakota global wheat models under the optimistic and pessimistic scenarios. The optimistic scenario provides the most economically desirable situation for the US wheat economy, with increases in US wheat exports to major importing countries, such as India, China and the former Soviet Union, and at the same time decreases in exportable surplus of wheat in major exporting countries, such as Canada, the European Union (EU) and Australia. The pessimistic scenario is the reverse case of the optimistic scenario.

Net income for North Dakota representative farms

Table 16.2 presents net farm income for large-, medium- and small-sized farms under the optimistic and pessimistic scenarios. Average income for North Dakota representative farms under the optimistic and pessimistic scenarios varies, depending upon sizes of the farms and regions where the farms are located. The net farm income for the large-sized farm under the optimistic scenario was US$136,000 in 1997, decreases to US$125,000 in 1998, and then increases gradually over the 2000–2007 period (Fig. 16.3). Net income in 2007 is US$186,000 for the large-sized farm, which is 37% higher than that in 1997. The net farm income for the medium-sized farm was US$86,000 in 1997, decreases to US$81,000 in 1999 and then increases gradually over the remaining forecast period. Net income in 2007 is US$113,000, which is 31% higher than that in 1997. Changes in the net farm income for the small-sized farm over the forecast period are similar to those for the large- and medium-sized farms, but the recovery rate for the 2000–2007 period is

Table 16.2. Net farm incomes for large-, medium- and small-sized farms under the optimistic and pessimistic scenarios ('000 US dollars).

	Optimistic scenario			Pessimistic scenario		
Year	Large	Medium	Small	Large	Medium	Small
1997	136	86	40	136	86	40
1998	125	81	37	103	71	34
1999	127	82	37	90	65	31
2000	128	84	37	91	66	30
2001	141	90	38	89	65	30
2002	150	94	40	95	68	30
2003	160	99	40	97	69	29
2004	166	102	40	104	72	30
2005	176	107	41	108	74	29
2006	188	113	42	113	77	30
2007	186	113	41	112	77	29
Average (1998–2007)	155	96	39	100	70	30

much smaller than for the other farms. As a result, the net farm income in 2007 (US$41,000) is similar to that in 1997 (US$40,000) for the small-sized farm. Average farm income for the 1998–2007 period under the optimistic scenario is US$154,000 for the large-sized farm, US$96,000 for the medium-sized farm, and US$39,000 for the small-sized farm.

Increases in net farm income from 1999 to 2007 for large- and medium-sized farms under the optimistic scenario are due mainly to

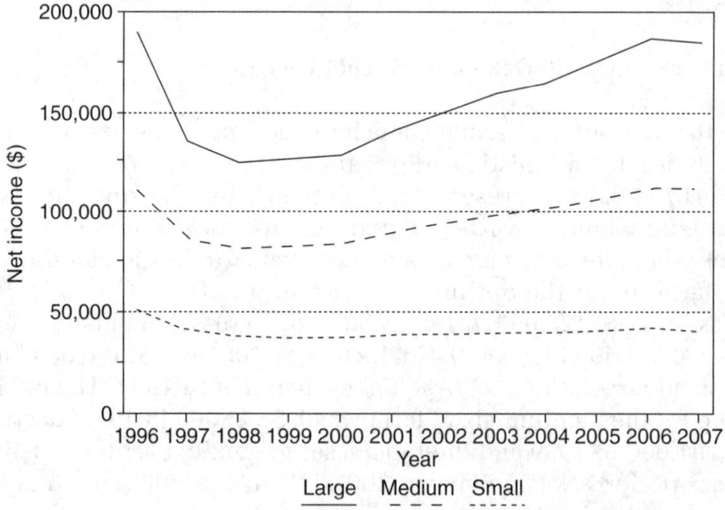

Fig. 16.3. Net income for North Dakota representative farms under the optimistic FAPRI scenario.

strong import demand for agricultural crops from developing countries. Crop production in the USA and around the world is predicted to be normal with annual trend line increases, while world demand for agricultural commodities is predicted to increase faster than supply mainly because of the expected increases in income and slow but steady growth in population in developing countries.

Under the pessimistic scenario, the net farm income for the large-sized farm was US$136,000 in 1997, reaches the lowest level (US$90,000) in 1999, and then increases gradually for the remaining period (Fig. 16.4). However, the income growth rate for the period under this scenario is slower than that under the optimistic scenario. Net farm income in 2007 is 6.8% smaller than that in 1997. Changes in the net farm income for the medium-sized farm are similar to those for the large-sized farms, but recovery rate is even slower than that for the large-sized farms, resulting in smaller farm income in 2007 (US$77,000) compared with that in 1997 (US$86,000). The net farm income for the small-sized farm was US$40,000 in 1997 and decreases to US$29,000 for the forecasting period. Average farm income under this scenario is US$100,000 for the large-sized farm, US$70,000 for the medium-sized farm, and US$30,000 for the small-sized farm.

In both scenarios, the net farm income for the small-sized farm is much smaller than those for other sizes of farm, indicating that farm size plays an important role in farm operation under the 1996 FAIR Act and globalized market places. The small-sized farm may not have the financial resilience to survive in a more market-orientated environment.

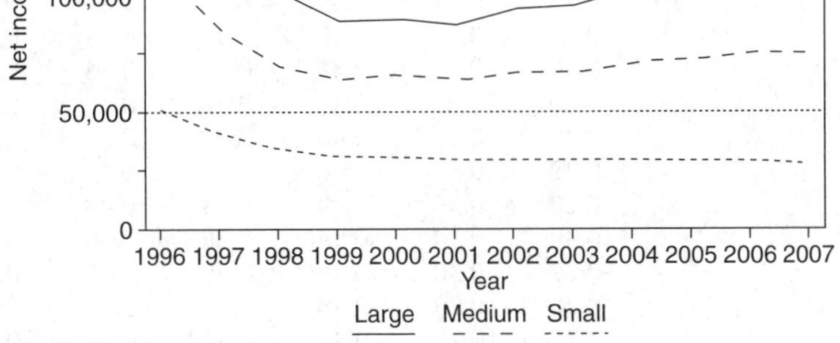

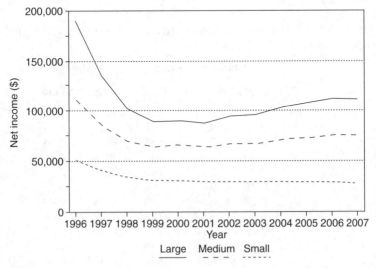

Fig. 16.4. Net income for North Dakota representative farms under the pessimistic FAPRI scenario.

Debt:asset ratio for North Dakota representative farms

Table 16.3 presents debt-to-asset ratios for large-, medium- and small-sized farms under the optimistic and pessimistic scenarios. Debt-to-asset ratios for all sizes of farm under the optimistic scenario are the highest in the 1999–2000 period due to the lower net farm incomes in 1998 and 1999. Debt-to-asset ratios under this scenario are predicted to decrease slowly for the remaining period. For the 1997–2007 period, the debt-to-asset ratios decrease from 0.29 to 0.27 for the large-sized farm, from 0.31 to 0.28 for the medium-sized farm, and from 0.39 to 0.36 for the small-sized farm (Fig. 16.5). The debt-to-asset ratios for the small-sized farm are much higher than those for other farms, but do not reach the critical level in farm operation.

Debt-to-asset ratios for all sizes of farm under the pessimistic scenario increase until 2004 and then decline slowly for the forecasting period. The debt-to-asset ratios for the 1997–2007 period under this scenario increase from 0.29 to 0.37 for the large farm, from 0.31 to 0.38 for the medium farm, and from 0.39 to 0.47 for the small farm (Fig. 16.6). The debt-to-asset ratios for the small farm are larger than those for other farms and also increase faster, but do not reach the level that imperils creditworthiness. Higher debt-to-asset ratios for the small farm, when coupled with meagre net farm income, suggest serious problems in sustaining the farm business unless substantial off-farm income is earned by the farm families. In addition, higher debt-to-asset ratios for the small farm clearly indicate farm size is an important factor affecting financial well-being under the 1996 FAIR Act.

Table 16.3. Debt-to-asset ratios for large-, medium- and small-sized farms under the optimistic and pessimistic scenarios.

	Optimistic scenario			Pessimistic scenario		
Year	Large	Medium	Small	Large	Medium	Small
1997	0.29	0.31	0.39	0.29	0.31	0.39
1998	0.30	0.32	0.40	0.32	0.33	0.41
1999	0.30	0.32	0.41	0.34	0.36	0.44
2000	0.30	0.32	0.41	0.36	0.37	0.45
2001	0.30	0.31	0.40	0.37	0.39	0.47
2002	0.29	0.31	0.40	0.38	0.39	0.48
2003	0.29	0.30	0.39	0.39	0.40	0.49
2004	0.30	0.30	0.39	0.39	0.40	0.49
2005	0.29	0.30	0.39	0.39	0.39	0.48
2006	0.28	0.29	0.38	0.39	0.39	0.48
2007	0.27	0.28	0.36	0.37	0.38	0.47
Average (1998–2007)	0.29	0.30	0.40	0.36	0.38	0.47

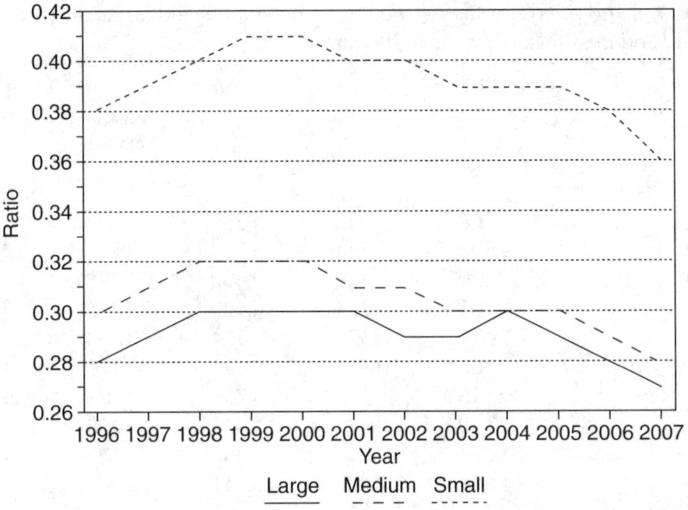

Fig. 16.5. Debt-to-asset ratios for North Dakota representative farms under the optimistic FAPRI scenario.

Land prices and cash rents

Land prices of the medium-sized farms in different regions in North Dakota under the optimistic and pessimistic scenarios are shown in Table 16.4. Land value differs over the regions under both the optimistic and pessimistic scenarios, the highest in the RRV and the lowest in the

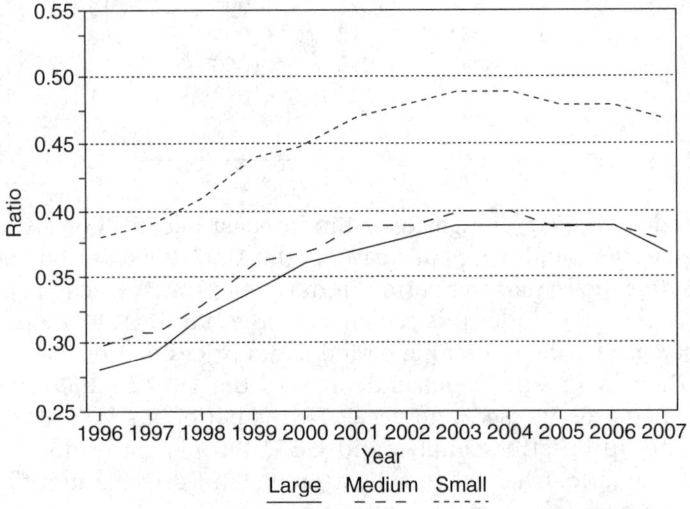

Fig. 16.6. Debt-to-asset ratios for North Dakota representative farms under the pessimistic FAPRI scenario.

Table 16.4. Land prices for large-, medium- and small-sized farms under the optimistic and pessimistic scenarios (dollars per ha).

Year	Red River Valley (RRV)	North Central (NC)	South Central (SC)	Western (West)	State average
Optimistic scenario					
1997	2664	1525	1586	1384	1789
1998	2592	1441	1737	1376	1787
1999	2530	1399	1690	1268	1722
2000	2461	1364	1599	1248	1668
2001	2436	1374	1574	1273	1665
2002	2362	1446	1661	1320	1698
2003	2345	1512	1754	1401	1752
2004	2380	1581	1846	1480	1821
2005	2454	1651	1960	1502	1890
2006	2612	1727	2041	1631	2004
2007	2859	1836	2108	1641	2110
Average (1998–2007)	2503	1532	1796	1416	1811
Pessimistic scenario					
1997	2664	1525	1586	1384	1789
1998	2666	1441	1737	1376	1787
1999	2456	1324	1574	1122	1619
2000	2271	1184	1324	895	1418
2001	2160	1109	1184	749	1300
2002	1967	1070	1097	598	1183
2003	1838	1050	1053	521	1117
2004	1769	1021	991	415	1050
2005	1735	1018	996	588	1085
2006	1804	1016	1060	707	1147
2007	2016	1035	1092	731	1218
Average (1998–2007)	2061	1127	1211	771	1292

West region. It also changes over the forecast period. For all regions except the RRV, land prices decrease for the 1997–2000 period and then increase for the remaining period under the optimistic scenario. Land prices in the RRV under this scenario decrease from 1997 to 2003 and then increase for the remaining period. Land prices for all sizes of farms under the pessimistic scenario decrease from 1997 to 2004 and then start to increase. Average land prices for the period are US$1811 per ha under the optimistic scenario and US$1290 per ha under the pessimistic scenario. Changes in state average land prices under the optimistic and pessimistic scenarios are shown in Fig. 16.7.

Cash rents under the optimistic scenario are the highest in 2000 due to the higher land prices in 1997, decrease for 2–3 years and then

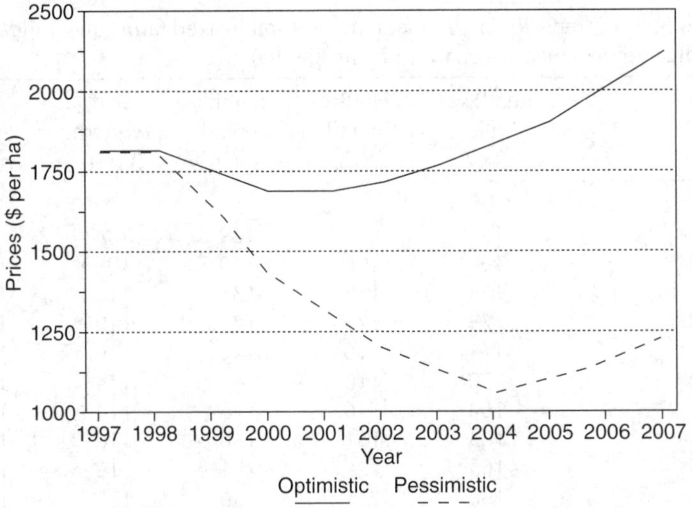

Fig. 16.7. State average land prices for medium-sized farms under optimistic and pessimistic scenarios.

increase over the remaining period, following land prices (Table 16.5). Cash rents in 2007 under this scenario are higher than those in 1997 in all regions. However, cash rents under the pessimistic scenario reach the highest level in 2000 and then decrease for the remaining period. Changes in cash rents under the optimistic and pessimistic scenarios are shown in Fig. 16.8.

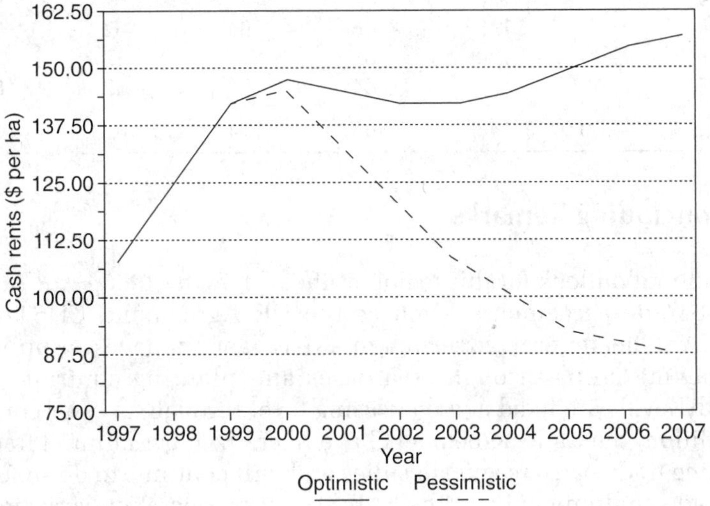

Fig. 16.8. State average cash rents for medium-sized farms under optimistic and pessimistic scenarios.

Table 16.5. Cash rents for large-, medium- and small-sized farms under the optimistic and pessimistic scenarios (dollars per ha).

Year	Red River Valley (RRV)	North Central (NC)	South Central (SC)	Western (West)	State average
Optimistic scenario					
1997	143	89	109	84	106
1998	161	106	119	106	124
1999	173	119	138	116	141
2000	178	121	141	119	146
2001	173	116	146	116	143
2002	170	116	146	114	141
2003	166	116	146	114	141
2004	163	121	148	116	143
2005	163	126	151	119	148
2006	166	131	156	121	153
2007	170	138	161	124	156
Average (1998–2007)	168	121	146	119	143
Pessimistic scenario					
1997	143	89	109	79	106
1998	161	106	119	91	124
1999	173	119	138	109	141
2000	178	119	138	109	143
2001	168	109	133	96	131
2002	158	101	124	91	119
2003	146	94	109	77	106
2004	136	89	101	67	99
2005	128	86	94	62	91
2006	124	86	91	57	89
2007	121	84	91	52	87
Average (1998–2007)	148	99	114	82	114

5. Concluding Remarks

Agricultural outlook for this region is affected by the 1996 FAIR Act and recent trade agreements, such as the UR Agreement, CUSTA and NAFTA. The federal government no longer manages supplies of programme crops through area bases and planting controls. Farm subsidy levels are fixed at a decreasing level through a 7-year contract. In addition, the trade agreements have liberalized agricultural trade by reducing trade barriers and subsidies and will continue to do so. Under this trade environment and the FAIR Act, farm operation is riskier and requires more efficiency, suggesting that larger-sized farms are better equipped to handle the problems than smaller-sized farms.

Large and medium farms can survive under both optimistic and pessimistic scenarios. Net farm income decreases until 1998 and 1999, and then increases gradually for the 2000–2007 period. However, income growth rates under the optimistic scenario are much faster than those under the pessimistic scenarios. The net farm income for the small farm decreases for the entire period under the pessimistic scenario, while it remains at the 1998 level under the optimistic scenario. This implies that small farms in both optimistic and pessimistic scenarios may not have the financial resilience to survive.

Increases in net farm income from 1999 to 2007 are mainly due to strong import demand for agricultural crops from developing countries. Crop production in the USA and around the world is predicted to be normal with annual trend line increases. On the other hand, the net farm income under the pessimistic scenario increases at a slower rate for the 1999–2007 period, mainly due to weak import demand for agricultural commodities in developing countries.

Land prices and cash rents under the optimistic scenario are predicted to increase in most years of the forecasting period, while under the pessimistic scenario they are predicted to decrease. As a result, land prices under the optimistic scenario they are 40% higher than those under the pessimistic scenario, while cash rents under the optimistic scenario are 26% higher.

The debt-to-asset ratios under the optimistic scenario are predicted to increase slowly until 1999 and then decrease. However, the debt-to-asset ratios under the pessimistic scenario will increase for the forecast period. The debt-to-asset ratios for the small farm are predicted to be higher than those for other farms under the optimistic and pessimistic scenarios, but do not reach levels that imperil creditworthiness. High debt-to-asset ratios for the small farm under both the optimistic and pessimistic scenarios clearly indicate farm size is an important factor affecting management efficiency of farm operation under the 1996 FAIR Act and current international market conditions.

Considering the financial crisis in South and South East Asia and sharp increases in agricultural production in Brazil and Argentina, the agricultural outlook under the pessimistic scenario may prevail and, therefore, small-sized farms may suffer most.

References

Benirschka, M. and Koo, W.W. (1995) *World Wheat Policy Simulation Model: Description and Computer Program Documentation.* Agricultural Economics Report No. 340, Department of Agricultural Economics, North Dakota State University, Fargo, North Dakota, USA.

Benirschka, M., Koo, W.W. and Lou, J. (1996) *World Sugar Policy Simulation Model: Description and Computer Program Documentation.* Agricultural Economics Report No. 356, Department of Agricultural Economics, North Dakota State University, Fargo, North Dakota, USA.

Conference Report (1996) Federal Agriculture Improvement and Reform Act of 1996. 25 March. United States House of Representatives and United States Senate, Washington DC, USA.

FAPRI Baseline Projections (1996) Food and Agricultural Policy Research Institute, Columbia, Missouri, USA.

North Dakota Agricultural Statistics (various issues) North Dakota Agricultural Statistics Service, Fargo, North Dakota, USA.

North Dakota Farm and Ranch Business Management Association (1993–1994) *Annual Reports 1993 and 1994.* North Dakota State Board for Vocational Education, Bismarck, North Dakota, USA.

Wailes, E. and Cramer, G. (1993) *World Rice Policy Simulation Model: Documentation.* University of Arkansas, Fayetteville, Arkansas, USA.

Yang, S. and Koo, W.W. (1996) Hicksian aggregation and price dynamics: test for a single price index in the US wheat markets. *Journal of Rural Development* 18, 227–242.

17

Prices, Net Returns and Land Use in Northern Great Plains Dryland Grain Production

John M. Antle, Susan M. Capalbo, James B. Johnson and Walter E. Zidack

Department of Agricultural Economics and Economics and Trade Research Center, Montana State University–Bozeman, USA

1. Introduction

The objective of this chapter is to examine the possible economic impacts on Northern Plains grain producers of changes in output prices for wheat and barley. These impacts include the decisions that producers make with respect to land use and variable input use, and the subsequent impacts on net returns. Economic impacts of price changes can differ substantially across regions in the USA due to spatial variability of soils, climate, crop mix and productivity, marketing conditions and economic base. But, even within a region such as the Northern Plains, there is substantial variability in agricultural production practices and physical characteristics of the resource base, which leads to different farm-level and sub-regional impacts. As a result, policy analysis needs to adequately address the spatial variability within a given region in order to assess the impacts of changes in prices or other economic variables.

This chapter focuses specifically on grain production in Montana. Wheat and barley account for approximately 50% of Montana's agricultural cash receipts. Volatility in grain prices and a dependence on climatic conditions provide for a high degree of variability in cash receipts and in net returns to Montana grain producers. The assessment of changes in net returns and land-use decisions are based on a field-scale stochastic simulation model of the dryland crop production system typical of the Northern Plains region. The model is based on statistically representative samples of producers and allows detailed analysis of the economic responses to output price changes and assessment of the

(eds J.M. Antle and V.H. Smith)

differential impacts of these changes in regions of Montana with differing productivity levels. This analysis also provides information on the distributional consequences of price changes on farms with differing productive resources. These distributional consequences are important in the Northern Plains region, where there is a relatively large number of farms whose long-term viability may be threatened by adverse changes in economic conditions, such as the long-term downward trend in real grain prices discussed in Chapter 3.

Most studies of economic impacts are based on representative farm models (for example, see Chapter 16). This chapter takes an alternative approach that utilizes site-specific survey data on input use decisions, land allocation, and prices. This information is used to estimate econometric production models, which in turn provide the basis for construction of a field-scale stochastic simulation model of producer decision-making. This simulation model accounts for spatial variations in productivity and management, including crop rotations. It is used to analyse changes in cost of production, net returns and land use for dryland grain producers in Montana, in response to changes in output prices predicted by larger-scale policy simulation models such as the Food and Agricultural Policy Research Institute (FAPRI) model discussed in Chapter 3.

The chapter is organized into four sections. The data and econometric models that were used to construct the field-scale stochastic simulation model of the crop production system are discussed in the next section. This is followed by a presentation of the empirical results of the simulation model and the results for alternative output price scenarios in section 3. The chapter concludes with a discussion of the long-term and distributional implications for grain production in the Northern Plains.

2. Econometric Estimation and Simulation of Costs, Returns and Land Use

This section describes econometric production models that were estimated using farm-level production data collected for statistically representative samples of Montana dryland grain farms, and a stochastic simulation model of the dryland cropping system in Montana that is based on those econometric models.

The data on which these models are based were collected by Montana State University in collaboration with the Montana Agricultural Statistics Service (Johnson *et al.*, 1997). The survey was designed to be statistically representative of the grain-producing areas of the state, stratified by the Major Land Resource Areas (MLRAs) shown in Fig. 17.1. Respondents were limited to farms operating 1000

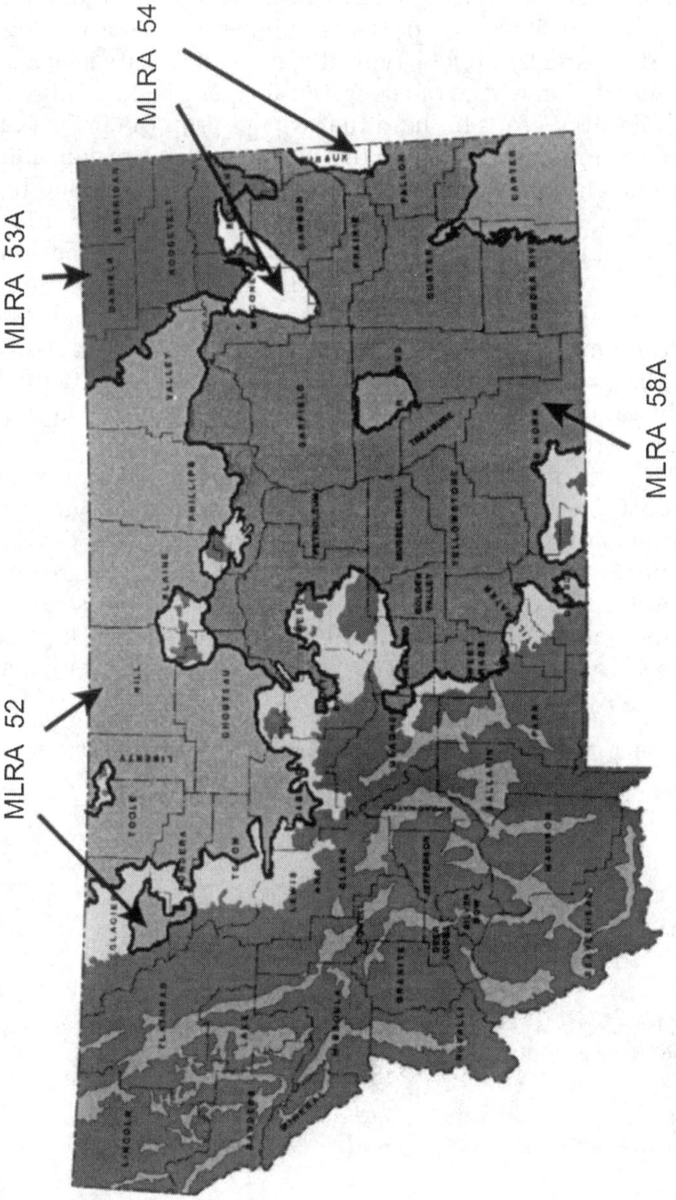

Fig. 17.1. Grain-producing areas in Montana stratified by the Major Land Resource Areas (MLRA).

or more acres (405 ha) of cropland, the minimum size deemed to be a viable commercial grain operation. Detailed production practice data were collected for up to five fields on each farm. The survey provided usable data for 425 farms. These data are described in detail in Johnson *et al.* (1998a, b, c, d). Table 17.1 presents summary statistics by crop, by cropping system, and by MLRA. Typically, many fields are managed in a crop–fallow rotation in order to conserve adequate soil moisture. The practice of planting crops on land that was in crop the prior year is referred to as recropping in much of the Northern Plains region, and we shall utilize this terminology here. There is very little cropland in the semiarid areas of this region that is continuously planted to crops, as would be the usual practice in the Corn Belt and other higher-rainfall regions of the country. The data in Table 17.1 show that there is substantial spatial variation in yields and costs of production between cropping systems (crop–fallow versus recrop) and among MLRAs. Within an MLRA the per hectare yield for a crop produced after fallow is generally 202–336 kg greater per hectare than the same crop produced under recrop conditions.

Short-term variable costs of production include seed cleaning and treatment costs; pesticide and fertilizer costs; crop insurance costs; machinery operating costs; and interest on operating costs. The short-term variable costs of production are usually $12–20 per ha greater for a crop produced under recrop conditions than for the same crop produced after fallow. Most of this per hectare difference in short-term variable costs is associated with higher per hectare costs for fertilizer for

Table 17.1. Summary statistics of the Montana Farm Management Survey, by crop and MLRA.

	Winter wheat		Spring wheat		Barley	
MLRA/item	Fallow	Recrop	Fallow	Recrop	Fallow	Recrop
MLRA 52						
Average yield (tonnes per ha)	3.1	2.5	2.6	2.4	4.1	4.0
Average STVC ($(1998) per ha)	99.8	116.6	81.1	94.9	85.5	100.8
MLRA 53A						
Average yield (tonnes per ha)	n/a	n/a	1.9	1.3	2.3	2.0
Average STVC ($(1998) per ha)	n/a	n/a	68.2	78.6	63.0	75.9
MLRA 54						
Average yield (tonnes per ha)	1.5	n/a	1.3	0.9	1.7	1.6
Average STVC ($(1998) per ha)	65.2	n/a	68.2	71.9	62.5	63.5
MLRA 58A						
Average yield (tonnes per ha)	2.4	2.3	1.8	1.5	2.9	2.6
Average STVC ($(1998) per ha)	99.1	119.1	81.0	100.8	84.5	104.8

STVC, short-term variable costs.
Source: Johnson *et al.* (1998a, b, c, d).

crops produced under recrop conditions. However, when the variable production costs associated with fallowing the cropland in the prior year are added to the current year's cost of production, the per tonne variable costs for crops produced after fallow are similar to the variable costs for the crop produced under recrop conditions (Johnson *et al.*, 1998a, b, c, d).

The average total costs per hectare include the per hectare ownership costs as well as the variable costs. The ownership costs associated with a crop produced on fallow should reflect ownership costs for both the current crop year and the year in which the field was fallowed. For example, winter wheat after fallow will have twice the ownership costs for winter wheat produced on recrop. Ownership costs were not collected in the 1996 Montana Cropping Practices Survey. These costs were approximated using average county-level Conservation Reserve Program (CRP) payment rates per hectare. The average payment rates that prevailed for CRP sign-ups 1–12, by MLRA, are shown in Table 17.2.

The MLRAs are delimited by the US Department of Agriculture (USDA) on such criteria as prevailing land use, elevation and topography, climate, water, soils and natural vegetation, so yields are expected to vary by MLRA. The total hectares in farms that were devoted to annually planted crops ranged from a low of 40% in MLRA 58A to a high of 67% in MLRA 52 (Johnson *et al.*, 1997). At the individual crop level it was observed that the 25.7% of the annually planted cropland in MLRA 52 was in spring wheat after fallow as compared with 29.4% in MLRA 53A, 28.7% in MLRA 54 and only 14.4% in MLRA 58A (Johnson *et al.*, 1998a, b, c, d). Spring wheat after fallow yields for the 1995 crop year were 2.63, 1.91, 1.30 and 1.83 tonnes per ha for MLRAs 52, 53A, 54 and 58A respectively. The 5-year average yields for these areas for the period 1991–1995 (based on county rather than field-level yields) are 2.29, 2.15, 2.02 and 2.06 tonnes per ha respectively. Thus, with the exception of MLRA 54, the yields for the 1995 crop year are within a reasonable range of the expected crop yields. MLRA 54 represents less than 10% of the dryland grain area in the state, and yields reported for any given year vary due to weather.

Table 17.2. Average CRP payment rate per hectare, CRP sign-ups 1–12 ($(1998) per ha).

	Winter wheat	Spring wheat	Barley
MLRA 52	114	111	114
MLRA 53A	86	89	89
MLRA 54	89	89	89
MLRA 58A	96	94	96

CRP, Conservation Reserve Program.

Expected returns were estimated using expected crop prices combined with expected yields and costs of production. Expected crop prices were defined as average prices received in a region net of transportation costs to the nearest grain elevator. Crop price data were collected from *USDA Market News, Montana Weekly Grain Summary* (various editions) on an area basis within Montana. Farm-gate prices were estimated as the area price net of transportation costs to the nearest grain elevator, using a minimum value of $3.67 per tonne for grain transported 48 km or less and increasing to around $5.51 per tonne for grain hauled from 48 to 129 km. This transport cost estimate was an average value obtained from a survey of grain hauliers in the region. This relationship also provided the basis for estimation of the farm-gate price under the alternative output price scenarios discussed below.

An econometric model was formulated to estimate expected production and variable costs of production associated with fertilizers, pesticides, seed, crop insurance and machinery operation. The general form of this model is:

$$y = s(p, w_f, w_p, area, fal, mlra, ins) \qquad 17.1$$

$$mc = m(p, w_f, w_p, area, fal, mlra, ins)$$

$$vc = c(y, w_f, w_p, mlra, ins)$$

where

y = crop output (tonnes)
mc = machinery operating costs ($)
vc = fertilizer and pesticide costs ($)
p = crop price ($ per tonne)
w_f = fertilizer price ($ per kg)
w_p = pesticide price ($ per kg active ingredient)
$area$ = size of field managed (ha)
fal = dummy variable indicating whether field was fallowed
$mlra$ = set of dummy variables for MLRAs
ins = dummy variable indicating if crop insurance was used.

In this model, seed costs and crop insurance costs are not modelled explicitly because they vary little by crop over the entire region. The crop insurance dummy is included to test for and estimate any effects of the use of crop insurance on variable costs of production.

For estimation, the system of equations was specified in log-linear form, and first-order conditions (share equations) from the cost function were included with linear homogeneity of the cost function and zero-degree homogeneity of the supply function. The system of Equations 17.1 was estimated for winter wheat, spring wheat and barley crops, based on the data described above. Details of the estimated models are discussed in Antle *et al.* (1998).

Using these econometric models, a stochastic simulation model was constructed according to the scheme presented in Fig. 17.2. The purpose of this model is to represent the *population* of production units in the region. A production unit is defined as a field, i.e. a parcel of land that is managed as a unit over time. The model simulates the farm manager's crop choice, and the related output and cost of production conditional on that crop choice, at the field scale. By operating at the field scale, the simulation can represent spatial differences in crop rotations and productivity, which give rise to significantly different economic outcomes in the region.

Following Fig. 17.2, each field in the data is described by total area, location and an associated set of location-specific prices paid and received by the farmer. Based on draws from sample distributions estimated from the data, a type of tillage, use of crop insurance and previous crop are selected to initialize the model. The econometric models are simulated to estimate expected output and cost of production and then to calculate expected returns above short-run variable costs of production for each crop alternative. Thus, these expected returns are interpreted as returns to family labour and management and capital ownership.

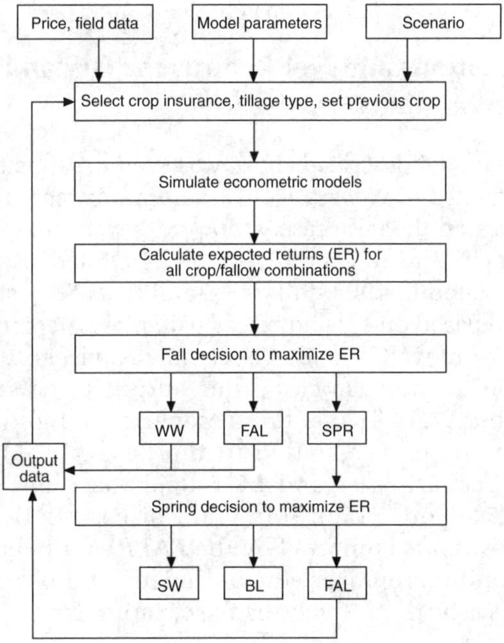

Fig. 17.2. Simulation model structure.

Based on the maximization of expected returns, a fall (autumn) decision is made to produce winter wheat (WW) or to postpone the production decision until spring (SPR). If winter wheat is not grown, the model advances to the spring decision, where either spring wheat (SW), barley (BL) or fallow (FAL) options are selected based on expected returns maximization. For expected returns calculations, it is assumed that if a field is fallowed in the current season then a crop is produced the following season, as is typically the case, with next season's expected returns discounted to the present. Likewise, for calculation of expected returns for crops on fallow, costs of production include the current costs of production plus the previous season's fallow costs compounded to the present. In addition to these crops, an alternative land use is allowed, which is defined as a non-crop use that is adopted when net returns above variable cost are negative. This category could correspond to idling the land (as opposed to fallow, which means the land is part of an ongoing annually planted crop rotation), use of the land for grazing or putting it in a conserving use.

It should be noted that there was little evidence of differences in yield risk associated with different cropping systems, thus providing support for the use of the risk-neutrality assumption in the modelling of farmer behaviour. Further details of the simulation model, including its validation, are found in Antle *et al.* (1998).

3. Land Allocations and Net Returns for Dryland Grain Production in Montana

The simulation model described above was used to estimate land-use patterns, costs and returns under a set of assumptions regarding crop prices and factor prices. In the base case, crop prices were set to correspond to those prevailing in the 1998 crop year, and 1995 factor prices from the survey were inflated to 1998 dollars assuming a 6% cost increase over this time period based on data on prices paid by farmers in the *Economic Report of the President* (Council of Economic Advisers, 1998).

In addition to the base case, four output price scenarios were simulated (Table 17.3). Two of these scenarios, H1 and H2, reflect an increase in grain prices relative to the base of 7.5% and 15.0% respectively. Scenarios L1 and L2 reflect the same proportionate decrease (−7.5% and −15.0%) in grain prices relative to the base. Based on the estimates reported by the FAPRI study (see Chapter 3), scenarios H2 and L2 represent the optimistic and pessimistic FAPRI grain price forecasts, respectively. In all scenarios, factor prices were left at the 1998 levels.

Table 17.4 shows the simulated crop land allocations for the base scenario and the four output price scenarios for the entire region. The

Table 17.3. Output price scenarios (per cent changes in 1998 output prices).

Scenario	Winter wheat	Spring wheat	Barley
Base	0	0	0
H1	+7.5	+7.5	+7.5
H2	+15.0	+15.0	+15.0
L1	−7.5	−7.5	−7.5
L2	−15.0	−15.0	−15.0

crops are winter wheat, spring wheat and barley, with each being grown on land that was previously fallowed or cropped, e.g. spring wheat after fallow (SWF) or spring wheat recropped (SWR). These data suggest that changes in output prices could alter the crop rotations and the allocation of land between the principal crops. With lower grain prices (scenarios L1 and L2), returns to investing in soil moisture by fallowing are reduced. Thus, with lower prices there will be less land fallowed, fewer hectares of crop produced after fallow, and more hectares of crop produced under recropped conditions. The amount of land fallowed each year declines to 26% under scenario L2, which is nearly a 20% reduction relative to the base scenario. When grain prices increase (scenarios H1 and H2), there is a slight shift toward more winter wheat and less spring wheat production. However, within the range of output prices considered in the simulation experiments, spring wheat remains the predominant crop in the region.

The regional variation in land use does not reflect the considerable spatial variation in land use across MLRAs. Table 17.5 shows the average land allocation within each MLRA for the changes in output prices. In MLRA 52, lower grain prices shift land allocation toward spring wheat and barley and less fallow. In MLRA 53A, lower grain prices increase recropping for spring wheat and a decline in the percentage of land allocated to fallow. In MLRA 54, the decision to fallow land is most influenced by output prices. At higher grain prices,

Table 17.4. Simulated cropland allocation for output price scenarios (%).

Scenario	WWF	WWR	SWF	SWR	BLF	BLR	FAL
Base	0.085	0.008	0.219	0.202	0.020	0.145	0.320
H1	0.107	0.005	0.196	0.209	0.014	0.140	0.330
H2	0.132	0.005	0.214	0.162	0.014	0.130	0.342
L1	0.086	0.011	0.195	0.217	0.019	0.169	0.302
L2	0.053	0.010	0.204	0.269	0.016	0.193	0.256

WW, winter wheat; SW, spring wheat; BL, barley; FAL, fallow; F, fallow; R, recropped.
Scenarios H1, H2, L1, L2 are explained in Table 17.3.

Table 17.5. Simulated cropland allocation, by MLRA, by output price scenario (%).

MLRA/scenario	WWF	WWR	SWF	SWR	BLF	BLR	FAL
MLRA 52							
Base	0.069	0.004	0.235	0.168	0.025	0.175	0.325
H1	0.098	0.004	0.202	0.161	0.029	0.179	0.327
H2	0.124	0.003	0.225	0.129	0.025	0.158	0.337
L1	0.072	0.003	0.221	0.155	0.023	0.207	0.316
L2	0.049	0.001	0.216	0.206	0.019	0.229	0.279
MLRA 53A							
Base	0.067	0.005	0.251	0.315	0.003	0.0568	0.302
H1	0.082	0	0.237	0.314	0	0.041	0.325
H2	0.078	0.003	0.260	0.256	0	0.039	0.365
L1	0.057	0.003	0.209	0.371	0.003	0.075	0.284
L2	0.018	0.005	0.228	0.433	0	0.073	0.244
MLRA 54							
Base	0.152	0.034	0.163	0.125	0.030	0.159	0.337
H1	0.176	0.019	0.118	0.202	0.004	0.168	0.313
H2	0.273	0.019	0.114	0.110	0.011	0.102	0.371
L1	0.171	0.068	0.118	0.133	0.023	0.171	0.316
L2	0.129	0.061	0.117	0.186	0.023	0.261	0.223
MLRA 58A							
Base	0.087	0.004	0.204	0.206	0.022	0.161	0.318
H1	0.103	0.002	0.196	0.201	0.009	0.146	0.344
H2	0.115	0.002	0.216	0.164	0.013	0.169	0.321
L1	0.083	0.002	0.188	0.230	0.023	0.184	0.291
L2	0.045	0	0.212	0.277	0.020	0.196	0.250

WW, winter wheat; SW, spring wheat; BL, barley; FAL, fallow; F, fallow; R, recropped.
Scenarios H1, H2, L1, L2 are explained in Table 17.3.

the proportion of fields that are fallowed increases, the proportion of fields planted to winter wheat increases, and the proportion of fields in spring wheat declines. The reverse is true as the grain prices fall relative to the baseline in this MLRA. Finally, in MLRA 58A higher (lower) grain prices tend to shift the land allocation toward (away from) winter wheat after fallow. The lower grain prices also result in a decline in the proportion of fields that are fallowed in this MLRA.

Table 17.6 shows the impacts of the output price scenarios on average net returns above variable costs per hectare by MLRA for fields that are allocated by the model to each crop. The pattern of returns reported in this table represents returns on fields that are allocated to a particular crop according to the maximum expected returns criterion. Net returns in Table 17.6 must be contrasted with the distribution of expected returns on all fields prior to the land allocation decision. To

Table 17.6. Simulated net returns above variable cost by MLRA ($1998 per ha) (number of fields in parentheses).

MLRA/ scenario	WWF	WWR	SWF	SWR	BLF	BLR
MLRA 52						
Base	344.0 (50)	198.4 (3)	356.3 (171)	255.5 (122)	319.3 (18)	259.2 (127)
H1	374.6 (71)	241.4 (3)	383.8 (147)	289.9 (117)	343.5 (21)	321.7 (130)
H2	413.4 (90)	263.4 (2)	411.7 (164)	328.2 (94)	383.3 (18)	346.4 (115)
L1	287.6 (54)	192.7 (2)	299.7 (161)	224.9 (113)	253.5 (17)	235.7 (151)
L2	253.5 (36)	165.6 (1)	261.7 (157)	183.8 (150)	253.3 (14)	199.2 (167)
MLRA 53A						
Base	156.7 (26)	132.0 (2)	199.4 (97)	144.6 (122)	174.0 (1)	120.8 (22)
H1	201.4 (32)	—	213.7 (92)	156.2 (122)	—	152.5 (16)
H2	224.2 (30)	148.3 (1)	238.2 (100)	181.6 (99)	—	167.5 (15)
L1	147.3 (22)	50.2 (1)	172.7 (81)	119.4 (144)	99.6 (1)	111.4 (29)
L2	115.4 (7)	50.9 (2)	145.3 (88)	103.5 (167)	—	88.2 (28)
MLRA 54						
Base	166.3 (40)	91.2 (9)	164.8 (43)	124.0 (33)	150.5 (8)	124.5 (42)
H1	211.8 (46)	154.7 (5)	177.2 (31)	127.0 (53)	142.3 (1)	145.5 (44)
H2	217.2 (42)	122.3 (5)	206.6 (30)	148.8 (29)	193.5 (3)	154.2 (27)
L1	135.4 (45)	79.8 (18)	135.7 (31)	102.3 (35)	120.6 (6)	97.4 (45)
L2	124.0 (34)	73.1 (16)	111.0 (31)	75.6 (49)	92.9 (6)	88.2 (69)
MLRA 58A						
Base	207.6 (48)	173.0 (2)	223.6 (113)	159.6 (114)	214.0 (12)	162.8 (89)
H1	249.8 (57)	199.4 (1)	249.3 (109)	177.4 (112)	212.5 (5)	191.3 (81)
H2	275.8 (64)	227.1 (1)	271.8 (120)	210.0 (91)	280.5 (7)	212.8 (94)
L1	172.2 (46)	49.2 (1)	182.6 (104)	140.1 (127)	163.3 (13)	142.1 (102)
L2	159.1 (25)	—	150.5 (118)	116.6 (154)	153.0 (11)	114.7 (109)

WW, winter wheat; SW, spring wheat; BL, barley; F, fallow; R, recropped.

illustrate, Fig. 17.3 shows the expected returns distributions for fields in MLRA 52 for winter wheat after fallow and spring wheat after fallow. The spring wheat distribution has a mean of about $110 and is somewhat concentrated about the mode, whereas the winter wheat distribution has a mean of about $90, and exhibits greater dispersion. As a result, the fields that are allocated to winter wheat are those in the positive tail of the distribution. Table 17.6 shows the mean expected returns on fields planted to winter wheat after fallow are nearly the same as the mean expected returns on fields planted to spring wheat after fallow in MLRA 52. This type of interrelationship between the expected returns of the different crops explains the patterns observed in Table 17.6. Generally, expected returns to spring wheat, the principal crop, are more symmetric and have a smaller dispersion than the returns of the competing crops.

To examine the distributional issues and the longer-term viability of grain production in Montana, information on the net returns above

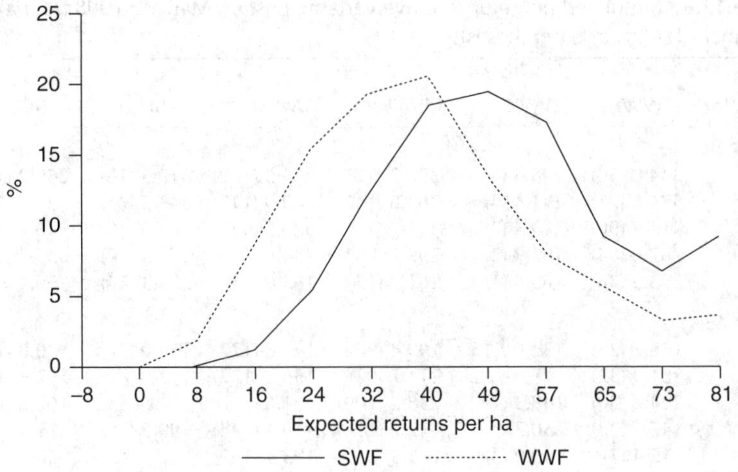

Fig. 17.3. Expected net returns distribution for winter wheat after fallow, and spring wheat after fallow, MLRA 52.

variable costs across all crops and rotations is provided. The mean net returns above variable costs for all crops and rotations, by MLRA, are shown in Table 17.7. These net returns are based on the simulated patterns for land use reported in Table 17.5, averaged across all crops and rotations. The net returns should be interpreted as the per hectare returns to land and management in each MLRA. It is also noted that these returns do not reflect any market transition payments that growers may receive under the terms of the 1996 Federal Agriculture Improvement and Reform (FAIR) Act.

The estimates reported in Table 17.7 indicate that there is substantial spatial variability in mean net returns for dryland grain producers in Montana and in the spread of the distributions. The more productive MLRA 52 earns greater returns per hectare relative to the other MLRAs in

Table 17.7. Simulated expected returns above variable cost, per hectare, by MLRA ($(1998) per ha) (standard deviation in parentheses).

	MLRA 52	MLRA 53A	MLRA 54	MLRA 58A
Base	292.87 (84.26)	162.00 (52.56)	137.88 (43.66)	181.89 (52.04)
H1	328.20 (86.07)	179.03 (51.60)	157.06 (57.67)	208.46 (62.74)
H2	367.15 (96.53)	203.49 (59.28)	183.48 (57.13)	235.07 (66.57)
L1	252.84 (70.82)	134.75 (43.37)	111.20 (36.67)	152.96 (44.75)
L2	213.52 (63.98)	113.27 (37.98)	92.42 (32.99)	127.73 (40.20)

Scenarios H1, H2, L1, L2 are explained in Table 17.3.

the study. For the base scenario, net returns above variable costs exceed the proxy used for ownership costs that was reported in Table 17.2 for all MLRAs. When grain prices fall to the low FAPRI price forecast (scenario L2), with the exception of MLRA 52, net returns are closer to the average 1995 CRP payment rates. If grain prices were to remain at this level or lower, dryland grain production would become economically marginal in these MLRAs. Long-term adjustments to lower grain prices would include a decline in land values, resulting in lower ownership costs relative to those reported in Table 17.2.

4. Conclusions

This chapter has analysed the economic impacts of alternative output price scenarios on dryland grain production in the northern Great Plains. Using a range of output prices which encompasses the FAPRI grain price projections, a spatially explicit stochastic simulation model of grain production in Montana was used to estimate the impacts on land allocation decisions and net returns pertinent to Montana and other Northern Plains production areas. This simulation model incorporates economic adaptations to changes in output prices in the form of changes in variable input use and land use. However, like other studies, the analysis does not incorporate farmers' long-run adaptations to higher or lower output prices in the form of changes in their machinery and other fixed capital. Thus, the estimated impacts of the price scenarios presented here should be interpreted as representative of short- to medium-run adaptations by farm decision makers. Long-run impacts would need to reflect the likely changes in the opportunity costs of land for each output price scenario.

This chapter has shown that net returns vary substantially by geographical location and by production practice for dryland grain production in Montana. A substantial portion of the land in production in Montana could become unprofitable at 1995/96 asset values if, and when, government market transition payments are phased out. If the long-term prices return to the level of the high FAPRI price projections, the outlook for grain producers in Montana and elsewhere improve. If prices fall to the levels predicted by the pessimistic FAPRI forecast, the outlook for Montana grain producers, especially in areas outside the north central part of the state, is less encouraging. The data in this analysis indicate that many grain-producing areas of the state could become economically marginal at the relatively low prices. The analysis also indicates that, by and large, the economically viable options for changing land uses are limited.

References

Antle, J.M., Capalbo, S.M., Johnson, J.B. and Zidack, W.E. (1998) *A Spatially-explicit, Econometrics-based Stochastic Simulation Model of Montana Dryland Grain Production.* Research Discussion Paper 21, Trade Research Center, Montana State University–Bozeman, Montana, USA.

Council of Economic Advisers (1998) *Economic Report of the President.* US Government Printing Office, Washington DC, USA.

Johnson, J.B., Zidack, W.E. Capalbo, S.M., Antle, J.M., Webb, D.F. (1997) *Farm-level Characteristics of Larger Central and Eastern Montana Farms with Annually-planted Dryland Crops.* Departmental Special Report No. 21, Department of Agricultural Economics and Economics, Montana State University–Bozeman, Montana, USA.

Johnson, J.B., Zidack, W.E., Capalbo, S.M., Antle, J.M. (1998a) *Production Costs for Annually-planted Crops Produced on Dryland Cropland, Northeastern Montana MLRA 53A.* Departmental Special Report No. 25, Department of Agricultural Economics and Economics, Montana State University–Bozeman, Montana, USA.

Johnson, J.B., Zidack, W.E., Capalbo, S.M., Antle, J.M. (1998b) *Production Costs for Annually-planted Crops Produced on Dryland Cropland, East Central Montana MLRA 54.* Departmental Special Report No. 26, Department of Agricultural Economics and Economics, Montana State University–Bozeman, Montana, USA.

Johnson, J.B., Zidack, W.E., Capalbo, S.M., Antle, J.M. (1998c) *Production Costs for Annually-planted Crops Produced on Dryland Cropland, Southeastern Montana MLRA 58A.* Departmental Special Report No. 27, Department of Agricultural Economics and Economics, Montana State University–Bozeman, Montana, USA.

Johnson, J.B., Zidack, W.E., Capalbo, S.M., Antle, J.M. (1998d) *Production Costs for Annually-planted Crops Produced on Dryland Cropland, Northern Montana MLRA 52.* Departmental Special Report No. 28, Department of Agricultural Economics and Economics, Montana State University–Bozeman, Montana, USA.

18

Synthesis and Implications

John M. Antle and Vincent H. Smith

Department of Agricultural Economics and Economics and Trade Research Center, Montana State University–Bozeman, USA

1. Introduction

This volume has provided a careful overview and detailed studies of the economic structure of world wheat markets and the major world wheat market economic issues that confront consumers, producers and policy makers: long-run trends in production and consumption; short-term price volatility and changes in stocks; and policies and institutions in the major importing and exporting countries and regions. The 16 studies presented in Chapters 2–17 also indicate the breadth of research that is being conducted on world wheat markets and the global importance of wheat as a major source of nutrition. In this concluding chapter we synthesize the insights these studies provide about the current state of world wheat markets and identify crucial unresolved questions about their behaviour over the first two decades of the 21st century.

2. Synthesis

As was shown in Chapter 1, the supply side of the global world wheat market is dominated by a small number of large exporting countries – Argentina, Australia, Canada, the European Community and the USA – while the demand side consists of a relatively large number of importing countries, none of which consistently has a dominant market share. This market structure means that the domestic and international trade policies of the five major wheat exporters generally have substantial impacts on global wheat markets, while the policies of individual importing countries tend to have smaller effects. These facts also explain why the research presented in this volume focuses more extensively on the policies and behaviour of the major exporting countries. However, in the 1990s, the behaviour of two importers – the former Soviet Union and China – has been of particular interest and relevance. Over the past 10 years, the former Soviet Union has shifted from being a substantial importer of wheat with about a 10% share of world wheat imports to being a modest importer with about a 2% share of world imports. In the 1990s China's wheat imports have been highly unstable, fluctuating from 12% to 2% of total world imports over a 3-year period. There have also been concerns about whether China's import demand will rise sharply over the next 15 years. Thus, the wheat markets of these two importing countries were examined in detail.

The general global patterns of production, consumption, and trade over the past four decades have been as follows. Between 1960 and 1998, global wheat production and consumption have increased by about 260%, from 42 million tonnes in 1960 to just under 600 million tonnes in 1998, while world exports and imports have expanded a little more slowly by about 250%, from about 41 million tonnes to about 100 million tonnes. In the 1990s world production and consumption have continued to expand. However, although there has been some degree of trade policy liberalization as a result of various bilateral and multilateral trade agreements, the volume of world wheat exports has remained relatively constant since 1990. This phenomenon is perhaps linked to the 'structural shift' in world wheat markets associated with economic and agricultural policy reform in the former Soviet Union, described by Goodwin and Grennes in Chapter 8, which resulted in a sharp decrease in net imports by that region.

The data on long-run trends in world prices presented in Chapter 3 provide clear evidence of what D. Gale Johnson describes in Chapter 2 as the great success story of agriculture in the latter half of the 20th century. Despite more than a doubling of world population, the supply of grain increased so rapidly that in real terms wheat and other grain prices declined substantially. Chapter 3 showed that the real price of wheat, in 1995 dollars, has declined from more than $800 per tonne in 1866 to between $110 and $145 per tonne in the late 1990s. If this trend continues, real wheat prices are likely to remain in the range of $75 to $145 per tonne well into the 21st century, following the extrapolation of the trend witnessed in the second half of the 20th century.

The long-term downward trend in real grain prices reflects the successful development and the dissemination of modern high-yielding seed varieties, increases in irrigated area and use of complementary agricultural chemicals and mechanical technology, discussed by Robert

Herdt in Chapter 6. This ongoing process of technological innovation and productivity growth has resulted in substantial competitive pressures on grain producers around the world, forcing those who have remained in agriculture to be increasingly productive and efficient. Johnson points out that the dramatic growth in global grain production and the consequent reductions in grain prices have greatly benefited the world's poor – in both rural and urban areas – who derive a large share of their food calories from wheat and other food grains.

D. Gale Johnson also observed that wheat prices were relatively stable during the 1960–1990 period (with the exceptions of the dramatic price spike in the mid-1970s caused by the Russian crop failure and related events and the more modest price spike in the mid-1990s associated with a global 15% shortfall in wheat production) because of the policies of the USA and other major exporting countries to hold large grain stocks. Widespread trade policy changes were initiated by the Uruguay Round General Agreement on Tariffs and Trade (GATT) negotiations, the provisions of the 1994 GATT Marakesh Agreement that created the World Trade Organization (WTO) in 1994 and several bilateral and multilateral trade agreements, such as the Canadian–US Free Trade Agreement (CUSTA, implemented in 1989), the North American Free Trade Agreement (NAFTA, implemented in 1993) and MERCOSUR (implemented in 1991). Significant changes were also made to domestic agricultural policies by major wheat-exporting countries in the early and mid-1990s, which reduced subsidies for wheat and other grains production, liberalized access to domestic markets for other wheat-producing countries and reduced governments' roles as holders of wheat and other grain stocks. These changes were perhaps most notable in Canada (as described and assessed by Carter and Wilson in Chapter 9 and Gardner in Chapter 12), the European Union (EU) (discussed by Rayner *et al.* in Chapter 10) and the USA (discussed by Gardner in Chapter 12).

One result of the international and domestic agricultural policy changes of the late 1980s and early 1990s has been that global grain stock-holding behaviour has changed. In Chapter 4, Carter *et al.* explored stock-holding behaviour in wheat and other world commodity markets and its links to price instability. The data they present suggest that in the mid- and later 1990s the average world stocks-to-use ratio has declined relative to the1970s and 1980s and that this decline has largely resulted from changes in stock-holding by government agencies in the USA and the EU. However, Carter *et al.* caution that many recent and current estimates of world stocks almost certainly fail to account accurately for private stock-holding by peasant farmers in China and may underestimate actual world stocks of wheat by as much as 80–120 million tonnes (an error of between 12% and 20% of current world production).

Regardless of whether current estimates of world stocks-to-use ratios are reasonably accurate, Carter *et al.* do point out that there has been an important shift in the link between changes in stocks-to-use ratios and volatility in world prices. In the early 1970s, when the world wheat stocks-to-use ratio declined from well above 30% to just under 20%, world wheat prices tripled. In the mid-1990s a similar change in the world stocks-to-use ratio resulted in only a 60% increase in world prices. Both D. Gale Johnson and Carter *et al.* suggest that this reduction in price volatility may in part be attributable to a shift away from the management of stocks by governments in the context of policies targeted towards managing domestic prices and ensuring domestic price stability. It may also be a consequence of the reductions in agricultural trade barriers that have taken place in the late 1980s and 1990s, which have created more integrated world markets for wheat and other grains.

A central issue for future trends in global wheat production and prices is whether the 20th century's Green Revolution in agricultural technology will be extended into the 21st century. Recent advances in biotechnology have led to considerable optimistic speculation about the potential of transgenic science and technology to extend the Green Revolution by addressing productivity constraints that could not be surmounted using conventional plant and animal breeding techniques. Robert Herdt's assessment (Chapter 6), however, is that currently there is little evidence that recent biotechnology innovations will have substantial effects on agricultural productivity with respect to grain production, with the possible exception of rice. However, both Herdt and D. Gale Johnson point out that there appears to be substantial potential for increases in the adoption of existing technology in parts of Africa and Latin America over the next three decades. Similarly, technological improvements based on conventional plant breeding, chemistry and related sciences are likely to extend the trends in productivity growth that have been experienced over the past 30 years well into the 21st century as long as global investments in agricultural research and development are sustained.

The domestic agricultural policies and trading practices of major producing and importing countries will also have substantial effects on the future of world wheat markets. In the case of China, Rozelle and Huang emphasize how little is known about its production, its consumption and the institutions that govern its global transactions. They raise important questions about China's ability to maintain investment in agricultural research and high rates of productivity growth. They also express a concern, shared by many in the academic community, about the productivity growth implications of the reductions in funding and changes in management of the world's second largest national agricultural research system that have been implemented in the 1990s. At the same time, however, Rozelle and Huang find evidence that urbanization and demographic changes are likely to slow the rate of growth in demand for food grains, with the net effect being relatively stable import demand in the period from 2000 to 2020. Their assessment of future developments in China's trade behaviour contrasts with those of some other analysts who have predicted that China's growing demand for imports could exert substantial upward pressure on world prices.

Russia is another potentially important actor in the world wheat market. Before the political and economic reforms of the late 1980s and early 1990s, the former Soviet Union was a major importer of feed grains. Subsidies for imported feed grains were eliminated in the early 1990s and, in addition, consumer subsidies for meat were removed. The net effect was a substantial reduction in the demand for feed grains, including wheat, in Russia and other parts of the former Soviet Union. Despite the fact that Russia's agricultural sector has substantial potential for expanded production, Goodwin and Grennes suggest that the country's nominal attempts to reform and privatize farming have not substantially changed the way resources are managed in Russian agriculture. Thus, the net effect of the breakup of the Soviet Union has been to make Russia essentially self-sufficient in grain production. Although Russia has the potential to be a significant exporter of wheat, that potential is not likely to be realized until substantive institutional reforms are implemented. Thus, in the short term, Goodwin and Grennes argue that Russia is unlikely be a large player (either as an exporter or an importer) in world wheat markets except in years when domestic production is well below average, when it may import some considerable amounts of wheat for human consumption.

The nature and consequences of behaviour of state trading enterprises present another set of thorny issues in the context of world wheat markets. Australia and Canada are two major exporting countries that market wheat exports through monopoly state trading agencies. Because they are significant players in the world market, the marketing practices of the Australian and Canadian Wheat Boards (AWB and CWB) have become contentious issues with their competitors, and have made state trading enterprises a likely topic for future multilateral trade negotiations held under the auspices of the WTO. With domestic policy reform, these organizations have also come under increased scrutiny in their own countries. In Chapter 9, Carter and Wilson raise important questions about whether, in fact, these organizations do have the ability to manipulate prices in the international market. They suggest that their own domestic markets suffer the most adverse economic consequences of their operations and that the effects of the AWB and the CWB on world prices and distortions in international patterns of trade may have been very modest. That the operations of the CWB do have some impact is confirmed by the finding reported by Gardner in Chapter 12 that feed wheat prices in Canada, as reflected by traded prices on the Winnipeg Exchange, are not integrated with traded wheat prices in the USA.

Since the early 1980s, the EU has emerged as a major wheat-exporting region. In Chapter 10, Rayner *et al.* provide compelling evidence that the EU will remain a major grain-exporting region for the foreseeable future. Moreover, they show that without substantial policy changes there is good reason to believe that the EU will be unable to meet its export subsidy reduction commitments under the provisions of the 1994 GATT agreement. Price supports for wheat and other cereals were cut by 36% between 1992 and 1995 under the MacSharry Reforms of the EU Common Agricultural Policy (CAP), and 5% land set-asides for cereals and oilseeds were mandated for the 1996/97 and 1997/98 crop years. However, wheat production in the EU has continued to increase because of improved yields and little reduction in the area planted to wheat (set-asides being satisfied by reduction in barley and other crop areas). To meet EU obligations, Rayner *et al.* indicate that the EU Commission, in its Agenda 2000 proposal for CAP reform, is proposing substantial further cuts in support price of the order of about 25%. Such cuts in EU intervention prices for wheat would reduce those support prices to about $123 (95.35 ecu) per tonne, well within the range for world wheat prices in the 1990s. Thus, in years when world wheat prices are not much below average, the EU may not need to use its export restitution policy to provide substantial export subsidies. However, as long as wheat yields continue to increase at their recent growth rates, these support price cuts may not have much impact on wheat production or planted area because they apply to both wheat and barley as well as other cereals crops and, in the 1990s, wheat has become a more profitable crop relative to barley.

North America (Canada and the USA) will continue to be the largest source of wheat exports well into the 21st century. A key question is whether Canada and the USA will be able to reform their domestic and trade policies successfully so as to maintain the cost-efficient production and transport of wheat and other grains to the rest of the world. The CUSTA and NAFTA created a framework for market integration but did not require Canada and the USA to eliminate inconsistencies between their respective policies. In Chapter 12, Gardner shows the two countries' wheat sectors share many similarities in technology and farm organization, but still differ significantly in their marketing and transportation systems. Moreover, while the 1988 CUSTA has encouraged increased trade between the two countries, in the 1990s the USA has effectively restricted wheat imports from Canada when, as in 1994, those imports have disrupted US domestic wheat markets.

The integration and performance of the US and Canadian grain markets depends not only on harmonization and convergence of agricultural policies but also on transportation policies. Fulton and

Gray (Chapter 14) examined the changes that have been taking place in the Canadian transportation system. As both they and Gardner note, the elimination of Canadian transportation subsidies in 1996 represented an important step towards market integration, but the continued existence of the CWB's monopoly over the storage and marketing system in Canada continues to cause significant friction between the two countries. This friction is evidenced by continued concerns on the part of producers in the USA about: (i) restricted access to the Canadian transportation and grain marketing system; (ii) the potential for ad hoc actions on the part of the CWB to generate sudden substantial and disruptive shifts in the pattern of trade between the two countries and the pattern of grain flows within the US grain handling and distribution system; and (iii) the CWB's periodic practice of marketing grain at substantial 'cut-price' discounts in third countries such as Chile and Brazil. These difficulties are compounded by a perceived lack of policy transparency; that is, the CWB operates Canada's wheat export policy but, as a state trading agency, provides no information about its discriminatory pricing and implicit targeted export subsidy practices on the grounds that it is really only a commercial entity and that its pricing information is a commercial trade secret. At the same time, Canadian wheat producers are concerned about the potential for the USA to affect world market prices through its explicit Export Enhancement Program (EEP) targeted export subsidy programme and about what are viewed as the substantial general subsidies received by US wheat producers in the form of market transition payments under the provisions of the 1996 Federal Agriculture Improvement and Reform (FAIR) Act. While these subsidies are 'GATT legal', rightly or wrongly they are widely viewed by Canadian farmers as encouraging US grain production.

Although Argentina has consistently been a wheat exporter in the 1980s and 1990s, Latin America has been a net importer of several million tonnes of wheat since the 1950s. In Chapter 13, Diaz-Bonilla showed that in Latin America wheat consumption and production have both grown substantially during the past four decades and amounted to about 20 million tonnes in the mid-1990s. Increased productivity, as well as market integration and trade and domestic general economic liberalization, resulted in economic growth that led to increased wheat consumption and trade in the region and, despite some adverse effects in countries such as Brazil because of reductions in domestic agricultural subsidies, production also expanded. The creation of MERCOSUR and shifts in Brazil's non-tariff wheat trade policies, however, have resulted in changes in the pattern of wheat trade in the southern part of the Western Hemisphere. By and large, in the 1990s imports by MERCOSUR countries from sources in other continents have decreased as, in the context of a preferential tariff structure for Argentinian wheat, they have switched to Argentina as their source of imports.

Correspondingly, Argentina now ships a much larger proportion of its total wheat exports to those countries. With the rate of growth in wheat consumption slowing, Latin America may attain net exporter status in the early part of the 21st century. However, there is considerable uncertainty about South America's future role in world wheat markets. On the demand side, political and financial uncertainties in Argentina and Brazil raise questions about the region's prospects for economic growth and wheat demand growth. On the supply side, limited investment in transport and market infrastructure continue to put the region's producers at a cost disadvantage relative to the other major producing regions of North America and Europe.

Taken together, this overview of world production and consumption suggests that there is little evidence to support the view that the long-term downward trend in real wheat prices discussed by D. Gale Johnson in Chapter 2 and by Antle *et al.* in Chapter 3 will be reversed in the early part of the 21st century. If, in real terms, world wheat prices continue their long-run downward trend, what does this portend for the future of wheat production in North America? In Chapters 16 and 17, two detailed studies focus on the economic prospects of grain producers in the Northern Plains region of the USA. Both studies find that the likely trend in wheat prices, combined with reductions in domestic subsidies, will put continuing economic pressure on smaller, less efficient farms in the region. However, these studies also show that the majority of acres in wheat production in the 1990s will remain sufficiently profitable to keep them in production for the foreseeable future. Despite the public discussion of a farm crisis in the region in the late 1990s, the data in Chapter 17 show that a majority of farms have low debt loads and can be operated profitably at prices within the likely ranges discussed in Chapter 3.

3. Questions for Future Research

This book has addressed a wide range of important economic issues in relation to world wheat markets. However, as each of the 16 studies included in this volume indicates, most of these issues are by no means completely resolved. First, there is considerable ambiguity about future trends in consumption and production in several major importing countries. In Russia, there are considerable ambiguities about future political developments, economic growth, and agricultural programmes. Thus it is not clear whether Russia will become a substantial net exporter or a modest and inconsistent net importer of wheat over the next two decades. In addition, while China appears likely to remain a net importer of wheat (buying between 2 and 15 million tonnes annually from the world market, depending on fluctuations in domestic harvests and domestic stocks), there is considerable uncertainty about whether productivity will continue to increase over the next two decades because of cut-backs in public agricultural research and development expenditures. Additional research is therefore needed on these issues.

A second unresolved question concerns the potential importance of current and future regional integration for patterns of trade and price in world wheat markets. The CUSTA, NAFTA and MERCOSUR have had important effects on patterns of trade in wheat in the Western Hemisphere. The implementation of CUSTA in 1989 and NAFTA in 1993 resulted in substantially expanded exports to the USA from Canada and to Mexico from the USA. Since the implementation of MERCOSUR, Argentina has become the major supplier of wheat to other member countries such as Brazil and Uruguay. Current initiatives to create a free-trade area of the Americas may have important implications for aggregate trade between North America, Central America and South America but the likely consequences of such a free-trade area are not well understood. Similarly, expansion of the EU to include Central European emerging democracies such as Poland, the Czech Republic, Hungary and Romania may also have substantial effects on European grain production and consumption, but again the consequences for world wheat prices and world wheat trading patterns are not clear.

A third important set of questions concerns whether changes in domestic and international agricultural policies will lead to more or less volatility in domestic and international prices. While there is some evidence that trade liberalization and shifts away from domestic policies targeted towards domestic price supports and price stabilization may have reduced the volatility of world wheat prices, it is not entirely clear whether the shift away from government stock-holding will lead to more or less instability in world wheat markets. In addition, it seems clear that very little is known about private stock-holding and its implications for domestic and international price stability in the markets for wheat or other grains.

Almost certainly, in relation to the economic well-being of the world's poor, the most critical unresolved questions with respect to wheat (and other food grains) revolve around whether the productivity growth rates experienced since the mid-1950s can be sustained in the 21st century. This fourth issue involves the links between agricultural research investments and agricultural productivity, which are still not well understood, especially with respect to the timing of the benefits provided by the research and the effects of different research management structures on research and output productivity. However, the worldwide slow-down in the rate of growth of such investments is a real cause for concern, as almost all studies have indicated that there are substantial social returns to agricultural research and development. In addition, there is considerable disagreement about the potential of new biotechnology to enhance crop yields. Nor is it clear whether current cropping practices are generating widespread resource degradation problems (although in some cases there is obvious cause for concern). Additional research is needed in all of these areas.

A fifth issue concerns what will happen to wheat consumption and production, and net imports in Africa and Asia. There is considerable evidence that as per capita incomes increase in low-income countries the demand for wheat-based products also increases, as does the demand for feed grains. There is also substantial scope for increased productivity. A better understanding of how these factors will evolve is needed.

A sixth set of issues involves unresolved questions about the role of quality in world wheat markets. Wilson and Dahl have presented some data that suggest a shift in demand by importing countries towards higher-quality wheats. However, the picture is far from clear and over the past decade only one country, South Korea, has unambiguously shifted its import purchases in that direction. Much more research is needed on this issue, especially in the context of developing countries that have enjoyed relatively rapid increases in per capita incomes and might be expected to increase their purchases of wheat with higher levels of protein and other higher-quality characteristics.

A final set of uncertainties is associated with future developments in agricultural trade policy and the effects of any such changes on world wheat markets. Agriculture is targeted for further trade liberalization in the year 2000 WTO GATT mini-round. However, it is by no means clear which of the major issues – export subsidies, the roles of export and import state trading enterprises, internal (domestic) support measures, market access and nominal tariff reductions, and sanitary and phytosanitary measures – will be taken up as central issues. Nor is it clear that, or to what degree, the participating countries will seek substantial reductions in tariff and non-tariff trade barriers. It remains to be seen whether there will be important quantitative consequences for world wheat markets from any given set of trade reforms in terms of average levels of output, consumption and prices or market volatility, and who will benefit most from those reforms.

As the studies presented here demonstrate, a great deal has been learned about world wheat markets. However, there is much more to be discovered about world wheat markets that will benefit policy makers, farmers, agri-business firms, food processors, and consumers in rich and poor countries. The challenges are both interesting and important and present an exciting agenda for future economic research.

Index